Rick Steves®

SCANDINAVIA

CONTENTS

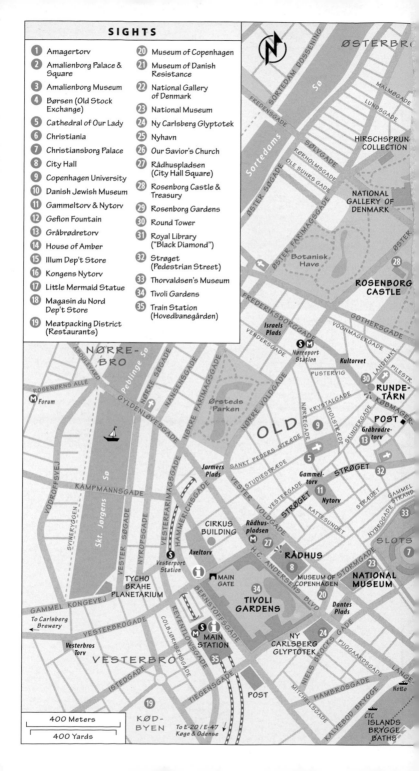

SIGHTS

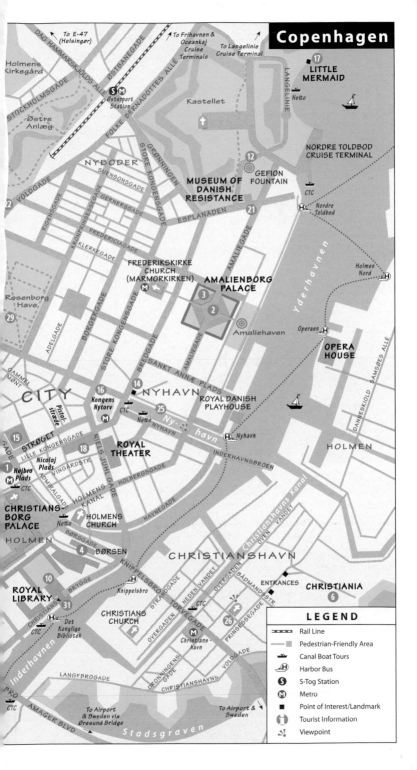

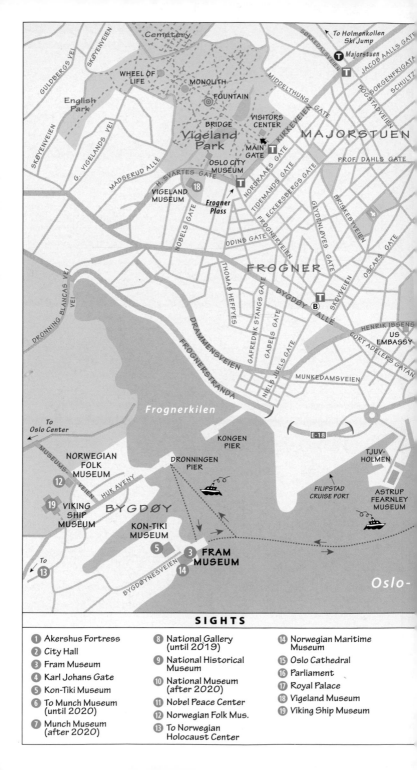

SIGHTS

1 Akershus Fortress

2 City Hall

3 Fram Museum

4 Karl Johans Gate

5 Kon-Tiki Museum

6 To Munch Museum (until 2020)

7 Munch Museum (after 2020)

8 National Gallery (until 2019)

9 National Historical Museum

10 National Museum (after 2020)

11 Nobel Peace Center

12 Norwegian Folk Mus.

13 To Norwegian Holocaust Center

14 Norwegian Maritime Museum

15 Oslo Cathedral

16 Parliament

17 Royal Palace

18 Vigeland Museum

19 Viking Ship Museum

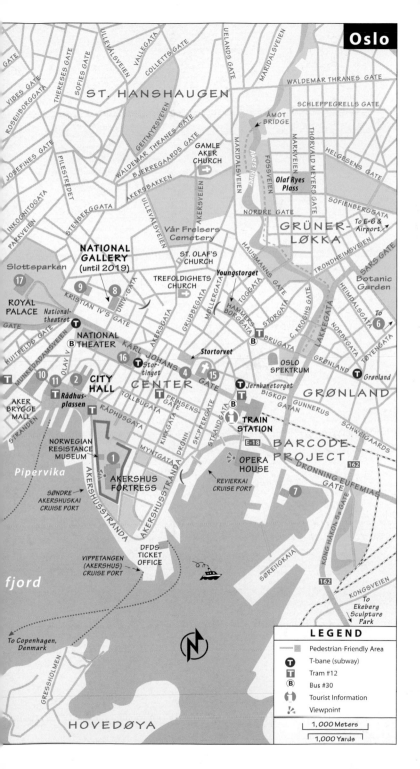

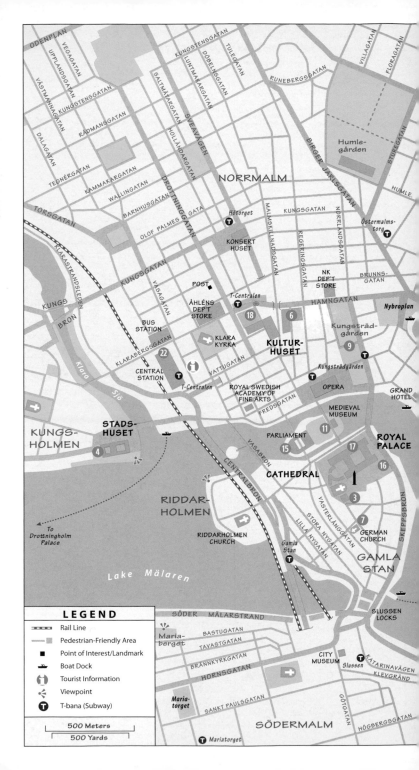

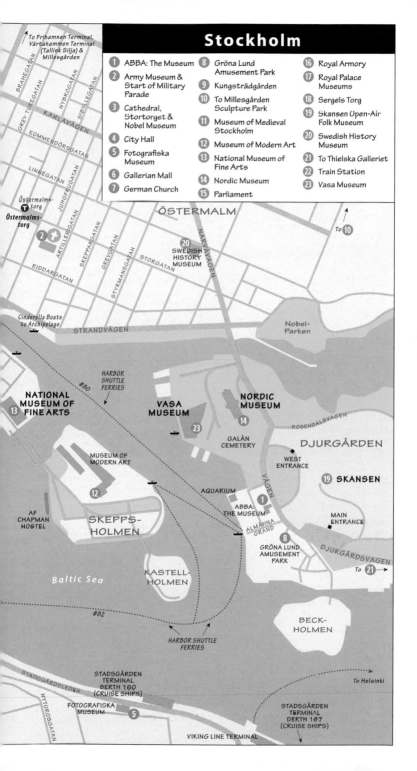

Stockholm

1. ABBA: The Museum
2. Army Museum & Start of Military Parade
3. Cathedral, Stortorget & Nobel Museum
4. City Hall
5. Fotografiska Museum
6. Gallerian Mall
7. German Church
8. Gröna Lund Amusement Park
9. Kungsträdgården
10. To Millesgården Sculpture Park
11. Museum of Medieval Stockholm
12. Museum of Modern Art
13. National Museum of Fine Arts
14. Nordic Museum
15. Parliament
16. Royal Armory
17. Royal Palace Museums
18. Sergels Torg
19. Skansen Open-Air Folk Museum
20. Swedish History Museum
21. To Thielska Galleriet
22. Train Station
23. Vasa Museum

To Frihamnen Terminal, Värtahammen Terminal (Tallink Silja) & Millesgården

BRAHEGATAN
GREV TUREGATAN
NYBROGATAN
SIBYLLEGATAN
KARLAVÄGEN
KOMMENDÖRSGATAN
LINNÉGATAN
JUNGFRUGATAN
Östermalms-torg
Östermalmstorg
ARTILLERIGATAN
SKEPPARGATAN
GREVGATAN
STYRMANSGATAN
STORGATAN
RIDDARGATAN

ÖSTERMALM

To 10

NARVAVÄGEN

SWEDISH HISTORY MUSEUM 20

Cinderella Boats to Archipelago
STRANDVÄGEN

Nobel-Parken

#80
HARBOR SHUTTLE FERRIES

NATIONAL MUSEUM OF FINE ARTS 13

VASA MUSEUM 23

NORDIC MUSEUM 14

ROSENDALSVÄGEN

GALÄN CEMETERY

DJURGÅRDEN

WEST ENTRANCE

VÄGEN

MUSEUM OF MODERN ART 12

AQUARIUM

19 SKANSEN

MAIN ENTRANCE

AF CHAPMAN HOSTEL

SKEPPS-HOLMEN

ABBA: THE MUSEUM 1

ALMÄNNA GRAND

GRÖNA LUND AMUSEMENT PARK 8

DJURGÅRDSVÄGEN

To 21

Baltic Sea

KASTELL-HOLMEN

BECK-HOLMEN

To Helsinki

#82

HARBOR SHUTTLE FERRIES

STADGÅRDSLEDEN

STADSGÅRDEN TERMINAL BERTH 160 (CRUISE SHIPS)

FOTOGRAFISKA MUSEUM 5

NYTORGSGATAN

STADSGÅRDEN TERMINAL BERTH 167 (CRUISE SHIPS)

VIKING LINE TERMINAL

Bergen

To Norwegian Fisheries Museum

SKOLTEN CRUISE TERMINAL

SKOLTEGRUNNS-KAIEN

INTERNATIONAL FERRIES

Harbor

SKUTEVIKSTORGET

Ⓑ

② BERGENHUS FORTRESS

E85

HÅKON'S HALL ⑨

ROSEN-KRANTZ TOWER ⑭

FESTNINGS-KAIEN

NORDNES

TOTEM POLE

AQUARIUM

①

STRANDGATEN

C. SUNDTS GATE

HARBOR FERRIES

POOL

SWIMMING BEACH

HAUGEVEIEN

Nordnesparken

STRANDSIDEN ✈

NYKIRKEN

NORDNESVEIEN

C. SUNDTS GATE

STRANDGATEN

HOLBERGSALLM.

HAUGEVEIEN

Puddefjorden

KLOSTERGATEN

SKOTTEGATEN

NØSTEGATEN

ENGEN

NØSTEGATEN

HURTIGRUTEN TERMINAL (COASTAL CRUISES)

555

TORBORG NEDREAASGATE

JEKTEVIKEN/DOKKEN CRUISE PORT

SIGHTS

① Aquarium
② Bergenhus Fortress
③ Bryggens Museum
④ Cathedral
⑤ Fish Market
⑥ Fløibanen Funicular
⑦ Fortress Museum
⑧ To Gamle Bergen
⑨ Håkon's Hall
⑩ Hanseatic Quarter & Museum
⑪ KODE Art Museums
⑫ Leprosy Museum
⑬ Ole Bulls Plass
⑭ Rosenkrantz Tower
⑮ St. Mary's Church
⑯ Theta Museum
⑰ Torgallmenningen (Main Square)
⑱ Bus to Ulriken643 Cable Car
⑲ Bybanen Tram to Troldhaugen, Fantoft Stave Church & Airport

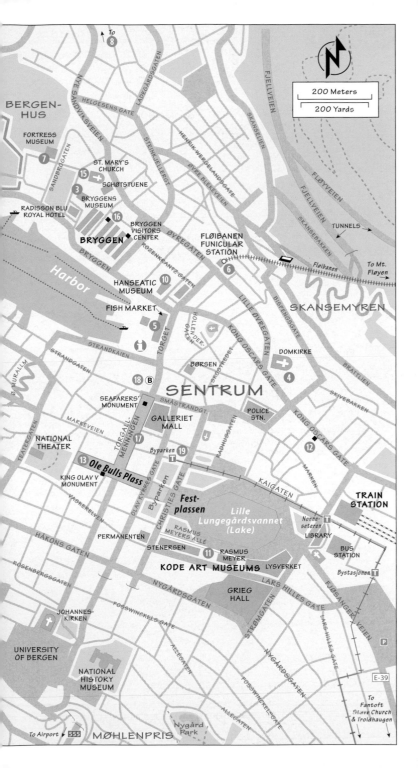

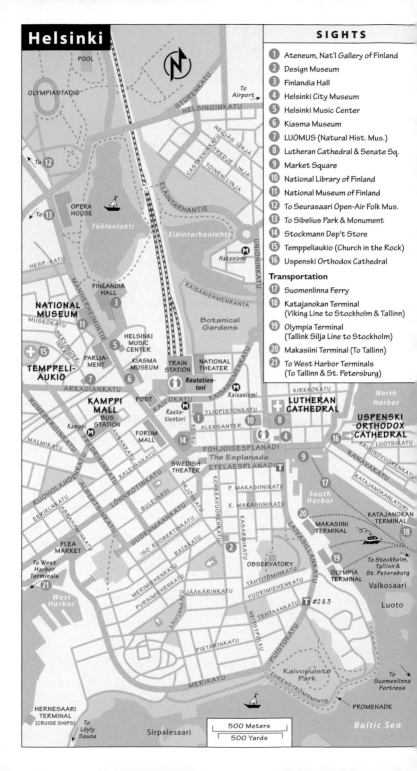

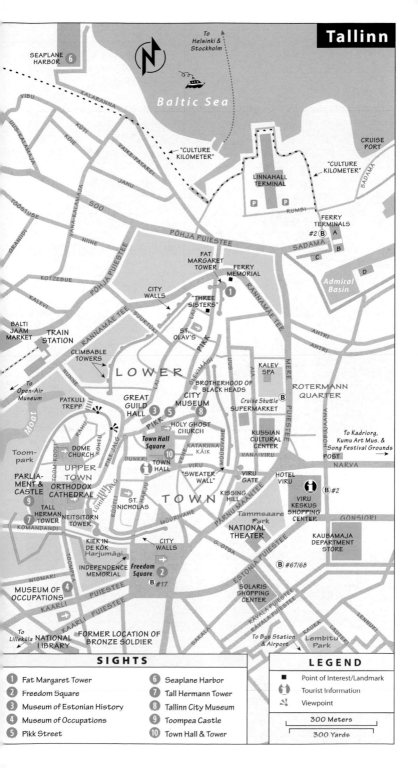

Tallinn

SIGHTS

1. Fat Margaret Tower
2. Freedom Square
3. Museum of Estonian History
4. Museum of Occupations
5. Pikk Street
6. Seaplane Harbor
7. Tall Hermann Tower
8. Tallinn City Museum
9. Toompea Castle
10. Town Hall & Tower

LEGEND

- ■ Point of Interest/Landmark
- ⓘ Tourist Information
- 🔭 Viewpoint

300 Meters

300 Yards

Join in the Viking fun

Helsinki harbor, Finland

Gamla Stan, Stockholm, Sweden

Rick Steves®

SCANDINAVIA

Welcome to Rick Steves' Europe

Travel is intensified living—maximum thrills per minute and one of the last great sources of legal adventure. Travel is freedom. It's recess, and we need it.

I discovered a passion for European travel as a teen and have been sharing it ever since—through my tours, public television and radio shows, and travel guidebooks. Over the years, I've taught thousands of travelers how to best enjoy Europe's blockbuster sights—and experience "Back Door" discoveries that most tourists miss.

This book offers you a balanced mix of Scandinavia's exciting capital cities and cozy small towns. Along with seeing Tivoli Gardens, Hans Christian Andersen's house, and *The Little Mermaid,* you'll take a bike tour of a sleepy, remote Danish isle, dock at a time-passed fjord village, and wander among eerie, prehistoric monoliths in Sweden. And for an exciting Baltic side trip, I've added my vote for the most interesting city in this corner of Europe—Tallinn, Estonia.

I advocate traveling simply and smartly. Take advantage of my money- and time-saving tips on sightseeing, transportation, and more. Try local, characteristic alternatives to expensive hotels and restaurants. In many ways, spending more money only builds a thicker wall between you and what you traveled so far to see.

We visit Scandinavia to experience it—to become temporary locals. Thoughtful travel engages us with the world, as we learn to appreciate other cultures and new ways to measure quality of life.

Judging by the positive feedback I receive from readers, this book will help you enjoy a fun, affordable, and rewarding vacation—whether it's your first trip or your tenth.

Happy travels!

Rick Steves

INTRODUCTION

Scandinavia—known for its stunning natural beauty, fun-loving cities, trend-setting design, progressive politics, high latitudes, and even higher taxes—is one of Europe's most enjoyable and most interesting corners. A visit here connects you with immigrant roots, modern European values, and the great outdoors like nowhere else. You'll gasp at breathtaking fjords, glide on a cruise ship among picturesque islands, and marvel at the efficiency and livability of its big cities. Yes, Scandinavia is expensive. But, delightfully, the best time to visit—summer—is also the best time to get good deals on the fancier hotels.

ABOUT THIS BOOK

Rick Steves Scandinavia is your smiling Swede, your Nordic navigator, and a personal tour guide in your pocket. This book is organized by destination. Each is a mini-vacation on its own, filled with exciting sights, strollable neighborhoods, affordable places to stay, memorable places to eat, and handy survival phrases.

In this book's chapters, you'll find these sections:

Planning Your Time suggests a schedule for how to best use your limited time.

Orientation has specifics on public transportation, helpful hints, local tour options, easy-to-read maps, and tourist information.

Sights describes the top attractions and includes their cost and hours. Major sights have self-guided tours.

The **Self-Guided Walks** take you through interesting neighborhoods, pointing out sights and fun stops.

Sleeping describes my favorite hotels, from good-value deals to cushy splurges.

Eating serves up a buffet of options, from inexpensive eateries to fancy restaurants.

Connections outlines your options for traveling to destinations by bus, train, plane, and boat. In car-friendly regions, I've also included route tips for drivers.

Country introductions give you an overview of each country's culture, history, current events, cuisine, language, and other useful practicalities.

The **Scandinavia: Past & Present** chapter introduces you to some key people and events in these nations' complicated pasts, making your sightseeing more meaningful.

The **Practicalities** chapter near the end of this book is a traveler's tool kit, with my best advice about money, sightseeing, sleeping, eating, staying connected, and transportation.

The **appendix** has the nuts-and-bolts: useful phone numbers and websites, a holiday and festival list, recommended books and films, a climate chart, and a handy packing checklist.

Browse through this book, choose your favorite destinations, and link them up. Then have a great trip! Traveling like a temporary local, you'll get the absolute most out of every mile, minute, and dollar. As you visit places I know and love, I'm happy that you'll be meeting some of my favorite Scandinavian people.

Planning

This section will help you get started on planning your trip—with advice on trip costs, when to go, and what you should know before you take off.

TRIP COSTS

Five components make up your trip costs: airfare to Europe, transportation in Europe, room and board, sightseeing and entertainment, and shopping and miscellany.

Airfare to Europe: A basic round-trip flight from the US to Copenhagen can cost, on average, $1,000-2,000, depending on where you fly from and when (cheaper in winter). Consider saving time and money in Scandinavia by flying into one city and out of another; for instance, into Copenhagen and out of Bergen. Overall, Kayak.com is the best place to start searching for international flights on a combination of mainstream and budget carriers.

Transportation in Europe: For a three-week whirlwind trip of my recommended destinations by public transportation, allow $650 per person. This pays for a second-class Scandinavia Eurail pass (4-country, 8 days in 1 month; offers a 20-40 percent discount on Stockholm-Helsinki or Helsinki-Tallinn boat fares), and the

Top Destinations in Scandinavia

extra boat rides that aren't discounted by the pass (such as Tallinn-Stockholm).

If you plan to rent a car, allow roughly $300 per week, not including tolls, gas, and supplemental insurance; add about $180 per person for the round-trip boat fare between Stockholm and Helsinki. Ferrying to and from Tallinn adds another $200. If you need the car for three weeks or more, leasing can save you money on insurance and taxes.

A short flight can be cheaper than the train (check www.skyscanner.com for intra-European flights).

Room and Board: You can manage comfortably in Scandinavia on an average of $140 a day per person for room and board. This allows $20 for lunch, $30 for dinner, and $90 for lodging (based on two people splitting the cost of a $180 double room that includes breakfast). Students and tightwads can enjoy Scandinavia for as little as $65 a day ($35 per hostel bed, $30 for groceries and snacks).

Sightseeing and Entertainment: In big cities, figure $10-20 per major sight (Oslo's Kon-Tiki Museum-roughly $12.50, Copenhagen's Tivoli Gardens-$17), $5 for minor ones (climbing towers), and $30-40 for splurge experiences (such as folk concerts, bus tours, and fjord cruises). Major cities have cards giving you free run of the public transit system and entrance to many sights for about $50-60/day.

An overall average of $45 per day works for most people. Don't

Scandinavia at a Glance

Denmark

▲▲▲Copenhagen Vibrant Danish capital city, with *The Little Mermaid,* old-time Tivoli Gardens amusement park, excellent National Museum, Renaissance King Christian IV's Rosenborg Castle, delightful pedestrian Strøget, and eye-opening hippie enclave at Christiania.

▲Near Copenhagen Great day-trip options: West to the Viking Ship Museum and Royal Cathedral at Roskilde, and north to Frederiksborg Castle—the "Danish Versailles"—in Hillerød, the Louisiana Art Museum in Humlebæk, and Kronborg Castle in Helsingør.

▲▲Central Denmark Peaceful isle of Ærø—perfect for a loop tour by bike or car—and home to Denmark's best-preserved 18th-century village—Ærøskøbing; and the busy town of Odense, with Hans Christian Andersen's childhood home and the nearby Funen Village open-air folk museum.

▲Jutland Family-friendly region with Legoland kids' adventure park; the tiny village of Jelling with historic rune stones; and Denmark's second-largest city, Aarhus, with its strollable pedestrian center, ARoS art museum, and Den Gamle By open-air folk museum.

Norway

▲▲Oslo Norway's sharp capital city, with its historic and walkable core, mural-lined City Hall, sculptures at Vigeland Park, and inspiring Nobel Peace Center, while the nearby Bygdøy district hosts museums dedicated to ships (Viking, *Fram,* and *Kon-Tiki*), traditional folk life, and the Holocaust.

▲▲▲Norway in a Nutshell A combination train, bus, and ferry trip to and through Norway's most spectacularly beautiful fjords—the Sognefjord and Nærøyfjord—passing pristine waterfalls, verdant forests, and take-your-breath-away scenery.

▲More on the Sognefjord Fjordside hamlet of Balestrand, a cozy home base for exploring nearby sights (including a medieval stave church), plus the serene Lustrafjord, with another stave church and a glacier you can walk on.

▲Gudbrandsdal Valley and Jotunheimen Mountains Lush green valley connecting northern and southern Norway, with touristy Lillehammer, the excellent Maihaugen Open-Air Folk Museum, and a rugged mountain range with some of this country's finest hikes and drives.

▲▲**Bergen** Salty port town and medieval capital of Norway, with lively fish market, colorful Hanseatic quarter (Bryggen), and a funicular to the top of Mount Fløyen with great views.

▲**South Norway** Harborside Stavanger—with its Petroleum Museum and nearby Pulpit Rock; time-passed and remote Setesdal Valley; and the port town of Kristiansand (connected by ferry to Denmark).

Sweden
▲▲▲**Stockholm** Bustling capital of Sweden, with its charming island core of Gamla Stan, Europe's original—and unsurpassed—Skansen open-air folk museum, the *Vasa* museum (17th-century warship), and the Nordic Museum's look at five centuries of Swedish lifestyles.

▲**Near Stockholm** Good day-trip options: Drottningholm Palace, the lavish royal residence with nearby Baroque-era theater; Sigtuna, Sweden's oldest town with rune stones and 18th-century buildings; and the university town of Uppsala, with its cathedral and Linnaeus Museum.

▲**Stockholm's Archipelago** Sweden's rocky garden of more than 30,000 islands, best seen on a boat trip from Stockholm.

▲**Southeast Sweden** Växjö, with a first-rate emigration museum and the Smålands Museum of glass-making; Kalmar, with its massive 12th-century Kalmar Castle and nearby holiday island of Öland; and the touristy "Kingdom of Crystal" Glass Country.

Finland
▲▲**Helsinki** Finland's capital city—an architectural delight for its Neoclassical and Art Nouveau buildings and churches—with Temppeliaukio, the stirring "Church in the Rock"; the fine National Museum of Finland; and an island fortress and open-air folk museum.

Estonia
▲▲**Tallinn** Russian-influenced, full-of-life capital of Estonia, with quaint Old Town center, remarkably intact medieval walls, and Estonian cultural sights contemporary art museum and parklike open-air museum).

INTRODUCTION

Scandinavia's Best
Three-Week Trip by Car

Day	Plan	Sleep in
1	Arrive in Copenhagen	Copenhagen
2	Copenhagen	Copenhagen
3	Copenhagen	Copenhagen
4	Sights near Copenhagen, into Sweden	Växjö
5	Växjö, Glass Country, Kalmar	Kalmar
6	Kalmar to Stockholm	Stockholm
7	Stockholm	Stockholm
8	Stockholm	Boat to Helsinki
9	Helsinki	Boat to Stockholm
10	Uppsala to Oslo	Oslo
11	Oslo	Oslo
12	Oslo	Oslo
13	Lillehammer, Gudbrandsdal Valley	Jotunheimen area
14	Jotunheimen Country	Lustrafjord area or Aurland
15	Sognefjord, Norway in a Nutshell	Bergen
16	Bergen	Bergen
17	Long drive south, Setesdal Valley	Kristiansand
18	Jutland, Aarhus, maybe Legoland	Aarhus (maybe Billund)
19	Jutland to Odense en route to Ærø	Ærøskøbing
20	Ærø	Ærøskøbing
21	Roskilde on the way into Copenhagen	Copenhagen

Flying into Copenhagen and out of Bergen (with a likely transfer in Copenhagen) can be wonderfully efficient; if you opt for this, see Jutland and Ærø sights near Copenhagen at the beginning of your trip.

skimp here. After all, this category is the driving force behind your trip—you came to sightsee, enjoy, and experience Scandinavia.

Shopping and Miscellany: Shopping can vary in cost from nearly nothing to a small fortune. Good budget travelers find that this category has little to do with assembling a trip full of lifelong and wonderful memories.

SIGHTSEEING PRIORITIES

So much to see, so little time. How to choose? Depending on the length of your trip, and taking geographical proximity into account, here are my recommended priorities:

4 days: Copenhagen, Stockholm (connected by a 5.5-hour express train)

6 days, add: Oslo

8 days, add: Norway in a Nutshell fjord trip, Bergen
10 days, add: Overnight cruise from Stockholm to Helsinki
14 days, add: Ærø, Odense, Roskilde, Frederiksborg (all in Denmark)
17 days, add: Aarhus (Denmark), Kalmar (Sweden)
21 days, add: Tallinn (Estonia) and more time in capitals
24 days, add: More Norwegian countryside or Stockholm's archipelago

The map and the three-week itinerary above includes most of the stops in the first 21 days.

WHEN TO GO

Summer is a great time to go. Scandinavia bustles and glistens under the July and August sun; it's the height of the tourist season,

Scandinavia's Best Three-Week Trip by Train and Boat

Day	Plan	Sleep in
1	Arrive in Copenhagen	Copenhagen
2	Copenhagen	Copenhagen
3	Copenhagen	Copenhagen
4	Roskilde, Odense, Ærø	Ærøskøbing
5	Ærø	Ærøskøbing
6	Ærø to Kalmar	Kalmar
7	Kalmar	Kalmar
8	Kalmar, early train to Stockholm	Stockholm
9	Stockholm	Stockholm
10	Stockholm, night boat to Helsinki	Boat
11	Helsinki	Helsinki
12	Helsinki, afternoon boat to Tallinn	Tallinn
13	Tallinn, night boat to Stockholm	Boat
14	Stockholm, afternoon train to Oslo	Oslo
15	Oslo	Oslo
16	Oslo	Oslo
17	Train and boat to Aurland	Aurland
18	Aurland to Bergen via fjord cruise	Bergen
19	Bergen	Bergen
20	Free day: more fjords, resting, or whatever	
21	Trip over	

If you want to see Legoland (near Billund) and the "bog man" (in Aarhus), visit these from Odense (closer) or Copenhagen. You could save lots of time by flying from Tallinn to Oslo.

when all the sightseeing attractions are open and in full swing. In many cases, things don't kick into gear until summer—beginning about June 20—when Scandinavian schools let out. Most local industries take July off, and the British and southern Europeans tend to visit Scandinavia in August. You'll notice crowds during these times, but up here "crowds" mean fun and action rather than congestion. At these northern latitudes, the days are long—on June 21 the sun comes up around 4:00 in Oslo and sets around 23:00. Things really quiet down when the local kids go back to school, around August 20.

"Shoulder-season" travel—in late May, early June, and September—lacks the vitality of summer but offers occasional good weather and minimal crowds. Norway in particular can be good from late May to mid-June, when the days are long but the tourist lines are short.

Winter is a bad time to explore Scandinavia unless winter

sports are high on your agenda. Like a bear, Scandinavia's metabolism slows down, and many sights and accommodations are closed or open on a limited schedule (especially in remote fjord towns). Business travelers drive hotel prices way up. Winter weather can be cold and dreary. Days are short, and nighttime will draw the shades on your sightseeing well before dinner. Christmastime activities (such as colorful markets and Copenhagen's festively decorated Tivoli Gardens) offer a brief interlude of warmth at this chilly time of year.

Before You Go

You'll have a smoother trip if you tackle a few things ahead of time. For more information on these topics, see the Practicalities chapter (and www.ricksteves.com, which has helpful travel tips and talks).

Make sure your passport is valid. If it's due to expire within six months of your ticketed date of return, you need to renew it. Allow up to six weeks to renew or get a passport (www.travel.state. gov).

Arrange your transportation. Book your international flights. Figure out your main form of transportation within Scandinavia: It's worth thinking about buying train tickets online in advance, getting a rail pass, renting a car, or booking cheap European flights. (You can wing it once you're there, but it may cost more.)

If you plan to take an **overnight boat** between major Scandinavian cities in summer or on weekends, book it in advance (Copenhagen to Oslo, page 114; Stockholm to Helsinki, page 623; Stockholm to Tallinn, page 678). If you're doing Norway in a Nutshell in July or August, make reservations for the Oslo-Myrdal train, and consider reservations for the Myrdal-Flåm train (see page 301).

Book rooms well in advance, especially if your trip falls during peak season or any major holidays or festivals.

Consider travel insurance. Compare the cost of the insurance to the cost of your potential loss. Check whether your existing insurance (health, homeowners, or renters) covers you and your possessions overseas.

Call your bank. Alert your bank that you'll be using your debit and credit cards in Europe. Ask about transaction fees, and get the PIN number for your credit card. You don't need to bring the local currency for your trip; you can withdraw cash from ATMs in Europe.

Use your smartphone smartly. Sign up for an international service plan to reduce your costs, or rely on Wi-Fi in Europe instead. Download any apps you'll want on the road, such as maps,

Budget Tips

While Scandinavia is expensive, transportation passes, groceries, alternative accommodations, and admissions are affordable (about what you'd pay in England or Italy). Being aware of your budget options will save you money.

Even though it's still possible to find midsummer hotel discounts, these discounts are generally offered only by the more expensive hotels. You'll save much more by staying in hostels like the Scandinavians do (many hostels have double rooms and great breakfasts).

The breakfasts offered at your lodgings are all-you-can-eat, and so hearty that you'll need only a sandwich for lunch. If you'd prefer more of a meal, the good news is that many restaurants offer lunch specials under $20. At many restaurants, tap water is served free, as are seconds on potatoes (so even if a restaurant's entrées cost $25, one entrée can easily make a complete dinner). Beer is very expensive, and wine is even more so (quench your thirst in Denmark, where alcohol isn't quite as pricey as it is farther north). Convenience and grocery stores offer a broad array of affordable to-go dishes, rescuing those shell-shocked by restaurant prices. You're never too far from a picnic-friendly park.

A Scandinavia rail pass can make train travel one of your smaller expenses; bus travel is even cheaper—and sometimes faster. At sights, ask about discounted admissions, as many discounts aren't posted.

The great scenery is free. When things are pricey, remind yourself you're not getting less for your travel dollar. Up here there simply aren't any lousy or cheap alternatives to classy, cozy, sleek Scandinavia. Even youth-hostel toilets are flushed by electronic sensors.

This book will help you save a shipload of money and days of headaches. Read it carefully. Many of the skills and tricks that are effective in Copenhagen work in Oslo and Stockholm as well.

translation, transit schedules, and Rick Steves Audio Europe (see sidebar).

Rip up this book! Turn chapters into mini guidebooks: Break the book's spine and use a utility knife to slice apart chapters, keeping gummy edges intact. Reinforce the chapter spines with clear wide tape; use a heavy-duty stapler; or make or buy a cheap cover (see the Travel Store at www.ricksteves.com), swapping out chapters as you travel.

Pack light. You'll walk with your luggage more than you think. Bring a single carry-on bag and a daypack. Use the packing checklist in the appendix as a guide.

Travel Smart

If you have a positive attitude, equip yourself with good information (this book), and expect to travel smart, you will.

Read—and reread—this book. To have an "A" trip, be an "A" student. Note opening hours of sights, closed days, crowd-beating tips, and whether reservations are required or advisable. Check the latest at www.ricksteves.com/update.

Be your own tour guide. As you travel, get up-to-date info on sights, reserve tickets and tours, reconfirm hotels and travel arrangements, and check transit connections. Visit local tourist information offices (TIs). Upon arrival in a new town, lay the groundwork for a smooth departure; confirm the train, bus, or road you'll take when you leave.

Outsmart thieves. Pickpockets abound in crowded places where tourists congregate. Treat commotions as smokescreens for theft. Keep your cash, credit cards, and passport secure in a money belt tucked under your clothes; carry only a day's spending money in your front pocket. Don't set valuable items down on counters or café tabletops, where they can be quickly stolen or easily forgotten.

Minimize potential loss. Keep expensive gear to a minimum. Bring photocopies or take photos of important documents (passport and cards) to aid in replacement if they're lost or stolen.

Guard your time and energy. Taking a taxi can be a good value if it saves you a long wait for a cheap bus or an exhausting walk across town. To avoid long lines, follow my crowd-beating tips, such as making advance reservations, or sightseeing early or late.

Prepare for border crossings. Border security between Norway, Sweden, Denmark, Finland, and Estonia may be a wave-through, but be prepared to show your passport. When you change countries, you change money (except between Finland and Estonia, which both use the euro), phone cards, and languages.

Be flexible. Even if you have a well-planned itinerary, expect changes, strikes, closures, sore feet, bad weather, and so on. Your Plan B could turn out to be even better.

Attempt the language. Many Scandinavians—especially in the tourist trade and in cities—speak English, but if you learn some of the local language, even just a few phrases, you'll get more smiles and make more friends. Practice the survival phrases at the end of each country section in this book, and even better, bring a phrase book.

INTRODUCTION

🎧 Rick Steves Audio Europe 🎧

My Rick Steves Audio Europe app makes it easy to download audio content to enhance your trip. Enjoy my audio tours of many of Europe's top destinations and a library of insightful  travel interviews from my public radio show with experts from Scandinavia and around the globe. The app and all of its content are entirely free. (And new content is added about twice a year.) You can download the app via Apple's App Store, Google Play, or Amazon's Appstore. For more info, see www.ricksteves.com/audioeurope.

Connect with the culture. Interacting with locals carbonates your experience. Enjoy the friendliness of the Scandinavian people. Ask questions; most locals are happy to point you in their idea of the right direction. Set up your own quest for the best *kringle,* stave church, or *smörgåsbord.* When an opportunity pops up, make it a habit to say "yes."

Scandinavia...here you come!

SCANDINAVIA

SCANDINAVIA

Scandinavia is Western Europe's least populated, most literate, most prosperous, most demographically homogeneous, most highly taxed, most socialistic, and least churchgoing corner. For the visitor, it's a land of Viking ships, brooding castles, salty harbors, deep green fjords, stave churches, and farmhouses—juxtaposed with the sleek modernism of its people-friendly cities.

Denmark, Norway, and Sweden are Scandinavia's core. They share a common linguistic heritage with Iceland, and a common history, religion, and culture with Finland and the Baltic nation of Estonia (both former Swedish colonies).

Emerging only slowly from under the glacial ice sheets, Scandinavia was the last part of Europe to be settled (its land mass is still rising from the ocean, rebounding from the press of the glaciers). Later, it was almost the last part of Europe to accept Christianity, and it's never quite forgotten its pagan roots, which live on in literature, place names, and the ancient runic alphabet. (For more background, see the Scandinavia Past & Present chapter.)

Scandinavia is blessed with natural beauty. The cavernous fjords of Norway's west coast are famous. Much of the region has mountains, lakes, green forests, and waterfalls. By contrast, low-lying Denmark has its rugged islands, salty harbors, and windswept, sandy coasts.

Climate-wise, Scandinavia has four distinct seasons. With Alaska-like latitudes, it's the "land of the midnight sun" in summer (18 hours of daylight) and of midafternoon darkness in winter (when there are just six hours between sunrise and sunset).

Most of Scandinavia is sparsely populated and very big. Sweden is the size of California, but has only a quarter the people (9.9 million). Just over 5 million Norwegians stretch out in Norway, where Oslo is as far from the northern tip of the country as it is from Rome. The exception is Denmark, which packs 5.6 million fun-loving Danes into a flat land the size of Switzerland.

Though each of the Scandinavian countries has its own language, there are some common threads. Danes and Norwegians can read each other's newspapers and can converse somewhat (but with difficulty because of thick accents). Swedes (whose written language is different) have a hard time with printed Danish and Norwegian, but can carry on simple conversations in those languages. Finns (whose language is not related at all) learn Swedish in school, thanks to Sweden's long historical presence in Finland. Estonian is similar to Finnish. Despite these common denominators, communication can be difficult due to one more factor—national pride. A Dane may simply pretend not to understand a Swede's request, and vice versa. If there's ever a language barrier, though, most Scandinavians can easily revert to their common second language—English.

It's not easy (and probably unwise) to make sweeping generalizations about a region's people, but here goes: In general, Scandinavians are confident, happy, healthy, and tall. They speak their minds frankly, even about taboo subjects like sex. They're strong individualists who cut others slack for their own eccentricities. They don't fawn on the rich and famous or look down on the down and out. At work, they're efficient and conscientious. They don't take cuts in line. They're well-educated, well-traveled, and worldly. Though reserved and super-polite at first, they have a good sense of humor and don't take life or themselves too seriously.

Scandinavians work hard, but they guard their leisure time fiercely. They like the out-of-doors, perhaps in keeping with the still-rural landscape they live in. For many, a weekend with the family at a (well-furnished) country cottage is all they need. Cycling, boating, and fishing are popular. Internationally, they're known for skiing, speed skating, hockey, and other winter sports. And, as with the rest of Europe, they're wild about football (soccer).

The region is a leader in progressive lifestyles, including recognizing same-sex partnerships. More than half the heterosexual couples in Denmark are "married" only because they've lived together for so long and have children. Wives and mothers generally have a job outside the home. While the state religion is Lutheran, only a small percentage of Scandinavians actually attend church

SCANDINAVIA

Scandi-hoovians You Might Know

Famous Danes

Hans Christian Andersen, writer of *The Ugly Duckling, The Little Mermaid,* etc.

Søren Kierkegaard, proto-existentialist philosopher

Bertel Thorvaldsen, sculptor

Karen Blixen, who wrote *Out of Africa* under pen name Isak Dinesen

Niels Bohr, physicist who described the atom as a tiny planetary system

Victor Borge, classical-music comedian

Arne Jacobsen, architect

Lars Ulrich, drummer for rock band Metallica

Nikolaj Coster-Waldau *(Game of Thrones),* Brigitte Nielsen, and Viggo Mortensen (half-Danish), actors

Carl Nielsen, composer

Lars von Trier, movie director

Morten Andersen, NFL placekicker and all-time leading scorer

Famous Norwegians

Eric the Red, first European settler in Greenland and father of Icelander Leif Eriksson, the Viking who discovered America

Edvard Grieg, Romantic composer

Edvard Munch, *The Scream* painter

Henrik Ibsen, playwright

Roald Amundsen, Arctic and Antarctic explorer

Gustav Vigeland, sculptor

Knute Rockne, football player and coach at University of Notre Dame

Sonja Henie, figure skater and movie actress

Thor Heyerdahl, explorer of *Kon-Tiki* fame

Jan Stenerud, NFL placekicker

other than at Easter or Christmas. Most are either indifferent or assertively secular.

Scandinavia is rich, with a very high standard of living (as American tourists learn the hard way). Norway has been blessed with offshore oil, Denmark with farmland, and Sweden and Finland with lush forests. They are all rich in fish. Alternative energy sources are important, especially hydroelectric and wind power. Given such pristine natural surroundings, the Scandinavians are environmentalists, committed to preserving their resources

Liv Ullmann, movie actress and director
Jo Nesbø, author of crime series featuring Oslo detective Harry
    Hole
Rick Steves, travel writer

Famous Swedes
Anders Celsius, inventor of the temperature scale
Carolus Linnaeus, botanist who developed taxonomic naming
    system
August Strindberg, playwright
Alfred Nobel, inventor of dynamite and the Nobel Peace Prize
Carl Milles, sculptor
Astrid Lindgren, children's author who created *Pippi Longstocking*
Ingmar Bergman, movie director
Ingrid Bergman, Greta Garbo, and Noomi Rapace, actresses
Max von Sydow and Stellan Skarsgård, actors
Dag Hammarskjöld, UN secretary general
Björn Borg and Stefan Edberg, tennis players
Hans Blix, UN weapons inspector
Annika Sörenstam and Jesper Parnevik, golfers
ABBA, pop-rock supergroup
Stieg Larsson, author of the *Millennium* trilogy

Famous Finns
Jean Sibelius, Romantic composer
Alvar Aalto, Modernist architect
Eliel Saarinen and son Eero, Modernist architects (the father
    known for his work in Finland, the son for his work in the US)
Esa-Pekka Salonen, classical conductor
Tove Jansson, author of the *Moomin* books
Linus Torvalds, creator of the Linux operating system
Kimi Räikkönen and Keke Rosberg, race car drivers

for future generations (except for the Norwegians' stubborn appetite for whaling).

Scandinavian society, carefully organized to maximize prosperity and happiness for everyone, is the home of cradle-to-grave security. Residents pay hefty taxes but get a hefty return. Children are educated. The old and sick are cared for. Cities are carefully planned to be clean, green, crime-free, and built on a human scale—with parks, fountains, public art, and pedestrian zones.

Generally speaking, citizens willingly share the burden for the common good. High taxes mean there's less of a gap between the very rich and the very poor, resulting in a less class-oriented society. Scandinavians are proud of this. If they seem a bit smug, you can't fault them, because statistics verify that they live longer, healthier, happier lives.

Scandinavia is also on the high-tech edge of the global economy. They practice a mix of free-market capitalism and enlightened socialism. In international business, they make their mark with telecommunications (Nokia from Finland, Ericsson from Sweden), Ikea furniture (originally from Sweden), Electrolux appliances (Sweden), and Lego toys (Denmark).

Politically, Denmark, Norway, and Sweden are constitutional monarchies with a figurehead monarch who cuts ribbons, works with parliament and a prime minister, and tries to stay out of the tabloids. Finland and Estonia have democratically elected presidents. The Scandinavian nations maintain close ties with each other. To some degree or other, they all participate in the European Union (though Norway is not a member, and only Finland and Estonia use the euro). Every election brings another debate about how closely they want to tie themselves to the rest of Europe. The Scandinavian nations have a reputation for international cooperation, exemplified by their leading role in the United Nations, and Sweden and Norway's Nobel Peace Prize.

All of Scandinavia's monarchs are descended from Oscar I, King of Sweden and Norway (and son of King Karl Johan XIV), through the House of Bernadotte: Denmark's Queen Margrethe II and Crown Prince Frederik (b. 1968), Sweden's King Carl XVI Gustaf and Crown Princess Victoria (b. 1977), and Norway's King Harald V and Crown Prince Håkon (b. 1973).

Artistically, Scandinavia is known for its serious playwrights (Henrik Ibsen and August Strindberg), brooding filmmakers (Ingmar Bergman), and gloomy painters (Edvard Munch), and more recently for its popular crime-thriller authors, Stieg Larsson and Jo Nesbø. Nordic mythology is familiar to the English-speaking world for its *Lord of the Rings*-style roots. Hans Christian Andersen, Astrid Lindgren, and Tove Jansson brought us children's tales. Less familiar are Scandinavia's people-friendly sculptors—Bertel Thorvaldsen, Gustav Vigeland, and Carl Milles— whose noble, realistic statues evoke the human spirit. Architecturally, Scandinavia continues to lead the way, with sleek modern buildings that fit in with the nat-
ural landscape. Late-20th-century Modernism (or Functionalism) had several Scandinavian champions, including Eero Saarinen and Alvar Aalto (Finland) and Arne Jacobsen (Denmark). Musically,

Scandinavia is known for classical composers like Grieg (Norway) and Sibelius (Finland) who celebrate the region's nature and folk tunes. Scandinavia's cities have thriving jazz scenes that rival America's. Oh yes, and then there's Scandinavia's biggest musical export—the '70s pop band from Sweden named ABBA.

The Scandinavian flair for art shines best in the design of everyday objects. They fashion chairs, lamps, and coffeemakers to be both functional and beautiful: sleek, with no frills, where the "beauty" comes from how well it works. In their homes, Scandinavians strive for a coziness that mixes modern practicality with traditional designs— carved wood and old flower-and-vine patterns.

Despite its ultramodern, progressive outlook, Scandinavia still honors its traditions. Parents tell kids the old folk tales about

grumpy, clever trolls, and gardeners dot their yards with friendly garden gnomes. At midsummer, you'll see locals in traditional clothes dancing around a maypole to the tunes of a folk band. At winter solstice and Christmas, they enjoy Yule cakes and winter beer. Scandinavia is sailing into the high-tech future on the hardy ship of its Viking past.

SCANDINAVIA

DENMARK

DENMARK

Danmark

Denmark is by far the smallest of the Scandinavian countries, but in the 16th century, it was the largest: At one time, Denmark ruled all of Norway and the three southern provinces of Sweden. Danes are proud of their mighty history and are the first to remind you that they were a lot bigger and a lot stronger in the good old days. And yet, they're a remarkably mellow, well-adjusted lot—organized without being uptight, and easygoing with a delightfully wry sense of humor.

In the 10th century, before its heyday as a Scan-superpower, Denmark was, like Norway and Sweden, home to the Vikings. More than anything else, these fierce warriors were known for their great shipbuilding, which enabled them to travel far. Denmark's Vikings journeyed west to Great Britain and Ireland (where they founded Dublin) and brought back various influences, including Christianity.

Denmark is composed of many islands, a peninsula (Jutland) that juts up from northern Germany, Greenland, and the Faroe Islands. The two main islands are Zealand (Sjælland in Danish), where Copenhagen is located, and Funen (Fyn in Danish), where Hans Christian Andersen (or, as Danes call him, simply "H. C.") was born. Out of the hundreds of smaller islands, ship-in-bottle-cute Ærø is my favorite. The Danish landscape

is gentle compared with the dramatic fjords, mountains, and vast lakes of other Scandinavian nations. Danes (not to mention Swedes and Norwegians) like to joke about the flat Danish landscape, saying that you can stand on a case of beer and see from one end of the country to the other. Denmark's highest point in Jutland is only 560 feet above sea level, and no part of the country is more than 30 miles from the sea.

In contrast to the rest of Scandinavia, much of Denmark is

DENMARK

arable. The landscape consists of rolling hills, small thatched-roof farmhouses, beech forests, and whitewashed churches with characteristic stairstep gables. Red brick, which was a favorite material of the nation-building King Christian IV, is everywhere—especially in major civic buildings such as city halls and train stations.

Like the other Scandinavian countries, Denmark is predominantly Lutheran, but only a small minority attend church regularly. The majority are ethnic Danes, and many (but certainly not all) of them have the stereotypical blond hair and blue eyes. Two out of three Danes have last names ending in "-sen." The assimilation of ethnic groups into this homogeneous society, which began in earnest in the 1980s, is a source of some controversy. But in general, most Danes have a live-and-let-live attitude and enjoy one of the highest standards of living in the world. Taxes are high in this welfare state, but education is free and medical care highly subsidized. Generous parental leave extends to both men and women.

DENMARK

Denmark Almanac

Official Name: Kongeriget Danmark—the Kingdom of Denmark—or simply Denmark.

Population: Denmark's 5.6 million people are mainly of Scandinavian descent, with immigrants—mostly Turkish, Polish, Syrian, German, and Iraqi—making up 12 percent of the population. Greenland is home to the indigenous Inuit, and the Faroe Islands to people of Nordic heritage. Most Danes speak both Danish and English, with a small minority speaking German, Inuit, or Faroese. The population is 76 percent Protestant (mostly Evangelical Lutheran), 4 percent Muslim, and 20 percent "other."

Latitude and Longitude: 56°N and 10°E, similar latitude to northern Alberta, Canada.

Area: 16,600 square miles, roughly twice the size of Massachusetts.

Geography: Denmark includes the Jutland peninsula in northern Europe. Situated between the North Sea and the Baltic Sea, it shares a 42-mile border with Germany. In addition to Greenland and the Faroe Islands, Denmark also encompasses over 400 islands (78 of which are inhabited). Altogether Denmark has 4,544 miles of coastline. The mainland is mostly flat, and nearly two-thirds of the land is cultivated.

Biggest Cities: Denmark's capital city, Copenhagen (pop. 1.2 million), is located on the island of Zealand (Sjælland). Aarhus (on the

Denmark, one of the most environmentally conscious European countries, is a front-runner in renewable energy, recycling, and organic farming. You'll see lots of modern windmills dotting the countryside. Wind power accounts for 36 percent of Denmark's energy today, with a goal of 50 percent by 2020. By 2050, the country hopes to free itself completely from its dependence on fossil fuels. About 60 percent of waste is recycled. In grocery stores, organic products are shelved right alongside nonorganic ones—for the same price.

Denmark's Queen Margrethe II is a very popular and talented woman who, along with her royal duties, has designed coins, stamps, and book illustrations. Danes gather around the TV on New Year's Eve to hear her annual speech to the nation and flock to the Royal Palace in Copenhagen on April 16 to sing her "Happy Birthday." Her son, mainland) has 310,000, and Odense (on Funen/Fyn) has 170,000.

Economy: Denmark's modern economy is holding its own, with a gross domestic product of just over $306 billion. Denmark's top exports include pharmaceuticals, machinery, and food products. It is also one of the world's leaders in exports of wind turbine technology. The GDP per capita is about $48,000.

Currency: 6 Danish kroner (DKK) = about $1.

Government: Denmark is a constitutional monarchy. Queen Margrethe II is the head of state, but the head of government is the prime minister, a post held since June 2015 by Lars Løkke Rasmussen. The 179-member parliament (Folketinget) is elected every four years.

Flag: Red with a white cross.

The Average Dane: He or she is 42 years old, has 1.7 children, and will live to be 79. Danes get five weeks of paid vacation per year, and their most popular vacation destination is Spain. Despite the cozy lifestyle, no European nation consumes more anti-depressants per capita except Iceland.

Crown Prince Frederik, married Australian Mary Donaldson in 2004. Their son Christian's birth in 2005 was cause for a national celebration (the couple now have four children).

The Danes are proud of their royal family and of the flag, a white cross on a red background. Legend says it fell from the sky during a 13th-century battle in Estonia, making it Europe's oldest continuously used flag. You'll see it everywhere—decorating cakes, on clothing, or fluttering in the breeze atop government buildings. It's as much a decorative symbol as a patriotic one.

You'll also notice that the Danes have an odd fixation on two animals: elephants and polar bears, both of which are symbols of national (especially royal) pride. The Order of the Elephant is the highest honor that the Danish monarch can bestow on someone; if you see an emblematic elephant, you know somebody very important is involved. And the polar bear represents the Danish protectorate of Greenland—a welcome reminder to Danes that their nation is more than just Jutland and a bunch of flat little islands.

From an early age, Danes develop a passion for soccer. You may see red-and-white-clad fans singing on their way to a match. Despite the country's small size, the Danish national team does well in international competition. Other popular sports include sailing, cycling, badminton, and team handball.

The Danish language, with its three extra vowels (Æ, Ø, and Å), is notoriously difficult for foreigners to pronounce. Even seemingly predictable consonants can be tricky. For example, the letter "d" is often dropped, so the word *gade* (street)—which you'll see, hear, and say constantly—is pronounced "gah-eh." Luckily for us, most Danes also speak English and are patient with thick-tongued foreigners. Danes have playful fun teasing tourists who make the brave attempt to say Danish words. The hardest phrase, *rød grød med fløde* (a delightful red fruit porridge topped with cream), is nearly impossible for a non-Dane to pronounce. Ask a local to help you.

Sample Denmark's sweet treats at one of the many bakeries you'll see. The pastries that we call "Danish" in the US are called *wienerbrød* in Denmark. Bakeries line their display cases with several varieties of *wienerbrød* and other delectable sweets. Try *kringle, snegle,* or *Napoleonshatte,* or find your own favorite. (Chances are it will be easier to enjoy than to pronounce.)

For a selection of useful Danish survival phrases, see page 28. Two important words to know are *skål* ("cheers," a ritual always done with serious eye contact) and *hyggelig* (pronounced HEW-geh-lee), meaning warm and cozy. Danes treat their home like a sanctuary and spend a great deal of time improving their gardens and houses—inside and out. Cozying up one's personal space (a national obsession) is something the Danes do best. If you have the opportunity, have some Danes adopt you during your visit so you can enjoy their warm hospitality.

Heaven to a Dane is returning home after a walk in a beloved beech forest to enjoy open-faced sandwiches washed down with beer among good friends. Around the *hyggelig* candlelit table, there will be a spirited discussion of the issues of the day, plenty of laughter, and probably a few good-natured jokes about the Swedes or Norwegians. *Skål!*

Danish Survival Phrases

The Danes tend to say words quickly and clipped. In fact, many short vowels end in a "glottal stop"—a very brief vocal break immediately following the vowel. While I haven't tried to indicate these in the phonetics, you can listen for them in Denmark...and (try to) imitate.

Three unique Danish vowels are *æ* (sounds like the *e* in "egg"), *ø* (sounds like the German *ö*—purse your lips and say "oh"), and *å* (sounds like the *o* in "bowl"). The letter *r* is not rolled—it's pronounced farther back in the throat, almost like a *w*. A *d* at the end of a word sounds almost like our *th;* for example, *mad* (food) sounds like "math." In the phonetics, ī sounds like the long *i* sound in "light," and bolded syllables are stressed.

English	Danish	Pronunciation
Hello. (formal)	*Goddag.*	goh-**day**
Hi. / Bye. (informal)	*Hej. / Hej-hej.*	hī / hī-hī
Do you speak English?	*Taler du engelsk?*	**tay**-lehr doo **eng**-elsk
Yes. / No.	*Ja. / Nej.*	yah / nī
Please. (May I?)*	*Kan jeg?*	kahn yī
Please. (Can you?)*	*Kan du?*	kahn doo
Please. (Would you?)*	*Vil du?*	veel doo
Thank you (very much).	*(Tusind) tak.*	(**too**-sin) tack
You're welcome.	*Selv tak.*	sehl tack
Can I help (you)?	*Kan jeg hjælpe (dig)?*	kahn yī **yehl**-peh (dī)
Excuse me. (to pass)	*Undskyld mig.*	**oon**-skewl mī
Excuse me. (Can you help me?)	*Kan du hjælpe mig?*	kahn doo **yehl**-peh mī
(Very) good.	*(Meget) godt.*	(**mī**-ehl) goht
Goodbye.	*Farvel.*	fah-**vehl**
zero / one / two	*nul / en / to*	nool / een / toh
three / four	*tre / fire*	tray / feer
five / six	*fem / seks*	fehm / sehks
seven / eight	*syv / otte*	syew / **oh**-deh
nine / ten	*ni / ti*	nee / tee
hundred	*hundred*	**hoo**-nuh
thousand	*tusind*	**too**-sin
How much?	*Hvor meget?*	vor **mī**-ehl
local currency: (Danish) crown	*(Danske) kroner*	(**dahn**-skeh) **kroh**-nah
Where is...?	*Hvor er...?*	vor ehr
...the toilet	*...toilettet*	toy-**leh**-teht
men	*herrer*	**hehr**-ah
women	*damer*	**day**-ah
water / coffee	*vand / kaffe*	van / **kah**-feh
beer / wine	*øl / vin*	uhl / veen
Cheers!	*Skål!*	skohl
Can I have the bill?	*Kan jeg få regningen?*	kahn yī foh **rī**-ning-ehn

*Because Danish has no single word for "please," they approximate that sentiment by asking "May I?", "Can you?", or "Would you?", depending on the context.

COPENHAGEN

København

Copenhagen, Denmark's capital, is the gateway to Scandinavia. It's an improbable combination of corny Danish clichés, well-dressed executives having a business lunch amid cutting-edge contemporary architecture, and some of the funkiest counterculture in Europe. And yet, it all just works so tidily together. With the Øresund Bridge connecting Sweden and Denmark (creating the region's largest metropolitan area), Copenhagen is energized and ready to dethrone Stockholm as Scandinavia's powerhouse city.

A busy day cruising the canals, wandering through the palace, and taking an old-town walk will give you your historical bearings.

Then, after another day strolling the Strøget (STROY-et, Europe's first and greatest pedestrian shopping mall), biking the canals, and sampling the Danish good life (including a gooey "Danish" pastry), you'll feel right at home. Live it up in Scandinavia's cheapest and most fun-loving capital.

PLANNING YOUR TIME

A first visit deserves a minimum of two days. Note that many sights are closed on Monday year-round or in the off-season.

Budget Itinerary Tip: Kamikaze sightseers on tight budgets see Copenhagen as a useful Scandinavian bottleneck. They sleep heading into town by train, tour the city during the day, and sleep on a boat or train as they travel north to their next destination. At the end of their Scandinavian travels, they do the same thing in reverse. The result is two days and no nights in Copenhagen (you can check your bag and take a shower at the train station). Considering the joy of Oslo and Stockholm, this isn't all that crazy if you have limited time (and can sleep on a moving train or boat). Consider taking a night train to Sweden with connections to Stockholm, or cruise up to Oslo on a night boat.

Day 1
Catch a 9:30 city walking tour with Richard Karpen (Mon-Sat mid-May–mid-Sept). After lunch, catch the relaxing canal-boat tour out to *The Little Mermaid* and back. Enjoy the rest of the afternoon tracing Denmark's cultural roots in the National Museum and visiting the Ny Carlsberg Glyptotek art gallery (Impressionists and Danish artists). Spend the evening following my "Copenhagen City Walk" and strolling with Copenhageners at the same time.

Day 2
At 10:00, go Neoclassical at Thorvaldsen's Museum, and tour the royal reception rooms at the adjacent Christiansborg Palace. After a *smørrebrød* lunch, spend the afternoon seeing Rosenborg Castle, with Denmark's crown jewels. Spend the evening at Tivoli Gardens.

Christiania—the hippie squatters' community—is not for everyone. But it's worth considering if you're intrigued by alternative lifestyles, or simply want a break from museums. During a busy trip, Christiania fits best in the evening.

Orientation to Copenhagen

Copenhagen is huge (with 1.2 million people), but for most visitors, the walkable core is the diagonal axis formed by the train station, Tivoli Gardens, Rådhuspladsen (City Hall Square), and the Strøget pedestrian street, ending at the colorful old Nyhavn sailors' harbor. Bubbling with street life, colorful pedestrian zones, and most of the city's sightseeing, the Strøget is fun. But also be sure to get off the main drag and explore. By doing things by bike or on foot, you'll stumble upon some charming bits of Copenhagen that many travelers miss. The city feels pretty torn up, as they are deep into a multiyear Metro expansion project, which will add 17 stations to their already impressive system.

Outside of the old city center are three areas of interest to tourists:

• To the north are Rosenborg Castle and Amalienborg Palace, with *The Little Mermaid* nearby.

• To the east, across the harbor, are Christianshavn (Copen-

The Story of Copenhagen

If you study your map carefully, you can read the history of Copenhagen in today's street plan. København ("Merchants' Harbor") was born on the little island of Slotsholmen—today

home to Christiansborg Palace—in 1167. What was Copenhagen's medieval moat is now a string of pleasant lakes and parks, including Tivoli Gardens. You can still make out some of the zigzag pattern of the moats and ramparts in the city's greenbelt.

Many of these fortifications—and several other landmarks—were built by Denmark's most memorable king. You need to remember only one character in Copenhagen's history: Christian IV. Ruling from 1588 to 1648, he was Denmark's Renaissance king and a royal party animal (see the "King Christian IV" sidebar, later). The personal energy of this "Builder King" sparked a Golden Age when Copenhagen prospered and many of the city's grandest buildings were erected. In the 17th century, Christian IV extended the city fortifications to the north, doubling the size of the city, while adding a grid plan of streets and his Rosenborg Castle. This "new town" was the district around the Amalienborg Palace.

In 1850, Copenhagen's 140,000 residents all lived within this defensive system. Building in the no-man's-land outside the walls was only allowed with the understanding that in the event of an attack, you'd burn your dwellings to clear the way for a good defense.

Most of the city's historic buildings still in existence were built within the medieval walls, but conditions became too crowded, and outbreaks of disease forced Copenhagen to spread outside the walls. Ultimately those walls were torn down and replaced with "rampart streets" that define today's city center: Vestervoldgade (literally, "West Rampart Street"), Nørrevoldgade ("North"), and Østervoldgade ("East"). The fourth side is the harbor and the island of Slotsholmen, where København was born.

hagen's "Little Amsterdam" district) and the alternative enclave of Christiania.

• To the west (behind the train station) is Vesterbro, a young and trendy part of town with lots of cafés, bars, and boutiques; the hip Meatpacking District (Kødbyen); and the Carlsberg Brewery (plus the picnic-friendly Frederiksberg Park).

Most of these sights are walkable from the Strøget, but taking a bike, bus, or taxi is more efficient. I rent a bike for my entire

COPENHAGEN

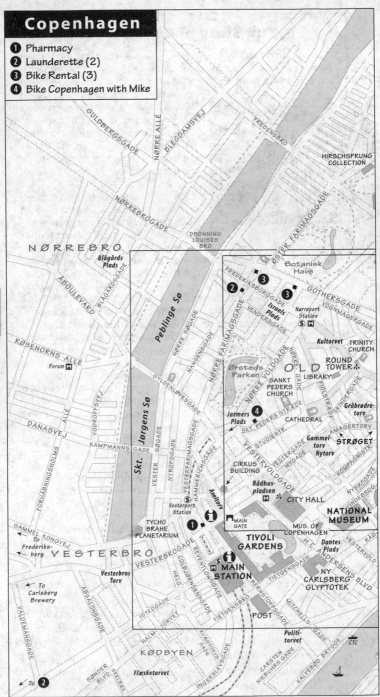

Copenhagen

1. Pharmacy
2. Launderette (2)
3. Bike Rental (3)
4. Bike Copenhagen with Mike

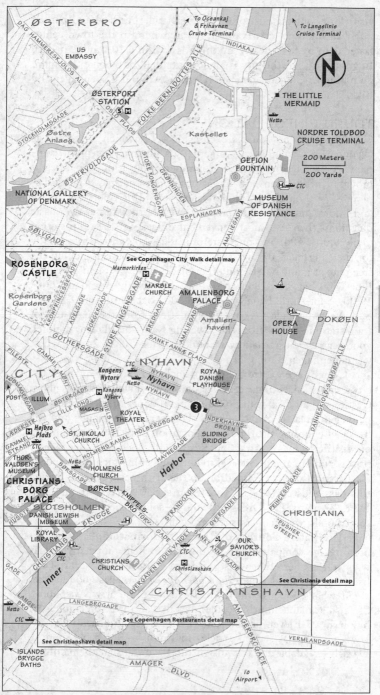

COPENHAGEN

visit (for about the cost of a single cab ride per day) and park it safely in my hotel courtyard. I get anywhere in the town center faster than by taxi (nearly anything is within a 10-minute pedal). In good weather, the city is an absolute delight by bike (for more on biking in Copenhagen, see "Getting Around Copenhagen: By Bike," later).

TOURIST INFORMATION

Copenhagen's questionable excuse for a TI, which bills itself as "Wonderful Copenhagen," is actually a blatantly for-profit company. As in a (sadly) increasing number of big European cities, it provides information only about businesses that pay a hefty display fee of thousands of dollars each year. This colors the advice and information the office provides. While they can answer basic questions, their two most convenient offices—at the train station (daily 9:00-17:00) and on Vesterbrogade—are worthwhile mostly for their big racks of advertising brochures—you can pick up the free map at many hotels and other places in town (main TI: May-June Mon-Sat 9:00-18:00, Sun until 14:00; July-Aug daily 9:00-19:00; Sept-April Mon-Fri 9:00-17:00, Sat until 16:00, closed Sun, Vesterbrogade 4A, just up the street from the main exit of train station—across from the towering Radisson Blu Royal Hotel, good Lagkagehuset bakery in building; tel. 70 22 24 42, www.visitcopenhagen.com).

Copenhagen Card: This card includes entry to many of the city's sights (including expensive ones, like Tivoli and Rosenborg Castle) and all local transportation in all zones of the greater Copenhagen area. It can save busy sightseers some money and the hassle of choosing the right transportation pass. If you're planning on visiting a lot of attractions (especially ones with steep entry prices) and are going to travel to outlying sights such as Kronborg Castle and Roskilde Cathedral, do the arithmetic to see if buying this pass adds up (389 DKK/24 hours, 550 DKK/48 hours, 660 DKK/72 hours, 890 DKK/120 hours—sold at the TI, online, and some hotels; www.copenhagencard.com).

Alternative Sources of Tourist Information: As the TI's bottom line competes with its mission to help tourists, you may want to seek out other ways to inform yourself. The weekly English-language newspaper, *The Copenhagen Post,* has good articles about what's going on in town. Read it online at www.cphpost.dk (also available in print, sometimes free at TI or some hotels, or buy it at a 7-Eleven or newsstand). The witty alternative website, www.aok.dk, has several articles in English (and many more in Danish—readable and very insightful if you translate them online).

ARRIVAL IN COPENHAGEN
By Train

The main train station is called Hovedbanegården (HOETH-bahn-gorn; look for *København H* on signs and schedules). It's a temple of travel and a hive of travel-related activity (and 24-hour thievery). Kiosks and fast-food eateries cluster in the middle of the main arrivals hall. From the main entrance, the **ticket office** is at the back of the station (Mon-Fri 7:00-20:00; Sat-Sun 8:00-18:00). If you need to make reservations for an upcoming high-speed train trip (required even of rail-pass holders), you could do it here.

Within the station, you'll find **baggage storage** (go down stairs at back of station marked *Bagagebokse;* lockers and check-room/*garderobe* both open long hours daily); pay **WCs** (right side of station; a branch of the recommended **Lagkagehuset** bakery (front of station); and lots more. At both the front and the back of the station, you'll find **ATMs.**

The tracks at the back of the station (tracks 9-10 and 11-12) are for the suburban train (S-tog).

Getting into Town: If you want to get right to sightseeing, you're within easy walking distance of downtown. Just walk out the front door and you'll run into one of the entrances for Tivoli amusement park; if you go around its left side and up a couple of blocks, you'll be at Rådhuspladsen, where my "Copenhagen City Walk" begins.

Hotels are scattered far and wide around town. It's best to get arrival instructions from your hotelier, but if you're on your own, here are some tips:

To reach hotels **behind the station,** slip out the back door—just go down the stairs at the back of the station marked *Reventlowsgade.*

For hotels **near Nørreport** (Ibsens and Jørgensen), ride the S-tog from the station two stops to Nørreport, within about a 10-minute walk of the hotels. Bus #14 also runs from near the train station to Nørreport.

For hotels **near Nyhavn** (71 Nyhavn and Bethel Sømandshjem), you can take the S-tog to Nørreport, then transfer to the Metro one stop to Kongens Nytorv, within a few minutes' walk of Nyhavn. Or you can take bus #66 to Nyhavn (or #26 from around the corner to Kongens Nytorv).

Note: If you're staying near Nørreport (or near Nyhavn, an easy Metro connection from Nørreport), check the train schedule carefully; many local trains (such as some from Roskilde and those from the airport) continue through the main train station to Nørreport Station, saving you an extra step.

By Plane
Copenhagen Airport (Kastrup)

Copenhagen's international airport is a traveler's dream, with a TI, baggage check, bank, ATMs, post office, shopping mall, grocery store, bakery, and more (airport code: CPH, airport tel. 32 31 32 31, www.cph.dk). The three check-in terminals are within walking distance of each other (departures screens tell you which terminal to go to). On arrival, all flights feed into one big lobby in Terminal 3. When you pop out here, a TI kiosk is on your left, taxis are out the door on your right, trains are straight ahead, and shops and eateries fill the atrium above you. You can use dollars or euros at the airport, but you'll get change back in kroner.

Getting Between the Airport and Downtown: Your options include the Metro, trains, and taxis. There are also buses into town, but the train/Metro is generally better.

The **Metro** runs directly from the airport to Christianshavn, Kongens Nytorv (near Nyhavn), and Nørreport, making it the best choice for getting into town if you're staying in any of these areas (36-DKK three-zone ticket, yellow M2 line, direction: Vanløse, 4-10/hour, 11 minutes to Christianshavn). The Metro station is located at the end of Terminal 3 and is covered by the roof of the terminal.

Convenient **trains** also connect the airport with downtown (36-DKK three-zone ticket, covered by rail pass, 4/hour, 12 minutes). Buy your ticket from the ground-level ticket booth (look for *DSB: Tickets for Train, Metro & Bus* signs) before riding the escalator down to the tracks. Track 2 has trains going into the city (track 1 is for trains going east, to Sweden). Trains into town stop at the main train station (signed *København H;* handy if you're sleeping at my recommended hotels behind the train station), as well as the Nørreport and Østerport stations. At Nørreport, you can connect to the Metro for Kongens Nytorv (near Nyhavn) and Christianshavn.

With the train/Metro trip being so quick, frequent, and cheap, I see no reason to take a taxi. But if you do, **taxis** are fast, civil, accept credit cards, and charge about 300 DKK for a ride to the town center.

By Boat or Cruise Ship

For information on Copenhagen's cruise terminals, see the end of this chapter.

HELPFUL HINTS

Pharmacy: Steno Apotek is across from the train station (open 24 hours, Vesterbrogade 6C, tel. 33 14 82 66, see the Copenhagen map, earlier, for location).

Blue Monday: As you plan, remember that most sights close on Monday, but these attractions remain open: Amalienborg Museum, Christiansborg Palace (closed Mon Oct-April), City Hall, Rosenborg Castle (generally closed Mon Jan-April and Nov-Dec), Round Tower, Royal Library, Our Savior's Church, Tivoli Gardens (generally closed late Sept-late March), both Harbor Baths (closed Oct-May), and various tours (canal, bus, walking, and bike). You can explore Christiania, but Monday is its rest day so it's unusually quiet and some restaurants are closed.

Laundry: Møntvask is a good coin-op laundry near Nørreport (daily 6:00-21:00, 50 yards from Ibsens Hotel at 86 Nansensgade). Another **Møntvask** is several blocks west of my train-station-area hotel listings (daily 7:00-21:00, Flensborggade 20). For both locations, see the Copenhagen map, earlier. *Vaskel* is wash, *tørring* is dry, and *sæbe* is soap.

Ferries: While in Copenhagen, book any ferries that you plan to take in Scandinavia. Visit a travel agent or book directly with the ferry company. For the Copenhagen-Oslo overnight ferry, contact **DFDS** or visit the **DSB Rejsebureau** at the main train station (see page 114 for details). For boats between Stockholm and Helsinki, see page 623. For the boat from Helsinki to St. Petersburg, see page 628.

Jazz Festival: The Copenhagen Jazz Festival—10 days in early July—puts the town in a rollicking slide-trombone mood. The Danes are Europe's jazz enthusiasts, and this music festival fills the town with happiness. The TI prints up an extensive listing of each year's festival events, or get the latest at www.jazz.dk. There's also a winter jazz festival in February.

GETTING AROUND COPENHAGEN
By Public Transit

It's easy to navigate Copenhagen, with its fine buses, Metro, and S-tog (a suburban train system with stops in the city). Be sure to pick up the *Bus, Train & Metro Guide* map at the TI for an overview of all your public transportation options. For a helpful website that covers public transport (nationwide) in English, consult www.rejseplanen.dk.

Tickets: The same tickets are used throughout the system. A 24-DKK, **two-zone ticket** gets you an hour's travel within the center—pay as you board buses, or buy from station ticket offices, convenience stores, or vending machines for the Metro. (Ticket machines should accept American credit cards with a chip, and most machines also take Danish cash; if the machine won't take your credit card, find a cashier.) Assume you'll be within the middle two zones unless traveling to or from the airport, which requires a **three-zone ticket** (36 DKK).

If you plan to ride transit in Copenhagen and to the outlying sights in one day, consider a **"24-hour ticket"** that covers all travel zones for 130 DKK.

If you're traveling exclusively in central Copenhagen, the **City Pass** is a good value (80 DKK/24 hours, 200 DKK/72 hours, covers travel within zones 1-4, including the airport). You can buy a pass at some train and Metro stations or use www.dinoffentligetransport. dk; it will be sent as a text message to your mobile phone. To travel throughout the greater Copenhagen region—including side-trips to Roskilde, Frederiksborg Castle, Louisiana Art Museum, and Kronborg Castle—you'll need to pay more (buy supplementary tickets at ticket machines or station ticket office).

For some visitors, the **Copenhagen Card** will be the best choice for its sheer convenience. It covers all public transportation in the greater Copenhagen area (including to Roskilde, Frederiksborg Castle, Louisiana Art Museum, etc.), canal boat tours, and admission to nearly all the major sights (see "Tourist Information," earlier).

Buses: While the train system is slick (Metro and S-tog, described later), its usefulness is limited for the typical tourist—but buses serve all of the major sights in town every five to eight minutes during daytime hours. If you're not riding a bike everywhere, get comfortable with the buses. Bus drivers are patient, have change, and speak English. City maps list bus routes. Locals are usually friendly and helpful. There's also a floating "Harbor Bus" (described on page 40).

Bus lines that end with "A" (such as #1A) use quiet, eco-friendly, electric buses that are smaller than normal buses, allowing access into the narrower streets of the Old Town. Designed for tourists, these provide an easy overview to the city center. Among these, the following are particularly useful:

Bus **#1A** loops from the train station up to Kongens Nytorv (near Nyhavn) and then farther north, to Østerport.

Bus **#2A** goes from Christianshavn to the city center, then onward to points west.

Bus **#6A** connects the station to Nørreport, but you'll need to catch it up around the corner on Vesterbrogade.

Other, non-"A" buses, which are bigger and tend to be more direct, can be faster for some trips:

Bus **#5C** connects the station more or less directly to Nørreport.

Bus **#14** runs from Nørreport (and near my recommended hotels) down to the city center, stopping near the Strøget, and eventually going near the main train station.

Bus **#26** runs a handy route right through the main tourist zone: train station/Tivoli to Slotsholmen Island to Kongens Nytorv (near Nyhavn) to the Amalienborg Palace/*Little Mermaid* area. It continues even farther north to one of the city's main cruise ports, but the line splits, so check with the driver to make sure you're on the right bus.

Bus **#66** goes from Nyhavn to Slotsholmen Island to Tivoli.

Metro: Copenhagen's Metro line, while simple, is super-futuristic and growing. For most tourists' purposes, only the airport and three consecutive stops within the city matter: Nørreport (connected every few minutes by the S-tog to the main train station), Kongens Nytorv (near Nyhavn and the Strøget's north end), and Christianshavn. Nearly all recommended hotels are within walking distance of the main train station or these three stops.

The city is hard at work on its Cityringen (City Circle) Metro line, which will intersect with its two existing lines. Eventually, the Metro will become far handier for tourists—linking the train station, Rådhuspladsen, Gammel Strand (near Slotsholmen Island), and Kongens Nytorv (near Nyhavn).

In the meantime, expect to see massive construction zones at each of those locations. For the latest on the Metro and route maps, see www.m.dk.

S-tog Train: The S-tog is basically a commuter line that links stations on the main train line through Copenhagen; for those visiting the city, the most important stops are the main train station and Nørreport (where it ties into the Metro system). Note that while rail passes are valid on the S-tog, it's probably not worth using a travel day. The S-tog is very handy for reaching many of the outlying sights described in the Near Copenhagen chapter.

By Boat

The hop-on, hop-off "Harbor Bus" (Havnebus) boat stops at the "Black Diamond" library, Christianshavn (near Knippels Bridge), Nyhavn, the Opera House, and the Nordre Toldbod cruise-ship pier, which is a short walk from *The Little Mermaid* site. The boat is part of the city bus system (lines #991 and #992) and covered by the tickets described earlier. Taking a long ride on this boat, from the library to the end of the line, is the "poor man's cruise"— without commentary, of course (runs 6:00-19:00). Or, for a true sightseeing trip, consider a guided harbor cruise (described later, under "Tours in Copenhagen").

By Taxi

Taxis are plentiful, easy to call or flag down, and pricey (35-DKK pickup charge and then about 15 DKK/kilometer—higher in evenings and on weekends). For a short ride, four people spend about the same by taxi as by bus. Calling 35 35 35 35 will get you a taxi within minutes...with the meter already well on its way.

By Bike

Cyclists see more, save time and money, and really feel like locals. With a bike, you have Copenhagen at your command. I'd rather have a bike than a car and driver at my disposal. Virtually every street has a dedicated bike lane (complete with bike signal lights). Warning: Police routinely issue hefty tickets to anyone riding on sidewalks or through pedestrian zones. Note also that bikes can't be parked just anywhere. Observe others and park your bike among other bikes. The simple built-in lock that binds the back tire is adequate.

Renting a Bike: Your best bet for renting a bike is often your hotelier: Many rent (or loan) decent bikes at fair rates to guests.

For an (often) better-quality bike and advice from someone with cycle expertise, consider one of these rental outfits in or near the city center (see the Copenhagen map, earlier, for locations).

Københavens Cyklebørs, near Nørreport Station, has a good selection of three-gear bikes (90 DKK/1 day, 170 DKK/2 days, 240 DKK/3 days, 450 DKK/week; Mon-Fri 10:00-17:30, Sat-Sun until 14:00, closed all day Sun in off-season; Gothersgade 157, tel. 33 14 07 17, www.cykelborsen.dk).

Cykelbasen, even closer to Nørreport, rents three- and seven-gear bikes (90 DKK/day, 450 DKK/week, includes lock; Mon-Fri 9:00-17:30, Sat until 14:30, closed Sun; Gothersgade 137, tel. 35 12 06 00, www.cykel-basen.dk, select "Info").

Copenhagen Bicycles, at the entrance to Nyhavn by the Inderhavnsbroen pedestrian/bicycle bridge, rents basic three-gear bikes (90 DKK/3 hours, 110 DKK/6 hours, 120 DKK/24 hours, includes lock, helmet-40 DKK, daily 8:30-17:30, Nyhavn 44, tel. 35 43 01 22, www.copenhagenbicycles.dk). They also offer guided tours in English and Danish (100 DKK, not including bicycle, April-Sept daily at 11:00, 2.5 hours).

Using City Bikes: The city's public bike-rental program **Bycyklen** lets you ride white, three-gear "smart bikes" (with GPS

and an electric motor) for 30 DKK/hour. You'll find them parked in racks near the train station, on either side of City Hall, and at many locations around town. Use the touchscreen on the handlebars to create an account. At their website (http://bycyklen.dk), you can locate docking stations, reserve a bike at a specific station, and create an account in advance. I'd use these bikes for a short hop here or there, but for more than a couple of hours, it's more cost-efficient to rent a regular bicycle.

Tours in Copenhagen

ON FOOT

Copenhagen is an ideal city to get to know by foot. You have several good options:

▲▲Hans Christian Andersen Tours by Richard Karpen

Once upon a time, American Richard Karpen visited Copenhagen and fell in love with the city. Now, dressed as writer Hans Christian

Andersen in a 19th-century top hat and long coat, he leads 1.5-hour tours that wander in and out of buildings, courtyards, back streets, and unusual parts of the old town. Along the one-mile route, he gives insightful and humorous background on the history, culture, and contemporary life of Denmark, Copenhagen, and the Danes—their core values, gender and economic equality, treatment of the elderly and children, health care, Vikings, royal family—along with the life and work of H. C. Andersen (140 DKK, kids under 12 free; departs from outside the TI, up the street from the main train station at Vesterbrogade 4A; mid-May-mid-Sept Mon-Sat at 9:30, none on Sun; Richard departs promptly—if you miss him try to catch up with the tour at the next stop at Rådhuspladsen).

Richard also gives excellent one-hour tours of **Rosenborg Castle** while in the role of Hans Christian Andersen (100 DKK, doesn't include castle entry, mid-May-mid-Sept Mon and Thu at 12:00, meet outside castle ticket office). No reservations are needed for any of Richard's scheduled tours—just show up.

You can also hire Richard for 1.5-hour private tours of the city or of Rosenborg Castle (price depends on number of participants, May-Sept, mobile 91 61 95 02, www.copenhagenwalks. com, copenhagenwalks@yahoo.com).

▲Daily City Walks by Red Badge Guides

Five local female guides work together, giving two-hour English-language city tours. Their walks mix the city's highlights, back lanes, history, art, and contemporary social issues, and finish at Amalienborg Palace around noon for the changing of the guard (100 DKK, daily mid-April-Sept at 10:00, departs from TI at Vesterbrogade 4A, just show up, pay direct, small groups, tel. 20 92 23 87, www.redbadgeguides.dk, redbadgeguides@gmail.com). They also offer private guided tours year-round upon request.

▲▲Copenhagen History Tours

Christian Donatzky, a charming Dane with a master's degree in history, runs a walking tour on Saturday mornings. In April and May, the theme is "Old Copenhagen" (covering the period from 1100-1600); in June and July, "King's Copenhagen" (1600-1800); and in August and September, "Hans Christian Andersen's Copenhagen" (1800-present). Those with a serious interest in Danish history will find these tours time well spent (90 DKK, Sat at 10:00, approximately 1.5 hours, small groups of 5-15 people, tours depart from statue of Bishop Absalon on Højbro Plads between the Strøget and Christiansborg Palace, English only, no reservations necessary—just show up, tel. 28 49 44 35, www.historytours.dk, info@historytours.dk).

BY BOAT

For many, the best way to experience the city's canals and harbor is by canal boat. Two companies offer essentially the same live, three-language, one-hour cruises. Both boats leave at least twice an hour from Nyhavn and Christiansborg Palace, cruise around the palace and Christianshavn area, and then proceed into the wide-open harbor. Best on a sunny day, it's a relaxing way to see *The Little Mermaid* and munch on a lazy picnic during the slow-moving narration.

▲Netto-Bådene

These inexpensive cruises cost about half the price of their rival, Canal Tours Copenhagen. Go with Netto; there's no reason to pay nearly double (40 DKK, mid-March-mid-Oct daily 10:00-17:00, runs later in summer, shorter hours in winter, sign at dock shows next departure, generally every 30 minutes, dress warmly—boats are open-top until Sept, tel. 32 54 41 02, www. havnerundfart.dk). Netto boats often make two stops where passengers can get off, then hop back on a later boat—at the bridge near *The Little Mermaid,* and at the Langebro bridge near Danhostel. Not every boat makes these stops; check the clock on the bridges for the next departure time.

Don't confuse the cheaper Netto and pricier Canal Tours Copenhagen boats: At Nyhavn, the Netto dock is midway down the canal (on the city side), while the Canal Tours Copenhagen dock is at the head of the canal. Near Christiansborg Palace, the Netto boats leave from Holmen's Bridge in front of the palace, while Canal Tours Copenhagen boats depart from Gammel Strand, 200 yards away. Boats leaving from Christiansborg are generally less crowded than those leaving from Nyhavn.

Canal Tours Copenhagen

This more expensive option does the same cruise as Netto for 75 DKK (daily March-late Oct 9:30-18:00, runs later in summer, shorter hours in winter, no tours Jan-Feb, boats are sometimes covered if it's raining, tel. 32 96 30 00, www.stromma.dk).

Canal Tours Copenhagen also runs audioguided hop-on, hop-off boat tours (99 DKK/48 hours, daily late May-mid-Sept 9:30-19:00), 1.5-hour evening **jazz cruises** (see "Nightlife in Copenhagen," page 94), and other theme cruises.

BY BUS
Hop-On, Hop-Off Bus Tours

Several buses with recorded narration circle the city for a basic 1.25- to 1.5-hour orientation, allowing you to get on and off as you like at the following stops: Tivoli Gardens, Gammel Strand near Christiansborg Palace, *The Little Mermaid*, Rosenborg Castle, Nyhavn sailors' quarter, and more. Cruise passengers arriving at

Hans Christian Andersen (1805-1875)

The author of such classic fairy tales as *The Ugly Duckling* was an ugly duckling himself—a misfit who blossomed. Hans Christian Andersen (called H. C., pronounced "hoe see" by the Danes) was born to a poor shoemaker in Odense. As a child he was gangly, high-strung, and effeminate. He avoided school because the kids laughed at him, so he spent his time in a fantasy world of books and plays. When his father died, the 11-year-old was on his own, forced into manual labor. He loved playing with a marionette theater that his father had made for him, sparking a lifelong love affair with the theater. In 1819, at the age of 14, he moved to Copenhagen to pursue an acting career and worked as a boy soprano for the

Royal Theater. When his voice changed, the director encouraged him to return to school. He dutifully attended—a teenager among boys—and eventually went on to the university. As rejections piled up for his acting aspirations, Andersen began to shift his theatrical ambitions to playwriting.

After graduation, Andersen won a two-year scholarship to travel around Europe, the first of many trips he'd make and write about. His experiences abroad were highly formative, providing inspiration for many of his tales. Still in his 20s, he published an obviously autobiographical novel, *The Improvisatore,* about a poor young man who comes into his own while traveling in Italy. The novel launched his writing career, and soon he was hobnobbing with the international crowd—Charles Dickens, Victor Hugo, Franz Liszt, Richard Wagner, Henrik Ibsen, and Edvard Grieg.

the Langelinie Pier can catch a hop-on, hop-off bus there; those arriving at the Oceankaj Pier can take a free shuttle provided by the hop-on, hop-off tour companies (or their own cruise shuttle) to *The Little Mermaid,* where they can pick up a hop-on, hop-off bus.

The same company runs **City Sightseeing**'s red buses and Strömma's green **Hop-On, Hop-Off** buses. Both offer a Mermaid route: City Sightseeing tickets, 195 DKK, are valid 72 hours, and Hop-On, Hop-Off tickets, 175 DKK, are good for 48 hours; other routes include the Carlsberg Brewery and Christiania area (pay driver, 2/hour, May-mid-Sept daily 9:30-18:00, shorter hours off-season, buses depart near the TI in front of the Radisson Blu Royal Hotel and at many other stops throughout city, www.city-sightseeing.dk or www.stromma.dk). Strömma's Hop-On, Hop-

Despite his many famous friends, Andersen remained a lonely soul who never married. He had very close male friendships and journaled about unrequited love affairs with several women, including the famous opera star of the day, Jenny Lind, the "Swedish Nightingale." Without a family of his own, he became very close with the children of his friends—and, through his fairy tales, with a vast extended family of kids around the world.

Though he wrote novels, plays, and travel literature, it was his fairy tales, including *The Ugly Duckling, The Emperor's New Clothes, The Princess and the Pea, The Little Mermaid, The Snow Queen,* and *The Red Shoes,* that made him famous in Denmark and abroad. They made him Denmark's best-known author, the "Danish Charles Dickens." Some stories are based on earlier folk tales, and others came straight from his inventive mind, all written in an informal, conversational style that was considered unusual and even surprising at the time.

Andersen's compelling tales appeal to children and adults alike. They're full of magic and touch on strong, universal emotions—the pain of being different, the joy of self-discovery, and the struggle to fit in. The ugly duckling, for example, is teased by his fellow ducks before he finally discovers his true identity as a beautiful swan. In *The Emperor's New Clothes,* a boy is derided by everyone for speaking the simple, self-evident truth that the emperor is fooling himself. J. K. Rowling said, "The indelible characters he created are so deeply implanted in our subconscious that we sometimes forget that we were not born with the stories." (For more on Andersen's famous story *The Little Mermaid*—and what it might tell us about his life—see page 61.)

By the time of his death, the poor shoemaker's son was wealthy, cultured, and had been knighted. His rise through traditional class barriers mirrors the social progress of the 19th century.

Off also offers a 245-DKK ticket that includes all tour routes and a cruise on their hop-on, hop-off canal boat.

Another operation—called **Red Buses**—does a similar Mermaid route (every 30-40 minutes, shorter hours off-season; 210 DKK/24 hours, www.redbuses.com).

BY BIKE
▲Bike Copenhagen with Mike
Mike Sommerville offers three-hour guided bike tours of the city. A Copenhagen native, Mike enjoys showing off his city to visitors, offering both historic background and contemporary cultural insights along the way (April-Sept daily at 10:00, second departure Fri-Sat at 14:30, must book all tours in advance; 300 DKK includes

bike rental, price same with or without a bike, 50-DKK discount with this book—maximum 2 discounts per book and must have book with you, cash only; participants must have good urban biking skills). All tours are in English and depart from his bike shop at Sankt Peders Straede 47, in the Latin Quarter (see the Copenhagen map in the Orientation section, earlier, for location). Mike also offers evening tours (19:00, 2.5 hours) and private tours; details at www.bikecopenhagenwithmike.dk.

Copenhagen City Walk

This self-guided walk takes about two hours. It starts at Rådhuspladsen (City Hall Square) and heads along the pedestrian street, the Strøget, through the old city, onto "Castle Island" (home of Christiansborg Palace), along the harbor promenade, and through Nyhavn, the sailors' quarter with the city's iconic canalfront houses. The walk officially ends at Kongens Nytorv ("King's New Square"), though you can continue another 10 minutes to Amalienborg Palace and then another 15 minutes beyond that to *The Little Mermaid*.

❶ Rådhuspladsen

Start from Rådhuspladsen, the bustling heart of Copenhagen, dominated by the tower of the City Hall. Today this square always

seems to be hosting some lively community event, but it was once Copenhagen's fortified west end. For 700 years, Copenhagen was contained within its city walls. By the mid-1800s, 140,000 people were packed inside. The overcrowding led to hygiene problems. (A cholera outbreak killed 5,000.) It was clear: The walls needed to come down...and they did. Those formidable town walls survive today only in echoes—a circular series of roads and the remnants of moats, which are now people-friendly city lakes (see the sidebar on page 31).

• *Stand 50 yards in front of City Hall and turn clockwise for a...*

Rådhuspladsen Spin-Tour: The **City Hall,** or Rådhus, is worth a visit (described on page 64). Old **Hans Christian Andersen** sits to the right of City Hall, almost begging to be in another photo (as he used to in real life). Climb onto his well-worn knee. (While up there, you might take off your shirt for a racy photo, as many Danes enjoy doing.)

He's looking at ❷ **Tivoli Gardens** (across the street), which he loved and which inspired him when writing some of his stories. Tivoli Gardens was founded in 1843, when magazine publisher

Georg Carstensen convinced the king to let him build a pleasure garden outside the walls of crowded Copenhagen. The king quickly agreed, knowing that happy people care less about fighting for democracy. Tivoli became Europe's first great public amusement park. When the train lines came, the station was placed just beyond Tivoli.

The big, glassy building with the *DI* sign is filled with the offices of Danish Industry—a collection of Danish companies whose logos you can see in the windows (plus the Irma grocery store at street level).

The big, broad boulevard is **Vesterbrogade** ("Western Way"), which led to the western gate of the medieval city (behind you, where the pedestrian boulevard begins). Here, in the traffic hub of this huge city, you'll notice...not many cars. Denmark's 180 percent tax on car purchases makes the bus, Metro, or bike a sweeter option. In fact, the construction messing up this square is part of a huge expansion of the Metro system.

Down Vesterbrogade towers the **Radisson Blu Royal Hotel,** Copenhagen's only skyscraper. Locals say it seems so tall because the clouds hang so low. When it was built in 1960, Copenhageners took one look and decided—that's enough of a skyline. Notice there are no other buildings taller than the five-story limit in the old center.

The golden ❸ **weather girls** (on the corner, high above Vesterbrogade) indicate the weather: on a bike (fair weather) or with an umbrella (foul). These two have been called the only women in Copenhagen you can trust, but for years they've been stuck in the almost-sunny mode...with the bike just peeking out. Notice that the red temperature dots max out at 28° Celsius (that's 82° Fahrenheit...a good memory aid: transpose 28 to get 82).

To the right, just down the street, is the Tiger Store (a popular local "dollar store"...nearly everything is super affordable). The next street (once the local Fleet Street, with the big newspapers) still has the offices for *Politiken* (the leading Danish newspaper) and the best bookstore in town, Boghallen.

As you spin farther right, three fast-food joints stand at the entry to the Strøget (STROY-et), Copenhagen's grand pedestrian boulevard—where we're heading next. Just beyond that and the Art Deco-style Palace Hotel (with a tower to serve as a sister to the City Hall) is the *Lur Blowers* **sculpture,** which honors the earliest warrior Danes. The *lur* is a curvy, trombone-sounding horn that was used to call soldiers to battle or to accompany pagan religious processions. The earliest bronze *lurs* date

Copenhagen City Walk

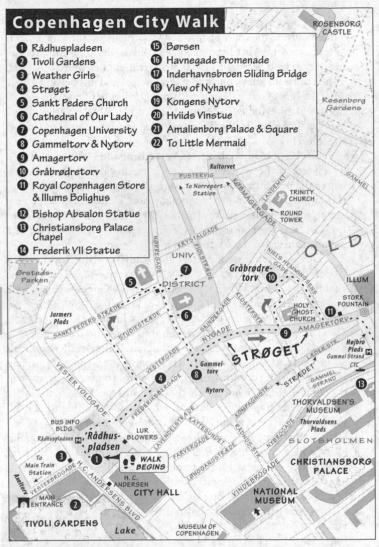

1. Rådhuspladsen
2. Tivoli Gardens
3. Weather Girls
4. Strøget
5. Sankt Peders Church
6. Cathedral of Our Lady
7. Copenhagen University
8. Gammeltorv & Nytorv
9. Amagertorv
10. Gråbrødretorv
11. Royal Copenhagen Store & Illums Bolighus
12. Bishop Absalon Statue
13. Christiansborg Palace Chapel
14. Frederik VII Statue
15. Børsen
16. Havnegade Promenade
17. Inderhavnsbroen Sliding Bridge
18. View of Nyhavn
19. Kongens Nytorv
20. Hviids Vinstue
21. Amalienborg Palace & Square
22. To Little Mermaid

as far back as 3,500 years ago. Later, the Vikings used a wood version of the *lur.* The ancient originals, which still play, are displayed in the National Museum.

• *Now head down the pedestrian boulevard (pickpocket alert).*

❹ The Strøget

The American trio of Burger King, 7-Eleven, and KFC marks the start of this otherwise charming pedestrian street. Finished in 1962, Copenhagen's experimental, tremendously successful, and much-copied pedestrian shopping mall is a string of lively (and

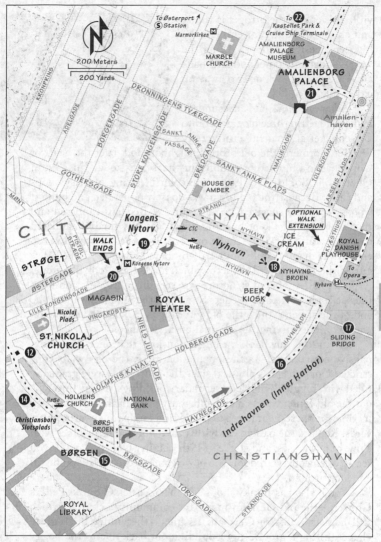

individually named) streets and lovely squares that bunny-hop through the old town from City Hall to the Nyhavn quarter, a 20-minute stroll away. Though the Strøget has become hamburgerized, historic bits and attractive pieces of old Copenhagen are just off this commercial can-can.

As you wander down this street, remember that the commercial focus of a historic street like the Strøget drives up the land value, which generally trashes the charm and tears down the old buildings. Look above the modern window displays and street-level advertising to discover bits of 19th-century character that still sur-

vive. This end of the Strøget is young
and cheap, while the far end has the
high-end designer shops. Along the
way, wonderfully quiet and laid-back
areas are just a block or two away on
either side.

After one block (at Kattesundet),
make a side-trip three blocks left into
Copenhagen's colorful **university
district.** Formerly the old brothel neighborhood, later the heart of
Copenhagen's hippie community in the 1960s, today this "Latin
Quarter" is SoHo chic. Enjoy the colorful string of artsy shops
and cafés. Because the old town was densely populated and built of
wood, very little survived its many fires. After half-timbered and
thatched buildings kept burning down, the city finally mandated
that new construction be made of stone. But because stone was so
expensive, many people built half-timbered structures, then disguised their facades with stucco, which made them look like stone.
Exposed half-timbered structures are seen in courtyards and from
the back sides. At Sankt Peders Stræde, turn right and walk to the
end of the street. Notice the old guild signs (a baker, a key maker,
and so on) identifying the original businesses here.

Along the way, look for large mansions that once circled expansive **courtyards.** As the population grew, the city walls constricted Copenhagen's physical size. The courtyards were gradually
filled with higgledy-piggledy secondary buildings. Today throughout the old center, you can step off a busy pedestrian mall and back
in time in these characteristic, half-timbered, time-warp courtyards. Replace the parked car with a tired horse and the bikes with
a line of outhouses, and you're in 19th-century Copenhagen. If you
see an open courtyard door, you're welcome to discreetly wander in
and look around.

You'll also pass funky shops and the big brick ❺ **Sankt Peders
Church**—the old German merchant community's church, which
still holds services in German. Its fine 17th-century brick grave
chapel (filling a ground-floor building out back due to the boggy
nature of the soil) is filled with fancy German tombs (open Wed-
Sat 11:00-15:00).

• *When Sankt Peders Stræde intersects with Nørregade, look right to find
the big, Neoclassical...*

❻ Cathedral of Our Lady (Vor Frue Kirche)

The obelisk-like **Reformation Memorial** across the street from
the cathedral celebrates Denmark's break from the Roman Catholic Church to become Lutheran in 1536. Walk around and study
the reliefs of great Danish reformers protesting from their pulpits.

The relief facing the church shows King Christian III presiding over the pivotal town council meeting when they decided to break away from Rome. As a young man, Prince Christian had traveled to Germany, where he was influenced by Martin Luther. He returned to take the Danish throne by force, despite Catholic opposition. Realizing the advantages of being the head of his own state church, Christian confiscated church property and established the state Lutheran Church. King Christian was crowned inside this cathedral. Because of the reforms of 1536, there's no Mary in the Cathedral of Our Lady. The other reliefs show the popular religious uprising, with people taking control of the word of God by translating the Bible from Latin into their own language.

Like much of this part of town, the church burned down in the British bombardment of 1807 and was rebuilt in the Neoclassical style. The cathedral's **facade** looks like a Greek temple. (Two blocks to the right, in the distance, notice more Neoclassicism—the law courts.) You can see why Golden Age Copenhagen (early 1800s) fancied itself a Nordic Athens. Old Testament figures (King David and Moses) flank the cathedral's entryway. Above, John the Baptist stands where you'd expect to see Greek gods. He invites you in...into the New Testament.

The **interior** is a world

of Neoclassical serenity (free, open daily 8:00-17:00). It feels like a pagan temple that now houses Christianity. The nave is lined by the 12 apostles, clad in classical robes—masterpieces by the great Danish sculptor Bertel Thorvaldsen (see sidebar, page 72). Each strikes a meditative pose, carrying his identifying symbol: Peter with keys, Andrew with the X-shaped cross of his execution, Matthew and John writing their books, and so on. They lead to a statue of the *Risen Christ* (see photo), standing where the statue of Zeus would have been: inside a temple-

COPENHAGEN

like niche, flanked by columns and topped with a pediment. Rather than wearing a royal robe, Jesus wears his burial shroud, opens his arms wide, and says, "Come to me." (Mormons will recognize this statue—a replica stands in the visitors center at Salt Lake City's Temple Square and is often reproduced in church publications.) The marvelous acoustics are demonstrated in free organ concerts Saturdays in July and August at noon. Notice how, in good Protestant style, only the front half of the pews are "reversible," allowing the congregation to flip around and face the pulpit (in the middle of the church) to better hear the sermon.

• *Head back outside. If you face the church's facade and look to the left (across the square called Frue Plads), you'll see...*

❼ Copenhagen University

Now home to nearly 40,000 students, this university was founded by the king in the 15th century to stop the Danish brain drain to

Paris. Today tuition is free (but room, board, and beer are not). Locals say it's easy to get in, but given the wonderful student lifestyle, very hard to get out.

Step up the middle steps of the university's big building; if the doors are open, enter a colorful lobby, starring Athena and Apollo. The frescoes celebrate high thinking, with themes such as the triumph of wisdom over barbarism. Notice how harmoniously the architecture, sculpture, and painting work together.

Outside, busts honor great minds from the faculty, including (at the end) Niels Bohr, a professor who won the 1922 Nobel Prize for theoretical physics. He evaded the clutches of the Nazi science labs by fleeing to America in 1943, where he helped develop the atomic bomb.

• *Rejoin the Strøget (one block downhill from the Reformation Memorial to the black-and-gold fountain) at the twin squares called...*

❽ Gammeltorv and Nytorv

This was the old town center. In Gammeltorv ("Old Square"), the Fountain of Charity (Caritas) is named for the figure of Charity on top. It has provided drinking water to locals since the early 1600s. Featuring a pregnant woman squirting water from her breasts next to a boy urinating, this was just too much for people of the Victorian Age. They corked both figures and raised the statue to what they hoped would be out of view. The exotic-looking kiosk was one of the city's first community telephone centers from the days before phones were privately owned. Look at the reliefs ringing its top: an airplane with bird wings (c. 1900) and two women talking on a newfangled telephonic device. (It was thought business would popularize the telephone, but actually it was women.)

While Gammeltorv was a place of happiness and merriment, Nytorv ("New Square") was a place of severity and judgment. Walk to the small raised area 20 yards in front of the old ancient-Greek-style former City Hall and courthouse. Do a 360. The square is Neoclassical (built mostly after the 1807 British bombardment). Read the old Danish on the City Hall facade: "With Law Shall

Man Build the Land." Look down at the pavement and read the plaque: "Here stood the town's *Kag* (whipping post) until 1780."

• *Now walk down the next stretch of the Strøget—called Nygade—to reach...*

❾ Amagertorv

This is prime real estate for talented street entertainers. Walk to the stately brick Holy Ghost Church (Helligåndskirken). The fine spire is typical of old Danish churches. Under the stepped gable was a medieval hospital run by monks (one of the oldest buildings in town, dating from the 12th century). Today the hospital is an antiques hall. In summer the pleasant courtyard is shared by a group of charities selling light bites and coffee.

Walk behind the church, down Valkendorfsgade—the street just before the church—and through a passage under the reddish-

colored building at #32 (if locked, loop back and go down Klosterstræde); here you'll find the leafy and beer-stained ❿ **Gråbrødretorv**. Surrounded by fine old buildings, this "Grey Friars' Square"—a monastic square until the Reformation made it a people's square—is a popular place for an outdoor meal or drink in the summer. At the end of the square, the street called Niels Hemmingsens Gade returns (past the recommended Copenhagen Jazz House, a good place for live music nightly) to the Strøget.

Once back on busy Strøget, turn left and continue down Amagertorv, with its fine inlaid Italian granite stonework, to the next square with the "stork" fountain (actually three herons). The Victorian WCs here (free, steps down from fountain) are a delight.

This square, Amagertorv, is a highlight for shoppers, with the

Copenhagen at a Glance

▲▲▲**Tivoli Gardens** Copenhagen's classic amusement park, with rides, music, food, and other fun. **Hours:** Late March-mid-Sept daily 11:00-23:00, Fri-Sat until 24:00, also open daily 11:00-22:00 for a week in mid-Oct and mid-Nov-New Year's Day. See page 62.

▲▲▲**National Museum** History of Danish civilization with tourable 19th-century Victorian Apartment. **Hours:** Museum—Tue-Sun 10:00-17:00, closed Mon; Victorian Apartment—English tours June-Sept Sat at 14:00, Danish tours Sat-Sun at 11:00, 12:00, and 13:00 year-round. See page 66.

▲▲▲**Rosenborg Castle and Treasury** Renaissance castle of larger-than-life "warrior king" Christian IV. **Hours:** Mid-June-mid-Sept daily 9:00-17:00; mid-April-mid-June and mid-Sept-Oct daily 10:00-16:00, except closed Mon in April; shorter hours and generally closed Mon rest of year. See page 76.

▲▲▲**Christiania** Colorful counterculture squatters' colony. **Hours:** Guided tours at 13:00 and 15:00 (daily July-Aug, only Sat-Sun rest of year). See page 85.

▲▲**Christiansborg Palace** Royal reception rooms with dazzling tapestries. **Hours:** Reception rooms, castle ruins, kitchen, and stables open daily except closed Mon in Oct-April. Hours vary by sight: Reception rooms 9:00-17:00, Oct-April from 10:00 (may close for royal events); ruins and kitchen 10:00-17:00; stables and carriage museum 13:30-16:00, longer hours possible in July. See page 69.

▲▲**Thorvaldsen's Museum** Works of the Danish Neoclassical sculptor. **Hours:** Tue-Sun 10:00-17:00, closed Mon. See page 71.

⓫ **Royal Copenhagen store**—stacked with three floors of porcelain—and **Illums Bolighus**—a fine place to ogle modern Danish design (see "Shopping in Copenhagen," later). A block toward the canal—running parallel to the Strøget—starts Strædet, which is a "second Strøget" featuring cafés and antique shops.

North of Amagertorv, a broad pedestrian mall called **Købmagergade** leads past a fine modern bakery (Holm's) to Christian IV's Round Tower and the Latin Quarter (university district). The recommended Café Norden overlooks the fountain—a good place for a meal or coffee with a view. The second floor offers the best vantage point.

• *Looking downhill from the fountain, about halfway to an imposing palace in the distance, you'll see a great man on a horse. Walk here to*

▲**City Hall** Copenhagen's landmark, packed with Danish history and symbolism and topped with a tower. **Hours:** Mon-Fri 9:00-16:00, some Sat 9:30-13:00, closed Sun. See page 64.

▲**Ny Carlsberg Glyptotek** Scandinavia's top art gallery, featuring Egyptians, Greeks, Etruscans, French, and Danes. **Hours:** Tue-Sun 11:00-18:00, Thu until 22:00, closed Mon. See page 65.

▲**Danish Jewish Museum** Exhibit tracing the 400-year history of Danish Jews, in a unique building by American architect Daniel Libeskind. **Hours:** Tue-Sun 10:00-17:00; Sept-May Tue-Fri 13:00-16:00, Sat-Sun 12:00-17:00; closed Mon year-round. See page 74.

▲**Amalienborg Museum** Quick and intimate look at Denmark's royal family. **Hours:** May-Oct daily 10:00-16:00, mid-June-mid-Sept until 17:00; Nov-April Tue-Sun 11:00-16:00, closed Mon. See page 75.

▲**Rosenborg Gardens** Park surrounding Rosenborg Castle, filled with statues and statuesque Danes. See page 82.

▲**National Gallery of Denmark** Good Danish and Modernist collections. **Hours:** Tue-Sun 11:00-17:00, Wed until 20:00, closed Mon. See page 82.

▲**Our Savior's Church** Spiral-spired church with bright Baroque interior. **Hours:** Church—daily 11:00-15:30 but may close for special services; tower—May-Sept Mon-Sat 9:30-19:00, Sun from 10:30; shorter hours off-season, closed mid-Dec-Feb and in bad weather. See page 84.

COPENHAGEN

view this statue of Copenhagen's founder, 🕑 *Bishop Absalon, shown in his Warrior Absalon get-up.*

From the bishop, you'll continue across a bridge toward the palace and the next statue—a king on a horse. As you cross the bridge, look right to see the City Hall tower, where this walk started. (A couple of the city's competing sightseeing boat tours depart from near here—see page 42.)

Christiansborg Palace and the Birthplace of Copenhagen

You're stepping onto the island of Slotsholmen ("Castle Island"), the easy-to-defend birthplace of Copenhagen in the 12th century. It's dominated by the royal palace complex. Christiansborg Palace (with its "three crowns" spire)—the imposing former residence of kings—is now the parliament building.

Ahead of you, the Neoclassical Lutheran church with the low dome is the ⓭ **Christiansborg Palace Chapel,** site of 350 years of royal weddings and funerals (free, only open Sun 10:00-17:00).

Walk to the next green copper equestrian statue. ⓮ **Frederik VII** was crowned in 1848, just months before Denmark got its constitution on June 5, 1849. (Constitution Day is celebrated with typical Danish understatement—stores are closed and workers get the day off.) Frederik, who then ruled as a constitutional monarch, stands in front of **Christiansborg Palace,** which Denmark's royal family now shares with its people's assembly (queen's wing on right, parliament on left; for information on visiting the palace, see page 69). This palace, the seat of Danish government today, is considered the birthplace of Copenhagen. It stands upon the ruins of Absalon's 12th-century castle (literally under your feet). The big stones between the statue and the street were put in for security after the 2011 terror attacks in Norway (in which 77 people were murdered, most of them teens and young adults). While Danes strive to keep government accessible, security measures like this are today's reality.

This is Denmark's power island, with the Folketing (Danish parliament), Supreme Court, Ministry of Finance (to the left), and ⓯ **Børsen**—the historic stock exchange (farther to the left, with the fanciful dragon-tail spire; not open to tourists). The eye-catching red-brick stock exchange was inspired by the Dutch Renaissance, like much of 17th-century Copenhagen. Built to promote the mercantile ambitions of Denmark in the 1600s, it was the "World Trade Center" of Scandinavia. The facade reads, "For the profitable use of buyer and seller." The dragon-tail spire with three crowns represents the Danish aspiration to rule a united Scandinavia—or at least be its commercial capital.

Notice Copenhagen's distinctive green copper spires all around you. Beyond the old stock exchange lies the island of **Christianshavn,** with its own distinct spire. It tops the Church of Our Savior and features an external spiral staircase winding to the top for an amazing view. While political power resided here on Slotsholmen, commercial power was in the merchant's district, Christianshavn (neighborhood and church described later, under "Sights in Copenhagen"). The Børsen symbolically connected Christianshavn with the rest of the city, in an age when trade was a very big deal.

• *Walk along the old stock exchange toward Christianshavn, but turn left at the crosswalk with the signal before you reach the end of the building. After crossing the street, go over the canal and turn right to walk along the harborfront promenade, enjoying views of Christianshavn across the water.*

⑯ Havnegade Promenade

The Havnegade promenade to Nyhavn is a delightful people zone with trampolines, harborview benches (a good place to stop, look

across the water, and ponder the trendy apartments and old-warehouses-turned-modern-office-blocks), and an ice-cream-licking ambience. Stroll several blocks from here toward the new **⑰ Inderhavnsbroen sliding bridge** for pedestrians and bikes. This "Kissing Bridge" (it's called that because the two sliding, or retractable, sections "kiss" when they come together) is designed to link the town center with Christianshavn and to make the modern Opera House (ahead on the right, across the water) more accessible to downtown. Walk until you hit the Nyhavn canal.

Across the way, at the end of Nyhavn canal, stands the glassy Royal Danish Theatre's Playhouse. While this walk finishes on Kongens Nytorv, the square at the head of this canal, you could extend it by continuing north along the harbor from the playhouse.

• *For now, turn left and walk to the center of the bridge over the canal for a...*

⑱ View of Nyhavn

Established in the 1670s along with Kongens Nytorv, Nyhavn ("New Harbor") is a recently gentrified sailors' quarter. (Hong Kong is the last of the nasty bars from the rough old days.) With its trendy cafés, jazz clubs, and tattoo shops (pop into Tattoo Ole at #17—fun photos, very traditional), Nyhavn is a wonderful place to hang out. The canal is filled with glamorous old sailboats of all sizes. Historic sloops are welcome to moor here in Copenhagen's ever-changing boat museum. Hans Christian Andersen lived and wrote his first stories here (in the red double-gabled building at #20).

From the bridge, take a few steps left to the cheap **beer kiosk** (on Holbergsgade, open daily until late). At this minimarket, let friendly manager Nagib give you a little lesson in Danish beer,

and then buy a bottle or can. Choose from Carlsberg (standard lager, 4.6 percent alcohol), Carlsberg Elephant (strong, 7.2 percent), Tuborg Grøn (standard lager, 4.6 percent), Tuborg Gold (stronger, 5.8 percent), and Tuborg Classic (dark beer, 4.6 percent). The cost? About 15 DKK, depending on the alcohol level. Take your beer out to the canal and feel like a local.

A note about all the public beer-drinking here: There's no more beer consumption here than in the US; it's just out in public. Many young Danes can't afford to drink in a bar, so they "picnic drink" their beers in squares and along canals, at a quarter of the price for a bottle.

If you crave **ice cream** instead, cross the bridge, where you'll find a popular place with freshly made waffle cones facing the canal (Vaffelbageren).

Now wander the quay, enjoying the frat-party parade of tattoos (hotter weather reveals more tattoos). Celtic and Nordic mythological designs are in (as is bodybuilding, by the looks of things). The place thrives—with the cheap-beer drinkers dockside and the richer and older ones looking on from comfier cafés.

• *Make your way to the head of the canal, where you'll find a minuscule amber museum, above the House of Amber (see "Shopping in Copenhagen," page 92).*

⓳ Kongens Nytorv

The "King's New Square" is home to the National Theater, French embassy, and venerable Hotel d'Angleterre, where VIPs and pop stars stay. In the mid-1600s the city expanded, pushing its wall farther east. The equestrian statue in the middle of the square celebrates Christian V, who made this square the city's geographical and cultural center. In 1676, King Christian rode off to reconquer the southern tip of Sweden and reclaim Denmark's

dominance. He returned empty-handed and broke. Denmark became a second-rate power, but Copenhagen prospered. In the winter this square becomes a popular ice-skating rink.

Across the square on the left, small glass pyramids mark the Metro. The **Metro** that runs underground here features state-of-the-art technology (automated cars, no driver...sit in front to watch the tracks coming at you). As the cars come and go without drivers, compare this system to the public transit in your town.

Wander into ⓴ **Hviids Vinstue,** the town's oldest wine cellar (from 1723, just beyond the Metro station, at #19, under a bar) to check out its characteristic dark and woody interior and fascinating old Copenhagen photos. It's a colorful spot for an open-face sandwich and a beer (three sandwiches and a beer for 79 DKK at lunchtime). Their wintertime *gløgg* (hot spiced wine) is legendary. Across the street, towering above the Metro station, is Magasin du Nord, the grandest old department store in town.

• *You've reached the end of this walk. But if you'd like to extend it by heading out to Amalienborg Palace and* The Little Mermaid, *retrace your steps to the far side of Nyhavn canal.*

Nyhavn to Amalienborg

Stroll along the canal to the Royal Danish Theatre's Playhouse and follow the harborfront promenade left from there to a large plaza dotted with outdoor cafés and benches, and views across the harbor. You'll then follow a delightful promenade to the modern fountain of Amaliehaven Park, immediately across the harbor from Copenhagen's slick Opera House. The striking Opera House is bigger than it looks—of its 14 floors, five are below sea level. Completed in 2005 by Henning Larsen, it was a $400 million gift to the nation from an oil-shipping magnate.

• *A block inland (behind the fountain) is the orderly...*

❹ Amalienborg Palace and Square

Queen Margrethe II and her husband live in the mansion to your immediate left as you enter the square from the harborside. (If the flag's flying, she's home.) The mansion across the street (on the right as you enter) is where her son and heir to the throne, Crown Prince Frederik, lives with his wife, Australian businesswoman Mary Donaldson, and their four children. The royal guesthouse palace is on the far left. And the palace on  the far right is the **Amalienborg Museum,** which offers an intimate look at royal living (described on page 75).

Though the guards change daily at noon, they do it with royal fanfare only when the queen is in residence (see page 75 for details). The royal guard often has a police escort when it marches through town on special occasions—leading locals to joke that theirs is "the only army in the world that needs police protection."

The equestrian statue of Frederik V is a reminder that this square was the centerpiece of a planned town he envisioned in 1750. It was named for him—Frederikstaden. During the 18th century, Denmark's population grew and the country thrived (as trade flourished and its neutrality kept it out of the costly wars impoverishing much of Europe). Frederikstaden, with its strong architectural harmony, was designed as a luxury neighborhood for the city's business elite. Nobility and other big shots moved in, but the king came here only after his other palace burned down in a 1794 fire.

Just inland, the striking Frederikskirke—better known as the

COPENHAGEN

Marble Church—was designed to fit this ritzy new quarter. If it's open, step inside to bask in its vast, serene, Pantheon-esque atmosphere (free, Mon-Thu 10:00-17:00, Fri-Sun 12:00-17:00; dome climb—35 DKK, mid-June-Aug daily at 13:00; off-season Sat-Sun at 13:00).

• *From the square, Amaliegade leads two blocks north to...*

Kastellet Park

In this park, you'll find some worthwhile sightseeing. The 1908 **Gefion Fountain** illustrates the myth of the goddess who was given one night to carve a hunk out of Sweden to make into Denmark's main island, Sjælland (or "Zealand" in English), which you're on. Gefion transformed her four sons into oxen to do the job, and the chunk she removed from Sweden is supposedly Vänern, Sweden's largest lake. If you look at a map showing Sweden and

Denmark, the island and the lake are, in fact, roughly the same shape. Next to the fountain is an Anglican church built of flint.

• *Climb up the stairs by the fountain and continue along the top of the rampart about five minutes to reach the harborfront site of the overrated, overfondled, and overphotographed symbol of Copenhagen,* Den Lille Havfrue, *or...*

㉒ *The Little Mermaid*

The Little Mermaid statue was a gift to the city of Copenhagen in 1909 from brewing magnate Carl Jacobsen (whose art collection forms the basis of the Ny Carlsberg Glyptotek). Inspired by a ballet performance of Andersen's story, Jacobsen hired the young sculptor Edvard Eriksen to immortalize the mermaid as a statue. Eriksen used his wife Eline as the model. The statue sat unappreciated for 40 years until Danny Kaye sang "Wonderful Copenhagen" in the movie *Hans Christian Andersen*, and the tourist board decided to use the mermaid as a marketing symbol for the city. For the non-Disneyfied *Little Mermaid* story—and insights into Hans Christian Andersen—see the sidebar. For more on his life, see page 44.

• *This is the end of our extended wonderful, wonderful "Copenhagen City Walk." From here you can get back downtown on foot, by taxi, on bus #1A from Store Kongensgade on the other side of Kastellet Park, or bus #26 from farther north, along Folke Bernadottes Allé.*

The Little Mermaid and Hans Christian Andersen

"Far out in the ocean, where the water is as blue as a corn-flower, as clear as crystal, and very, very deep..." there lived a young mermaid. So begins one of Hans Christian Andersen's best-known stories. The plot line starts much like the Disney movie, but it's spiced with po-etic description and philosoph-ical dialogue about the immor-tal soul.

The mermaid's story goes like this: One day, a young mermaid spies a passing ship and falls in love with a hand-some human prince. The ship is wrecked in a storm, and she saves the prince's life. To be with the prince, the mermaid asks a sea witch to give her human legs. In exchange, she agrees to give up her voice and the chance of ever return-ing to the sea. And, the witch tells her, if the prince doesn't marry her, she will immediately die heartbroken and without an immortal soul. The mermaid agrees, and her fish tail becomes a pair of beautiful but pain ful legs. She woos the prince—who loves her in return—but he eventually marries another. Heartbroken, the mermaid pre-pares to die. She's given one last chance to save herself: She must kill the prince on his wedding night. She sneaks into the bedchamber with a knife...but can't bear to kill the man she loves. The mermaid throws herself into the sea to die. Sud-denly, she's miraculously carried up by the mermaids of the air, who give her an immortal soul as a reward for her long-suffering love.

The tale of unrequited love mirrors Andersen's own sad love life. He had two major crushes—one of them for the fa-mous opera singer Jenny Lind—but he was turned down both times, and he never married. He had plenty of interest in sex but likely died a virgin. He had close brotherly and motherly relations with women but stayed single, had time to travel and write, and maintained a childlike wonder about the world to his dying days.

Sights in Copenhagen

NEAR THE TRAIN STATION

Copenhagen's great train station, the Hovedbanegården, is a fascinating mesh of Scandinavian culture and transportation efficiency. From the station, delightful sights fan out into the old city. The following attractions are listed roughly in order from the train station to Slotsholmen Island.

▲▲▲Tivoli Gardens

The world's grand old amusement park—since 1843—is 20 acres, 110,000 lanterns, and countless ice-cream cones of fun. You pay

one admission price and find yourself lost in a Hans Christian Andersen wonderland of rides, restaurants, games, marching bands, roulette wheels, and funny mirrors. A roller coaster screams through the middle of a tranquil Asian food court, and the Small World-inspired Den Flyvende Kuffert ride floats through Hans Christian Andersen fairy tales. It's a children's fantasyland midday, but it becomes more adult-oriented later on. With or without kids, this place is a true magic kingdom. Tivoli doesn't try to be Disney. It's wonderfully and happily Danish. (Many locals appreciate the lovingly tended gardens.) I find it worth the admission just to see Danes—young and old—at play.

As you stroll the grounds, imagine the place in the mid-1800s, when it was new. Built on the site of the old town fortifications (today's lake was part of the old moat), Tivoli was an attempt to introduce provincial Danes to the world (for example, with the Asian Pavilion) and to bring people of all classes together.

Cost: 110-120 DKK, free for kids under 8. To go on rides, you must buy ride tickets (from booth at entrance or from machines

in the park—machines take credit card only, 25 DKK/ticket, color-coded rides cost 1-4 tickets apiece); or you can buy a multiride pass for 230 DKK. If you'll be using at least eight tickets, buy the ride pass instead. To leave and come back later, you'll have to buy a 35-DKK re-entry ticket before you exit.

Hours: Late March-mid-Sept daily 11:00-23:00, Fri-Sat until 24:00. In winter, Tivoli opens daily 11:00-22:00 from mid-Oct to early Nov for Halloween, from mid-Nov to New Year's Day for a Christmas market with *gløgg* (hot spiced wine) and ice-skating on Tivoli Lake, and during most of Feb. Dress warmly for chilly evenings any time of year. There are lockers by each entrance.

Information: Tel. 33 15 10 01, www.tivoli.dk.

Getting There: Tivoli is across Bernstoffsgade from the train station. If you're catching a late train, this is *the* place to spend your last Copenhagen hours.

Entertainment at Tivoli: Upon arrival (through main entrance, on left in the service center), pick up a map and look for the events schedule. Take a moment to plan your entertainment for the evening. Events are generally spread between 15:00 and 23:00; the 19:30 concert in the concert hall can be as little as 75 DKK or more than 1,000 DKK, depending on the performer (box office tel. 33 15 10 01). If the Tivoli Symphony is playing, it's worth paying for. The ticket box office is outside, just to the left of the main entrance (daily 10:00-20:00; if you buy a concert ticket you get into Tivoli for free).

Free concerts, pantomime theater, ballet, acrobats, puppets, and other shows pop up all over the park, and a well-organized visitor can enjoy an exciting evening of entertainment without spending a single krone beyond the entry fee. Friday evenings feature a (usually free) rock or pop show at 22:00. People gather around the lake 45 minutes before closing time for the "Tivoli Illuminations." Fireworks blast a few nights each summer. The park is particularly romantic at dusk, when the lights go on.

Eating at Tivoli: Inside the park, expect to pay amusement-park prices for amusement-park-quality food. Still, a meal here is part of the fun. **$$ Søcafeen** serves traditional open-face sandwiches and main courses in a fun beer garden with lakeside ambience. They allow picnics if you buy a drink (and will rent you plates and silverware for 10 DKK/person). **$$$ Mazzoli's Caffé & Trattoria,** in a circular building near the lake, serves classic Italian fare and pizza. **$$$ Færgekroen Bryghus** offers a quiet, classy lakeside escape from the amusement-park intensity, with traditional dishes washed down by its own microbrew (open-face sandwiches, seafood, pub grub). They host live piano on Friday, as well as Saturday evenings from 20:00, often resulting in an impromptu sing-along

COPENHAGEN

with a bunch of very happy Danes. **$$$ Wagamama,** a modern pan-Asian slurpathon from the UK, serves healthy noodle dishes (at the far back side of the park, also possible to enter from outside). **$$$ Fru Nimb** offers a large selection of open-face sandwiches in a garden setting. The kid-pleasing **$$$ Piratiriet** lets you dine on a pirate ship. For cheaper fare, look for a *pølse* (sausage) stand. And if you're longing for something sweet, **Cakenhagen** serves classic Danish cakes and pastries that you can wash down with a cup of tea—or champagne.

For something more upscale, consider the complex of Nimb restaurants, in the big Taj Mahal-like pavilion near the entrance facing the train station. For dinner, **$$$$ Nimb Bar 'n' Grill** is a definite splurge, grilling up creative international meat and seafood dishes. **$$$$ Nimb Brasserie,** sharing the same lobby, serves rustic French classics.

And if these options aren't enough, check out the eateries in the glassy new Tivoli Food Hall (facing the train station) that promises "fast gourmet food."

▲City Hall (Rådhus)

This city landmark, between the train station/Tivoli and the Strøget, is free and open to the public (including a public WC). You can wander throughout the building and into the peaceful garden out back. It also offers private tours and trips up its 345-foot-tall tower.

Cost and Hours: Free to enter building, Mon-Fri 9:00-16:00; you can usually slip in Sat 9:30-13:00 when weddings are going on, or join the Sat tour; closed Sun. Guided English-language tours—50 DKK, 45 minutes, gets you into more private, official rooms; Mon-Fri at 13:00, Sat at 10:00. Tower by escort only—30 DKK, 300 steps for the best aerial view of Copenhagen, Mon-Fri at 11:00 and 14:00, Sat at 12:00, closed Sun. Tel. 33 66 33 66.

Visiting City Hall: It's draped, inside and out, in Danish symbolism. The city's founder, Bishop Absalon, stands over the door. Absalon (c. 1128-1201)—bishop, soldier, and foreign-policy wonk—was King Valdemar I's right-hand man. In Copenhagen, he drove out pirates and built a fort to guard the harbor, turning a miserable fishing village into a humming Baltic seaport. The polar bears climbing on the rooftop symbolize the giant Danish protectorate of Greenland. Six night watchmen flank the city's gold-and-green seal under the Danish flag.

Step inside. The info desk (on the left as you enter) has racks

of tourist information (city maps and other brochures). The building and its huge tower were inspired by the City Hall in Siena,
Italy (with the necessary bad-weather addition of a glass roof).
Enormous functions fill this grand hall (the iron grate in the center
of the floor is an elevator for bringing up 1,200 chairs), while the
marble busts of four illustrious local boys—fairy-tale writer Hans
Christian Andersen, sculptor Bertel Thorvaldsen, physicist Niels
Bohr, and the building's architect, Martin Nyrop—look on. Underneath the floor are national archives dating back to 1275, popular with Danes researching their family roots.

As you leave, pop into the amazing clock opposite the info
desk. Jens Olsen's World Clock, built from 1943 to 1955, was the
mother of all astronomical clocks in precision and function. And
it came with something new: tracking the exact time across the
world's time zones. One of its gears does a complete rotation only
every 25,753 years.

▲Ny Carlsberg Glyptotek

Scandinavia's top art gallery is an impressive example of what beer
money can do. Brewer Carl Jacobsen (son of J. C. Jacobsen, who

funded the Museum of Na-
tional History at Frederiksborg
Castle) was an avid collector
and patron of the arts. (Carl
also donated *The Little Mermaid* statue to the city.) His
namesake museum has intoxi-
cating artifacts from the ancient world, along with some
fine art from our own times. The next time you sip a Carlsberg beer,
drink a toast to Carl Jacobsen and his marvelous collection. *Skål!*

Cost and Hours: 95 DKK, free on Tue; open Tue-Sun 11:00-
18:00, Thu until 22:00, closed Mon; behind Tivoli at Dantes Plads
7, tel. 33 41 81 41, www.glyptoteket.com. It has a classy **$$$** caf-
eteria under palms, as well as a rooftop terrace with snacks, drinks,
and city views.

Visiting the Museum: Pick up a floor plan as you enter to
help navigate the confusing layout. For a chronological swing,
start with Egypt (mummy coffins and sarcophagi, a 5,000-year-old
hippo statue), Greece (red-and-black painted vases, statues), the
Etruscan world (Greek-looking vases), and Rome (grittily realistic
statues and portrait busts).

The sober realism of 19th-century Danish Golden Age paint-
ing reflects the introspection of a once powerful nation reduced
to second-class status—and ultimately embracing what made it
unique. The "French Wing" (just inside the front door) has Rodin

statues. A heady, if small, exhibit of 19th-century French paintings (in a modern building within the back courtyard) shows how Realism morphed into Impressionism and Post-Impressionism, and includes a couple of canvases apiece by Géricault, Delacroix, Monet, Manet, Millet, Courbet, Degas, Pissarro, Cézanne, Van Gogh, Picasso, Renoir, and Toulouse-Lautrec. Look for art by Gauguin—from before Tahiti (when he lived in Copenhagen with his Danish wife and their five children) and after Tahiti. There's also a fine collection of modern (post-Thorvaldsen) Danish sculpture.

Linger with marble gods under the palm leaves and glass dome of the very soothing winter garden. Designers, figuring Danes would be more interested in a lush garden than in classical art, used this wonderful space as leafy bait to cleverly introduce locals to a few Greek and Roman statues. (It works for tourists, too.) One of the original *Thinker* sculptures by Rodin (wondering how to scale the Tivoli fence?) is in the museum's backyard.

Museum of Copenhagen (Københavns Museum)

This museum offers an entertaining and creative telling of the story of Copenhagen, from its origins to contemporary culture.

Cost and Hours: May be closed when you visit, when open likely 40 DKK, daily 10:00-17:00, kitty-corner to the National Museum at Stormgade 18, tel. 33 21 07 72, www.copenhagen.dk.

▲▲▲National Museum

Focus on this museum's excellent and curiously enjoyable Danish collection, which traces this civilization from its ancient beginnings. Its prehistoric collection is the best of its kind in Scandinavia. Exhibits are laid out chronologically and are eloquently described in English.

Cost and Hours: 75 DKK, Tue-Sun 10:00-17:00, closed Mon, mandatory lockers, enter at Ny Vestergade 10, tel. 33 13 44 11, www.natmus.dk. The **$$** café overlooking the entry hall serves coffee, pastries, and lunch.

Visiting the Museum: Pick up the museum map as you enter, and head for the Danish history exhibit. It fills three floors, from the bottom up: prehistory, the Middle Ages and Renaissance, and modern times (1660-2000).

Danish Prehistory: Start before history did, in the Danish Prehistory exhibit (on the right side of the main entrance hall). Follow the room numbers in order, working counterclockwise around the courtyard and through the millennia.

In the Stone Age section, you'll see primitive tools and still-clothed skeletons of Scandinavia's reindeer hunters. The oak coffins were originally covered by burial mounds (called "barrows"). People put valuable items into the coffins with the dead, such as a

folding chair (which, back then, was a real status symbol). In the farming section, ogle the ceremonial axes and amber necklaces.

The Bronze Age brought the sword (several are on display). The "Chariot of the Sun"—a small statue of a horse pulling the sun across the

sky—likely had religious significance for early Scandinavians (whose descendants continue to celebrate the solstice with fervor). In the same room are those iconic horned helmets. Contrary to popular belief (and countless tourist shops), these helmets were not worn by the Vikings, but by their predecessors—for ceremonial purposes, centuries earlier. In the next room are huge cases filled with still-playable *lur* horns (see page 47).

Another room shows off a collection of well-translated rune stones proclaiming heroic deeds.

This leads to the Iron Age and an object that's neither Iron nor Danish: the 2,000-year-old Gundestrup Cauldron of art-textbook

fame. This 20-pound, soup-kitchen-size bowl made of silver was found in a Danish bog, but its symbolism suggests it was originally from either Thrace (in northeast Greece) or Celtic Ireland. On the sides, hunters slay bulls, and gods cavort with stags, horses, dogs, and dragons. It's both mysterious and fascinating.

Prehistoric Danes were fascinated by bogs. To make iron, you need ore—and Denmark's many bogs provided that critical material in abundance, leading people to believe that the gods dwelled there. These Danes appeased the gods by sacrificing valuable items (and even people) into bogs. Fortunately for modern archaeologists, bogs happen to be an ideal environment for preserving fragile objects. One bog alone—the Nydam bog—has yielded thousands of items, including three whole ships.

No longer bogged down in prehistory, the people of Scandinavia came into contact with Roman civilization. At about this time, the Viking culture rose; you'll see the remains of an old warship. The Vikings, so feared in most of Europe, are still thought of fondly here in their homeland. You'll notice the descriptions straining to defend them: Sure, they'd pillage, rape, and plunder. But they also founded thriving, wealthy, and cultured trade towns. Love the Vikings or hate them, it's impossible to deny their massive reach—Norse Vikings even carved runes into the walls of the Hagia Sophia church (in today's Istanbul).

Middle Ages and Renaissance: Next, go upstairs and follow signs to Room 101 to start this section. You'll walk through the

Middle Ages, where you'll find lots of bits and pieces of old churches, such as golden altars and *aquamaniles*, pitchers used for ritual handwashing. The Dagmar Cross is the prototype for a popular form of crucifix worn by many Danes (Room 102, small glass display case—with colorful enamel paintings). Another cross in this case (the Roskilde Cross, studded with gemstones) was found inside the wooden head of Christ displayed high on the opposite wall. There are also exhibits on tools and trade, weapons, drinking horns, and fine, wood-carved winged altarpieces. Carry on to find a fascinating room on the Norse settlers of Greenland, material on the Reformation, and an exhibit on everyday town life in the 16th and 17th centuries.

Modern Times: The next floor takes you through the last few centuries, with historic toys and a slice-of-Danish-life (1660-2000)

gallery where you'll see everything from rifles and old bras to early jukeboxes. You'll learn that the Danish Golden Age (which dominates most art museums in Denmark) captured the everyday pastoral beauty of the countryside, celebrated Denmark's smallness and peace-loving nature, and mixed in some Nordic mythology. With industrialization came the labor movement and trade unions. After delving into the World Wars, Baby Boomers, creation of the postwar welfare state, and the

"Depressed Decade" of the 1980s (when Denmark suffered high unemployment), the collection is capped off by a stall that, until recently, was used for selling marijuana in the squatters' community of Christiania.

The Rest of the Museum: If you're eager for more, there's plenty left to see. The National Museum also has exhibits on the history of this building (the Prince's Palace), a large ethnology collection, antiquities, coins and medallions, temporary exhibits, and a good children's museum. The floor plan will lead you to what you want to see.

▲National Museum's Victorian Apartment

The National Museum inherited an incredible Victorian apartment just around the corner. The wealthy Christensen family managed to keep its plush living quarters a 19th-century time capsule until the granddaughters passed away in 1963. Since then, it's been part of the National Museum, with all but two of its rooms looking just as they did in the late Victorian days.

Cost and Hours: 50 DKK, required one-hour tours leave from the National Museum reception desk (in English, June-Sept Sat only at 14:00; in Danish Sat-Sun at 11:00, 12:00, and 13:00 year-round).

ON SLOTSHOLMEN ISLAND

This island, where Copenhagen began in the 12th century, is a short walk from the train station and Tivoli, just across the bridge from the National Museum. It's dominated by Christiansborg Palace and several other royal and governmental buildings. Note that my "Copenhagen City Walk" (earlier) cuts right through Slotsholmen and covers other landmarks on the island (see page 55).

▲▲Christiansborg Palace

A complex of government buildings stands on the ruins of Copenhagen's original 12th-century fortress: the parliament, Supreme Court, prime minister's office, royal reception rooms, royal library, several museums, and royal stables. Although the current palace dates only from 1928 and the royal family moved out 200 years ago, this building—the sixth to stand here in 800 years—is rich with tradition.

Four palace sights (the reception rooms, old castle ruins, stables, and kitchen) are open to the public, giving us commoners a glimpse of the royal life.

Cost and Hours: Reception rooms-90 DKK, castle ruins, stables, and kitchen-50 DKK each; a combo-ticket for all four-150 DKK. All sights are open daily (except in Oct-April, when they're closed on Mon) but have different hours: reception rooms open 9:00-17:00, Oct-April from 10:00 (may close for royal events); ruins and kitchen open 10:00-17:00; stables and carriage museum open 13:30-16:00—longer hours possible in July.

Information: Tel. 33 92 64 92, www.christiansborg.dk.

Visiting the Palace: From the equestrian statue in front, go through the wooden door; the entrance to the ruins is in the corridor on the right, and the door to the reception rooms is out in the next courtyard, also on the right.

Royal Reception Rooms: While these don't rank among Europe's best palace rooms, they're worth a look. This is still the place where Queen Margrethe II impresses visiting dignitaries. The information-packed, hour-long English tours of the rooms are excellent (included in ticket, daily at 15:00). At other times, you'll wander the rooms on your own in a one-way route, reading the sparse English descriptions. As you slip-slide on protect-the-floor slippers through 22 rooms, you'll gain a good feel for Danish history, royalty, and politics. Here are a few highlights:

After the Queen's Library you'll soon enter the grand Great Hall, lined with boldly colorful (almost gaudy) tapestries. The palace highlight is this dazzling set of modern tapestries—Danish-designed but Gobelin-made in Paris. This gift, given to the queen on her 60th birthday in 2000, celebrates 1,000 years of Danish history, from the Viking age to our chaotic times...and into the future. Borrow the laminated descriptions for blow-by-blow explanations of the whole epic saga. The Velvet Room is where royals privately greet VIP guests before big functions.

In the corner room on the left, don't miss the family portrait of King Christian IX, which illustrates why he's called the "father-in-law of Europe"—his children eventually became, or married into, royalty in Denmark, Russia, Greece, Britain, France, Germany, and Norway.

In the Throne Room you'll see the balcony where new monarchs are proclaimed (most recently in 1972). And at the end, in the Hall of Giants (where you take off your booties among heroic figures supporting the building), you'll see a striking painting of Queen Margrethe II from 2010 on her 70th birthday. The three playful lions, made of Norwegian silver, once guarded the throne and symbolize absolute power—long gone since 1849, when Denmark embraced the notion of a constitutional monarch.

Castle Ruins: An exhibit in the scant remains of the first fortress built by Bishop Absalon, the 12th-century founder of Copenhagen, lies under the palace. A long passage connects to another set of ruins, from the 14th-century Copenhagen Castle. There's precious little to see, but it is, um, old and well-described. A video covers more recent palace history.

Royal Stables and Carriages Museum: This facility is still home to the horses that pull the queen's carriage on festive days, as well as a collection of historic carriages. While they're down from 250 horses to about a dozen, the royal stables are part of a strong tradition and, as the little video shows, will live on.

Royal Kitchen: Unless you're smitten with old ladles and shiny copper pots and pans, I'd skip this exhibit.

▲▲Thorvaldsen's Museum

This museum, which has some of the best swoon-worthy art you'll see anywhere, tells the story and shows the monumental work of

the great Danish Neoclassical sculptor Bertel Thorvaldsen (see sidebar). Considered Canova's equal among Neoclassical sculptors, Thorvaldsen spent 40 years in Rome. He was lured home to Copenhagen with the promise to showcase his work in a fine museum, which opened in the revolutionary year of 1848 as Denmark's first public art gallery. Of the 500 or so sculptures Thorvaldsen completed in his life—including 90 major statues—this museum has most of them, in one form or another (the plaster model used to make the original or a copy done in marble or bronze).

Cost and Hours: 50 DKK, free on Wed, Tue-Sun 10:00-17:00, closed Mon, includes excellent English audioguide on request, located in Neoclassical building with colorful walls next to Christiansborg Palace.

Information: Tel. 33 32 15 32, www.thorvaldsensmuseum.dk.

Visiting the Museum: The ground floor showcases his statues. After buying your ticket, go straight in and ask to borrow a free audioguide at the desk. This provides a wonderful statue-by-statue narration of the museum's key works.

Just before the audioguide desk, turn left into the Great Hall, which was the original entryway of the museum. It's filled with replicas

COPENHAGEN

Bertel Thorvaldsen (1770-1844)

Bertel Thorvaldsen was born, raised, educated, and buried in Copenhagen, but his most productive years were spent in Rome. There he soaked up the prevailing style of the time: Neoclassical. He studied ancient Greek and Roman statues, copying their balance, grace, and impassive beauty. The simple-but-noble style suited the patriotism of the era, and Thorvaldsen got rich off it. Public squares throughout Europe are dotted with his works, celebrating local rulers, patriots, and historical figures looking like Greek heroes or Roman conquerors.

In 1819, at the height of his fame and power, Thorvaldsen returned to Copenhagen. He was asked to decorate the most important parts of the recently bombed, newly rebuilt Cathedral of Our Lady: the main altar and nave. His *Risen Christ* on the altar (along with the 12 apostles lining the nave) became his most famous and reproduced work—without even realizing it, most people imagine the caring features of Thorvaldsen's Christ when picturing what Jesus looked like.

The prolific Thorvaldsen depicted a range of subjects. His grand statues of historical figures (Copernicus in Warsaw, Maximilian I in Munich) were intended for public squares. Portrait busts of his contemporaries were usually done in the style of Roman emperors. Thorvaldsen carved the Lion Monument, depicting a weeping lion, into a cliff in Luzern, Switzerland. He did religious statues, like the *Risen Christ.* Thorvaldsen's most accessible works are from Greek mythology—*The Three Graces,* naked *Jason with the Golden Fleece,* or Ganymede crouching down to feed the eagle Jupiter.

Though many of his statues are of gleaming white marble, Thorvaldsen was not a chiseler of stone. Like Rodin and Canova, Thorvaldsen left the grunt work to others. He fashioned a life-size model in plaster, which could then be reproduced in marble or bronze by his assistants. Multiple copies were often made, even in his lifetime.

Thorvaldsen epitomized the Neoclassical style. His statues assume perfectly balanced poses—maybe even a bit stiff, say critics. They don't flail their arms dramatically or emote passionately. As you look into their faces, they seem lost in thought, as though contemplating deep spiritual truths.

In Copenhagen, catch Thorvaldsen's *Risen Christ* at the Cathedral of Our Lady, his portrait bust at City Hall, and the full range of his long career at the Thorvaldsen's Museum.

of some of Thorvaldsen's biggest and grandest statues—national heroes who still stand in the prominent squares of their major cities (Munich, Warsaw, the Vatican, and others). Two great equestrian statues stare each other down from across the hall; while they both take the classic, self-assured pose of looking one way while pointing another (think Babe Ruth calling his home run), one of them (Jozef Poniatowski) is modeled after the ancient Roman general Marcus Aurelius, while the other (Bavaria's Maximilian I) wears modern garb.

Then take a spin through the smaller rooms that ring the central courtyard. Each of these is dominated by one big work—mostly classical subjects drawn from mythology. At the far end of the building stand the plaster models for the iconic *Risen Christ* and the 12 Apostles (the final marble versions stand in the Cathedral of Our Lady— see page 50). Peek into the central courtyard to see the  planter-box tomb of Thorvaldsen himself (who died in 1844). Continue into the next row of rooms: In the far corner room look for Thorvaldsen's (very flattering) self-portrait, leaning buffly against a partially finished sculpture.

Downstairs you'll find a collection of plaster casts (mostly ancient Roman statues that inspired Thorvaldsen) and a video about his career.

Upstairs, get into the mind of the artist by perusing his personal possessions and the private collection of paintings from which he drew inspiration.

Royal Library

Copenhagen's "Black Diamond" (Den Sorte Diamant) library is a striking, supermodern building made of shiny black granite, leaning over the harbor at the edge of the palace complex. From the inviting lounge chairs, you can ponder this stretch of harborfront, which serves as a showcase for architects. Inside, wander through the old and new sections, catch the fine view from the "G" level, read a magazine, and enjoy a classy—and pricey—lunch.

Cost and Hours: Free, special exhibits generally 50 DKK; Mon-Fri 8:00-21:00, Sat 9:00-19:00; July-Aug Mon-Sat 8:00-19:00, reading room hours vary, closed Sun year-round; tel. 33 47 47 47, www.kb.dk.

▲Danish Jewish Museum (Dansk Jødisk Museum)

In a striking building by American architect Daniel Libeskind, this museum offers a very small but well-exhibited display of 400 years of the life and impact of Jews in Denmark.

Cost and Hours: 60 DKK; Tue-Sun 10:00-17:00; Sept-May Tue-Fri 13:00-16:00, Sat-Sun 12:00-17:00; closed Mon year-round; behind "Black Diamond" library at Proviantpassagen 6—enter from the courtyard behind the red-brick, ivy-covered building.

Information: Tel. 33 11 22 18, www.jewmus.dk.

Visiting the Museum: Frankly, the architecture overshadows the humble exhibits. Libeskind—who created the equally conceptual Jewish Museum in Berlin, and whose design is the basis for the redevelopment of the World Trade Center site in New York City—has literally written Jewish culture into this building. The floor plan, a seemingly random squiggle, is actually in the shape of the Hebrew characters for *Mitzvah*, which loosely translated means "act of kindness."

Be sure to watch the two introductory films about the Jews' migration to Denmark, and about the architect Libeskind (12-minute loop total, English subtitles, plays continuously). As you tour the collection, the uneven floors and asymmetrical walls give you the feeling that what lies around the corner is completely unknown... much like the life and history of Danish Jews. Another interpretation might be that the uneven floors give you the sense of motion, like waves on the sea—a reminder that despite Nazi occupation in 1943, nearly 7,000 Danish Jews were ferried across the waves by fishermen to safety in neutral Sweden.

NEAR THE STRØGET
Round Tower

Built in 1642 by Christian IV, the tower connects a church, library, and observatory (the oldest functioning observatory in Europe) with a ramp that spirals up to a fine view of Copenhagen (though the view from atop Our Savior's Church is far better—see page 84).

Cost and Hours: 25 DKK, nothing to see inside but the ramp and the view; tower—daily 10:00-20:00, Oct-April Thu-Mon 10:00-18:00, Tue-Wed until 21:00; observatory—summer Sun 13:00-16:00, mid-Oct-mid-March Tue-Wed 18:00-21:00; just off the Strøget on Købmagergade.

AMALIENBORG PALACE AND NEARBY

For more information on this palace and nearby attractions, including the famous *Little Mermaid* statue, see the end of my "Copenhagen City Walk" (page 60).

▲Amalienborg Museum (Amalienborgmuseet)

While Queen Margrethe II and her husband live quite privately in one of the four mansions that make up the palace complex, another mansion has been open to the public since 1994. It displays the private studies of four kings of the House of Glucksborg, who ruled from 1863-1972 (the immediate predecessors of today's queen). Your visit won't take long—you'll see six to eight rooms on each of two floors—but it affords an intimate and unique peek into Denmark's royal family. On the first floor you'll see the private study of each of the last four kings of Denmark. They feel particularly lived-in—with cluttered pipe collections and bookcases jammed with family pictures—because they were. It's easy to imagine these blue-blooded folks just hanging out here, even today. The earliest study, Frederik VIII's (c. 1869), feels much older and more "royal"—with Renaissance gilded walls, heavy drapes, and a polar bear rug. On the second floor, your visit includes the Gothic library designed for dowager Queen Caroline Amalie, the cheery gala hall (the palace's largest room) with statues by Bertel Thorvaldsen, and a hall gleaming with large gilt-bronze table decorations.

Cost and Hours: 95 DKK, 145-DKK combo-ticket includes Rosenborg Palace—available on the website or at Rosenborg only; May-Oct daily 10:00-16:00, mid-June-mid-Sept until 17:00; Nov-April Tue-Sun 11:00-16:00, closed Mon; with your back to the harbor, entrance is at the far end of the square on the right; tel. 33 15 32 86, www.dkks.dk.

Amalienborg Palace Changing of the Guard

This noontime event is boring in the summer, when the queen is not in residence—the guards just change places. (This goes on for quite a long time—no need to rush here at the stroke of noon, or to crowd in during the first few minutes; you'll have plenty of good photo ops.) If the queen's at home (indicated by a flag flying above her home), the changing of the guard is accompanied by a military band.

Museum of Danish Resistance (Frihedsmuseet)

This museum tells the story of Denmark's Nazi-resistance struggle (1940-1945). While relatively small, the museum rewards those who take the time to read the English explanations and understand the fascinating artifacts. The building was destroyed by fire in 2013. The collection was saved, but the museum may still be closed during your visit—check details at their website (located on Churchillparken between Amalienborg Palace and the *Little Mermaid* site; bus #1A or #15 from downtown/Tivoli/train station stops right in front, a 10-minute walk from Østerport S-tog station, or bus #26 from Langelinie cruise port or downtown; tel. 41 20 62 91, www.frihedsmuseet.dk).

ROSENBORG CASTLE AND NEARBY
▲▲▲Rosenborg Castle (Rosenborg Slot) and Treasury

This finely furnished Dutch Renaissance-style castle was built by King Christian IV in the early 1600s as a summer residence. Rosenborg was his favorite residence and where he chose to die. Open to the public since 1838, it houses the Danish crown jewels and 500 years of royal knickknacks. While the old palace interior is a bit dark and not as immediately impressive as many of Europe's later Baroque masterpieces, it has a certain lived-in charm. It oozes the personality of the fascinating Christian IV and has one of the finest treasury collections in Europe. For more on Christian, read the sidebar.

Cost and Hours: 110 DKK, 145-DKK combo-ticket includes Amalienborg Museum; mid-June-mid-Sept daily 9:00-17:00; mid-April-mid-June and mid-Sept-Oct daily 10:00-16:00, except closed Mon in April; shorter hours and generally closed Mon rest of the year; mandatory lockers take 20-DKK coin, which will be returned; Metro or S-tog: Nørreport, then 5-minute walk on Østervoldgade and through park.

Information: Tel. 33 15 32 86, www.dkks.dk.

Tours: Richard Karpen leads fascinating one-hour tours in Hans Christian Andersen garb (100 DKK plus entry fee, mid-May-mid-Sept Mon and Thu at 12:00, meet outside castle ticket office—no reservations needed; see listing on page 41). Or take the following self-guided tour that I've woven together from the highlights of Richard's walk. You can also use the palace's free Wi-Fi to follow the "Konge Connect" step-by-step tour through the palace highlights (with audio/video/text explanations for your smartphone or tablet—bring earphones; instructional brochure at ticket desk).

➔ **Self-Guided Tour:** Buy your ticket, then head back out

King Christian IV:
A Lover and a Fighter

King Christian IV (1577-1648) inherited Denmark at the peak of its power, lived his life with the exuberance of the age, and went to his grave with the country in decline. His legacy is ob-

vious to every tourist—Rosenborg Castle, Frederiksborg Palace, the Round Tower, Christianshavn, and on and on. Look for his logo adorning many buildings: the letter "C" with a "4" inside it and a crown on top. Thanks to both his place in history and his passionate personality, Danes today regard Christian IV as one of their greatest monarchs.

During his 50-year reign, Christian IV reformed the government, rebuilt the army, established a trading post in India, and tried to expand Denmark's territory. He took Kalmar from Sweden and captured strategic points in northern Germany. The king was a large man who also lived large. A skilled horseman and avid hunter, he could drink his companions under the table. He spoke several languages and gained a reputation as outgoing and humorous. His lavish banquets were legendary, and his romantic affairs were numerous.

But Christian's appetite for war proved destructive. In 1626, Denmark again attacked northern Germany, but was beaten back. In late 1643, Sweden launched a sneak attack, and despite Christian's personal bravery (he lost an eye), the war went badly. By the end of his life, Christian was tired and bitter, and Denmark was drained.

The heroics of Christian and his sailors live on in the Danish national anthem, "King Christian Stood by the Lofty Mast."

COPENHAGEN

and look for the *castle* sign. You'll tour the ground floor room by room, then climb to the third floor for the big throne room. After a quick sweep of the middle floor, finish in the basement (enter from outside) for the jewels.

• *Begin the tour on the palace's ground floor (turn right as you enter), in the Winter Room.*

Ground Floor: Here in the wood-paneled **Winter Room,** all eyes were on King Christian IV. Today, your eyes should be on him, too. Take a close look at his bust by the fireplace (if it's not here, look for it out in the corridor by the ticket taker). Check this guy out—fashionable braid, hard drinker, hard lover, energetic statesman, and warrior king. Christian IV was dynamism in the flesh, wearing a toga: a true Renaissance guy. During his reign, Copenhagen doubled in size. You're surrounded by Dutch paintings (the Dutch had a huge influence on 17th-century Denmark). Note the smaller statue of the 19-year-old king, showing him jousting jauntily on his coronation day. In another case, the golden astronomical clock—with musical works and moving figures—did everything you can imagine. Flanking the fireplace (opposite where you entered), beneath the windows, look for the panels in the tile floor that could be removed to let the music performed by the band in the basement waft in. (Who wants the actual musicians in the dining room?) The audio holes were also used to call servants.

The **study** (or "writing closet," nearest where you entered) was small (and easy to heat). Kings did a lot of corresponding. We know a lot about Christian because 3,000 of his handwritten letters survive. The painting on the right wall shows Christian at age eight. Three years later, his father died, and little Christian technically ascended the throne, though Denmark was actually ruled by a regency until Christian was 19. A portrait of his mother hangs above

the boy, and opposite is a portrait of Christian in his prime—having just conquered Sweden—standing alongside the incredible coronation crown you'll see later.

Going back through the Winter Room, head for the door to Christian's **bedroom.** Before entering, notice the little peephole

in the door (used by the king to spy on those in this room—well-camouflaged by the painting, and more easily seen from the other side), and the big cabinet doors for Christian's clothes and accessories, flanking the bedroom door (notice the hinges and keyholes). Heading into the bedroom, you'll see paintings showing the king as an old man...and as a dead man. (Christian died in this room.) In the case are the clothes he wore at his finest hour. During a naval battle against Sweden (1644), Christian stood directing the action when an explosion ripped across the deck, sending him sprawling and riddling him with shrapnel. Unfazed, the 67-year-old monarch bounced right back up and kept going, inspiring his men to carry on the fight. Christian's stubborn determination during this battle is commemorated in Denmark's national anthem. Shrapnel put out Christian's eye. No problem: The warrior king with a knack for heroic publicity stunts had the shrapnel bits removed from his eye and forehead and made into earrings as a gift for his mistress. The earrings hang in the case with his blood-stained clothes (easy to miss, right side). Christian lived to be 70 and fathered 25 children (with two wives and three mistresses). Before moving on, you can peek into Christian's private bathroom—elegantly tiled with Delft porcelain.

Proceed into the **Dark Room.** Here you'll see wax casts of royal figures. This was the way famous and important people were portrayed back then. The chair is a forerunner of the whoopee cushion. When you sat on it, metal cuffs pinned your arms down, allowing the prankster to pour water down the back of the chair (see hole)—making you "wet your pants." When you stood up, the chair made embarrassing tooting sounds.

The **Marble Room** has a particularly impressive inlaid marble floor. Imagine the king meeting emissaries here in the center, with the emblems of Norway (right), Denmark (center), and Sweden (left) behind him.

The end room, called the **King's Chamber,** was used by Christian's first mistress. Notice the ceiling painting, with an orchestra looking down on you as they play.

The long **stone passage** leading to the staircase exhibits an intriguing painting (by the door to the King's Chamber) show-

ing the crowds at the coronation of Christian's son, Frederik III. After Christian's death, a weakened Denmark was invaded, occupied, and humiliated by Sweden (Treaty of Roskilde, 1658). Copenhagen alone held out through the long winter of 1658-1659 (the Siege of Copenhagen), and Sweden eventually had to withdraw from the country. During the siege, Frederik III distinguished himself with his bravery. He seized upon the resulting surge of popularity as his chance to be anointed an absolute, divinely ordained monarch (1660). This painting marks that event—study it closely for slice-of-life details. Next, near the ticket taker, a sprawling family tree makes it perfectly clear that Christian IV comes from good stock. Notice the tree is labeled in German—the second language of the realm.

• *The queen had a hand-pulled elevator, but you'll need to hike up two flights of stairs to the throne room.*

Throne Room (Third Floor): The **Long Hall**—considered one of the best-preserved Baroque rooms in Europe—was great for banquets. The decor trumpets the accomplishments of Denmark's great kings. The four corners of the ceiling feature the four continents known at the time. (America—at the far-right end of the hall

as you enter—was still considered pretty untamed; notice the decapitated head with the arrow sticking out of it.) In the center, of course, is the proud seal of the Danish Royal Family. The tapestries, designed for this room, are from the late 1600s. Effective propaganda, they show the Danes defeating their Swedish rivals on land and at sea. The king's throne—still more propaganda for two centuries of "absolute" monarchs—was made of "unicorn horn" (actually narwhal tusk from Greenland). Believed to bring protection from evil and poison, the horn was the most precious material in its day. The queen's throne is of hammered silver. The 150-pound lions are 300 years old.

The small room to the left holds a delightful **royal porcelain** display with Chinese, French, German, and Danish examples of the "white gold." For five centuries, Europeans couldn't figure out how the Chinese made this stuff. The difficulty in just getting it back to Europe in one piece made it precious. The Danish pieces, called "Flora Danica" (on the left as you enter), are from a huge royal set showing off the herbs and vegetables of the realm.

• *Heading back down, pause at the middle floor, which is worth a look.*

Middle Floor: Circling counterclockwise, you'll see more fine clocks, fancy furniture, and royal portraits. The queen enjoyed her royal lathe (with candleholders for lighting and pedals to spin it hidden away below; in the Christian VI Room). The small mirror room (up the stairs from the main hall) was where the king played Hugh Hefner—using mirrors on the floor to see what was under those hoop skirts. In hidden cupboards, he had a fold-out bed and a handy escape staircase.

• *Back outside, turn right and find the stairs leading down to the...*

Royal Danish Treasury (Castle Basement): The palace was a royal residence for a century and has been the royal vault right up until today. As you enter, first head to the right, into the **wine cellar,** with thousand-liter barrels and some fine treasury items. The first room has a vast army of tiny golden soldiers, and a wall lined with fancy rifles. Heading into the next room, you'll see fine items of amber (petrified tree resin, 30-50 million years old) and ivory. Study the large box made of amber (in a freestanding case, just to the right as you enter)—the tiny figures show a healthy interest in sex.

Now head back past the ticket taker and into the main part of the treasury, where you can browse through exquisite royal knickknacks.

The diamond- and pearl-studded **saddles** were Christian

IV's—the first for his coronation, the second for his son's wedding. When his kingdom was nearly bankrupt, Christian had these constructed lavishly—complete with solid-gold spurs—to impress visiting dignitaries and bolster Denmark's credit rating.

The next case displays **tankards.** Danes were always big drinkers, and to drink in the top style, a king had narwhal steins (#4030). Note the fancy Greenland Inuit (Eskimo) on the lid (#4023). The case is filled with exquisitely carved ivory. On the other side of that case, what's with the mooning snuffbox (#4063)? Also, check out the amorous whistle (#4064).

Drop by the case on the wall in the back-left of the room: The 17th century was the age of **brooches.** Many of these are made of freshwater pearls. Find the fancy combination toothpick and ear spoon (#4140). Look for #4146: A queen was caught having an affair after 22 years of royal marriage. Her king gave her a special present: a golden ring—showing the hand of his promiscuous queen shaking hands with a penis.

Step downstairs, away from all this silliness. Passing through the serious vault door, you come face-to-face with a big, jeweled **sword.** The tall, two-handed, 16th-century coronation sword was drawn by the new king, who cut crosses in the air in four directions, symbolically promising to defend the realm from all attacks. The cases surrounding the sword contain everyday items used by the king (all solid gold, of course). What looks like a trophy case of gold records is actually a collection of dinner plates with amber centers (#5032).

Go down the steps. In the center case is Christian IV's **coronation crown** (from 1596, seven pounds of gold and precious stones, #5124), which some consider to be the finest Renaissance crown in Europe. Its six tallest gables radiate symbolism. Find the symbols of justice (sword and scales), fortitude (a woman on a lion with a sword), and charity (a nursing woman—meaning the king will love God and his people as a mother loves her child). The pelican,  which according to medieval legend pecks its own flesh to feed its young, symbolizes God sacrificing his son, just as the king would make great sacrifices for his people. Climb the footstool to look inside—it's as exquisite as the outside. The shields of various Danish provinces remind the king that he's surrounded by his realms.

Circling the cases along the wall (right to left), notice the fine enameled lady's goblet with traits of a good woman spelled out in

Latin (#5128) and above that, an exquisite prayer book (with hand-written favorite prayers, #5134). In the fifth window, the big solid-gold baptismal basin (#5262) hangs above tiny oval silver boxes that contained the royal children's umbilical cords (handy for protection later in life, #5272); two cases over are royal writing sets with wax, seals, pens, and ink (#5320).

Go down a few more steps into the lowest level of the treasury and last room. The two **crowns** in the center cases are more modern (from 1670), lighter, and more practical—just gold and diamonds without all the symbolism. The king's crown is only four pounds, the queen's a mere two.

The cases along the walls show off the **crown jewels.** These were made in 1840 of diamonds, emeralds, rubies, and pearls from earlier royal jewelry. The saber (#5540) shows emblems of the realm's 19 provinces. The sumptuous pendant features a 19-carat diamond cut (like its neighbors) in the 58-facet "brilliant" style for maximum reflection (far-left case, #5560). Imagine these on the dance floor. The painting shows the anointing of King Christian V at the Frederiksborg Castle Chapel in 1671. The crown jewels are still worn by the queen on special occasions several times a year.

▲Rosenborg Gardens

Rosenborg Castle is surrounded by the royal pleasure gardens and, on sunny days, a minefield of sunbathing Danish beauties and picnickers. While "ethnic Danes" grab the shade, the rest of the Danes worship the sun. When the royal family is in residence, there's a daily changing-of-the-guard miniparade from the Royal Guard's barracks adjoining Rosenborg Castle (at 11:30) to Amalienborg Palace (at 12:00). The Queen's Rose Garden (across the moat from the palace) is a royal place for a picnic. The fine statue of Hans Christian Andersen in the park—erected while he was still alive (and approved by him)—is meant to symbolize how his stories had a message even for adults (gardens open daily 7:00-dusk).

▲National Gallery of Denmark
(Statens Museum for Kunst)

This museum fills a stately building with Danish and European paintings from the 14th century through today. It's particularly worthwhile for the chance to be immersed in great art by the Danes, and to see its good collection of French Modernists, all well-described in English.

Cost and Hours: 110 DKK, Tue-Sun 11:00-17:00, Wed until 20:00, closed Mon, Sølvgade 48, tel. 33 74 84 94, www.smk.dk.

Visiting the Museum: The ground floor holds special exhibits; the second floor has collections of Danish and Nordic artists from 1750 to 1900, and European art from 1300 to 1800; and the Danish and International Art after 1900 is spread between the second and third floors. Museum upgrades may force the temporary closure of some exhibition rooms.

Head first to the Danish and Nordic artists section, and pick up the excellent floor plan that suggests a twisting route through

the collection. Take the time to read the descriptions in each room, which put the paintings into historical context. In addition to Romantic works by well-known, non-Danish artists (such as the Norwegian J. C. Dahl and the German Caspar David Friedrich), this is a chance to learn about some very talented Danish painters not well-known outside their native land. Make a point to meet the "Skagen Painters," including Anna Ancher, Michael Ancher, Peder Severin Krøyer, and others (find them in the section called "The Modern Breakthrough I-II"). This group, with echoes of the French Impressionists, gathered in the fishing village of Skagen on the northern tip of Denmark, surrounded by the sea and strong light, and painted heroic folk-fishermen themes in the late 1800s. Also worth seeking out are the canvases of Laurits Andersen Ring, who portrayed traditional peasant scenes with modern style; and Jens Ferdinand Willumsen, who pioneered "Vitalism" (celebrating man in nature). Other exhibits are cleverly organized by theme, such as gender or the body.

In the 20th-century section, the collection of early French Modernism is particularly impressive (with works by Matisse, Picasso, Braque, and more). This is complemented with works by Danish artists, who, inspired by the French avant-garde, introduced new, radical forms and colors to Scandinavian art.

CHRISTIANSHAVN

Across the harbor from the old town, Christianshavn—the former merchant's district—is one of the most delightful neighborhoods in town to explore. It offers pleasant canalside walks and trendy restaurants, along with two things to see: Our Savior's Church (with its fanciful tower) and Christiania, a colorful alternative-living community. Before visiting, make sure to read the background on Christianshavn, which helps explain what you'll see (see sidebar).

Your first look at the island will likely be its main square. Christianshavns Torv has a Metro stop, an early Copenhagen phone kiosk (from 1896), a fine bakery across the street (Lagkage-huset), and three statues celebrating Greenland. A Danish protectorate since 1721, Greenland, with 56,000 people, is represented by two members in the Danish parliament. The square has long been a hangout for Greenlanders, who appreciate the cheap beer and long hours of the big supermarket fronting the square.

▲Our Savior's Church (Vor Frelsers Kirke)

Following a recent restoration, the church gleams inside and out. Its bright Baroque interior (1696) is shaped like a giant cube. The magnificent pipe organ is supported by elephants (a royal symbol of the prestigious Order of the Elephant). Looking up to the ceiling, notice elephants also sculpted into the stucco of the dome, and a little one hanging from the main chandelier. Best of all, you can climb the unique spiral spire (with an outdoor staircase winding up to its top—398 stairs in all) for great views of the city and of the Christiania commune below.

Cost and Hours: Church interior-free, open daily 11:00-15:30 but may close for special services; church tower-40 DKK Mon-Thu, 45 DKK Fri-Sun; May-Sept Mon-Sat 9:30-19:00, Sun from 10:30; shorter hours off-season, closed mid-Dec-Feb and in bad weather; bus #2A, #19, or Metro: Christianshavn, Sankt Annægade 29, tel. 41 66 63 57, www.vorfrelserskirke.dk.

❸ Spin-Tour from the Top of Our Savior's Church: Climb up until you run out of stairs. As you wind back down, look for these landmarks:

The modern windmills are a reminder that Denmark generates 36 percent of its power from wind. Below the windmills is a great aerial view of the Christiania commune. Beyond the windmills, across Øresund (the strait that separates Denmark and Sweden), stands a shuttered Swedish nuclear power plant. The lone skyscraper in the distance—the first and tallest skyscraper in Scandinavia—is in Malmö, Sweden. The Øresund Bridge made Malmö an easy 35-minute bus or train ride from Copenhagen (it's become a bedroom community, with much cheaper apartments making the commute worthwhile).

Farther to the right, the big red-roof zone is Amager Island. Five hundred years as the city's dumping grounds earned Amager the nickname "Crap Island." Circling on, you come to the towering

Christianshavn: Then and Now

Christianshavn—Copenhagen's planned port—was vital to Danish power in the 17th and 18th centuries. Denmark had always been second to Sweden when it came to possession of natural resources, so the Danes tried to make up for it by acquiring resource-rich overseas colonies. They built Christianshavn (with Amsterdam's engineering help) to run the resulting trade business—giving this neighborhood a "little Amsterdam" vibe today.

Since Denmark's economy was so dependent on trade, the port town was the natural target of enemies. When the Danes didn't support Britain against Napoleon in 1807, the Brits bombarded Christianshavn. In this "blackest year in Danish history," Christianshavn burned down. That's why today there's hardly a building here that dates from before that time.

Christianshavn remained Copenhagen's commercial center until the 1920s, when a modern harbor was built. Suddenly, Christianshavn's economy collapsed and it became a slum. Cheap prices attracted artsy types, giving it a bohemian flavor. In 1971, squatters set up shop in an old military camp in Christianshavn and created their own community called Christiania, which still survives today (see below).

Over the past few decades, Christianshavn has had a resurgence, and these days, prices are driven up by wealthy locals (who pay about 60 percent of their income in taxes) spending too much for apartments, renting them cheaply to their kids, and writing off the loss. Demand for property is huge. Today the neighborhood is inhabited mostly by rich students and young professionals, living in some of the priciest real estate in town.

Radisson Blu Royal Hotel. The area beyond it is slated to become a forest of skyscrapers—the center of Europe's biomedical industry.

Downtown Copenhagen is decorated with several striking towers and spires. The tower capped by the golden ball is a ride in Tivoli Gardens. Next is City Hall's pointy brick tower. The biggest building, with the three-crown tower, is Christiansborg Palace. The Børsen (old stock exchange) is just beyond, with its unique dragon-tail tower. Behind that is Nyhavn. Just across from that and the Royal Danish Theatre's Playhouse is the dramatic Opera House (with the flat roof and big, grassy front yard).

▲▲▲Christiania

In 1971, the original 700 Christianians established squatters' rights in an abandoned military barracks just a 10-minute walk from the Danish parliament building. Two generations later, this "free city" still stands—an ultra-human mishmash of idealists, hippies, potheads, nonmaterialists, and happy children (900 people, 200 cats,

200 dogs, 2 parrots, and 17 horses). There are even a handful of Willie Nelson-type seniors among the 180 remaining here from the original takeover. And an amazing thing has happened: The place has become the second-most-visited sight among tourists in Copenhagen, behind Tivoli Gardens. Move over, *Little Mermaid*.

"Pusher Street" (named for the sale of soft drugs here) is Christiania's main drag. Get beyond this touristy side of Christiania, and you'll find a fascinating, ramshackle world of moats and earthen ramparts, alternative housing, cozy tea houses, carpenter shops, hippie villas, children's playgrounds, peaceful lanes, and people who believe that "to be normal is to be in a straitjacket." A local slogan claims, *"Kun døde fisk flyder med strømmen"* ("Only dead fish swim with the current").

Hours and Tours: Christiania is open all the time but quiet (and some restaurants closed) on Mondays, which is its rest day (though "resting" from what, I'm not sure). Guided tours leave from the main entrance (50 DKK, July-Aug daily at 13:00 and 15:00; Sat-Sun only the rest of the year, just show up, 1.5 hours, in English and Danish, info tel. 32 95 65 07, www.rundvisergruppen.dk). You're welcome to snap photos, except on Pusher Street (but ask residents before you photograph them).

The Community: Christiania is broken into 14 administrative neighborhoods on a former military base. Most of the land, once owned by Denmark's Ministry of Defense, has been purchased by the Christiania community; the rest of it is leased from the state (see the sidebar for details). Locals build their homes but don't own them—individuals can't buy or sell property. When someone moves out, the community decides who will be invited in to replace that person. A third of the adult population works on the outside, a third works on the inside, and a third doesn't work much at all.

There are nine rules: no cars, no hard drugs, no guns, no explosives, and so on. The Christiania flag is red and yellow because when the original hippies took over, they found a lot of red and yellow paint onsite. The three yellow dots in the flag are from the three "i"s in "Christiania" (or, some claim, the "o"s in "Love, Love, Love").

The community pays the city about $1 million a year for utili-

Christiania

To
Holmen
& Opera
House

Peaceful
walk to
residential
areas

BROBERGSGADE

OVERGADEN

MAIN
ENTRANCE
GATE

THE
GRAY
HALL

REFSHALEVEJ

To
Christianshavns
Canal

PRINSESSE GADE

CHRISTIANIA

OTHER
ENTRANCE

7

6

1

"PUSHER STREET"

4

LANGGADEN

5

BADMANDSSTRÆDE

To Our
Savior's
Church

SANKT ANNÆ GADE

3

2

PATH

ULRIKS-
BASTION
RAMPARTS

OTHER
ENTRANCE

Stadsgraven
(former moat)

Rabbit
Island

To
Airport

100 Meters

100 Yards

1 Carl Madsens Plads	**5** Morgenstedet Vegetarian Café
2 Green Hall	**6** Spiseloppen Restaurant
3 Nemoland	**7** Tour Departure Point
4 Månefiskeren Café	

ties and has about $1 million a year more to run its local affairs. A few "luxury hippies" have oil heat, but most use wood or gas. The ground here was poisoned by its days as a military base, so nothing is grown in Christiania. There's little industry within the commune (Christiania Cykler, which builds fine bikes, is an exception—www.pedersen-bike.dk). A phone chain provides a system of communal security (they have had bad experiences calling the police). Each September 26, the day the first squatters took over the barracks in 1971, Christiania has a big birthday bash.

Tourists are entirely welcome here, because they've become a major part of the economy. Visitors react in very different ways to the place. Some see dogs, dirt, and dazed people. Others see a haven of peace, freedom, and no taboos. It's true that this free city isn't always pretty. But watching parents here raise their children with Christiania values makes me a believer in this social experiment. My take: Giving alternative-type people a place to be alternative is a kind of alternative beauty that deserves a place.

Christiania Documentary: For a fascinating, one-hour insight into Christiania, watch the 2011 documentary *Christiania: 40 Years of Occupation*. This film, produced by Seattle production company Bus No. 8, does a wonderful job of chronicling the his-

The Fight for Christiania

Ever since several hundred squatters took over an unused military camp in 1971, Christiania has been a political hot potato. No one in the Danish establishment wanted it. And no one had the nerve to mash it.

Part of Christiania's history has been ongoing government attempts to shut the place down. At first, city officials looked the other way because back then, no one cared about the land. But skyrocketing Christianshavn land values brought pressure to open Christiania to market forces. By the 1980s, the neighborhood had become gentrified, and both the city and developers were eyeing the land Christiania's hippies were squatting on. And when Denmark's conservative government took over in 2001, they vowed to  "normalize" Christiania (with pressure from the US), with police regularly conducting raids on pot sellers.

Things were looking grim for the Christianians until 2012, when the Danish government offered to sell most of the land to the residents at below the market rate, and offered guaranteed loans. In exchange, the Christianians had to promise to upgrade and maintain water, sewage, and electrical services, and preserve rights of way and "rural" areas. Accepting the offer, Christianians formed a foundation—Freetown Christiania—to purchase and control the property. The parts of Christiania that were not sold are leased to the residents and are still owned by the state.

For many Christianians, it's an ironic, capitalistic twist that they now own property, albeit collectively. They even sell symbolic Christiania "shares" to help pay for the land. And, every adult over age 18 now owes a monthly rent that goes toward paying off the loans and to support services. But on the flip side, this is the greatest degree of security Christiania has ever experienced in its four-plus decades of existence. Even so, mistrust of the establishment is by no means dead, and there are still those who wonder what the government might be up to next.

tory of Europe's oldest still-existing squatters' community. Today, this community is closing in on the 50-year mark and is still going strong—but it hasn't been easy. See www.busno8.com for details.

Visiting Christiania: The main entrance is down Prinsessegade, behind the Our Savior's Church spiral tower. Passing under the gate, take Pusher Street directly into the community. The first square—a kind of market square (souvenirs and marijuana-related stuff)—is named Carl Madsens Plads, honoring the lawyer who took the squatters' case to the Danish supreme court in 1976 and won. Beyond that is Nemoland (a food circus, on the right). A huge warehouse called the Green Hall (Den Grønne Hal) is a recycling center and hardware store (where people get most of their building materials) that does triple duty as a nighttime concert hall and as a craft center for kids. If you go up the stairs between Nemoland and the Green Hall, you'll climb up to the ramparts that overlook the canal. As you wander, be careful to distinguish between real Christianians and Christiania's motley guests—drunks (mostly from other countries) who hang out here in the summer for the freedom. Part of the original charter guaranteed that the community would stay open to the public.

On the left beyond the Green Hall, a lane leads to the Månefiskeren café, and beyond that, to the Morgenstedet vegetarian restaurant (the best place for a simple, friendly meal; see "Eating in Christiania," next page). Beyond these recommended restaurants, you'll find yourself lost in the totally untouristy, truly local

residential parts of Christiania, where kids play in the street and the old folks sit out on the front stoop—just like any other neighborhood. Just as St. Mark's Square isn't the "real Venice," the hippie-druggie scene on Pusher Street isn't the "real Christiania"—you can't say you've experienced Christiania until you've strolled these back streets.

A walk or bike ride through Christiania is a great way to see how this community lives. When you leave, look up—the sign above the gate says, "You are entering the EU."

Smoking Marijuana: Pusher Street was once lined with stalls selling marijuana, joints, and hash. Residents intentionally destroyed the stalls in 2004 to reduce the risk of Christiania being disbanded by the government. (One stall was spared and is on display at the National Museum.) Today, the stalls are back, and you'll

likely hear whispered offers of "hash" during your visit. During my last visit there was a small, pungent stretch of Pusher Street, dubbed the "Green Light District," where pot was being openly sold (signs acknowledged that this activity was still illegal, and announced three rules here: 1. Have fun; 2. No photos; and 3. No running—"because it makes people nervous"). However, purchasing and smoking may buy you more time in Denmark than you'd planned—possession of marijuana remains illegal.

About hard drugs: For the first few years, junkies were tolerated. But that led to violence and polluted the mellow ambience residents envisioned. In 1979, the junkies were expelled—an epic confrontation in the community's folk history now—and since then the symbol of a fist breaking a syringe is as prevalent as the leafy marijuana icon. Hard drugs are emphatically forbidden in Christiania.

Eating in Christiania: The people of Christiania appreciate good food and count on tourism as a big part of their economy. Consequently, there are plenty of decent eateries. Most of the restaurants are open from lunchtime until late and are closed on Monday (the community's weekly holiday). **Pusher Street** has a few grungy but tasty falafel stands, as well as a popular burger bar. **$ Nemoland** is the hangout zone—a fun collection of stands peddling Thai food, burgers, *shawarma,* and other fast hippie food with great, tented outdoor seating. Its stay-a-while atmosphere comes with backgammon, foosball, bakery goods, and fine views from the ramparts. **$$ Månefiskeren** ("Moonfisher Bar") looks like a modern-day Brueghel painting, with billiards, chess, snacks, and drinks. **$$ Morgenstedet** ("Morning Place") is a good, cheap vegetarian café with a mellow, woody interior and a rustic patio outside (left after Pusher Street). **$$$$ Spiseloppen** is *the* classy, good-enough-for-Republicans restaurant in the community (described on page 108). While there are lots of public concerts at the open-air Nemoland stage, for a music club experience, consider **Musik Loppen** (which has live music almost nightly, under the Spiseloppen restaurant).

GREATER COPENHAGEN
Harbor Baths
Swimming in the middle of a large city is unthinkable in most of the world, yet the enterprising Danes have made it happen. On a warm summer day there's no better way to see Copenhageners at play than to visit one of the city's Harbor Baths. The two

most centrally located baths are Havnebadet Fisketorvet, next to the Fisketorvet Mall behind Kødbyen, and Islands Brygge, just south of the Langebro bridge and Christianshavn.

The baths are open to all to enjoy a refreshing saltwater dip. How refreshing? Water temperatures peak at 65 degrees in August, which should be no problem for those with Viking blood. Though the baths are located in former industrial areas, the water is monitored, and the quality is as good as what you'll find at the pristine beaches around Copenhagen. On the rare occasions it dips below acceptable levels, the baths are closed.

Cost and Hours: Free, open long hours June-Sept (lifeguards on duty 11:00-19:00).

Information: Havnebadet Fisketorvet, tel. 30 89 04 70; Islands Brygge, tel. 30 89 04 69.

Getting There: Havnebadet Fisketorvet—from Kødbyen, head east on Dybbølsbro, across the train tracks to the Fisketorvet Mall. Skirt the mall to the left, following the wide promenade toward the water and you'll soon see the baths on the left. Islands Brygge—from Fisketorvet Mall, cross the Inner Harbor on the Bryggebroen pedestrian and bicycle bridge. On the other side, follow the waterside promenade north to the baths (best on a bike). Or, if coming from the main train station area, head east over Langebro bridge, then head a short distance south—you can't miss the baths. From Christianshavn, follow the ramparts west to where they meet the Inner Harbor. Pass under Langebro bridge, and you'll see the baths.

Visiting the Baths: The Havnebadet Fisketorvet is actually a huge, semisubmerged barge containing three pools: one for children, another for diving (from one-, two-, and three-meter-high boards), and an Olympic-size swimming pool. Here you'll be hemmed in on three sides by glassy modern office buildings and the Fisketorvet Mall.

The much busier Islands Brygge facility consists of five pools (two suitable for kids) and a prow-shaped diving platform offering three- and five-meter leaps into the water. The shore is one big cobbled promenade backed by a grassy area that's great for sunbathing, barbecues, and people-watching.

Carlsberg Brewery

Denmark's beloved source of legal intoxicants is Carlsberg. About 1.5 miles west of Rådhuspladsen (City Hall Square), Carlsberg welcomes you to its visitors center for a self-guided tour, a free beer, and a small gift. Mostly, it's a ruse to ply you with a beer and get you into their substantial gift shop. For a more in-depth visit, take the guided tour or do the beer tasting, though both cost extra.

Cost and Hours: 100 DKK, daily 10:00-20:00, Oct-April until 17:00; half-hour guided tour—50 DKK, in English at 13:00, 14:00, and 15:00; beer tasting—75 DKK, at 12:00, 14:00, and 16:00; catch the local train to Carlsberg Station or bus #26 (get off at the Kammasvej stop and walk five minutes), or take a free shuttle from near the Vesterbrogade TI (where the hop-on, hop-off buses stop); enter at Gamle Carlsbergvej 11 around corner from brewery entrance, tel. 33 27 12 82, www.visitcarlsberg.dk.

Nearby: The manicured gardens of the sprawling Frederiksberg Park (Frederiksberg Have) and adjacent Southern Field (Søndermarken) make a lovely setting for a picnic.

Open-Air Folk Museum (Frilandsmuseet)

This park, located north of Copenhagen in the suburb of Lyngby, is part of the National Museum. It's filled with traditional Danish architecture and folk culture, farm animals, and gardens. Bring a picnic or dine at the on-site restaurant.

Cost and Hours: 65 DKK; May-mid-Oct Tue-Sun 10:00-16:00, July-mid-Aug until 17:00, closed Mon and off-season; S-tog: Sorgenfri and 10-minute walk to Kongevejen 100 in Lyngby (see the Near Copenhagen map in the following chapter); tel. 41 20 64 55, http://natmus.dk.

Bakken

Danes gather at Copenhagen's *other* great amusement park, Bakken, situated in the Dyrehaven forest about a 10-minute drive north of the city.

Cost and Hours: Free entry, 269 DKK for all-ride pass; late June-mid-Aug daily 12:00-24:00, shorter hours April-late June and mid-Aug-mid-Sept, closed mid-Sept-March; S-tog: Klampenborg, then walk 10 minutes through the woods (see the Near Copenhagen map in the following chapter); tel. 39 63 73 00, www.bakken.dk.

Dragør

If you don't have time to get to the idyllic island of Ærø (see the Central Denmark chapter), consider the eight-mile trip south of Copenhagen to the fishing village of Dragør, near the airport (bus #350S from Nørreport). For information, see www.visit-dragoer.dk.

Shopping in Copenhagen

Shops are generally open Monday through Friday from 10:00 to 19:00 and Saturday from 9:00 to 16:00 (closed Sun). While big department stores dominate the scene, many locals favor the characteristic, small artisan shops and boutiques.

Uniquely Danish souvenirs to look for include intricate paper cuttings with idyllic motifs of swans, flowers, or Christmas themes; mobiles with everything from bicycles to Viking ships (look for the quality Flensted brand); and the colorful artwork of Danish artist Bo Bendixen (posters, postcards, T-shirts, and more). Jewelry lovers look for amber, known as the "gold of the North." Globs of this petrified sap wash up on the shores of all the Baltic countries.

If you buy anything substantial (minimum 300 DKK, about $50) from a shop displaying the **Danish Tax-Free Shopping** emblem, you can get a refund of the Value-Added Tax, roughly 20 to 25 percent of the purchase price (VAT is "MOMS" in Danish). If you have your purchase mailed, the tax can be deducted from your bill. For details, see "Getting a VAT Refund" on page 700.

WHERE TO SHOP

Consider the following stores, markets, and neighborhoods:

For a street's worth of shops selling **"Scantiques,"** wander down Ravnsborggade from Nørrebrogade.

Copenhagen's colorful **flea markets** are small but feisty and surprisingly cheap (May-Nov Sat 8:00-14:00 at Israels Plads; May-Sept Fri and Sat 8:00-17:00 along Gammel Strand and on Kongens Nytorv). For other street markets, ask at the TI.

The city's top **department stores** (Illum at Østergade 52, and Magasin du Nord at Kongens Nytorv 13) offer a good, if expensive, look at today's Denmark. Both are on the Strøget and have fine cafeterias on their top floors. The department stores and the Politiken Bookstore on Rådhuspladsen have a good selection of maps and English travel guides.

The section of the Strøget called **Amagertorv** is a highlight for shoppers. The **Royal Copenhagen** store here sells porcelain on three floors (Mon-Fri 10:00-19:00, Sat 10:00-18:00, Sun 11:00-16:00). The first floor up features figurines and collectibles. The second floor has a second-quality department for discounts, proving that "even the best painter can miss a stroke." Next door, **Illums Bolighus** shows off three floors of modern Danish design (Mon-Sat 10:00-19:00, Fri until 20:00, Sun 11:00-18:00).

House of Amber has a shop and a tiny two-room museum with about 50 examples of prehistoric insects trapped in the amber (remember *Jurassic Park*?) under magnifying glasses. You'll also see remarkable items made of amber, from necklaces and chests to Viking ships and chess sets (25 DKK, daily May-Sept 9:00-19:30, Oct-April 10:00-17:30, at the top of Nyhavn at Kongens Nytorv 2). If you're visiting Rosenborg Castle, you'll see the ultimate examples of amber craftsmanship in its treasury.

Nightlife in Copenhagen

For the latest event and live music listings, check at the TI and pick up *The Copenhagen Post* (comes out weekly, read online or pick up free copy at TI and some hotels, also sold at newsstands, www.cphpost.dk).

Nightlife Neighborhoods: The **Meatpacking District,** which I've listed for its restaurants (see page 111), is also one of the city's up-and-coming destinations for bars and nightlife. On warm evenings, **Nyhavn** canal becomes a virtual nightclub, with packs of young people hanging out along the water, sipping beers. **Christiania** always seems to have something musical going on after dark. **Tivoli** has evening entertainment daily from mid-April through late September (see page 62).

Music Venues: Copenhagen Jazz House is a good bet for live jazz (two stages, closed Mon, Niels Hemmingsensgade 10, tel. 33 15 47 00, schedule at www.jazzhouse.dk). For blues, try the **Mojo Blues Bar** (nightly 20:00-late, music starts at 21:30, Løngangsstræde 21c, tel. 33 11 64 53, schedule in Danish at www.mojo.dk). For locations, see the Copenhagen Restaurants map later in this chapter.

Jazz Cruises: Canal Tours Copenhagen offers 1.5-hour jazz cruises along the canals of Copenhagen. You can bring a picnic dinner and drinks on board and enjoy a lively night on the water surrounded by Danes (150 DKK and up, June-mid-Sept Thu and Sun at 19:00, no tours mid-Sept-May, departs from Canal Tours Copenhagen dock at Nyhavn, tel. 32 96 30 00). Call to reserve on July and August evenings; otherwise try arriving 20 to 30 minutes in advance, www.stromma.dk.

Sleeping in Copenhagen

I've listed a few big business-class hotels, the best budget hotels in the center, and a few backpacker dorm options.

Big Copenhagen hotels have an exasperating pricing policy. Their high rack rates are charged only about 20 or 30 days a year (unless you book in advance and don't know better). As hotels are swamped at certain times, they like to keep their gouging options open. Therefore, you'll need to check their website for deals or be bold enough to simply show up and use the TI's booking service to find yourself a room on their push list (ask at their desk, 100-DKK fee). The TI swears that, except for maybe 10 days a year, you can land yourself a deeply discounted room in a three- or four-star business-class hotel in the center. That means a 1,500-DKK double with American-style comfort for about 1,000 DKK, including a big buffet breakfast.

Sleep Code

Hotels are classified based on the average price of a typical en suite double room with breakfast in high season.

$$$$	**Splurge:** Most rooms over 1,100 DKK
$$$	**Pricier:** 900-1,100 DKK
$$	**Moderate:** 700-900 DKK
$	**Budget:** 500-700 DKK
¢	**Backpacker:** Under 500 DKK
RS%	**Rick Steves discount**

Unless otherwise noted, credit cards are accepted, hotel staff speak basic English, and free Wi-Fi is available. Comparison-shop by checking prices at several hotels (on each hotel's own website, on a booking site, or by email). For the best deal, *always book directly with the hotel.* Ask for a discount if paying in cash; if the listing includes **RS%,** request a Rick Steves discount.

HOTELS IN CENTRAL COPENHAGEN

All of these hotels are big and modern, with elevators and non-smoking rooms. Beware: Many hotels have rip-off phone rates even for local calls.

Near Nørreport

$$$$ Ibsens Hotel is a stylish 118-room hotel with helpful staff, located in a charming neighborhood away from the main train station commotion and a short walk from the old center (consider splurging on a larger room—smaller rooms can be very tight, great bikes-150 DKK/24 hours, pay parking, Vendersgade 23, S-tog and Metro: Nørreport—to find Vendersgade after surfacing from the Metro, head for the five-story brown building with the green copper dome, tel. 33 13 19 13, www.ibsenshotel.dk, hotel@ibsenshotel.dk).

$$$ Hotel Jørgensen is a friendly little 30-room hotel in a great location just off Nørreport, kitty-corner from the bustling Torvehallerne KBH food market. With fresh and tidy rooms and a welcoming lounge, it's a fine option, though the halls are a narrow, tangled maze (Rømersgade 11, tel. 33 13 81 86, www.hoteljoergensen.dk, hoteljoergensen@mail.dk). They also rent ¢ dorm beds.

Near Nyhavn

$$$$ 71 Nyhavn has 130 rustic but very classy rooms in a pair of beautifully restored, early-19th-century brick warehouses located at the far end of the colorful Nyhavn canal. With a professional, polite staff, lots of old brick and heavy timbers, and plenty of style, it's

Copenhagen Hotels

1. Ibsens Hotel
2. Hotel Jørgensen
3. 71 Nyhavn
4. Hotel Bethel Sømandshjem
5. Axel Hotel
6. 66 Guldsmeden
7. Star Hotel
8. Hotel Nebo
9. Wake Up Copenhagen
10. Cabinn (4)
11. Danhostel Copenhagen City
12. Copenhagen Downtown
13. To Danhostel Copenhagen Amager

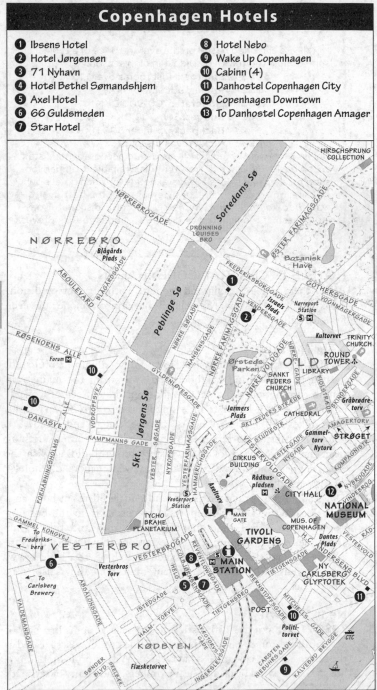

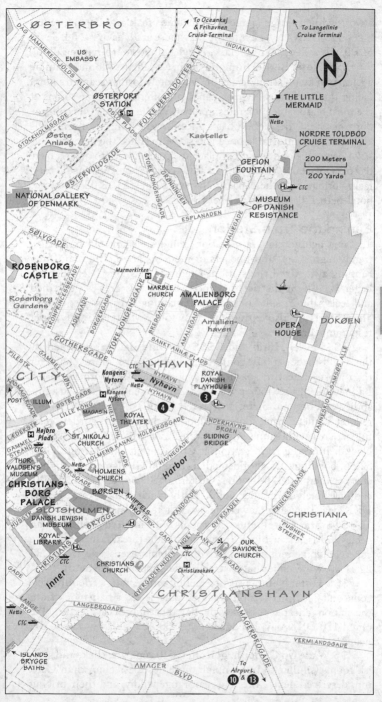

a worthwhile splurge (some rates include breakfast, air-con, rental bikes-125 DKK/day, next to the Playhouse at Nyhavn 71, tel. 33 43 62 00, www.71nyhavnhotel.dk, 71nyhavnhotel@arp-hansen.dk).

$$$ Hotel Bethel Sømandshjem ("Seamen's Home"), run by a Lutheran association, is a calm and stately former seamen's hotel facing the boisterous Nyhavn canal and offering 29 cozy rooms at the most reasonable rack rates in town. While the decor is college-dorm-inspired, the hotel boasts a kind, welcoming staff and feels surprisingly comfortable once you settle in. Plus, the colorful Nyhavn neighborhood is a great place to "come home" to after a busy day of sightseeing. Book long in advance (Metro: Kongens Nytorv, facing bridge over the canal at Nyhavn 22, tel. 33 13 03 70, www.hotel-bethel.dk, info@hotel-bethel.dk).

Behind the Train Station

The area behind the train station mingles elegant old buildings, trendy nightspots, and pockets of modern sleaze. The main drag running away from the station, Istedgade, has long been Copenhagen's red-light district; but increasingly, this area is gentrified and feels safe (in spite of the few remaining harmless sex shops). These hotels are also extremely handy to the Meatpacking District restaurant zone.

$$$$ Axel Hotel and **$$$$ 66 Guldsmeden,** operated by the Guldsmeden ("Dragonfly") company, have more character than most—a restful spa-like ambience decorated with imported Balinese furniture, four-poster beds, and an emphasis on sustainability and organic materials. (**Axel:** breakfast extra, 189 rooms, request a quieter back room overlooking the pleasant garden, restful spa area with sauna and hot tub-295 DKK/person per stay, a block behind the train station at Colbjørnsensgade 14, tel. 33 31 32 66, booking@hotelguldsmeden.com; **66 Guldsmeden:** slightly cheaper than Axel, 64 rooms, Vesterbrogade 66, tel. 33 22 15 00, carlton@hotelguldsmeden.com). Both hotels rent bikes for 150 DKK/day. They share a website: www.hotelguldsmeden.com.

$$$ Star Hotel rents 134 rooms with modern Scandinavian decor and is just a block from the station (breakfast extra, nice courtyard, bike rental-130 DKK/day, Colbjørnsensgade 13, tel. 33 22 11 00, www.copenhagenstar.dk, star@copenhagenstar.dk).

$$$ Hotel Nebo, a secure-feeling refuge with a friendly welcome and 84 comfy if a bit creaky rooms, is just a half-block from the station (cheaper rooms with shared bath, breakfast extra, bike rental-120 DKK/day, Istedgade 6, tel. 33 21 12 17, www.nebo.dk, nebo@nebo.dk).

$$ Wake Up Copenhagen offers 510 compact, slick, and stylish rooms (similar to but a notch more upscale-feeling than Cabinn, described next). The rates can range wildly, and their pricing structure is like the airlines' in that the further ahead and less flexibly you book, the less you pay). Rooms that are higher up—with better views and quieter—are also more expensive. It's in a desolate no-man's-land behind the station, between the train tracks and the harbor—about a 15-minute walk from the station or Tivoli, but ideal for biking (breakfast extra, air-con, bike rental, Carsten Niebuhrs Gade 11, tel. 44 80 00 00, www.wakeupcopenhagen. com, wakeupcopenhagen@arp-hansen.dk).

A DANISH MOTEL 6

$ Cabinn is a radical innovation and a great value, with several locations in Copenhagen (as well as Odense, Aarhus, and elsewhere):

identical, mostly collapsible, tiny but comfy, cruise-ship-type staterooms, all bright, molded, and shiny, with TV, coffeepot, shower, and toilet. Each room has a single bed that expands into a twin-bedded room with one or two fold-down bunks on the walls. It's tough to argue with this kind of efficiency (family rooms available, breakfast extra, easy pay parking, www.cabinn.com). The best of the bunch is **Cabinn City,** with 350 rooms and a great central location (a short walk south of the main train station and Tivoli at Mitchellsgade 14, tel. 33 46 16 16, city@cabinn.com). Two more, nearly identical Cabinns are a 15-minute walk northwest of the station: **Cabinn Copenhagen Express** (86 rooms, Danasvej 32, tel. 33 21 04 00, express@cabinn.com) and **Cabinn Scandinavia** (201 rooms, family rooms, Vodroffsvej 55, tel. 35 36 11 11, scandinavia@cabinn.com). The largest is **Cabinn Metro,** near the Ørestad Metro station (710 rooms, family rooms, on the airport side of town at Arne Jakobsens Allé 2, tel. 32 46 57 00, metro@cabinn.com).

ROOMS AND APARTMENTS

At about 650 DKK or more per double, renting a room in a private home can be a great value. It offers a peek into Danish domestic life, and the experience can be as private or as social as you wish. These accommodations usually don't include breakfast, but you'll have access to the kitchen. **$ Bed & Breakfast Denmark** has served as a clearinghouse for local B&Bs since 1992. Peter Eberth and his staff rent piles of good local rooms in central apartments and take a 20-30 percent cut (the "deposit" you pay) but monitor quality. Their website lets you choose the type and location and gives you the necessary details when you pay (tel. 39 61 04 05, www.bbdk.dk).

Another great option is **AirBnB,** which offers scores of accommodations and options all over town, including rooms in private homes as well as apartments where you have privacy, can prepare your own meals, and come and go as you like (www.airbnb.com).

HOSTELS

¢ **Danhostel Copenhagen City,** an official HI hostel, is the hostel of the future. This huge harborside 16-story skyscraper is clean,

modern, nonsmoking, and a 10-minute walk from the train station and Tivoli. Some rooms on higher floors have panoramic views over the city (available on a first-come, first-served basis). This is your best bet for a clean, basic, and inexpensive room with private baths in the city center (private rooms and family rooms available, breakfast extra, elevator, rental bikes, H. C. Andersens Boulevard 50, tel. 33 11 85 85, www.danhostelcopenhagencity.dk, copenhagencity@danhostel.dk).

¢ **Copenhagen Downtown** is beautifully located on a pleasant street right in the city center, a few steps from Slotsholmen Island and two blocks from the Strøget. Its 300 beds are a bit institutional, but it promises free dinner and comes with a guest kitchen and a colorful, fun hangout bar, which doubles as the reception (private rooms available, breakfast extra, no curfew, Vandkunsten 5, tel. 70 23 21 10, www.copenhagendowntown.com, info@copenhagendowntown.com).

¢ **Danhostel Copenhagen Amager,** an official HI hostel, is on the edge of town (private rooms available, breakfast extra, family rooms, no curfew, excellent facilities, Vejlands Allé 200, tel. 32 52 29 08, www.danhostelcopenhagen.dk, copenhagen@danhostel.dk). To get from downtown to the hostel, take the Metro (Metro: Bella Center, then 10-minute walk).

Eating in Copenhagen

CHEAP MEALS

For a quick lunch, try a *smørrebrød*, a *pølse*, or a picnic. Finish it off with a pastry.

Smørrebrød

Denmark's 300-year-old tradition of open-face sandwiches survives. Find a *smørrebrød* takeout shop and choose two or three that look good (about 35 DKK each). You'll get them wrapped and

Restaurant Price Code

I've assigned each eatery a price category, based on the average cost of a typical main course. Drinks, desserts, and splurge items (steak and seafood) can raise the price considerably.

$$$$	**Splurge:** Most main courses over 150 DKK
$$$	**Pricier:** 100-150 DKK
$$	**Moderate:** 50-100 DKK
$	**Budget:** Under 50 DKK

In Denmark, a *pølsevogn* or other takeout spot is **$**; a sit-down café is **$$**; a casual but more upscale restaurant is **$$$**; and a swanky splurge is **$$$$**.

ready for a park bench. Add a cold drink, and you have a fine, quick, and very Danish lunch. Tradition calls for three sandwich courses: herring first, then meat, and then cheese. Downtown, you'll find these handy local alternatives to Yankee fast-food chains. They range from splurges to quick stop-offs.

COPENHAGEN

Between Copenhagen University and Rosenborg Castle

My three favorite *smørrebrød* places are particularly handy when connecting your sightseeing between the downtown Strøget core and Rosenborg Castle.

$$ Restaurant Schønnemann is the foodies' choice—it has been written up in international magazines and frequently wins awards for "Best Lunch in Copenhagen." It's a cozy cellar restaurant crammed with small tables—according to the history on the menu, people "gather here in intense togetherness." The sand on the floor evokes a bygone era when passing traders would leave their horses out on the square while they lunched here. You'll need to reserve to get a table, and you'll pay a premium for their *smørrebrød* (two lunch seatings Mon-Sat: 11:30-14:00 & 14:15-17:00, closed Sun, no dinner, Hauser Plads 16, tel. 33 12 07 85, www.restaurantschonnemann.dk).

$$ Café Halvvejen is a small mom-and-pop place serving traditional lunches and open-face sandwiches in a woody and smoke-stained café, lined with portraits of Danish royalty. You can eat inside or at an outside table in good weather (food served Mon-Sat 12:00-15:00, closed Sun, next to public library at Krystalgade 11, tel. 33 11 91 12). In the evening, it becomes a hip and smoky student hangout, though no food is served.

$ Slagteren ved Kultorvet, a few blocks northwest of the uni-

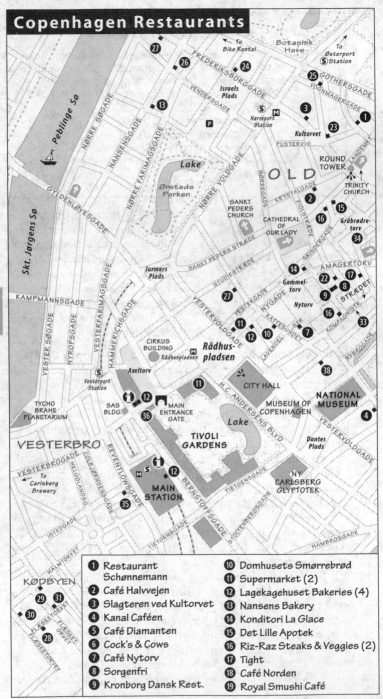

Copenhagen Restaurants

1. Restaurant Schønnemann
2. Café Halvvejen
3. Slagteren ved Kultorvet
4. Kanal Caféen
5. Café Diamanten
6. Cock's & Cows
7. Café Nytorv
8. Sorgenfri
9. Kronborg Dansk Rest.
10. Domhusets Smørrebrød
11. Supermarket (2)
12. Lagekagehuset Bakeries (4)
13. Nansens Bakery
14. Konditori La Glace
15. Det Lille Apotek
16. Riz-Raz Steaks & Veggies (2)
17. Tight
18. Café Norden
19. Royal Smushi Café

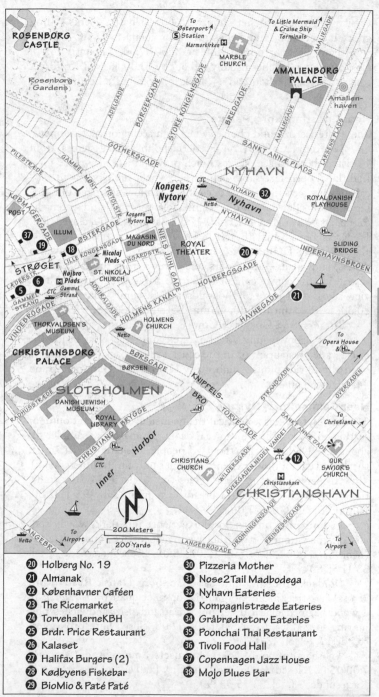

COPENHAGEN

20 Holberg No. 19
21 Almanak
22 Københavner Caféen
23 The Ricemarket
24 TorvehallerneKBH
25 Brdr. Price Restaurant
26 Kalaset
27 Halifax Burgers (2)
28 Kødbyens Fiskebar
29 BioMio & Paté Paté
30 Pizzeria Mother
31 Nose2Tail Madbodega
32 Nyhavn Eateries
33 Kompagnistræde Eateries
34 Gråbrødretorv Eateries
35 Poonchai Thai Restaurant
36 Tivoli Food Hall
37 Copenhagen Jazz House
38 Mojo Blues Bar

versity, is a small butcher shop with bowler-hatted clerks selling good, inexpensive sandwiches to go for about 45 DKK. Choose from ham, beef, or pork (Mon-Fri 8:00-17:30, Sat until 15:00, closed Sun, sandwiches usually sell out by 13:00; just off Kultorvet square at Frederiksborggade 4, look for gold bull's head hanging outside).

Near Christiansborg Palace
These eateries are good choices when sightseeing on Slotsholmen.

$$ Kanal Caféen, on Frederiksholms Kanal across from Christiansborg Palace, serves lunch only and is a nice place for a traditional open-face sandwich. Inside, you'll rub elbows with locals in what feels like the cozy confines of a low-ceilinged old sailing ship; outside you can dine right above the canal and watch the tour boats go by (Mon-Fri 11:30-17:00, Sat until 15:00, closed Sun, Frederiksholms Kanal 18, tel. 33 11 57 70).

$$ Café Diamanten serves open-face sandwiches, warm dishes, and salads—and pours microbrews from the tap. Take a seat inside the comfy café or under the parasols out front, with a view across the square to Thorvaldsen's Museum (Mon-Fri 10:00-20:30, Sat-Sun until 19:00, Gammel Strand 50, tel. 33 93 55 45).

Burgers: $$$ Cock's & Cows is a trendy burger-and-cocktail bar with a happy, young vibe on an elegant street. Eat inside the brick-walled restaurant or in the courtyard out back (some burgers piled almost ridiculously high, daily 11:30-21:30, Gammel Strand 34, tel. 69 69 60 00).

Near Gammeltorv/Nytorv
$$ Café Nytorv has a nautical theme inside and pleasant outdoor seating on Nytorv. There's a great deal on a *smørrebrød* sampler for about 230 DKK—perfect for two people to share (if you smile, they'll serve it for dinner even though it's only on the lunch menu). This "Copenhagen City Plate" gives you a selection of the traditional sandwiches and extra bread on request (daily 9:00-22:00, Nytorv 15, tel. 33 11 77 06).

$$ Sorgenfri offers a local experience in a dark, woody spot just off the Strøget—give the herring open-face sandwich a try (Mon-Sat 11:00-20:45, Sun 12:00-18:00, Brolæggerstræde 8, tel. 33 11 58 80).

Or duck (literally) into **$$ Kronborg Dansk Restaurant,** across the street from Sorgenfri, for finer-quality *smørrebrød* in a wood-beamed nautical setting (meat and fish sandwiches plus herring specialties, Mon-Sat 11:00-17:00, closed Sun, Brolæggerstræde 12, tel. 33 13 07 08).

Another option is **$$ Domhusets Smørrebrød** (Mon-Fri 7:00-15:00, closed Sat-Sun, off the City Hall end of the Strøget at Kattesundet 18, tel. 33 15 98 98).

The *Pølse*

The famous Danish hot dog, sold in *pølsevogne* (sausage wagons) throughout the country, is another typically Danish institution

that has resisted the onslaught of our global, prepackaged, fast-food culture. Study the photo menu for variations. These are fast, cheap, tasty, and, like their American cousins, almost worthless nutritionally. Even so, what the locals call the "dead man's finger" is the dog Danish kids love to bite.

There's more to getting a *pølse* than simply ordering a "hot dog" (which in Copenhagen simply means a sausage with a bun on the side, generally the worst bread possible). The best is a *ristet* (or grilled) hot dog *med det hele* (with the works). Employ these other handy phrases: *rød* (red, the basic boiled weenie), *medister* (spicy, better quality), *knæk* (short, stubby, tastier than *rød*), *brød* (a bun, usually smaller than the sausage), *svøb* ("swaddled" in bacon), *Fransk* (French style, buried in a long skinny hole in the bun with sauce). *Sennep* is mustard and *ristet løg* are crispy, fried onions. Wash everything down with a *sodavand* (soda pop).

By hanging around a *pølsevogn*, you can study this institution. Denmark's "cold feet cafés" are a form of social care: People who have difficulty finding jobs are licensed to run these wiener mobiles. As they gain seniority, they are promoted to work at more central locations. Danes like to gather here for munchies and *pølsesnak*—the local slang for empty chatter (literally, "sausage talk"). And traditionally, after getting drunk, guys stop here for a hot dog and chocolate milk on the way home—that's why the stands stay open until the wee hours.

Picnics

Throughout Copenhagen, small delis *(viktualiehandler)* sell fresh bread, tasty pastries, juice, milk, cheese, and yogurt (drinkable, in tall liter boxes). Two of the largest supermarket chains are **Irma** (in the glassy DI—Danish Industry—building on Vesterbrogade next to Tivoli) and **Super Brugsen. Netto** is a cut-rate outfit with the cheapest prices and a good bakery section (located on Rådhuspladsen at Vestergade). And, of course, there's the ever-present **7-Eleven** chain, with branches seemingly on every corner; while you'll pay a bit more here, there's a reason they're called "convenience" stores—and they also serve pastries and hot dogs.

COPENHAGEN

Dine with the Danes

For a unique experience and a great opportunity to meet locals in their homes, consider having this organization arrange a dinner for you with a Danish family. You get a homey two-course meal with lots of conversation. Some effort is made to match your age, interests, and occupations. Book online at least two weeks in advance (450 DKK/person, www.facebook.com/DineWithTheDanes, dinewiththedanes@msn.com). Fill out an online questionnaire, and you'll soon be contacted via Facebook or by email.

Pastry

The golden pretzel sign hanging over the door or windows is the Danes' age-old symbol for a bakery. Danish pastries, called *wienerbrød* ("Vienna bread") in Denmark, are named for the Viennese bakers who brought the art of pastry-making to Denmark, where the Danes say they perfected it. Try these bakeries: **Lagkagehuset** (multiple locations around town; the handiest options include one right in the train station, another nearby inside the Vesterbrogade TI, one along the Strøget at Frederiksborggade 21, and another on Torvegade just across from the Metro station in Christianshavn) and **Nansens** (on corner of Nansensgade and Ahlefeldtsgade, near Ibsens Hotel). **Emmerys,** a trendy, gluten-free, Starbucks-like organic bakery and café, has more than 20 branches around Copenhagen, and sells good pastries and sandwiches. For a genteel bit of high-class 1870s Copenhagen, pay a lot for a coffee and a fresh Danish at **Konditori La Glace,** just off the Strøget at Skoubogade 3.

RESTAURANTS

I've listed restaurants in four areas: the downtown core, the funky Christianshavn neighborhood across the harbor, near Nørreport, and in the trendy Meatpacking District behind the main train station.

Downtown Core

$$$$ Det Lille Apotek ("The Little Pharmacy") is a candlelit place with seating spread among its four themed "parlours." It's been popular with locals for 200 years, and today it's a hit with tourists, serving open-face sandwiches at lunchtime and traditional dinners in the evening (nightly from 17:30, just off the Strøget, between Frue Church and Round Tower at Store Kannikestræde 15, tel. 33 12 56 06).

$$ Riz-Raz Steaks & Veggies has two locations in Copenhagen: around the corner from the canal boat rides at Kompagnistræde 20 (tel. 33 15 05 75) and across from Det Lille Apotek at Store Kannikestræde 19 (tel. 33 32 33 45). At both places, you'll find a combination of burgers and meat dishes as well as vegetarian, including an all-you-can-eat Middle Eastern/Mediterranean/vegetarian buffet lunch for 90 DKK (great falafel, daily 11:30-16:00) and a bigger dinner buffet for 100 DKK (16:00-24:00). Use lots of plates and return to the buffet as many times as you like.

$$$ Tight resembles a trendy gastropub, serving an eclectic international array of food and drink (Canadian, Aussie, French, and burgers, with Danish microbrews) in a split-level maze of hip rooms that mix old timbers and brick with bright colors (daily 17:00-22:00, just off the Strøget at Hyskenstræde 10, tel. 33 11 09 00).

$$$$ Café Norden, very Danish with modern "world cuisine," seasonal menus, good light meals, and fine pastries, is a big, venerable institution overlooking Amagertorv by the heron fountain. It's family-friendly, with good seats outside on the square, in the busy ground-floor interior, or with more space and better views upstairs (great people-watching from the window seats). Order at the bar—it's the same price upstairs or down (huge splittable portions, daily 9:00-24:00, Østergade 61, tel. 33 11 77 91).

$$$ Royal Smushi Café is a hit with dainty people who like the idea of small, gourmet, open-face sandwiches served on Royal Copenhagen porcelain. You can sit in their modern chandeliered interior or the quiet courtyard (daily 10:00-18:00, next to Royal Copenhagen porcelain store at Amagertorv 6, tel. 33 12 11 22).

$$ Holberg No. 19, a cozy Argentinian-run café with classic ambience, sits just a block off the tourist crush of the Nyhavn canal. With a loose and friendly vibe, it offers more personality and lower prices than the tourist traps along Nyhavn (no real kitchen but reasonably priced salads and sandwiches—some with an international twist, quiche, selection of wines and beers, order at the bar, Mon-Fri 8:00-22:00, Sat 10:00-20:00, Sun 10:00-18:00, Holberg 19, tel. 33 14 01 90).

$$$ Almanak, on the waterfront promenade near the entrance to Nyhavn, dishes artfully prepared (and tasty) open-face sandwiches and main courses in a cool and sleek restaurant and on its outdoor terrace facing the Inner Harbor. Look for the long green building on the promenade with a big sign on the roof that reads *The Standard* (Tue-Sun 12:00-22:00, closed Mon, Havnegade 44, tel. 72 14 88 08).

$$$ Københavner Caféen, cozy and old-fashioned, feels like a ship captain's dining room. The staff is enthusiastically traditional, serving local dishes and elegant open-face sandwiches for a good value. Lunch specials (80-100 DKK) are served until 17:00, when the more expensive dinner menu kicks in (daily, kitchen closes at 22:00, at Badstuestræde 10, tel. 33 32 80 81).

$$$ The Ricemarket, an unpretentious Asian fusion bistro, is buried in a modern cellar between the Strøget and Rosenborg Castle. It's a casual, more affordable side-eatery of a popular local restaurant, and offers a flavorful break from Danish food (seven-dish family-style meal for 285 DKK, daily 12:00-22:00, Hauser-gade 38 near Kultorvet, tel. 35 35 75 30).

$$ Illum and **Magasin du Nord** department stores serve cheery, reasonable meals in their cafeterias. At Illum, eat outside at tables along the Strøget, or head to the elegant glass-domed top floor (Østergade 52). Magasin du Nord (Kongens Nytorv 13) also has a great grocery and deli in the basement.

Also try **Café Nytorv** at Nytorv 15 or **Sorgenfri** at Brolæg-gerstræde 8 (both are described under "Smørrebrød," earlier).

Christianshavn

This neighborhood is so cool, it's worth combining an evening wander with dinner. It's a 10-minute walk across the bridge from the old center, or a 3-minute ride on the Metro. Choose one of my listings (for locations, see the Christianshavn map, next page), or simply wander the blocks between Christianshavns Torv, the main square, and the Christianshavn Canal—you'll find a number of lively neighborhood pubs and cafés.

$$$$ Ravelinen Restaurant, on a tiny island on the big road 100 yards south of Christianshavn, serves traditional Danish food to happy local crowds. Dine indoors or on the lovely lakeside ter-race (which is tented and heated, so it's comfortable even on blus-tery evenings). This is like Tivoli without the kitsch and tourists. They offer a shareable "Cold Table" meal for 280 DKK at lunch only (mid-April-late Dec daily 11:30-21:00, closed off-season, Torvegade 79, tel. 32 96 20 45).

$ Lagkagehuset is everybody's favorite bakery in Christian-shavn. With a big selection of pastries, sandwiches, excellent fresh-baked bread, and award-winning strawberry tarts, it's a great place for breakfast or picnic fixings (takeout coffee, daily 6:00-19:00, Torvegade 45). For other locations closer to the town center, see page 106 under "Pastry."

Ethnic Strip on Christianshavn's Main Drag: Torvegade, which is within a few minutes' walk of the Christianshavn Metro station, is lined with appealing and inexpensive ethnic eateries, in-cluding Italian, cheap kebabs, Thai, Chinese, and more. **$$ Spicy Kitchen** serves cheap and good Indian food—tight and cozy, it's a hit with locals (daily 17:00-23:00, Torvegade 56).

In Christiania: $$$$ Spiseloppen ("The Flea Eats") is a wonderfully classy place in Christiania. It serves great 140-DKK

Christianshavn

1 Ravelinen Restaurant
2 Lagkagehuset Bakery
3 Spicy Kitchen
4 Spiseloppen Restaurant

vegetarian meals and 185-250-DKK meaty ones by candlelight. It's gourmet anarchy—a good fit for Christiania, the free city/squatter town (Tue-Sun 17:00-22:00, kitchen closes at 21:00, closed Mon, reservations often necessary Fri-Sat; 3 blocks behind spiral spire of Our Savior's Church, on top floor of old brick warehouse, turn right just inside Christiania's main gate, enter the wildly empty warehouse, and climb the graffiti-riddled stairs; tel. 32 57 95 58, http://spiseloppen.dk). Other, less-expensive Christiania eateries are listed on page 90.

Near Nørreport

$$$ TorvehallerneKBH is in a pair of modern, glassy market halls right on Israel Plads. Survey both halls and the stalls on the square before settling in. In addition to produce, fish, and meat stalls, it has several inviting food counters where you can sit to eat a meal, or grab something to go. I can't think of a more enjoyable place in Copenhagen to browse for a meal than this upscale food court (pricey but fun, with quality food; Mon-Thu 10:00-19:00, Fri until 20:00, Sat until 18:00, Sun 11:00-17:00, some places closed Mon; Frederiksborggade 21).

$$-$$$ Brdr. Price Restaurant—an elegant, highly regarded bistro serving creative Danish and international meals just across from Rosenborg Castle—is good for a dressy splurge in their

A Culinary Phe-noma-non

Foodies visiting Denmark probably already know that Copenhagen is home to one of the planet's top-rated restaurants. *Restaurant* magazine named Noma the "Best Restaurant in the World" for several years, making it *the* reservation to get in the foodie universe. Chef René Redzepi is a pioneer in the burgeoning "New Nordic" school of cooking, which combines modern nouvelle cuisine and molecular gastronomy techniques with locally sourced (and, in some cases, foraged) ingredients from Denmark and other Nordic lands. So, while they use sophisticated cooking methods, they replace the predictable French and Mediterranean ingredients with Nordic ones. The restaurant's name comes from the phrase *nordisk mad* (Nordic food). Noma closed for several years so it may have lost its official ranking—but it reopened with new energy. The seasonal menu focuses on seafood in winter; vegetables in early summer to early fall; and game and forest fare (like berries, mushrooms, nuts, and wild plants) from fall to January.

But Noma, northeast of the Opera House at Refshalevej 96, is not cheap. The menu runs 2,250 DKK; accompanying wines add 1,100 DKK to the bill (there is a student package for 1,000 DKK). A couple going for the whole shebang is looking at spending more than $1,000. And even if you're willing to take the plunge, you have to plan ahead—around three months in advance. Check their website (www.noma.dk) for the latest procedure; you can also put your name on their waiting list.

If you can't commit that far out (or don't want to spend that much), many of the top restaurants in Copenhagen (including Kødbyens Fiskebar, listed on page 111) are run by former chefs from Noma—giving you at least a taste of culinary greatness.

downstairs restaurant, or for classy lighter meals in their upstairs bistro (daily 12:00-22:00, Rosenborggade 15, tel. 38 41 10 20, www.brdr-price.dk).

$$$ Kalaset, in a funky daylight basement with mismatched furniture, bubbles with a youthful energy and is a local favorite. The creative, internationally inspired menu is constantly evolving, and the decent portions are prepared "the way our grandmothers taught us" (daily specials, outdoor seating available, daily 10:00-late, Vendersgade 16, kitty-corner from the recommended Ibsens Hotel, tel. 33 33 00 35).

$$ Halifax, part of a small local chain, serves up "build-your-own" burgers, where you select a patty, a side dish, and a dipping sauce for your fries (Mon-Sat 11:30-22:00, Sun until 21:00, Frederiksborggade 35, tel. 33 32 77 11). They have another location just off the Strøget (at Larsbjørnsstræde 9).

Meatpacking District (Kødbyen)

Literally "Meat Town," Kødbyen is an old warehouse zone huddled up against the train tracks behind the main station. Danes raise about 25 million pigs a year (five per person), so there's long been lots of "meatpacking." Today, much of the meatpacking action is diners chowing down.

There are three color-coded sectors in the district—brown, gray, and white—and each one is a cluster of old industrial buildings. At the far end is the white zone (Den Hvide Kødby), which has been overtaken by some of the city's most trendy and enjoyable eateries, which mingle with the surviving offices and warehouses of the local meatpacking industry. All of the places I list here are within a few steps of each other (except for the Mother pizzeria, a block away).

The curb appeal of this area is zilch (it looks like, well, a meatpacking district), but inside, these restaurants are bursting with life, creativity, and flavor. While youthful and trendy, this scene is also very accessible. Most of these eateries are in buildings with old white tile; this, combined with the considerable popularity of this area, can make the dining rooms quite loud. These places can fill up, especially on weekend evenings, when it's smart to reserve ahead.

It's a short stroll from the station: If you go south on the bridge called Tietgens Bro, which crosses the tracks just south of the station, and carry on for about 10 minutes, you'll run right into the area. Those sleeping in the hotels behind the station just stroll five minutes south. Or you can ride the S-tog to the Dybbølsbro stop.

$$$$ Kødbyens Fiskebar ("Fish Bar") is one of the first and still the most acclaimed restaurant in the Meatpacking District. Focusing on small, thoughtfully composed plates of modern Nordic seafood, the Fiskebar has a stripped-down white interior with a big fish tank and a long cocktail bar surrounded by smaller tables. It's extremely popular (reservations are essential), and feels a bit too trendy for its own good. While the prices are high, so is the quality; diners are paying for a taste of the "New Nordic" style of cooking that's so in vogue here (in summer daily from 17:30, in winter generally closed Sat-Sun; Flæsketorvet 100, tel. 32 15 56 56, http://fiskebaren.dk).

$$$$ BioMio, in the old Bosch building, serves rustic Danish, vegan, and vegetarian dishes, plus meat and fish. It's 100 percent organic, and the young boss, Rune, actually serves diners (daily 12:00-22:00, Halmtorvet 19, tel. 33 31 20 00, http://biomio.dk).

$$$ Paté Paté, next door to BioMio, is a tight, rollicking bistro in a former pâté factory. While a wine bar at heart—with a good selection of wines by the glass—it has a fun and accessible menu of creative modern dishes and a cozy atmosphere rare in the Meatpacking District. Ideally diners choose about three dishes per person and share (Mon-Sat from 17:30, closed Sun, Slagterboderne 1, tel. 39 69 55 57, www.patepate.dk).

$$$ Pizzeria Mother is named for the way the sourdough for their crust must be "fed" and cared for to flourish. You can taste that care in the pizza, which has a delicious tangy crust. Out front are comfortable picnic benches, while the interior curls around the busy pizza oven with chefs working globs of dough that will soon be the basis for your pizza (daily 11:00-23:00, a block beyond the other restaurants listed here at Høkerboderne 9, tel. 22 27 58 98).

$$ Nose2Tail Madbodega (*mad* means "food") prides itself on locally sourced, sustainable cooking, using the entire animal for your meal (hence the name). You'll climb down some stairs into an unpretentious white-tiled cellar (Mon-Sat 18:00-24:00, closed Sun, Flæsketorvet 13A, tel. 33 93 50 45, http://nose2tail.dk).

Other Central Neighborhoods to Explore

To find a good restaurant, try simply window-shopping in one of these inviting districts.

Nyhavn's harbor canal is lined with a touristy strip of restaurants set alongside its classic sailboats. Here thriving crowds are served mediocre, overpriced food in a great setting. On any sunny day, if you want steak and fries (130 DKK) and a 65-DKK beer, this can be fun. On Friday and Saturday, the strip becomes the longest bar in the world.

Kompagnistræde is home to a changing cast of great little eateries. Running parallel to the Strøget, this street has fewer tourists and lower rent, and encourages places to compete creatively for the patronage of local diners.

Gråbrødretorv ("Grey Friars' Square") is perhaps the most popular square in the old center for a meal. It's like a food court, especially in good weather, with a variety of international dining options outside and in. The French-inspired steakhouse **$$$$ Bøf & Ost** is pricey but good, serving elegant beef and veal dishes—even pigeon—and a wide selection of French and Danish cheeses (daily 11:00-22:00). Across the square, **$$$ Huks Fluks** enjoys a sunny location, dishing up southern European small plates, main courses, and shareable portions, and specializes in ham (daily 11:00-22:00).

Istedgade and the surrounding streets behind the train station (just above the Meatpacking District) are home to an assortment of inexpensive ethnic restaurants. You will find numerous places serving kebabs, pizza, Chinese, and Thai (including tasty meals at **$$ Poonchai Thai Restaurant**—across the street from Hotel Nebo at Istedgade 1). The area can be a bit seedy, especially right behind the station, but walk a few blocks away to take your pick of inexpensive, ethnic eateries frequented by locals.

Copenhagen Connections

BY PUBLIC TRANSPORTATION
From Copenhagen by Train to: Hillerød/Frederiksborg Castle (6/hour, 40 minutes on S-tog), **Roskilde** (7/hour, 30 minutes), **Humlebæk/Louisiana Art Museum** (3/hour, 30 minutes), **Helsingør** (3/hour, 45 minutes), **Odense** (3/hour, 1.5 hours), **Ærøskøbing** (2/hour Mon-Sat, hourly on Sun, 2.5 hours to Svendborg with a transfer in Odense, then 1.25-hour ferry crossing to Ærøskøbing—see page 160 for info on ferry), **Billund/Legoland** (2/hour, 2-2.5 hours to Vejle, then bus to Billund—see page 187), allow 3.5 hours total), **Aarhus** (2/hour, 3 hours), **Malmö** (3-5/hour, 40 minutes), **Stockholm** (almost hourly, 5-6 hours on high-speed train, some with a transfer at Malmö or Lund, reservation required; overnight service available but requires a change in Hässleholm or Lund), **Växjö** (hourly, 2.5 hours), **Kalmar** (hourly, 3.5-4 hours, most direct, some transfer in Alvesta), **Oslo** (4/day, 8-9 hours, transfer at Göteborg; also overnight boat option, see next page), **Hamburg** (3/day direct, 5 hours, 2 more with transfer, reservation required in summer; from Hamburg, connections run to **Berlin** (2 more hours, railway also operates 2 direct Copenhagen-Berlin buses, 7.5 hours), **Amsterdam** (5.5 more hours, change at Osnabrück), and **Frankfurt/Rhine** (hourly, 3.5 more hours). Train info tel. 70 13 14 15 (for English, press 1 for general information and tickets, and 2 for international trains). DSB (or Danske Statsbaner) is Denmark's national railway, www.rejseplanen.dk.

By Bus: Taking the bus to **Stockholm** is cheaper but more time-consuming than taking the train (1/day, 9.5 hours, longer for overnight trips, www.swebus.se).

BY CRUISE SHIP
More than half a million people visit Copenhagen via cruise ship each year. For a wealth of online information for cruise-ship passengers, see www.cruisecopenhagen.com. For more in-depth cruising information, pick up my *Rick Steves Scandinavian & Northern European Cruise Ports* guidebook.

Most cruise ships use one of two terminals, both north of downtown—**Oceankaj,** the farther port;

and **Langelinie,** about a mile closer to downtown. Another, smaller cruise port, **Nordre Toldbod,** is just south of *The Little Mermaid* and within easy walking distance (25 minutes) of Nyhavn. **Frihavnen** ("Freeport"), about three miles north of downtown, is used only on rare occasions. There are no ATMs at the piers. There is a tiny TI at Oceankaj, but none at other cruise ports.

Getting Downtown: Many cruise lines run **shuttle buses** between the port and town; if they're available, consider a shuttle for the convenience and time saved.

Langelinie is about a 10- to 15-minute walk from a **train** station on Copenhagen's S-tog suburban rail line, where you can take a train headed downtown. From Langelinie, you can also **walk** or take a **hop-on, hop-off** bus into town. There's also a hop-on, hop-off bus connection at Oceankaj. Taking a **taxi** to downtown is easy but expensive from any port (about 275 DKK from Oceankaj, 175 DKK from Langelinie).

Public buses are possible but a hassle. From Oceankaj, bus #27 connects to bus #26 at the Østerport train station and into the city center. From Langelinie, bus #26 runs directly to various points in downtown Copenhagen. See "Getting Around Copenhagen" at the beginning of the chapter for more bus information.

BY OVERNIGHT BOAT TO OSLO

Luxurious DFDS Seaways cruise ships leave daily from Copenhagen at 16:30 and arrive in Oslo at 9:45 the next day (17-hour sailing). They also depart from Oslo at 16:30 for the return to Copenhagen, allowing you to spend about seven hours in Norway's capital if doing it as a day trip (see page 291 for info on departing from Oslo).

Cruise Costs: Cabins vary dramatically in price depending on the day and season (most expensive on weekends and late June-mid-Aug; cheapest on weekdays and Oct-April). For example, a bed in a four-berth "Seaways" shoehorn economy cabin starts at 325 DKK/person one-way for four people traveling together (370 DKK/person with a window); a luxurious double "Commodore class" cabin higher on the ship starts at 850 DKK/person one-way (and includes a TV, minibar, and breakfast buffet).

Onboard Services: DFDS Seaways operates two ships on this route—the MS *Pearl Seaways* and the MS *Crown Seaways*. Both offer all the cruise-ship luxuries: big buffets for breakfast and dinner, gourmet restaurants, bars, a kids' playroom, pool, hot tub, sauna, casino, nightclubs, and tax-free shopping. All shops and restaurants accept credit cards as well as euros, dollars, and Danish, Swedish, and Norwegian currency.

Reservations: Reservations are smart in summer and on weekends. Advance bookings get the best prices. Book online or call DFDS Seaway's Danish office (Mon-Fri 9:00-16:30, closed Sat-Sun, tel. 33 42 30 10, www.dfdsseaways.us) or visit the **DSB Rejsebureau** at the main train station.

Port Details: The **Copenhagen Ferry Terminal** (a.k.a. DFDS Terminalen) is a short walk north of *The Little Mermaid*. The terminal is open daily 9:00-17:00 (luggage lockers available). Boarding is from 15:15 to 16:15.

Getting Downtown: Shuttle buses marked either *Axel Torv* or *Nørreport* meet arriving ships from Oslo (22 DKK—buy on DFDS website in advance, tickets not sold on buses). The Axel Torv bus drops you at Axel Torv—near Tivoli, the main train station, recommended hotels, and the start of my "Copenhagen City Walk." Buses marked *Nørreport* drop you at Øster Voldgade 2C—next to Nørreport Station (near recommended hotels). From here you can ride the Metro one stop to Kongens Nytorv at Nyhavn (and more recommended hotels).

To reach the ferry terminal *from* the city, catch the shuttle bus marked *DFDS Terminal* near Nørreport Station at Øster Voldgade 2C (22 DKK—buy on DFDS website in advance, tickets not sold on buses, daily at 14:45, 15:15, and 15:45). Or take the S-tog from downtown in the direction of Hellerup or Hillerød to the Nordhavn Station. Exit the station, cross under the tracks, and hike toward the water; you'll see the ship on your right.

NEAR COPENHAGEN

*Roskilde • Frederiksborg Castle • Louisiana Art Museum •
Kronborg Castle*

Copenhagen's the star, but there are several worthwhile sights nearby on its island (called Zealand), and the public transportation system makes side-tripping a joy. Visit Roskilde's great Viking ships and royal cathedral. Tour Frederiksborg, Denmark's most spectacular castle, and slide along the cutting edge at Louisiana Art Museum—a superb collection with a coastal setting as striking as its art. At Helsingør, do the dungeons of Kronborg Castle before heading on to Sweden.

PLANNING YOUR TIME

The area's essential sights are Roskilde's cathedral (with the tombs of Danish royalty) and its Viking ships, along with Frederiksborg Castle. Each destination takes a half-day, and each one is an easy commute from Copenhagen in different directions (30- or 40-minute train ride, then a 20-minute walk or short bus ride). If you're really fast and well-organized, you could visit both Roskilde and Frederiksborg with public transportation in a day (see "The Zealand Blitz," later).

If you're choosing between castles, Frederiksborg is the beautiful showpiece with the opulent interior, and Kronborg—darker and danker—is more typical of the way most castles really were. Both are dramatic from the outside, but Kronborg—overlooking the raging sea channel to Sweden—has a more scenic setting. Castle collectors can hit both in a day (see the two-castle day plan, later).

Drivers can visit these sights on the way into or out of Copenhagen. By train, do day trips from Copenhagen, then sleep while traveling to and from Copenhagen to Oslo (by boat, or by train

Near Copenhagen

Kattegat

To Oslo

Gilleleje

To Göteborg, Oslo & Kalmar

E-6

To Stockholm, Växjö & Kalmar

E-4

KRONBORG CASTLE

Helsingborg

Helsingør

Esrum Sø

SWEDEN

205

Hunde-sted

Arresø

6

FREDENSBORG PALACE

LOUISIANA ART MUSEUM

Humle-bæk

To Rørvig

FREDERIKSBORG CASTLE

Frederiks-sund

Hillerød

Rungsted

Øresund

Ise-fjord

201

152

E-47

BAKKEN

E-6

OPEN-AIR FOLK MUSEUM

ZEALAND

Klampenborg

Roskildefjord

Ballerup

E-47

Copenhagen

See detail maps in this area

Saltholm

Lund

Roskilde

21

Høje Tåstrup

E-20

TUNNEL

ØRESUND

Malmö

23

Lejre

Øm

E-20

Amager

Kastrup

Dragør

BRIDGE

Limhamn

E-20

14

To Holbæk

E-47

DENMARK

Køge Bugt

To Ystad

To Ringsted, Odense, Ærø, Aarhus & Germany

10 Kilometers

10 Miles

via Malmö, Sweden) or Stockholm (by train via Malmö). Consider getting a Copenhagen Card (see page 34), which covers your transportation to all of the destinations in this chapter, as well as admission to Roskilde Cathedral, Frederiksborg Castle, Kronborg Castle, and Louisiana Art Museum (but not the Roskilde Viking Ship Museum). Each train ride is just long enough for a relaxed picnic.

The Zealand Blitz—Roskilde Cathedral, Viking Ship Museum, and Frederiksborg Castle in a Day: If you have limited time and are well-organized, you can see the highlights of Zealand in one exciting day. Here's the plan (all times are rough, train connections take about 30-40 minutes, trains depart about every 10 minutes): Leave Copenhagen by train at 8:00, arrive in Roskilde at 8:30, wander through the town and be at the cathedral when it opens at 9:00 (later on Sun and in off-season). At 10:00, after an hour in the cathedral, stroll down to the harborfront to tour the Viking Ship Museum. They can call a taxi for you to return to the station for a 13:00 train back to Copenhagen. Buy a picnic lunch at Roskilde's station and munch your lunch on the train. Catch a 14:00 train from Copenhagen to Hillerød; there you'll catch the bus to Frederiksborg Castle, arriving at 15:00. This gives you two hours to enjoy the castle before it closes at 17:00 (earlier in off-season). Browse through Hillerød before catching a train at 18:00 to return to Copenhagen. You'll be back at your hotel by 19:00.

A Two-Castle Day (plus Louisiana) by Public Transportation: You can see both Frederiksborg and Kronborg castles, plus Louisiana Art Museum, in one busy day. (This works best Tue-Fri, when Louisiana is open until 22:00.) Take the train from Copenhagen to Hillerød (leaving about 9:00), then hop on the awaiting bus to Frederiksborg Castle; you'll hear the 10:00 bells and be the first tourist inside. Linger in the sumptuous interior for a couple of hours, but get back to the station in time for a midday train (about 12:30 or 13:00) to Helsingør, a 15-minute walk from Kronborg Castle. Either munch your picnic lunch on the train, or—if it's a nice day—save it for the ramparts of Kronborg Castle. If you're castled out, skip the interior (saving the ticket price, and more time for Louisiana) and simply enjoy the Kronborg grounds and Øresund views before catching a train south toward Copenhagen. Hop off at Humlebæk for Louisiana.

GETTING AROUND

All of these sights except Roskilde are served by Copenhagen's excellent commuter-train (S-tog) system (covered by Eurail Pass; Copenhagen Card; and "24-hour ticket" and "7-day FlexCard"—both of which include greater Copenhagen; not covered by City Pass, which includes only zones 1-4—see page 37). All of the train connections (including the regional train line to Roskilde, which is covered by the Copenhagen Card) depart from the main train station; but be aware that most lines also stop at other Copenhagen stations, which may be closer to your hotel (for example, the Nørreport Station is near the recommended Ibsens and Jørgensen hotels). Check schedules carefully to avoid needlessly going to the main train station.

At the main train station, S-tog lines do not appear on the overhead schedule screens (which are for longer-distance destinations); simply report to tracks 9-10 to wait for your train (there's a schedule at the head of those tracks).

If renting a car, see "Route Tips for Drivers" at the end of the chapter for more information.

Roskilde

Denmark's roots, both Viking and royal, are on display in Roskilde (ROSS-killa), a pleasant town 18 miles west of Copenhagen. The town was the seat of the bishop and the residence of Danish royalty until 1450, when these shifted to Copenhagen. In its day, Roskilde was the second biggest city in the country. Today the town that introduced Christianity to Denmark in A.D. 980 is much smaller, except for the week of its famous rock/jazz/folk festival—northern Europe's largest—when 100,000 fans pack the place and it becomes one of Denmark's biggest cities again

(early July, www.roskilde-festival.dk). Wednesday and Saturday are flower/flea/produce market days (8:00-14:00).

GETTING THERE

Roskilde is an easy side-trip from Copenhagen by train (7/hour, 30 minutes). Trains headed to Ringsted, Nykøbing, or Lindholm may not stop in Roskilde (which is an intermediate stop you won't see listed on departure boards)—confirm in advance. Returning to Copenhagen, hop on any train in the direction of Østerport or København H.

Orientation to Roskilde

TOURIST INFORMATION

Roskilde's helpful TI is on the main square, next to the cathedral (Mon-Fri 10:00-16:00, Sat until 13:00, closed Sun; Stændertorvet 1, tel. 46 31 65 65, www.visitroskilde.com).

ARRIVAL IN ROSKILDE

There are no lockers at the train station (or nearby), but the TI—about a five-minute walk away—will take your bags for a few hours if you ask nicely. Free WCs are right next door to the TI.

From the train station, consider this circular route: First you'll head to the TI, then the cathedral, and finally down to the Viking Ship Museum on the harborfront. Exit straight out from the station, and walk down to the bottom of the square. Turn left (at the Super Brugsen supermarket) on the pedestrianized shopping street,

Algade (literally "the street for all"). After walking down this main drag about four blocks, you emerge into the main square, Stænder-torvet, with the TI and the cathedral. After visiting the cathedral, you'll head about 10 minutes downhill (through a pleasant park) to the Viking Ship Museum: Facing the cathedral facade, turn left and head down the tree-lined path through the park. When you emerge at the roundabout (avoiding the temptation to eat a "Viking Pizza"), continue straight through it to reach the museum.

If you want to go directly from the station to the Viking Ship Museum, you can ride a bus; see page 124.

Sights in Roskilde

▲▲Roskilde Cathedral

Roskilde's imposing 12th-century, twin-spired cathedral houses the tombs of nearly all of the Danish kings and queens (39 royals in all; pick up the included guidebook as you enter). If you're a fan of Danish royalty or of evolving architectural styles, it's thrill-ing; even if you're neither, Denmark's "Westminster Abbey" is still interesting. It's a stately, modern-looking old church with great marble work, paintings, wood carvings, and an engaged congregation that makes the place feel very alive (par-ticularly here in largely unchurched Scan-dinavia). A big museum and welcome center are in the works.

Cost and Hours: 60 DKK, includ-ed with Copenhagen Card; April-Sept Mon-Sat 9:00-18:00, Sun 12:30-17:00; Oct-March Tue-Sat 10:00-16:00, Sun from 12:30, closed Mon; often closed for funerals and on Sat-Sun afternoons for baptisms and weddings; free organ con-certs offered July-Aug Thu at 20:00; tel. 46 35 16 24, www. roskildedomkirke.dk.

◐ Self-Guided Tour: Begun in the 1170s by Bishop Absa-lom (and completed in 1280), Roskilde Cathedral was cleared of its side chapels and altars by the Reformation iconoclasts—leaving a blank slate for Danish royals to fill with their tombs. The highlight here is slowly strolling through a half-millennium's worth of royal chapels, representing a veritable textbook's worth of architectural styles.

• *Before entering, walk around the outside of the cathedral.*

Exterior, King's Door, and Tomb of Frederik IX: Notice the big bricks, which date from the 12th century, and how the cathe-

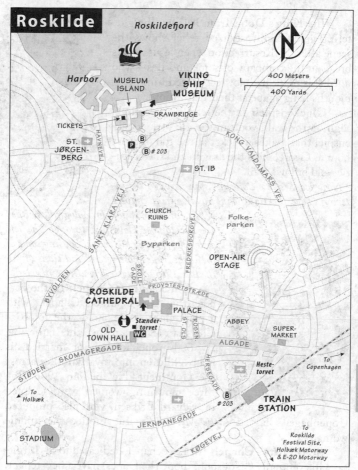

dral is built on the highest ground in town. Face the towering west facade. The main door—called the King's Door—was installed in 2010 and depicts scenes from the ministry of Jesus. This door is used by the congregation only to leave special services; the only people who may enter through this door are members of the royal family.

Find the freestanding brick chapel to the left. This holds the remains of Denmark's last king, Frederik IX (1899-1972), and his wife Ingrid (parents of the current queen, born in 1940). While all of the other monarchs are inside, Frederik—who was an avid sailor in his youth—requested to be buried here, with a view of the harbor.

• *Now go around the right side, buy a ticket, and go inside. First, head to the middle of the nave to look at...*

The King's Door, from Inside: The glittering-gold, highly stylized relief shows the scene after the Resurrection when Jesus breaks bread in the company of some apostles—who until this point had not recognized him (their mouths hang agape at their realization).

Glockenspiel: In the rear of the church, high on the wall, you can see the little glockenspiel that makes a racket at the top of every hour as George kills the dragon and the centuries-old billows wail.

• *Now we'll take a clockwise spin through the interior to see the significant royal burial chapels.*

While this tour is not chronological, neither are the tombs. Continue through the left aisle and into the big chapel housing some of the cathedral's most recent additions (from the late 19th through early 20th centuries).

Glücksburger Chapel: In the corner, the Glücksburger Chapel, with a plain light dome, holds the tomb of Christian IX, nicknamed the "father-in-law of Europe" for how he married his many children into royal families across the Continent. He died in 1906. The three mourning women were sculpted by Edvard Eriksen, who also produced Copenhagen's famed *Little Mermaid* statue (notice the middle woman).

St. Birgitta's Chapel: The next chapel, dedicated to St. Birgitta, will eventually ("Not soon," hope the Danes) have a new tenant: It has been restored to house the tomb of the current queen, Margrethe II, and her husband Henrik. She teamed up with an artist to design her own tomb (there's a model on display). Her body will reside in the stepped area at the bottom, upon which stand three columns representing the far-flung Danish holdings: one made of basalt from the Faroe Islands, another of marble from Greenland, and the third of stone from Denmark proper. Topping the columns are elephants (symbols of Danish royalty) and a semitransparent glass tomb, symbolizing the unpredictability of life and how death, like a seed, is a new beginning.

St. Andrew's Chapel: The next chapel, a modern addition to the church, is dedicated to St. Andrew and has a glittering mosaic over the altar. But pre-Reformation frescoes (1511) peek through the Protestant whitewash. Standing in front of this chapel, look across the nave to see the gorgeous 16th-century Baroque organ.

Christian IV Chapel: The next, larger chapel (up the stairs behind the small wooden organ) dates from the era of Christian IV, the larger-than-life 17th-century king who created modern Denmark. Christian also left his mark on Roskilde Cathedral, building the altarpiece, pulpit, distinctive twin towers...and this chapel. Walk around the stately yet humble tombs, marvel at the painting, and consider the huge personality of the greatest king in Danish history. In here you'll see a fine statue of the king, by Bertel Thorvaldsen; a large 3-D painting with Christian IV wearing his trademark eye patch, after losing his eye in battle; and his rather austere tomb (black with silver trim, surrounded by several others). Great he was...until his many wars impoverished his once-mighty country.

• *Head into the nave and climb up the stairs into the choir area.*

The Nave, Choir, and High Altar: Take in the gorgeous gilded altarpiece and finely carved stalls. The three-winged altarpiece, carved in 1560 in Antwerp, shows scenes from Christ's last week. The fine carvings above the chairs in the choir feature scenes from the Old Testament on one side and the New Testament on the other.

Tomb of Margrethe I: Behind the altar is the ornately decorated tomb of Margrethe I, the Danish queen who added Nor-

way to her holdings by marrying Norwegian King Håkon VI in 1363. Legend holds that buried in a nearby brick pilaster are the supposed remains of Harold (read the Latin: *Haraldus*) Bluetooth, who ruled more than a millennium ago (r. 958-985 or 986), made Roskilde the capital of his realm, and converted his subjects to Christianity.

• *Now explore the apse (the area behind the altar).*

Apse: Go down the stairs, walk over the well-worn tombs of 500-year-old aristocrats who had the money to buy prime tomb space, and go through the little door. Circle around the apse, noticing more fine tombs behind Margrethe's.

• *Hooking back around toward the front, dip into the many more chapels you'll pass, including...*

Frederik V's Chapel: The grand, textbook Neoclassical tomb of Frederik V has white pillars, gold trim, and mourning maidens—representing Norway and Denmark—in ancient Greek gowns. You'll also pass a room housing elaborate, canopied Baroque tombs. Imagine: Each king or queen commissioned a tomb that suited his or her time—so different, yet all so grand.

Christian I's Chapel: The next chapel, with the tomb of

Christian I, has a stone column marking the heights of visiting monarchs such as Prince Charles. The *P* is for the giant Russian czar Peter the Great—clearly the tallest.

• *Leaving the cathedral, turn right and walk downhill for 10 minutes along a peaceful tree-lined lane that will eventually take you to the harbor and the Viking Ship Museum.*

▲▲▲Viking Ship Museum (Vikingeskibsmuseet)

Vik literally means "shallow inlet," and "Vikings" were the people who lived along those inlets. Roskilde—and this award-winning museum—are strategically located along one such inlet. (They call it a "fjord," but it's surrounded by much flatter terrain than the Norwegian fjords.) Centuries before Europe's Age of Exploration, Viking sailors navigated their sleek, sturdy ships as far away as the Mediterranean, the Black Sea, the Persian Gulf, and the

Americas. This museum displays five different Viking ships, which were discovered in the Roskilde fjord and painstakingly excavated, preserved, and pieced back together beginning in the 1960s. The ships aren't as intact or as evocative as those in Oslo (see page 251), but this museum does a better job of explaining shipbuilding. The outdoor area (on "Museum Island") continues the experience, with a chance to see modern-day Vikings creating replica ships, chat with an old-time rope maker, and learn more about the excavation. The English descriptions are excellent—it's the kind of museum where you want to read everything.

Cost and Hours: 130 DKK, not covered by Copenhagen Card; daily May-mid-Oct 10:00-17:00, Nov-April until 16:00, tel. 46 30 02 00, www.vikingeskibsmuseet.dk.

Tours: Free 45-minute tours in English run mid-June-Aug daily at 12:00 and 15:00; May-mid-June and Sept Sat-Sun at 12:00; none off-season.

Boat Ride: The museum's workshop has re-created working replicas of all five of the ships on display here, plus others. For an extra 100 DKK, you can go for a fun hour-long sail around Roskilde's fjord in one of these replica Viking vessels (you'll row, set sail, and row again; frequent departures—up to 7/day—in summer, fewer off-season, ask about schedule when you arrive or call ahead).

Eating: Café Knarr serves salads, sandwiches, and "planks" of Viking tapas with ingredients the Vikings knew (decent prices, open daily 10:00-17:00).

Getting There: It's on the harbor at Vindeboder 12. From the train station, catch bus #203 toward Boserup (2/hour, 24 DKK,

7-minute ride). From the cathedral, it's a 10-minute downhill walk. The museum desk can call a taxi (120 DKK) when you want to go back to the station, or take the bus back.

Visiting the Museum: The museum has two parts: the Viking Ship Hall, with the remains of the five ships; and, across the draw-bridge, Museum Island with workshops, replica ships, a café, and more exhibits. There are ticket offices at each location; it's best to start with the Viking Ship Hall.

As you enter the **Viking Ship Hall,** check the board for the day's activities and demonstrations (including shipbuilding, weaving, blacksmithing, and minting). Consider buying the 24-DKK guidebook and request the 14-minute English movie shown in the lobby's cinema.

Your visit is a one-way walk. You'll first see the five ships, then go through the preservation exhibit, the kids' zone with a video about the modern voyage of the *Sea Stallion,* and finally the popular shop.

The core of the exhibit is the remains of five ships, which were deliberately sunk a thousand years ago to block an easy channel into this harbor (leaving open only the most challenging approach—virtually impossible for anyone but a local to navigate). The ships, which are named for the place where they were found (Skuldelev), represent an impressively wide range of Viking shipbuilding technology. *Skuldelev 1* is a big, sail-powered ocean-going trade ship made in Norway, with a crew of six to eight men and room for lots of cargo; it's like the ship Leif Eriksson took to America 1,000 years ago. *Skuldelev 2* is a 100-foot-long, 60-oar longship made in the Viking city of Dublin; loaded with 65 or 70 bloodthirsty warriors, it struck fear into the hearts of foes. It's similar to the ones depicted in the Bayeux Tapestry in Normandy, France. *Skuldelev 3* is a modest coastal trader that stayed closer to home (wind-powered with oar backup, similar to #1 in design and also made in Norway). *Skuldelev 5* is a smaller longship—carrying about 30 warriors, it's the little sibling of #2. And *Skuldelev 6* is a small fishing vessel—a row/sail hybrid that was used for whaling and hunting seals. (There's no #4 because they originally thought #2 was two different ships...and the original names stuck.)

Exhibits in the surrounding rooms show the 25-year process of excavating and preserving the ships, explain a step-by-step attack and defense of the harbor, and give you a chance to climb aboard a couple of replica ships for a fun photo op. You'll also see displays describing the re-creation of the *Sea Stallion*, a replica of the big longship (#2) constructed by modern shipbuilders using ancient techniques. A crew of 65 rowed this ship to Dublin in 2007 and then back to Roskilde in the summer of 2008. You can watch a 20-minute film of their odyssey.

Leaving the hall, cross the drawbridge to **Museum Island.** Replicas of all five ships—and others—bob in the harbor; you can

actually climb on board the largest, the *Sea Stallion* (if in port). At the boatyard, watch modern craftsmen re-create millennium-old ships using the original methods and materials. Poke into the various workshops, with exhibits on tools and methods. The little square called *Tunet* ("Gathering Place") is ringed by traditional craft shops—basket maker, rope maker, blacksmith, wood carver—which are sometimes staffed by workers doing demonstrations. In the archaeological workshop, exhibits explain how they excavated and preserved the precious timbers of those five ships.

Frederiksborg Castle

Frederiksborg Castle, rated ▲▲, sits on an island in the middle of a lake in the cute town of Hillerød. This grandest castle in Scandinavia is often called the "Danish Versailles." Built from 1602 to 1620, Frederiksborg was the castle of Denmark's King Christian IV. Much of it was reconstructed after an 1859 fire, with the normal Victorian over-the-top flair, by the brewer J. C. Jacobsen and his Carlsberg Foundation.

You'll still enjoy some of the magnificent spaces of the castle's heyday: the breathtaking grounds and courtyards, the sumptuous chapel, and the regalia-laden Great Hall. But most of the place was turned into a fine museum in 1878. Today it's the Museum of National History, taking you on a chronological walk through the story of Denmark from 1500 until now (the third/top floor covers modern times). The countless musty paintings are a fascinating scrapbook of Danish history—it's a veritable national portrait gallery, with images of great Danes from each historical period of the last half-millennium.

A fine path leads around the lake, with ever-changing views of the castle. The traffic-free center of Hillerød is also worth a wander.

Tourist Information: Hillerød's TI, with information on the entire North Zealand region, is in the freestanding white house next to the castle parking lot (to the left as you face the main castle gate; July-mid-Sept Mon-Sat 10:00-16:00, shorter hours in June, closed mid-Sept–May, Frederiksværksgade 2A, tel. 49 21 13 33, www.visitnordsjaelland.com). Because the TI is inside an art gallery, if the TI is "closed" while the gallery is open, you can still slip inside and pick up a town map and brochures.

GETTING THERE

By Train: From Copenhagen, take the S-tog to Hillerød (line E, 6/hour, 40 minutes, bikes go free on S-tog trains).

From the Hillerød station, you can enjoy a pleasant 20-minute walk to the castle, or catch **bus #301** or **#302** (free with S-tog ticket or Copenhagen Card, buses are to the right as you exit station, ride three stops to Frederiksborg Slot bus stop; as buses go in two directions from here, confirm direction with driver).

If **walking,** just follow the signs to the castle. Bear left down the busy road (Jernbanegade) until the first big intersection, where you'll turn right. After a couple of blocks, where the road curves to the left, keep going straight; from here, bear left and downhill to the pleasant square Torvet, with great views of the castle and a café pavilion. At this square, turn left and walk through the pedestrianized shopping zone directly to the castle gate.

Linking to Other Sights: If continuing directly to Helsingør (with Kronborg Castle), hop on the regional train (departs from track 16 at Hillerød station, Mon-Fri 2/hour, Sat-Sun 1/hour, 30 minutes). From Helsingør, it's a quick trip on the train to the town of Humlebæk (where you'll find Louisiana Art Museum).

By Car: Drivers will find easy parking at the castle (for driving directions, see "Route Tips for Drivers" at the end of this chapter).

ORIENTATION TO FREDERIKSBORG CASTLE

Cost and Hours: 75 DKK, included with Copenhagen Card; daily April-Oct 10:00-17:00, Nov-March 11:00-15:00.

Tours: Take advantage of the free, informative, one-hour iPod audioguide; ask for it when you buy your ticket—it's also available as a smartphone app. My self-guided tour zooms in on the highlights, but the audioguide is more extensive. There are also posted explanations and/or borrowable English descriptions in many rooms. Daily English-language, 30-minute highlights tours leave at 14:00 (included in admission).

NEAR COPENHAGEN

Information: Tel. 48 26 04 39, www.dnm.dk.

Eating: You can picnic in the castle's moat park or enjoy the **$$-$$$ Spisestedet Leonora** at the moat's edge (*smørrebrød,* sandwiches, salads, hot dishes, open daily 10:00-17:00, slow service). Or, better, walk into the town center near the bus stop.

➲ SELF-GUIDED TOUR

The castle's included audio tour is excellent, and you can almost follow it in real time for a one-hour blitz of the palace's highlights. Use my self-guided tour to supplement the audioguide.

The Castle Approach

From the entrance of the castle complex, it's an appropriately regal approach to the king's residence. You can almost hear the clopping of royal hooves as you walk over the moat and through the first island (which housed the stables and small businesses needed to support a royal residence). Then walk down the winding (and therefore easy-to-defend) lane to the second island, which was home to the domestic and foreign ministries. Finally, cross over the last moat to the main palace, where the king lived.

Fountain of Neptune Courtyard

Survey the castle exterior from the Fountain of Neptune. Christian IV imported Dutch architects to create this "Christian IV style," which you'll see all over Copenhagen. The brickwork and sandstone are products of the local clay and sandy soil. The building, with its horizontal lines, triangles, and squares, is generally in Renaissance style, but notice how this is interrupted by a few token Gothic elements on the church's facade. Some say this homey touch was to let the villagers know the king was "one of them."

• *Step over the last moat, through the ornate gate, and into the castle grounds. Go in the door in the middle of the courtyard to buy your ticket, pick up your free audioguide, and put your bag in a locker (mandatory). Pick up a free floor plan; room numbers will help orient you on this tour. You'll enter the Knights' Parlor, also called The Rose, a long room decorated as it was during the palace's peak of power. Go up the stairs on the left side of this hall to the...*

Royal Chapel

Christian IV wanted to have the grandest royal chapel in Europe. For 200 years the coronation place of Danish kings, this chapel is still used for royal weddings (and is extremely popular for commoner weddings—book long in advance). The chapel is nearly all original, dating back to 1620. As you walk around the upper level, notice the graffiti scratched on the windowpanes by the diamond rings of royal kids visiting for the summer back in the 1600s. Most of the coats of arms show off noble lineage—with a few exceptions we'll get to soon. At the far end of the chapel, the wooden organ is from 1620, with its original hand-powered bellows. (Hymns play on the old carillon at the top of each hour.)

Scan the hundreds of coats of arms lining the walls. These belong to people who have received royal orders from the Danish crown (similar to Britain's knighthoods). While most are obscure princesses and dukes, a few interesting (and more familiar) names show up just past the organ. In the first window bay after the organ, look for the distinctive red, blue, black, and green shield of South Africa—marking Nelson Mandela's coat of arms. (Notice he was awarded the highly prestigious Order of the Elephant, usually reserved for royalty.) Around the side of the same column (facing the chapel interior), find the coats of arms for Dwight D. Eisenhower (with the blue anvil and the motto "Peace through understanding"), Winston Churchill (who already came from a noble line), and Field Marshal Bernard "Monty" Montgomery. Around the far side of this column is the coat of arms for France's wartime leader, Charles de Gaulle.

Leaving the chapel, you step into the king's private oratory, with evocative Neo-Romantic paintings (restored after a fire) from the mid-19th century.

• *You'll emerge from the chapel into the museum collection. But before seeing that, pay a visit to the Audience Room: Go through the door in the left corner marked Audienssalen, and proceed through the little room to the long passageway (easy to miss).*

Audience Room

Here, where formal meetings took place, a grand painting shows the king as a Roman emperor firmly in command (with his two sons prominent for extra political stability). This family is flanked by Christian IV (on the left) and Frederik III (on the right). Christian's military victories line the walls, and the four great continents—Europe, North America, Asia, and Africa—circle the false cupola (notice it's just an attic). Look for the odd trapdoor in one corner with a plush chair on it. This was where they could majestically lower the king to the exit.

• *Now go back to the museum section, and proceed through the numbered rooms.*

Museum Collection

Spanning three floors and five centuries, this exhaustive collection juxtaposes portraits, paintings of historical events, furniture, and other objects from the same time period, all combining to paint a picture of a moment in Danish history. While fascinating, the collection is huge, so I've selected only the most interesting items to linger over.

First Floor: Proceed to **Room 26,** which is focused on the Reformation. The case in the middle of the room holds the first Bible translated into Danish (from 1550—access to the word of God was a big part of the Reformation). Over the door to the next room is the image of a monk, Hans Tausen, invited by the king to preach the new thinking of the Reformation...sort of the "Danish Martin Luther." Also note the effort noble families put into legitimizing themselves with family trees and family seals.

Pass through Rooms 27, 28, and 29, and into **Room 30**—with paintings telling the story of Christian IV (for more on this dy-

namic Renaissance king, who built this castle and so much more, see page 77). Directly across from the door you entered is a painting of the chancellor on his deathbed, handing over the keys to the kingdom to a still-wet-behind-the-ears young Christian IV—the beginning of a long and fruitful career. On the right wall is a painting of Christian's coronation (the bearded gentleman looking out the window in the upper-left corner is Carlsberg brewer and castle benefactor J. C. Jacobsen—who, some 300 years before his birth, was probably not actually in attendance). Room 31 covers the royal family of Charles IV, while the smaller, darkened corner Room 32 displays the various Danish orders; find the most prestigious, the Order of the Elephant.

• *Hook back through Room 30, go outside on the little passage, and climb up the stairs.*

Second Floor: Go to the corner **Room 39,** which has a fascinating golden globe designed to illustrate Polish astronomer Nicolaus Copernicus' bold new heliocentric theory (that the sun, not the earth, was the center of our world). Look past the constellations to see the tiny model of the solar system at the very center, with a brass ball for the sun and little figures holding up symbols for each of the planets. The mechanical gears could actually make this model move to make the illustration more vivid.

Continue into one of the castle's most jaw-dropping rooms, the **Great Hall** (Room 38). The walls are lined with tapestries and royal portraits (including some modern ones, near the door). The

remarkable wood-carved ceilings include panels illustrating various industries. The elevated platform on the left was a gallery where musicians could play without getting in the way of the revelry.

Head back out and walk back along the left side of the hall. You can go quickly through the rooms numbered in the 40s and 50s (though pause partway down the long hallway; on the left, find the optical-illusion portrait that shows King Frederik V when viewed from one angle, and his wife when viewed from another). At the far end of this section, **Room 57** has a portrait of Hans Christian Andersen. Notice that fashion styles have gotten much more modern...suits and ties instead of tights and powdered wigs. It's time to head into the modern world.

• *Find the modern spiral staircase nearby. Downstairs are late 19th century exhibits—which are skippable. Instead, head up to the top floor.*

Third Floor: This staircase puts you right in the middle of the modern collection. From here, the museum's focus shifts, focusing more on the art and less on the history. Highlights include:

The Art Critics, showing four past-their-prime, once-rambunctious artists themselves, now happily entrenched in the art institution, leaning back to critique a younger artist's work.

A room focusing on Denmark's far-flung protectorate of Greenland, with a porcelain polar bear and portraits of explorers.

A room of distinctive Impressionist/Post-Impressionist paintings, with a Danish spin.

The *Ninth of April, 1940,* showing the (ultimately unsuccessful) Danish defense against Nazi invaders on that fateful date.

A room focusing on the royal family, with a life-size, photorealistic portrait of the beloved Queen Margrethe II. Facing her is her daughter-in-law, Mary Donaldson—who, in this portrait at least, bears a striking resemblance to another young European royal.

Peter Carlsen's *Denmark 2009*—a brilliant parody of Eugène Delacroix's famous painting *Liberty Leading the People* (a copy of the inspiration is on the facing wall).

Carlsen has replaced the stirring imagery of the original with some dubious markers of contemporary Danish life: football flags, beer gut, shopping bags, tabloids, bikini babes, even a Christiania flag. It's a delightfully offbeat (and oh-so-Danish) note to end our visit to this seriously impressive palace.

NEAR THE CASTLE: HILLERØD TOWN

While there's not much here, the pedestrianized commercial zone is pleasant enough. It's best visited from the castle. Slotsgade, the main street, leads away from the castle bus stop toward the train station and is lined with shops and cafés. An inviting Scandinavian sweater shop is right at the bus stop. And if you feel like a little (very little) cruise, a tiny ferry leaves from a pier next to the castle and stops at the castle garden across the lake (30 DKK, free with Copenhagen Card, 2/hour, 30 minutes).

Louisiana Art Museum

This is Scandinavia's most-raved-about modern-art museum. Located in the town of Humlebæk, beautifully situated on the coast 18 miles north of Copenhagen, Louisiana is a holistic place that masterfully mixes its art, architecture, and landscape.

Getting There: Take the train from Copenhagen toward Helsingør, and get off at Humlebæk (3/hour, 30 minutes). It's a pleasant 10-minute walk (partly through a forest) to the museum: Exit the station and immediately go left onto Hejreskor Allé, a residential street; when the road curves right, continue straight along the narrow footpath through the trees. After you exit the trail, the museum is just ahead and across the street (at Gammel Strandvej 13).

If you're arriving by train from **Helsingør,** take the pedestrian underpass beneath the tracks, then follow the directions above. Louisiana is also connected to Helsingør by bus #388 (runs hourly, stops right at museum as well as at Humlebæk).

If you're coming from **Frederiksborg Castle,** you have two options: You can catch the Lille Nord train from Hillerød to Helsingør, then change there to a regional train heading south to Humlebæk (1-2/hour, 30 minutes). Alternately, you can take the S-tog toward Copenhagen and Køge, get off at Hellerup, then catch a regional train north toward Helsingør to reach Humlebæk (6/hour, 30 minutes).

Cost and Hours: 125 DKK, included with Copenhagen Card; Tue-Fri 11:00-22:00, Sat-Sun until 18:00, closed Mon; tel. 49 19 07 19, www.louisiana.dk.

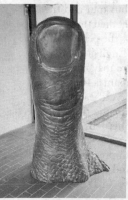

Cuisine Art: The **$$$** cafeteria, with indoor and outdoor seating, has reasonably priced sandwiches and welcomes picnickers who buy a drink.

Visiting the Museum: Wander from famous Chagalls and Picassos to more obscure art (everything is post-1945). Poets spend days here nourishing their creative souls with new angles, ideas, and perspectives. Even those who don't think they're art lovers can get sucked into a thought-provoking exhibit and lose track of time. There's no permanent exhibit; they constantly organize their substantial collection into ever-changing arrangements, augmented with borrowed and special exhibits (check www.louisiana. dk for the latest). An Andy Warhol *Marilyn Monroe* you see on one visit may not be there the next. (One favorite item, French sculptor César's *The Big Thumb*—which is simply a six-foot-tall bronze thumb—isn't going anywhere, since any time they move it, patrons complain.) There's no audioguide, but everything is labeled in English.

Outside, a delightful sculpture garden sprawls through the grounds, downhill toward the sea. The views over the Øresund, one of the busiest passages in the nautical world, are nearly as inspiring as the art. The museum's floor plan is a big loop, and the seaward side is underground—so as not to block the grand views. It's fun to explore the grounds, peppered with sculptures and made accessible by bridges and steps. There are sculptures by Alexander Calder, Jean Dubuffet, Joan Miró, and others.

Taken as a whole, the museum is a joy to explore. What you see from the inside draws you out, and what you see from the outside draws you in. The place can't be rushed. Linger and enjoy.

Kronborg Castle

Kronborg Castle is located in Helsingør, a pleasant, salty Danish seaside town that's often confused with its Swedish sister, Helsingborg, just two miles across the channel. Kronborg Castle (also called Elsinore, the Anglicized version of Helsingør) is a ▲▲ sight famous for its tenuous (but profitable) ties to Shakespeare. Most of the "Hamlet"

castle you'll see today—a darling of every big-bus tour and travelogue—was built long after the historical Hamlet died (more than a thousand years ago), and Shakespeare never saw the place. But this Renaissance castle existed when a troupe of English actors performed here in Shakespeare's time (Shakespeare may have known them). These days, various Shakespearean companies from around the world perform *Hamlet* in Kronborg's courtyard each August. Among the actors who've donned tights here in the title role are Laurence Olivier, Christopher Plummer, Kenneth Branagh, and Jude Law.

To see or not to see? The castle is most impressive from the outside. The free grounds between the walls and sea are great for picnics, with a close-up view of the strait between Denmark and

Sweden. If you're heading to Sweden, Kalmar Castle (described in the Southeast Sweden chapter) is a better medieval castle. And in Denmark, Frederiksborg (described earlier), which was built as an upgrade to this one, is far more opulent inside. But if Kronborg is handy to your itinerary—or you never met a castle you didn't like—it's worth a visit...even if just for a short romp across the ramparts (no ticket required). Many big-bus tours in the region stop both here and at Frederiksborg (you'll recognize some of the same fellow tourists at both places)—not a bad plan if you're a castle completist.

Tourist Information: The town of Helsingør has a TI (Mon-Fri 10:00-16:00, until 17:00 in summer, closed Sat-Sun except for short midday hours in summer; tel. 49 21 13 33, www.visithelsingor.dk), a medieval center, the ferry to Sweden, and lots of Swedes who come over for the lower-priced alcohol.

GETTING THERE

Helsingør is a 45-minute train ride from Copenhagen (3/hour). Exit the station out the front door: The TI is on the little square to your left, and the castle is dead ahead along the coast (about a 15-minute walk). Between the station and the castle, you'll pass through a harborfront zone with the town's cultural center and maritime museum (described later).

ORIENTATION TO KRONBORG CASTLE

Cost and Hours: 140 DKK June-Aug, 90 DKK Sept-May, 20 percent discount with Maritime Museum ticket, included with Copenhagen Card; open June-Sept daily 10:00-17:30, Oct-May daily 11:00-16:00 except closed Mon in Nov-March; tel. 33 95 42 00, www.kongeligeslotte.dk.

Tours: Free 30-minute **tours** in English are offered of the casements and of the royal apartments (1-2/day; call or check online for times). You can download a free **audioguide** to your mobile device. Dry English descriptions are posted throughout the castle.

VISITING THE CASTLE

Approaching the castle, pretend you're an old foe of the king, kept away by many layers of earthen ramparts and moats—just when you think you're actually at the castle, you find there's another gateway or waterway to pass. On the way in, you'll pass a small model of the complex to help get your bearings.

On a sunny day, you could have an enjoyable visit to Kronborg just walking around these grounds and playing "king of the castle," without buying a ticket. Many do.

Follow the signs into the ticket desk, buy your ticket, stick your bag in a locker (insert a 20-DKK coin, which will be returned), and head upstairs. You'll pop out at the beginning of the royal apartments.

Royal Apartments

Visitors are able to walk through one-and-a-half floors of the complex. The first few rooms are filled with high-tech exhibits, using touchscreens and projected videos to explain the history of the place. You'll learn how, in the 1420s, Danish King Eric of Pomerania built a fortress here to allow for the collection of "Sound Dues," levied on any passing ship hoping to enter the sound of Øresund. This proved hugely lucrative, eventually providing up to two-thirds of Denmark's entire income. By the time of Shakespeare, Kronborg was well-known both for its profitable ability to levy these dues, and for its famously lavish banquets—what better setting for a tale of a royal family unraveling?

Continuing into the apartments themselves, you'll find that the interior is a shadow of its former self; while the structure was

rebuilt by Christian IV after a 1629 fire, its rooms were never returned to their former grandeur, making it feel like something of an empty shell. And yet, there are still some fine pieces of furniture and art to see. Frederik II ruled Denmark from the king's chamber in the 1570s; a model shows how it likely looked back in its heyday. After passing through two smaller rooms, you come to the queen's chamber; from there, stairs lead up to the queen's gallery, custom-built for Queen Sophie to be able to quickly walk directly from her chambers to the ballroom or chapel. Follow her footsteps into the ballroom, a vast hall of epic proportions decorated by a series of paintings commissioned by Christian IV (explained by the board near the entry). At the far end, a model (enlivened by seemingly holographic figures) illustrates how this incredible space must have looked in all its original finery. Beyond the ballroom, the "Little Hall" is decorated with a fine series of tapestries depicting Danish monarchs. Then wind through several more royal halls, chambers, and bedrooms on your way back down into the courtyard. Once there, go straight across and enter the chapel. The enclosed gallery at the upper-left was the private pew of the royal family.

Øresund Region

When the Øresund (UH-ra-soond) Bridge, which connects Denmark and Sweden, opened in July of 2000, it created a dynamic new metropolitan area. Almost overnight, the link forged an economic power with the 12th-largest gross domestic product in Europe. The Øresund region has surpassed Stockholm as the largest metro area in Scandinavia. Now 3.7 million Danes and Swedes—a highly trained and highly technical workforce—are within a quick commute of each other.

The bridge opens up new questions of borders. Historically, southern Sweden (the area across from Copenhagen, called Skåne) had Danish blood. It was Danish for a thousand years before Sweden took it in 1658. Notice how Copenhagen is the capital on the fringe of its realm—at one time it was in the center.

The 10-mile-long link, which has a motorway for cars (the toll is about 375 DKK) and a two-track train line, ties together the main islands of Denmark with Europe and Sweden. The $4 billion project consisted of a 2.5-mile-long tunnel, an artificial island called Peberholm, and a 5-mile-long bridge. With speedy connecting trains, Malmö in Sweden is now an easy half-day side-trip from Copenhagen (about 120 DKK each way, 3-5/hour, 35 minutes). The train drops you at the "Malmö C" (central) station right in the heart of Malmö, and all the important sights are within a short walk.

Citing security concerns and ongoing waves of immigration, Sweden has tightened controls at select border crossings. This means that anyone traveling from Denmark to Sweden on the Øresund Bridge needs to carry a passport, which will likely be checked by Swedish police.

Casements

You'll enter the underground part of the castle through a door on the main courtyard (diagonally across from the chapel). While not particularly tight, these passages are very dark (and a good place to use your mobile phone flashlight). This extensive network of dank cellars is a double-decker substructure that once teemed with activity. The upper level, which you'll see first, was used as servants' quarters, a stable, and a storehouse. The lower level was used to train and barrack soldiers during wartime (an efficient use of so much prime, fortified space). As you explore this creepy,

labyrinthine, nearly pitch-black zone (just follow the arrows), imagine the miserably claustrophobic conditions the soldiers lived in, waiting to see some action.

The most famous "resident" of the Kronborg casements was Holger Danske ("Ogier the Dane"), a mythical Viking hero revered by Danish children. The story goes that if the nation is ever in danger, this Danish superman will awaken and restore peace and security to the land (like King Arthur to the English, Barbarossa to the Germans, and Wenceslas to the Czechs). While this legend has been around for many centuries, Holger's connection to Kronborg was cemented by a Hans Christian Andersen tale, so now everybody just assumes he lives here. In

one of the first rooms, you'll see a famous, giant statue of this sleeping Viking...just waiting for things to get *really* bad.

NEAR THE CASTLE: MARITIME MUSEUM OF DENMARK

Fans of nautical history and modern architecture should consider a visit to this museum, built within the old dry docks adjacent to the castle and designed by noted Danish firm BIG (Bjarke Ingels Group). Cutting-edge exhibits journey through Denmark's rich seafaring tradition, from the days of tall-masted sailing ships to the container-ship revolution, in which Danish shipping company Maersk is a world leader. Topics include life on board, wartime challenges, the globalization of trade, navigation, and maritime traditions (including tattoos!) in popular culture.

Cost and Hours: 110 DKK, included with Copenhagen Card, 25 percent discount with Kronborg Castle ticket; daily July-Aug 10:00-18:00, Sept 11:00-17:00, shorter hours off-season; café, tel. 49 21 06 85, www.mfs.dk.

Near Copenhagen Connections

ROUTE TIPS FOR DRIVERS

Copenhagen to Hillerød (45 minutes) to Helsingør (30 minutes): Just follow the town-name signs. Leave Copenhagen following signs for *E-47* and *Helsingør*. The freeway is great. *Hillerød* signs lead to the Frederiksborg Castle (not to be confused with the nearby Fredensborg Palace) in the pleasant town of Hillerød. Follow signs to *Hillerød C* (for "center"), then *slot* (for "castle"). Though the E-47 freeway is the fastest, the Strandvejen coastal road (152) is pleasant, passing some of Denmark's grandest mansions (including that of author Karen Blixen of *Out of Africa* fame).

Copenhagen to Sweden: The 10-mile Øresund Bridge conveniently links Denmark with Sweden (toll about 375 DKK), giving drivers and train travelers a direct route from Copenhagen to Malmö, Sweden (see sidebar, earlier). Swedish authorities have tightened border security, so be sure to carry your passport on any trip from Denmark to Sweden.

If you're heading to Sweden from Kronborg Castle—or if you're simply nostalgic for the pre-bridge days—the Helsingør-Helsingborg ferry putters across the Øresund Channel (follow signs to *Helsingborg, Sweden*—freeway leads to dock). Buy your ticket as you roll on board (about 360 DKK one-way for car, driver, and up to nine passengers). Reservations are free but not usually necessary, as ferries depart frequently (2-4/hour; tel. 33 15 15 15, or book online at www.scandlines.dk; also see www.hhferries.se). If you arrive early, you can probably drive onto any ferry. The 20-minute Helsingør-Helsingborg ferry ride gives you just enough time to enjoy the view of the Kronborg "Hamlet" castle, be impressed by the narrowness of this very strategic channel, and exchange any leftover Danish kroner into Swedish kronor (the ferry exchange desk's rate is decent).

In Helsingborg, follow signs for *E-4* and *Stockholm*. The road is good, traffic is light, and towns are all clearly signposted. At Ljungby, road 25 takes you to Växjö and Kalmar. Entering Växjö, skip the first Växjö exit and follow the freeway into *Centrum*, where it ends. It takes about four hours total to drive from Copenhagen to Kalmar.

NEAR COPENHAGEN

CENTRAL DENMARK

Ærø • Odense

The sleepy isle of Ærø is the cuddle after the climax. It's the perfect time-passed world in which to wind down, enjoy the seagulls, and take a day off. Wander the unadulterated cobbled lanes of Denmark's best-preserved 18th-century town. Get Ærø-dynamic and pedal a rented bike into the essence of Denmark. Settle into a world of sailors, who, after the invention of steam-driven boat propellers, decided that building ships in bottles was more their style.

Between Ærø and Copenhagen, drop by bustling Odense, home of Hans Christian Andersen. Its Hans Christian Andersen House is excellent, and with more time, you can also enjoy its other museums (town history, trains, folk) and stroll the car-free streets of its downtown.

PLANNING YOUR TIME

Allow four hours to get from Copenhagen to Ærø (not counting a possible stopover in Odense). All trains stop in Roskilde (with its Viking Ship Museum—see previous chapter) and Odense (see the end of this chapter). On a quick trip, you can leave Copenhagen in the morning and do justice to both towns en route to Ærø. (With just one day, Odense and Roskilde together make a long but doable day trip from Copenhagen.)

While out of the way, Ærø is worth the journey. Once there, you'll want two nights

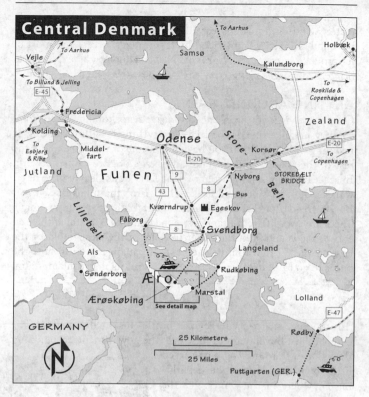

Central Denmark

and a day to properly enjoy it (for details, see "Planning Your Time" for Ærøskøbing, later).

Ærø

This small (22 by 6 miles) island on the south edge of Denmark is as salty and sleepy as can be. A typical tombstone reads: "Here lies Christian Hansen at anchor with his wife. He'll not weigh until he stands before God." It's the kind of island where baskets of strawberries sit in front of houses—for sale on the honor system.

Ærø statistics: 7,000 residents, 500,000 visitors and 80,000 boaters annually, 350 deer, seven pastors, no crosswalks, and three police officers. The three big industries are farming (wheat and dairy), shipping, and tourism—in that order. Twenty percent of the Danish fleet still resides on Ærø, in the town of Marstal. But jobs are scarce, the population is slowly dropping, and family farms are consolidating into larger units.

Ærø, home to several windmills and one of the world's largest solar power plants, is going "green." They hope to become completely wind- and solar-powered. Currently, about half the island's heat and electricity is provided by renewable sources, and most of its produce is organically grown. New technology is expected to bring Ærø closer to its goal within the next few years.

GETTING AROUND ÆRØ

On a short visit, you won't need to leave Ærøskøbing, except for a countryside bike ride, if you like—everything is within walking or pedaling distance. But if you have more time or want to explore the rest of the island, you can take advantage of Ærø's **bus** network. Buses leave from a stop just above the ferry dock (leaving the ferry, walk up about a block and look right). Ærø's main bus line, Jesper Bus, is free (Mon-Fri hourly until about 19:00; Sat-Sun 3-4/day). There are two different branches—one going to Marstal at the east end of the island, and the other to Søby in the west (look for the town name on the front of the bus). The main reason to take the bus is to go to Marstal on a rainy day to visit its maritime museum.

Ærøskøbing

Ærøskøbing is Ærø's village in a bottle. It's small enough to be cute, but just big enough to feel real. The government, recognizing the value of this amazingly preserved little town, prohibits modern building anywhere in the center. It's the only town in Denmark protected in this way. Drop into the 1680s, when Ærøskøbing was the wealthy home port of a hundred windjammers. The many Danes and Germans who come here for the tranquility—washing up the cobbled main drag in waves with the landing of each boat—call it the fairy-tale town. The Danish word for "cozy," *hyggelig*, describes Ærøskøbing perfectly.

Ærøskøbing is simply a pleasant place to wander. Stubby little porthole-type houses, with their birth dates displayed in proud decorative rebar, lean on each other like drunk, sleeping sailors. Wander under flickering old-time lamps. Snoop around town. It's OK. Peek into living rooms (if people want privacy, they shut their drapes). Notice the many "snooping mirrors" on the houses—antique locals are following your every move. The harbor now caters to holiday yachts, and on midnight low tides you can almost hear the crabs playing cards.

The town economy, once rich with the windjammer trade, hit the rocks in modern times. Kids 15 to 18 years old go to a boarding school in Svendborg; many don't return. About a third of Ærø's population is over age 60. And even though young couples on the island are having more babies, it's not enough to prevent a net population decline.

PLANNING YOUR TIME

You'll regret not setting aside a minimum of two nights for your Ærøskøbing visit. In a busy day you can "do" everything you like—except relax. If ever a place was right for recreating, this is it. I'd arrive in time for an evening stroll and dinner (and, when it's running, the Night Watchman's tour—see "Nightlife in Ærøskøbing," later). The next morning, do the island bike tour, returning by midafternoon. You can see the town's three museums in less than two hours (but note that they all close early—by 15:00 or 16:00), then browse the rest of your daylight away. Your second evening is filled with options: Stroll out to the summer huts for sunset, watch the classic sailing ships come in to moor for the evening (mostly Dutch and German boats crewed by vacationers), watch a movie in the pint-sized town cinema, go bowling with local teens, or check out live music in the pub.

Note that during the off-season (basically Sept-May), the town can be quite dead, but efforts are being made by local business owners to enliven the shorter days of fall and winter. Though several shops and restaurants close during the off-season, restaurant owners are trying to keep some dining establishments open on a rotating basis, so there should always be someplace to get a meal.

Orientation to Ærøskøbing

Ærøskøbing is tiny. Everything's just a few cobbles from the ferry landing.

TOURIST INFORMATION

The TI, which faces the ferry landing, has all the services you'd expect from a larger town's TI, including free Wi-Fi (late-June-mid-Aug Mon-Fri 9:00-18:00, Sat 10:00-18:00, Sun 10:00-15:00; off-season Mon-Fri 10:00-16:00, closed Sat-Sun; tel. 62 52 13 00, www.aeroe.dk).

HELPFUL HINTS

Money: The town's only ATM is at the blue building by the ferry dock, facing the TI.

Laundry: You'll find limited self-service laundry facilities at Ærøskøbing's marinas, on either side of the ferry dock.

Ferries: See "Ærøskøbing Connections" on page 160.

Bike Rental: Pilebækkens Cykler rents bikes year-round at the gas station at the top of town. Manager Janne hands out free

CENTRAL DENMARK

cykel maps so you can't get lost (seven-speed bikes-75 DKK/day, 150 DKK/2 days, 200 DKK/3 days; electric bikes also available—book a day ahead, deposit required; Mon-Fri 9:00-16:30, Sat until 13:00, closed Sun except July-Aug—when it's open 9:00-1:30; from Torvet Square, go through green door at Søndergade end of square, past garden to next road, in the gas station at Pilebækken 7; tel. 62 52 11 10). **Andelen Guesthouse** rents good, clean bikes too (100 DKK/day, Søndergade 28A, see "Sleeping in Ærøskøbing," later"). The campground also rents bikes. Most people on Ærø don't bother locking up their bikes—if your rental doesn't have a lock, don't fret.

Shopping: The town is speckled with cute little shops. Each July, local artisans show their creations in a warehouse facing the ferry landing.

Ærøskøbing Walk

This self-guided stroll, rated ▲▲▲, is ideal when the sun is low, the shadows long, and the colors rich. Start at the harbor.

Harbor: First, loiter around the harbor, where German and Dutch pleasure boaters come into port each evening. Because Ærø is only nine miles across the water from Germany, the island is popular with Germans who regularly return to this peaceful retreat on their grand old sailboats.

• *From the harbor and TI, walk up the main street a block and go left on...*

Smedegade: This is the poorest street in town, with the most architectural and higgledy-piggledy charm. Have a close look at the "street spies" on the houses—clever mirrors letting old women inside keep an eye on what's going on outside. The ship-in-a-bottle Bottle Peter Museum is on the right (described later, under "Sights in Ærøskøbing"). Notice the gutters—some protect only the doorway. Locals find the rounded modern drainpipes less charming than the old-school ones with hard angles. Appreciate the finely carved old

doors. Each is proudly unique—try to find two the same. Number 37 (on the left, after Arnfeldt Hotel), from the 18th century, is

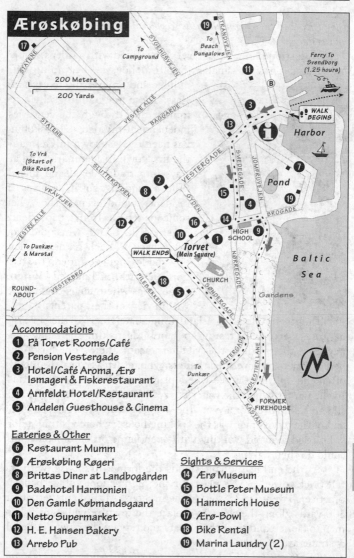

Ærøskøbing

200 Meters
200 Yards

To Campground
To Beach Bungalows
Ferry To Svendborg (1.25 hours)
WALK BEGINS
Harbor
To Vrå (Start of Bike Route)
Pond
To Dunkær & Marstal
High School
Torvet (Main Square)
WALK ENDS
Church
Baltic Sea
ROUND-ABOUT
Gardens
To Dunkær
Former Firehouse

Accommodations
❶ På Torvet Rooms/Café
❷ Pension Vestergade
❸ Hotel/Café Aroma, Ærø Ismageri & Fiskerestaurant
❹ Arnfeldt Hotel/Restaurant
❺ Andelen Guesthouse & Cinema

Eateries & Other
❻ Restaurant Mumm
❼ Ærøskøbing Røgeri
❽ Brittas Diner at Landbogården
❾ Badehotel Harmonien
❿ Den Gamle Købmandsgaard
⓫ Netto Supermarket
⓬ H. E. Hansen Bakery
⓭ Arrebo Pub

Sights & Services
⓮ Ærø Museum
⓯ Bottle Peter Museum
⓰ Hammerich House
⓱ Ærø-Bowl
⓲ Bike Rental
⓳ Marina Laundry (2)

Ærøskøbing's cutest house. Its tiny dormer is from some old ship's poop deck. The plants above the door have a traditional purpose—to keep this part of the house damp and slow to burn in case of fire.

Smedegade ends at the Folkehøjskole (folk high school). Inspired by the Danish philosopher Nikolaj Gruntvig—who wanted people to be able to say, "I am good at being me"—it offers people of any age the benefit of government-subsidized cultural education (music, art, theater, and so on).

• Jog left, then turn right after the school, and stroll along the peaceful, harborside...

Molestien Lane: This gravel path is lined with gardens, a quiet beach, and a row of small-is-beautiful houses—beginning with

humble and progressing to captain's class. These fine buildings are a reminder that through the centuries, independent-minded Ærøskøbing has been the last town in Germany, the first town in Denmark...and always into trade—legal and illegal. (The smuggling spirit survives in residents' blood even today. When someone returns from a trip, friends eagerly ask, "And what did you bring back?") Each garden is cleverly and lovingly designed. The harborfront path, nicknamed "Virgin's Lane," was where teens could court within view of their parents.

The dreamy-looking island immediately across the way is a nature preserve and a resting spot for birds making their long journey from the north to the Mediterranean. There's one lucky bull here (farmers raft over their heifers, who return as cows). Rainbows often end on this island—where plague victims were once buried. In the winter, when the water freezes (about once a decade), locals slip and slide over for a visit. The white building you can see at the end of the town's pier was the cooking house, where visiting sailors (who tried to avoid working with open flame on flammable ships) could do their baking.

At the end of the lane stands the former firehouse (with the tall brick tower, now a place for the high school garage band to practice). Twenty yards before the firehouse, a trail cuts left about 100 yards along the shore to a place the town provides for fishermen to launch and store their boats and tidy up their nets. A bench is strategically placed to enjoy the view.

• Follow the rutted lane inland, back past the firehouse. Turn right and walk a block toward town. At the first intersection, take a right onto...

Østergade: This was Ærøskøbing's east gate. In the days of German control, all island trade was legal only within the town. All who passed this point would pay various duties and taxes at a tollbooth that once stood here.

As you walk past the traditional houses, peer into living rooms. Catch snatches of Danish life. (After the bend, you can see right through the windows to the sea.) Ponder the beauty of a society with such a keen sense of civic responsibility that fishing permits entrust you "to catch only what you need." You're welcome to pick berries where you like...but "no more than what would fit in your hat."

The wood on these old houses prefers organic coverings to modern paint. Tar painted on beams as a preservative blisters in the sun. An old-fashioned paint of chalk, lime, and clay lets old houses breathe and feel more alive. (It gets darker with the rain and leaves a little color on your fingers.) Modern chemical paint has much less personality.

The first square (actually a triangle, at #55) was the old goose market. Ærøskøbing—born in the 13th century, burned in the 17th, and rebuilt in the 18th—claims (believably) to be the best-preserved town from that era in Denmark. The original plan, with 12 streets laid out by its founder, survives.

• *Leaving the square, stay left on...*

Søndergade: Look for wrought-iron girders on the walls, added to hold together bulging houses. (On the first corner, at #55,

notice the nuts that could be tightened like a corset to keep the house from sagging.) Ærøskøbing's oldest houses (check out the dates)—the only ones that survived a fire during a war with Sweden—are #36 and #32. At #32, the hatch upstairs was where masts and sails were stored for the winter. These houses also have some of the finest doors in town (and in Ærøskøbing, that's saying something). The red on #32's door is the original paint job—ox blood, which, when combined with the tannin in the wood, really lasts. The courtyard behind #18 was a parking lot in pre-car days. Farmers, in town for their shopping chores, would leave their horses here. Even today, the wide-open fields are just beyond.

• *Wander down to Ærøskøbing's main square.*

Torvet Square: Notice the two hand pumps, which still work. Until 1951, towns-people came here for their water. The linden tree is the town symbol. The rocks around it celebrate the reunion of a big chunk of southern Denmark (including this island), which was ruled by Germany from 1864 to 1920. See the town seal featuring a linden tree, over the door of the old City Hall (now the library, with Internet stations in former prison cells). Read the Danish on the wall: "With law shall man a country build."

• *Our walk is over. Continue straight (popping into recommended Restaurant Mumm, the best place in town, to make a reservation for dinner). You'll return to the main street (Vestergade) and—just when you need it—the town bakery (to the left). But, if you're ready to launch right into a bike ride, instead go through the green door to the right of City Hall to reach one of the town's bike-rental places (listed earlier, under "Helpful Hints").*

Sights in Ærøskøbing

MUSEUMS

Ærøskøbing's three tiny museums cluster within a few doors of each other just off Torvet Square. While quirky and fun (and with sketchy English handouts), these museums would be much more interesting and worthwhile if they translated their Danish descriptions for the rare person on this planet who doesn't speak *Dansk*. (Your gentle encouragement might help get results.) In July, they organize daily chatty tours.

Ærø Museum (Ærøskøbing Bymuseum)

This museum, which may be closed for renovation during your visit, fills two floors of an old house with the island's history, from seafaring to farming. Be on the lookout  for household objects (such as pottery, kitchenware, and tools), paintings, a loom from 1683, an 18th-century peasant's living room with colorful furniture, and gear from a 100-year-old pharmacy. There's also a fun diorama showing an aerial view of Ærøskøbing in 1862—notice the big gardens behind nearly every house. (This museum carries on the tradition with its own garden out back—be sure to go out and explore it before you leave.)

Cost and Hours: 40 DKK; July-Aug Mon-Fri 10:00-16:00, Sat-Sun 11:00-15:00; mid-April-June and Sept-mid-Oct Mon-Sat 11:00-15:00, closed Sun; shorter hours and closed Sat-Sun off-season; Brogade 3, tel. 62 52 29 50, www.arremus.dk.

▲Bottle Peter Museum (Flaske-Peters Samling)

This fascinating house has 750 different bottled ships. Old Peter Jacobsen, who made his first bottle at 16 and his last at 85, created some 1,700 ships-in-bottles in his lifetime. He bragged that he drank the contents of each bottle...except those containing milk. This museum opened in 1943, when the mayor of Ærøskøbing offered Peter and his wife a humble home in exchange for the right to display his works. Bottle Peter died in 1960 (and is most likely buried in a glass bottle), leaving a lifetime of tedious little creations for visitors to squint and marvel at.

Cost and Hours: 40 DKK; July-Aug daily 10:00-16:00; May-June and Sept Mon-Sat 11:00-15:00, closed Sun; off-season call for viewing appointment; Smedegade 22, tel. 81 55 59 72.

Visiting the Museum: In two buildings facing each other across a cobbled courtyard, you'll see rack after rack of painstaking models in bottles and cigar boxes. Some are "right-handed" and some are "left-handed" (referring to the direction the bottle faced, and therefore which hand the model maker relied on to execute the fine details)—Bottle Peter could do it all.

In the entrance building, you'll see Peter's "American collection," which he sold to a Danish-American collector so he could have funds to retire. One of Peter's favorites was the "diver-bottle"—an extra-wide bottle with two separate ship models inside: One shipwreck on the "ocean floor" at the bottom of the bottle, and, above that, a second one floating on the "surface." A video shows the artist at work, and nearby you can see some of his tools.

The second building has some English panels about Peter's life (including his mischievous wit, which caused his friends great anxiety when he had an audience with the king) and the headstone he designed for his own grave: a cross embedded with seven ships-in-bottles, representing the seven seas he explored in his youth as a seaman.

Hammerich House (Hammerichs Hus)

These 12 funky rooms in three houses are filled with 200- to 300-year-old junk.

Cost and Hours: 40 DKK, late July-Aug Mon-Fri 12:00-15:00, otherwise ask for access at the Ærø Museum, closed off-season, Gyden 22.

ÆRØ ISLAND BIKE RIDE (OR CAR TOUR)

This 15-mile trip shows you the best of this windmill-covered island's charms. The highest point on the island is only 180 feet above sea level, but the wind can be strong and the hills seem long and surprisingly steep.

As a bike ride, it's good exercise, though it may be more exhausting than fun if you've done only light, recreational cycling

Ærø Island Bike Ride

To Svendborg

100 KM
50 MI
DENMARK
Odense • Cope.
Ærø
GER.

To Søby

Urehoved

BEACH
BUNGALOWS
CAMPING

GÆSTGIVERI
BREGNINGE
CHURCH
Bregninge

Borgnæs

DIKE

Drejø

Ommels-
hoved

Synneshøj

Vrå

Ærøskøbing
(start & end bike ride)

Lilleø

SHORTCUTS BACK
TO ÆRØSKØBING

VINDEBALLE KRO
Vindeballe

Stokkeby

Olde

Lille
Rise

Kragnæs

Vodrup
Klint
(Cliffs)

Tranderup

TINGSTEDET
DOLMEN
BREWERY

Store
Rise

Dunkær

To Marstal
& Maritime
Museum

Baltic Sea

2 Kilometers

2 Miles

Vejnæs Nakke

at home. You'll pay more for seven gears instead of five, but it's worth it.

Rent your bike in town (see "Helpful Hints," earlier), and while my map and instructions work, a local cycle map is helpful (free loaner maps if you rent from Pilebækkens Cykler, or buy one at the TI). Bring along plenty of water, as there are few opportunities to fill up (your first good chance is at the WC at the Bregninge church; there are no real shops until downtown Bregninge).

• *Leave Ærøskøbing to the west on the road to Vrå (Vråvejen, signed Bike Route #90). From downtown, pedal up the main street (Vestergade) and turn right on Vråvejen; from the bike-rental place on Pilebækken, just turn right and pedal straight ahead—it turns into Vråvejen.*

Leaving Ærøskøbing: You'll see the first of many U-shaped farmhouses, typical of Denmark. The three sides block the wind and store cows, hay, and people. *Gård* (farm) shows up in many local surnames.

At Øsemarksvej, bike along the coast in the protection of the dike built in 1856 to make the once-salty swampland to your left farmable. While the weak soil is good for hay and little else, they get the most out of it. Each winter, certain grazing areas flood with seawater. (Some locals claim this makes their cows produce fatter milk and meat.) As you roll along the dike, the land on your left is about eight feet below sea level. The little white pump house— alone in the field—is busy each spring and summer.

• *At the T-junction, go right (over the dike) toward...*

Borgnæs: The traditional old "straw house" (50 yards down, on left) is a café and shop selling fresh farm products. Just past that, a few roadside tables sell farm goodies on the honor system. Borgnæs is a cluster of modern summer houses. In spite of huge demand, a weak economy, and an aging population, development like this is no longer allowed.

• *Keep to the right (passing lots of wheat fields); at the next T-junction, turn right, following signs for Ø.* Bregningemark *(don't turn off for* Vindeballe*). After a secluded beach, head inland (direction: Ø. Bregninge). Pass the island's only water mill, and climb uphill over the island's 2,700-inch-high summit toward Bregninge. The tallest point on Ærø is called Synneshøj (probably means "Seems High" and it sure does—if you're even a bit out of shape, you'll feel every one of those inches).*

Gammelgård: Take a right turn marked only by a *Bike Route #90* sign. The road deteriorates (turns to gravel—and can be slushy

if there's been heavy rain, so be careful). You'll wind scenically and sometimes steeply through "Ærø's Alps," past classic thatched-roofed "old farms" (hence the name of the lane— Gammelgård).

• *At the modern road, turn left (leaving Bike Route #90) and pedal to the big village church. Before turning left to roll through Bregninge, visit the church.*

Bregninge Church: The interior of the 12th-century Bregninge church is still painted as a Gothic church would have been.

Find the painter's self-portrait (behind the pulpit, right of front pew). Tradition says that if the painter wasn't happy with his pay, he'd paint a fool's head in the church (above third pew on left). Note how the fool's mouth—the hole for a rope tied to the bell—has been worn wider and wider by centuries of ringing. (During services, the ringing bell would call those who were ill and too contagious to be allowed into the church to come for communion—distributed through the square hatches flanking the altar.)

The altarpiece—gold leaf on carved oak—is from 1528, six

years before the Reformation came to Denmark. The cranium carved into the bottom indicates it's a genuine master-piece by Claus Berg (from Lübeck, Germany). This Crucifixion scene is such a commotion, it seems to cause Christ's robe to billow up. The soldiers who tradition-ally gambled for Christ's robe have traded their dice for knives. Even the three wise men (lower right; each perhaps a Danish king) made it to this Crucifixion. Notice the escaping souls of the two thieves—the one who converted on the cross being car-ried happily to heaven, and the other, with its grim-winged escort, heading straight to hell. The scene at lower left—a disciple with a bare-breasted, dark-skinned woman feeding her child—symbolizes the Great Commission: "Go ye to all the world." Since this is a Catholic altarpiece, a roll call of saints lines the wings. During the restoration, the identity of the two women on the lower right was unknown, so the lettering—even in Latin—is clearly gibberish. Take a moment to study the 16th-century art on the ceiling (for example, the crucified feet ascending, leaving only footprints on earth). In the narthex, a list of pastors goes back to 1505. The current pastor (Agnes) is the first woman on the list.

• *Now's the time for a bathroom break (public WC in the churchyard). If you need some food or drink, pop in to the* **$$$ Gæstgiveri Bregninge** *restaurant, to the right of the church as you face it (lunch and dinner, May-mid-Sept Wed-Thu 12:00-17:00, Fri-Sun until 21:00, closed Mon-Tue and in the off-season, guest rooms available, tel. 30 23 65 55, www.gaestgiveri.dk). Then roll downhill through...*

Bregninge: As you bike through what is supposedly Denmark's "second-longest village," you'll pass many more U-shaped *gårds*. Notice how the town is in a gully. Imagine pirates trolling along the coast, looking for church spires marking unfortified villages. Ærø's 16 villages are all invisible from the sea—their church spires carefully designed not to be viewable from sea level.

• *About a mile down the main road is Vindeballe. Just before the main part of the village (soon after you pass the official* Vindeballe *sign and the* din fart *sign—which tells you "your speed"), take the* Vodrup Klint *turnoff to the right.*

Vodrup Klint: A road leads downhill (with a well-signed jog to the right) to dead-end at a rugged bluff called Vodrup Klint (WC, picnic benches). If I were a pagan, I'd worship here for the sea, the wind, and the chilling view. Notice how the land steps in sloppy slabs down to the sea. When saturated with water, the

slabs of clay that make up the
land here get slick, and entire
chunks can slide.

Hike down to the foamy
beach (where you can pick up
some flint, chalk, and wild
thyme). While the wind at
the top could drag a kite-flyer,
the beach below can be ideal

for sunbathing. Because Ærø is warmer and drier than the rest of
Denmark, this island is home to plants and animals found nowhere
else in the country. This southern exposure is the warmest area.
Germany is dead ahead.

• *Backtrack 200 yards and follow the signs to* Tranderup. *On the way,
you'll pass a lovely pond famous for its bell frogs and happy little duck
houses.*

*Popping out in Tranderup, you can backtrack (left) about 300 yards
to get to the traditional* **$$$ Vindeballe Kro**—*a handy inn for a stop if
you're hungry or thirsty (lunch served daily July–mid-Aug 12:00–14:00,
dinners served daily year-round 18:00–21:00, tel. 62 52 16 13, www.
vindeballekro.dk).*

*If you're tired or if the weather is turning bad, you can shortcut
from here back to* **Ærøskøbing**: *Go down the lane across the street from
the Vindeballe Kro, and you'll zip quickly downhill across the island to
the dike just east of Borgnæs; turn right and retrace your steps back into
town.*

But there's much more to see. To continue our pedal, head on into...

Tranderup: Still following signs for *Tranderup,* stay on Tran-
derupgade parallel to the big road through town. You'll pass a
lovely farm and a potato stand. At the main road, turn right. At the
Ærøskøbing turnoff (another chance to bail out and head home),
side-trip 100 yards left to the big stone (commemorating the re-
turn of the island to Denmark from Germany in 1750) and a grand
island panorama. Claus Clausen's rock (in the picnic area, next to
WC) is a memorial to an extremely obscure pioneer who was born
in Ærø, emigrated to America, and played a role in shaping the
early history of Scandinavian Lutheranism in the US.

• *Return to the big road (continuing in direction: Marstal), pass through
Olde, pedal past FAF (the local wheat farmers' co-op facility), and head
toward Store Rise (STOH-reh REE-zuh), the next church spire in the
distance. Think of medieval travelers using spires as navigational aids.*

Store Rise Prehistoric Tomb, Church, and Brewery: Thirty
yards after the Stokkeby turnoff, follow the rough, tree-lined path
on the right to the Langdysse (Long Dolmen) Tingstedet, just be-
hind the church spire. This is a 6,000-year-old **dolmen,** an early
Neolithic burial place. Though Ærø once had more than 200 of

these prehistoric tombs, only 13 survive. The site is a raised mound the shape and length (about 100 feet) of a Viking ship, and archaeologists have found evidence that indicates a Viking ship may indeed have been burned and buried here.

Ting means assembly spot. Imagine a thousand years ago: Viking chiefs representing the island's various communities gathering here around their ancestors' tombs. For 6,000 years, this has been a holy spot. The stones were considered fertility stones. For centuries, locals in need of virility chipped off bits and took them home (the nicks in the rock nearest the information post are mine).

Tuck away your chip and carry on down the lane to the Store Rise **church.** Inside you'll find little ships hanging in the nave, a fine 12th-century altarpiece, a stick with offering bag and a ting-a-ling bell to wake those nodding off (right of altar), double seats (so worshippers can flip to face the pulpit during sermons), and Martin Luther in the stern keeping his Protestant hand on the rudder. The list in the church allows today's pastors to trace their pastoral lineage back to Doctor Luther himself. (The current pastor, Janet, is the first woman on the list.) The churchyard is circular—a reminder of how churchyards provided a last refuge for humble communities under attack. Can you find anyone buried in the graveyard whose name doesn't end in "-sen"?

Next follow the smell of hops (or the *Rise Bryggeri* signs) to Ærø's **brewery.** Located in a historic brewery 400 yards beyond the Store Rise church, it welcomes visitors with free samples of its various beers. The Ærø traditional brews are available in pilsner (including the popular walnut pilsner), light ale, dark ale, and a typical dark Irish-style stout. The Rise organic brews come in light ale, dark ale, and walnut (daily July-Aug 10:00-15:00; shorter hours Sept-mid-Oct, closed mid-Oct-June; tel. 62 52 11 32, www.risebryggeri.dk).

• *From here, climb back to the main road and continue (direction: Marstal) on your way back home to Ærøskøbing. The three 330-foot-high modern windmills on your right are communally owned and, as they are a nonpolluting source of energy, state-subsidized. At Dunkær (3 miles from Ærøskøbing), take the small road, signed* Lille Rise, *past the topless windmill. Except for the Lille Rise, it's all downhill from here, as you coast past great sea views back home to Ærøskøbing.*

Huts at the Sunset Beach: Still rolling? Bike past the campground along the Urehoved beach (*strand* in Danish) for a look at the coziest little beach houses you'll never see back in the "big is beautiful" US. This is Europe, where small is beautiful, and the

concept of sustainability is neither new nor subversive. (For
more details, see "Beach Bun-
galow Sunset Stroll," later.)

RAINY-DAY OPTIONS
Ærø is disappointing but not
unworkable in bad weather.
In addition to the museums listed earlier, you could check out the
evening options under "Nightlife in Ærøskøbing" (later), many of
which are good in bad weather. Or hop on the free bus to Marstal
to visit its maritime museum.

Marstal Maritime Museum (Marstal Søfartsmuseum)
To learn more about the island's seafaring history, visit this fine
museum in the dreary town of Marstal. You'll see plenty of model
ships, nautical paintings (including several scenes by acclaimed
painter Carl Rasmussen), an original ship's galley, a re-created
wheelhouse (with steering and navigation equipment), a collection
of exotic goods brought back from faraway lands, and a children's
area with a climbable mast. Designed by and for sailors, the museum presents a warts-and-all view of the hardships of the seafaring
life, rather than romanticizing it.

Cost and Hours: 60 DKK; June-Aug daily 9:00-17:00; mid-
April-May and Sept-Oct daily 10:00-16:00; shorter hours and
closed Sun off-season; Prinsensgade 1, tel. 62 53 23 31, www.
marmus.dk.

Getting There: Ride the free Jesper Bus from Ærøskøbing all
the way to the harbor in Marstal, where you'll find the museum. It's
about a 20-minute trip.

Nightlife in Ærøskøbing

These activities are best done in the evening, after a day of biking
around the island.

▲▲Beach Bungalow Sunset Stroll
At sunset, stroll to Ærøskøbing's sand beach. Facing the ferry

dock, go left, following the
harbor. Upon leaving the town,
you'll pass the Netto supermarket (convenient for picking up snacks, beer, or wine),
a minigolf course, and a children's playground. In the rosy
distance, past a wavy wheat
field, is Vestre Strandvejen—a

row of tiny, Monopoly-like huts facing the sunset. These beach escapes are privately owned on land rented from the town (no overnight use, WCs at each end). Each is different, but all are stained with merry memories of locals enjoying themselves Danish-style. Bring a beverage or picnic. It's perfectly acceptable—and very Danish—to borrow a porch for your sunset sit. From here, it's a fine walk out to the end of Urehoved (as this spit of land is called).

Town Walk with Night Watchman

On summer evenings in July and August, the night watchman leads visitors through town. It's a fine time to be outside, meeting other travelers (30 DKK, starts 21:00 at Torvet Square—just show up, English tours Wed and Sat).

Cinema

The cute little 30-seat Andelen Theater (in the Andelen Guesthouse—a former grain warehouse) plays movies in their original language (Danish subtitles, closed Mon and in July—when it hosts a jazz festival, new titles begin every Tue). It's run in a charming community-service kind of way. The management has installed heat, so tickets no longer come with a blanket (near Torvet Square at Søndergade 28A, tel. 62 52 17 11).

Bowling

Ærø-Bowl is a six-lane alley in a modern athletic club at the edge of town. In this old-fashioned town, where no modern construction is allowed in the higgledy-piggledy center, this hip facility is a magnet for young people. One local told me, "I've never seen anyone come out of there without a smile" (hot dogs, junk food, arcade games, kids on dates; Tue-Thu 16:00-22:00, later on Fri-Sat, shorter hours off-season, closed Sun-Mon, Statene 42A, tel. 62 52 23 06).

Pub

Arrebo Pub bills itself as "probably the best bar in town." Maybe that's because it's the *only* one in town. In any case, it attracts a young crowd and is the place to go for live music and beer, but there's no food (open daily from 13:00, at the bottom of Vestergade, near ferry dock).

Sleeping in Ærøskøbing

The accommodations scene here is boom or bust. Summer weekends and all of July are packed (book long in advance). It's absolutely dead in the winter. These places come with family-run personality, and each is an easy stroll from the ferry landing.

IN ÆRØSKØBING

$$$$ På Torvet ("On the Square") is a cheery hotel/café/wine shop that's bringing a lively new spirit to the town square. Owners Gunnar and Lili rent 11 modern, sparkling apartments, each with a private bathroom, and several with a kitchen (Torvet 7, tel. 62 52 40 50, www.paatorvet.dk, info@paatorvet.dk). The recommended café serves breakfast and lunch with seating inside and out on Torvet Square (see "Eating in Ærøskøbing," later). They also sell wine and specialty foods, and the grand piano in the dining area is ready for you to tickle its ivories.

$$$ Pension Vestergade is your best home away from home in Ærøskøbing. It's lovingly run by Susanna Greve and her daughters, Henrietta and Celia. Su-
sanna, who's fun to talk with and is always ready with a cup of tea, has a wealth of knowl-edge about the town's his-tory and takes good care of her guests. Built in 1784 for a sea captain's daughter, this creaky, sagging, and venerable eight-room place—with each room

named for its particular color scheme—is on the main street in the town center. Picnic in the back garden and get to know Til-lie, the live-in dog. Reserve well in advance (RS%, payment via TransferWise app or cash, cuddly hot-water bottles, shared bath-rooms, Vestergade 44, tel. 62 52 22 98, www.vestergade44.com, pensionvestergade44@post.tele.dk).

$$$ Hotel Aroma offers four bright, cheery, and modern rooms—two standard doubles and two large family rooms with kitchens—above the recommended Café Aroma (shared bath-room, laundry facilities, roof terrace, on Vestergade, just up the street from the ferry dock, open mid-April-Aug, closed in off-sea-son, tel. 62 52 40 02, mobile 40 40 26 84, www.cafe-aroma.dk).

$$$ Arnfeldt Hotel, formerly Det Lille Hotel, was once a 19th-century captain's home. Now owned by an energetic hus-band-and-wife team, Morten and Katrine Arnfeldt, this cozy hotel offers six clean and tidy, freshly renovated rooms with shared baths (Smedegade 33, tel. 62 52 23 00, ma@arnfeldtgroup.com).

$$ Andelen Guesthouse, run by Englishman Adam, is brimming with a funky nautical charm. An old warehouse that's been converted into a hotel, it has five guest rooms that share two bathrooms and one two-level family room with private bath (no breakfast—but can be purchased nearby at På Torvet Café, free entry to downstairs movie theater, nice rental bikes-100 DKK/

day, pay laundry, Søndergade 28A, mobile 61 26 75 11, www. andelenguesthouse.com, info@andelenguesthouse.com).

OUTSIDE OF ÆRØSKØBING

$$ Vindeballe Kro, about three miles from Ærøskøbing, is a traditional inn in Vindeballe at the island's central crossroads. Maria and Steen rent 10 straightforward, well-kept rooms (free parking; for location, see the Ærø Island Bike Ride map; tel. 62 52 16 13, www.vindeballekro.dk, mail@vindeballekro.dk). They also have a restaurant (described earlier, under "Ærø Island Bike Ride").

¢ **Ærø Campground** is set on a fine beach a few minutes' walk out of town. This three-star campground offers a lodge with a fireplace, campsites, cabins, and bike rental (open April-mid-Oct; facing the water, follow waterfront to the left; tel. 62 52 18 54, www. aeroecamp.dk, info@aeroecamp.dk).

Eating in Ærøskøbing

Ærøskøbing has a handful of charming and hardworking little eateries. Business is so light that chefs and owners come and go constantly, making it tough to predict the best value for the coming year. As each place has a distinct flavor, I'd spend 20 minutes enjoying the warm evening light and do a strolling survey before making your choice. I've listed only the serious kitchens. Note that almost everything closes by 21:00—don't wait too late to eat (if you'll be taking a later ferry from Svendborg to Ærø, either eat before your boat trip or call ahead to reserve a place...otherwise you're out of luck). During the winter, some of my recommended restaurants take turns staying open, so you should be able to find a decent place to eat (the TI posts a list of restaurant opening days and times).

$$$$ Restaurant Mumm is where visiting yachters go for a good and classy meal. Portions are huge, and on balmy days their garden terrace out back is a hit. Call ahead to reserve or book online (daily specials, starters, main courses, daily 18:00-21:00, shorter hours and closed Sun-Tue in off-season, near Torvet Square at Søndergade 12, tel. 62 52 12 12, www.mumm.restaurant).

$$ Pä Torvet Café, right on Torvet Square, offers a tasty lunch menu, with hearty portions that are stylishly presented. Dine in the cozy café or out on the square (daily May-mid-Sept 12:00-15:30, shorter hours off-season, tel. 62 52 40 50).

$$ Café Aroma, a reasonably priced Danish café that feels like a rustic old diner, has a big front porch filled with tables and good entrées, sandwiches, and burgers. Ask about the daily special, which will save you money and is not listed on the menu. Order at the bar (mid-April-Aug Thu-Mon 11:00-20:00, closed Tue-Wed and in off-season, on Vestergade, just up from the ferry dock, tel. 62 52 40 02). They also run a delicious ice-cream shop; a high-quality, pricey fish restaurant next door (**Fiskerestaurant,** open July only); and produce gourmet handmade licorice just across the street.

$$ Ærøskøbing Røgeri serves wonderful smoked-fish meals on paper plates. With picnic tables facing the harbor, it's great for a light meal. Eat there or find a pleasant picnic site at the beach or at the park behind the fish house. A smoked-fish dinner with potato salad, bread, and a couple of cold Carlsbergs or Ærø brews are a well-earned reward after a long bike ride (daily April-mid-Oct 11:00-19:00, mid-June-mid-Aug 10:00-21:00, Havnen 15, tel. 62 52 40 07).

$$$$ Brittas Diner at Landbogården prides itself on serving "honest and special" dishes using local ingredients in its changing menu (meat, fish, international dishes, Tue-Sun 17:30-21:00, closed Mon, near the top of Vestergade at #54, tel. 23 92 41 30).

Hotel Restaurants: Two hotels in town have dining rooms with good but expensive food; I'd eat at the restaurants I've listed above, unless they're closed. But in a pinch, try these: **$$$ Badehotel Harmonien** serves Italian dishes and wood-fired pizza, and owns the best location in town, with views of the sea from its bright and lively perch (pizza made right in the dining room, Thu-Tue 17:30-22:00, closed Wed, tel. 42 50 00 05). **$$$$ Arnfeldt Hotel** offers gourmet meals using local ingredients. After stints in London and Copenhagen, chef Morten Arnfeldt is bringing upscale dining to Ærø, serving internationally inspired dishes in an inviting dining room and garden (four-course dinners, reservations required, Smedegade 33, tel. 62 52 23 00).

SNACKS, PICNICS, AND DESSERT
Here are some places for lighter fare.

Market for Local Specialties: At **Den Gamle Købmandsgaard** ("The Old Merchants' Court") on Torvet Square you'll find a remarkable selection of mostly locally sourced and produced foods, including meat, sausage, salami, bread, fruit, honey, jam, chocolate, beer, cigars, and whiskey—which is distilled on-site (ask about tours and tastings). Grab a seat in their café for lunch or cake (Mon-Sat 10:00-17:30, closed Sun, Torvet 5, tel. 20 24 30 07).

Grocery: The **Netto** supermarket has picnic fixings and drinks, including chilled beer and wine—handy for walks to the little huts on the beach at sunset (daily 7:00-22:00, kitty-corner from ferry dock).

Bakery: Ærøskøbing's old-school **H. E. Hansen** bakery sells fresh bread and delicious pastries, plus cheese, yogurt, and drinks

(Tue-Fri 7:00-17:00, Sat-Sun until 14:00, closed Mon, top of Vestergade).

Ice Cream: The ice-cream shop at Café Aroma, **Ærø Ismageri,** serves good, flavorful ice cream—try gooseberry beer (made from Ærø stout—way better than it sounds), or the local favorite, the "Ærø Special"—walnut ice cream with maple syrup (daily mid-April-Aug 9:00-23:00, closed Sept-mid-April, just up from the ferry dock).

Ærøskøbing Connections

ÆRØ-SVENDBORG FERRY

The ferry ride between **Svendborg,** with connections to Copenhagen, and **Ærøskøbing,** on the island of Ærø, is a relaxing 1.25-hour crossing. Just get on, and the crew will come to you for payment. American credit cards with a chip work (2.50-DKK surcharge), or you can pay cash (218 DKK round-trip per person, 476 DKK round-trip per car—not including driver/passengers, ferry not covered by or discounted with rail pass, significant off-season discounts). You can leave the island via any of the three different Ærø ferry routes.

The ferry always has room for walk-ons, but drivers should reserve a spot in advance, especially on weekends and in summer. During these busy times, reserve as far ahead as you can—ideally at least a week in advance. Car reservations by phone or email are free and easy—simply give your name and license-plate number. If you don't know your license number (i.e., you're reserving from home and haven't yet picked up your rental car), try asking nicely if they're willing to just take your name. They may want you to call them with the number when you pick up your car, but if that's not practical, you can usually just tell the attendant your name before you drive onto the boat. Ferries depart daily in summer (roughly 10/day in each direction). Call or look online for the schedule (office open Mon-Fri 8:00-15:30, Sat-Sun 9:00-15:00, tel. 62 52 40 00, www.aeroe-ferry.dk, info@aeroe-ferry.dk).

Drivers with reservations just drive on (be sure to get into the *med* reservations line). If you won't use your car in Ærø, park it in Svendborg (big, safe lot two blocks in from ferry landing, or at the far end of the harbor near the Bendix fish shop). On Ærø, parking is free.

Trains Connecting with Ærø-Svendborg Ferry

The train from **Odense** dead-ends at the Svendborg harbor (2/hour Mon-Sat, hourly on Sun, 45 minutes; don't get off at Svendborg Vest Station—wait until you get to the end of the line, called simply "Svendborg").

Arriving in Svendborg: It takes about 10 minutes to walk from the station to the dock (5 minutes if you walk briskly). Don't dawdle—the boat leaves stubbornly on time, even if trains are running late. I recommend taking a train from Odense that arrives about 30 minutes before your ferry departure to give yourself time to absorb delays and find your way. If you're cutting it close, be ready to hop off the train and walk swiftly.

To get from the Svendborg train station to the dock, turn left after exiting the train, following the sidewalk between the tracks and the station, then take a left (across the tracks) at the first street, Brogade. Head a block downhill to the harbor, make a right, and the ferry dock is ahead, across from Hotel Ærø. If you arrive early, you can head to the waiting room in the little blue building across the street from the hotel. There are several carry-out restaurants along Brogade, and a few hotels overlooking the ferry line have restaurants.

Departing from Svendborg: All Svendborg trains go to Odense (where you can connect to Copenhagen or Aarhus). A train tends to leave shortly after the ferry arrives (a tight connection—it's a good idea to buy your train ticket in advance instead of making a mad rush to use the one ticket machine at the station). To reach the train from the Svendborg ferry dock, pass Hotel Ærø and continue a block along the waiting lane for the ferry, turn left and go up Brogade one block, then take a right and follow the sidewalk between the tracks and the train station. Look for a train signed *Odense* waiting on the single track.

Odense

Founded in A.D. 988 and named after Odin (the Nordic Zeus), Odense is the main city of the big island of Funen (Fyn in Danish) and the birthplace of storyteller Hans Christian Andersen (whom the Danes call simply H. C., pronounced "hoe see"; for more on the author, see the Copenhagen chapter). Although the author was born here in poverty and left at the tender age of

14 to pursue a career in the theater scene of Copenhagen, H. C. is Odense's favorite son—you'll find his name and image all over town. He once said, "Perhaps Odense will one day become famous because of me." Today, Odense (OH-then-za) is one of Denmark's most popular tourist destinations.

Orientation to Odense

As Denmark's third-largest city, with 170,000 people, Odense is big and industrial. But its old center, tidy and neatly urbanized, re-

tains some pockets of the fairy-tale charm it had in the days of H. C. Everything is within easy walking distance, except for the open-air folk museum.

The train station sits at the north end of the town center. A few blocks south runs the main pedestrian shopping bou-

levard, Vestergade. Near the eastern end of this drag, and a couple of blocks up, is a tight tangle of atmospheric old lanes, where you'll find the Hans Christian Andersen Museum and Møntergården, Odense's urban history museum.

TOURIST INFORMATION

The TI is in the Town Hall (Rådhuset), the big brick palace overlooking the square at the east end of the Vestergade pedes-

trian street (July-Aug Mon-Fri 9:30-18:00, Sat 10:00-15:00, Sun 11:00-14:00; shorter hours and closed Sun off-season; tel. 63 75 75 20, www. visitodense.com). For all the information needed for a longer stop, pick up their excellent and free *Odense* guide. If you plan to visit multiple sights, consider the **Odense Pass,**

which covers the Hans Christian Andersen Museum, urban history museum, art museum, railway museum, and open-air folk museum. It saves you money if you visit at least three sights (169 DKK/24 hours, buy at TI).

ARRIVAL IN ODENSE

The train station is located in the Bånegard Center, a large shopping complex, which also holds the bus station, library, shops, eateries, and a movie theater. For a quick visit, check your luggage at the train station (pay lockers in corridor next to DSB Resjebureau

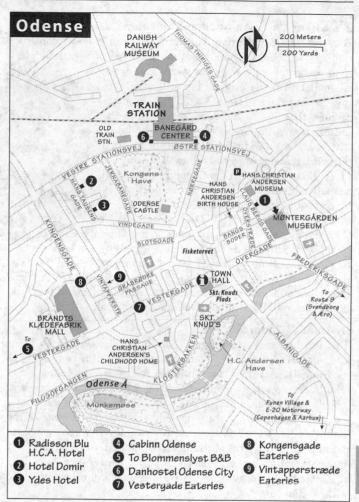

Odense

DANISH RAILWAY MUSEUM

TRAIN STATION

OLD TRAIN STN.

BANEGÅRD CENTER

6 4

ØSTRE STATIONSVEJ

VESTRE STATIONSVEJ

Kongens Have

2

3

ODENSE CASTLE

VINDEGADE

SLOTSGADE

Fisketorvet

HANS CHRISTIAN ANDERSEN BIRTH HOUSE

HANS CHRISTIAN ANDERSEN MUSEUM

1

MØNTERGÅRDEN MUSEUM

FREDERIKSGADE

TOWN HALL

Skt. Knuds Plads

8

9

GRÅBRØDRE PASSAGE

VESTERGADE

7

BRANDTS KLÆDEFABRIK MALL

5

VESTERGADE

HANS CHRISTIAN ANDERSEN'S CHILDHOOD HOME

SKT. KNUD'S

KLØSTERBAKKEN

H.C. Andersen Have

ALBANIGADE

To Route 9 (Svendborg & Ærø)

Odense Å

FILOSOFGANGEN

Munkemose

To Funen Village & E-20 Motorway (Copenhagen & Aarhus)

200 Meters
200 Yards

1 Radisson Blu H.C.A. Hotel
2 Hotel Domir
3 Ydes Hotel
4 Cabinn Odense
5 To Blommenslyst B&B
6 Danhostel Odense City
7 Vestergade Eateries
8 Kongensgade Eateries
9 Vintapperstræde Eateries

CENTRAL DENMARK

office), pick up a free town map inside the ticket office, jot down the time your train departs, and hit the town (follow signs to *Odense Centrum*).

To get to the **TI,** turn right out of the station, cross the busy road, then cut through the Kongens Have (King's Garden) park and head down Jernabanegade. When you come to Vestergade, take a left and follow this fine pedestrian street 100 yards to the TI.

Sights in Odense

Note that some of Odense's museums charge higher admission (about 15-20 DKK extra) during school holidays.

▲▲▲Hans Christian Andersen Museum

As a new Hans Christian Andersen Museum is under construction into 2020, the museum has moved some of its exhibits to a temporary venue a few blocks away. This space is smaller than the original but still offers "an insight into Andersen's life through a number of clues that link to the poet's art"—check the museum's website for the latest info. The home where Andersen was born, a part of the original museum, remains open to visitors. And another H. C. house, the writer's childhood home (with a small exhibit of its own), is a few blocks from here at Munkemøllestræde 3.

Cost and Hours: 110 DKK combo-ticket (125 DKK in summer) includes Andersen's birthplace, childhood home, and the Møntergården Museum with the Fyrtøjet ("Tinderbox") children's activity center; daily 10:00-16:00, July-late-Aug until 17:00, Claus Bergs Gade 11 (next to the recommended Radisson Blu H. C. A. Hotel), tel. 65 51 46 01, www.museum.odense.dk.

Fyrtøjet ("Tinderbox")

This fun hands-on center for children, based on works by Hans Christian Andersen, is in a temporary location (through 2020) as its original site at the Hans Christian Andersen Museum is being rebuilt. As a result, there may be changes to what's described here (check their website for updates). Normally, the centerpiece is Fairytale Land, with giant props and sets inspired by one of the author's tales. Kids can dress up in costumes and get their faces painted at the "magical wardrobe," act out a fairy tale, and do arts and crafts in the "atelier." Ask about performances (generally daily at 12:00 and 14:00; some are in Danish only, but others are done without dialogue).

Cost and Hours: 80 DKK for ages 3-69 (free to other ages), higher prices during holidays; July-mid-Aug daily 10:00-17:00; shorter hours and closed Mon-Thu off-season; at the Møntergården Museum in the Nyborgladen building, Møntestræde 1, tel. 66 14 44 11, www.museum.odense.dk.

▲Møntergården (Urban History Museum)

This well-presented museum fills several medieval buildings with exhibits on the history of Odense. You'll time-travel from prehistoric times (lots of arrow, spear, and ax heads) through to 1660, when the king stripped the town of its independent status. The main exhibit, "Life of the City," fills a stately 17th-century, red house (Falk Gøyes Gård) with a high-tech, well-presented exhibit about Odense in medieval and Renaissance times, covering historical events as well as glimpses of everyday life. Wedged along the side of this building is a surviving medieval lane; at the far end are four minuscule houses that the city used to house widows and orphaned students who couldn't afford to provide for themselves. It's fascinating to squeeze into these humble interiors and imagine that people lived in these almshouses through 1955 (open only in summer, but at other times you can ask at the ticket desk to have them unlocked). A new museum building with expanded exhibits may be open by the time you visit.

Cost and Hours: 50 DKK, Tue-Sun 10:00-16:00, closed Mon; Møntestræde 1, tel. 65 51 46 01, www.museum.odense.dk.

▲Danish Railway Museum (Danmarks Jernbanemuseum)

Conveniently (and appropriately) located directly behind the train station, this is an ideal place to kill time while waiting for a train—and is worth a look for anyone who enjoys seeing old locomotives and train cars. Here at Denmark's biggest (and only official) rail museum, the huge roundhouse is filled with classic trains, while up-stairs you'll walk past long

display cases of model trains and enjoy good views down onto the trains. The information is in English, picnicking is encouraged, and there are lots of children's activities.

Cost and Hours: 65 DKK, more during special exhibits, daily 10:00-16:00; Dannebrogsgade 24—just exit behind the station, near track 7/8, and cross the street; tel. 66 13 66 30, www.railmuseum.dk.

▲Funen Village/Den Fynske Landsby Open-Air Museum

The sleepy gathering of 26 old buildings located about two miles out of town preserves the 17th- to 19th-century culture of this region. During the summer, you'll meet people dressed in period costumes who recount what life was like in 19th-century Funen as they perform their daily chores. Dozens of farm animals also bring to life the sounds—and smells—of the era. Families can enjoy tales of Hans Christian Andersen performed on an outdoor stage (mid-July-mid-Aug). Explanations in the buildings are sparse, so buy the guidebook to help make your visit meaningful.

Cost and Hours: 85 DKK July-Aug, 60 DKK rest of the year; July-Aug daily 10:00-18:00 except closes at 17:00 last half of Aug; April-June and Sept-late Oct Tue-Sun 10:00-17:00, closed Mon; closed late Oct-March; bus #110 or #111 from Odense Station, or

CENTRAL DENMARK

take train to Fruens Bøge Station and walk 15 minutes; tel. 65 51 46 01, www.museum.odense.dk.

Sleeping in Odense

Demand (and prices) are higher in Odense on weekdays and in winter; in summer and on weekends, you can often get a better deal.

$$$ Radisson Blu H. C. A. Hotel is big, comfortable, and impersonal, with 145 rooms near the Hans Christian Andersen sights. It's older but nicely updated, and offers great rates every day through the summer (elevator, Claus Bergs Gade 7, tel. 66 14 78 00, www.radissonblu.com/hotel-odense, hcandersen@radissonblu. com).

$$ Hotel Domir has 35 tidy, basic, stylish little rooms along its tiny halls. It's located on a quiet side street just a few minutes from the train station and features extra soundproofing (elevator, limited pay parking, Hans Tausensgade 19, tel. 66 12 14 27, www. domir.dk, booking@domir.dk). They also run **$ Ydes Hotel,** just down the street, with industrial and metallic simplicity (breakfast extra).

$ Cabinn Odense brings its no-frills minimalist economy to town, with 201 simple, comfy, and modern rooms (breakfast extra, elevator, pay parking for small cars only, next to the station at Østre Stationsvej 7, tel. 63 14 57 00, www.cabinn.com, odense@cabinn. com). For more about this chain, see page 99.

$ Blommenslyst B&B rents four rooms in two private guest-houses just outside Odense (breakfast extra, 10-minute drive from town center, Ravnebjerggyden 31, tel. 65 96 81 88, www. blommenslyst.dk, ingvartsen-speth@post.tele.dk, Marethe and Poul Erik Speth).

Hostel: ¢ Danhostel Odense City is a huge, efficient hostel towering above the train station (private rooms available, elevator, reception open 8:00-12:00 & 16:00-20:00 but self-service check-in kiosk at other times, Østre Stationsvej 31, tel. 63 11 04 25, http:// odensedanhostel.dk, info@cityhostel.dk).

Eating in Odense

Odense's main pedestrian shopping streets, **Vestergade** and **Kongensgade,** offer the best atmosphere and most options for lunch and dinner.

Vintapperstræde is an alleyway full of restaurants just off Vestergade (look for the ornamental entryway). Choose from Danish, Mexican, Italian, and more. Study the menus posted outside each restaurant to decide, then grab a table inside or join the locals at an outdoor table.

Odense Connections

From Odense by Train to: Copenhagen (3/hour, 1.5 hours, some go directly to the airport), **Aarhus** (2/hour, 1.5 hours), **Billund/Legoland** (2/hour, 50-minute train to Vejle, then transfer to bus—see page 187; allow 2 hours total), **Svendborg/Ærø ferry** (2/hour Mon-Sat, hourly Sun, 45 minutes, to Svendborg dock; Ærø ferry—roughly 10/day, 1.25 hours), **Roskilde** (2/hour, 70 minutes).

ROUTE TIPS FOR DRIVERS

Aarhus or Billund to Ærø: Figure about two hours to drive from Billund (or 2.5 hours from Aarhus) to Svendborg. The freeway takes you over a bridge to the island of Funen (or *Fyn* in Danish); from Odense, take the highway south to Svendborg.

Leave your car in Svendborg (at the convenient long-term parking lot two blocks from the ferry dock or at the far end of the harbor near the Bendix fish shop) and sail for Ærø (see page 160 for ferry details). Cars need reservations but walk-on passengers don't.

Ærø to Copenhagen via Odense: From Svendborg, drive north on Route 9, past Egeskov Castle, and on to Odense. To visit the open-air folk museum just outside Odense (Den Fynske Landsby), leave Route 9 just south of town at Højby, turning left toward Dalum and the Odense campground (on Odensevej). Look for *Den Fynske Landsby* signs (near the train tracks, south edge of town). If you're going directly to the Hans Christian Andersen Museum (in temporary quarters through 2020), follow the signs.

Continuing toward Copenhagen, you'll take the world's third-longest suspension bridge (Storebælt Bridge, 245-DKK toll, 12.5 miles long). Follow signs marked *København* (Copenhagen). If you're following my three-week itinerary by car: When you get to Ringsted, signs point you to Roskilde—aim toward the twin church spires and follow signs for *Vikingskibene* (Viking ships). Otherwise, if you're heading to Copenhagen or the airport, stay on the freeway, following signs to *København C* or to *Dragør/Kastrup Airport*.

JUTLAND

Aarhus • Legoland • Jelling

Jutland (Jylland—pronounced "YEW-lan"—in Danish) is the part of Denmark that juts up from Germany. It's a land of windswept sandy beaches, inviting lakes, Lego toys, moated manor houses, and fortified old towns. In Aarhus, the lively and student-filled capital of Jutland, you can ogle the artwork in one of Denmark's best art museums, experience centuries-old Danish town life in its open-air folk museum, and meet a boggy prehistoric man. After you wander the pedestrian street, settle in for a drink along the canalside people zone. This region is particularly family-friendly. Make a pilgrimage to the most famous land in all of Jutland: the pint-sized kids' paradise, Legoland. The nearby village of Jelling is worth a quick stop to see the ancient rune stones known as "Denmark's birth certificate."

PLANNING YOUR TIME

Aarhus makes a natural stop for drivers connecting Kristiansand, Norway and Hirtshals, Denmark by ferry. Trains also link Aarhus to Hirtshals, as well as to points south, such as Odense and Copenhagen. Allow one day and an overnight to enjoy this busy port town.

Families will likely want a whole day at Legoland (near the town of Billund), while historians might consider a brief detour to Jelling, just 10 minutes off the main Billund-Vejle road. Both are best by car but doable by public transportation.

Aarhus

Aarhus (OAR-hoos, sometimes spelled Århus), Denmark's second-largest city, has a popu-
lation of 310,000 and calls itself the "World's Smallest Big
City." I'd argue it's more like
the world's biggest little town:
easy to handle and easy to like.
Aarhus is Jutland's capital and
cultural hub. Its Viking found-
ers settled here—where a river
hit the sea—in the eighth cen-
tury, calling their town Aros. Today, modern Aarhus bustles with
an important university, an inviting café-lined canal, a bursting-
with-life pedestrian boulevard (Strøget), a collection of top-notch
museums (modern art, open-air folk, and prehistory/ethnography),
and an adorable "Latin Quarter" filled with people living very, very
well. Aarhus, a pleasant three-hour train ride from Copenhagen,
is well worth a stop.

Orientation to Aarhus

Aarhus lines up along its tranquil canal—formerly a busy highway—called Åboulevarden, which runs through the middle of
town. The cathedral and lively Latin Quarter are directly north of
the canal, while the train station is about five blocks to the south
(along the main pedestrianized shopping street—the Strøget). The
main museums are scattered far and wide: The ARoS art museum
is at the western edge of downtown, the Den Gamle By open-air
folk museum is a bit farther to the northwest, and the Moesgård
Museum (prehistory and ethnography) is in the countryside far to
the south.

TOURIST INFORMATION

The Aarhus TI is in Dokk1, a library/cultural center at the Aarhus
Harbor (generally Mon-Thu 10:00-19:00, Fri until 17:00, Sat-Sun
until 16:00). There's also a branch near the bus station at Fredensgade 45 and one in the summer on the main square. All branches
share a telephone number and website (tel. 87 31 50 10, www.
visitaarhus.com).

ARRIVAL IN AARHUS

At Aarhus' user-friendly **train** station, all tracks feed into a concourse, with ticket offices (*billetsalg;* open Mon-Fri 7:00-18:00, Sat-

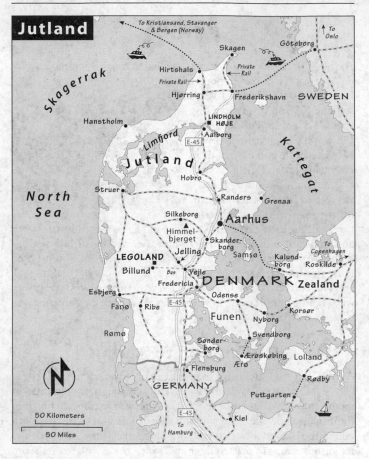

Jutland

To Kristiansand, Stavanger
& Bergen (Norway)

To Oslo

Skagerrak

Skagen

Göteborg

Hirtshals

Private
Rail

Private Rail →

Hjørring

Frederikshavn

SWEDEN

Hanstholm

LINDHOLM
HØJE

Limfjord

Aalborg

E-45

Jutland

Kattegat

Hobro

North
Sea

Struer

Randers

Grenaa

Silkeborg

Aarhus

Himmel-
bjerget

Skander-
borg

To
Copenhagen

LEGOLAND

Jelling

Samsø

Kalund-
borg

Roskilde

Billund

Bus

Vejle

DENMARK

Zealand

Fredericia

Esbjerg

Odense

Fanø

Ribe

E-45

Funen

Korsør

Rømø

Nyborg

Sønder-
borg

Svendborg

Ærøskøbing

Lolland

Flensburg

Ærø

GERMANY

Rødby

Puttgarten

50 Kilometers

E-45

Kiel

50 Miles

To
Hamburg

Sun 10:15-17:00) and a waiting room between tracks 2-3 and 4-5. A side entrance (marked *Bruun's Galleri*) takes you directly into a shopping mall; the other entrance (under the clock) leads into the blocky main terminal hall, with pay lockers, fast food, and ticket machines. Near the main doors, screens show departure times for upcoming city and regional buses.

To get into town, it's a pleasant 10-minute walk: Exit straight ahead, cross the street, and proceed up the wide, traffic-free shopping street known as the Strøget, which takes you directly to the canal, cathedral, and start of my "Aarhus Walk."

If arriving by **car** or **cruise ship,** see "Aarhus Connections," later.

GETTING AROUND AARHUS

The sights mentioned in my self-guided walk, along with the ARoS art museum, are all within a 15-minute **walk;** the Den Gamle By open-air folk museum is a few minutes farther, but still walkable. The Moesgård Museum and Tivoli Friheden amusement park are best reached by bus. While Aarhus has a new light-rail line, the route is of little use to tourists.

You can buy **bus** tickets from the coin-op machines on board the bus (a 20-DKK, 2-zone ticket covers any of my recommended sights, and is good for 2 hours). Bus drivers are friendly and speak English.

A few local buses leave from in front of the train station, but most depart around the corner, along Park Allé in front of the Town Hall. Bus #3A to the Den Gamle By open-air folk museum leaves from a stop across the street from the station. Other buses leave from in front of the Town Hall, about two blocks away: Cross the street in front of the station, turn left and walk to the first major corner, then turn right up Park Allé; the stops are in front of the blocky Town Hall (with the boxy tower, on the left). From here, bus #16 goes to the Tivoli Friheden amusement park; and bus #18 goes to the Moesgård Museum. To find your bus stop, look for the handy diagram at the start of the Strøget.

Taxis are easy to flag down but pricey (45-DKK drop fee).

HELPFUL HINTS

Sightseeing Pass: The **Aarhus Card** provides small discounts on major sights and free entry to some minor sights, and includes public transportation. This can be a money-saver for busy sightseers (299 DKK/24 hours, 499 DKK/48 hours, purchase at hotels, the Dokk1 TI, or at www.visitaarhus.com).

Festival: The 10-day **Aarhus Festival,** which takes place in late summer (Aug-Sept), fills the city's streets and venues with music, dance, food, kids' activities, and much more (www.aarhusfestuge.dk).

Laundry: An unstaffed, coin-op launderette *(mønt-vask)* is four short blocks south of the train station, on the square in front of St. Paul's Church (daily 7:00-21:00, bring lots of coins, M.P. Bruunsgade 64).

Aarhus Walk

This quick little self-guided walk acquaints you with the historic center, covering everything of sightseeing importance except the three big museums (modern art, prehistory, and open-air folk). You'll begin at the cathedral, check out the modest sights in its vicinity, wander the cute Latin Quarter, take a stroll down the "most beautiful street" in Aarhus, and end at the canal (for walking route, see the "Aarhus Center" map). After touring the impressive cathedral, the rest of the walk should take about an hour.

Aarhus Center

Self-Guided Walk
1. Aarhus Cathedral
2. Cathedral Square
3. Hotel Royal
4. Viking Museum
5. Aarhus Theater
6. Church of Our Lady
7. Møllestien
8. Canal (Åboulevarden)

200 Meters
200 Yards

Botanical Gardens

DEN GAMLE BY FOLK MUSEUM

MAIN ENTRANCE

Mølleparken

AROS ART MUSEUM

GODSBANEGÅRD

CONCERT HALL

Rådhuspladsen

TOWN HALL

Banegårds-pladsen

Accommodations
9. Villa Provence
10. The Mayor Hotel
11. Hotel Guldsmeden
12. Hotel Ritz
13. Cabinn
14. To Danhostel Aarhus
15. City Sleep-In

Eateries & Other
16. Lecoq
17. Den Rustikke
18. Pilhkjær
19. Carlton Brasserie
20. Sota
21. Åboulevarden Canal Eateries
22. A Hereford Beefstouw
23. Teater Bodega
24. To Launderette

JUTLAND

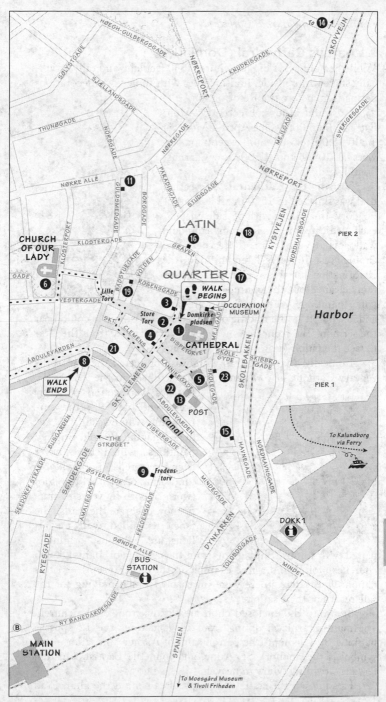

• *Start by touring Aarhus Cathedral.*

▲▲Aarhus Cathedral (Domkirke)

While Scandinavia's biggest church (330 feet long and tall) is typically stark-white inside, it also comes with some vivid decorations dating from before the Reformation.

Cost and Hours: Free entry; Mon-Sat 9:30-16:00; Oct-April Mon-Sat 10:00-15:00; closed Sun except for services at 10:00 and 17:00; www.aarhus-domkirke.dk.

Visiting the Cathedral: The cathedral was finished in 1520 in all its Catholic glory. Imagine it with 55 side chapels, each dedicated to a different saint and wallpapered with colorful frescoes. Bad timing. Just 16 years later, in 1536, the Reformation hit this region and Protestants cleaned out the church—side altars gone, paintings whitewashed over—and added a pulpit in the middle of the nave so parishioners could hear the sermon. The front pews were even turned away from the altar to face the pulpit (a problem for weddings today).

Ironically, that Lutheran whitewash protected the fine 16th-century Catholic art. When it was peeled back in the 1920s, the

frescoes were found perfectly preserved. In 1998, the surrounding whitewash was redone, making the old original paintings, which have never been restored, pop. Noble tombs that once lined the floor (worn smooth by years of traffic) now decorate the walls. The fancy text-filled wall medallions are epitaphs, originally paired with tombs. Ships hang from the ceilings of many Danish churches (you'll find a fine example in the left transept)—in this nation of seafarers, there were invariably women praying for the safe return of their sailors.

Step into the enclosed choir area at the front of the church. The main altarpiece, dating from 1479, features the 12 apostles flanking St. Clement (the patron saint of Aarhus and sailors—his symbol is the anchor), St. Anne, and John the Baptist. On top, Jesus is crowning Mary in heaven.

Head down the stairs to the apse area behind the altar. Find

the model of the altarpiece, which
demonstrates how the polyptych
(many-paneled altarpiece) you
just saw can be flipped to different
scenes throughout the church year.

Also in this area, look for the
fresco in the aisle (right of altar, facing windows) that shows a three-
part universe: heaven, earth (at
Mass), and—under the thick black
line—purgatory...an ugly land with
angels and devils fighting over
souls. The kid on the gallows illustrates how the medieval Church
threatened even little children with
ugly damnation. Notice the angels
trying desperately to save the damned. Just a little more money to
the Church and...I...think...we...can...pull...Grandpa...OUT.

An earlier Romanesque church—just as huge—once stood
on this spot. As you exit, notice the tiny, pointy-topped window
in the back-right. It survives with its circa-1320 fresco from that
earlier church. Even back then—when the city had a population
of 1,000—the church seated 1,200. Imagine the entire community (and their dogs) assembled here to pray and worship their way
through the darkness and uncertainty of medieval life.

• *Then, standing at the cathedral door, survey the...*

Cathedral Square

The long, triangular square is roughly the shape of the original Viking town from A.D. 770. Aarhus is the Viking word for "mouth

of river." The river flows to your left
to the beach, which—before modern
land reclamation—was just behind
the church. The green spire peeking
over the buildings dead ahead is the
Church of Our Lady (which we'll
visit later on this walk). Fifty yards
to the right, the nubile caryatids by
local artist Hans Krull decorate the
entry to the **Hotel Royal** and town casino. (Krull's wildly decorated bar is just beyond, down the stairs at the corner.) Also nearby
(around the corner from the cathedral) is the fine **Occupation Museum 1940-1945,** about the Danish resistance during World War
II (described later, under "Sights in Aarhus").

• *Fifty yards to the left of the church (as you face the square), in the basement of the Nordea Bank, is the tiny...*

JUTLAND

Viking Museum

When excavating the site for the bank building in 1960, remains of Viking Aarhus were uncovered. Today you can ride an escalator down to the little bank-sponsored museum showing a surviving bit of the town's original boardwalk in situ (where it was found), Viking artifacts, and a murder victim (missing his head)—all well-described in English.

Cost and Hours: Free, open bank hours: Mon-Fri 10:15-16:00, Thu until 17:00, closed Sat-Sun.

• *Leaving the bank, walk straight ahead along the substantial length of the cathedral (brides have plenty of time to reconsider things during their procession) to the fancy building opposite.*

Aarhus Theater

This ornate facade, with its flowery stained glass, is Danish Art Nouveau from around 1900. Under the tiny balcony is the town

seal, featuring towers, the river, St. Clement with his anchor, and St. Paul with his sword. High above, on the roofline, crouches the devil. The local bishop made a stink when this "house of sin" was allowed to be built facing the cathedral. The theater builders had the last say, finishing their structure with this smart-aleck devil triumphing (this was a hit with the secular, modern locals).

• *Return to the square in front of the cathedral.*

Latin Quarter

The higgledy-piggledy old town encompasses the six or eight square blocks in front of the cathedral and to the right. Latin was never spoken here—the area was named in the 1960s after the cute, boutique-ish, and similarly touristy zone in Paris. Though Aarhus' canal strip is a newer trendy spot, the Latin Quarter is still great for shopping, cafés, and strolling. Explore these streets: Volden (named for the rampart), Graven (moat), and Badstuegade

("Bath Street"). In the days when fires routinely decimated towns, bathhouses—with their open fires necessary to heat the water—were located outside the walls. Back in the 15th century, finer people bathed monthly, while everyday riff-raff took their "Christmas bath" once a year.

• Back at the far end of Cathedral Square, side-trip away from the cathedral to the green spire of the...

Church of Our Lady (Vor Frue Kirke)

The smart brick building you see today is in the Dutch Renaissance style from the early 16th century, but this local "Notre-Dame" is the

oldest church in town. After Christianity came to Viking Denmark in 965, a tiny wooden church was built here. Step down into the crypt of today's church (below the main altar). This evocative arcaded space (c. 1060) was originally an 11th-century stone rebuild of the first church (and only discovered in 1955). Four rune stones were also discovered on this site. Back upstairs, find the graphic crucifix, with its tangled thieves flanking Christ, which was carved and painted by a Lübeck artist in 1530. As at Aarhus Cathedral, the church's whitewashed walls are covered with fine epitaph medallions with family portraits. Step through the low door behind the rear pew (on the right with your back to the altar) into the peaceful cloister. With the Reformation, this became a hospital. Today, it's a retirement home for lucky seniors.

Cost and Hours: Free; Mon-Fri 10:00-16:00, Sat until 14:00; closed Sun, www.aarhusvorfrue.dk.

• Walk west on Vestergade to the next street, Grønnegade. Turn left, then take the next right onto...

Møllestien

Locals call this quiet little cobbled lane the "most beautiful street in Aarhus." The small, pastel cottages—draped in climbing roses

and hollyhock in summer—date from the 18th century. Notice the small mirrors on one of the windows. Known as "street spies," they allow people inside to inconspicuously watch what's going on outside.

*• At the end of the lane, head left toward the canal. The park on your right, **Mølleparken**, is a good spot for a picnic. The big, boxy building with the rainbow ring on top is the **ARoS** art museum (described later)—consider visiting it now, or backtrack here when the walk is over.*

When you reach the canal, turn left and walk about four blocks toward the cathedral spire until you get to the concrete pedestrian bridge.

Canal (Åboulevarden)

You're standing on the site of the original Viking bridge. The open sea was dead ahead. A protective harbor was behind you. When the town was attacked, the bridge on this spot was raised, ships were tucked safely away, and townsmen stood here to defend their fleet. Given the choice, they'd let the town burn and save their ships.

In the 1930s, the Aarhus River was covered over to make a new road—an event marked by much celebration. In the 1980s, locals reconsidered the change, deciding that the road cut a boring, people-mean swath through the center of their town. They removed the road, artfully canalized the river, and created a new people zone—the town's place to see and be seen. This strip of modern restaurants ensures the street stays as lively as possible even after the short summer.

• *Your walk is over. Retreating back up the canal takes you to the **ARoS** art museum, then to the **Den Gamle By** open-air folk museum. Following the canal ahead takes you past the best of the Aarhus canal zone. Crossing the canal bridge and going straight (with a one-block jog left) gets you to the Strøget pedestrian boulevard, which leads all the way to the train station (where you can catch a bus—either at the station or the Town Hall nearby—to Tivoli Friheden amusement park, the Den Gamle By open-air folk museum, or the Moesgård Museum). All of these sights are described in the next section.*

Sights in Aarhus

▲▲ARoS

The ARoS Aarhus Art Museum is a must-see sight, both for the building's architecture and for its knack for making cutting-edge art accessible and fun. Everything is described in English. Square and unassuming from the outside, the bright white interior—with its spiral staircase winding up the museum's eight floors—is surprising. The building has two sections, one for the exhibits and one for administration. The halves are divided by a vast atrium, which is free to enter if you just want to peek at the building itself (or to visit the gift shop or café). But to see any of the items described later, you'll have to buy a ticket. In addition to the permanent collections that I've described, the museum displays an impressive

JUTLAND

range of temporary exhibits—be sure to find out what's on during your visit.

Cost and Hours: 130 DKK; Tue-Sun 10:00-17:00, Wed until 22:00; closed Mon, ARoS Allé 2, tel. 87 30 66 00, www.aros.dk.

Cuisine Art: The **$$** lunch café on the museum's ground floor serves light meals, while the **$$$** wine and food hall on the top floor features regional specialties from local producers.

Visiting the Museum: After entering at the fourth-floor lobby, buy your ticket, pick up a museum floor plan, and walk two

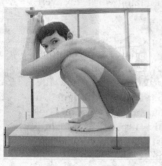

floors down the spiral staircase (to floor 2) to find one of the museum's prized pieces: the squatting sculpture called **Boy** (by Australian artist Ron Mueck)—15 feet high, yet astonishingly realistic, from the wrinkly skin on his elbows to the stitching on his shorts.

Next, head down to the lowest level. Here, amid black walls, artists from around the world (including Tony Oursler, Elmgreen & Dragset, and James Turrell) exhibit their immersive works of light and sound in each of nine spaces *(De 9 Rum)*. In this unique space, you're plunged into the imagination of the artists.

Now ride the elevator all the way to the top floor (floor 8), then climb up the stairs (or ride a different elevator) to the rooftop.

Here you can enjoy the museum's icon: Olafur Eliasson's **Your Rainbow Panorama**, a 150-yard-long, 52-yard-diameter circular walkway enclosed in glass that gradually incorporates all the different colors of the spectrum. The piece provides 360-degree views over the city, while you're immersed in mind-bending, highly saturated hues. (It's "your" panorama because you are experiencing the colors.) It's a striking contrast to the mostly dark and claustrophobic works you've just seen in the nine spaces down below—yet, like those, it's all about playing with light. It's also practical—from a distance, it can be used by locals throughout the city as a giant compass (provided they know which color corresponds with which direction).

Back on floor 8, stroll through the manageable permanent collection of works from 1770 to 1930. Paintings dating from the **Danish Golden Age** (1800-1850) are evocative of the dewy-eyed Romanticism that swept Europe during that era: pastoral scenes of flat Danish countryside and seascapes, slices of peasant life, aristocratic portraits, "postcards" from travels to the Mediterranean world, and poignant scenes of departures and arrivals at Danish seaports. The **Danish Modernist** section, next, mostly feels derivative of big-name artists (you'll see the Danish answers to Picasso, Matisse, Modigliani, and others).

Continue down the spiral staircase, past various temporary exhibits. On floor 5, take a spin through the **classic art gallery**, featuring temporary art and multimedia installations. Like the rest of this museum, these high-concept, navel-gazing works are well-presented and very accessible.

▲▲Den Gamle By

"The Old Town" open-air folk museum has 75 half-timbered houses and craft shops. Unlike other Scandinavian open-air museums

that focus on rural folk life, Den Gamle By is designed to give you the best possible look at Danish urban life in centuries past. A fine botanical garden is next door.

Cost and Hours: Because peak-season days offer more activities, the cost depends on the time of year, from 75 DKK off-season to 135 DKK during busy times. Open daily 10:00-17:00, until 18:00 in July-mid-Aug; shorter hours off-season; after hours, the buildings are locked, but the peaceful park is open. Tel. 86 12 31 88, www.dengamleby.dk.

Getting There: Stroll 20 minutes up the canal from downtown, or catch a bus from near the train station: Bus #3A departs directly across the street from the station; otherwise use the transit route planner at www.rejseplanen.dk.

Eating: This is a perfect place to enjoy a picnic lunch (bring your own, or order a lunch packet at the reception desk by the ticket booth)—outdoor and indoor tables are scattered around the grounds. The only eatery in the park open year-round is the cheery indoor/outdoor **$$ Simonsens Have,** an inviting cafeteria serving affordable light meals. In peak season, you'll have many other options, including *pølse* and other snack stands, a bakery, a café next to the ticket kiosk, and another café in the 1970s neighborhood.

Visiting the Museum: At the ticket desk, pick up the free map of the grounds; also pick up the flier listing what's on (and plan your time around those options). Though each building is described with a plaque, and there are maps throughout the park, the guide-booklet (small fee) is a worthwhile investment and a nice souvenir.

The grounds reward an adventurous spirit. They're designed

to be explored, so don't be too shy to open doors or poke into seemingly abandoned courtyards—you may find a chatty docent inside, telling their story, answering questions, or demonstrating an old-timey handicraft. Follow sounds and smells to discover a whole world beyond the main streets.

The main part of the exhibit focuses on the 18th and 19th centuries. You'll start by heading up Navnløs, then hanging a right at Vestergade (passing a row house and a flower garden with samples for sale) to the canal. Head straight over the bridge and hike up the cute street lined with market stalls, shops, and a bakery until you pop out on the main square, Torvet. The building on the left side of Torvet, the Mayor's House (from 1597), contains a museum upstairs featuring home interiors from 1600 to 1850, including many with gorgeously painted walls. At the top of Torvet is the Mintmaster's Mansion, the residence of a Copenhagen noble (from 1683). Enter around back to tour the boldly colorful, 18th-century Baroque rooms. Under the heavy timbers of the attic is an exhibit about the history of this restored building.

Continuing out the far end of Torvet on Søndergade, you enter the 20th century. The streets and shops here evoke the year 1927, including a hardware store and (down Havbogade) a brewery where you can often buy samples (in the courtyard behind). At the end of Søndergade (on the left) is the Legetøj toy museum, with two floors of long hallways crammed with nostalgic playthings.

Walking into the next zone, you come to a street scene from 1974, with re-created apartments, a radio and TV repair shop, a hairdresser, a gynecology clinic, and a jazz bar where you can order a beer or pastry. In the Udstillinger building, you'll find the Danish Poster Museum (a delightful collection of retro posters) and the Gallery of Decorative Arts (porcelain, clocks, and silverware).

Occupation Museum 1940-1945

Nazi occupiers used Aarhus' police station as their Gestapo headquarters throughout World War II. It was the scene of tortures and executions. Today, it's a fine exhibit telling the story of the resistance and what it was like to live here under Nazi rule. You'll learn of heroic acts of sabotage, find out how guns were dropped out of British airplanes in the night, and see underground newspapers that kept occupied Danes connected and in the know. Sadly, much of the exhibit is without English descriptions (though free loaner English info sheets are available).

Cost and Hours: 30 DKK; June-Aug Tue-Sun 11:00-16:00, closed Mon; Sept-May Sat-Sun and Tue 11:00-16:00, closed Mon and Wed-Fri; facing the cathedral, it's around to the left, just off Cathedral Square at Mathilde Fibigers Have 2; tel. 86 18 42 77, www.besaettelsesmuseet.dk.

▲▲Moesgård Museum

This museum, dedicated to prehistory and ethnography, is housed in a state-of-the art venue, south of Aarhus in the suburb of Højbjerg. The building juts dramatically from a hill, with grass growing on a sloping roof that visitors can walk on.

Cost and Hours: 140 DKK; Tue-Sun 10:00-17:00, Wed until 21:00, closed Mon; café, tel. 87 16 10 16, www.moesmus.dk.

Getting There: The museum is located outside Aarhus at Moesgård Allé 15 in Højbjerg, in a lush, wooded park sprawling down to the sea. It's a pricey taxi trip or easy, cheap bus ride: Bus #18 leaves Aarhus from directly in front of the Town Hall on Park Allé (around the corner from the train station). On weekdays, the bus runs three to four times hourly during the museum's opening times (2/hour on Sat-Sun, ride 20 minutes to end of line, covered by bus ticket that includes zone 2, see www.midttrafik.dk for bus details). Once at the museum, carefully check what time the return bus departs (posted at the bus stop, or ask at the ticket desk).

Visiting the Museum: Divided into three main periods—the Bronze Age (1800 to 500 B.C.), Iron Age (500 B.C. to A.D. 800), and Viking Age (A.D. 700 to 1050), the prehistory section features lots of real artifacts (primitive tools and pottery, plenty of spearheads and arrowheads), all well-described in English, along with an impressive collection of rune stones.

But the highlight is the well-preserved body of an Iron Age man. Believing that the gods dwelled in the bogs, prehistoric people threw offerings (such as spearheads) into the thick peat. The peat did a remarkable job of preserving these artifacts, many of which are now on display in the museum. The prehistoric people also sacrificed humans to the bog gods—resulting in the incredibly intact Graub-alle Man, the world's best-preserved "bog-corpse." Reclining in his stately glass tomb, the more than 2,000-year-old "bog man" looks like a fellow half his age. He still has his skin, nails, hair, and even the slit in his throat he got at the sacrificial banquet (back in 300 B.C.). Spend some time with this visitor from the past. The story of his discovery (in a Jutland peat bog in 1952) and conservation is also interesting.

The Grounds: The museum sits on the pleasant grounds of the Moesgård Manor; while the manor itself is closed to the public, its grounds are fun to explore. Behind the museum, a two-mile-long circular trail stretches down to a fine beach. This "Prehistoric Trackway" runs past a few model Viking buildings, including a 12th-century stave church.

Tivoli Friheden Amusement Park

The local Tivoli, about a mile south of the Aarhus train station, offers great fun for the family.

Cost and Hours: 90-120 DKK for entry only, 250-350 DKK includes rides; July-early Aug 11:30-20:00, longer hours in late July, weekends only and shorter hours off-season, closed Oct-April except for special events; bus #16 from Park Allé near Town Hall, tel. 86 14 73 00, www.friheden.dk.

Sleeping in Aarhus

Aarhus has a good variety of lodgings. My recommendations range from charming hotels with personality to backpacker-friendly hostel bunks.

$$$$ Villa Provence, named for owners Steen and Annette's favorite vacation destination, is a *petit* taste of France in the center of Aarhus, and makes a very cozy and convenient home base. Its 40 fun-yet-tasteful rooms, decorated with antique furniture and old French movie posters, surround a quiet courtyard. The pub across the street can get noisy on weekends, so ask for a room facing away from the street (pay parking, 10-minute walk from station, near Åboulevarden at the end of Fredensgade, Fredens Torv 12, tel. 86 18 24 00, www.villaprovence.dk, hotel@villaprovence.dk).

$$$$ The Mayor Hotel, affiliated with the Best Western chain, rents 162 sleek, well-furnished, business-class rooms 100 yards from the station (elevator, free fitness room, pay parking, Banegårdspladsen 14, tel. 87 32 01 00, www.themayor.dk, hotel@themayor.dk).

$$$ Hotel Guldsmeden ("Dragonfly") is a small, welcoming, and clean hotel with 27 rooms, fluffy comforters, a delightful stay-awhile garden, and a young, disarmingly friendly staff. A steep staircase takes you to the best rooms, while the cheaper rooms (five rooms sharing two bathrooms) are in a ground-floor annex behind the garden (RS%, 15-minute walk in Aarhus' quiet Latin Quarter at Guldsmedgade 40, tel. 86 13 45 50, www.guldsmedenhotels.com, aarhus@guldsmedenhotels.com).

$$$ Hotel Ritz, across the street from the station, offers 67 clean, bright rooms done in Art Deco style (elevator, Banegård-spladsen 12, tel. 86 13 44 44, www.hotelritz-aarhus.com, mail@hotelritz.dk).

$$ Cabinn, overlooking the atmospheric Åboulevarden canal, is extremely practical. Rooms are minimalist yet comfy, and service is no-nonsense (family rooms, breakfast extra, pay parking—reserve ahead, rooms overlook boisterous canal or quieter courtyard, at Kannikegade 14 but main entrance on the canal at Åboulevarden 38, tel. 86 75 70 00, www.cabinn.dk, aarhus@cabinn.dk). For more on this chain, see page 99.

¢ Danhostel Aarhus, an official HI hostel, is near the water two miles out of town (served by several buses from the train station—see website for details, Marienlundsvej 10, tel. 86 21 21 20, www.aarhusdanhostel.dk, info@aarhusdanhostel.dk).

¢ City Sleep-In, a creative independent hostel, has a shared kitchen, fun living and games room, laundry service, and lockers. It's on a busy road facing the harbor (with thin windows—expect some street noise), a 15-minute hike from the station. It's pretty grungy, but is the only centrally located hostel option in town (private rooms available, elevator, no curfew; reception open daily 8:00-11:00 & 16:00-22:00, Fri-Sat until 23:00; Havnegade 20, tel. 86 19 20 55, www.citysleep-in.dk, sleep-in@citysleep-in.dk).

Eating in Aarhus

Affluent Aarhus has plenty of great little restaurants. My listings are in the old town, within a few minutes' stroll from the cathedral.

IN AND NEAR THE LATIN QUARTER

The streets of the Latin Quarter are teeming with hardworking and popular eateries. The street called Mejlgade, along the eastern edge of downtown, has a smattering of youthful, trendy restaurants that are just far enough off the tourist trail to feel local. Look for a variety of fixed-price, three-course dinners—some affordable, others a splurge.

$$$$ Lecoq is a pricey favorite. Chef/owner Troels Thomsen and his youthful gang (proud alums from a prestigious Danish cooking school) serve up a fresh twist on traditional French cuisine in a single Paris-pleasant yet unassuming 10-table room. They pride themselves on their finely crafted presentation. Reservations are smart (daily 11:30-15:00 & 17:30-21:30, Graven 16, tel. 86 19 50 74, www.cafe-lecoq.dk).

$$$$ Den Rustikke is a French-style brasserie offering mostly French dishes (including affordable fixed-price meals), either in the rollicking interior or outside, under a cozy colonnade (daily 11:30-15:00 & 17:00-late, Mejlgade 20, tel. 86 12 00 95, www.denrustikke.dk).

$$$$ Pilhkjær is a bit more expensive and sedate, filling a cellar with elegantly casual atmosphere. The menu, which changes daily and can include fish, meat, or vegetarian offerings, is available only as a full-course meal—there's no à la carte option (Tue-Thu 17:30-22:30, Fri-Sat 17:30-23:30, closed Sun-Mon; at the end of a long courtyard at Mejlgade 28, tel. 86 18 23 30, www.pihlkjaer-restaurant.dk).

$$$ Carlton Brasserie, facing a pretty square, is a solid bet for good Danish and international food in classy (verging on stuffy) surroundings. The restaurant has tables on the square, with more formal seating in back (Mon-Sat from 12:00, closed Sun, Rosensgade 23, tel. 86 20 21 22).

A few short blocks farther from the action (past the Church of Our Lady), **$$$ Sota** is a local favorite for sushi, to eat in or take away. This sleek, split-level, Tokyo-Scandinavian hybrid is in a half-timbered old house (Mon-Thu 16:00-22:00, Fri-Sat 12:00-23:00, closed Sun, reservations recommended, Vestergade 48, tel. 86 47 47 88, www.sotasushibar.dk).

ALONG ÅBOULEVARDEN CANAL

The canal running through town is lined with trendy eateries—all overpriced unless you value making the scene with the locals (and all open daily until late). They have indoor and canalside seating with heaters and blankets, so diners can eat outdoors even when it's cold. Before settling in, cruise the entire strip, giving special consideration to **$$ Cross Café** (with red awnings, right at main bridge) and **$$ Ziggy,** both of which are popular for salads, sandwiches, burgers, and drinks; and **$$$ Grappa,** a classy Italian place with pastas and pizzas, as well as pricier plates. Several places along here serve basic breakfast buffets.

NEAR THE CATHEDRAL

These places, while a bit past their prime and touristy, are convenient and central.

$$$$ A Hereford Beefstouw, in the St. Clement's Brewery building facing the cathedral, is a bright, convivial, fun-loving, and woody land of happy eaters and drinkers. Choose from a hearty

JUTLAND

menu and eat amid shiny copper beer vats. If you're dropping by for a brew, they have enticing beer snacks and spicy little *ølpølse* sausages (hearty dinners such as steak, ribs, burgers, and fish; Mon-Thu and Sun 17:30-23:00, Fri-Sat 12:00-24:00, Kannikegade 10, tel. 86 13 53 25, www.beefstouw.com/aarhus).

$$$ Teater Bodega is the venerable best bet for traditional Danish—where local men go for "food their wives won't cook." While a bit tired and old-fashioned for Aarhus' trendy young student population, it's a sentimental favorite for old-timers. Facing the theater and cathedral, it's dressy and draped in theater memorabilia (open-face sandwiches at lunch only, Mon-Sat 11:30-21:30, Sun 12:00-20:00, Skolegade 7, tel. 86 12 19 17, www.teaterbodega. dk).

Aarhus Connections

BY PUBLIC TRANSPORTATION
From Aarhus by Train to: Odense (2/hour, 1.5 hours), **Copenhagen** (2/hour, 3.5 hours), **Ærøskøbing** (6-7/day, transfer to ferry in Svendborg, allow 5 hours total), **Billund/Legoland** (3/hour; 45-minute train to Vejle, then transfer to bus—described later, allow 2 hours total), **Hamburg,** Germany (2 direct/day, more with transfers, 5 hours).

You can take the train from Aarhus to **Hirtshals,** where you can catch the **ferry to Norway** on the Color Line (www.colorline. com) or Fjordline (www.fjordline.com). Trains depart Aarhus hourly and take about 2.5 hours (to meet the Color Line ferry, transfer at Hjørring and continue to Hirtshals Havn; note that rail passes don't cover the Hjørring-Hirtshals train, but do give a 50 percent discount; buy your ticket in Hjørring or on board).

ROUTE TIPS FOR DRIVERS
From the Ferry Dock at Hirtshals to Jutland Destinations: From the dock in Hirtshals, drive south (signs to *Hjørring, Ålborg*). It's about 2.5 hours to Aarhus. (To skip Aarhus, skirt the center and follow E-45 south.) To get to downtown **Aarhus,** follow signs to the center, then *Domkirke.* Park in the pay lot across from the cathedral. Signs all over town direct you to Den Gamle By open-air folk museum. From Aarhus, it's 60 miles to Billund/Legoland (go south on Skanderborg Road and get on E-45; follow signs to *Vejle, Kolding*). For **Jelling,** take the *Vejle N* exit and follow signs to *Vejle,* then veer right on the ring road (following signs to *Skovgade*), then follow Route 442 north. For **Legoland,** take the *Vejle S* exit for Billund (after *Vejle N*—it's the first exit after the dramatic Vejlefjord bridge).

Legoland

Legoland is Scandinavia's top kids' sight. If you have a child (or are a child at heart), it's a fun stop.
This huge park is a happy combination of rides, restaurants, trees, smiles, and 33 million Lego bricks creatively arranged into such wonders as Mount Rushmore, the Parthenon, "Mad" King Ludwig's castle, and the Statue of Liberty. It's

a Lego world here, as everything is cleverly related to this popular toy. If your time in Denmark is short, or if your family has already visited a similar Legoland park in California, England, or Germany, consider skipping the trip. But if you're in the neighborhood, a visit to the mothership of all things Lego will be a hit with kids ages two through the pre-teens.

GETTING THERE

Legoland, located in the town of Billund, is easiest to visit by car (see "Route Tips for Drivers," earlier), but doable by public transportation. The nearest train station to Billund is Vejle. Trains arrive at Vejle from **Copenhagen** (2/hour, 2.5 hours), **Odense** (2/hour, 1 hour), and **Aarhus** (3/hour, 45 minutes). At Vejle, catch buses #43 or #143 to travel the remaining 25 miles to Billund (30-45 minutes). For train and bus details, see www.rejseplanen.dk.

ORIENTATION TO LEGOLAND

Cost: 359 DKK for adults, 339 DKK for kids ages 3-12. Advance tickets, often available at a discount, are sold online at www.legoland.dk (reduced-price family tickets also available), and at many Danish locations (stores, hotels, and TIs), including the Dagli' Brugsen store in Vandel, just west of Billund. Legoland generally doesn't charge in the evening (free after 19:30 in July and late Aug, otherwise after 17:30).

Hours: Generally April-Oct daily 10:00-18:00, later on weekends and for much of July-Aug, closed Nov-March and Wed-Thu in Sept-mid-Oct. Activities close an hour before the park, but it's basically the same place after dinner as during the day, with fewer tour groups. Confirm exact hours before heading out.

Information: Tel. 75 33 13 33, www.legoland.dk.

Crowd-Beating Tips: Legoland is crowded during the Danish summer school vacation, from early July through mid-August.

To bypass the ticket line, purchase tickets online in advance (simply scan them at the entry turnstile).

Money-Saving Deals: If a one-day visit is not enough, you can pay 488 DKK for a two-day ticket. If you hate waiting in lines, consider shelling out for a Q-bot, which allows you to book ahead and skip the queue for some popular attractions (available at select times).

Eating: Surprisingly, the park's restaurants don't serve Lego-lamb, but there are plenty of other food choices. Prices are high, so consider bringing a picnic to enjoy at one of the several spots set aside for bring-it-yourselfers.

BACKGROUND

Lego began in 1932 in the workshop of a local carpenter who named his wooden toys after the Danish phrase *leg godt* ("play well"). In 1949, the company started making the plastic interlocking building bricks for which they are world famous. Since then, Lego has continued to expand its lineup and now produces everything from Ninjago ninja warriors to motorized models, Clikits jewelry, board games, video games—many based on popular movies (*Lego Star Wars, Lego Harry Potter,* etc.)—making kids drool in languages all around the world. *The Lego Movie,* a hit animated feature released in 2014, kicked off a series of Lego-themed films, and *Beyond the Brick: A Lego Brickumentary* looks at the toy's enduring popularity. According to the company, each person on this planet has, on average, 62 Lego blocks.

VISITING LEGOLAND

Legoland is divided into eight different "worlds" with fun themes such as Adventure Land, Pirate Land, and Knight's Kingdom.

Pick up a brochure at the entrance and make a plan using the colorful 3-D map. You can see it all in a day, but you'll be exhausted. The Legoredo section (filled with Wild West clichés Europeans will enjoy more than Americans) merits just a quick look, though your five-year-old might enjoy roasting a biscuit-on-a-stick around the fire with a tall, blond park employee wearing a Native American headdress.

A highlight for young and old alike is Miniland (near the entrance), where landscaped gardens are filled with carefully constructed Lego landscapes and cityscapes. Anyone who has ever picked up a Lego block will marvel at seeing representations of

the world's famous sights, including Danish monuments, Dutch windmills, German castles, and an amazing version of the Norwegian harbor of Bergen. Children joyfully watch as tiny Lego boats ply the waters and Lego trains chug merrily along the tracks. Nearby, kids can go on mellow rides in child-size cars, trains, and boats. A highlight of Miniland is the Traffic School, where young drivers (ages 7-13) learn the rules of the road and get a souvenir license. (If interested in this popular attraction, make a reservation upon arrival.)

More rides are scattered throughout the park. While the rides aren't thrilling by Disneyland standards, most kids will find some-

thing to enjoy (parents should check the brochure for strictly enforced height restrictions). The Falck Fire Brigade ride in Lego City invites family participation as you team up to put out a (fake) fire. The Temple is an Indiana Jones-esque Egyptian-themed treasure hunt/shoot-'em-up, and the Dragon roller coaster takes you in and around a medieval castle. Note that on a few rides (including the Pirate Splash Battle), you'll definitely get wet. Special walk-in, human-sized dryers help you warm up and dry off.

The indoor museum features company history, high-tech Lego creations, a great doll collection, and a toy exhibit full of mechanical wonders from the early 1900s, many ready to jump into action with the push of a button. A Lego playroom encourages hands-on fun, and a campground is across the street if your kids refuse to move on.

Nearby: Those looking for water fun with a tropical theme can check out the Aquadome (one of Europe's largest water parks), located outside Legoland in Billund at the family resort of Lalandia (www.lalandia.dk).

SLEEPING NEAR LEGOLAND

$$$$ Legoland Hotel adjoins Legoland (family rooms and deals, tel. 79 51 13 50, www.hotellegoland.dk, reservation@legoland.dk).

$$$$ Legoland Holiday Village offers cabins, camping, and motel rooms that sleep up to eight people (Ellehammers Allé 2, tel. 79 51 13 50, www.legoland-village.dk, reservation@legoland.dk).

$$ Hotel Svanen is close by, in Billund (Nordmarksvej 8, tel. 75 33 28 33, www.hotelsvanen.dk, billund@hotelsvanen.dk).

Nearby: In a forest just outside of Billund, Erik and Mary Sort run **$ Gregersminde,** a B&B with a great setup: six double rooms (some with shared bath), plus a cottage that sleeps up to six people. Guests enjoy a huge living room, a kitchen, lots of Lego toys, and a kid-friendly yard (breakfast extra, rental bikes, leave Billund on Grindsted Road, turn right on Stilbjergvej, go a half-mile to Stilbjergvej 4B, tel. 61 27 33 23, www.gregersminde.dk, info@gregersminde.dk).

Jelling

On your way to or from Legoland, consider a short side-trip to the tiny village of Jelling (pronounced "YELL-ing"), a place of immense importance in Danish history. Here you'll find two rune stones, set next to a 900-year-old church that's flanked by two enormous, man-made burial mounds. The two stones are often called "Denmark's birth certificate"—the first written record of Denmark's status as a nation-state. An excellent (and free) museum lies just across the street.

Two hours is ample for a visit. If pressed for time, an hour is enough to see the stones and take a quick look at the museum. Note that the museum is closed on Monday.

Jelling is too small for a TI, but the museum staff can answer most questions. If you're here around lunchtime, Jelling is a great spot for a picnic. There are several central eateries and a café and WC inside the museum, and another WC in the parking lot near the North Mound.

Getting There: Drivers can easily find Jelling, just 10 minutes off the main Vejle-Billund road (see "Route Tips for Drivers" under "Aarhus Connections"). Train travelers coming from Copenhagen or Aarhus must change in Vejle, which is connected to Jelling by hourly trains (direction: Herning) and bus #211.

Jelling Walk

Denmark is proud of being Europe's oldest monarchy and of the fact that Queen Margrethe II, the country's current ruler, can trace her lineage back 1,300 years to Jelling. This short, self-guided walk explores this sacred place.

• Begin your visit at the...

Kongernes Jelling Museum: Inside this modern, light-filled building you'll find informative exhibits, historical models of the area, and replicas of the rune stones. Kids will love the room in the back on the ground level where they can write their name in the runic alphabet—and the gift shop bristling with wooden swords and Viking garb (free, June-Aug Tue-Sun 10:00-17:00, Sept-May Tue-Sun 12:00-16:00, closed between Christmas and New Year's and on Mon year-round, café, tel. 75 87 23 50, http://natmus.dk/kongernes-jelling).

• Cross the street and walk through the graveyard to examine the actual...

Rune Stones: The stones stand just south of the church. The modern bronze-and-glass structure is designed to protect the stones from the elements while allowing easy viewing.

The smaller stone was erected by King Gorm the Old (a.k.a. Gorm the Sleepy), who ruled Denmark for 40 years in the ninth

century. You probably don't read runic so I'll translate: *"King Gorm made this monument in memory of Thyra, his wife, Denmark's salvation."* These are the oldest recorded words of a Danish king, and the first time that the name Denmark is used to describe a country and not just the region.

The **larger stone** was erected by Gorm's son, Harald Bluetooth, to honor his parents, commemorate the conquering of Denmark and Norway, and mark the conversion of the Danes to Christianity. (Today's Bluetooth wireless technology takes its name from Harald, who created the decidedly non-wireless connection between the Danish and Norwegian peoples.)

Harald was a shrewd politician who had practical reasons for being baptized. He knew that if he declared Denmark to be a Christian land, he could save it from possible attack by the predatory German bishops to the south. The inscription reads: *"King Harald ordered this monument made in memory of Gorm, his father, and in memory of Thyra, his mother; that Harald who won for himself all of Denmark and Norway and made the Danes Christian."*

This large stone has three sides. One side reveals an image of Jesus and a cross, while the other has a serpent wrapped around a lion. This is important imagery that speaks to the transition from Nordic

paganism to Christianity. These designs carved into the rock were once brightly painted.

• *Go around the back of the church and climb the steps to the 35-foot-high, grass-covered...*

North Mound: According to tradition, Gorm was buried in a chamber inside this mound, with his queen Thyra interred in the smaller mound to the south. But excavations in the 1940s turned up no royal remains in either mound. (In the 1970s, what is believed to be Gorm's body was discovered below the church.) Scan the horizon and mentally remove the trees. Imagine the commanding view this site had in the past. Look north to stones that trace the outline of a ship. Below you lies a graveyard with typically Danish well-manicured plots.

• *Now descend the stairs to the...*

Church: Within the sparse interior, note the ship model hanging from the ceiling, a holdover from a pre-Christian tradition seeking a safe journey for ship and crew. The church, which dates from around 1100, is decorated with restored frescoes. A zigzag motif is repeated in the modern windows and the inlaid floor. The metal "Z" in the floor marks the spot where Gorm's body lies.

More Jutland Sights

NORTHEAST OF BILLUND
Himmelbjerget and Silkeborg

If you're connecting the Billund and Jelling area with Aarhus, consider this slower but more scenic route north through the idyllic Danish Lake District. (With less time, return to Vejle and take the E-45 motorway.)

Himmelbjerget, best seen by car, lies in the middle of Jutland near the town of Silkeborg. Both are about an hour northeast of Billund (22 miles west of Aarhus). Silkeborg is accessible by train from Aarhus with a change in Skanderborg.

Denmark's landscape is vertically challenged when compared to its mountainous neighbors Norway and Sweden. If you have a hankering to ascend to one of the country's highest points, consider a visit to the 482-foot-tall **Himmelbjerget,** which translates loftily as "The Heaven Mountain." That may be overstating it, but by Danish standards the view's not bad. One can literally drive to the top, where a short trail leads to an 80-foot-tall brick tower. Climb the **tower** for a commanding view. Clouds roll by above a patchwork of green and gold fields while boats ply the blue waters of the lake below. You may see the vintage paddle steamers make the hour-long trip between Himmelbjerget and Silkeborg in season (the dock is accessed by a short hike from the tower down to the lake).

Silkeborg, in the center of the Danish Lake District, has an excellent freshwater aquarium/exhibit/nature park called **AQUA** that's worth a visit, especially if you're traveling with kids (tel. 89 21 21 89, www.visitaqua.dk). Also in Silkeborg, modern-art lovers will enjoy the **Museum Jorn Silkeborg,** featuring colorful abstract works by Asger Jorn—a prominent member of the 1960s' COBRA movement—plus other Danish and foreign art (tel. 86 82 53 88, www.museumjorn.dk).

SOUTHWEST OF BILLUND
▲Ribe

A Viking port 1,000 years ago, Ribe, located about 30 miles southwest of Billund, is the oldest, and possibly the loveliest, town in Denmark. It's an entertaining mix of cobbled lanes and leaning medieval houses, with a fine **cathedral** boasting modern paintings under Romanesque arches. The **TI** is on the main square (Torvet 3, tel. 75 42 15 00, www.visitribe.com). **$ Weis Stue,** a smoky, low-ceilinged, atmospheric inn across from the church, rents primitive rooms with a shared bath and serves good meals (no breakfast, tel. 75 42 07 00, www.weis-stue.dk). Take the free **Night Watchman** tour (daily May-mid-Oct, www.visitribe.com).

WEST OF BILLUND
North Sea Coast

If beautiful beaches and WWII-era bunkers sound appealing, consider this side trip, worth ▲▲ on a nice day. Just an hour or so west from Legoland is a land of rolling dunes, wide sandy beaches and big waves. It's often windy and the water can be brisk but the Danes who flock here in the summer don't mind. You can make a strategic strike to Blåvand and back in half a day but allow a whole day to fully experience the coast. Bring your swimsuit!

Blåvand ("BLOW-van") is a popular beach destination a little over an hour west of Billund (take highway 30, then 475 to Varde, then follow highway 471). Turn left at Oksby on Tane Hedevej to reach the **Tirpitz Museum.** This striking structure, designed by Danish "starchitect" Bjarke Ingels, is built into the dunes and connected by tunnel to a German bunker that was part of Hitler's Atlantic Wall that stretched from Norway down to Spain. Look for the exhibit on amber (the "Gold of the North" washes up on local beaches) and an amazing amber model of the Sydney Opera House, which was designed by Dane Jørn Utzon (tel. 72 10 84 85, http://vardemuseerne.dk/museum/tirpitz). To reach the wide beach, backtrack through Oksby and follow Fyrvej to the light-house.

Just 20 minutes north is the low-key beach town of **Vejers Strand,** where the main drag dead-ends at the beach. **$$$$ Knud-edyb,** a famous local restaurant, offers good seafood and on-site smoked fish (reservations smart, tel. 75 27 67 67). **$$$ Klithjem Badehotel** provides nice rooms just steps from the sea (two-night minimum but you might get lucky, closed Oct-April, tel. 40 18 17 26, www.klithjembadehotel.dk).

The dunes along the coast hide many other bunkers. Along with Blåvand, you'll find an easy-to-access observation post and troop bunker at **Hvide Sande,** a

harbor town one hour north that straddles the entrance to a wide bay. After crossing the bridge, park in the lot on the right where you'll find a TI, plus some shops and restaurants. Cross the road and climb the Troldbjerg Hill, heading toward a large mast and a flagpole to find the sights.

More evocative and isolated are the bunkers 20 minutes further north at Houvig Strand. Along the way you'll pass dozens of sum-mer houses, many with thatched roofs and Danish flags flapping in the breeze. Turn left at the *Houvig Strand* sign, and park in the lot, where a path leads through the dunes to the beach. One bunker is just in front of you and several others lie a 10-minute walk to the right. Be careful exploring these tilting concrete structures up close, as shifting sands covering rusty metal rebar can make them treacherous. From Houvig Strand it's a 90-minute drive back to Billund via Ringkøping.

NORWAY

NORWAY

Norge

Norway is stacked with superlatives—it's the most mountainous, most scenic, and most prosperous of all the Scandinavian countries. Perhaps above all, Norway is a land of intense natural beauty, its famously steep mountains and deep fjords carved out and shaped by an ancient ice age.

Norway is also a land of rich harvests—timber, oil, and fish. In fact, its wealth of resources is a major reason why Norwegians have voted *"nei"* to membership in the European Union. They don't want to be forced to share fishing rights with EU countries.

The country's relatively recent independence (in 1905, from Sweden) makes Norwegians notably patriotic and proud of their traditions and history. They have a reputation for insularity, and controversially have tightened immigration laws over the past several years.

Norway's Viking past (c. A.D. 800-1050) can still be seen today in the country's 28 remaining stave churches—with their decorative nods to Viking ship prows—and the artifacts housed in Oslo's Viking Ship Museum.

The Vikings, who also lived in present-day Denmark and Sweden, were great traders, shipbuilders, and explorers. However, they are probably best known for their infamous invasions, which terrorized much of Europe. The sight of their dragon-prowed ships on the horizon struck fear into the hearts of people from Ireland to the Black Sea.

Named for the Norse word *vik,* which means "fjord" or "inlet," the Vikings sailed their sleek, seaworthy ships on extensive voyages, laden with amber and furs for trading—and weapons for fighting. They traveled up the Seine and deep into Russia, through the Mediterranean east to Constantinople, and across the Atlantic to Greenland and even "Vinland" (Canada). In fact, they touched the soil of the Americas centuries before Columbus, causing proud "ya sure ya betcha" Scandinavian immigrants in the US to display bumper stickers that boast, "Columbus used a Viking map!"

History and Hollywood have painted a picture of the Vikings

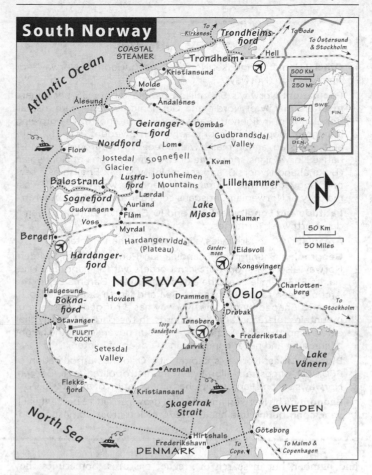

South Norway

To Kirkenes
Trondheims-fjord
To Bodø
To Östersund & Stockholm
COASTAL STEAMER
Atlantic Ocean
Trondheim
Hell
Kristiansund
Molde
500 KM
250 MI
Ålesund
Åndalsnes
SWE.
Geiranger-fjord
Dombås
FIN.
NOR.
Gudbrandsdal Valley
Nordfjord
Lom
DEN.
Florø
Sognefjell
Jostedal Glacier
Kvam
Balestrand
Lustra-fjord
Jotunheimen Mountains
Lillehammer
Sognefjord
Lærdal
N
Gudvangen
Aurland
Flåm
Lake Mjøsa
Bergen
Voss
Myrdal
Hamar
50 Km
Hardangervidda (Plateau)
Garder-moen
Eidsvoll
50 Miles
Hardanger-fjord
Kongsvinger
Haugesund
NORWAY
Charlotten-berg
Bokna-fjord
Hovden
Drammen
Oslo
To Stockholm
Stavanger
Drøbak
PULPIT ROCK
Torp Sandefjord
Tønsberg
Setesdal Valley
Larvik
Frederikstad
Flekke-fjord
Arendal
Lake Vänern
Kristiansand
Skagerrak Strait
SWEDEN
North Sea
Hirtshals
Göteborg
Frederikshavn
To Cope.
To Malmö & Copenhagen
DENMARK

as fierce barbarians, an image reinforced by the colorful names of leaders like Sven Forkbeard, Erik Bloodaxe, and Harald Bluetooth.

Unless you're handy with an ax, these don't sound like the kind of men you want to hoist a tankard of mead with. They kept slaves and were all-around cruel (though there is no evidence that they forced their subjects to eat lutefisk). But the Vikings also had a gentle side. Many were farmers, fishermen, and craftsmen who created delicate works with wood and metal. Faced with a growing population constrained by a lack of arable land, they traveled south not just to rape, pillage,

NORWAY

Norway Almanac

Official Name: Kongeriket Norge—"The Kingdom of Norway"—or simply Norge (Norway).

Population: Norway's 5.3 million people (about 35 per square mile) are mainly of Nordic and Germanic heritage, with a small population of indigenous Sami people in the north. The growing immigrant population is primarily from Sweden, Poland, Lithuania, Pakistan, and Somalia, with a recent wave from Syria. Most native Norwegians speak one of two official forms of Norwegian (Bokmål and Nynorsk), and the majority speak English as a second language. While church attendance is way down, the vast majority of Norwegian Christians consider themselves Lutheran.

Latitude and Longitude: 62°N and 10°E, similar latitude to Canada's Northwest Territories.

Area: 148,700 square miles, slightly larger than Montana.

Geography: Sharing the Scandinavian Peninsula with Sweden, Norway also has short northern borders with Finland and Russia. Its 51,575-mile coastline extends from the Barents Sea in the Arctic Ocean to the Norwegian Sea and North Sea in the North Atlantic. Shaped by glaciers, Norway has a rugged landscape of mountains, plateaus, and deep fjords. In the part of Norway that extends north of the Arctic Circle, the sun never sets at the height of summer, and never comes up in the deep of winter.

Biggest Cities: Norway's capital city, Oslo, has a population of 660,000; almost a million live in its metropolitan area. Bergen, Norway's second-largest city, has a population of about 275,000.

Economy: The Norwegian economy grows around 2 percent each year, contributing to a healthy $370 billion gross domestic prod-

and plunder, but in search of greener pastures. Sometimes they stayed and colonized, as in northeast England, which was called the "Danelaw," or in northwest France, which became known as Normandy ("Land of the North-men").

The Vikings worshiped many gods and had a rich tradition of mythology. Epic sagas were verbally passed down through generations or written in angular runic writing. The sagas told the heroic tales of the gods, who lived in Valhalla, the Viking heaven, presided over by Odin, the god of both wisdom and war. Like the Egyptians, the Vikings believed in life after death, and chieftains were often buried in their ships within burial mounds, along with prized possessions such as jewelry, cooking pots, food, and Hagar the Horrible cartoons.

Like the Greeks and Etruscans before them, the Vikings never organized on a large national scale and eventually faded away due to bigger, better-organized enemies and the powerful influence of uct and a per capita GDP of $69,200. Its primary export is oil—Norway is the world's seventh-largest oil exporter, making it one of the world's richest countries. By law, the country must save a portion of the oil revenue; the fund is currently worth almost $1 trillion.

Currency: 8 Norwegian kroner (NOK) = about $1.

Government: As the leader of Norway's constitutional monarchy, King Harald V has largely ceremonial powers. In September 2017, Norwegian voters reelected a center-right coalition government, which has been led by Prime Minister Erna Solberg since 2013. Leader of the Conservative Party, Solberg is Norway's second woman prime minister (after the Labor Party's Gro Harlem Brundtland). Solberg's party shares power with the far-right Progress Party, which wants to restrict immigration and cut taxes. Norway's legislative body is the Stortinget (Parliament), with 169 members elected for four-year terms.

Flag: Red with a blue Scandinavian cross outlined in white.

The Average Norwegian: He or she is 39 years old, has 1.85 children, and will live to be 82. The average Norwegian feels very safe compared to other Europeans—only Iceland has a lower murder rate.

Christianity. By 1150, the Vikings had become Christianized and assimilated into European society. But their memory lives on in Norway.

Beginning in the 14th century, Norway came under Danish rule for more than 400 years, until the Danes took the wrong side in the Napoleonic Wars. The Treaty of Kiel forced Denmark to cede Norway to Sweden in 1814. Sweden's rule of Norway lasted until 1905, when Norway voted to dissolve the union. Like many European countries, Norway was taken over by Germany during World War II. April 9, 1940, marked the start of five years of Nazi occupation, during which a strong resistance movement developed, hindering some of the Nazi war efforts.

Each year on May 17, Norwegians celebrate their idealistic 1814 constitution with fervor and plenty of flag-waving. Men and women wear folk costumes *(bunads)*, each specific to a region of Norway. Parades are held throughout the country. The parade in Oslo marches past the Royal Palace, where the royal family waves to the populace from their balcony. While the king holds almost zero political power (Norway has a parliament chaired by a prime minister), the royal family is still highly revered and respected.

Several holidays in spring and early summer disrupt transportation schedules: the aforementioned Constitution Day (May 17), Ascension Day (in May or June, 39 days after Easter), and Whitsunday and Whitmonday (a.k.a. Pentecost and the following day, in May or June, 50 days after Easter).

High taxes contribute to Norway's high standard of living. Norwegians receive cradle-to-grave social care: university education, health care, nearly yearlong paternity leave, and an annual six weeks of vacation. Norwegians feel there is no better place than home. Norway regularly shows up in first place on the annual UN Human Development Index.

Visitors enjoy the agreeable demeanor of the Norwegian people—friendly but not overbearing, organized but not uptight, and with a lust for adventure befitting their gorgeous landscape. Known for their ability to suffer any misfortune with an accepting (if a bit pessimistic) attitude, Norwegians are easy to get along with.

Despite being looked down upon as less sophisticated by their Scandinavian neighbors, Norwegians are proud of their rich folk traditions—from handmade sweaters and folk costumes to the small farms that produce a sweet cheese called *geitost*. Less than 7 percent of the country's land is arable, resulting in numerous small farms. The government recognizes the value of farming, especially in the remote reaches of the country, and provides rich subsidies to keep this tradition alive. These subsidies would not be allowed if Norway joined the European Union—yet another reason the country remains an EU hold-out.

Appropriate for a land with countless fjords and waterfalls, Norway is known for its pristine water. Norwegian-bottled artisanal water has an international reputation for its crisp, clean taste. Although the designer Voss water—the H2O of choice for Hollywood celebrities—comes with a high price tag, the blue-collar

Olden is just as good. (The tap water is actually wonderful, too—and much cheaper.)

While the Norwegian people speak a collection of mutually understandable dialects, the Norwegian language has two official forms: *bokmål* (book language) and *nynorsk* (New Norse). During the centuries of Danish rule, people in Norway's cities and upper classes adopted a Danish-influenced style of speech and writing (called Dano-Norwegian), while rural language remained closer to Old Norse. After independence, Dano-Norwegian was renamed *bokmål,* and the rural dialects were formalized as *nynorsk,* as part of a nationalistic drive for a more purely Norwegian language. Despite later efforts to combine the two forms, *bokmål* remains the most commonly used, especially in urban areas, books, newspapers, and government agencies. Students learn both.

The majority of the population under 70 years of age also speaks English, but a few words in Norwegian will serve you well. For starters, see the Norwegian survival phrases at the end of this chapter. If you visit a Norwegian home, be sure to leave your shoes at the door; indoors is usually meant for stocking-feet only. At the end of a meal, it's polite to say "Thanks for the food"—*"Takk for maten"* (tahk for MAH-ten). Norwegians rarely feel their guests have eaten enough food, so be prepared to say *"Nei, takk"* (nay tahk; "No, thanks"). You can always try *"Jeg er mett"* (yay ehr met; "I am full"), but be careful not to say *"Jeg er full"*—"I am drunk."

STAVE CHURCHES

Norway's most distinctive architecture is the stave church. These medieval houses of worship—tall, skinny, wooden pagodas with dragon's-head gargoyles—are distinctly Norwegian and palpably historic, transporting you right back to the Viking days. On your visit, make it a point to visit at least one stave church.

Stave churches are the finest architecture to come out of medieval Norway. Wood was plentiful and cheap, and locals had an expertise with woodworking (from all that boat-building). In 1300, there were as many as 1,000 stave churches in Norway. After a 14th-century plague, Norway's population dropped, and many churches fell into disuse or burned down. By the 19th century, only a few dozen stave churches survived. Fortunately, they became recognized as part of the national heritage and were protected. Virtually all of Norway's surviving stave churches have been rebuilt or renovated, with painstaking attention to the original details.

A distinguishing feature of the "stave" design is its frame of tall, stout vertical staves (Norwegian *stav*, or "staff"). The churches typically sit on stone foundations, to keep the wooden structure away from the damp ground (otherwise it would rot). Most stave churches were made of specially grown pine, carefully prepared before being felled for construction. As the trees grew, the tips and most of the branches were cut off, leaving the trunks just barely alive to stand in the woods for about a decade. This allowed the sap to penetrate the wood and lock in the resin, strengthening the wood while keeping it elastic. Once built, a stave church was slathered with black tar to protect it from the elements.

Stave churches are notable for their resilience and flexibility. Just as old houses creak and settle over the years, wooden stave churches can flex to withstand fierce winds and the march of time. When the wind shifts with the seasons, stave churches groan and moan for a couple of weeks...until they've adjusted to the new influences, and settle in.

Even after the Vikings stopped raiding, they ornamented the exteriors of their churches with warlike, evil spirit-fighting dragons reminiscent of their ships. Inside, a stave church's structure makes you feel like you're huddled under an overturned ship. The churches are dark, with almost no windows (aside from a few small "portholes" high up). Typical decorations include carved, X-shaped crossbeams; these symbolize the cross of St. Andrew (who was crucified on such a cross). Round, Romanesque arches near the tops of the staves were made from the "knees" of a tree, where the roots bend to meet the trunk (typically the hardest wood in a tree). Overall, these churches are extremely vertical: the beams inside and the roofline outside both lead the eye up, up, up to the heavens.

Most surviving stave churches were renovated during the Reformation (16th and 17th centuries), when they acquired more horizontal elements such as pews, balconies, pulpits, altars, and other decorations to draw attention to the front of the church. In some (such as the churches in Lom and Urnes), the additions make the church feel almost cluttered. But the most authentic (including Hopperstad near Vik) feel truly medieval. These time-machine churches take visitors back to early Christian days: no pews (worshippers stood through the service), no pulpit, and a barrier between the congregation and the priest, to symbolically separate the physical world from the spiritual one. Incense filled the church, and the priest and congregation chanted the service back and forth to each other, creating an otherworldly atmosphere that likely made worshippers feel close to God. (If you've traveled in Greece, Russia, or the Balkans, Norway's stave churches might remind you of Orthodox churches, which reflect the way all Christians once worshipped.)

When traveling through Norway, you'll be encouraged to see stave church after stave church. Sure, they're interesting, but there's no point in spending time seeing more than a few of them. Of Norway's 28 remaining stave churches, seven are described in this book. The easiest to see are the ones that have been moved to open-air museums in Oslo and Lillehammer. But I prefer to appreciate a stave church in its original fjords-and-rolling-hills setting. My two favorites are both near Sognefjord: Borgund and Hopperstad. They are each delightfully situated, uncluttered by more recent additions, and evocative as can be. Borgund is in a pristine wooded valley, while Hopperstad is situated on a fjord. Borgund comes with the only good adjacent stave church museum. (Most stave churches on the Sognefjord are operated by the same preservation society; for more details, see www.stavechurch.com.)

Other noteworthy stave churches include the one in Lom, near the Jotunheimen Mountains, which is one of Norway's biggest, and is indeed quite impressive. The Urnes church, across from Solvorn, is technically the oldest of them all—but it's been thoroughly renovated in later ages (it is still worth considering, however, if only for its exquisite carvings and the fun excursion to get to it; see the More on the Sognefjord chapter). The Fantoft church, just outside Bergen, burned down in 1992, and the replica built to replace it has none of the original's magic. The stave church in Undredal (see the Norway in a Nutshell chapter) advertises itself as the smallest. I think it's also the dullest.

Norwegian Survival Phrases

Norwegian can be pronounced quite differently from region to region. These phrases and phonetics match the mainstream Oslo dialect, but you'll notice variations. Vowels can be tricky: *å* sounds like "oh," *æ* sounds like a bright "ah" (as in "apple"), and *u* sounds like the German *ü* (purse your lips and say u). Certain vowels at the ends of words (such as *d* and *t*) are sometimes barely pronounced (or not at all). In some dialects, the letters *sk* are pronounced "sh." In the phonetics, ī sounds like the long i in "light," and bolded syllables are stressed.

English	Norwegian	Pronunciation
Hello. (formal)	*God dag.*	goo dahg
Hi. / Bye. (informal)	*Hei. / Ha det.*	hī / hah deh
Do you speak English?	*Snakker du engelsk?*	**snahk**-kehr dew **eng**-ehlsk
Yes. / No.	*Ja. / Nei.*	yah / nī
Please.	*Vær så snill.*	vayr soh sneel
Thank you (very much).	*(Tusen) takk.*	(**tew**-sehn) tahk
You're welcome.	*Vær så god.*	vayr soh goo
Can I help you?	*Kan jeg hjelpe deg?*	kahn yī **yehl**-peh dī
Excuse me.	*Unnskyld.*	**ewn**-shuld
(Very) good.	*(Veldig) fint.*	(**vehl**-dee) feent
Goodbye.	*Farvel.*	fahr-**vehl**
zero / one / two	*null / en / to*	newl / ayn / toh
three / four	*tre / fire*	treh / **fee**-reh
five / six	*fem / seks*	fehm / sehks
seven / eight	*syv / åtte*	seev / **oh**-teh
nine / ten	*ni / ti*	nee / tee
hundred	*hundre*	**hewn**-dreh
thousand	*tusen*	**tew**-sehn
How much?	*Hvor mye?*	voor **mee**-yeh
local currency: (Norwegian) crown	*(Norske) kroner*	(**norsh**-keh) **kroh**-nehr
Where is...?	*Hvor er...?*	voor ehr
...the toilet	*...toalettet*	toh-ah-**leh**-teh
men	*menn / herrer*	mehn / **hehr**-rehr
women	*damer*	**dah**-mehr
water / coffee	*vann / kaffe*	vahn / **kah**-feh
beer / wine	*øl / vin*	uhl / veen
Cheers!	*Skål!*	skohl
The bill, please.	*Regningen, takk.*	**rī**-ning-ehn tahk

OSLO

While Oslo is the smallest of the Scandinavian capitals, this brisk little city offers more sightseeing thrills than you might expect. As an added bonus, you'll be inspired by a city that simply has its act together.

Sights of the Viking spirit—past and present—tell an exciting story. Prowl through the remains of ancient Viking ships, and marvel at more peaceful but equally gutsy modern boats (the *Kon-Tiki, Ra II, Fram,* and *Gjøa*). Dive into the traditional folk culture at the Norwegian open-air folk museum, and get stirred up by the country's heroic spirit at the Norwegian Resistance Museum. For a look at modern Oslo, tour the striking City Hall, peek at sculptor Gustav Vigeland's people-pillars, ascend the exhilarating Holmenkollen Ski Jump, wander futuristic promenades, walk all over the Opera House, and celebrate the world's greatest peacemakers at the Nobel Peace Center.

Situated at the head of a 60-mile-long fjord, surrounded by forests, and populated by more than a half-million people, Oslo is Norway's cultural hub. For 300 years (1624-1924), the city was called Christiania, after Danish King Christian IV. With independence, it reverted to the Old Norse name of Oslo. As an important port facing the Continent, Oslo has been one of Norway's main cities for a thousand years and the de facto capital since around 1300. Still, Oslo has always been small by European standards; in 1800, Oslo had just 10,000 people—one-fiftieth the size of Paris or London.

But Oslo experienced a growth spurt with the Industrial Age, and in 50 years (from 1850 to 1900) its population exploded from about 10,000 to about 250,000. Most of "old Oslo" dates from this period, when the city's many churches and grand buildings were built of stone in the Historicism styles (neo-Gothic and neo-Romanesque) of the late 19th century. Oslo's onetime industrial zone—along the Akers River—has now been reclaimed as a cutting-edge park, with a lush river valley filled with spiffed-up brick warehouses and (on a sunny day) hundreds of sunbathing Norwegian hipsters.

Today the city sprawls out from its historic core to encompass nearly a million people in its metropolitan area, about one in five Norwegians. Oslo's port hums with international shipping and a sizeable cruise industry. Its waterfront, once traffic-congested and slummy, has undergone an extreme urban make-over—with ultramodern yet people-friendly residential zones replacing gritty shipyards. A nearly complet-ed 5.5-mile pedestrian promenade stretches the length of its harbor.

And Oslo just continues to grow: Near the Opera House sprouts a development called the "Barcode Project"; its sleek and distinc-tive collection of high-rise office buildings resemble the bars in a UPC code. The metropolis feels as if it's rushing to prepare for an Olympics-like deadline. But it isn't—it just wants to be the best city it can be.

And yet, it's delightful easy to escape the futuristic downtown and harbor area to a sprawling, green, and pastoral countryside—dotted with parks and lakes, and surrounded by hills and forests. For the visitor, Oslo is an all-you-can-see *smörgåsbord* of historic sights, trees, art, and Nordic fun.

PLANNING YOUR TIME

Oslo offers an exciting slate of sightseeing thrills. Ideally, spend two days, and leave on the night boat to Copenhagen, or on the scenic "Norway in a Nutshell" train to Bergen the third morning. Keep in mind that the National Gallery and the Vigeland Museum (at Vigeland Park) are closed on Monday. Spend the two days like this:

Day 1: Take my self-guided "Oslo Walk." Tour the Akershus Fortress and the Norwegian Resistance Museum, and catch the City Hall tour (offered June-Aug; off-season, tour it on your own). Spend the afternoon at the National Gallery (for Norwegian art-ists) or at the Holmenkollen Ski Jump and museum (to enjoy some wilderness).

Day 2: Ferry across the harbor to Bygdøy and tour the *Fram*, *Kon-Tiki*, and Viking Ship museums. Spend the afternoon at the

Norwegian Folk Museum. Finish the day at Vigeland Park, enjoying Gustav Vigeland's statues.

With More Time: You could easily fill a third day: Slow things down, go for a lazy hike up the Akers River (and eat at the trendy Mathallen Oslo food hall), and/or head out to the islands in the Oslofjord.

In the evening, you could enjoy a pricey dinner by the harbor or near Karl Johans Gate. Or venture to the more appealing, more affordable, and less touristy dining zones around Youngstorget, Mathallen, and Olaf Ryes Plass.

Orientation to Oslo

Oslo (pop. 660,000) is easy to manage. Most sights are contained within the monumental, homogenous city center. Much of what you'll want to see clusters in three easy-to-connect zones: **downtown,** around the harbor and the main boulevard, Karl Johans Gate (with the Royal Palace at one end and the train station at the other); in the **Bygdøy** (big-duhy) district, a 10-minute ferry ride across the harbor; and **Vigeland Park** (with Gustav Vigeland's statues), about a mile behind the palace.

With more time, head out of the core to see the more colorful neighborhoods: Majorstuen and Frogner feel "uptown," with chic boutiques, elegant homes, and lots of parks. Grünerløkka—and the adjacent Akers River park—is hipster central, with the foodie-paradise Mathallen and plenty of bohemian cafés. Youngstorget, a quick walk north of Karl Johans Gate, is local-feeling, mostly residential, and packed with tempting restaurants. And Grønland, behind the train station, is the multiethnic immigrants' zone.

TOURIST INFORMATION

The big, high-tech Visit Oslo office is in the Østbanehallen—the traditional-looking building next to the central train station. Standing in the square (Jernbanetorget) by the tiger statue and facing the train station, you'll find the TI's entrance in the red-painted section between the station and Østbanehallen. You can also enter the TI from inside the train station (July-Aug Mon-Sat 8:00-19:00, Sun 9:00-18:00; May-June and Sept daily 9:00-18:00; slightly shorter hours Oct-April; tel. 81 53 05 55, www.visitoslo.com).

At the TI, pick up these freebies: an Oslo map (with a helpful public-transit map on the back); the annual *Oslo Guide* (a handy overview of museums, eating, and nightlife); *U.F.O.* (the exhibition guide, listing current museum events); and the *What's On Oslo* monthly (with updated museum prices and hours, and an extensive events listing). If you're traveling on, pick up the *Bergen Guide* and

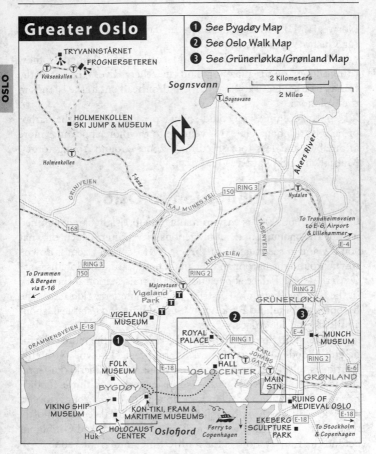

Greater Oslo

1. See Bygdøy Map
2. See Oslo Walk Map
3. See Grünerløkka/Grønland Map

TRYVANNSTÅRNET
FROGNERSETEREN
Voksenkollen

Sognsvann

2 Kilometers
2 Miles

HOLMENKOLLEN
SKI JUMP & MUSEUM

Holmenkollen

Akers River

GRINIVEIEN

T-bane

KAJ MUNKS VEI

RING 3

150

Nydalen

TÅSENVEIEN

To Trondheimsveien
to E-6, Airport
& Lillehammer

E-4

168

RING 3
150

KIRKEVEIEN

RING 2

RING 2

To Drammen
& Bergen
via E-16

Majorstuen

Vigeland
Park

GRÜNERLØKKA

E-4

VIGELAND
MUSEUM

ROYAL
PALACE

RING 1

MUNCH
MUSEUM

DRAMMENSVEIEN E-18

1

FOLK
MUSEUM

E-18

CITY
HALL

OSLO CENTER

KARL
JOHANS
GATE

RING 2

E-6

BYGDØY

MAIN
STN.

GRØNLAND

VIKING SHIP
MUSEUM

KON-TIKI, FRAM &
MARITIME MUSEUMS

Ferry to
Copenhagen

RUINS OF
MEDIEVAL OSLO

E-18

Huk

HOLOCAUST
CENTER Oslofjord

EKEBERG
SCULPTURE
PARK

To Stockholm
& Copenhagen

information for the rest of Norway, including the useful, annual *Fjord Norway Travel Guide*.

Oslo Pass: Sold at the TI, this pass covers the city's public transit, ferry boats, and entry to nearly every major sight—all described in a useful handbook (395 NOK/24 hours, 595 NOK/48 hours, 745 NOK/72 hours; big discounts for kids ages 4-15 and seniors age 67 and over). Do the math before buying: Add up the individual costs of the sights you want to see and compare to the cost of an Oslo Pass. Students with an ISIC card may be better off without the pass.

ARRIVAL IN OSLO
By Train

The central train station (Oslo Sentralstasjon, or "Oslo S" for short) is slick and helpful. You'll find free Wi-Fi, ATMs, two Forex exchange desks, and luggage storage. The station is plugged into a lively modern shopping mall called Byporten (Mon-Fri 10:00-21:00, Sat until 20:00, closed Sun), where just inside the entrance you'll find a cheap Bit sandwich shop with seating. Inside the station is a well-stocked Co-op Prix grocery store (long hours Mon-Sat, closed Sun), a small Joker supermarket (long hours daily), and a Vinmonopolet liquor store (Oslo's most central place to buy wine or liquor—which is sold only at Vinmonopolet stores, Mon-Thu 10:00-18:00, Fri from 9:00, Sat 9:00-15:00, closed Sun). The TI is in the Østbanehallen, right next to the train station.

For tickets and train info, you can go to the station's ticket office located between tracks 8 and 9 (Mon-Fri 7:30-20:00, Sat-Sun 10:00-18:00—opens at 7:45 on summer weekends). At this ticket office, you can buy domestic and Norway in a Nutshell tickets, and pick up leaflets on the Flåm and Bergen Railway (Bergensbanen). Only the station office sells international tickets. Domestic tickets can also be bought from the TI (same price) and at the red ticket machines (marked *NSB*); the blue machines (marked *SJ*) are for tickets to Sweden.

By Plane or Boat

For details on arriving in Oslo by plane or cruise ship, see the end of this chapter.

HELPFUL HINTS

Theft Alert: Pickpockets are a problem in Oslo, particularly in crowds on the street and on subways and buses. Oslo's street population loiters around the train station; you may see aggressive panhandlers there and along Karl Johans Gate. While a bit unnerving to some travelers, locals consider this rough-looking bunch harmless (but keep an eye on your wallet). To call the police, dial 112.

Money: Banks in Norway don't change money. Use ATMs or the Forex exchange office at the train station.

Post Office: It's in the train station.

Pharmacy: Jernbanetorgets Vitus Apotek is open 24 hours daily (across from train station on Jernbanetorget, tel. 23 35 81 00).

Laundry: Billig Vask & Rens ("Cheap Wash & Clean") is near Vår Frelsers Cemetery, a half-mile north of the train station (self-serve open daily 8:00-21:00; full-serve Mon-Fri 9:00-18:00, Sat 10:00-15:00, closed Sun; on the corner of Wessels Gate and Ullevålsveien, Ullevålsveien 15, catch bus #37 from station, tel. 41 64 08 33).

Bike Rental: Oslo isn't the best city for cycling. It's quite hilly, downtown streets are congested with buses and trams, and the city lags behind other Scandinavian capitals in bike lanes. But if you'd like wheels, the best spot is **Viking Biking,**

run by American Curtis (160 NOK/8 hours, 200 NOK/24 hours, includes helmet and lock, daily 9:30-18:00, Nedre Slottsgate 4, tel. 41 26 64 96, www.vikingbikingoslo.com; see "Tours in Oslo," later, for their guided bike tours). The city also has a public bike-rental system

that lets you grab basic **city bikes** out of locked racks at various points around town (works with a smartphone, details at www.oslobysykkel.no/en).

Movies: The domed **Colosseum Kino** in Majorstuen, one of northern Europe's largest movie houses with 1,500 seats, is a fun place to catch a big-time spectacle. Originally built in 1928, this now high-tech, four-screen theater shows first-run films in their original language (Fridtjof Nansens Vei 6, a short walk west from Marjorstuen T-bane station, www.oslokino.no).

GETTING AROUND OSLO
By Public Transit

Oslo is a big city, and taxi fares are exorbitant. Commit yourself to taking advantage of the excellent transit system, made up of buses, trams, ferries, and a subway (*Tunnelbane,* or T-bane for short; see the "Sightseeing by Public Transit" sidebar). The system is run by Ruter, which has a transit-information center below the tall, skinny, glass tower in front of the central train station (Mon-Fri 7:00-20:00, Sat-Sun 8:00-18:00, tel. 177 or 81 50 01 76, www.ruter.no).

Schedules: To navigate, use the public transit map on the back of the free TI city map, or download the RuterReise app. The system runs like clockwork, with schedules clearly posted and followed. Most stops have handy electronic reader boards showing the time remaining before the next tram arrives (usually less than 10 minutes).

Tickets: A different app—called RuterBillett—lets you buy tickets on your phone (with your credit card) rather than having to buy paper tickets; however, it may not work with American cards, and requires Wi-Fi or data to work. **Individual tickets** work on buses, trams, ferries, and the T-bane for one hour (33 NOK at machines, transit office, Narvesen kiosks, convenience stores such as 7-Eleven or Deli de Luca, or with the RuterBillett app—or a hefty 55 NOK from the driver). Other options include the **24-hour ticket** (90 NOK; buy at machines, transit office, or on RuterBillett app; good for unlimited rides in 24-hour period) and the **Oslo Pass**

OSLO

Sightseeing by Public Transit

With a transit pass or an Oslo Pass, take full advantage of the T-bane and the trams. Just spend five minutes to get a grip on the system, and you'll become amazingly empowered. Here are the T-bane stations you're likely to use:

Jernbanetorget (central station, bus and tram hub, express train to airport)

Stortinget (top of Karl Johans Gate, near Akershus Fortress)

Nationaltheatret (National Theater, also a train station, express train to airport, near City Hall, Aker Brygge, Royal Palace)

Majorstuen (walk to Vigeland Sculpture Park, trendy shops on Bogstadveien, Colosseum cinema)

Grønland (colorful immigrant neighborhood, cheap and fun restaurant zone, bottom of Grünerløkka district; the underground mall in the station is a virtual trip to Istanbul)

Holmenkollen (famous ski jump, city view)

Frognerseteren (highest point in town, jumping-off point for forest walks and bike rides)

Sognsvann (idyllic lake in forest outside of town)

Trams and buses that matter:

Trams #11 and #12 ring the city (stops at central station, fortress, harborfront, City Hall, Aker Brygge, Vigeland Park, Bogstadveien, National Gallery, and Stortorvet)

Trams #11, #12, and #13 to Olaf Ryes Plass (center of Grünerløkka district)

Trams #13 and #19, and bus #31 (south and parallel to Karl Johans Gate to central station)

Bus #30 (Olaf Ryes Plass in Grünerløkka, train station, near Karl Johans Gate, National Theater, and Bygdøy, with stops at each Bygdøy museum)

(gives free run of entire system; described earlier). Validate your ticket by holding it next to the card reader when you board.

By Taxi

Taxis come with a 150-NOK drop charge (yes, that's nearly $20 just to get in the car) that covers you for three or four kilometers—about two miles (more on evenings and weekends). Taxis are a good value only if you're with a group. If you use a minibus taxi, you are welcome to negotiate an hourly rate. To get a taxi, wave one down, find a taxi stand, or call 02323.

Tours in Oslo

Oslofjord Cruises

A fascinating world of idyllic islands sprinkled with charming vacation cabins is minutes away from the Oslo harborfront. For locals, the fjord is a handy vacation getaway. Tourists can get a glimpse of this island world by public ferry or tour boat. Cheap ferries regularly connect the nearby islands with downtown (free with Oslo Pass).

Several tour boats leave regularly from pier 3 in front of City Hall. **Båtservice** has a relaxing and scenic 1.5-hour hop-on, hop-off service, with recorded multilingual commentary. It departs from the City Hall dock (215 NOK, daily at 9:45, 11:15, 12:45, and 14:15; departs 30 minutes earlier from the Opera House and 30 minutes later from Bygdøy; tel. 23 35 68 90, www.boatsightseeing. com). They won't scream if you bring something to munch. They also offer two-hour fjord tours with lame live commentary (299 NOK, 3/day late March-mid-Oct, may run on winter weekends), a "Summer Evening on the Fjord" dinner cruise on a sailing ship (420 NOK, no narration; "shrimp buffet" is just shrimp, bread, and butter; daily mid-June-Aug 19:00-22:00), and jazz and blues-themed cruises.

Guided Walking Tour

Oslo Guideservice offers 1.5-hour historic "Oslo Promenade" walks from mid-May through August (200 NOK, free with Oslo Pass; Mon, Wed, and Fri at 17:30; leaves from harbor side of City Hall, confirm departures at TI, tel. 22 42 70 20, www.guideservice. no).

Local Guides

You can hire a private guide for around 2,000 NOK for a two- to three-hour tour. I had a good experience with **Oslo Guideservice** (2,000 NOK/2 hours, tel. 22 42 70 20, www.guideservice.no); my guide, Aksel, had a passion for both history and his hometown of Oslo. Or try **Oslo Guidebureau** (tel. 22 42 28 18, www. osloguidebureau.no, info@osloguide.no).

Bike Tours

Viking Biking gives several different guided tours in English, including a three-hour Oslo Highlights Tour that includes Bygdøy beaches and a ride up the Akers River (350 NOK, May-Sept daily at 14:00, Nedre Slottsgate 4, tel. 41 26 64 96, www.vikingbikingoslo. com). They also rent bikes; see "Helpful Hints," earlier. If you'd rather walk, check out their "Viking Hiking" forest-to-fjord and island hikes.

Bus Tours

While a bus tour can help you get your bearings, most of Oslo's sightseeing is concentrated in a few discrete zones that are well-connected by the public transportation—making pricey bus tours a lesser value. Consider my self-guided tram tour (later) instead.

Båtservice, which runs the harbor cruises, offers four-hour **bus tours** of Oslo, with stops at the ski jump, Bygdøy museums, and Vigeland Park (410 NOK, daily at 10:30, departs from next to City Hall, longer tours available, tel. 23 35 68 90, www.boatsightseeing. com). **HMK** also does daily city bus tours (330 NOK/2.5 hours, 450 NOK/4.5 hours, departs from next to City Hall, tel. 22 78 94 00, www.hmk.no).

Open Top Sightseeing runs **hop-on, hop-off bus tours** (300 NOK/all day, 18 stops, www.city-sightseeing.com; every 30 minutes from City Hall, English headphone commentary, buy ticket from driver). Be aware that you may wait up to an hour at popular stops (such as Vigeland Park) for a chance to hop back on.

Oslo Tram Tour

Tram #12, which becomes tram #11 halfway through its loop (at Majorstuen), circles the city from the train station, lacing together many of Oslo's main sights. Apart from the practical value of being able to hop on and off as you sightsee your way around town (trams come by at least every 10 minutes), this 40-minute trip gives you a fine look at parts of the city you wouldn't otherwise see.

This tour starts at the main train station, at the traffic-island tram stop located immediately in front of the Ruter transit office tower. The route makes almost a complete circle and finishes at Stortorvet (the cathedral square), dropping you off a three-minute walk from where you began the tour.

Starting out, you want tram #12 as it leaves from the second set of tracks, going toward Majorstuen. Confirm with your driver that the particular tram #12 you're boarding becomes tram #11 and finishes at Stortorvet; some turn into tram #19 instead, which takes a different route. If yours becomes #19, simply hop out at Majorstuen and wait for the next #11. (If #11 is canceled due to construction, leave #12 at Majorstuen and catch #19 through the center back to the train station, or hop on the T-bane, which zips every few minutes from Majorstuen to the National Theater—closest to the harbor and City Hall—and then to the station).

Here's what you'll see and places where you might want to hop out:

From the **station,** you'll go through the old grid streets of 16th-century Christiania, King Christian IV's planned Renaissance town. After the city's 17th fire, in 1624, the king finally got fed up. He decreed that only brick and stone buildings would be permitted in the city center, with wide streets to serve as fire breaks.

You'll turn a corner at the **fortress** (Christiana Torv stop; get off here for the fortress and Norwegian Resistance Museum), then head for **City Hall** (Rådhus stop). Next comes the harbor and up-scale **Aker Brygge** waterfront neighborhood (jump off at the Aker Brygge stop for the harbor and restaurant row). Passing the harbor, you'll see on the left a few old shipyard buildings that still survive. Then the tram goes uphill, past the **House of Oslo** (a mall of 20 shops highlighting Scandinavian interior design; Vikatorvet stop) and into a district of ugly 1960s buildings (when elegance was replaced by "functionality"). The tram then heads onto the street Norwegians renamed **Henrik Ibsens Gate** in 2006 to commemorate the centenary of Ibsen's death, honoring the man they claim is the greatest playwright since Shakespeare.

After Henrik Ibsens Gate, the tram follows Frognerveien through the chic **Frogner neighborhood.** Behind the fine old facades are fancy shops and spendy condos. Here and there you'll see 19th-century mansions built by aristocratic families who wanted to live near the Royal Palace; today, many of these house foreign embassies. Turning the corner, you roll along the edge of **Frogner Park** (which includes **Vigeland Park,** featuring Gustav Vigeland's sculptures), stopping at its grand gate (hop out at the Vigeland-sparken stop).

Ahead on the left, a statue of 1930s ice queen Sonja Henie marks the arena where she learned to skate. Turning onto Bog-stadveien, the tram usually becomes #11 at the Majorstuen stop. **Bogstadveien** is lined with trendy shops, restaurants, and cafés—it's a fun place to stroll and window-shop. (You could get out here and walk along this street all the way to the Royal Palace park and the top of Karl Johans Gate.) The tram veers left before the palace, passing the **National Historical Museum** and stopping at the **National Gallery** (Tullinløkka stop). As you trundle along, you may notice that lots of roads are ripped up for construction. It's too cold to fix the streets in winter, so, when possible, the work is done in summer. Jump out at **Stortorvet** (a big square filled with flower stalls and fronted by the cathedral and the big GlasMagasinet department store). From here, you're a three-minute walk from the station, where this tour began.

Oslo Walk

This self-guided stroll, worth ▲▲, covers the heart of Oslo—the zone where most tourists find themselves walking—from the train station, up the main drag, and past City Hall to the harborfront. Allow a brisk 45 minutes without stops.

OSLO

Train Station: Start at the plaza just outside the main entrance of Oslo's central train station (Oslo Sentralstasjon), near the statue of the **tiger** prowling around out front. This alludes to the town's nickname of Tigerstaden ("Tiger Town"), and commemorates

the 1,000th birthday of Oslo's founding, celebrated in the year 2000. In the 1800s, Oslo was considered an urban tiger, leaving its mark on the soul of simple country folk who ventured into the wild and crazy New York City of Norway.

In the middle of the plaza, look for the tall, skinny, glass ❶ **Ruter tower** that marks the public transit office. From here, trams zip to City Hall (harbor, boat to Bygdøy), and the underground subway (T-bane, or *Tunnelbane*—look for the *T* sign to your right) goes to Vigeland Park (statues) and Holmenkollen. Tram #12—featured in the self-guided tram tour described earlier—leaves from directly across the street.

The green building behind the Ruter tower is a shopping mall called **Byporten** (literally, "City Gate," see big sign on rooftop), built to greet those arriving from the airport on the shuttle train. Oslo's 37-floor pointed-glass **skyscraper,** the Radisson Blu Plaza Hotel, pokes up behind that. The hotel's 34th-floor SkyBar welcomes the public with air-conditioned views and pricey drinks. The tower was built with reflective glass so that, from a distance, it almost disappears. The area behind the Radisson—the lively and colorful "Little Karachi," centered along a street called Grønland—is where many of Oslo's immigrants settled. It's become a vibrant nightspot, offering a fun contrast to the predictable Norwegian cuisine and culture.

Oslo allows hard-drug addicts and prostitutes to mix and mingle in the station area. (While it's illegal to buy sex in Norway, those who sell it are not breaking the law.) Troubled young people come here from small towns in the countryside for anonymity and community. The two cameras near the top of the Ruter tower monitor drug deals. Signs warn that this is a "monitored area," but victimless crimes proceed while violence is minimized. (Watch your valuables here.)

• *Note that you are near the Opera House if you'd like to side-trip there now (through the park to the right of the station). Otherwise, turn your back to the station. You're now looking (across the street) up Norway's main drag, called…*

Karl Johans Gate: This grand boulevard leads directly from the train station to the Royal Palace. The street is named for the

OSLO

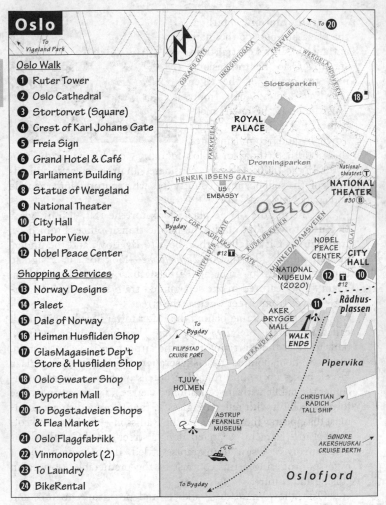

Oslo

Oslo Walk

1. Ruter Tower
2. Oslo Cathedral
3. Stortorvet (Square)
4. Crest of Karl Johans Gate
5. Freia Sign
6. Grand Hotel & Café
7. Parliament Building
8. Statue of Wergeland
9. National Theater
10. City Hall
11. Harbor View
12. Nobel Peace Center

Shopping & Services

13. Norway Designs
14. Paleet
15. Dale of Norway
16. Heimen Husfliden Shop
17. GlasMagasinet Dep't Store & Husfliden Shop
18. Oslo Sweater Shop
19. Byporten Mall
20. To Bogstadveien Shops & Flea Market
21. Oslo Flaggfabrikk
22. Vinmonopolet (2)
23. To Laundry
24. Bike Rental

French general Jean Baptiste Bernadotte, who was given a Swedish name, established the current Swedish dynasty, and ruled as a popular king (1818-1844) during the period after Sweden took Norway from Denmark.

Walk three blocks up Karl Johans Gate. This stretch is sometimes called **"Desolation Row"** by locals because it has no soul—just shops greedily devouring tourists' money. If you visit in the snowy winter, you'll walk on bare concrete: Most of downtown Oslo's pedestrian streets are heated.

• *Hook right around the curved old brick structure of an old market and walk to the...*

   2 Oslo Cathedral (Domkirke): This Lutheran church is the third cathedral Oslo has had, built in 1697 after the second one

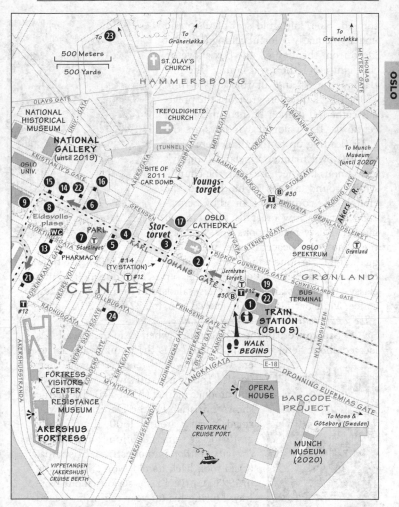

burned down. It's where Norway commemorates its royal marriages and deaths. Seventy-seven deaths were mourned here following a tragic bombing and mass shooting in July 2011 (see the "In Cold Blood" sidebar, later). In the grass in front of the cathedral, you may see a plastic heart on a pole—a semipermanent memorial to the victims.

Look for the cathedral's cornerstone (near the base of the steeple), a thousand year-old carving from Oslo's first and long-gone cathedral showing how the forces of good and evil tug at each of us. Look high up on the tower. The tiny square windows midway up the copper cupola were once the lookout quarters of the fire watchman.

Step inside (daily 10:00-16:00, open overnight on Fri) beneath

the red, blue, and gold seal of Oslo and under an equally colorful ceiling (late Art Deco from the 1930s). The box above on the right is for the royal family. The fine Baroque pulpit and altarpiece date from 1700. The chandeliers are from the previous cathedral (which burned in the 17th century). The colorful windows in the choir (leading up to the altar) were made in 1910 by Emanuel Vigeland (Gustav's less famous brother). Leaving the church, stroll around to the right, behind the church. The **courtyard** is lined by a circa-1850 circular row of stalls from an old market. Rusty meat hooks now decorate the lamps of a peaceful café, which has quaint tables around a fountain. The atmospheric **$$$$ Café Bacchus,** at the far left end of the arcade, serves food outside and in a classy café downstairs (sandwiches, salads, full meals, good cakes, coffee, Mon-Sat 11:30-22:30, closed Sun, tel. 22 33 34 30).

• *The square that faces the cathedral is called...*

❸ **Stortorvet:** In the 17th century, when Oslo's city wall was located about here, this "Big Square" was the point where farm-

ers were allowed to enter and sell their goods. Today it's still lively as a flower and produce market (Mon-Fri). The statue shows Christian IV, the Danish king who ruled Norway around 1600, dramatically gesturing at some geraniums. He named the city, rather immodestly, Christiania. (Oslo took back its old Norse name only in 1925.) Christian was serious about Norway. During his 60-year reign, he visited it 30 times (more than all other royal visits combined during 300 years of Danish rule). The big GlasMagasinet department store is a landmark on this square.

• *Return to Karl Johans Gate, and continue up the boulevard past street performers, cafés, shops, and hordes of people. At the next corner, Kongens Gate leads left, past the 17th-century grid-plan town to **Akershus Fortress** (described in "Sights in Oslo," later). But we'll continue hiking straight up to the crest of the hill, enjoying some of the buskers along the way.*

Pause at the wide spot in the street just before Akersgata (near the T-bane stop) to appreciate the...

❹ **Crest of Karl Johans Gate** (Egertorget): Look back at the train station. A thousand years ago, the original (pre-1624) Oslo was located at the foot of the wooded hill behind the station (described later). Now look ahead to the **Royal Palace** in the distance, which was built in the 1830s "with nature and God behind it and the people at its feet." If the flag flies atop the palace, the king is in the country. For details on visiting the palace, see the listing later, under "Sights in Oslo."

Karl Johans Gate, a parade ground laid out in about 1850 from here to the palace, is now the axis of modern Oslo. Each May 17, Norway's Constitution Day, an annual children's parade turns this street into a sea of marching student bands and costumed young flag-wavers, while the royal family watches from the palace balcony. Since 1814, Norway has preferred peace. Rather than celebrating its military on the national holiday, it celebrates its children.

In the middle of the small square, the *T* sign marks a stop of the T-bane (Oslo's subway). W. B. Samson's bakery is a good place for a quick, affordable lunch, with a handy cafeteria line (WC in back)—duck inside and be tempted by the pastries. Two traditional favorites are *kanelboller* (cinnamon rolls) and *skolebrød* ("school bread," with an egg-and-cream filling).

High overhead, the big neon ❺ **Freia sign** (dating from 1911) trumpets another sweet Norwegian treat. Norway's answer to Cadbury, the Norwegian chocolatier Freia is beloved...or it was, until it was bought by an American company. Still, the local factory is partly operational, and nostalgic Norwegians will always think of Freia as "a little piece of Norway."

From here, the street called **Akersgata** (on the right) kicks off a worthwhile stroll past the site of the July 2011 bombing, the national cemetery, and through a parklike river gorge to the Mathallen food hall and the trendy Grünerløkka quarter (an hour-long walk, described later, under "Sights in Oslo").

Continuing down Karl Johans Gate: People-watching is great along Karl Johans Gate, but remember that if it's summer, half of the city's regular population is gone—vacationing in their cabins or farther away—and the city center is filled mostly with visitors.

Hike two blocks farther down Karl Johans Gate, passing the big brick Parliament building (on the left). On your right, seated in the square, is a bearded, tubby statue of the 19th-century painter Christian Krohg.

If you'd like to get a city view (and perhaps some pricey refreshment), enter the glass doors facing the street at #27 (not the bank entrance at the corner) and take the elevator to the eighth-floor rooftop bar, aptly named Eight (cocktails-150 NOK, beers-90 NOK).

A few doors farther down Karl Johans Gate, just past the Freia

OSLO

Browsing

Oslo's pulse is best felt by strolling. Three good areas are along and near the central Karl Johans Gate, which runs from the train station to the palace (follow my self-guided "Oslo Walk"); in the trendy harborside Aker Brygge mall, a glass-and-chrome collection of sharp cafés, fine condos, and polished produce stalls (really lively at night, tram #12 from train station); and along Bogstadveien, a bustling shopping street with no-nonsense modern commerce, lots of locals, and no tourists (T-bane to Majorstuen and follow this street back toward the palace and tourist zone). While most tourists never get out of the harbor/Karl Johans Gate district, the real, down-to-earth Oslo is better seen elsewhere, in places such as Bogstadveien. The bohemian, artsy Grünerløkka district, described on page 258, is good for a daytime wander.

---

shop (selling that favorite Norwegian chocolate at only slightly inflated prices), the venerable **Grand Hotel** (Oslo's celebrity hotel—Nobel Peace Prize winners sleep here) overlooks the boulevard.

• *Politely ask the waiter at the Grand Café—part of the Grand Hotel—if you can pop inside for a little sightseeing (he'll generally let you).*

❻ **Grand Café:** This historic café was for many years the meeting place of Oslo's intellectual and creative elite (playwright Henrik Ibsen was a regular here). While it's been renovated, it still has some beautiful old artwork—including (at the far back) a wall-length **mural** showing Norway's literary and artistic clientele—from a century ago—enjoying this fine hangout. On the far left, find Ibsen, coming in as he did every day at 13:00. Edvard Munch is on the right, leaning against the window behind the waiter, looking pretty drugged. Names are on the sill beneath the mural.

• *For a cheap bite with prime boulevard seating, continue past the corner to Deli de Luca, a convenience store with a super selection of takeaway food and a great people-watching perch. Across the street, a little park faces Norway's...*

❼ **Parliament Building** (Stortinget): Norway's parliament meets here (along with anyone participating in a peaceful protest outside). *Stortinget*—from an old Viking word—basically means "Big Gathering." Built in 1866, the building seems to counter the Royal Palace at the other end of Karl Johans Gate. If the flag's flying, parliament's in session. Today the king is a figurehead, and Norway is run by a unicameral parliament and a prime minister. Guided tours of the Stortinget are offered for those interested in Norwegian government (free, 1 hour, typically Sat mornings, may be more frequent in summer—check schedule at www.stortinget. no, enter on Akersgata—on the back side of the building).

• *Cross over into the long median park. On your left, notice the red, white, and blue coin-op public WCs. (Free WCs are inside the Paleet shopping mall, on the right side of the boulevard).*

   Enjoying the park, stroll toward the palace, past the fountain. Pause at the...

❽ **Statue of Wergeland:** The poet Henrik Wergeland helped inspire the national resurgence of Norway during the 19th century. Norway won its independence from Denmark in 1814, but within a year it lost its freedom to Sweden. For nearly a century, until Norway won independence in 1905, Norwegian culture and national spirit was stoked by artistic and literary patriots like Wergeland. In the winter, the pool here is frozen and covered with children happily ice-skating.

   Across the street behind Wergeland stands the ❾ **National Theater** and statues of Norway's favorite playwrights: Ibsen and Bjørnstjerne Bjørnson. Across Karl Johans Gate, the pale yellow building is the first university building in Norway, dating from 1854. A block behind that is the National Gallery, with Norway's best collection of paintings (self-guided tour on page 234).

   Take a moment here to do a 360-degree spin to notice how quiet and orderly everything is. People seem content—and, according to most surveys, Norwegians are among the happiest people on earth. If you ask them why, their hunch is that it's because they live collectively. The Vikings would famously share one large bowl of mead, passing it around the circle. Nobody—no matter how big, angry, hairy, or smelly—gulped more than his share. They all made sure that everyone got some.

   In modern times, Norwegians at the dinner table are still mindful when helping themselves not to take too much: They mentally ration enough for the people who come after them. It's a very considerate—and a very Norwegian—way of thinking. (Similarly, upper-Midwesterners in the US are familiar with the "Minnesota Slice": The Scandinavian-American tendency to carve off a little sliver of the last slice of pie, rather than take the entire thing for themselves.)

• *Facing the theater, turn left and follow Roald Amundsens Gate to the towering brick...*

❿ **City Hall** (Rådhuset): Built mostly in the 1930s with contributions from Norway's leading artists, City Hall is full

Oslo at a Glance

▲▲▲**City Hall** Oslo's artsy 20th-century government building, lined with huge, vibrant, municipal-themed murals, best visited with included tour. **Hours:** Daily 9:00-16:00, until 18:00 June-Aug; 3 tours/day June-Aug. See page 225.

▲▲▲**National Gallery** Norway's cultural and natural essence, captured on canvas. **Hours:** Tue-Fri 10:00-18:00, Thu until 19:00, Sat-Sun 11:00-17:00, closed Mon. See page 234.

▲▲▲**Vigeland Park** Set in sprawling Frogner Park, with tons of statuary by Norway's greatest sculptor, Gustav Vigeland, and the studio where he worked (now a museum). **Hours:** Park—always open; Vigeland Museum—Tue-Sun 10:00-17:00, Sept-April 12:00-16:00, closed Mon year-round. See page 242.

▲▲▲**Fram Museum** Captivating exhibit on the Arctic exploration ships *Fram* and *Gjøa.* **Hours:** Daily June-Aug 9:00-18:00, May and Sept 10:00-17:00, Oct and March-April until 16:00; Nov-Feb Mon-Fri 10:00-15:00, Sat-Sun until 16:00. See page 252.

▲▲**Norwegian Folk Museum** Norway condensed into 150 historic buildings in a large open-air museum. **Hours:** Daily 10:00-18:00—grounds open until 20:00; mid-Sept-mid-May Mon-Fri 11:00-15:00, Sat-Sun until 16:00, but most historical buildings closed. See page 250.

▲▲**Norwegian Resistance Museum** Gripping look at Norway's tumultuous WWII experience. **Hours:** Mon-Sat 10:00-17:00, Sun from 11:00; Sept-May Mon-Fri until 16:00, Sat-Sun from 11:00. See page 230.

▲▲**Viking Ship Museum** An impressive trio of ninth-century Viking ships, with exhibits on the people who built them. **Hours:** Daily 9:00-18:00, Oct-April 10:00-16:00. See page 251.

▲▲**Kon-Tiki Museum** Adventures of primitive *Kon-Tiki* and *Ra II*

of great art and is worth touring (see listing later, under "Sights in Oslo"). The mayor has his office here (at the base of one of the two 200-foot towers), and every December 10, this building is where the Nobel Peace Prize is presented. The semicircular square facing the building, called Fridtjof Nansens Plass, was designed to evoke Il Campo, the main square in Siena, Tuscany. Just like Oslo, Siena's main building (dominating Il Campo) is its City Hall.

For the City Hall's best exterior art, step up into the U-shaped ships built by Thor Heyerdahl. **Hours:** Daily 9:30-18:00, March-May and Sept-Oct 10:00-17:00, Nov-Feb until 16:00. See page 255.

▲**Oslo Opera House** Stunning performance center that's helping revitalize the harborfront. **Hours:** Foyer and café/restaurant open Mon-Fri 10:00-23:00, Sat from 11:00, Sun 12:00-22:00; Opera House tours—3/day year-round. See page 233.

▲**Akershus Fortress Complex and Tours** Historic military base and fortified old center, with guided tours, a ho-hum castle interior, and the excellent Norwegian Resistance Museum (listed earlier). **Hours:** Park generally open daily 6:00-21:00—until 18:00 in winter; one-hour tour daily July-mid-Aug, weekends-only off-season. See page 229.

▲**Norwegian Maritime Museum** A briny voyage through Norway's rich seafaring heritage. **Hours:** Daily 10:00-17:00; Sept-mid-May Tue-Sun until 16:00, closed Mon. See page 255.

▲**Ekeberg Sculpture Park** Hilly, hikeable 63-acre forest park with striking contemporary art and city views. See page 264.

▲**Edvard Munch Museum** Works of Norway's famous Expressionistic painter. **Hours:** Daily 10:00-17:00, early Oct-early May until 16:00. See page 263.

▲**Grünerløkka** Oslo's trendy former working-class district, with bustling cafés and pubs. See page 258.

▲**Aker Brygge and Tjuvholmen** Oslo's harborfront promenade, and nearby trendy Tjuvholmen neighborhood with Astrup Fearnley Museum, upscale galleries, shops, and cafés. See page 229.

▲**Holmenkollen Ski Jump and Ski Museum** Dizzying vista and a schuss through skiing history, plus a zip line off the top. **Hours:** Daily 9:00-20:00, May and Sept 10:00-17:00, Oct-April until 16:00. See page 265.

courtyard and circle it clockwise, savoring the colorful woodcuts in the arcade. Each shows a scene from Norwegian mythology, well-explained in English: Thor with his billy-goat chariot, Ask and Embla (a kind of Norse Adam and Eve), Odin on his eight-legged horse guided by ravens, the swan maidens shedding their swan disguises, and so on.

Facing City Hall, circle around its right side (through a lovely garden) until you reach the front. Like all of the statues adorning the building, the **six figures** facing the waterfront—dating from a period of Labor Party rule in Norway—celebrate the nobility of the working class. Norway, a social democracy, believes in giving respect to the workers who built their society and made it what it is, and these laborers are viewed as heroes.

• *Walk to the...*

❶ Harbor: Over a decade ago, you would have dodged several lanes of busy traffic to reach Oslo's harborfront. Today, the traffic passes beneath your feet in tunnels. In addition, the city has made its town center relatively quiet and pedestrian-friendly by levying a 34-NOK toll on every car entering town. (This system, like a similar one in London, subsidizes public transit and the city's infrastructure.)

At the water's edge, find the shiny metal plaque (just left of center) listing the contents of a sealed time capsule planted in 2000 out in the harbor in the little Kavringen lighthouse straight ahead (to be opened in 1,000 years).

Head to the end of the stubby pier (just to the right). This is the ceremonial "enter the city" point for momentous occasions. One such instance was in 1905, when Norway gained its independence from Sweden and a Danish prince sailed in from Copenhagen to become the first modern king of Norway. Another milestone event occurred at the end of World War II, when the king returned to Norway after the country was liberated from the Nazis.

• *Stand on that important pier and give the harbor a sweeping counterclockwise look.*

Harborfront Spin-Tour: Oslofjord is one big playground, with 40 city-owned, parklike islands. Big white cruise ships—a large part of the local tourist economy—dock just under the Akershus Fortress on the left. (The big, boxy building clinging to the top of the fortress—just under the green steeple—is the excellent Norwegian Resistance Museum.) Just this side of the fort's impressive 13th-century ramparts, a **statue of FDR** grabs the shade. He's here in gratitude for the safe refuge the US gave to members of the royal family (including the young prince, Harald, who is now Norway's king) during World War II—while the king and his government-in-exile waged Norway's fight against the Nazis from London.

Panning left, enjoy the grand view of City Hall. The yellow building farther to the left was the old West Train Station; today it houses the **❷ Nobel Peace Center,** which celebrates the work of Nobel Peace Prize winners. Just to the left and behind that is the construction site for the new home of the National Museum, including the fine art collection of the National Gallery (slated to open in 2020).

The next pier over is the launchpad for harbor boat tours and the shuttle boat to the Bygdøy museums. At the base of this pier, the glassy box is a new fish market, serving a mix of locals and tourists. You may see a fisherman mooring his boat near here, selling shrimp from the back. Also in this area, look for a bright-orange container box—an information point for Oslo's impressive harbor promenade, the nearly complete 5.5-mile walkway that runs the entire length of the city's futuristic harborfront.

Along the right side of the harbor, shipyard buildings (this was the former heart of Norway's once-important shipbuilding industry) have been transformed into **Aker Brygge**—Oslo's thriving restaurant/shopping/nightclub zone (see "Eating in Oslo").

Just past the end of Aker Brygge is a new housing development—dubbed Norway's most expensive real estate—called **Tjuvholmen.** It's anchored by the Astrup Fearnley Museum, an international modern art museum complex designed by renowned architect Renzo Piano (most famous for Paris' Pompidou Center).

An ambitious urban renewal project called Fjord City (Fjordbyen)—which kicked off years ago with Aker Brygge, and led to the construction of Oslo's dramatic Opera House—has made remarkable progress in turning the formerly industrial waterfront into a flourishing people zone.

• *From here, you can stroll out Aker Brygge and through Tjuvholmen to a tiny public beach at the far end; tour City Hall; visit the Nobel Peace Center; hike up to Akershus Fortress; take a harbor cruise (see "Tours in Oslo," earlier); or catch a boat across the harbor to the museums at Bygdøy (from pier 3). All of these sights are described in detail in the following section.*

Sights in Oslo

NEAR THE HARBORFRONT
▲▲▲City Hall (Rådhuset)

In 1931, Oslo tore down a slum and began constructing its richly decorated City Hall. It was finally finished—after a WWII delay—in 1950 to celebrate the city's 900th birthday. Norway's leading artists all contributed to the building, which was an avant-garde thrill in its day. City Halls, rather than churches, are the dominant buildings in Scandinavian capitals. The prominence of this building on the harborfront makes sense in this most humanistic, yet least churchgoing, northern end of the Continent. Up here, people pay high taxes, have high expectations, and are generally satisfied with what their governments do with their money.

Cost and Hours: Free, daily 9:00-16:00—until 18:00 June-Aug, free and fine WC in the basement, tel. 23 46 12 00.

Tours: Only in the summer months (June-Aug), the City Hall offers 50-minute guided tours daily at 10:00, 12:00, and 14:00.

❍ Self-Guided Tour: For descriptions of the building's exterior features and symbolism, see the City Hall section of my "Oslo Walk," earlier. On this tour, we'll focus on the interior.

The visitor entrance is on the Karl Johans Gate side (away from the harbor). You'll step into a cavernous **main hall,** which feels like a temple to good government, with its altar-like murals celebrating "work, play, and civic administration." It's decorated with 20,000 square feet of bold and colorful Socialist Realist murals celebrating a classless society, with everyone—town folk, country folk, and people from all walks of life—working harmoniously for a better society. The huge murals take you on a voyage through the collective psyche of Norway, from its simple rural beginnings through the scar tissue of the Nazi occupation and beyond. Filled with significance and symbolism—and well-described in English—the murals become even more meaningful with the excellent guided tours.

First, turn around and face the mural over the door you came in, which celebrates the **traditional industries** of Norway (from left to right): the yellow-clad fisherman (standing in his boat, glancing nervously at a flock of seagulls), the factory worker (with his heavy apron), the blue-clad sailor (he's playing with exotic beads acquired through distant trade), the farmer (in a striped dress, with a bushel under her arm), and the miner (lower right, lifting a heavy rock). Flanking these figures are portraits of two important Norwegians: On the far right is Bjørnstjerne Bjørnson (1832-1910), a prominent poet and novelist whose works pluck the patriotic heartstrings of Norwegians. And on the far left is Fridtjof Nansen (1861-1930), the famous Arctic explorer (you can learn more about him at the Fram Museum on Bygdøy). Here Nansen is seen shedding the heavy coat of his most famous endeavor—polar exploration—as he embarks on his "second act": Once retired from seafaring, he advocated for the dissolution of Norway's union with Sweden—which took place in 1905, making Norway fully independent.

Now turn 180 degrees and face the hall's main mural, which emphasizes **Oslo's youth** participating in community life—and rebuilding the country after Nazi occupation. Across the bottom, the slum that once cluttered up Oslo's harborfront is being cleared out to make way for this building. Above that, scenes show Norway's pride in its innovative health care and education systems. Left of center, near the top, Mother Norway stands next to a church—reminding viewers that the Lutheran Church of Norway (the official state religion) provides a foundation for this society. On the right, four forms represent the arts; they illustrate how creativity springs from children. And in the center, the figure of Charity is surrounded by Culture, Philosophy, and Family.

The **"Mural of the Occupation"** lines the left side of the hall, tucked under the balustrade. Scan it from left to right to see the

story of Norway's WWII experience: First, the German blitzkrieg overwhelms the country. Men head for the mountains to organize a resistance movement. Women huddle around the water well, traditionally where news is passed, while Quislings (traitors named after the Norwegian fascist who ruled the country as a Nazi puppet) listen in. While Germans bomb and occupy Norway, a family gathers in their living room. As a boy clenches his fist (showing determination) and a child holds the beloved Norwegian flag, the Gestapo steps in. Columns are toppled to the ground, symbolizing how Germans shut down the culture by closing newspapers and the university. Two resistance soldiers stand up against a wall—about to be executed by firing squad. A cell of resistance fighters (wearing masks and using nicknames, so if tortured they can't reveal their compatriots' identities) plan a sabotage mission. Finally, prisoners are freed, the war is over, and Norway celebrates its happiest day: May 17, 1945—the first Constitution Day after five years under Nazi control.

While gazing at these murals, keep in mind that the Nobel Peace Prize is awarded in this central hall each December (though the general Nobel Prize ceremony occurs in Stockholm's City Hall). You'll see photos of this event in the little foyer with the strollers (on the right from where you entered). You can see videos of the ceremony and acceptance speeches in the adjacent Nobel Peace Center (listed next).

At the base of the grand marble staircase is a mural of the 11th-century **St. Hallvard,** the patron saint of Oslo. Above his head, he holds his symbol—three arrows—and he rests a millstone on his knee. As the story goes, Hallvard took pity on a pregnant woman (the naked woman in front of him) who had been wrongly accused of theft by three men. They attempted to escape, but the accusers killed the woman, shot Hallvard with three arrows, tied a millstone around his neck, and tossed him into the fjord. Miraculously, he survived (or perhaps rose from the dead). This story of compassion in the face of injustice swayed Norwegians at a time when Christianity was making its bid to be the country's main religion.

In front of the mural is a **bell** from the ship that brought Norway's royal family back home after World War II—landing at the pier right in front of City Hall.

Now head up the stairs and explore several **ceremonial rooms,** each well-described in English. The wood-paneled Munch Room is dominated by the artist's oil painting *Life*. Circle around the gallery to the City Council Assembly Room, where Oslo's leadership steers the agenda of this impressive city. Notice the "three arrows and millstone" motif, recalling St. Hallvard. The city council acts collectively as a virtual "mayor"—a system, originating here in Oslo in 1986, called "parliamentary metropolitan government." Notice how this room evokes the semicircular shape of the square where you entered. Out in the hall, you'll pass gifts from visiting heads of state (*gave fra* means "gift from").

Nearby: Fans of the explorer Fridtjof Nansen might enjoy taking a break for a bite and a coffee or beer across the street at **Fridtjof,** an atmospheric bar filled with memorabilia from Nansen's Arctic explorations. A model of his ship, the *Fram,* hangs from the ceiling, and 1894 photos and his own drawings are upstairs (Mon-Sat 12:00 until late, Sun 14:00-22:00, Nansens Plass 7, tel. 93 25 22 30).

Nobel Peace Center (Nobels Fredssenter)

This museum, housed in the former West Train Station (Vestbanen), poses the question, "What is the opposite of conflict?" It celebrates the 800-some past and present Nobel Peace Prize winners with touchscreen exhibits (with good English explanations).

Cost and Hours: 100 NOK; daily 10:00-18:00, closed Mon Sept-mid-May; includes English guided tours at 14:00 and 15:00—off-season weekends only at 14:00; Brynjulfs Bulls Plass 1, tel. 48 30 10 00, www.nobelpeacecenter.org.

Visiting the Center: The ground floor is dominated by generally good, thought-provoking temporary exhibits. The permanent collection upstairs is modest: First you'll step into "The Nobel Field," a sea of lights and touchscreens profiling various past prizewinners (from Teddy Roosevelt to Mother Theresa). Next, "The Nobel Chamber" has a big virtual book that invites you to learn more about the life and work of Alfred Nobel, the Swedish inventor of dynamite, who initiated the prizes—perhaps to assuage his conscience. While it's a nice museum, unless the temporary exhibits intrigue you, save your time and money for the better Nobel Prize Museum in Stockholm.

▲Aker Brygge and Tjuvholmen

Oslo's harborfront was dominated by the **Aker Brygge** shipyard until it closed in 1986. In the late 2000s, it became the first finished part of a project (called Fjordbyen, or Fjord City) to convert the central stretch of Oslo's harborfront into a people-friendly park and culture zone. Today's Aker Brygge is a stretch of trendy, if over-priced, yacht-club style restaurants facing a fine promenade—just the place to join in on a Nordic paseo on a balmy summer's eve.

The far end of Aker Brygge is marked by a big black anchor from the wreck of the German warship *Blücher*, sunk by Norwegian forces near Drøbak while heading for Oslo during the Nazi invasion on April 9, 1940. From there a bridge crosses over onto **Tjuvholmen** (where they hung thieves back in the 17th century). This is a planned futuristic community, with the trendiest and costliest apartments in town, private moorings for luxury jet boats, boardwalks with built-in seating to catch the sun, elegant shops and cafés, and the striking, wood-clad, glass-roofed **Astrup Fearnley Museum of Modern Art** (good temporary exhibits of contemporary art, closed Mon, www.afmuseet.no). On the harbor side of the museum, find the grassy little knob of land with an appealing sculpture park. This area is well worth a wander—and don't be afraid to explore the back lanes away from the waterfront. As you stroll through Tjuvholmen, admire how, while the entire complex feels cohesive, each building has its own personality.

Eating: Dining here is appealing, but be prepared to pay royally for the privilege. Choose from many restaurants, or—to eat on a budget—take advantage of the generous public benches, lounge chairs, and picnic tables that allow people who can't afford a fancy restaurant meal to enjoy the best seats of all (grocery stores are a block away from the harborfront views). For recommendations, see "Eating in Oslo," later.

▲AKERSHUS FORTRESS COMPLEX

This parklike complex of sights scattered over Oslo's fortified old center is still a military base. (You'll see uniformed members of the Royal Guard keeping watch, because the castle is a royal mausoleum.) But the public is welcome, and as you dodge patrol guards and vans filled with soldiers, you'll see the castle, war memorials, the Norwegian Resistance Museum, and cannon-strewn ramparts affording fine harbor views and picnic perches. There's an unimpressive changing of the guard—that's singular "guard," as in just one—daily at 13:30 (at the parade ground, deep in the castle complex). The park is generally open daily 6:00-21:00 (until

18:00 in winter), but because the military is in charge here, times can change without warning. Expect bumpy cobblestone lanes and steep hills. To get here from the harbor, follow the stairs (which lead past the FDR statue) to the park.

Getting Oriented: It's a sprawling complex. You can hike up the stairs by the FDR statue on the harbor, or (less steeply) from the grid of streets just east of City Hall. As you hike up toward the ramparts, go through the gate smack in the middle of the complex (rather than hooking up around to the right). You'll pop out into an inner courtyard. The visitors center (described next) is to the left, and the other sights are through the gate on the right. Heading through this gate, you'll curl up along a tree-lined lane, then pass the Norwegian Resistance Museum on your right (capping the ramparts). The entrance to the castle is dead ahead. There are terrific harbor views (often filled with a giant cruise ship) from the rampart alongside the Resistance Museum.

Fortress Visitors Center: Stop here to pick up the fortress trail and site map, quickly browse through a modest exhibit tracing the story of Oslo's fortifications from medieval times, use the free WCs, and consider catching a tour (daily July-mid-Aug 11:00-17:00, until 16:00 in shoulder season, shorter hours off-season, tel. 23 09 39 17, www.akershusfestning.no).

Fortress Tours: The 60-NOK, hour-long English walking tours of the grounds help you make sense of the most historic piece of real estate in Oslo (July-mid-Aug daily in English at 13:00, weekends-only off-season; departs from Fortress Visitors Center, call ahead to confirm tour is running).

▲▲Norwegian Resistance Museum (Norges Hjemmefrontmuseum)

This fascinating museum tells the story of Norway's WWII experience: appeasement, Nazi invasion (they made Akershus one of their headquarters), resistance, liberation, and, finally, the return of the king. With good English descriptions, this is an inspirational look at how the national spirit can endure total occupation by a malevolent force. While the exhibit grows a bit more old-fashioned with each passing year, for those with an appetite for WWII history and the patience to read the displays, it's still both riveting and stirring. Norway had the fiercest resistance movement in Scandinavia, and this museum shows off their (hard-earned) pride.

Cost and Hours: 60 NOK; Mon-Sat 10:00-17:00, Sun from 11:00; Sept-May Mon-Fri 10:00-16:00, Sat-Sun from 11:00; next to castle, overlooking harbor, tel. 23 09 31 38, www.forsvaretsmuseer.no.

Visiting the Museum: It's a one-way, chronological, can't-get-lost route. As you enter the exhibit, you're transported back to 1940, greeted by an angry commotion of rifles aimed at you. A German notice proclaiming "You will submit or die" is bayonetted onto a gun in the middle. A **timeline** on the right wall traces the brief history of skirmishes between Nazi and improvised Norwegian forces following the invasion on April 9, 1940. This ends abruptly on June 10, when the Norwegian government officially capitulates.

On the left, you'll see the German ultimatum to which King Haakon VII gave an emphatic "No." A video screen nearby plays the radio address by Vidkun Quisling, the fascist Nasjonal Samling (National Union Party) politician who declared himself ruler of Norway on the day of the invasion. (Today, Quisling's name remains synonymous with "traitor"—the Norwegian version of Benedict Arnold.)

Head **downstairs** and take some time with the in-depth exhibits. Various displays show secret radios, transmitters, and underground newspapers. The official name for the resistance was Milorg (for "Military Organization")—but Norwegians affectionately referred to the ragtag, guerilla force as simply *gutta på skauen* ("the boys in the forest"). Look for the display case explaining wartime difficulty and austerity in Norway. Red knit caps were worn by civilians to show solidarity with the resistance—until the hats were outlawed by Nazi officials. In the same case, notice the shoes made of fish skin, and the little row of *erstatning* (ersatz, or replacement) products. With the Nazi occupation, Norway lost its trade partners, and had to improvise.

You'll also learn about the military actions against the occupation. British-trained special forces famously blew up a strategic heavy water plant (a key part of the Nazis' atomic bomb program)—still fondly recalled by Norwegians, and immortalized in the not-so-accurate 1965 Kirk Douglas film *The Heroes of Telemark*. Nearby, see the case of crude but effective homemade weapons, and the German machine used to locate clandestine radio stations. Exhibits explain how the country coped with 350,000 occupying troops; how airdrops equipped a home force of 40,000 so they were ready to coordinate with the Allies when liberation was imminent; and the happy day when the resistance army came out of the forest, and peace and freedom returned to Norway. Liberation day was May 8, 1945...but it took a few days to pull together the celebration, which coincided neatly with the 17th of May—Constitution Day. (That's partly why May 17 is still celebrated so fiercely today.)

Back **upstairs,** notice the propaganda posters trying to recruit Norwegians to the Nazi cause and "protect the eastern border" from the Soviets and communism. A more recent addition to the museum (downstairs) considers the many Norwegians who did choose to cooperate with (and profit from) the Nazis.

The museum is particularly poignant because many of the patriots featured inside were executed by the Germans right outside the museum's front door; a **stone memorial** marks the spot. (At war's end, the traitor Vidkun Quisling was also executed at the fortress, but at a different location.)

Akershus Castle

Although it's one of Oslo's oldest buildings, the castle overlooking the harbor is mediocre by European standards; the big, empty rooms recall Norway's medieval poverty. The first fortress here was built by Norwegians in 1299. It was rebuilt much stronger by the Danes in 1640 so the Danish king (Christian IV) would have a suitable and safe place to stay during his many visits. When Oslo was rebuilt in the 17th century, many of the stones from the first Oslo cathedral were reused here, in the fortress walls.

Cost and Hours: 100 NOK, includes audioguide; Mon-Sat 10:00-16:00, Sun from 12:00; Sept-April Sat-Sun 12:00-17:00 only, closed Mon-Fri; tel. 23 09 35 53. Note that renovation work may affect these hours or close the castle; check locally.

Visiting the Castle: From the old kitchen, where the ticket desk and gift shop are located, you'll follow a one-way circuit of rooms open to the public. Descend through a secret passage to the dungeon, crypt, and royal tomb. Emerge behind the altar in the chapel, then walk through echoing rooms including the Daredevil's Tower, Hall of Christian IV (with portraits of Danish kings of Norway on the walls), and Hall of Olav V.

Old Christiania

In the mid-1600s, the ruling Danes had the original Oslo leveled and built a more modern grid-planned city. They built with stone so it wouldn't burn, and located the new city just below the castle so it was easier to control and defend. They named it Christiania, after their king. The checkerboard neighborhood between the castle and the cathedral today—aptly called Kvadraturen—marks that original Christiania town. There's little to see, but curious tourists can wander through this sleepy zone (between the castle and Karl Johans Gate) and look for some 17th-century buildings. Bits of Christiania's original Dutch Renaissance-style buildings survive. (Norwegian builders, accustomed to working with wood, lacked skill with stone, so the Danes imported Dutch builders.) The area's main square, Christiania Torv (near the recommended Café Skansen), is marked by a modern fountain called "The Glove." The sculpture of Christian IV's glove points as if to indicate, "This is where we'll build my city." The old City Hall, now the Gamle Raadhus restaurant, survives.

ON THE WATERFRONT, NEAR THE TRAIN STATION

▲Oslo Opera House (Operahuset Oslo)

Opened in 2008, Oslo's striking Opera House was a huge hit. The building angles up from the water on the city's eastern harbor, across the highway from the train station. Its boxy, low-slung, glass center holds a state-of-the-art 1,400-seat main theater with a 99-piece orchestra "in the pit," which can rise to put the orchestra "on the pedestal." The season is split between opera and ballet.

Cost and Hours: Foyer and café/restaurant open Mon-Fri 10:00-23:00, Sat from 11:00, Sun 12:00-22:00.

Tours: Year-round, you can take a fascinating 50-minute guided tour of the stage, backstage area, and architecture (100 NOK; usually 3 tours/day in English—generally at 11:00, 12:00, and 14:00; reserve online at www.operaen.no, tel. 21 42 21 00).

Daytime Mini-Concerts: For a few weeks in the summer, the Opera House offers sporadic one-hour daytime "Concerts at the Balcony" (70 NOK, many days in late July at 14:00).

Getting There: You'll find it on Bjørvika, the next harbor over from City Hall and Akershus Fortress—just below the train station.

Visiting the Opera House: Information-packed, 50-minute tours explain what makes this one of the greenest buildings in Europe and why Norwegian taxpayers helped foot the half-billion-dollar cost for this project—to make high culture (ballet and opera) accessible to the younger generation and a stratum of society who normally wouldn't care. You'll see a workshop employing 50 people who hand-make costumes, and learn how the foundation of 700 pylons set 40 or 50 meters deep support the jigsaw puzzle of wood, glass, and 36,000 individual pieces of marble. The construction masterfully integrates land and water, inside and outside, nature and culture.

The jutting white marble planes of the Opera House's roof double as a public plaza. You feel a need to walk all over it. The

Opera House is part of a larger harbor-redevelopment plan that includes rerouting traffic into tunnels and turning a once-derelict industrial zone into an urban park. If you hike all the way to the top of the building (watch your footing—it's slippery when wet), you can peek over the back railing to see the high-rise development known as the "Barcode Project." The new Munch Museum (likely opening in 2020) resides in the futuristic Lambda building on the adjacent pier.

DOWNTOWN MUSEUMS
▲▲▲National Gallery (Nasjonalgalleriet)

While there are many schools of painting and sculpture displayed in Norway's National Gallery, focus on what's uniquely Norwegian. Paintings come and go in this museum, but you're sure to see plenty that showcase the harsh beauty of Norway's landscape and people. A thoughtful visit here gives those heading into the mountains and fjord country a chance to pack along a little of Norway's cultural soul. Tuck these images carefully away with your goat cheese—they'll sweeten your explorations.

The gallery also has several Picassos, a noteworthy Impressionist collection, a Van Gogh self-portrait, and some Vigeland statues. Its many raving examples of Edvard Munch's work, including one of his famous *Scream* paintings, make a trip to the Munch Museum unnecessary for most. It has about 50 Munch paintings in its collection, but only about a third are on display. Be prepared for changes, but don't worry—no matter what the curators decide to show, you won't have to scream for Munch's masterpieces.

Cost and Hours: 100 NOK, free on Thu; Tue-Fri 10:00-18:00, Thu until 19:00, Sat-Sun 11:00-17:00, closed Mon; obligatory lockers, Universitets Gata 13, tel. 21 98 20 00, www.nasjonalmuseet. no. Pick up the guidebooklet to help navigate the collection.

Tours: Invest 50 NOK in the thoughtful, evocative audio-guide, which supplements my self-guided tour.

Eating: The richly ornamented **$$ French Salon café** offers an elegant break (150-NOK lunches).

Closure and Move: The gallery is scheduled to close in September 2019, when the collection will move to a new purpose-built home in the new National Museum near the harbor, behind the Nobel Peace Center (not far from City Hall, likely opening in 2020). Confirm details locally. As the museum is in flux, you may find even more changes to the collection than usual.

National Gallery—Upper Floor

❶ DAHL — View from Stalheim

❷ DAHL — Hellefossen near Hokksund

❸ FEARNLEY — The Labro Falls at Kongsberg

❹ TIDEMAND & GUDE — Bridal Procession on the Hardangerfjord

❺ PETERSSEN — Christian II

❻ KROHG — Sick Girl

❼ KROHG — Albertine to See the Police Surgeon

❽ WERENSKIOLD — Peasant Burial

❾ SOHLBERG — Winter Night in the Mountains

❿ MUNCH — Self Portrait with a Cigarette

⓫ MUNCH — Madonna

⓬ MUNCH — The Scream

⓭ MUNCH — Dance of Life

⓮ MUNCH — Puberty

⓯ MUNCH — The Sick Child

➲ Self-Guided Tour

This easy-to-handle museum gives an effortless tour back in time and through Norway's most beautiful valleys, mountains, and fjords, with the help of its Romantic painters (especially Johan Christian Dahl).

• *Go up the stairs, pausing at the top of the...*

Stairwell—Norway Past and Present

Two historical paintings by Christian Krohg hang in the stairwell, offering a helpful backstory to the collection we're about to see. Over the stairs is a big, dynamic painting of Viking explorer **Leiv Eiriksson** (Leif Eriksson), on rough seas. He was born in Iceland, lived most of his life in Greenland, and was very likely the first European to set foot in the Americas (specifically, today's Newfoundland). At this point, the Vikings rule one of the biggest territories on earth...and it's about to get that much bigger.

Now turn right, as we tumble from Norway's high-water mark

to its lowest: *Struggle for Survival* (1889). Desperately poor, grub-by, almost animal-like Norwegian children and mothers clamor for a scrap of food. This is the context of much of the art you're about to see: Norway is part of Denmark for four centuries, then part of Sweden for nearly a century. Norwegians felt like second-class citizens in their own homeland...their cities weren't really theirs. Seeking a sense of national pride, they looked to nature: fjords, mountains, villages.

• *To see some of that, step into Room 24, and turn left into Room 13.*

Landscape Paintings and Romanticism

Landscape painting has always played an important role in Nor-wegian art, perhaps because Norway provides such an awesome and varied landscape to inspire artists. The style reached its peak during the Romantic period in the mid-1800s, which stressed the beauty of unspoiled nature. (This passion for landscapes sets Nor-way apart from Denmark and Sweden.) After 400 years of Dan-ish rule, the soul of the country was almost snuffed out. But with semi-independence and a constitution in the early 1800s, there was a national resurgence. Even though the cities and palaces still felt foreign (which is why you'll rarely see those depicted in art), Norwegians could claim their countryside as their own. Romantic paintings featuring the power of Norway's natural wonders and the toughness of its salt-of-the-earth folk came into vogue.

• *On the right wall as you enter is...*

❶ **Johan Christian Dahl**, *View from Stalheim*, **1842:** This painting epitomizes the Norwegian closeness to nature. It shows a view very similar to the one that 21st-century travelers enjoy on their Norway in a Nutshell excursion (see that chapter): mountains, rivers, and farms clinging to hillsides. Painted in 1842, it's quint-essential Romantic style. Nature rules—the background is as de-tailed as the foreground, and you are sucked in.

Johan Christian Dahl (1788-1857) is considered the father of Norwegian Romanticism. Romantics such as Dahl (and Turner, Beethoven, and Lord Byron) put emotion over rationality. They reveled in the power of nature—death and pessimism ripple through their work, though in this scene a double rainbow and a splash of sunlight give hope of a better day. The birch tree—stand-ing boldly front and center—is a standard symbol for the politically downtrodden Norwegian people: hardy, weathered, but defiantly sprouting new branches. In the mid-19th century, Norwegians were awakening to their national identity. Throughout Europe, na-tionalism and Romanticism went hand in hand.

Find the farm buildings huddled near the cliff's edge, smoke rising from chimneys, and the woman in traditional dress tending her herd of goats, pausing for a moment to revel in the glory of nature. It reminds us that these farmers are hardworking, independent, small landowners. There was no feudalism in medieval Norway. People were poor...but they owned their own land. You can almost taste goat cheese.

• *Look at the other works in Rooms 13 and 12. Dahl's paintings and those by his Norwegian contemporaries, showing heavy clouds and glaciers, repeat these same themes—drama over rationalism, nature pounding humanity. Human figures are melancholy. Norwegians, so close to nature, are fascinated by those plush, magic hours of dawn and twilight. The dusk makes us wonder: What will the future bring?*

In particular, focus on the painting to the right of the door marked 13.

❷ **Dahl, *Hellefossen near Hokksund*, 1838:** Another typical Dahl setting: romantic nature and an idealized scene. A fisherman checks on wooden baskets designed to catch salmon migrating up the river. In the background, a water-powered sawmill slices trees into lumber. Note another Dahl birch tree at the left, a subtle celebration of the Norwegian people and their labor.

• *Now continue into Room 12. On the right is...*

❸ **Thomas Fearnley, *The Labro Falls at Kongsberg*, 1837:** Man cannot control nature or his destiny. The landscape in this painting is devoid of people—the only sign of humanity is the jumble of sawn logs in the foreground. A wary eagle perched on one log seems to be saying, "While you can cut these trees, they'll always be mine."

• *Continue to the end of Room 12, and turn left into Room 14. On the left is...*

❹ **Adolph Tidemand and Hans Gude, *Bridal Procession on the Hardangerfjord*, 1848:** This famous painting shows the ultimate Norwegian scene: a wedding party with everyone decked out in traditional garb, heading for the stave church on the quintessential fjord (Hardanger). It's a studio work and a collaboration: Hans Gude painted the landscape, and Adolph Tidemand painted the people. Study their wedding  finery. This work trumpets the greatness of both the landscape and Norwegian culture.

• *Also in Room 14, on the opposite wall, is an example of...*

The Photographic Eye

At the end of the 19th century, Norwegian painters traded the emotions of Romanticism for more slice-of-life detail. This was the end of the Romantic period and the beginning of Realism. With the advent of photography, painters went beyond simple realism and into extreme realism.

❺ Eilif Peterssen, *Christian II*, 1875: The Danish king signs the execution order for the man who'd killed the king's beloved mistress. With camera-like precision, the painter captures the whole story of murder, anguish, anger, and bitter revenge in the king's set jaw and steely eyes.

• *Go through Room 15 and into Room 16. Take time to browse the paintings.*

Vulnerability

Death, disease, and suffering were themes seen again and again in art from the late 1800s. The most serious disease during this period was tuberculosis (which killed Munch's mother and sister).

❻ Christian Krohg, *Sick Girl*, 1880: Christian Krohg (1852-1925) is known as Edvard Munch's inspiration, but to Norwegians, he's famous in his own right for his artistry and giant personality. This extremely realistic painting shows a child dying of tuberculosis, as so many did in Norway in the 19th century. The girl looks directly at you. You can almost feel the cloth, with its many shades of white.

• *And just to the right of this painting, find...*

❼ Krohg, *Albertine to See the Police Surgeon*, c. 1885-1887: Krohg had a sharp interest in social justice. In this painting, Albertine, a sweet girl from the countryside, has fallen into the world of prostitution in the big city. She's the new kid on the Red Light block in the 1880s, as Oslo's prostitutes are pulled into the police clinic for their regular checkup. Note her traditional dress and the disdain she gets from the more experienced girls. Krohg has buried his subject in this scene. His technique requires the viewer to find her, and that search helps humanize the prostitute.

• *Facing these paintings in Room 16 is...*

❽ Erik Werenskiold, *Peasant Burial*, 1883-1885: While Monet and the Impressionists were busy abandoning the realistic style, Norwegian artists continued to embrace it. In this painting, you're invited to participate. A dead man's funeral is attended by a group of famers and peasants, but only one is a woman—the widow. Their faces speak volumes about the life of toil here. A com-

mon thread in Norwegian art is the cycle—the tough cycle—of life. There's also an interest in everyday experiences.
• *Continue through Room 17 and into Room 18.*

Atmosphere

Landscape painters were often fascinated by the phenomena of nature, and the artwork in this room takes us back to this ideal from the Romantic Age. Painters were challenged by capturing atmospheric conditions at a specific moment, since it meant making quick sketches outdoors, before the weather changed yet again.
• *On the right wall as you enter is...*

❾ Harald Sohlberg, *Winter Night in the Mountains*, 1914: Harald Sohlberg was inspired by this image while skiing in the

mountains in the winter of 1899. Over the years, he attempted to re-create the scene that inspired this remark: "The mountains in winter reduce one to silence. One is overwhelmed, as in a mighty, vaulted church, only a thousand times more so."
• *Follow the crowds into Room 19, the Munch room.*

Turmoil

Room 19 is filled with works by Norway's single most famous painter, Edvard Munch (see sidebar). Norway's long, dark winters and social isolation have produced many gloomy artists, but none gloomier than Munch. He infused his work with emotion and expression at the expense of realism. After viewing the paintings in general, take a look at these in particular (listed in clockwise order).

❿ Edvard Munch, *Self Portrait with a Cigarette*, 1895: This painting may not be on view, but the description is worth reading regardless, to set the context for the Munch collection. In this self-portrait, Munch is spooked, haunted—an artist working, immersed in an oppressive world. Indefinable shadows inhabit the background. His hand shakes as he considers his uncertain future. (Ironic, considering he created his masterpieces during this depressed period.) After eight months in a Danish clinic, he found peace—and lost his painting power. Afterward, Munch never again painted another strong example of what we love most about his art.

⓫ Munch, *Madonna*, 1894-1895: Munch had a tortured relationship with women. He never married. He dreaded and struggled with love, writing that he feared if he loved too much, he'd lose his

Edvard Munch (1863-1944)

Edvard Munch (pronounced "moonk") is Norway's most famous and influential painter. His life was rich, complex, and sad. His father was a doctor who had a nervous breakdown. His mother and sister both died of tuberculosis. He knew suffering. And he gave us the enduring symbol of 20th-century pain, *The Scream*.

He was also Norway's most forward-thinking painter, a man who traveled extensively through Europe, soaking up the colors of the Post-Impressionists and the curves of Art Nouveau. He helped pioneer a new style—Expressionism—using lurid colors and wavy lines to "express" inner turmoil and the angst of the modern world.

After a nervous breakdown in late 1908, followed by eight months of rehab in a clinic, Munch emerged less troubled—but a less powerful painter. His late works were as a colorist: big, bright, less tormented...and less noticed.

painting talent. This painting is a mystery: Is she standing or lying? Is that a red halo or some devilish accessory? Munch wrote that he would strive to capture his subjects at their holiest moment. His alternative name for this work: *Woman Making Love*. What's more holy than a woman at the moment of conception?

⑫ **Munch, *The Scream*, 1893:** Munch's most famous work shows a man screaming, capturing the fright many feel as the

human "race" does just that. The figure seems isolated from the people on the bridge—locked up in himself, unable to stifle his scream. Munch made four versions of this scene, which has become *the* textbook example of Expressionism. On one, he graffitied: "This painting is the work of a madman." He explained that the painting "shows today's society, reverberating within me...making me want to scream." He's sharing his internal angst. In fact, this Expressionist masterpiece is a breakthrough painting; it's angst personified.

⓭ Munch, *Dance of Life*, 1899-1900: In this scene of five dancing couples, we glimpse Munch's notion of femininity. To him, women were a complex mix of Madonna and whore. We see Munch's take on the cycle of women's lives: She's a virgin (discarding the sweet flower of youth), a whore (a jaded temptress in red), and a widow (having destroyed the man, she is finally alone, aging, in black). With the phallic moon rising on the lake, Munch demonizes women as they turn men into green-faced, lusty monsters.

⓮ Munch, *Puberty*, 1894-1895: One of the artist's most important non-*Scream* canvases reveals his ambivalence about women (see also his *Madonna*, earlier). This adolescent girl, grappling with her emerging sexuality, covers her nudity self-consciously. The looming shadow behind her—frighteningly too big and amorphous—threatens to take over the scene. The shadow's significance is open to interpretation—is it phallic, female genitalia, death, an embodiment of sexual anxiety...or Munch himself?

⓯ Munch, *The Sick Child*, 1896: The death of Munch's sister in 1877 due to tuberculosis likely inspired this painting. The girl's face melts into the pillow. She's becoming two-dimensional, halfway between life and death. Everything else is peripheral, even her despairing mother saying good-bye. You can see how Munch scraped and repainted the face until he got it right.

• *Our tour is over, but there's more to see in this fine collection. Take a break from Nordic gloom and doom by visiting Rooms 15 and 23 (adjoining each other, in the middle of the museum)—with works by Impressionist and Post-Impressionist artists...even Munch got into the spirit with his Parisian painting, titled* Rue Lafayette. *You'll see lesser-known, but still beautiful, paintings by non–Norwegian big names such as Picasso, Modigliani, Monet, Manet, Van Gogh, Gauguin, Renoir, and Cézanne.*

Near the National Gallery
Royal Palace (Slottet)
Set at the top of Karl Johans Gate, the Neoclassical Royal Palace is home to Norway's King Harald V and Queen Sonja. Completed in 1849, it was extensively (and expensively) renovated in 2001. To quell controversy the public is now invited inside each summer with a one-hour guided tour.

Cost and Hours: 135 NOK, English tours 4/day late June-mid-Aug, tickets go on sale in March and fill fast—it's smart to book in advance at www.ticketmaster.no, or by calling 81 53 31 33, www.kongehuset.no.

National Historical Museum (Historisk Museum)
Directly behind the National Gallery and just below the palace is a fine Art Nouveau building offering an easy (if underwhelming)

peek at Norway's history. It includes the country's top collection of Viking artifacts, displayed in low-tech, old-school exhibits with barely a word of English.

Cost and Hours: 100 NOK, same ticket covers Viking Ship Museum for 48 hours; open Tue-Sun 10:00-17:00, mid-Sept–mid-May 11:00-16:00; closed Mon year-round; Frederiks Gate 2, tel. 22 85 19 00, www.khm.uio.no.

Visiting the Museum: The ground floor has medieval and Viking Age artifacts from around Norway. Ogle the gorgeous carved doors from stave churches (with their filigree-like details). Look for the little door to the easy-to-miss Viking section, where you'll find the museum's hidden highlight: the only intact, authentic Viking helmet ever found in Scandinavia (with an eye mask; it's unceremoniously jammed into a crowded display case). Upstairs is an exhibit about life for the Sami (previously known to outsiders as Laplanders) and other Arctic cultures. It's fun to peek in the cutaway igloo for a glimpse at Inuit lifestyles. There's also a modest anthropological exhibit about indigenous peoples of the Americas. In this overview of the past, a few Egyptian mummies and Norwegian coins through the ages are tossed in for good measure.

FROGNER PARK

The sprawling Frogner Park anchors an upscale neighborhood of the same name, 1.5 miles west of the city center. Here you'll find a breathtaking sculpture park and two museums. The Frognerbadet swimming pool is nearby (see "Escapes from the City," later).

▲▲▲Vigeland Park

Within Oslo's vast Frogner Park is Vigeland Park, containing a lifetime of work by Norway's greatest sculptor, Gustav Vigeland

(see sidebar). In 1921, he made a deal with the city. In return for a great studio and state support, he'd spend his creative life beautifying Oslo with this sculpture garden. From 1924 until his death in 1943 he worked on-site, designing 192 bronze and granite statue groupings—600 figures in all, each nude and unique. Vigeland even planned the landscaping.

Today the park is loved and respected by the people of Oslo (no police, no fences—and no graffiti). At once majestic, hands-on, entertaining, and deeply moving, why this sculpture park isn't considered one of Europe's top artistic

Gustav Vigeland (1869-1943)

Gustav Vigeland's father was a carpenter in the city of Mandal, in southern Norway. Vigeland grew up carving wood, and showed promise. And so, as a young man, he went to Oslo to study sculpture, then supplemented his education with trips abroad to Europe's art capitals. Back home, he carved out a successful, critically acclaimed career feeding newly independent Norway's hunger for homegrown art.

During his youthful trips abroad, Vigeland had frequented the studio of Auguste Rodin, admiring Rodin's naked, restless, intertwined statues. Like Rodin, Vigeland explored the yin/yang relationship of men and women. Also like Rodin, Vigeland did not personally carve or cast his statues. Rather, he formed them in clay or plaster, to be executed by a workshop of assistants. Vigeland's sturdy humans capture universal themes of the cycle of life—birth, childhood, romance, struggle, child-rearing, growing old, and death.

sights, I can only guess. In summer, this is a tempting destination in the late afternoon—after the museums have closed and there's still plenty of daylight to go. (But if you want to visit the nearby Vigeland Museum, be aware that it closes at 17:00.) Vigeland Park is more than great art: It's a city at play. Appreciate its urban Norwegian ambience.

Cost and Hours: The garden is always open and free. The park is safe (cameras monitor for safety) and lit in the evening.

Getting There: Tram #12—which leaves from the central train station, Rådhusplassen in front of City Hall, Aker Brygge, and other points in town—drops you off right at the park gate (Vigelandsparken stop). Tram #19 (with stops along Karl Johans Gate) takes you to Majorstuen, a 10-minute walk to the gate (or you can change at Majorstuen to tram #12 and ride it one stop to Vigelandsparken).

Information and Services: For an illustrated guide and fine souvenir, consider the 120-NOK book in the **visitors center** (Besøkssenter) on your right as you enter. The modern **$$ cafeteria** has sandwiches and light meals (indoor/outdoor seating, daily 9:00-20:30 in summer, shorter hours off-season), plus books, gifts, and pay WCs.

➋ **Self-Guided Tour:** The park is huge, but this visit is a snap. Here's a quick, four-stop, straight-line, gate-to-monolith tour.

• *Begin by entering the park through the grand gates, from Kirkeveien (with the tram stop). In front of the visitors center, look at the...*

Gustav Vigeland Statue: Vigeland has his hammer and chisel in hand...and is drenched in pigeon poop. Consider his messed-up life. He lived with his many models. His marriages failed. His

children entangled his artistic agenda. He didn't age gracefully. He didn't name his statues, and refused to explain their meanings. While those who know his life story can read it clearly in the granite and bronze, I'd forget Gustav's troubles and see his art as observations on the bittersweet cycle of life in general—from a man who must have had a passion for living.

• *Now walk 100 yards toward the fountain and the pillar.*

Bridge: The 300-foot-long bridge is bounded by four granite columns: Three show a man fighting a lizard, the fourth shows a woman submitting to the lizard's embrace. Hmmm. (Vigeland was familiar with medieval mythology, where dragons represent man's primal—and sinful—nature.)

But enough lizard love; the 58 bronze statues along the bridge are a general study of the human body. They capture the joys of life (and, on a sunny day, so do the Norwegians and tourists filling the park around you). Many deal with relationships between people. In the middle, on the right, find the circular statue of a man and woman going round and round—perhaps the eternal attraction and love between the sexes. But directly opposite, another circle feels like a prison—man against the world, with no refuge.

On your left, see the famous *Sinnataggen,* the hot-headed little boy and a symbol of the park. (Notice his left hand is worn shiny from too many hand-holdings.) It's said Vigeland gave a boy chocolate and then took it away to get this reaction. Look below the angry toddler, to the lower terrace—with eight bronze infants circling a head-down fetus.

• *Continue through a rose garden to the earliest sculpture unit in the park.*

Fountain: Six giants hold a fountain, symbolically toiling with the burden of life, as water—the source of life—cascades steadily around them. Twenty tree-of-life groups surround the fountain. Four clumps of trees (on each corner) show humanity's relationship to nature and the seasons of life: childhood, young love, adulthood, and winter.

Take a quick swing through life, starting on the right with youth. In the branches you'll see a swarm of children (Vigeland

called them "geniuses"): A boy
sits in a tree, boys actively climb
while most girls stand by quietly, and a girl glides through the
branches wide-eyed and ready
for life...and love. Circle clockwise to the next stage: love
scenes. In the third corner, life

becomes more complicated: a sad woman in an animal-like tree, a
lonely child, a couple plummeting downward (perhaps falling out
of love), a man desperately clinging to his tree, and finally an angry
man driving away babies. The fourth corner completes the cycle, as
death melts into the branches of the tree of life and you realize new
geniuses will bloom.

The 60 bronze reliefs circling the basin develop the theme
further, showing man mixing with nature and geniuses giving the
carousel of life yet another spin. Speaking of another spin, circle
again and follow these reliefs.

The pattern in the pavers surrounding the basin is a maze—
life's long and winding road with twists, dead ends, frustrations,
and, ultimately, a way out. If you have about an hour to spare, enter
the labyrinth (on the side nearest the park's entrance gate, there's a
single break in the black border) and follow the white granite path
until (on the monolith side) you finally get out. (Tracing this path
occupies older kids, affording parents a peaceful break in the park.)
• *Or you can go straight up the steps to the...*

Monolith: The centerpiece of the park—a teeming monolith
of life surrounded by 36 groups of granite statues—continues Vige-

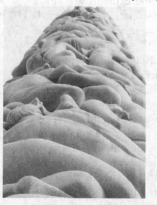

land's cycle-of-life motif. The figures are
hunched and clearly earthbound, while
Vigeland explores a lifetime of human
relationships. At the center, 121 figures
carved out of a single block of stone rock-
et skyward. Three stone carvers worked
daily for 14 years, cutting Vigeland's full-
size plaster model into the final 180-ton,
50-foot-tall erection.

Circle the plaza, once to trace the
stages of life in the 36 statue groups, and a
second time to enjoy how Norwegian kids
relate to the art. The statues—both young
and old—seem to speak to children.

Vigeland lived barely long enough to see his monolith raised.
Covered with bodies, it seems to pick up speed as it spirals skyward. Some people seem to naturally rise. Others struggle not to
fall. Some help others. Although the granite groups around the

monolith are easy to understand, Vigeland left the meaning of the monolith itself open. Like life, it can be interpreted many different ways.

From this summit of the park, look a hundred yards farther, where four children and three adults are intertwined and spinning in the Wheel of Life. Now, look back at the entrance. If the main gate is at 12 o'clock, the studio where Vigeland lived and worked—now the Vigeland Museum—is at 2 o'clock (see the green copper tower poking above the trees). His ashes sit in the top of the tower in clear view of the monolith. If you liked the park, visit the Vigeland Museum (described next), a delightful five-minute walk away, for an intimate look at the art and how it was made.

▲▲Vigeland Museum

This palatial city-provided studio was Gustav Vigeland's home and workplace for the last two decades of his life. The high south-facing

windows provided just the right light. Vigeland, who had a deeply religious upbringing, saw his art as an expression of his soul. He once said, "The road between feeling and execution should be as short as possible." Here, immersed in his work, Vigeland supervised his craftsmen like a father, from 1924 until his death in 1943.

Today it's filled with plaster casts and studies of many of the works you'll see in the adjacent park—shedding new light on that masterpiece, and allowing you to see familiar pieces from new angles. It also holds a few additional works, and explains Vigeland's creative (and technical) process. While his upstairs apartment is usually closed to the public, it is open a few times a year—check the website to find out when.

Cost and Hours: 80 NOK; Tue-Sun 10:00-17:00, Sept-April 12:00-16:00, closed Mon year-round; bus #20 or tram #12 to Frogner Plass, Nobels Gate 32, tel. 23 49 37 00, www.vigeland. museum.no.

Visiting the Museum: It's all on one floor, roughly arranged chronologically, which you'll see in an easy clockwise loop. **Rooms I-III** explain Vigeland's development, including his early focus on biblical themes. In *Accused* (1891), Cain flees with his family, including their dog. But gradually, Vigeland grew more interested in the dynamics that dictate relationships in families, and between men and women. In these first rooms, look for two particularly touching sculptures in marble (a medium you won't often see used by Vigeland): *Mother and Child* (1909) and *Young Man and Woman* (1906).

Room IV is a long hall of portrait busts, which Vigeland often created without payment—he considered this task an opportunity to practice. While most of the busts don't depict famous people, you will see King Oscar II and Arctic explorer Fridtjof Nansen. **Room V** continues this theme, with a few portraits (mostly full-body) of more recognizable figures: Beethoven, Ibsen, Wergeland, Bjørnson.

Room VI, with a 1942 self-portrait, explains the process by which Vigeland created his statues. See his tools displayed in a case, and read the explanation: Using the "sand casting" method, Vigeland would make a small plaster model, which guided his workers in creating a metal "skeleton." Vigeland would then bring the skeleton to life with soft clay—which he enjoyed using because its pliability allowed him to be spontaneous in his creativity. Once the clay piece was finished, plaster and sand were used to create a plaster cast, used for the final bronze piece. For his stone works, they used a "pointing machine" to painstakingly measure the exact nuances of Vigeland's contours. Examples of using both methods (including five different versions of the famous "angry baby" bronze) are displayed around the room.

Room VII holds temporary exhibits, while **Room VIII** features the full-sized plaster models for the park's bronze fountain. The large **Room IX** has more pieces from the park, including a one-fifth-scale model of the fountain (used to win the Oslo City Council's support for the project) and the four dragon statues that top the bridge's pillars (high up and difficult to see in the park, but fascinating up close).

Room X is the dramatic climax of the museum, with a model of the entire park, and the life-size plaster models for the Monolith—in three pieces, making it easy to scrutinize the details. You'll also see wrought-iron chained dragons—originally designed as a feature for the park gates—and several plaster models for the statues that surround the Monolith. Notice the many little "freckles" on these statues, left behind by the pointer used by craftsmen to replicate Vigeland's work. The museum finishes with more temporary exhibits (in Rooms XI and XII).

Nearby: Across the street from the Vigeland Museum is the **Oslo City Museum** (Oslo Bymuseum)—a modest, hard-to-be-thrilled-about exhibit that tells the story of Oslo. For a quick overview of the city while escaping the rain, watch the 15-minute English video (free, Tue-Sun 11:00-16:00, closed Mon, in Frogner Manor Farm across street from Vigeland Museum, tel. 23 28 41 70, www.oslomuseum.no).

BYGDØY NEIGHBORHOOD

This thought-provoking and exciting cluster of sights, worth ▲▲, is on a parklike peninsula just across the harbor from downtown Oslo. It provides a busy and rewarding half-day (at a minimum) of sightseeing.

Here, within a short walk, are six major sights (listed in order of importance): the **Norwegian Folk Museum,** an open-air museum with traditional wooden buildings from all corners of the country, a stave church, and a collection of 20th-century urban buildings; the **Viking Ship Museum,** showing off the best-preserved Viking ships in existence; the **Fram Museum,** showcasing the modern Viking spirit with the *Fram,* the ship of Arctic-exploration fame, and the *Gjøa,* the first ship to sail through the Northwest Passage; the **Kon-Tiki Museum,** starring the *Kon-Tiki* and the *Ra II,* in which Norwegian explorer Thor Heyerdahl proved that early civilizations—with their existing technologies—could have crossed the oceans; the **Norwegian Maritime Museum,** interesting mostly to old salts, has a wonderfully scenic movie of Norway; and the **Norwegian Holocaust Center,** memorializing the Holocaust in Norway.

Getting to Bygdøy: Sailing from downtown to Bygdøy is fun, fast, and gets you in a seafaring mood. Ride the Bygdøy **ferry**—marked *Public Ferry Bygdøy Museums*—from pier 3 in front of City Hall (45 NOK one-way at the ticket desk, 60 NOK on board; 65 NOK round-trip at the ticket desk; covered by Oslo Pass; 3/hour, 10-15-minute trip; runs mid-May-Aug daily 8:55-20:55, fewer sailings spring and fall, doesn't run mid-Oct-mid-March). Boats generally leave from downtown at :05, :25, and :45 past each hour. In summer, avoid the nearby (much more expensive) tour boats.

For a less memorable approach, you can take **bus** #30 (from train station, National Theater, or in front of City Hall, direction: Bygdøy; 20-minute trip).

Returning to Oslo: Note that after 17:00, bus and boat departures back to downtown are sparse. If returning by ferry, get to the dock a little early—otherwise the boat is likely to be full, and you'll have to wait for the next sailing.

Getting Around Bygdøy: The Norwegian Folk and Viking Ship museums are a 10-minute walk from the ferry's first stop (Dronningen). The other boating museums (Fram, Kon-Tiki, and Maritime) are at the second ferry stop, in an area called Bygdøynes. The Holocaust Center is off Fredriksborgveien, about halfway between these two museum clusters. All Bygdøy sights are within

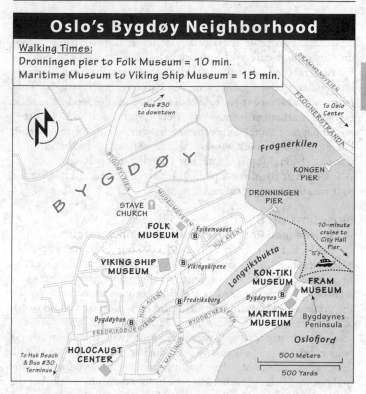

Oslo's Bygdøy Neighborhood

Walking Times:
Dronningen pier to Folk Museum = 10 min.
Maritime Museum to Viking Ship Museum = 15 min.

a pleasant (when sunny) 15-minute walk of each other. The walk gives you a picturesque taste of suburban Oslo.

City bus #30 connects the sights four times hourly in this order: Norwegian Folk Museum, Viking Ship Museum, Kon-Tiki Museum, Norwegian Holocaust Center. (For the Holocaust Center, you'll use the Bygdøyhus stop a long block away; tell the bus driver you want the stop for the "HL-Senteret.") The bus turns around at its final stop (Huk), then passes the sights in reverse order on its way back to the city center.

Planning Your Day: If the weather's good, hit the Folk Museum first (before it gets too hot). If it's ugly out—but may get better—begin with the mostly indoor boat museums at Bygdøynes. The marginally interesting Holocaust Center is a bit of a detour, and skippable if you're short on time. The Bygdøynes museums offer a 10 percent discount if you buy tickets for all three at the same time; decide before you buy your first ticket, and save a few bucks. The major museums all have free lockers, Wi-Fi, and WCs.

Eating at Bygdøy: Each of the museum areas has **$** food options. At the boat museum cluster (Bygdøynes), you'll find the **Framheim Café** inside the Fram Museum; the little **Cargo Café**

window with hot dogs and ice cream outside the Kon-Tiki Museum; and two more substantial eateries at the Maritime Museum: an **indoor café** with sandwiches and soup, and the outdoor **Fjordterrassen Café,** with hot dogs and deep-fried fish and veggie burgers, and tables overlooking the harbor. The Norwegian Folk Museum has a decent **Kafe Arkadia** at its entrance, and a fun little **farmers market** stall across the street (produce, drinks, yogurt— just enough to forage a healthy lunch). The Viking Ship Museum has an outdoor **snack window** selling shrimp and salmon sandwiches. The Holocaust Center has a small **café** upstairs.

Beach at Bygdøy: A popular beach is located at Huk, on the southwest tip of the peninsula.

Museums on Bygdøy
▲▲Norwegian Folk Museum (Norsk Folkemuseum)
Brought from all corners of Norway, 150 buildings have been re-assembled here on 35 acres. While Stockholm's Skansen was the first museum of this kind to open to the public, this collection is a bit older, started in 1881 as the king's private collection (and the inspiration for Skansen). The folk museum is most lively (and worth ▲▲▲) June through mid-August, when buildings are open and staffed with attendants in period clothing (who'll happily answer your questions—so ask many). And during peak season you'll also see craftspeople doing their traditional things and barnyard animals roaming about. Otherwise, the indoor museum is fine, but the park is just a pleasant walk past lots of locked-up log cabins.

Cost and Hours: 130 NOK, daily 10:00-18:00—grounds open until 20:00; mid-Sept-mid-May park open Mon-Fri 11:00-15:00, Sat-Sun until 16:00 but most historical buildings closed; Museumsveien 10, bus #30 stops immediately in front, tel. 22 12 37 00, www.norskfolkemuseum.no.

Visiting the Museum: Think of the visit in three parts: the park sprinkled with old buildings, the re-created old town, and the folk-art museum. As you enter, you'll cut through the courtyard with the museum to reach the open-air sections.

Upon arrival, pick up the site map and review the list of the day's activities, concerts, and guided tours (on a video screen near the ticket desk). In summer, there are two guided tours in English per day; the Telemark Farm hosts a small daily fiddle-and-folk-dance show; and a folk music-and-dance show is held each Sunday. If you don't take a tour, invest in a guidebook and ask questions of the informative attendants stationed in buildings throughout the park.

The **park** is loaded with mostly log-built, sod-roofed cabins from various parts of Norway (arranged roughly geographically). Be sure to go inside the buildings. The evocative Gol stave church, at the top of a hill at the park's edge, is worth the climb. Built in 1212 in Hallingdal and painstakingly reconstructed here, it has a classic design and, inside, beautiful-yet-primitive wood paintings on the apse walls (c. 1452). If you won't make it to a stave church elsewhere on your trip, this is a must. (For more on stave churches, see page 201.)

Back near the entrance building, the **old town** has a variety of homes and shops that focus on urban lifestyles. It's worth exploring the tenement building, in which you can explore intimate, fully furnished apartments from various generations and lifestyles—1905, 1930, 1950, 1979, and even a Norwegian-Pakistani apartment.

In the **museum,** the ground floor beautifully presents woody, colorfully painted, and exactingly carved folk art; traditional Norwegian knitting; and weapons. Upstairs are exquisite-in-a-peasant-kind-of-way folk costumes. I'd skip the sleepy collection of Norwegian church art (in an adjoining building). But don't miss the best Sami culture exhibit I've seen in Scandinavia (across the courtyard in the green building, behind the toy exhibit). Everything is thoughtfully explained in English. A new exhibit showing various slices of Oslo life is scheduled to open in 2019.

▲▲Viking Ship Museum (Vikingskiphuset)

In this impressive museum, you'll gaze with admiration at two finely crafted, majestic oak Viking ships dating from the 9th and

10th centuries, and the scant remains of a third vessel. Along with the two well-preserved ships, you'll see the bones of Vikings buried with these vessels and remarkable artifacts that may cause you to consider these notorious raiders in a different light. Over a thousand years ago, three things drove Vikings on their far-flung raids: hard economic times in their bleak homeland, the lure of prosperous and vulnerable communities to the south, and a mastery of the sea. There was a time when most frightened Europeans closed every prayer with, "And deliver us from the Vikings, Amen." Gazing up at the prow of one of these sleek, time-stained vessels, you can almost hear the screams and smell the armpits of those redheads on the rampage.

Cost and Hours: 100 NOK, ticket also covers the National

Historical Museum in downtown Olso for 48 hours; daily 9:00-18:00, Oct-April 10:00-16:00; Huk Aveny 35, tel. 22 13 52 80, www.khm.uio.no.

Visitor Information: The museum doesn't offer tours, but everything is well-described in English. You can use the free Wi-Fi to download a free, informative audio tour app. You probably don't need the little museum guidebook—it repeats exactly what's already posted on the exhibits.

Visiting the Museum: Focus on the two well-preserved ships, starting with the *Oseberg*, from A.D. 834. With its ornate carving and impressive rudder, it was likely a royal pleasure craft. It seems designed for sailing on calm inland waters during festivals, but not in the open ocean.

The *Gokstad*, from A.D. 950, is a practical working boat, capable of sailing the high seas. A ship like this brought settlers to the west of France (Normandy was named for the Norsemen). And in such a vessel, explorers such as Eric the Red hopscotched from Norway to Iceland to Greenland and on to what they called Vinland—today's Newfoundland in Canada. Imagine 30 men hauling on long oars out at sea for weeks and months at a time. In 1892, a replica of this ship sailed from Norway to America in 44 days to celebrate the 400th anniversary of Columbus *not* discovering America.

You'll also see the ruins of a third vessel, the **Tune Ship** (c. A.D. 910), which saw service only briefly before being used as the tomb for an important chieftain. In this hall, every 20 minutes, the lights dim and a wrap-around film plays on the walls around the ship for five minutes—with dramatic virtual footage of the Vikings and their fleet.

The ships tend to steal the show, but don't miss the hall displaying **jewelry and personal items** excavated along with the ships. The ships and related artifacts survived so well because they were buried in clay as part of a gravesite. Many of the finest items were not actually Viking art, but goodies they brought home after raiding more advanced (but less tough) people. Still, there are lots of actual Viking items, such as metal and leather goods, that give insight into their culture. Highlights are the cart and sleighs, ornately carved with scenes from Viking sagas.

▲▲▲Fram Museum (Frammuseet)

Under its distinctive A-frame roof, this museum holds the 125-foot, steam- and sail-powered ship that took modern-day Vikings Roald Amundsen and Fridtjof Nansen deep into the Arctic and Antarctic, farther north and south than any vessel had gone before. In an adjacent A-frame is Amundsen's *Gjøa,* the first ship to sail through the Northwest Passage. Together, the exhibit spins a fascinating tale of adventure, scientific exploration, and human determination...all at subzero temperatures.

Cost and Hours: 100 NOK; daily June-Aug 9:00-18:00, May and Sept 10:00-17:00, Oct and March-April until 16:00; Nov-Feb Mon-Fri 10:00-15:00, Sat-Sun until 16:00; Bygdøynesveien 36, tel. 23 28 29 50, www.frammuseum.no.

Visiting the Museum: Stepping into the museum, you're immediately bow-to-bow with the 128-foot *Fram.* Before diving in, remember that there are two parts to the museum: The *Fram,* which you're looking at, and to the left through a tunnel, the smaller *Gjøa.* I'd see the *Gjøa* first, because it's a better lead-up to the main event, and because it features a short film that's a fine introduction to the entire museum.

Crossing through the tunnel to the *Gjøa,* you'll learn about the search for the Northwest Passage (that long-sought-after trade route through the Arctic from the Atlantic to the Pacific). Exhibits tell the story of how Roald Amundsen and a crew of six used this motor- and sail-powered ship to successfully navigate the Northwest Passage (1903-1906). Exhibits describe their ordeal as well as other Arctic adventures, such as Amundsen's 1925 flight to 88 degrees north (they had to build a runway out of ice to take off and return home); and his 1926 airship (zeppelin) expedition from Oslo over the North Pole to Alaska. This section also features a 100-seat cinema showing an excellent 15-minute film about the exploration of the earth's polar regions (shows every 15 minutes).

Now return to the *Fram,* and peruse the exhibits—actual artifacts and profiles of the brave explorers and their crew. The upper floor focuses on Nansen's voyages to the North Pole on the *Fram,* including an early kayak, a full-size stuffed polar bear, and a model of the ship. Here you can cross a gangway to explore the *Fram*'s claustrophobic but fascinating interior. A simulated "Northern Lights Show," best viewed from the *Fram*'s main deck, is presented every 20 minutes.

Exhibits on the middle floor focus on Admundsen, who picked up where Nansen left off and explored the South Pole. You'll see an actual dogsled Admundsen's team used, and a small model of the motorized sled used by the rival Scott expedition. Also featured are a tent like the one Amundsen used, reconstructed shelves from his Arctic kitchen, models of the *Fram,* and a "polar simulator" plunging visitors into a 15° Fahrenheit environment.

The Fram Museum: From Pole to Pole

The Fram Museum tells the tale of two great Norwegian explorers, Fridtjof Nansen and Roald Amundsen.

Early polar explorers focused on the Northwest Passage, believing the Arctic could hold a highly lucrative trade route between the Atlantic and the Pacific oceans. Englishman John Franklin famously led a failed expedition looking for the Northwest Passage in 1845; two ships and 129 men were never seen again. Many others attempted and failed—more than a thousand sailors were lost in the search.

A generation later, with the Northwest Passage conquered by Amundsen, explorers (inspired by tales of Franklin and his ilk) became determined to reach the North Pole.

Fridtjof Nansen (1861-1930) prepared for his North Pole expedition by crossing the inland ice of Greenland in six weeks in 1888—hand-pulling sledges all the way—and then spent the winter learning from Inuit people he met. Nansen also commissioned the *Fram,* which was purpose-built for Arctic exploration—with its rounded hull, it was designed to be stuck in the ice without being crushed. (The downside was that it got tossed around in fierce waves.) It even had a windmill that could power electric lights. In the end, the *Fram* went on three major expeditions. In each one, the crew set out knowing they'd be living in subzero temperatures for three to five years.

The *Fram*'s maiden voyage was Nansen's search for the North Pole (1893-1896). He believed that, due to the natural drifting of the northern ice cap, a ship encased in ice would simply be carried by currents to the North Pole. For three years, the *Fram* drifted, trapped in the Arctic ice. While he didn't reach the North Pole, Nansen made better progress than anyone before him.

Then, **Otto Sverdrup** (1854-1930) took the helm of the *Fram* and advanced Nansen's progress (riding icebergs from 1898 until 1902), but he didn't make it all the way, either.

Finally, **Roald Amundsen** (1872-1928)—who had already successfully sailed the Northwest Passage—made plans to reach the North Pole in the *Fram* in 1910. Amundsen's crew (and financiers) believed he was heading north. But when word came that American explorer Frederick Cook had already accomplished that feat, Amundsen decided to head south instead. He sailed the *Fram* to Antarctica, and set out to reach the South Pole (1910-1912). Amundsen and his team were in a race to the pole with Englishman Robert Falcon Scott and his men, who had arrived at a different location aboard the ship *Terra Nova.* Amundsen beat Scott to the South Pole by about a month. And, unlike Scott, Amundsen made it home alive.

The *Fram* expeditions coincided with the nascent Norwegian independence movement—and became a proud patriotic symbol of the Norwegian people.

▲▲Kon-Tiki Museum (Kon-Tiki Museet)

Next to the *Fram* is a museum housing the *Kon-Tiki* and the *Ra II*, the ships built by the larger-than-life anthropologist, seafarer, and adventurer Thor Heyerdahl (1914-2002). Heyerdahl and his crew used these ships—constructed entirely without modern technology—to undertake tropical voyages many had thought impossible. Both ships are well-displayed and described in English. This museum—more lighthearted than the other boat-focused exhibits—puts you in a castaway mood.

Cost and Hours: 100 NOK, daily 9:30-18:00, March-May and Sept-Oct 10:00-17:00, Nov-Feb until 16:00, Bygdøynesveien 36, tel. 23 08 67 67, www.kon-tiki.no.

Background: Thor Heyerdahl believed that early South Americans could have crossed the Pacific to settle Polynesia. To prove his point, in 1947 Heyerdahl and five crewmates constructed the *Kon-Tiki* raft out of balsa wood, using only premodern tools and techniques—and adorned with a giant image of the sun god Kon-Tiki on the sail. They set sail from Peru on the tiny craft, surviving for 101 days on fish, coconuts, and sweet potatoes (which were native to Peru). About 4,300 miles later, they arrived in Polynesia. (While Heyerdahl proved that early South Americans *could* have made this trip, anthropologists doubt they did.) The *Kon-Tiki* story became a best-selling book and award-winning documentary (and helped spawn the "Tiki" culture craze in the US). Funded by the *Kon-Tiki* success, Heyerdahl went on to explore Easter Island (1955), and then turned his attention to another voyage—this time across the Atlantic. In 1970, Heyerdahl's *Ra II* made a similar 3,000-mile journey from Morocco to Barbados—on a vessel made of reeds—to prove that Africans could have populated the Americas.

Visiting the Museum: You'll see both the *Kon-Tiki* and the *Ra II*, and learn about Heyerdahl's other adventures (including Easter Island and the *Ra I*, which sank partway into its journey). Everything's well-described in English and very kid-friendly. In the basement, you'll see the bottom of the vessel with a life-size model of a whale shark (the largest fish on earth) and other marine life that the crew observed at sea. Nearby, a small theater continuously plays a 10-minute documentary about the voyage; every day at 12:00, they show the full-length (67-minute), Oscar-winning 1950 documentary film *Kon-Tiki*.

▲Norwegian Maritime Museum (Norsk Maritimt Museum)

If you're into the sea and seafaring, this museum is a salt lick, providing a wide-ranging look at Norway's maritime heritage through exhibits, art, and a panoramic film soaring over Norway's long and varied coastline.

Cost and Hours: 100 NOK; daily 10:00-17:00; Sept-mid-May Tue-Sun until 16:00, closed Mon; Bygdøynesveien 37, tel. 22 12 37 00, www.marmuseum.no.

Visiting the Museum: On the ground floor, you'll see a collection of small vessels, temporary exhibits, and an exhibit called *At Sea (Til Sjøs)*, exploring what life is like on the ocean, from Viking days to the present. If you appreciate maritime art, the collection in the gallery should float your boat. Downstairs is *The Ship (Skipet)*, tracing two millennia of maritime development. You'll see a 2,200-year-old dugout boat, heft various materials used to make ships, and pilot model boats in a little lagoon. Nearby, watch the wrap-around, 20-minute movie *The Ocean: A Way of Life* (look for *Supervideografen* signs). Dated but still dramatic—and quite relaxing—it swoops you scenically over Norway's diverse coast, showing off fishing townscapes, shiplap villages, industrial harbors, and breathtaking scenery from here all the way to North Cape in a comfy theater (starts at the top and bottom of the hour). Upstairs, past the library, the *Norway Is the Sea* exhibit considers how technology has transformed the way Norwegians earn their living at sea.

Norwegian Holocaust Center (HL-Senteret)

Located in the stately former home of Nazi collaborator Vidkun Quisling—whose name is synonymous with "complicit in atrocities"—this museum and study center offers a high-tech look at the racist ideologies that fueled the Holocaust. It's designed primarily for Norwegians, but you can borrow a tablet with English translations of the exhibits. The ground floor displays historical documents about the rise of anti-Semitism and personal effects from Holocaust victims. The exhibits continue downstairs; near the end of the exhibit, the names of 760 Norwegian Jews killed by the Nazis are listed in a bright, white room. Out front, the *Innocent Questions* glass-and-neon sculpture shows an old-fashioned punch card, reminding viewers of how the Norwegian puppet government collected seemingly innocuous information before deporting its Jews.

Cost and Hours: 70 NOK; daily 10:00-18:00; Sept-May Mon-Fri 10:00-16:00, Sat-Sun from 11:00; Huk Aveny 56—take bus #30 to the Bygdøyhus stop and follow brown *HL-Senteret* signs, tel. 22 84 21 00, www.hlsenteret.no.

GRÜNERLØKKA AND GRØNLAND DISTRICTS

Oslo's Grünerløkka district is trendy, and workaday Grønland is emerging as a fun spot. The Akers River bisects Grünerløkka. You can connect the dots by taking my self-guided "Up Akers River and Down Grünerløkka Walk."

In Cold Blood

Norway likes to think of itself as a quiet, peaceful nation on the edge of Europe after all, its legislators award the Nobel Peace Prize. So the events of July 22, 2011—when an anti-immigration fanatic named Anders Behring Breivik set off a car bomb in Oslo, killing eight, and then traveled to a summer camp where he shot and killed 69 young people and counselors—had a profound effect on the country's psyche.

Unlike other European nations, Norway had escaped 21st-century terrorism until Breivik's attack. When the public learned that the man behind the bombing and gunfire was a native Norwegian—dressed in a policeman's uniform—who hunted down his victims in cold blood, it became a national nightmare. Though Norwegians are often characterized as stoic, there was a huge outpouring of grief. Bouquets flooded the square in front of Oslo Cathedral.

Arrested after the shootings, Breivik was described by police as a gun-loving fundamentalist obsessed with what he saw as the "threat" of multiculturalism and immigration to Norwegian values. His targets were the Norwegian government and politically active youths—some only 14 years old—at an island summer camp sponsored by Norway's center-left party.

Norway has a big and growing immigrant community. More than 11 percent of today's citizens are not ethnic Norwegians, and a quarter of Oslo's residents are immigrants. These "new Norwegians" have provided a much-needed and generally appreciated labor force, filling jobs that wealthy natives would rather not do.

Horrified by Breivik's actions, many Norwegians went out of their way to make immigrants feel welcome after the attack. But there is some resentment in a country that is disinclined to be a melting pot. There have been scuffles between Norwegian gangs and immigrant groups. Another source of friction is the tough love Norwegians feel they get from their government compared to the easy ride offered to needy immigrants: "They even get pocket money in jail!"

The country strengthened its immigration laws in 2014, but Norway seems determined not to let the July 22 massacre poison its peaceful soul. Calls for police to start carrying weapons or to reinstate the death penalty were quickly rejected. "Breivik wanted to change Norway," an Oslo resident told me. "We're determined to keep Norway the way it was."

Akers River

This river, though only about five miles long, powered Oslo's early industry: flour mills in the 1300s, sawmills in the 1500s, and Norway's Industrial Revolution in the 1800s. A walk along the river not only spans Oslo's history, but also shows the contrast the city offers. The bottom of the river (where this walk doesn't go)—bordered by the high-rise Oslo Radisson Blu Plaza Hotel and the "Little Pakistan" neighborhood of Grønland—has its share of drunks and drugs, reflecting a new urban reality in Oslo. Farther up, the river valley becomes a park as it winds past decent-size waterfalls and red-brick factories. The source of the river (and Oslo's drinking water) is the pristine Lake Maridal, situated at the edge of the Nordmarka wilderness. The idyllic recreation scenes along Lake Maridal are a favorite for nature-loving Norwegians.

▲Grünerløkka

The Grünerløkka district is the largest planned urban area in Oslo. It was built in the latter half of the 1800s to house the legions of workers employed at the factories powered by the Akers River. The first buildings were modeled on similar places built in Berlin. (German visitors observe that there's now more turn-of-the-20th-century Berlin here than in present-day Berlin.) While slummy in the 1980s, today it's trendy. Locals sometimes refer to it as "Oslo's Greenwich Village." Although that's a stretch, it is a bustling area with lots of cafés, good spots for a fun meal, and few tourists.

Getting There: Grünerløkka can be reached from the center of town by a short ride on tram #11, #12, or #13, or by taking the interesting walk described next.

▲Trendy Riverside Oslo: Up Akers River and Down Grünerløkka Walk

While every tourist explores the harborfront and main drag of Oslo, few venture north into this neighborhood that evokes the Industrial Revolution. Once housing poor workers, it now attracts Norwegian hipsters and foodie tourists. This hike up the Akers River, finishing in the stylish Grünerløkka district, shines a different, more livable, and more appealing light on Oslo than the staid and touristy central zone. Allow about an hour at a brisk pace, including a fair bit of up and down and a 20-minute detour en route.

While there are a few "sights" along this walk, they're all skippable—making this a fun experience on a sunny early evening, after the museums have closed, when Oslo's young people are out enjoying their riverside park. (Several excellent dining opportunities are along or near this walk.)

Begin the walk by leaving Karl Johans Gate where it crests (alongside the Parliament building, by the T-bane stop), and head

OSLO

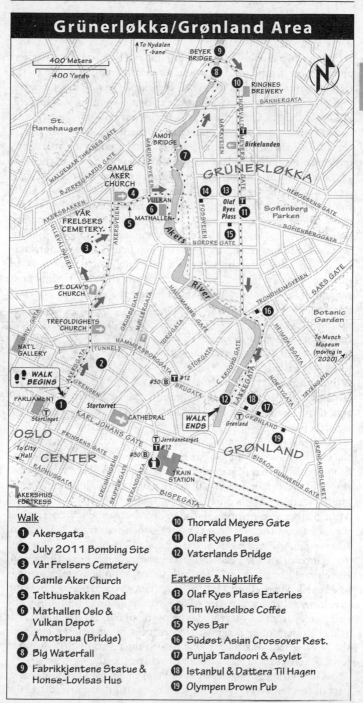

Grünerløkka/Grønland Area

400 Meters
400 Yards

↑To Nydalen
T-bane

BEYER
BRIDGE ⑨

St.
Hanshaugen

⑧

⑩ RINGNES
BREWERY

SANNERGATA

ÅMOT
BRIDGE

WALDEMAR THRANES GATE

MARIDALSVEIEN

BJERREGAARDS GATE

GAMLE
AKER
CHURCH ④

AKERSBAKKEN

VÅR
FRELSERS
CEMETERY

③

ULLEVÅLSVEIEN

AKERSVEIEN

⑤

VULKAN ⑥

MATHALLEN

⑦

Akers

THORVALD MEYERS GATE

MARKVEIEN

Birkelunden

GRÜNERLØKKA

⑭

FOSSVEIEN

⑬
Olaf
Ryes
Plass ⑪

⑮

NORDRE GATE

HØGESENS GATE

Sofienberg
Parken

SOFIENBERGGATA

River

HAUSMANNS GATE

ST. OLAV'S
CHURCH

TREFOLDIGHETS
CHURCH

UNIV. GATA

NAT'L
GALLERY

GRUBBEGATA

MØLLERGATA

HAMMERSBORGGATA

(TUNNEL)

TORGGATA

②

AKERSGATA

GRENSEN

WALK
BEGINS

PARLIAMENT
①

Stortinget

Stortorvet

KARL JOHANS GATE

CATHEDRAL

OSLO

PRINSENS GATE

DRONNINGENS GATE

To City
Hall

CENTER

RÅDHUSGATA

AKERSHUS
FORTRESS

SKIPPERGATE

STRANDGATA

#50 B T #12

BRUGATA

STORGATA

WALK
ENDS

Jernbanetorget
T #12

#50 B

i

TRAIN
STATION

BISPEGATA

TRONDHEIMSVEIEN

SARS GATE

Botanic
Garden

To Munch
Museum
(moving in
2020)

⑯

HEIMDALSGATA

C. KROGHS GATE

LAKKEGATA

⑫

NORBYGATA

⑱
⑰

T GRØNLAND

Grønland

URTEGATA

GRØNLAND

⑲

BISKOP GUNNERUS GATE

GRØNLANDSLEIRET

Walk

① Akersgata
② July 2011 Bombing Site
③ Vår Frelsers Cemetery
④ Gamle Aker Church
⑤ Telthusbakken Road
⑥ Mathallen Oslo &
   Vulkan Depot
⑦ Åmotbrua (Bridge)
⑧ Big Waterfall
⑨ Fabrikkjentene Statue &
   Honse-Lovisas Hus
⑩ Thorvald Meyers Gate
⑪ Olaf Ryes Plass
⑫ Vaterlands Bridge

Eateries & Nightlife

⑬ Olaf Ryes Plass Eateries
⑭ Tim Wendelboe Coffee
⑮ Ryes Bar
⑯ Südøst Asian Crossover Rest.
⑰ Punjab Tandoori & Asylet
⑱ Istanbul & Dattera Til Hagen
⑲ Olympen Brown Pub

up ❶ **Akersgata**—Oslo's "Fleet Street," lined with major newspaper companies.

After two blocks, at **Apotekergata,** you'll notice stout barriers blocking car traffic, and may see some construction work to the right. Continue into the big plaza. ❷ Behind the tall, blocky building, on Grubbegata, was where a car bomb went off on July 22, 2011 (see the "In Cold Blood" sidebar). Four buildings in the area suffered structural damage—including the long, low-lying one to the left (it's slated to be torn down and replaced; if it's still there, notice the Picasso mural on the side). You may also see (on the right as you face the big building) a small visitors center marked *22. julisenteret,* with photographs and information about the event. Along the street, notice the row of newspaper headlines under shattered glass. These were displayed in a newspaper office's window just down Akersgata, and have been preserved here—symbolizing how, for Oslo residents, time stood still on that fateful Friday morning.

Continuing straight past this somber site, you'll approach the massive brick Trefoldighets Church. Passing that, angle right onto the uphill street called **Akersveien,** along the side of the pointy-steepled St. Olav's Church. Hiking up this quiet street, you'll pass some traditional wooden houses. This is what much of "Christiania" (as Oslo was then called) looked like in the early 20th century; after World War II, most of this classic architecture was torn down in favor of modern construction.

After passing a square with a big pool, watch on the left for the entrance gate to the ❸ **Vår Frelsers (Our Savior's) Cemetery.** Stop at the big metal map just inside the gate to chart your course through the cemetery: You'll go through the light-green Æreslunden section—with the biggest plots and VIP graves (including Munch, Ibsen, Bjørnson, and many of the painters whose works you can see in the National Gallery)—then veer right to return to Akersveien, using the exit at the far end (#13).

Once oriented, head into the cemetery and bear right, into the elevated, walled area. The tall, green, canopied grave belongs to **Henrik Wergeland** (1808-1845), Norway's national poet and instrumental in creating its May 17th celebrations (including the children's parade). Wergeland is beloved not only for his poetry, but as a champion of civil rights: He spent his life fighting a clause in the Norwegian constitution that denied the rights of citizenship to Jews. A few years after his death, it was removed.

Go up the path to the right of Wergeland, into the uppermost part of the cemetery. Bear left with the path, then turn left again.

You'll pass the grave of painter Christian Krohg on your left, then reach the grave of the great Expressionist painter, **Edvard Munch** (1863-1944).

At Munch's 10 o'clock, walk under the drooping tree to the tall, obelisk-topped tomb—that of **Henrik Ibsen** (1828-1906), the great Norwegian playwright. Notice the hammer engraved in his tomb, an allusion to an Ibsen poem that spoke of a man chipping away inside a cave. This represents the determination of Ibsen the artist—who would walk the streets of Oslo, lost in thought, painstakingly crafting his next masterpiece in his mind.

Facing Ibsen's grave, turn left and walk toward the yellow house, exiting through the nearby gate. Turn left and walk 100 yards up Akersveien to the Romanesque ❹ **Gamle Aker Church** (from the 1100s)—the oldest building in Oslo. The church, which fell into ruins and has been impressively rebuilt, is rarely open and is pretty bare inside except for a pulpit and baptismal font from the 1700s.

On the little terrace just below the church, notice the **stone marker** indicating 639 kilometers to Nidaros Cathedral in Trondheim—the burial place of the great Norwegian king/saint, Olav II (995-1030). Olav was instrumental in Christianizing Norway, and his tomb in Trondheim was the focus of Norway's main medieval pilgrimage route. Walking half the length of Norway by foot offered forgiveness of sins. Like the Camino de Santiago in northern Spain, this pilgrimage route—long forgotten—is again en vogue, not only for spiritual reasons, but for anyone who simply wants a long walk with time to think. If you're up for a slightly longer walk than this one, the modern pilgrimage office is in the pink, half-timbered building across the street.

From the church, backtrack 20 yards, head left at the red hydrant, and go downhill on the steep ❺ **Telthusbakken** road toward the huge, gray former grain silos (now student housing). This delightful lane is lined with colorful old wooden houses: Constructed by people who were too poor to meet the no-wood fire-safety building codes within the city limits, so they built in what used to be suburbs. Also notice the little neighborhood garden patches on the right (through the fence).

At the bottom of Telthusbakken, you'll reach busy **Maridalsveien** street. Cross it and turn left to the trendy, modern Vulkan shopping center. Follow the driveway just in front of Vulkan as it curls down behind the building and to the recommended ❻ **Mathallen**—a foodie paradise, with more than a dozen stalls selling every kind of cuisine imaginable, and lots of outdoor tables filling an inviting plaza. (For more on Mathallen—including several great eateries here—see "Eating in Oslo," later.)

Find the **bridge** over the river at the near end of Mathallen (just follow the sound of the waterfall). You'll pop out into a beautiful little square. Turn left just before the playground, and walk along the river (with the silo housing on your right). At the waterfall, look down on your left to see fish ladders—which allow salmon and sea trout to make their way back upstream to spawn. Farther along, enjoy a little stretch of **boardwalk** that's cantilevered to stick out over the waterfall.

The lively **Grünerløkka** district is just to your right. But if you have 20 minutes and a little energy, detour upstream first, then hook back down. Continuing along the river, you'll pass a log bridge on your left, then a few rusty *lur* horns on your right, before you come to yet another **bridge**—this one loaded down with "love locks." Cross this bridge, turn right, and continue following the riverside path uphill.

Just above the next waterfall, cross ❼ **Åmotbrua,** a big white springy suspension footbridge from 1852 (moved here in 1958). Keep hiking uphill along the river.

At the base of the next ❽ **big waterfall,** cross over again to the large brick buildings, hiking up the stairs to the **Beyer Bridge** (above the falls) and ❾ *Fabrikkjentene,* a statue of four women laborers. They're pondering the textile factory where they and 700 others toiled long and hard. This gorge was once lined with the water mills that powered Oslo through its 19th-century Industrial Age boom.

Look back (on the side you just left) at the city's two biggest former textile factories. Once you could tell what color the fabric was being dyed each day by the color of the river. Just beyond them, between the two old factories, is a small light-gray building housing the **Labor Museum** (Arbeidermuseet, free; Tue-Sun 11:00-16:00, closed Mon; mid-Aug-late June Sat-Sun only; borrow English handout). Inside you'll see old photos that humanize the life of laborers there, and an 1899 photo exhibit by Edvard Munch's sister, Inger Munch.

The tiny red house just over and below the bridge—the **Honse-Lovisas Hus** cultural center—makes a good rest-stop (Tue-Sun 11:00-16:00, closed Mon, coffee and waffles). Continue past the red house to the red-brick Ringnes Brewery and follow ❿ **Thorvald Meyers Gate** downhill directly into the heart of Grünerløkka. First you'll go through a few blocks of modern, tidy apartment buildings. Then you'll pass a park (Birkelunden) with a tram stop and a gazebo. The next stretch of Thorvald Meyers Gate is lined with several inviting bars and cafés with outdoor seating. And a few short blocks farther is Grünerløkka's main square, ⓫ **Olaf Ryes Plass**—a happening place to grab a meal or drink (see "Eating in Oslo," later). Trams take you from here back to the center.

• *To continue exploring, you could keep going straight past Olaf Ryes Plass and continue walking until you reach a T-intersection with a busy road (Trondheimsveien). From there (passing the recommended Südøst Asian Crossover Restaurant) you can catch a tram back to the center, or drop down to the riverside path and follow it downstream to* ⓬ *Vaterlands bridge in the Grønland district. From here the train station is a five-minute walk down Stenersgata.*

Grønland

With the Industrial Revolution, Oslo's population exploded. The city grew from an estimated 10,000 in 1850 to 250,000 in 1900. The T-bane's Grønland stop deposits you in the center of what was the first suburb to accommodate workers of Industrial Age Oslo. If you look down side streets, you'll see fine 19th-century facades from this period. While the suburb is down-and-dirty like working-class and immigrant neighborhoods in other cities, Grønland is starting to emerge as a trendy place for eating out and after-dark fun. Locals know you'll get double the food and lots more beer for the kroner here (see "Eating in Oslo," later). If you'd enjoy a whiff of Istanbul, make a point to wander through the underground commercial zone at the Grønland station (easy to visit even if you're not riding the T-bane).

EAST OF DOWNTOWN
▲Edvard Munch Museum (Munch Museet)

The only Norwegian painter to have had a serious impact on European art, Munch (pronounced "moonk") is a surprise to many who visit this fine museum—displaying the emotional, disturbing, and powerfully Expressionistic work of this strange and perplexing man. In 2020, the museum is scheduled to move to a brand-new, state-of-the-art location in the Lambda building, on a little spit in the harbor next to the Opera House; before then, you may find it at its original location a mile east of downtown (Tøyengata 53; ride the T-bane to Tøyen or bus #20 to Munchmuseet). Either way, you'll see an extensive collection of paintings, drawings, lithographs, and photographs.

If the collection is still in the inconveniently located old building—or if it's out of view entirely during the transition—never fear. You can see an arguably better (more concise and thoughtfully arranged) collection of a dozen great Munch paintings, including *The Scream,* at the National Gallery (described earlier and also slated to soon close and move to a new location). In this time of flux, if you must see Munch, check at the TI for a location that's open. For more on Munch, see page 240.

Cost and Hours: Likely 100 NOK; daily 10:00-17:00, early May-early Oct until 16:00; confirm hours and location, tel. 23 49 35 00, www.munchmuseet.no.

▲Ekeberg Sculpture Park

In 2013, this piece of wilderness—on a forested hill over town, with grand city views—was transformed into a modern sculpture park. The art collector who financed the park loves women and wanted his creation to be a "celebration of femininity." While that vision was considered a bit ill-advised and was scaled back, the park is plenty feminine and organic.

Getting There: The park, always open and free, is a 10-minute tram ride southeast of the center (at the train station, catch tram #18 from platform E, or #19 from platform C; take either one in the direction of Ljabru). Ride just a few stops to Ekebergparken, right at the park's entrance.

Background: This location (literally "Oak Hill") is historic: There's evidence that Stone Age people lived here 7,000 years ago; a spot in this park is said to be where Edvard Munch was first inspired to paint *The Scream* (the viewpoint is marked *Utsiktspunkt Skrik* on maps); and in World War II, it held a Nazi military cemetery. In 2013, real estate tycoon Christian Ringnes (grandson of Norwegian brewery tycoons, who—like Coors in Denver and Carlsberg in Copenhagen—have lots of money for grand city projects) paid to turn the wooded area into a park. Norwegians tend to be skeptical of any fat cat giving something to the city...what's the real motive? They note that the park's popularity attracts more business to the fancy Ringnes-owned restaurant within. Others disagreed with the decision to replace nature with a man-made park. But critics are getting over their concerns, and today the people of Oslo are embracing this lovely 63-acre mix of forest and contemporary art.

Visiting the Park: A visit here involves lots of climbing on trails through the trees. While some people come for the statues (35 in all, including some by prominent artists such as Dalí, Rodin, Renoir, Vigeland, and Damien Hirst), others simply enjoy a walk in nature...and most agree that the views of Oslo's fast-emerging harbor scene (the Opera House and Barcode Project) may be the highlight. From the tram stop, hike up to the little cluster of buildings (including the visitors center, where you can pick up a map and join a 1.5-hour guided walk in English—see schedule at www.ekebergparken.com). In this area, you can see the first of the sculptures. For views and more art, keep heading up the hill to the restaurant...and beyond. Maps, suggesting various walking routes, are posted throughout the park.

Nearby: The faint **ruins of medieval Oslo** (free, always open) are between the harbor and Ekeberg Park—you can get a peek of them as you rumble past on the tram. While underwhelming for most, history buffs can spend a few minutes wandering a park with a few scant foundations of the 11th-century town—back when it was 3,000 people huddled around a big stone cathedral, seat of the Norwegian bishop. The arcade of a 13th-century Dominican monastery still stands (office of today's Lutheran bishop). To get there, hop off at the St. Halvards Plass tram stop; the ruins are across the street from the bus stop.

ESCAPES FROM THE CITY

Oslo is surrounded by a vast forest dotted with idyllic little lakes, huts, joggers, bikers, and sun-worshippers. One of the easiest escapes is simply to grab a beach towel and ride T-bane line #6 to its last stop, Sognsvann, and join the lakeside scene of Norwegians at play. A pleasant trail leads around the lake. To go farther afield, consider these options.

▲Holmenkollen Ski Jump and Ski Museum

The site of one of the world's oldest ski jumps (from 1892), Holmenkollen has hosted many championships, including the 1952 Winter Olympics. To win the privilege of hosting the 2011 World Ski Jump Championship, Oslo built a bigger jump to match modern ones built elsewhere—futuristic, cantilevered, and Olympic-standard. For skiers and winter-sports fans, a visit here is worth ▲▲.

Cost and Hours: 130-NOK ticket includes museum and viewing platform at top of jump; zipline-600 NOK, ski simulator-95 NOK; daily 9:00-20:00, May and Sept 10:00-17:00, Oct-April until 16:00; tel. 22 92 32 64, www.skiforeningen.no.

Getting There: T-bane line #1 gets you out of the city, through the hills, forests, and mansions that surround Oslo, and to the jump (4/hour, 25 minutes, direction: Frognerseteren). From the Holmenkollen station, you'll hike steeply up the road 15 minutes to the ski jump. (Getting back down is more like 10 minutes. Note T-bane departure times before you leave.) For more details—including a slightly longer, but more scenic, approach—see "Near the Ski Jump," later.

Visiting Holmenkollen: You'll enter the complex directly under the ramp. First you'll tour the **ski museum,** which traces the evolution of the sport, from 4,000-year-old rock paintings to crude

1,500-year-old wooden sticks to the slick and quickly evolving skis of modern times, including a fun exhibit showing the royal family on skis. You'll see gear from Roald Amundsen's famous trek to the South Pole, including the stuffed remains of Obersten ("The Colonel"), one of his sled dogs. Exhibits show off lots and lots of historic skis, gear, and video clips of great moments in skiing. Kids love the downhill ski-breeze simulator...basically a superpowered fan that blasts you in the face with fierce wind.

Near the end of the museum exhibits, look for the sign up to the **ski jump.** The tilted elevator takes you up to the top (on a sunny day, you may have to wait your turn for the elevator). Stand right at the starting gate, just like an athlete, and get a feel for this daredevil sport. The jump empties into a 30,000-seat amphitheater. Climb the stairs up to the rooftop deck; when it's clear, you'll see one of the best possible views of Oslo. While the view is exciting from the top, even more thrilling is the **zip-line** ride that sends daredevils screaming (literally) down over the jump to the landing area at the very bottom in 30 heart-stopping seconds.

As you ponder the jump, consider how modern athletes continually push the boundaries of their sport. The first champion here in 1892 jumped 21 meters (nearly 69 feet). In 1930 it took a 50-meter jump to win. In 1962 it was 80 meters, and in 1980 the champ cracked 100 meters. And, most recently, a jump of 140 meters (459 feet) took first place.

To cap your Holmenkollen experience, you can step into the **simulator** (or should I say stimulator?) and fly down the ski jump and ski in a virtual downhill race. My legs were exhausted after the five-minute terror. It's located at the lower level of the complex, near the entry of the ski museum. Outside, have fun watching a candid video of those shrieking inside.

Near the Ski Jump

For an easy downhill jaunt through the Norwegian forest, with a woodsy coffee or meal break in the middle, stay on the T-bane past Holmenkollen to the end of the line at Frognerseteren. From there, follow signs five minutes downhill on the gravel path to the recommended **Frognerseteren Hovedrestaurant,** a fine traditional eatery with a sod roof, reindeer meat on the griddle, an affordable cafeteria, and a city view over more sod rooftops.

From the restaurant, head down to the little sod-roofed village and look for the *Holmenkollen 1.6* sign to the right. Follow the wide, reddish gravel path through the woods (don't be distracted by the many side-paths, which are for mountain bikers—speaking of which, keep an eye out for bicycles zipping across your path). After about 20 minutes, you'll come to a paved roller-ski course (use the gravel path alongside), then pass between the wooden Holmenkollen village church and the top of a different ski jump (Midtstubak-ken). Soon you'll see the glassy swoop of Holmenkollen on your right; the entrance to the jump is at the base of the ramp.

On your way back to the Holmenkollen T-bane stop, you'll pass the recommended **Holmenkollen Restaurant,** with a similar view, but without Frognerseteren's pewter-and-antlers folk theme—or pretense. For details on both restaurants, see "Eating in Oslo," later.

Oslofjord Island Beaches

On a hot day, it seems the busy ferry scene at Oslo's harborfront is primarily designed to get locals out of their offices and onto the cool, green islands across the harbor so they can take a dip in the fjord, enjoy a little beach time, or simply stroll and enjoy views of the city. The larger Hovedøya offers good beaches, the ruins of a Cistercian monastery from 1147, some old cannons from the early 1800s, a marina, and a café. Little Gressholmen has good swimming, easy wandering to a pair of connected islands, and Gressholmen Kro, a rustic café dating to the 1930s.

Getting to the Islands: From Aker Brygge, catch ferry #B1, #B2, or #B3 to Hovedøya, or ferry #B4 to Gressholmen (both covered by city transit passes and Oslo Pass, ticket machines at dock). For schedules and fare info, check www.ruter.no.

Beach at Bygdøy: There's also a beach at Huk on the Bygdøy peninsula; take the direct boat from pier 3 in front of City Hall or bus #30. Once there, if you head left, you'll find a clothed beach, and to the right is a nude beach.

Mountain Biking

Mountain-biking possibilities are endless (as you'll discover if you go exploring without a good map). Consider taking your bike on the T-bane (free outside of rush hour, otherwise half the normal adult fare) to the end of line #1 (Frognerseteren, 30 minutes from National Theater) to gain the most altitude possible. Then follow the gravel roads (mostly downhill but with some climbing) past several dreamy lakes to Sognsvann at the end of T-bane line #6. Farther east, from Maridalsvannet, a bike path follows the Akers River all the way back into town. (The TI has details.) While Oslo isn't much on bike rentals, you can rent quality bikes at Viking Biking (listed under "Helpful Hints," earlier).

Amusement Parks and Wet Fun

The giant **Tusenfryd** amusement complex, just out of town, offers a world of family fun. It's sort of a combination Norwegian Disneyland/Viking Knott's Berry Farm, with more than 50 rides, plenty of entertainment, and restaurants (closed off-season, tel. 64

97 66 99, www.tusenfryd.no, ride bus #500 from behind Oslo's train station).

Oslo also offers a variety of water play. Located near Vigeland Park, the **Frognerbadet** has three outdoor pools, a waterslide, high dives, a cafeteria, and lots of young families (open mid-May-late Aug, closed off-season, Middelthunsgate 28, tel. 23 27 54 50).

Tøyenbadet, a modern indoor/outdoor pool complex with a 330-foot-long waterslide, also has a gym and sauna (northeast of downtown at Helgengate 90, tel. 23 30 44 70). Oslo's free botanical gardens are nearby.

NEAR OSLO
▲Eidsvoll Manor

During the Napoleonic period, control of Norway changed from Denmark to Sweden. This ruffled the patriotic feathers of Norway's Thomas Jeffersons and Ben Franklins, and on May 17, 1814, Norway's constitution was written and signed in this stately mansion (in the town of Eidsvoll Verk, north of Oslo). While Sweden still ruled, Norway had more autonomy than ever. To get ready for the bicentennial of Norway's constitution, the manor itself was restored to how it looked in 1814. A visitors center in the nearby Wergeland House tells the history of Norway's march to independence with 21st-century high-tech touches. Your ticket also includes an English tour, offered every day year-round at 12:30.

Cost and Hours: 125 NOK; daily 10:00-17:00; Sept-April Tue-Fri 10:00-15:00, Sat-Sun 11:00-16:00, closed Mon; tel. 63 92 22 10, www.eidsvoll1814.no.

Getting There: Eidsvoll is 45 minutes from Oslo by car (take road E-6 toward Trondheim, turn right at *Eidsvolls Bygningen* sign, free parking). You can also take the train to the Eidsvoll Verk station (2/hour, 30 minutes plus 20-minute walk). If you're driving from Oslo to Lillehammer and the Gudbrandsdal Valley, the manor is right on the way and worth a stop.

Drøbak

This delightful fjord town is just an hour from Oslo by bus (2/hour, bus #500 from behind the train station) or ferry (70 NOK one-way, 2/day weekends only spring and fall, also 1/day weekdays mid-June-mid-Aug, check at pier 1 or ask at Oslo TI). Consider taking the 1.25-hour boat trip down, exploring the town, having dinner, and taking the bus back (either trip is covered by a 2-zone, 53-NOK ticket). TI tel. 64 93 50 87, www.visitdrobak.no.

For holiday cheer year-round, stop into **Tregaarden's Julehuset** Christmas shop, right off Drøbak's main square (closed Christmas-Feb, tel. 64 93 41 78, www.julehus.no). Then wander out past the church and cemetery on the north side of town to a pleasant park. Looking out into the fjord, you can see the old **Oscarsborg Fortress,** where Norwegian troops fired cannons and torpedoes to sink Hitler's warship, *Blücher.* The attack bought enough time for Norway's king and parliament to escape capture and eventually set up a government-in-exile in London during the Nazi occupation of Norway (1940-1945). Nearby, a monument is dedicated to the commander of the fortress, and one of *Blücher*'s anchors rests aground (the other is at Aker Brygge in Oslo). A 100-NOK round-trip summer ferry shuttles visitors from the town harbor.

Eating in Drøbak: With outdoor seating, **$$$$ Restaurant Skipperstuen** is a pricey but good option for dinner overlooking the fjord and all the Oslo-bound boat traffic (Mon-Sat 12:00-22:00, Sun until 20:00; off-season closed Mon-Tue; Havnebakken 11, tel. 64 93 07 03, www.skipperstuen.no).

Shopping in Oslo

Shops in Oslo are generally open 10:00-18:00 or 19:00. Many close early on Saturday and all day Sunday. Shopping centers are open Monday through Friday 10:00-21:00, Saturday 9:00-18:00, and are closed Sunday. Remember, when you make a purchase of 315 NOK or more, you can get the 25 percent tax refunded when you leave the country (see page 700). Here are a few favorite shopping opportunities many travelers enjoy, but not on Sunday, when they're all closed. For locations, see the map on page 216.

Norway Designs, just outside the National Theater, shows off the country's sleek, contemporary designs in clothing, kitchenware, glass, textiles, jewelry—and high prices (Stortingsgata 12, T-bane: Nationaltheatret, tel. 23 11 45 10).

Paleet is a mall in the heart of Oslo, with 30 shops on three levels and a food court in the basement (Karl Johans Gate 37, tel. 23 08 08 11).

Dale of Norway, considered Norway's biggest and best maker of traditional and contemporary sweaters, offers its complete collection at their "concept store" in downtown Oslo (Karl Johans Gate 45, tel. 97 48 12 07).

Heimen Husfliden has a superb selection of authentic Norwegian sweaters, *bunads* (national costumes), traditional jewelry, and other Norwegian crafts (top quality at high prices, Rosenkrantz Gate 8, tel. 23 21 42 00).

GlasMagasinet is one of Oslo's oldest and fanciest department stores (top-end, good souvenir shop, near the cathedral at Stortorvet 9, tel. 22 82 23 00).

The Husfliden Shop, in the basement of the GlasMagasinet department store (listed earlier), is popular for its Norwegian-made sweaters, yarn, and colorful Norwegian folk crafts (tel. 22 42 10 75).

The Oslo Sweater Shop has competitive prices for a wide range of Norwegian-made sweaters, including Dale brand (in Radisson Blu Scandinavia Hotel at Tullinsgate 5, tel. 22 11 29 22).

Byporten, the big, splashy mall adjoining the central train station, is filled with youthful and hip shops, specialty stores, and eateries (Jernbanetorget 6, tel. 23 36 21 60).

The street named **Bogstadveien** is considered to have the city's trendiest boutiques and chic, high-quality shops (stretches from behind the Royal Palace to Majorstuen near Vigeland Park).

Oslo's Flea Market makes Saturday morning a happy day for those who brake for garage sales (at Vestkanttorvet, March-Nov only, two blocks east of Frogner Park at the corner of Professor Dahl's Gate and Neubergsgate).

Oslo Flaggfabrikk sells quality flags of all shapes and sizes, including the long, pennant-shaped *vimpel*, seen fluttering from flagpoles all over Norway (a 11.5-foot *vimpel* dresses up a boat or cabin wonderfully, near City Hall at Hieronymus Heyerdahlsgate 1, entrance on Tordenskioldsgate—on the other side of the block, tel. 22 40 50 60).

Vinmonopolet stores are the only places where you can buy wine and spirits in Norway. The most convenient location is at the central train station. Another location, not far from Stortinget, is at Rosenkrantz Gate 11. The bottles used to be kept behind the counter, but now you can actually touch the merchandise. Locals say it went from being a "jewelry store" to a "grocery store." (Light beer is sold in grocery stores, but strong beer is still limited to Vinmonopolet shops.)

Sleeping in Oslo

Oslo's hotel rates are particularly susceptible to supply-and-demand fluctuation. You may find deals on weekends and during some parts of the summer, but even then, conventions or special meetings can cause hotel prices to double overnight. Since it's so hard to predict trends, the only way to know is to check hotel websites, or a booking engine, for the dates you want to visit, and see who's offering a discount. For convenience and modern comfort, I like the Thon Budget Hotels. For lower prices, consider a cheap hotel or a hostel.

NEAR THE TRAIN STATION AND KARL JOHANS GATE

These accommodations are within a 15-minute walk of the station. While some streets near the station can feel a bit sketchy, these

Sleep Code

Hotels are classified based on the average price of a typical en suite double room with breakfast in high season.

$$$$	**Splurge:**	Most rooms over 1,500 NOK
$$$	**Pricier:**	1,200-1,500 NOK
$$	**Moderate:**	900-1,200 NOK
$	**Budget:**	600-900 NOK
¢	**Hostel/Backpacker:**	Under 600 NOK
RS%	**Rick Steves discount**	

Unless otherwise noted, credit cards are accepted, and free Wi-Fi is available. Comparison-shop by checking prices at several hotels (on each hotel's own website, on a booking site, or by email). For the best deal, *always book directly with the hotel.* Ask for a discount if paying in cash; if the listing includes **RS%,** request a Rick Steves discount.

hotels are secure and comfortable. Parking in a central garage will run you about 250-300 NOK per day.

Thon Hotels

This chain of business-class hotels (found in big cities throughout Norway) knows which comforts are worth paying for, and which are not. They offer little character, but provide maximum comfort per *krone* in big, modern, conveniently located buildings. Each hotel has a cheery staff and lobby, tight but well-designed rooms, free Wi-Fi, free coffee in the lobby, and a big buffet breakfast. All are nonsmoking and have elevators and central air-conditioning.

Thon's **$$$$** "City Hotels" are a cut above their **$$$** "Budget Hotels" and are generally more expensive. Because Thon Hotels base their prices on demand, their rates vary wildly (my price ratings are based on average summer rates). You may be able to find a City hotel that's discounted below the cost of the Budget hotels. Both Budget and City hotels are usually cheaper during the summer. In Budget hotels, all rooms lack phones and minifridges; also, rooms with double beds are a bit bigger than twin-bedded rooms for the same price.

Book by phone or online (central booking tel. 81 55 24 00, www.thonhotels.no). For the best prices, check the "price calendar" on the Thon Hotels website. Booking via the Thon website gets you a 10 percent "Thon WebDeal" discount (with some exceptions) if you prepay, and with no option to change or cancel your reservation 24 hours after booking. Of the more than a dozen Thon Hotels in Oslo, I find the following most convenient:

Thon City Hotel Rosenkrantz Oslo offers 152 modern, comfortable, stylish rooms in a central location two blocks off Karl Jo-

Oslo Hotels

1. Thon City Hotel Rosenkrantz Oslo
2. Thon City Hotel Terminus
3. Thon City Hotel Cecil
4. Thon City Hotel Spectrum
5. Thon Budget Hotel Astoria
6. Thon City Hotel Munch
7. Thon City Hotel Oslo Panorama
8. Comfort Hotel Karl Johan
9. Hotell Bondeheimen
10. Perminalen Hotel
11. Citybox Oslo
12. P-Hotel
13. To Saga Hotel Oslo; Cochs & Ellingsen's Pensjonats
14. Anker Hostel

hans Gate. Its eighth-floor lounge offers views of the Royal Palace park. They offer a free light supper every evening for guests—making this an even better value than it seems. If you want to splurge, this is the place to do it (Rosenkrantz Gate 1, tel. 23 31 55 00, www.thonhotels.no/rosenkrantzoslo, rosenkrantzoslo@thonhotels.no).

Thon City Hotel Terminus is similar but just a five-minute walk from the station; along with the Rosenkrantz, it offers a free light evening meal for guests (Steners Gate 10, tel. 22 05 60 00, www.thonhotels.no/terminus, terminus@thonhotels.no).

Thon City Hotel Cecil, ideally located near the Parliament building a block below Karl Johans Gate, has 110 efficient, comfortable rooms ringing a tall, light-filled, breakfast-room atrium (Stortingsgata 8, tel. 23 31 48 00, www.thonhotels.no/cecil, cecil@thonhotels.no).).

Thon City Hotel Spectrum has 187 rooms just behind Oslo Spektrum concert arena. It's on a pedestrianized street, next door to a handy grocery store. Rooms facing the street can be noisy on weekends (Brugata 7; leave station out north entrance toward bus terminal, go across footbridge and down the stairs on the left,

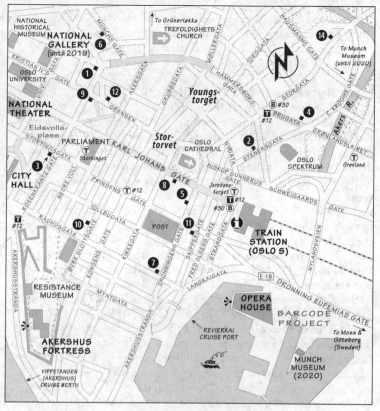

pass by tall glass Radisson Blu Plaza Hotel and walk to the other side of the park; tel. 23 36 27 00, www.thonhotels.no/spectrum, spectrum@thonhotels.no).

Thon Budget Hotel Astoria, with 180 rooms, has the least charm of my recommended Thon Hotels, but it's well-located and perfectly serviceable (2 blocks in front of station, 50 yards off Karl Johans Gate, Dronningens Gate 21, tel. 24 14 55 50, www. thonhotels.no/astoria, astoria@thonhotels.no).

Thon City Hotel Munch has 180 rooms in a location that's quiet but still relatively central, a few blocks from the National Gallery. Some rooms have hardwood floors, others have carpets. Because it's transitioning from "Budget" to "City" class, its prices are a bit lower and therefore a good value (Munchs Gate 5, tel. 23 21 96 00, www.thonhotels.no/munch, munch@thonhotels.no).

Thon City Hotel Oslo Panorama was a 15-story attempt at a downtown condominium building (the condos didn't work, so now it's a 118-room hotel). While higher rooms are more expensive, even those reserving a cheap room often get bumped up. If you request anything higher than the fourth floor, you'll likely enjoy a bigger room, perhaps with a tiny balcony and/or a kitch-enette (just off Dronningens Gate at Rådhusgata 7, about 6 blocks from station, tel. 23 31 08 00, www.thonhotels.no/oslopanorama, oslopanorama@thonhotels.no).

More Hotels near the Train Station

$$$$ Comfort Hotel Karl Johan fills a mod building with 181 tight rooms, across from the cathedral near the train-station end of Karl Johans Gate. It feels new (from 2016), with sleek, somewhat minimalist decor and a trendy lobby that tries a little too hard to be hip and funky. Light sleepers should request a quiet room (elevator, Karl Johans Gate 12, tel. 23 01 03 50, www.nordicchoicehotels. com).

$$$ Hotell Bondeheimen ("Farmer's Home") is a historic hotel run by the farmers' youth league, *Bondeungdomslaget*. It once housed the children of rural farmers attending school in Oslo. Its 145 rooms have all the comforts of a modern hotel (elevator, Rosenkrantz Gate 8, tel. 23 21 41 00, www.bondeheimen.com, bookingoffice@ bondeheimen.com). This almost-100-year-old building is also home to the Kaffistova cafeteria (see "Eating in Oslo") and the Heimen Husfliden shop (see "Shopping in Oslo").

$$ Perminalen Hotel, designed for military personnel on leave, also rents 15 rooms to tourists. It's perfectly central, spar-tan, and inexpensive. Spliced invisibly into a giant office block on a quiet street, they have the same fair prices all year—making it an excellent deal when the city is busy and rates are sky-high. All of the doubles are bunk beds (some seventh-floor rooms have tiny bal-conies, elevator, tram #12, #13, or #19 from station to Øvre Slott-sgate stop, Øvre Slottsgate 2, tel. 24 00 55 00, www.perminalen. com, post.perminalen@iss.no). They also have single beds in dorms segregated by sexes (with lockers and breakfast). Its cheap mess hall is open nightly for dinner, and for lunch on weekdays.

$$ Citybox Oslo has 217 simple, basic rooms at a good price, in a nondescript urban zone a short walk from the train station. While services are minimal (self-check-in), the public areas are in-viting (breakfast extra, Prinsens Gate 6, tel. 21 42 04 80, www. citybox.no).

$$ P-Hotel rents 93 cheaply designed, well-worn but afford-able rooms. It's a lesser value than the polished Thon hotels, but may have rooms when others are full (or charging higher rates). You get a basic breakfast delivered each morning. Avoid late-night street noise by requesting a room high up or in the back (some sixth-floor rooms have balconies, Grensen 19, T-bane: Stortinget, tel. 23 31 80 00, www.p-hotels.com, oslo@p-hotels.no).

THE WEST END

This pleasant, refined-feeling residential neighborhood is a long walk or a short tram ride from downtown, tucked between the Royal Palace and Frogner Park. The busy main drag of this area is Hegdehaugsveien, lined with tram tracks, busy shops, and restaurants and cafés. The pensions listed here are affordable, but are plagued by street and tram noise—try requesting a quiet room. Saga Hotel is quieter and more upscale.

$$$$ Saga Hotel Oslo feels elegant, with a trendy lobby and gold-trim furnishings. The 47 rooms are comfortable, and the location—in a posh residential area is appealing (Eilert Sundts Gate 39, tel. 22 55 44 90, www.sagahotels.no).

$$ Ellingsen's Pensjonat rents 24 bright, cheery rooms with fluffy down comforters. About half of their rooms have shared bathrooms, which cost less. It's in a residential neighborhood four blocks behind the Royal Palace (breakfast extra, nonsmoking, tram #19 from central station to Rosenborg stop, near Uranienborg church at Holtegata 25, tel. 22 60 03 59, www.ellingsenspensjonat.no, post@ellingsenspensjonat.no, Peter and Emelie).

$ Cochs Pensjonat is cheap and cozy, with 90 dated, simple rooms, many with kitchenettes (cheaper rooms with shared bath, discounts for breakfast at nearby cafés, elevator; T-bane: Nationaltheatret, exit to Parkveien, and 10-minute walk through park; or more-convenient tram #11 to Homansbyen or #17 or #18 to Dalsbergstien; Parkveien 25, tel. 23 33 24 00, www.cochs.no, booking@cochs.no, three generations of the Skram family).

PRIVATE HOMES

To find a room in a private home, which can save you money but at the cost of being farther from the center, try Airbnb or www.bbnorway.com. Sleeping downtown puts you close to the main sights, but carefully check reviews for noise troubles (many loud discos are in the center). The upscale area behind the Royal Palace (Frogner and Majorstuen neighborhoods) gives you a posh address in Oslo. And for proximity to the trendy dining scene, look in the part of Grünerløkka near the river.

HOSTELS

¢ Anker Hostel, a huge student dorm open to travelers of any age, offers 250 rooms, including 34 of Oslo's best cheap doubles. The hostel also offers bunks in dorm rooms. Though it comes with the ambience of a bomb shelter, each of its rooms is spacious, simple, clean, and has a small kitchen (sheets and towels extra, elevator, no breakfast, pay parking; tram #12 or #13, or bus #30 or #31 from central station, bus and tram stop: Hausmannsgate; or 15-minute walk from station; Storgata 55, tel. 22 99 72 00, www.ankerhostel. no, hostel@anker.oslo.no).

¢ **Haraldsheim Youth Hostel (IYHF),** a huge, modern hostel open all year, comes with a grand view, 315 beds—most of them in four-bed rooms...and a long commute (2.5 miles out of town). They also offer private rooms (sheets extra, from Oslo's central train station catch bus #31 or tram #17 to Sinsenkrysset, or T-bane lines #4 or #5 to Sinsen, then 5-minute uphill hike to Haraldsheimveien 4, tel. 22 22 29 65, www.haraldsheim.no, oslo.haraldsheim@ hihostels.no). Eurailers can train to the hostel with their rail pass (2/hour, to Grefsen and walk 10 minutes).

SLEEPING ON A TRAIN OR BOAT

Norway's trains and ferries offer ways to travel while sleeping. The eight-hour night train between Bergen and Oslo leaves at about 23:00 in each direction (nightly except Sat). The overnight cruise between these Nordic capitals is a clever way to avoid a night in a hotel and to travel while you sleep, saving a day in your itinerary (see "Oslo Connections," later).

Eating in Oslo

Eating out is expensive in Oslo. How do average Norwegians afford their high-priced restaurants? They don't eat out much. This is one city in which you might want to settle for simple or ethnic meals— you'll save a lot and miss little. Many menus list small and large plates. Because portions tend to be large, choosing a small plate or splitting a large one makes some otherwise pricey options reasonable. You'll notice many locals just drink free tap water, even in fine restaurants.

Splurge for a hotel that includes breakfast, or pay for it if it's optional. At around 80 NOK, a Norwegian breakfast fit for a Viking is a good deal. Picnic for lunch or dinner. Basements of big department stores have huge, first-class supermarkets with lots of alternatives to sandwiches for picnic dinners. The little yogurt tubs with cereal come with collapsible spoons. Wasa crackers and meat, shrimp, or cheese spread in a tube are cheap and pack well. The central station has a Joker supermarket with long hours. Some supermarkets have takeout food that is discounted just before closing—showing up just before 20:00 or so to buy some roast chicken could be your cheapest meal in Oslo. My favorite meals in Oslo are picnic dinners harborside.

Oslo's One-Time Grills

Norwegians are experts at completely avoiding costly restaurants. "One-time grills," or *engangsgrill,* are the rage for locals

on a budget. For about 25 NOK, you get a disposable outdoor cooker consisting of an aluminum tray, easy-to-light charcoal, and a flimsy metal grill. All that's required is a sunny evening, a grassy park, and a group of friends. During balmy summer evenings, the air in Oslo's city parks is thick with the smell of disposable (and not terribly eco-friendly) grills. It's fun to see how prices for this kind of "dining" aren't that bad in the supermarket: Norwegian beer-28 NOK/half-liter, potato salad-30 NOK/tub, cooked shrimp-50 NOK/half kilo, "ready for grill" steak-two for 120 NOK, *grill pølse* hot dogs-75 NOK per dozen, *lomper* (Norwegian tortillas for wrapping hot dogs)-20 NOK per stack, and the actual grill itself.

Bars are also too expensive for the average Norwegian. Young night owls drink at home before *(forspiel)* and after *(nachspiel)* an evening on the town, with a couple of hours, generally around midnight, when they go out for a single drink in a public setting. A beer in a bar costs about $10 for a half-liter (compared to $6 in Ireland and $2 in the Czech Republic), while they can get a six-pack for about twice that price in a grocery store.

You'll save by getting takeaway food from a restaurant rather than eating inside. (The tax on takeaway food is 12 percent, while restaurant food is 24 percent.) Fast-food restaurants ask if you want to take away or not before they ring up your order on the cash register. Even McDonald's has a two-tiered price list.

Oslo is awash with little budget eateries (modern, ethnic, fast food, pizza, department-store cafeterias, and so on). **Deli de Luca,** a cheery convenience store chain that's notorious for having a store on every key corner in Oslo, is a step up from the similarly ubiquitous 7-Elevens and Narvesens. Most are open 24/7, selling sandwiches, pastries, sushi, and to-go boxes of warm pasta or Asian noodle dishes. You can fill your belly here for about 80 NOK. Some outlets (such as the one at the corner of Karl Johans Gate and Rosenkrantz Gate) have seating on the street or upstairs. Beware: Because this is still a *convenience* store, not everything is well-priced. Convenience stores—while convenient—charge double what supermarkets do.

OSLO

Restaurant Price Code

I've assigned each eatery a price category, based on the average cost of a typical main course. Drinks, desserts, and splurge items (steak and seafood) can raise the price considerably.

$$$$ **Splurge:** Most main courses over 175 NOK
$$$ **Pricier:** 125-175 NOK
$$ **Moderate:** 75-125 NOK
$ **Budget:** Under 75 NOK

In Norway, a Deli de Luca or other takeout spot is **$**; a sit-down café is **$$**; a casual but more upscale restaurant is **$$$**; and a swanky splurge is **$$$$**.

KARL JOHANS GATE STRIP

Strangely, **Karl Johans Gate**—the most Norwegian of boulevards—is lined with a strip of good-time American chain eateries and sports bars where you can get ribs, burgers, and pizza, including T.G.I. Fridays and the Hard Rock Café. **$$ Egon Restaurant** offers a daily 110-NOK all-you-can-eat pizza deal (available Tue-Sat 11:00-18:00, Sun-Mon all day)—though the rest of their menu is overpriced. Each place comes with great sidewalk seating and essentially the same prices.

$$$$ Grand Café is perhaps the most venerable place in town, with genteel decor described on page 220. They have a seasonal menu, with high-end Nordic, French, and international dishes. Reserve a window, and if you hit a time when there's no tour group, you're suddenly a posh Norwegian (Mon-Fri 11:00-23:00, Sat-Sun 12:00-23:00, Karl Johans Gate 31, tel. 98 18 20 00).

$ Deli de Luca, just across from the Grand Café, offers good-value food and handy seats on Karl Johans Gate. For a fast meal with the best people-watching view in town, you may find yourself dropping by here repeatedly (for 70 NOK you can get a calzone, or a portion of chicken noodles, beef noodles, or chicken vindaloo with rice—ask to have it heated up, open 24/7, Karl Johans Gate 33, tel. 22 33 35 22).

$$ Kaffebrenneriet is a good local coffeehouse chain serving quality coffee drinks and affordable sandwiches, salads, and pastries. Convenient locations include in the park along Karl Johans Gate at #24, closer to the cathedral and train station at Karl Johans Gate 7, behind the cathedral at Storgata 2, facing the back of the Parliament building at Akersgata 16, and next to City Hall at Hieronymus Heyerdahls Gate 1. Most have similar hours (typically Mon-Fri 7:00-19:00, Sat 9:00-18:00, closed Sun).

$$ United Bakeries, next to the Paleet mall, is a quiet bit of Norwegian quality among sports bars, appreciated for its 80-NOK sandwiches, salads, light weekday lunches, and fresh pastries

Norwegian Cuisine

Traditional Norwegian cuisine doesn't rank very high in terms of excitement. But the typical diet of meat, fish, and potatoes is evolving to incorporate more diverse products, and the food here is steadily improving. Fresh produce, colorful markets, and efficient supermarkets abound in Europe's most expensive corner.

In this land of farmers and fishermen, traditional recipes are built on ingredients like potatoes, salmon, or beef. A favorite tart/sweet condiment is lingonberry jam, which cuts through a heavy, salty meat dish. Some traditional places also serve *lefse*—a soft flatbread made from potatoes, milk, and flour.

Norway's national dish is *Fårikål,* a lamb or mutton stew with cabbage, peppercorns, and potatoes. This dish is so popular that the last Thursday in September is *Fårikål* day in Norway. There's really no need for a recipe, so every stew turns out differently—and every grandma claims hers is the best.

Because of its long, cold winters, Norway relies heavily on the harvesting and preservation of fish. Smoked salmon, called *røkt laks,* is prepared by salt-curing the fish and cold-smoking it, ensuring the temperature never rises above 85°F. This makes the texture smooth and almost raw. *Bacalao* is another favorite: salted and dried cod that is rehydrated and rinsed in water before cooking. You'll often find *bacalao* served with tomatoes and olives. Stockfish *(tørrfisk),* usually cod, is hung on wooden racks to air-dry (rather than salt-cure), creating a kind of "fish jerky" that goes well with beer. *Klippfisk* is yet another variation, which is partly air-dried on rocks along the shoreline, then further salt-cured.

Some Norwegians serve lutefisk around Christmas time, but you'll rarely see this salty, pungent dish on the menu. Instead, try the more pleasant *fiskekake,* a small white fish cake made with cream, eggs, milk, and flour. You can find these patties year-round.

For a break from seafood, try local specialties such as reindeer meatballs, or pork-and-ground beef meat cakes called *kjøttkaker.* True to Scandinavian cuisine, *kjøttkaker* are usually slathered in a heavy cream sauce.

Dessert and coffee after a meal are essential. *Bløtkake,* a popular delight on Norway's Constitution Day (May 17), is a layered cake drizzled with strawberry juice, covered in whipped cream, and decorated with fresh strawberries. The cloudberry *(multe),* which grows in the Scandinavian tundra, makes a unique jelly that tastes delicious on vanilla ice cream, or even whipped into a rich cream topping for heart-shaped waffles. Norwegians are proud of their breads and pastries, and you'll never be too far from a bakery that sells an almond-flavored *kringle* or a cone-shaped *krumkake* cookie filled with whipped cream.

OSLO

Oslo Restaurants

1. Egon Restaurant & United Bakeries
2. Grand Café
3. Deli de Luca
4. Kaffebrenneriet
5. Kaffistova
6. Theatercaféen
7. Café Skansen
8. Engebret Café
9. Solsiden
10. Fenaknoken Deli
11. Aker Brygge Eateries
12. Groceries (2)
13. Youngstorget Eateries
14. Illegal Burger Bar
15. Torggata North Eateries
16. Peloton
17. Torggata South Eateries
18. To Lofotstua; Curry & Ketchup Indian

(seating inside and out, Mon-Fri 7:30-20:00, Sat 9:00-18:00, Sun 11:00-17:00).

$$$ **Kaffistova,** a block off the main drag, is where my thrifty Norwegian grandparents always took me. And it remains almost unchanged since the 1970s. This alcohol-free cafeteria still serves simple, hearty, and typically Norwegian (read: bland) meals for a good price (big portions of Norwegian meatballs, Mon-Fri 11:00-21:00, Sat-Sun until 19:00, Rosenkrantz Gate 8, tel. 23 21 41 00).

$$$$ **Theatercaféen,** since 1900 the place for Norway's illuminati to see and be seen (note the celebrity portraits adorning the walls), is a swanky splurge steeped in Art Nouveau elegance (Mon-Sat 11:00-23:00, Sun 15:00-22:00, in Hotel Continental at Stortingsgata 24, across from National Theater, tel. 22 82 40 50).

NEAR AKERSHUS FORTRESS

$$$$ **Café Skansen** is a delightful spot for a quality meal—especially in good weather, when its leafy, beer garden-like terrace fills with a convivial, mostly local crowd. Or huddle in the old-time interior, and dig into classic Norwegian dishes. They serve more

OSLO

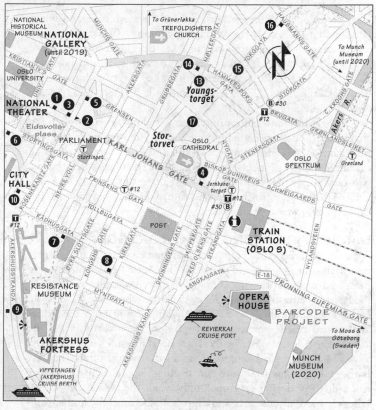

affordable lunches until 16:00, and good salads anytime (Mon-Fri 11:00-23:00, Sat-Sun 12:00-22:00, Rådhusgata 32, tel. 24 20 13 11).

$$$$ Engebret Café is a classic old restaurant in a 17th-century building in the Christiania section of town below the fortress. Since 1857, it's been serving old-fashioned Norse food (reindeer is always on the menu) in a classic

old Norwegian setting. In good weather, you can sit out on the delightful square with a gurgling fountain (Mon-Fri 11:30-23:00, Sat from 17:00, closed Sun and most of July, Bankplassen 1, tel. 22 82 25 25).

$$$$ Solsiden ("Sunny Side"), filling a glassed-in former warehouse on the embankment just under the fortress, is a local favorite for a harborfront splurge. You'll dig into fish and seafood meals in an open, unpretentious, nautical-themed, blue-and-white interior that doesn't distract from the cooking. Think of this as a less posh-feeling alternative to the Aker Brygge scene across the harbor. Reserve ahead, and ask for a table with a view (May-mid-Sept daily 16:30-22:00, in peak times they do two dinner seatings—at 20:00 and 22:30, Akershusstranda 13, tel. 22 33 36 30, www.solsiden.no).

Top-End Picnic Shopping: Near City Hall, **Fenaknoken** is a characteristic deli specializing in gourmet Norwegian products—from salmon and lefse to moose salami and dried fish. If you value authentic quality products over price, this is the place to assemble a blowout Norwegian picnic to enjoy out along the harbor (Mon-Fri 10:00-17:00, Sat until 13:30, closed Sun, Tordenskioldsgate 12, tel. 22 42 34 57, www.fenaknoken.no).

HARBORSIDE DINING IN AKER BRYGGE

Aker Brygge, the harborfront development near City Hall, is popular with businesspeople and tourists. While it isn't cheap, its inviting cafés and restaurants with outdoor, harborview tables make for a memorable waterfront meal. Before deciding where to eat, walk the entire lane (including the back side), considering both the brick-and-mortar places (some with second-floor view seating) and the various floating options. Nearly all are open for lunch and dinner.

$$$$ Lekter'n Lounge, right on the water, offers the best harbor view (rather than views of strolling people). This trendy bar has a floating dining area open only when the weather is warm. It serves hamburgers, fish-and-chips, salads, mussels, and shrimp buckets (all outdoors, Stranden 3, tel. 22 83 76 46). If you go just for drinks, the sofas make you feel right at home, and a DJ adds to the ambience.

$$$$ Rorbua ("Fisherman's Cabin") is a lively yet cozy eatery tucked back into this otherwise modern stretch of restaurants. The specialty is food from Norway's north, such as whale and reindeer. Inside, it's extremely woody with a rustic charm and candlelit picnic tables surrounded by harpoons and old B&W photos. While the à la carte dinners start at around 300 NOK, a hearty daily special with coffee for 175 NOK is one of the city's best restaurant deals (daily 12:30-23:00, Stranden 71, tel. 22 83 64 84).

$$$$ Lofoten Fiskerestaurant serves fish amid a dressy yacht-club atmosphere at the end of the strip. While it's beyond the people-watching action, it's comfortable even in cold and blustery weather because of its heated atrium, which makes a meal here practically outdoor dining. Reservations are a must, especially for a harborside window table (daily 11:00-23:00, Stranden 75, tel. 22 83 08 08, www.lofoten-fiskerestaurant.no).

Budget Tips: If you're on a budget, try a hot dog from a *pølse* stand or get a picnic from a nearby grocery store and grab a bench along the boardwalk. The **Co-op Mega** grocery store—in the middle of the mall a few steps behind all the fancy restaurants—has salads, warm takeaway dishes (sold by weight), and more (turn in about midway down the boardwalk, Mon-Sat 8:00-22:00, Sun 9:00-20:00). Farther down is a **Joker mini-grocery,** just over the bridge and to the right on Lille Stranden in Tjuvholmen (Mon-Sat 8:00-22:00, Sun from 11:00).

NEAR YOUNGSTORGET

Central Oslo's most appealing dining zone percolates just a 10-minute stroll north of Karl Johans Gate, around the otherwise nondescript urban square named Youngstorget. This aptly named square feels fresh and trendy, although it's tucked between all-business high-rises and Thon hotels. The square itself has several fine options, but the streets leading off it are also worth a browse—especially Torggata, lined with a couple dozen eclectic options more tempting than anything in the touristy downtown.

On Youngstorget

First, check out the hipster **food carts** that are often parked in the middle of the square, which can be a great spot for a quick, affordable al fresco bite. But to settle in for a more serious meal, you have plenty of choices.

Three good options cluster at the base of the towering, red-brick headquarters of the Arbeiderpartiet (Labor Party). **$$$ Fiskeriet** started as a small fish counter (with stacks of dried cod) before expanding into a full-blown restaurant. It has a concise but tempting menu of simple fish-focused dishes, including fish-and-chips, and seating either in the tiled interior or out on the square (Mon-Fri 11:00-21:00, Sat from 12:00, closed Sun, Youngstorget 2b, tel. 22 42 45 40, www.fiskeriet.com). Next door, **$$$$ Taverna'n** is an industrial-strength eatery with a big, rustic/trendy interior plus outdoor dining, a fun energy, and a menu of pastas, fish dishes, grill meals, and pizza—which they call "skorpe" (Mon-Fri 11:00-late, Sat from 12:00, Sun 13:00-22:00, Youngstorget 1, tel. 40 01 74 37). Rounding out the scene is **$$ Internasjonalen,** a bar with a checkerboard-tile-and-red-leather interior, a wall of lit-up liquor bottles, inviting outdoor tables on the square, and cheap sandwiches (Mon-Sat 10:00-late, Sun from 16:00, Youngstorget 2a, tel. 46 82 52 40).

From any of the above, you can gaze across the square to the pinkish, crenellated former police station that was headquarters for the notorious Nazi security service during the occupation—and where traitor Vidkun Quisling surrendered to Norwegian police at war's end. Its former stables, in the arcades just below, are filled with more bars and eateries (cozy **Fyret** has a great selection of aquavit and open-face sandwiches, while **Politiker'n** has ample outdoor seating). And finally, if you were to hike up to the old police station and turn right (at the uphill corner of the square), you'd find **$$$ Illegal Burger Bar**—the best-regarded of Oslo's many trendy burger joints, with a long, creative menu of gourmet burgers (daily 14:00-late, Møllergata 23, tel. 22 20 33 02).

On Torggata, North of Youngstorget

For even more options, simply stroll from Youngstorget up Torggata and comparison-shop menus, ignoring the American fast-food chains and keeping an eye out for these places (listed in order as you head north): A short block up Badstugata (on the left) is the high-end **$$$$ Arakataka,** serving refined New Nordic dishes in an elegant setting (450-NOK tasting *menu,* daily from 16:00, Mariboes Gate 7b, tel. 23 32 83 00, www.arakataka.no). Nearby is **$$ Pisco,** with affordable Peruvian and Latin American meals, and across the street is **Tilt Bar,** a pinball-themed dive filling what used to be the old public bathhouse. Back on Torggata at #18, you'll pass **$$$ Troys Burger** (Mon-Sat from 11:00, Sun from 14:00). A block farther up, on the corner at #30, **$$$ Taco República** has impressively authentic and delicious Mexican food in a tight, lively, colorful, casual setting. As servings are small, you may need several dishes to fill up (Tue-Thu 16:00-22:00, Fri 15:00-24:00, Sat from 12:00, Sun 14:00-22:00, closed Mon, tel. 40 05 76 65). Just past that, at #32, **$$ Crowbar** is an industrial-mod microbrewery with an easy-to-miss self-service counter upstairs serving cheap falafel and kebabs (Sun-Fri 15:00-late, Sat from 13:00, tel. 21 38 67 57). And finally, up at the corner (at #36), **$$$ Peloton** is a casual and inviting *sykkelcafe*—a bright, cheery "bicycle café" serving pizza and long list of beers, with a bike shop in the back (Mon 8:00-18:00, Tue-Fri until 24:00, Sat 10:00-24:00, Sun 12:00-23:00, tel. 92 15 61 81).

On Torggata, South of Youngstorget

The stretch of Torgatta to the south, where it connects Youngstorget to Karl Johans Gate, feels less residential and more shopping-oriented. But it's also lined with a fun variety of eateries as well—most of which double as hard-partying nightspots into the wee hours. **$$$ Cafe Sør,** a few steps south of Youngstorget, has a cool ramshackle vibe and an affordable menu of salads and sandwiches. It becomes a lively dance club after hours (Mon-Sat 10:00-late, Sun from 12:00, Torggata 11, tel. 41 46 30 47). Nearby, the *Strøget* sign marks the entrance to a courtyard that's jammed with lively eateries, bars, cafés, and clubs. This courtyard is a fun place to browse for a meal or drink by day, or to find a lively nightlife scene after hours. In here, **$$$$ Habibi** has an old cafeteria vibe, a menu of Palestinian mezes, and warbling Middle Eastern music. **Angst** is an achingly hip bar with brooding, atmospheric decor and a live DJ after 23:00.

DINING NEAR VIGELAND PARK

$$$$ Lofotstua Restaurant feels transplanted from the far northern islands it's named for. Kjell Jenssen and his son, Jan Hugo, proudly serve up fish Lofoten-style. Evangelical about fish, they will patiently explain to you the fine differences between all the local varieties, with the help of a photo-filled chart. They serve only the freshest catch, perfectly—if simply—prepared. And if you want meat, they've got it: whale or seal (Mon-Fri 15:00-21:30, closed Sat-Sun, generally closed in July, 5-minute walk from Vigeland Park's main gate, tram #12, in Majorstuen at Kirkeveien 40, tel. 22 46 93 96). This place is packed daily in winter for their famous lutefisk.

$$$ Curry and Ketchup Indian Restaurant is filled with locals enjoying hearty, decent meals for about 130 NOK. This happening place requires no reservations and feels like an Indian market, offering a flavorful meal near Vigeland's statues (daily 14:00-23:00, a 5-minute walk from Vigeland Park's main gate, tram #12, in Majorstuen at Kirkeveien 51, tel. 22 69 05 22).

TRENDY DINING AT THE BOTTOM OF GRÜNERLØKKA

These spots are located on the map on page 259.

Oslo's Foodie Epicenter: Mathallen and Vulkan

This fast-emerging zone, on the bank of the Akers River (and covered on my "Akers River and Grünerløkka Walk"), has recently put Oslo on the foodie map. In the appealing Akers River valley, several old brick industrial buildings and adjoining new construction house a busy hive of culinary activity that's an easy walk or tram ride from downtown (it's a 5-minute walk from the tram stop at Olaf Ryes Plass, described later).

The anchor of this area is **Mathallen Oslo**—once a 19th-century factory, now spiffed up and morphed into a riverside market with a mix of produce stalls and enticing eateries all sharing food-circus-type seating in the middle (Tue-Wed and Sat 10:00-19:00, Thu-Fri until 20:00, Sun 11:00-17:00, closed Mon, some restaurants open longer, www.mathallenoslo.no).

Inside, and ringing the perimeter, you'll find a world of options: tapas, Italian, sushi, tacos and tequila, pizza, Asian street food, Paradis gourmet ice cream, and so on. Most places have high-quality meals in the 150-200-NOK range. **$$$ Ma Poule** is a French wine bar with tasty light meals. **$$$ Atelier Asian Tapas** dishes up small plates and full meals. Or browse the market vendors: **Ost & Sånt** is a high-end Norwegian farm cheese counter with generous free samples. **Smelt Ostesmørbrød** sells fresh breads, pastries, and sandwiches. **The Cupcake & Pie Co.** serves sweet and savory pies. Upstairs, don't miss the taco shop and the sprawling **Hitchhiker** wine bar.

More places face the outside of the hall, including—overlooking the bridge—**$$$$ Lucky Bird** fried chicken and ribs, **$$$$ Smelteverket** ("global tapas" with wonderful views over the river), and more. Still can't decide? For me, the winner may be **$$$$ Vulkanfisk,** with indoor and outdoor seating and a tempting menu of relatively well-priced and elegantly executed fish and seafood dishes: mussels, fish-and-chips, fish soup, garlic scampi, etc. (Tue-Sat 10:00-22:00, Sun until 20:00, closed Mon, tel. 21 39 69 58, www.vulkanfisk.no). For just a drink, consider the suntrap outdoor patio bar in **Dansens Hus** (the national dance theater), facing Vulkanfisk from across the street.

Just uphill is the **Vulkan Depot,** a small shopping mall with a trendy food court including Sapporo Ramen Bar, an Italian grocery store, a florist, a pharmacy, the Aetat co-working space (where independent contractors can rent a desk), and a big Rema 1000 supermarket.

Olaf Ryes Plass

Grünerløkka's main square (and the streets nearby) is lined with inviting eateries and has a relaxed, bohemian-chic vibe. To get here, hop on tram #11, #12, or #13. The top edge of the square has several pubs selling beer-centric food to a beer-centric crowd. Before choosing, simply wander and survey your options: Quesadilla (Mexican fare), Parkteatret (a classic café), Fontés (tapas), Eldhuset (barbecue), the charming little Grünerhaven café kiosk in the park itself, and perhaps the most appealing choice, **$$$ Villa Paradiso Pizzeria.** Youthful and family-friendly, it has a rustic interior and a popular terrace overlooking the square and people scene (Olaf Ryes Plass 8, tel. 22 35 40 60). Just past Villa Paradiso, a block to the west (toward the Mathallen scene described earlier), sits Oslo's most renowned third-wave coffee shop, named simply **Tim Wendelboe** for its celebrity-barista owner. If you're a coffee pilgrim wanting to caffeinate in style...do it here (Mon-Fri 8:30-18:00, Sat-Sun 11:00-17:00, Grüners Gate 1).

The bottom of the leafy square is more focused on nightlife, including **Ryes** (a dive bar famous for its cheap happy-hour beer and 1950s Americana theme). From here, it's fun to stroll south on lively Thorvald Meyers Gate back toward downtown, passing a few cheap international eateries (**Miss Gin** Vietnamese street food,

Bislett kebab house, and **Trattoria Popolare,** with affordable pastas and sprawling outdoor seating perfectly situated to catch the sun's final rays). Eventually you'll run into the place described next.

Between Olaf Ryes Plass and Downtown: Originally a big bank, **$$$$ Südøst Asian Crossover Restaurant** now fills its vault with wine (which makes sense, given Norwegian alcohol prices). Today it's popular with young Norwegian professionals as a place to see and be seen. It's a fine mix of Norwegian-chic, high-ceilinged, woody ambience inside with a trendy menu, and a big riverside terrace outdoors with a more casual menu. Diners enjoy its setting, smart service, and modern creative Asian-fusion cuisine. Reservations are wise, especially on weekends. They're particularly popular on Sundays, when they offer an all-you-can-eat buffet for a relatively affordable 200 NOK (daily 11:00-24:00, Sun buffet until 21:00, at bottom of Grünerløkka, tram #11, #12, or #17 to Trondheimsveien 5, tel. 23 35 30 70).

EATING CHEAP AND SPICY IN GRØNLAND

The street called Grønland leads through this colorful immigrant neighborhood (a short walk behind the train station or T-bane: Grønland; see the map on page 259). After the cleanliness and orderliness of the rest of the city, the rough edges and diversity of people here can feel like a breath of fresh air. Whether you eat here or not, the street is fun to explore. In Grønland, backpackers and immigrants munch street food for dinner. Cheap and tasty *börek* (savory phyllo pastry with feta, spinach, or mushroom) is sold hot and greasy to go for 25 NOK.

$$ Punjab Tandoori is friendly and serves hearty meals (lamb and chicken curry, tandoori specials). I like eating outside here with a view of the street scene (daily 11:00-23:00, Grønland 24).

$$ Istanbul Restaurant is clean and simple, with a decorative interior, outdoor seating, cheap kebabs, and affordable plates of Turkish food (Mon-Fri 10:00-24:00, Sat-Sun from 11:00, Grønland 14, tel. 23 40 90 22).

$$$ Asylet is more expensive and feels like it was here long before Norway ever saw a Pakistani. This big, traditional eatery—like a Norwegian beer garden—has a rustic, cozy interior and a cobbled backyard filled with picnic tables (burgers, pub food, hearty dinner salads, daily 11:00-23:30, Grønland 28, tel. 22 17 09 39).

$$$ Dattera Til Hagen feels like a college party. It's a lively scene filling a courtyard with graffiti, picnic tables, and benches under strings of colored twinkle lights. If it's too cold, hang out inside. Locals like it for the tapas, burgers, salads, and Norwegian microbrews on tap (daily 11:00-late, Grønland 10, tel. 22 17 18 61). On weekends after 22:00, it becomes a disco.

$$$$ Olympen Brown Pub is a dressy dining hall that's a

blast from the past. You'll eat in a spacious, woody saloon with big dark furniture, faded paintings of circa-1920 Oslo lining the walls, and huge chandeliers. It's good for solo travelers, because sharing the long dinner tables is standard practice. They serve hearty, pricey plates and offer a huge selection of beers. Traditional Norwegian cuisine is served downstairs, while upstairs on the rooftop, the food is grilled (daily 11:00-late, Grønlandsleiret 15, tel. 22 17 28 08).

NEAR THE SKI JUMP, HIGH ON THE MOUNTAIN

You can combine a trip into the forested hills surrounding the city with lunch or dinner and get a chance to see the famous Holmen-kollen Ski Jump up close (described earlier, under "Sights in Oslo").

Frognerseteren Hovedrestaurant, nestled high above Oslo (and 1,387 feet above sea level), is a classy, sod-roofed old restaurant. Its packed-when-it's-sunny terrace, offering a commanding view of the city, is a popular stop for its famous apple cake and coffee. The **$$ self-service café** is affordable for hearty plates of classic Norwegian dishes, with indoor and outdoor seating (Mon-Sat 11:00-22:00, Sun 11:00-21:00). The elegant view **$$$$ restaurant** is quite expensive and more formal, with antler chandeliers—ideally, reserve ahead for evening dining (reindeer specials, Mon-Fri 12:00-22:00, Sat from 13:00, Sun 13:00-21:00, tel. 22 92 40 40, www.frognerseteren.no).

$$$$ Holmenkollen Restaurant, below the ski jump and a five-minute hike above the Holmenkollen T-bane stop, is a practical alternative to Frognerseteren. Woody but modern, it's slightly cheaper and also has a grand Oslofjord view, but without the folk charm and affordable self-service option. I'd eat here only if you need a solid meal near the ski jump and aren't heading up to Frog-nerseteren (Tue-Sat 12:00-21:00, Sun 13:00-19:00, Holmenkoll-veien 119, tel. 22 13 92 00).

Oslo Connections

BY TRAIN, BUS, OR CAR

For train information, call 61 05 19 10 and press 9 for English. For international trains, press 3. Even if you have a rail pass, reservations are required (or strongly recommended) for express and other long-distance journeys. If you have a first-class rail pass, you can get a free "Komfort" class seat reservation for long-distance trains if you book it in Norway; if you have a second-class pass, you'll pay about 50 NOK for a reservation, or 90 NOK to upgrade to "Komfort." Note that private trains (like the Flåmsbana Myrdal-Flåm connection for the "Norway in a Nutshell" route) are not fully covered by rail passes (for details on this complex connection, see the Norway in a Nutshell chapter).

Be warned that international connections from Oslo are often in flux. Schedules can vary depending on the day of the week, so carefully confirm the specific train you need and purchase any required reservations in advance. Most trips from Oslo to Copenhagen require a change in Sweden.

From Oslo by Train to Stockholm: The speedy X2000 train zips from downtown to downtown in about 5.5 hours, runs several times daily, and requires reservations (160 NOK in first class, 65 NOK in second class; first class often comes with a hot meal, fruit bowl, and unlimited coffee). Note that through 2020, construction on this line will likely interrupt service, in which case you'll take the slower SJ InterCity train (recommended 35-NOK reservation in either class). There may also be (slower) connections possible with a change in Göteborg.

By Train to Bergen: Oslo and Bergen are linked by a spectacularly scenic train ride (3-5/day, 7 hours, overnight possible daily except Sat). Many travelers take it as part of the **Norway in a Nutshell** route, which combines train, ferry, and bus travel in an unforgettably beautiful trip. For information on times and prices, see the Norway in a Nutshell chapter.

By Train to: Lillehammer (almost hourly, 2.5 hours), **Kristiansand** (5/day, 4.5 hours, overnight possible), **Stavanger** (5/day, 8 hours, overnight possible), **Copenhagen** (2/day, 8.5 hours, transfer at Göteborg, more with multiple changes).

By Bus to Stockholm: Taking the bus to Stockholm is cheaper but slower than the train (3/day, 8 hours, www.swebus.se).

By Car to the Jotunheimen Mountains: See "Route Tips for Drivers" on page 356.

BY PLANE
Oslo Airport
Oslo Lufthavn, also called Gardermoen, is about 30 miles north of the city center and has a helpful 24-hour information center (airport code: OSL, tel. 91 50 64 00, www.osl.no).

The fastest and cheapest way to get into the city center is by **train.** Exiting the baggage claim, turn left and head to the far end of the building. Here you'll see two options: local trains (NSB) take about 25 minutes to downtown (93 NOK, 2/hour, covered by rail passes, cheaper if you have an Oslo Pass, buy ticket at machines or pay a little extra to buy it at the counter); the private, competing Flytoget train is only a few minutes faster but costs nearly double (180 NOK, 4/hour, runs roughly 5:00-24:00, not covered by rail passes, www.flytoget.no; simply swipe your credit card at the gate, then swipe it again when you get off). Monitors show the next several departures; unless you are in a big hurry or enjoy paying double, I'd stick with the NSB trains. Note that for either type of train, some departures only go as far as the central train station, while others continue—for no extra charge—to the National Theater station (which is closer to most recommended hotels). Unfortunately, this isn't clearly indicated on the screen; to spare yourself a transfer (or save some extra walking), ask whether your train continues to the National Theater.

Flybuss airport buses stop directly outside the arrival hall and make several downtown stops, including the central train station (180 NOK one-way, 3/hour, 40 minutes, tel. 67 98 04 80)—but since it costs more than the train and takes twice as long, it's hard to justify taking the bus.

Taxis take about 45 minutes to downtown, and vary in price depending on the company; figure 600-900 NOK on weekdays, more on weekends or after hours. An interactive screen at the information desk (near the trains) lets you comparison-shop prices and order a cab. Given the high price and long trip, I'd take a taxi only if you're traveling with a group or have lots of luggage.

Sandefjord Airport Torp

Ryanair, WizzAir, and other discount airlines use this airport (airport code: TRF, tel. 33 42 70 00, www.torp.no), 70 miles south of Oslo. You can take a bus into downtown Oslo (220 NOK, www.torpekspressen.no). If you're going from Oslo *to* Sandefjord, note that buses depart Oslo's central bus terminal (next to the train station) about three hours before all flight departures.

BY CRUISE SHIP

Oslo has three cruise ports, described next. For more in-depth cruising information, pick up my *Rick Steves Scandinavian & Northern European Cruise Ports* guidebook.

Getting Downtown: To varying degrees, all of Oslo's cruise ports are within walking distance of the city center—but from the farthest-flung port, Filipstad, your best option is to take advantage of your cruise line's shuttle bus, even if you have to pay for it (most drop off by the Nobel Peace Center, near City Hall on the harborfront). No public transit serves the ports, but Open Top Sightseeing's hop-on, hop-off bus tours meet arriving cruise ships at or near all ports (pricey but con-

venient; see "Tours in Oslo," near the beginning of this chapter). A taxi into town from any of the ports costs 150 NOK minimum.

Once you arrive at the City Hall/harbor area, you can simply walk up the street behind City Hall to find Karl Johans Gate, and the National Gallery; hop on tram #12 (ride it toward Majorstuen to reach Vigeland Park—get off at the Vigelandsparken stop; or ride it toward Disen to reach the train station—use the Jernbanetorget stop); or take the shuttle boat from below City Hall across the harbor to the museums on Bygdøy.

Port Details: Akershus, right on the harbor below Akershus Fortress, has two berths: **Søndre Akershuskai,** a bit closer to town, and **Vippetangen,** at the tip of the peninsula. Both are within an easy 10-minute walk of City Hall (just stroll with the harbor on your left). **Revierkai,** around the east side of the Akershus Fortress peninsula, faces Oslo's striking, can't-miss-it Opera House. From the Opera House, cross the busy street to the train station and the start of my self-guided "Oslo Walk," or head up the street called Rådhusgata to City Hall.

Filipstad is just west of downtown, next to the Tjuvholmen development (around the far side of Aker Brygge from City Hall). From here, it's best to take the cruise-line shuttle bus into town. But if you do choose to hoof it, it's a dull 20-minute walk: Exiting the port, turn right at the roundabout, then head to the busy highway and follow the path to the right and signs to *sentrum*. Your ship's upper deck provides the perfect high-altitude vantage point for scouting your options before disembarking.

BY OVERNIGHT BOAT TO COPENHAGEN

Consider connecting Oslo and Copenhagen by cruise ship. The boat leaves daily from Oslo at 16:30 (arrives in Copenhagen at 9:45 the following morning; going the other way, it departs Copenhagen at 16:30 and arrives in Oslo at 9:45; about 17 hours sailing each way). The boat leaves Oslo from the far (Opera House) side of the Akershus Fortress peninsula (take bus #60 to Vippetangen from the train station, 2-4/hour, get off at Vippetangen stop and follow signs to DFDS ticket office at Akershusstranda 31). Boarding is from 15:15 to 16:15. From Oslo, you'll sail through the Oslofjord—not as dramatic as Norway's western fjords, but impressive if you're not going to Bergen. On board are gourmet restaurants, dinner and breakfast buffets, cafés, nightclubs, tax-free shops, a casino, children's activities, a sauna, hot tub, and swimming pool. This is fun and convenient, but not as swanky as the Stockholm-Helsinki cruise (see the Helsinki chapter).

You can take this cruise one-way or do a round-trip from either city. Book online or by phone (from Norway, call DFDS Seaways' Denmark office: Mon-Fri 9:00-16:30, closed Sat-Sun, tel. 00 45 33 42 30 10, www.dfdsseaways.us). Book in advance for the best prices. For more specifics and sample prices, see "By Overnight Boat to Oslo" on page 114.

NORWAY IN A NUTSHELL

A Scenic Journey to the Sognefjord

While Oslo and Bergen are the big draws for tourists, Norway is first and foremost a place of unforgettable natural beauty. There's a certain mystique about the "land of the midnight sun," but you'll get the most scenic travel thrills per mile, minute, and dollar by going west from Oslo rather than north.

Norway's greatest claims to scenic fame are her deep, lush fjords. Three million years ago, an ice age made this land as inhabitable as the center of Greenland. As the glaciers advanced and cut their way to the sea, they gouged out long grooves—today's fjords.

The entire west coast is slashed by stunning fjords, and the Sognefjord—Norway's longest (120 miles) and deepest (1 mile)—is tops. The seductive Sognefjord has tiny but tough ferries, towering canyons, and isolated farms and villages marinated in the mist of countless waterfalls.

A series of well-organized and spectacular bus, train, and ferry connections—appropriately nicknamed "Norway in a Nutshell"—lays Norway's beautiful fjord country before you on a scenic platter. With the Nutshell, you'll delve into two offshoots of the Sognefjord, which make an upside-down "U" route: the Aurlandsfjord and the Nærøyfjord. You'll link the ferry ride to the rest of Norway with two trains and a bus: The main train is an express route that takes you through stark and icy scenery above the tree line. To get from the express train down to the ferry, you'll catch an old-fashioned slow train one way (passing waterfalls and forests) and a bus the other way (offering fjord views and more waterfalls). All connections are designed for tourists, explained in English, convenient, and easy. At the start of the fjord, you'll go through the town of Flåm (a transit hub), then pass briefly by the workaday town of

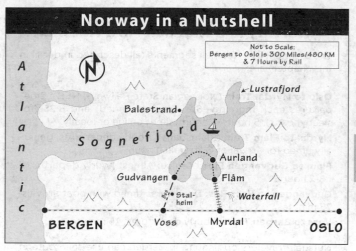

Norway in a Nutshell

Not to Scale:
Bergen to Oslo is 300 Miles/480 KM
& 7 Hours by Rail

A t l a n t i c

Lustrafjord

Balestrand

S o g n e f j o r d

Aurland

Gudvangen

Flåm

Bus · Stal-heim

Waterfall

BERGEN

Voss

Myrdal

OSLO

Aurland and the hamlet of Undredal (by taking the Nutshell trip segments at your own pace, you can visit the latter two fjord towns on your own; all are described in this chapter).

This region enjoys mild weather for its latitude, thanks to the warm Gulf Stream. (When it rains in Bergen, it just drizzles here.) But if the weather is bad, don't fret. I've often arrived to gloomy weather, only to enjoy sporadic splashes of brilliant sunshine all day long.

Recently the popularity of the Nutshell route has skyrocketed. And the 2005 completion of the longest car tunnel in the world (15 miles between Flåm and Lærdal) rerouted the main E-16 road between Bergen and Oslo through this idyllic fjord corner. All of this means that summer comes with a crush of crowds, dampening some of the area's magic. Unfortunately, many tourists are overcome by Nutshell tunnel-vision, and spend so much energy scurrying between boats, trains, and buses that they forget to simply enjoy the fjords. Relax—you're on vacation.

PLANNING YOUR TIME

Even the blitz tourist needs a day for the Norway in a Nutshell trip. With more time, sleep in a town along the fjord, and customize your fjord experience to include sights outside the Nutshell.

Day 1: The Nutshell works well as a single day (one-way between Oslo and Bergen, or as a long day-trip loop from either city). If you're without a car and want to make efficient use of your time, organize your trip so that it begins in Oslo and ends in Bergen (or vice versa).

Day 2: If you have enough time, spend the night somewhere on the Sognefjord—either along the Nutshell route itself (in Flåm

"Norway in a Nutshell" in a Nutshell

The essential five Nutshell segments (all described in detail in this chapter) are:

Oslo to Myrdal Train (Norwegian State Railways, NSB): 2 departures each morning—6:25 (recommended) and 8:25 (for sleepyheads), 5 hours. Confirm times online or locally.

Myrdal to Flåm Train (Flåmsbana): Hourly departures, generally timed for arrival of Oslo train, 1 hour.

Flåm to Gudvangen Fjord Cruise: Almost hourly departures, 1.5-2 hours.

Gudvangen to Voss Bus: Departures timed with boat arrivals, 75 minutes.

Voss to Bergen Train: Hourly departures, 75 minutes.

Nutshell travelers originating in Bergen can use this route in reverse.

or Aurland; accommodations listed later), or in another, even more appealing fjordside town (such as Balestrand or Solvorn, both described in the next chapter).

With More Time: The Sognefjord deserves more than a day. If you can spare the time, venture off the Nutshell route. You can easily connect to some non-Nutshell towns (such as Balestrand) via ferry or express boat. Drivers can improve on the Nutshell by taking a northern route: From Oslo, drive through the Gudbrandsdal Valley, go over the Jotunheimen Mountains, then along the Lustrafjord to Kaupanger; from there, you can experience the Sognefjord on a car ferry ending in Gudvangen, and drive the remainder of the Nutshell route to Bergen. (Most of these sights, and the ferry connections, are covered in the next two chapters.) For more tips, see the "Beyond the Nutshell" sidebar.

Orientation to the Nutshell

The most exciting single-day trip you could make from Oslo or Bergen is this circular train/boat/bus/train jaunt through fjord country.

Local TIs (listed throughout this chapter) are well-informed about your options, and they sell tickets for various segments of the trip. At TIs, train stations, and hotels, look for souvenir-worthy

brochures with photos, descriptions, and exact times.

Route Overview

The basic idea is this: Take a train
halfway across the mountainous
spine of Norway, make your way
down to the Sognefjord for a boat
cruise, then climb back up out of the
fjord to rejoin the main train line.
Each of these steps is explained in
the self-guided "Nutshell Tour" in
this chapter. Transportation along
the Nutshell route is carefully coor-

dinated. If any segment of your journey is delayed, the transportation for the next segment will wait for you (because everyone on
board is catching the same connection).

Doing the Nutshell one-way between Oslo and Bergen (or
vice versa) is most satisfying—you'll see the whole shebang, and it's
extremely efficient if you're connecting the two cities anyway. It's
also possible to do most of the route in a round-trip loop from either Bergen or Oslo. Doing the round-trip from Bergen is cheaper,
but it doesn't include the majestic train ride between Myrdal and
Oslo. The round-trip from Oslo includes all the must-see sights but
it's a very long day (you leave Oslo at 6:25 and don't get back until
22:35).

When to Go

The Nutshell trip is possible all year. In the summer (June-Aug),
the connections are most convenient, the weather is most likely to
be good...and the route is at its most crowded. Outside of this time,
sights close and schedules become more challenging. Some say the
Nutshell is most beautiful in winter, though schedules are severely
reduced.

Nutshell Itineraries
Oslo-Bergen

You must take one of two morning departures (6:25 or 8:25) to
do the entire trip from Oslo to Bergen in a day. I recommend the
earlier departure to enjoy an hour more free time in Flåm and generally fewer crowds. This itinerary shows typical sample times for
summer travel; confirm exact times before your trip (www.nsb.no
for trains, www.kringom.no for buses and ferries):

- Train from Oslo to Myrdal: 6:25-11:34
- Flåmsbana train from Myrdal to Flåm: 12:13-13:10
- Free time in Flåm: 13:10-15:15

- Boat from Flåm to Gudvangen: 15:15-17:30
- Bus from Gudvangen to Voss: 17:45-19:00
- Train from Voss to Bergen: 19:38-21:00

If you leave Oslo on the later train, you can either arrive in Bergen at the same time (with less free time in Flåm) or have more time in Flåm and Voss and arrive later (22:30).

Other Options

Here are other one-day options for doing the Nutshell in the summer. Confirm specific times before your trip.

Bergen-Oslo: Train departs Bergen-8:43, arrives Voss-9:56; bus departs Voss-10:10, arrives Gudvangen-11:20; boat departs Gudvangen-11:45, arrives Flåm-13:15; Flåmsbana train departs Flåm-16:05, arrives Myrdal-17:03; train departs Myrdal-17:54, arrives Oslo-22:35.

Day-Trip Loop from Oslo: Train departs Oslo-6:25, arrives Myrdal-11:34; Flåmsbana train departs Myrdal-12:13, arrives Flåm-13:10; boat departs Flåm-14:00, arrives Gudvangen-15:30; bus departs Gudvangen-15:40, arrives Voss-16:55; train departs Voss-17:11, arrives Oslo-22:35.

Day-Trip Loop from Bergen: Train departs Bergen-8:43, arrives Voss-9:56; bus departs Voss-10:10, arrives Gudvangen-11:20; boat departs Gudvangen-11:45, arrives Flåm-13:15; Flåmsbana train departs Flåm-14:50, arrives Myrdal-15:46; train departs Myrdal-17:30, arrives Bergen-19:56.

Buying Tickets

The easiest way to purchase Nutshell tickets is to buy a package from Fjord Tours—it will save you time and the trouble of planning your itinerary. However, you're locked into their schedule and the package price can be more expensive than buying individual tickets.

On your own, you can often find discounts for the train and can choose the cheapest ferry—possibly saving up to 500 NOK. You also have more flexibility—you choose how much time you spend in Flåm and what time you arrive in Bergen or Oslo. However, you have to plan your itinerary and buy tickets for each leg of your journey—that's five separate tickets for a one-way trip between Oslo and Bergen.

If you have a rail pass, or if you're a student or a senior (68 or older), you'll save money by booking the Nutshell on your own.

Whether you are doing a package deal or buying tickets on your own, in summer book well in advance—four to five weeks is best. Train tickets on the Nutshell route from or back to Oslo can sell out in high season (June-Aug), as can some departures on the ferry from Flåm.

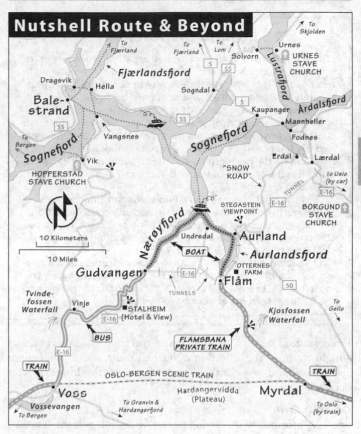

Nutshell Route & Beyond

Package Deals

Fjord Tours sells the Nutshell package at all Norwegian State Railways (NSB) stations, including Oslo and Bergen, or through their offices in Norway (tel. 55 55 76 60, www.fjordtours.com, booking@fjordtours.com). With these packages, all your departures are fixed. You can choose between two different types of ferries: Classic, about a 2-hour ride on an old car ferry that just carries foot passengers; or Premium, 1.5 hours on a hybrid catamaran. Unless you are in a hurry (though why hurry through the fjords?), take the Classic ferry.

Here are the prices (as of press time) for Nutshell packages on the Classic ferry:
- One-way from Bergen or Oslo-1,690 NOK
- Round-trip from Oslo via Voss-2,760 NOK
- Round-trip from Bergen via Myrdal-1,440 NOK
- Round-trip from Flåm-1,010 NOK

Packages on the Premium ferry cost 250-500 NOK extra.

Beyond the Nutshell

The Sognefjord is the ultimate natural thrill Norway has to offer, and there's no doubt that the Nutshell route outlined in this chapter is the most efficient way to see it quickly. Unfortunately, its trains, buses, and boats are thronged with other visitors who have the same idea.

Travelers with a bit more time, and the willingness to chart their own course, often have a more rewarding Sognefjord experience. It's surprisingly easy to break out of the Nutshell and hit the northern part of the Sognefjord (for example, using the Bergen-Vik-Balestrand-Aurland-Flåm express boat, described on page 332).

In the next chapter, you'll find some tempting stopovers on the north bank of the Sognefjord, including adorable fjordside villages (such as Balestrand and Solvorn), evocative stave churches (Hopperstad and Urnes), and a chance to get up close to a glacier (at the Nigard Glacier).

Read up on your options, then be adventurous about mixing and matching the fjordside attractions that appeal to you most. Ideally, use the Nutshell as a springboard for diving into the Back Door fjords of your travel dreams.

Fjord Tours also sells a Nutshell round-trip from Oslo that includes a night train, a "Sognefjord in a Nutshell" tour, and a "Sognefjord and Nærøyfjord in a Nutshell" tour—see www.fjordtours.com for details.

On Your Own

Specific information on buying tickets for each leg of the Nutshell route is explained later, under their individual listings. In general, you can buy train tickets (including the Flåmsbana) at the NSB train stations in Oslo or Bergen or online at www.nsb.no. For the best deal, look for nonrefundable "minipris" tickets. You can buy Flåm-Gudvangen ferry tickets with one of two companies: The Fjords (more sailings, www.visitflam.com) or Lustrabaatane (cheaper prices, www.lustrabaatane.no). You can't buy tickets in advance for the Gudvangen-Voss bus; there's always room but you must pay the driver in cash. If you're a student or senior, always ask about discounts.

Rail Pass Discounts: If you have any rail pass that includes Norway, the Oslo-Bergen train is covered (except a 50-NOK reservation fee for second class; free for first-class passholders); you also get a 30 percent discount on the Flåmsbana train. You still have to pay full fare for the boat cruise and the Gudvangen-Voss bus. Your total one-way cost between Oslo and Bergen: about 650 NOK with a first-class pass, 700 NOK with a second-class pass.

Travel Tips

Luggage: Transporting luggage on the Nutshell is no big deal, as the connections require almost no walking: At Myrdal, you just cross the platform; in Flåm, you walk 50 yards from the train to the dock; in Gudvangen, the bus meets the ferry at the dock; in Voss, the bus drops you at the train station. If you want to check your bag during your free time in Flåm, use the baggage-check cabin at the head of the train track, across the lane from the boat dock.

An alternative to carrying your luggage is **Porterservice AS**. They pick up your luggage at your hotel, transport it via the train between Oslo and Bergen, and drop it off at your next hotel by 21:00 (250 NOK/piece, mobile 90 61 00 09, www.porterservice. no).

Eating: Options along the route aren't great—on the Nutshell I'd consider food just as a source of nutrition and forget about fine dining. You can buy some food on the fjord cruises (hot dogs, burgers, and pizza) and the Oslo-Bergen train. Depending on the timing of your layovers, Myrdal, Voss, or Flåm are your best lunch-stop options (the Myrdal and Flåm train stations have decent cafeterias, and other eateries surround the Flåm and Voss stations)—although you won't have a lot of time there if you're making the journey all in one day. Your best bet is to pack picnic meals and munch en route. If catching an early train in Oslo, the station has a handy grocery store open at 5:00 (6:00 on Sun).

Cruise-Ship Passengers: Tiny Flåm—in the heart of Nutshell country—is an increasingly popular destination for huge cruise ships. If arriving in Flåm by cruise ship, see my *Scandinavian & Northern European Cruise Ports* book for details on how to approach the Nutshell during your day in port.

Nutshell Tour

If you only have one day for this region, it'll be a thrilling one—worth ▲▲▲. The following self-guided segments of the Nutshell route are narrated from Oslo to Bergen. If you're going the other way, hold the book upside down.

▲▲Oslo-Bergen Train (Via Myrdal)

The Oslo-Bergen route—called "Bergensbanen" by Norwegians—is simply the most spectacular train ride in northern Europe. The entire railway, an amazing engineering feat completed in 1909, is 300 miles long; peaks at 4,266 feet, which, at this Alaskan latitude, is far above the tree line; goes under 18 miles of snow sheds; trundles over 300 bridges; and passes through 200 tunnels in just under seven hours. To celebrate the Bergensbanen centennial in 2009, Norwegian TV mounted cameras on the outside of the train and broadcast the entire trip—and more than a million Norwegians tuned in (search for "Bergensbanen" on YouTube and you can watch it too).

Cost and Reservations: Here are the one-way fares for various segments: Oslo-Bergen-950 NOK, Oslo-Myrdal-781 NOK, Myrdal-Voss-126 NOK, Myrdal-Bergen-309 NOK, Voss-Bergen-204 NOK. You can save money on these fares if you book "minipris" tickets in advance at www.nsb.no. If you have difficulty paying for your ticket with a US credit card online, use PayPal or call 61 05 19 10—press 9 for English, and you'll be given a web link where you can finish your transaction. In peak season, get reservations for this train four to five weeks in advance.

Second-class rail-pass holders pay just 50 NOK to reserve, and first-class passholders pay nothing. If you have a second-class rail pass or ticket, you can pay 90 NOK to upgrade to "Komfort" class, with more legroom, extra comfortable seats, free coffee and tea, and an outlet for your laptop (book online or ask the conductor when you board).

Schedule: This train runs three to five times per day, including two morning departures (overnight possible except Sat). The segment from Oslo to Myrdal takes about five hours; going all the way to Bergen takes seven hours.

Route Narration: The scenery crescendos as you climb over Norway's mountainous spine. After a mild three hours of deep woods and lakes, you're into the barren, windswept heaths and glaciers. Here's what you'll see traveling westward from Oslo: Leaving Oslo, you pass through a six-mile-long tunnel and stop in Drammen, Norway's fifth-largest town. The scenery stays low-key and woodsy up Hallingdal Valley until you reach Geilo, a popular ski resort. Then you enter a land of big views and tough little cabins. Finse, at about 4,000 feet, is the highest stop on the line. At several towns, the conductor may announce how many minutes the train will be stopped there. This gives you a few fun moments to get out, stretch, take a photograph, and look around.

Before Myrdal, you enter the longest high-mountain stretch of railway in Europe. Much of the line is protected by snow tun-

nels. The scenery gets more dramatic as you approach Myrdal (MEER-doll). Just before Myrdal, look to the right and down into the Flåm Valley, where the Flåmsbana branch line winds its way down to the fjord. Nutshell travelers get off at Myrdal.

▲▲Myrdal-Flåm Train (Flåmsbana)

The little 12-mile spur line leaves the Oslo-Bergen line at Myrdal (2,800 feet), which is nothing but a scenic high-altitude train junc-

tion with a decent cafeteria. Before boarding, pick up the free, multilingual souvenir pamphlet with lots of info on the trip (or see www. flaamsbana.no). Video screens onboard and sporadic English commentary on the loudspeakers explain points of interest, but there's not much to say—it's all about the scen-

ery. If you're choosing seats, you'll enjoy slightly more scenery if you sit on the left going down.

Cost and Reservations: 360 NOK one-way (rail-pass holders pay 250 NOK), 480 NOK round-trip. You can book one-way tickets on www.nsb.no; the cheapest round-trip tickets are on www. visitflam.com. You also can buy tickets onboard the train or at the Flåmsbana stations in Flåm. Train staff in Oslo may tell you that the Flåmsbana is booked—don't worry, it very rarely fills. Even if it's standing-room only, you can usually squeeze in. Simply get to Myrdal and hop on the train.

However, morning trains ascending from Flåm to Myrdal (when there are several cruise ships in port) can sell out. In summer, if you want to leave Flåm in the morning, try buying your ticket the night before or right when the Flåm ticket office opens (at 7:00). The best plan is to buy your Flåmsbana ticket at the same time you buy your other train tickets.

Schedule: The train departs in each direction nearly hourly.

Route Narration: From Myrdal, the Flåmsbana train winds down to Flåm (sea level) through 20 tunnels (more than three

miles' worth) in 55 thrilling minutes. It's party time on board, and the engineer even stops the train for photos at the best waterfall, Kjosfossen. According to a Norwegian legend, Huldra (a temptress) lives behind these falls and tries to lure men to the rocks with her singing... look out for her...and keep a wary eye on your partner.

The train line is an even more impressive feat of engineering when you realize it's not a cogwheel train—it's held to the tracks only by

steel wheels, though it does have five separate braking systems.

▲▲▲Flåm-Gudvangen Fjord Cruise

The Flåmsbana train deposits you at Flåm, a scenic, functional transit hub at the far end of the Aurlandsfjord. If you're doing the Nutshell route nonstop, follow the crowds and hop on the sightseeing boat that'll take you to Gudvangen. With minimal English narration, the boat takes you close to the goats, sheep, waterfalls, and awesome cliffs.

Cruise Options: There are two boat companies to choose from— The Fjords (www.visitflam.com) and Lustrabaatane (www.lustrabaatane.com). The Fjords has a Classic option that takes more than two hours. It stops at Aurland, Undredal, Dyrdal, and Styvi, which is handy if you want to hop off and on along the way—though you'll need to buy separate tickets for each leg of your trip, and it'll end up costing you more (be sure to notify the ticket seller where you want to get off, to make certain they'll stop). The other option is their Premium ferry, a hybrid catamaran that's faster, silent, and more expensive. It takes about 1.5 hours nonstop between Flåm and Gudvangen.

The cheapest option is the Lustrabaatane ferry—a slow boat that takes about two hours—similar to the Classic ferry, but with no stops.

I much prefer the slower boats because the price is lower, you have more time to savor the scenery, and the bus connection in Gudvangen is immediate and reliable.

Cost and Reservations: For the whole route (Flåm-Gudvangen), you'll pay 250-645 NOK one-way depending on the ferry

(435-705 NOK round-trip). Reservations may be necessary on busy days in summer. Buy your ticket in Flåm as soon as you know which boat you want or in advance at each boat company's website. Beware: The ticket desk at the Flåm Visitors Center is The Fjords boat desk, and they'll sell you a boat ticket implying it's your only option. Tickets for Lustrabaatane are sold at the nearby TI.

Schedule: In summer (June-Aug), boats run multiple times daily in both directions—Classic ferry (2/day), Premium ferry (5/day), Lustrabaatane ferry (2/day). Specific departure times can vary, but generally boats leave Flåm starting at 8:00, with a last departure at 19:00. From Gudvangen, the first boat is generally

The Facts on Fjords

The process that created the majestic Sognefjord began during an ice age about three million years ago. A glacier up to 6,500 feet thick slid downhill at an inch an hour, following a former river valley on its way to the sea. Rocks embedded in the glacier gouged out a steep, U-shaped valley, displacing enough rock material to form a mountain 13 miles high. When the climate warmed up, the ice age came to an end. The melting glaciers retreated and the sea level rose nearly 300 feet, flooding the valley now known as the Sognefjord. The fjord is more than a mile deep, flanked by 3,000-foot mountains—for a total relief of 9,300 feet. Waterfalls spill down the cliffs, fed by runoff from today's glaciers. Powdery sediment tinges the fjords a cloudy green, the distinct color of glacier melt.

Why are there fjords on the west coast of Norway, but not, say, on the east coast of Sweden? The creation of a fjord requires a setting of coastal mountains, a good source of moisture, and a climate cold enough for glaciers to form and advance. Due to the earth's rotation, the prevailing winds in higher latitudes blow from west to east, so chances of glaciation are ideal where there is an ocean to the west of land with coastal mountains. When the winds blow east over the water, they pick up a lot of moisture, then bump up against the coastal mountain range, and dump their moisture in the form of snow—which feeds the glaciers that carve valleys down to the sea.

You can find fjords along the northwest coast of Europe—including western Norway and Sweden, Denmark's Faroe Islands, Scotland's Shetland Islands, Iceland, and Greenland; the northwest coast of North America (from Puget Sound in Washington state north to Alaska); the southwest coast of South America (Chile); the west coast of New Zealand's South Island; and on the continent of Antarctica.

As you travel, bear in mind that, while we use the word "fjord" to mean only glacier-cut inlets, Scandinavians often use it in a more general sense to include bays, lakes, and lagoons that weren't formed by glacial action.

at 9:30, with a last departure at 17:45. See www.kringom.no for schedules covering both ferry lines.

Your only concern is that the Nutshell bus from Gudvangen to Voss may not meet the last departure of the day (check locally); the worst-case scenario is that you'd need to catch the regular commuter bus to Voss, which makes more stops and doesn't take the razzle-dazzle Stalheimskleiva corkscrew road.

Route Narration: You'll cruise up the lovely **Aurlandsfjord,** motoring by the town of **Aurland** (a good home base, but only a few boats stop here), pass the towns of **Undredal, Dyrdal,** and **Styvi** (possible stops here on limited sailings by request), and hang a left at the stunning **Nærøyfjord.** The cruise ends at the apex of the Nærøyfjord, in **Gudvangen.**

The trip is breathtaking in any weather. For the last hour, as you sail down the Nærøyfjord, camera-clicking tourists scurry around struggling to get a photo that will catch the magic. Waterfalls turn the black cliffs into bridal veils, and you can nearly reach out and touch the cliffs of the Nærøyfjord. It's the world's narrowest fjord: six miles long and as little as 820 feet wide and 40 feet deep. On a sunny day, the ride is one of those fine times—like when you're high on the tip of an Alp—when a warm camaraderie spontaneously combusts between the strangers who've come together for the experience.

▲Gudvangen-Voss Bus

Nutshellers get off the boat at Gudvangen and take the 25-mile bus ride to Voss. Gudvangen is little more than a boat dock and giant tourist kiosk. If you want, you can

browse through the grass-roofed souvenir stores and walk onto a wooden footbridge—then catch your bus. While some buses—designed for commuters rather than sightseers—take the direct route to Voss, buses tied to the Nutshell schedule take a super-scenic detour via Stalheim (described later). If you're a waterfall junkie, sit on the left.

Cost: 115 NOK, pay on board, cash only, no rail pass discounts. Reservations are not necessary.

Schedule: Buses meet each ferry, or will show up usually within an hour. (Confirm this in advance if you plan to take the last boat of the day—the ferry crew can call ahead to be sure the bus waits for you.)

Route Narration: First the bus takes you up the **Nærøydal** and through a couple of long tunnels. Then you'll take a turnoff to drive past the landmark **Stalheim Hotel** for the first of many spectacular views back into fjord country. Though the hotel dates from 1885, there's been an inn here since about 1700, where the royal mailmen would change horses. The hotel is geared for tour groups (genuine trolls sew the pewter buttons on the sweaters), but the priceless view from the backyard is free. Drivers should be sure to stop here for the view and peruse the hotel's living room to survey the art showing this perch in the 19th century.

Leaving the hotel, the bus wends its way down a road called **Stalheimskleiva,** with a corkscrew series of switchbacks flanked by a pair of dramatic waterfalls. With its 18 percent grade, it's the steepest road in Norway.

After winding your way down into the valley, you're back on the same highway. The bus goes through those same tunnels again, then continues straight on the main road through pastoral countryside to Voss. You'll pass a huge lake, then follow a crystal-clear, surging river. Just before Voss, look to the right for the wide **Tvindefossen waterfall,** tumbling down its terraced cliff. Drivers will find the grassy meadow and flat rocks at its base ideal for letting the mist fog their glasses and enjoying a drink or snack (be discreet, as "picnics are forbidden").

Voss

The Nutshell bus from Gudvangen drops you at the Voss train station, which is on the Oslo-Bergen train line. This connection is generally not well-coordinated; you'll likely have 40 minutes or so to kill before the next train to Bergen.

Visiting Voss: A plain town in a lovely lake-and-mountain setting, Voss lacks the striking fjordside scenery of Flåm, Aurland, or Undredal, and is basically a home base for summer or winter sports (Norway's Winter Olympics teams often practice here). Voss surrounds its fine, 13th-century church with workaday streets— busy with both local shops and souvenir stores—stretching in several directions. Fans of American football may want to see the humble monument to player and coach Knute Rockne, who was born in Voss in 1888; look for the metal memorial plaque on a rock near the train station.

Voss' helpful **TI** is a five-minute walk from the train station— just head toward the church and stay on the right; the TI is down the street past the City Hall signed *Voss Tinghus* (Mon-Sat 9:00-18:00, Sun 10:00-17:00; off-season until 16:00 and closed Sat-Sun; Skulegata 14, mobile 40 61 77 00, www.visitvoss.no).

Drivers should zip right through Voss, but two miles outside town, you can stop at the **Mølstertunet Folk Museum,** which has 16 buildings showing off farm life in the 17th and 18th centuries (80 NOK; daily 10:00-17:00, Sept-mid-May until 15:00 and closed Sat; Mølstervegen 143, tel. 47 47 97 94, www.vossfolkemuseum. no).

▲Voss-Bergen Train

The least exciting segment of the trip—but still pleasantly scenic—

this train chugs 60 miles along the valley between the midsize town of Voss and Bergen. For the best scenery, sit on the right side of the train if coming from Oslo, or the left side if coming from Bergen. Between Voss and Dale, you'll pass several scenic lakes; near Bergen, you'll go along the Veafjord.

Cost: 204 NOK, fully covered by rail passes that include Norway. Reservations aren't necessary for this leg.

Schedule: Unlike the long-distance Oslo-Bergen journey, this line is also served by more frequent commuter trains (about hourly, 75 minutes).

Voss-Oslo Train: Note that if you're doing the Nutshell round-trip loop from Oslo, you should catch the train from Voss (rather than Bergen) back to Oslo. The return trip takes six hours and costs 860 NOK; reservations are strongly recommended four to five weeks ahead in peak season.

Flåm

Flåm (pronounced "flome")—where the boat and Flåmsbana train meet, at the head of the Aurlandsfjord—feels more like a transit junction than a village. But its striking setting, easy transportation connections, and touristy bustle make it appealing as a home base for exploring the nearby area.

Orientation to Flåm

Most of Flåm's services are in a modern cluster of buildings in and around the train station, including the TI, train ticket desk, public WC, cafeteria, and souvenir shops. Just outside the station, the little red shed at the head of the tracks serves as a **left-luggage desk** (daily 8:00-19:00, on your right as you depart the train, ring bell if nobody's there), and displays a chart of the services you'll find in the station. The **boat dock** for fjord cruises is just beyond the end of the tracks. Surrounding the station are a Co-op Marked **grocery store** (with a basic pharmacy and post office inside, Mon-Fri 8:00-20:00, Sat-Sun 10:00-18:00, shorter hours off-season) and a smattering of hotels, travel agencies, and touristy restaurants. Aside from a few scattered farmhouses and some homes lining the road, there's not much of a town here. (The extremely sleepy old

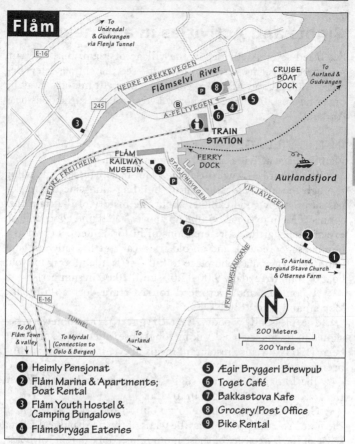

Flåm

1. Heimly Pensjonat
2. Flåm Marina & Apartments; Boat Rental
3. Flåm Youth Hostel & Camping Bungalows
4. Flåmsbrygga Eateries
5. Ægir Bryggeri Brewpub
6. Toget Café
7. Bakkastova Kafe
8. Grocery/Post Office
9. Bike Rental

town center—where tourists rarely venture, and which you'll pass on the Flåmsbana train—is a few miles up the river, in the valley.)

Tourist Information: Inside the train station you'll find the TI and the Flåm Visitors Center.

The **visitors center** sells tickets for The Fjords ferries to Gudvangen (but not its rival, Lustrabaatane), the Flåmsbana train, regular train tickets, and other tours in the area (daily 7:00-19:00, shorter hours Sept-April, tel. 57 63 14 00, www.visitflam.com).

At the **TI** you can purchase tickets for the Lustrabaatane ferry to Gudvangen, the express boat to Bergen, FjordSafari, Njord Seakayak Adventures, and other tours. The TI also hands out schedules for buses, boats, and trains; a diagram of the train-station area, identifying services available in each building; a map of Flåm and the surrounding area, marked with suggested walks and hikes; and information on Bergen or Oslo (daily 8:30-18:00, Oct-March 9:00-15:00, mobile 99 23 15 00, https://en.sognefjord.no).

Sights and Activities in and near Flåm

I've listed several activities in the village of Flåm. But the main reason people come here is to leave it—see the options later. Because Aurland and Flåm are close together (10 minutes away by car or bus, or 20 minutes by boat), I've also listed attractions near Aurland.

IN THE VILLAGE

Flåm's village activities are all along or near the pier.

The **Flåm Railway Museum** (Flåmsbana Museet), sprawling through the long old train station building alongside the tracks, has surprisingly good exhibits about the history of the train that connects Flåm to the main line up above. You'll find good English explanations, artifacts, re-creations of historic interiors (such as a humble schoolhouse), and an old train car. It's the only real museum in town and a good place to kill time while waiting for your boat or train (free, daily 9:00-17:00, until 20:00 in summer).

A pointless and overpriced **tourist train** does a 45-minute loop around Flåm (130 NOK).

The pleasantly woody **Ægir Bryggeri,** a microbrewery designed to resemble an old Viking longhouse, offers tastes of its five beers (150 NOK; also restaurant meals in evening with a matching beer menu).

The TI hands out a map suggesting several **walks and hikes** in the area, starting from right in town.

Consider renting a **boat** to go out on the peaceful waters of the fjord. You can paddle near the walls of the fjord and really get a sense of the immensity of these mountains. You can rent rowboats, motorboats, and paddleboats at the little marina across the harbor. If you'd rather have a kayak, **Njord Seakayak Adventures** does kayak tours, but won't rent you one unless you're certified (mobile 91 32 66 28, www.seakayaknorway.com).

FROM OR NEAR FLÅM
▲▲▲Cruising Nærøyfjord

The most scenic fjord I've seen anywhere in Norway is about an hour from Flåm (basically the last half of the Flåm-Gudvangen trip). If you've driven to Flåm, didn't book a Nutshell tour, or are staying overnight, here are several ways to cruise it.

The Fjords Tours: This private company runs several trips from Flåm; their most popular is a ferry ride to Gudvangen and a bus ride back to Flåm (435-705 NOK, 4-hour round-trip, departs Flåm at 10:00, 12:00, 16:00, and 18:00, fewer off-season, choose slower Classic ferry for best viewing).

Another offering, the World Heritage Cruise, is a boat trip up the Nærøyfjord, stopping at Bleiklindi, Bakka, Styvi, and Dyrdal. You can leave the boat to visit these villages and hop on when the boat returns. It's possible to hike about four miles between Bleiklindi and Styvi with this option (350 NOK, 3 hours, multiple departures daily June-Aug). They also do a variation on this trip with a 45-minute stop in the village of Undredal for lunch and a goat-cheese tasting (750 NOK, June-Aug only); a bus ride up to the thrilling Stegastein viewpoint (a concrete-and-wood viewing pier sticking out from a mountainside high above Aurland, 290 NOK); and more. For details, drop by the Flåm Visitors Center inside the train station, call 57 63 14 00, or see www.visitflam.com.

FjordSafari to Nærøyfjord: FjordSafari takes little groups out onto the fjord in small, open Zodiac-type boats with an English-speaking guide. Participants wear full-body weather suits, furry hats, and spacey goggles (making everyone on the boat look like crash-test dummies). As the boat rockets across the water, you'll be thankful for the gear, no matter what the weather. Their two-hour Flåm-Gudvangen-Flåm tour focuses on the Nærøyfjord, and gets you all the fjord magnificence you can imagine (790 NOK, several departures daily). Their three-hour tour is the same but adds a stop in Undredal, where you can see goat cheese being made, sample it, and wander that sleepy village (890 NOK, one departure daily May-Aug, fewer off-season, kids get discounts, mobile 99 09 08 60, www.fjordsafari.com, Maylene). Skip the 1.5-hour "basic" tour, which just barely touches on the Nærøyfjord.

▲Flåm Valley Bike Ride or Hike

For the best single-day land activity from Flåm, take the Flåms-bana train to Myrdal, then hike or mountain-bike along the road

(half gravel, half paved) back down to Flåm (2-3 hours by bike, gorgeous water-falls, great mountain scenery, and a cute church with an evocative graveyard, but no fjord views).

Walkers can hike the best two hours from Myrdal to Blomheller, and catch the train from there into the valley. Or, without riding the train, you can simply walk up the valley 2.5 miles to the church and a little farther to a waterfall. Whenever you get tired hiking up or down the valley, you can hop on the next train. Pick up the helpful map with this and other hiking options (ranging from easy to strenuous) at the Flåm TI.

Bikers can rent good mountain bikes from the cabin next to the Flåm train station (180 NOK/2-hour minimum, 350 NOK/

day, includes helmet; daily May-June 9:00-18:00, July-Sept 8:00-20:00, closed off-season). It costs 100 NOK to take a bike to Myrdal on the train.

Otternes Farms

This humble but magical cluster of four centuries-old farms is about three miles from Flåm (easy for drivers; a decent walk or bike ride otherwise). It's a ghost village perched high on a ridge, up a twisty gravel road midway between Flåm and Aurland. These traditional time-warp houses and barns date from the time before emigration decimated the workforce, coinage replaced barter, and industrialized margarine became more popular than butter—all

of which left farmers to eke out a living relying only on their goats and the cheese they produced. Until 1919 the only road between Aurland and Flåm passed between this huddle of 27 buildings, high above the fjord. First settled in 1522, farmers lived here until the 1990s.

OVER (OR UNDER) THE MOUNTAINS, TO LÆRDAL AND BORGUND

To reach these sights, you'll first head along the fjord to Aurland (described later). Of the sights below, the Lærdal Tunnel, Stegastein viewpoint, and Aurlandsvegen "Snow Road" are best for drivers. The Borgund Stave Church can be reached by car, or by bus from Flåm or Aurland.

Lærdal Tunnel

Drivers find that this tunnel makes connecting Flåm and Lærdal a snap. It's the world's longest road-vehicle tunnel, stretching 15 miles between Aurland and Lærdal as part of the E-16 highway. It also makes the wonderful Borgund Stave Church (described later) less than an hour's drive from Aurland. The downside to the tunnel is that it goes beneath my favorite scenic drive in Norway (the Aurlandsvegen "Snow Road," described next). But with about two hours, you can drive through the tunnel to Lærdal and then return via the "Snow Road," with the Stegastein viewpoint as a finale, before dropping back into Aurland.

▲▲Stegastein Viewpoint and Aurlandsvegen "Snow Road"

With a car, clear weather, and a little nerve, consider twisting up the mountain behind Aurland on route 243 for about 20 minutes to a magnificent view over the Aurlandsfjord. A viewpoint called Stegastein—which looks like a giant, wooden, sideways number "7"—provides a platform from which you can enjoy stunning views across the fjord and straight down to Aurland. Immediately beyond the viewpoint, you leave the fjord views and enter the beautifully desolate mountaintop world of the Aurlandsvegen "Snow Road." When this narrow ribbon of a road finally hits civilization on the other side, you're a mile from the Lærdal tunnel entrance and about 30 minutes from the fine Borgund Stave Church.

▲▲Borgund Stave Church

About 16 miles east of Lærdal, in the village of Borgund, is Norway's most-visited and one of its best-preserved stave churches.

Dating from around 1180, the interior features only a few later additions, including a 16th-century pulpit, 17th-century stone altar, painted decorations, and crossbeam reinforcements.

Cost and Hours: 90 NOK, buy tickets in museum across street, daily June-Aug 8:00-20:00, May and Sept 10:00-17:00, closed Oct-April. The museum has a shop and a fine little **$$ cafeteria** serving filling and tasty lunches. Tel. 57 66 81 09, www.stavechurch.com.

Getting There: It's about a 30-minute **drive** east of Lærdal, on E-16 (the road to Oslo—if coming from Aurland or Flåm, consider taking the scenic route via the Stegastein viewpoint, described earlier). There's also a convenient **bus** connection: The bus departs Flåm and Aurland around midday (direction: Lillehammer) and heads for the church, with a return bus departing Borgund in mid-afternoon (170-NOK round-trip, get ticket from driver, about 1 hour each way with about 1 hour at the church, bus runs daily May-Sept, tell driver you want to get off at the church).

Visiting the Church: Explore the dimly lit interior, illuminated only by the original, small, circular windows up high. The oldest and most authentic item in the church is the stone baptismal font. In medieval times, priests conducting baptisms would go outside to shoo away the evil spirits from an infant before bringing it inside the church for the ritual. (If infants died before being baptized, they couldn't be buried in the churchyard, so parents would put their bodies in little coffins and hide them under the church's floorboards to get them as close as possible to God.)

Notice the X-shaped crosses of St. Andrew (the church's patron), carvings of dragons, and medieval runes. Borgund's church also comes with one of this country's best stave-church history museums, which beautifully explains these icons of medieval Norway.

Sleeping in Flåm

My recommended accommodations are away from the tacky train-station bustle, but a close enough walk to be convenient. The first two places are located along the waterfront a quarter-mile from the station: Walk around the little harbor (with the water on your left) for about 10 minutes. It's more enjoyable to follow the level, waterfront dock than to hike up the main road.

$$$$ Heimly Pensjonat, with 22 straightforward rooms, is clean, efficient, and the best small hotel in town. Sit on the porch with new friends and watch the clouds roll down the fjord. Prices include breakfast and a three-course dinner (family rooms, doubles are mostly twins, closed off-season, tel. 57 63 23 00, post@heimly. no).

$$$ Flåm Marina and Apartments, perched right on the fjord, is ideal for families and longer stays. They offer one standard double and 10 new-feeling, self-catering apartments that each sleep 2-5 people. All units offer views of the fjord with a balcony, kitchenette, and small dining area (no breakfast, café serving lunch and dinner open during high season, boat rental, laundry facilities, next to the guest harbor just below Heimly Pensjonat, tel. 57 63 35 55, www.flammarina.no, booking@flammarina.no).

¢-$$ Flåm Youth Hostel and Camping Bungalows, voted Scandinavia's most beautiful campground, is run by the friendly Håland family, who rent the cheapest beds in the area (sheets and towels included in hostel but extra in cabins, showers extra, no meals but kitchen access, laundry, apple grove, mobile 94 03 26 81, www.flaam-camping.no, camping@flaam-camping.no). It's a five-minute walk toward the valley from the train station: Cross the bridge and turn left up the main road; then look for the hostel on the right.

Eating in Flåm

Dining options beyond your hotel's dining room or kitchenette are expensive and touristy. Don't aim for high cuisine here—go practical. Almost all eateries are clustered near the train station complex. Hours can be unpredictable, flexing with the season, but you can expect these to be open daily in high season. Places here tend to close pretty early (especially in shoulder season)—don't wait too long for dinner.

The **Flåmsbrygga** complex, sprawling through a long building toward the fjord from the station, includes a hotel, the affordable **$$ Furukroa Caféteria** (daily 8:00-20:00 in season, sandwiches, fast-food meals, and pizzas), and the pricey **$$$$ Flåmstova Restaurant** (breakfast and lunch buffet, sit-down dinner service). Next door is their fun, Viking-longhouse-shaped brewpub, **$$$ Ægir Bryggeri** (daily 17:00-22:00, local microbrews, Viking-inspired meals). **$$ Toget Café,** with seating in old train cars, prides itself on using as many locally sourced and organic ingredients as possible. **$$ Bakkastova Kafe,** at the other end of town, feels cozier. Housed in a traditional Norwegian red cabin just above the Fretheim Hotel, with a view terrace, it serves sandwiches, salads, and authentic Norwegian fare (daily 12:00-16:00).

Aurland

A few miles north of Flåm, Aurland is more of a real town and less of a tourist depot. While it's nothing exciting (Balestrand is more lively and appealing, and Solvorn is cuter—see next chapter), it's a good, easy-going fjordside home base. And thanks to its location—on the main road and boat lines, near Flåm—it's relatively handy for those taking public transportation.

Getting There: Aurland is an easy 10-minute drive or bus trip from Flåm. If you want to stay overnight in Aurland, note that every train (except the late-night one) arriving in Flåm connects with a bus or boat to Aurland (in summer: bus-11/day, 10 minutes, 60 NOK; ferry-4/day, 20 minutes, 165 NOK). The Flåm-Gudvangen Classic ferry doesn't always have a scheduled stop at Aurland, but they're willing to stop there if you ask—so it's possible to continue the Nutshell route from Aurland without backtracking to Flåm. Boat tickets can be bought aboard the ferry in Aurland or at www.visitflam.com. The Bergen-Balestrand-Flåm express boat stops in Aurland (for details, see the next chapter).

Orientation to Aurland

From Aurland's dingy boat dock area, walk one block up the paved street into the heart of town. On your right is the Spar supermarket (handy for picnic supplies) and Marianne Bakeri and Café (at the bridge). To your left is the Vangsgården Guest House and, behind it, Aurland Fjordhotel. To reach the TI, go straight ahead and bear right, then look behind the white church (800 years old and worth a peek). The bus stop, with buses to Flåm, is in front of the TI. For attractions near Aurland, see "Sights and Activities in and near Flåm," earlier.

Tourist Information: The TI stocks English-language brochures about hikes and day trips from the area, and sells local maps (daily 9:00-16:00, closed Sat-Sun in off-season; behind the white church—look for green-and-white *i* sign; mobile 91 79 41 64, https://en.sognefjord.no).

Sleeping in Aurland

$$$$ Aurland Fjordhotel is big, modern, and centrally located. While it has a business-hotel vibe, most of its 30 rooms come with gorgeous fjord-view balconies (tel. 57 63 35 05, www.aurland-fjordhotel.com, post@aurland-fjordhotel.com, Steinar Kjerstein).

$$$ Vangsgården Guest House, closest to the boat landing, is a complex of old buildings dominating the old center of Aurland and run from one reception desk (Wi-Fi in main building, tel. 57 63 35 80, www.vangsgaarden.no, vangsgaarden@alb.no, open all year, Astrid). The main building is a simple, old guesthouse offering basic rooms and a fine old-timey living room. Their old-fashioned **Aabelheim Pension** is Aurland's best *koselig* (cozy)-like-a-farmhouse place (same prices). And lining the waterfront are their six adorable wood **$$$$** cabins with balconies, kitchen, bathroom, and two bedrooms (sleeps 2-6 people, sheets and breakfast extra, book 2 months in advance). The owners also run the recommended Duehuset Pub and rent bikes.

NEAR AURLAND

$$ Skahjem Gard is an active farm run by Aurland's former deputy mayor, Nils Tore. He's converted his old sheep barn into seven spic-and-span family apartments with private bathrooms and kitchenettes, each sleeping up to four people (sheets and towels included, two miles up the valley—road #50, follow *Hol* signs, mobile 95 17 25 67, nskahjem@online.no). It's a 25-minute walk from town, but Nils will pick up and drop off travelers at the ferry. This is best for families and foursomes with cars.

¢ Winjum Huts, about a half-mile from Aurland's dock, rents 14 basic cabins on a peaceful perch overlooking the majestic fjord. The washhouse/kitchen is where you'll find the toilets and showers. Follow the road uphill past the Aurland Fjordhotel; the huts are after the first hairpin curve (apartment available, sheets extra, showers extra, no food available—just beer, mobile 41 47 47 51).

Eating in Aurland

$$$ Marianne Bakeri and Café is a basic little bakery/café serving the best-value food in town. It's a block from the main square, at the bridge over the river. Sit inside or on its riverside terrace (sandwiches, pizza, and quiche; daily 10:00-17:00, mobile 90 51 29 78).

$$$ Duehuset Pub ("The Dove's House"), run by Vangsgården Guest House, serves up decent food in the center of town (daily 15:00-23:00, only open Fri Sun for dinner in off-season).

The **$$$$ Aurland Fjordhotel** is your only alternative for splurges (dinner buffet, daily 19:00-22:00, shorter hours off-season, bar open later, tel. 57 63 35 05).

For cheap eats on dockside benches, gather a picnic at the **Spar** supermarket (Mon-Fri 9:00-20:00, Sat until 18:00, closed Sun).

Undredal

This almost impossibly remote community is home to about 80 people and 400 goats. A huge percentage of the town's former

population (300 people) emigrated to the US between 1850 and 1925. Undredal was accessible only by boat until 1988, when the road from Flåm opened. There's not much in the town, which is famous for its church and its goat cheese, but I'll never forget the picnic I had on the ferry wharf. While appealing, Undredal is quiet (some say better from the boat) and difficult to reach—you'll have to be patient to connect to other towns. For more information on the town, see www.undredal.no.

Getting There: The 15-minute drive from Flåm is mostly through a tunnel. By sea, you'll sail past Undredal on the Flåm-Gudvangen boat (you can request a stop). To get the ferry to pick you up in Undredal, turn on the blinking light (though some express boats will not stop).

Visiting Undredal: Undredal has Norway's smallest still-used **church,** seating 40 people for services every fourth Sunday. The original church was built in 1147 (look for the four original stave pillars inside). It was later expanded, pews added, and the interior painted in the 16th century in a way that resembles the traditional Norwegian *rosemaling* style (which came later). You can get in only with a 30-minute tour (70 NOK, June-mid-Aug daily 10:00-17:00, less in shoulder season, closed Oct-April, mobile 95 29 76 68).

Undredal's farms exist to produce **cheese.** The beloved local cheese comes in two versions: brown and white. The brown version is unaged and slightly sweet, while the white cheese has been aged and is mild and a bit salty. For samples, visit the Undredalsbui grocery store at the harbor (Mon-Fri 9:00-16:30, Sat until 15:00, Sun 12:00-16:00, shorter hours and closed Sun off-season).

Sleeping in Undredal: This sleepy town can accommodate maybe a dozen visitors a night. **$ Undredal Overnatting** rents four modern, woody, comfortable rooms and two apartments. The reception is at the café on the harbor, while the accommodations are at the top of town (sheets included, breakfast extra, tel. 57 63 30 80, www.visitundredal.no, visit@undredal.no).

MORE ON THE SOGNEFJORD

Balestrand • The Lustrafjord • Scenic Drives

Norway's world of fjords is decorated with medieval stave churches, fishing boats, cascading waterfalls, dramatic glaciers, and brightly painted shiplap villages. Travelers in a hurry zip through the fjords on the Norway in a Nutshell route (see previous chapter). Their heads spin from all the scenery, and most wish they had more time on the Sognefjord. If you can linger in fjord country, this chapter is for you.

Snuggle into the fjordside village of Balestrand, which has a variety of walking and biking options and a fun local arts scene. Balestrand is also a handy jumping-off spot for adventures great and small, including a day trip up the Fjærlandsfjord to gaze at a receding tongue of the Jostedal Glacier, or across the Sognefjord to the truly medieval-feeling Hopperstad Stave Church. Farther east is the Lustrafjord, a tranquil branch of the Sognefjord offering drivers an appealing concentration of visit-worthy sights. On the Lustrafjord, you'll enjoy enchanting hamlets with pristine fjord views (such as Solvorn), historic churches (including Norway's oldest stave church at Urnes and the humble village Dale Church in Luster), an opportunity to touch and even hike on a glacier (the Nigard), and more stunning fjord views.

This region is important to the people of Norway. After four centuries under Danish rule, the soul of the country was nearly lost. With partial independence and its own constitution in the early 1800s, the country experienced a resurgence of national pride. Urban Norwegians headed for the fjord country here in the west. Norway's first Romantic painters and writers were drawn to Balestrand, inspired by the unusual light and dramatic views of mountains plunging into the fjords. The Sognefjord, with its many branches, is featured in more Romantic paintings than any other fjord.

PLANNING YOUR TIME

If you can spare a day or two off the Norway in a Nutshell route, spend it here. Balestrand is the best home base, especially if you're

relying on public transportation (it's well-connected by express boat both to the Nutshell scene and to Bergen). If you have a car, consider staying in the heart of the Lustrafjord region in sweet little Solvorn (easy ferry connection to the Urnes Stave Church and a short drive to the Nigard Glacier). As fjord home bases go, Balestrand and Solvorn are both better—but less convenient—than Flåm or Aurland on the Nutshell route.

With one night in this area, you'll have to blitz the sights on the way between destinations; with two nights, you can slow your pace (and your pulse) to enjoy the fjord scenery and plenty of day-trip possibilities.

Balestrand

The pleasant fjord town of Balestrand (pop. 1,300) has a long history of hosting tourists, thanks to its landmark Kviknes Hotel. But

it also feels real and lived-in, making Balestrand a nice mix of cuteness and convenience. The town is near, but not *too* near, the Nutshell bustle across the fjord—and yet it's an easy express-boat trip away if you'd like to dive into the Nuttiness. In short, consider Balestrand a worthwhile detour from the typical fjord visit—al-

lowing you to dig deeper into the Sognefjord, just like the glaciers did during the last ice age.

With two nights, you can relax and consider some day trips: Cruise up the nearby Fjærlandsfjord for a peek at a distant tongue of the ever-less-mighty Jostedal Glacier, or head across the Sognefjord to the beautiful Hopperstad Stave Church in Vik. Balestrand also has outdoor activities for everyone, from dreamy fjordside strolls and strenuous mountain hikes to wildly scenic bike rides. For dinner, splurge on the memorable *smörgåsbord*-style *store koldt bord* dinner in the Kviknes Hotel dining room, then sip coffee from its balcony as you watch the sun set (or not) over the fjord.

PLANNING YOUR TIME
Balestrand's key advantage is its easy express-boat connection to Bergen, offering an alternative route to the fjord from the typical Nutshell train-bus combo. Consider zipping here on the Bergen boat, then continuing on via the Nutshell route.

One night is enough to get a taste of Balestrand. But spending two nights buys you some time for day trips. Note that the first flurry of day trips departs early, around 7:30-8:00 (includes the boat to Vik/Hopperstad Stave Church or the full-day Fjærlandsfjord glacier excursion), and the next batch departs around noon (the half-day Fjærlandsfjord glacier excursion and the last boat to Flåm). If you wait until after 12:00 to make your choice, you'll miss the boat...literally.

Balestrand pretty much shuts down from mid-September through mid-May—when most of the activities, sights, hotels, and restaurants listed here are likely closed.

Orientation to Balestrand

Most travelers arrive in Balestrand on the express boat from Bergen or Flåm. The tidy harbor area has a TI, two grocery stores, a couple of galleries, a town history museum, and a small aquarium devoted to marine life found in the fjord. The historic wooden Kviknes Hotel and its ugly modern annex dominate Balestrand's waterfront.

Even during tourist season, Balestrand is quiet. How quiet? The police station closes on weekends. And it's tiny—from the harbor to the Balestrand Hotel is a five-minute stroll, and you can walk from the aquarium to Kviknes Hotel in less time than that.

Balestrand became accessible to the wider world in 1858 when an activist minister (from the church you see across the fjord from town) brought in the first steamer service. That put Balestrand on the Grand Tour map of the Romantic Age. Even the German *Kaiser* chose to summer here. Today, people from around the world come here to feel the grandeur of the fjord country and connect with the essence of Norway.

TOURIST INFORMATION
At the TI, located next to the Joker supermarket at the harbor, pick up the free, helpful *Outdoor Activities in Balestrand* brochure. If

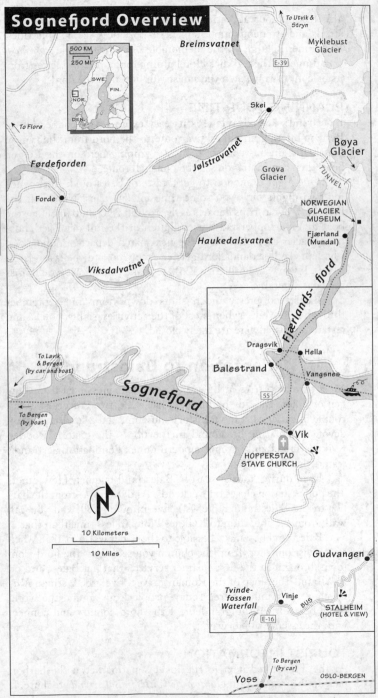

Sognefjord Overview

500 KM
250 MI

SWE.
FIN.
NOR.
DEN.

To Utvik & Stryn

Breimsvatnet

Mykiebust Glacier

E-39

Skei

To Florø

Bøya Glacier

Førdefjorden

Jølstravatnet

TUNNEL

Grova Glacier

Forde

NORWEGIAN GLACIER MUSEUM

Fjærland (Mundal)

Haukedalsvatnet

Viksdalvatnet

Fjærlands-fjord

Dragsvik

Hella

Balestrand

Vangsnes

To Lavik & Bergen (by car and boat)

Sognefjord

55

To Bergen (by boat)

Vik

HOPPERSTAD STAVE CHURCH

N

10 Kilometers

10 Miles

Gudvangen

Tvinde-fossen Waterfall

Vinje

BUS

STALHEIM (HOTEL & VIEW)

E-16

To Bergen (by car)

OSLO-BERGEN

Voss

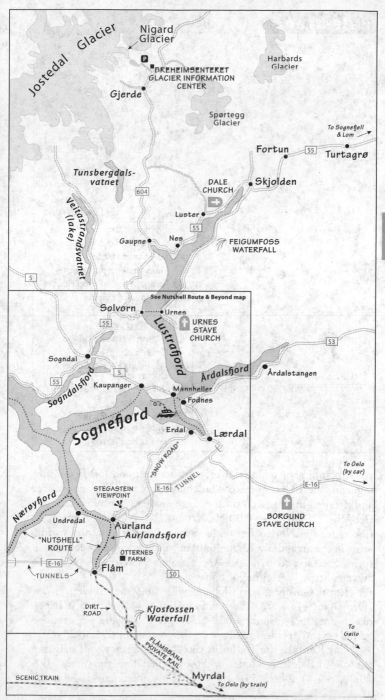

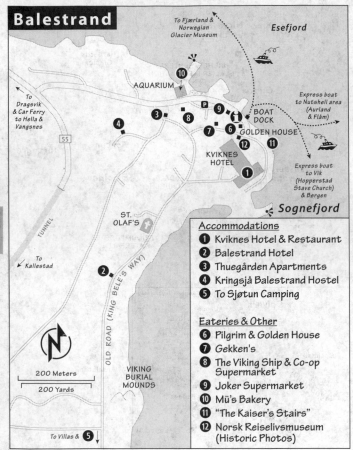

Balestrand

To Fjærland &
Norwegian
Glacier Museum

Esefjord

AQUARIUM

10

P 9

BOAT
DOCK

Express boat
to Nutshell area
(Aurland
& Flåm)

3

8

i

GOLDEN HOUSE

To
Dragsvik
& Car Ferry
to Hella &
Vangsnes

4

55

7

6

12

11

KVIKNES
HOTEL

1

Express boat
to Vik
(Hopperstad
Stave Church)
& Bergen

Sognefjord

TUNNEL

ST.
OLAF'S

To
Kallestad

2

OLD ROAD (KING BELE'S WAY)

Accommodations
1 Kviknes Hotel & Restaurant
2 Balestrand Hotel
3 Thuegården Apartments
4 Kringsjå Balestrand Hostel
5 To Sjøtun Camping

N

200 Meters

200 Yards

VIKING
BURIAL
MOUNDS

Eateries & Other
6 Pilgrim & Golden House
7 Gekken's
8 The Viking Ship & Co-op
   Supermarket
9 Joker Supermarket
10 Mü's Bakery
11 "The Kaiser's Stairs"
12 Norsk Reiselivsmuseum
   (Historic Photos)

To Villas & 5

you're planning on a longer hike, consider the good 150-NOK hiking map. The TI has numerous brochures about the Sognefjord area and detailed information on the more challenging hikes. It offers free Wi-Fi, rents bikes (100 NOK/hour, 270 NOK/day), and sells tickets for the Norled ferry and various fjord, kayak, and fishing tours in the area (daily 10:00-16:00 in summer, closed weekends in spring and fall and all of Oct-April; mobile 94 87 75 01—answered all year, https://en.sognefjord.no).

Local Guide: Bjørg Bjøberg, who runs the Golden House (Det Gylne Hus) art gallery, knows the town well and is happy to show visitors around (1,000-1,500 NOK/2 hours per group—gather several people and divvy up the cost, mobile 91 56 28 42).

Car Rental: The **Balholm Car Rental** agency will deliver a car to your Balestrand hotel, and they'll pick it up, too (daily 8:00-20:00, tel. 41 24 82 53, www.leigebil.no, booking@leigebil.no).

Also, the Kviknes Hotel can arrange a one-day car rental for you (tel. 57 69 42 00).

Sights in Balestrand

Balestrand Harborfront Stroll

The tiny harbor stretches from the aquarium to the big, old Kviknes Hotel. Stroll its length, starting at the aquarium (described later) and little marina. Across the street, at The Viking Ship shack, a German woman named Carola sells German sausages with an evangelical zeal (see "Eating in Balestrand," later). A couple of doors down, the Spindelvev ("Spider's Web") shop sells handicrafts made by people with physical and mental disabilities. A local home for the disabled was closed in the 1980s, but many of its former residents stayed in Balestrand because the government gave them pensions and houses in town.

Then, in the ugly modern strip mall, you'll find the TI, supermarket, and a community bulletin board with the schedule for the summer cinema (the little theater, 800 yards away, runs films nightly in their original language). On the corner is the Golden House art gallery and museum (described later). Behind it—and built into solid rock—is the boxy new moss-covered home of the Norwegian Travel Museum (Norsk Reiselivsmuseum), featuring photos showing this part of Norway over the past 150 years, interactive exhibits, and souvenirs. And just beyond that is the dock where the big Bergen-Sognefjord express catamaran ties up.

Across the street is a cute white house (at #8), which used to stand at the harborfront until the big Joker supermarket and Kviknes Hotel, with its modern annex, partnered to ruin the town center. This little house was considered historic enough to be airlifted 100 yards to this new spot. It's flanked by two other historic buildings, which house a gallery and an artisans' workshop.

Farther along, find the rust-red building that was the waiting room for the 19th-century steamer that first brought tourism to town. Walk a few steps farther, and stop at the tall stone monument erected to celebrate the North Bergen Steamship Company. Its boats first connected Balestrand to the rest of the world in 1858. In front of the monument, some nondescript concrete steps lead into the water. These are "The Kaiser's Stairs," built for the German emperor, Kaiser Wilhelm II, who made his first summer visit (complete with navy convoy) in 1899 and kept returning until the outbreak of World War I.

Behind the monument stands one of the largest old wooden buildings in Norway, Kviknes Hotel. It was built in the 1870s and faces the rare little island in the fjord, which helped give the town its name: "Balestrand" means the strand or promenade in front of an island. (The island is now connected to the hotel's front yard and is part of a playground for its guests.) Hike up the black driveway that leads from the monument to the hotel's modern lobby. Go inside and find (to your left) the plush old lounge, a virtual painting gallery. All the pieces are by artists from this area, celebrating the natural wonder of the fjord country—part of the trend that helped 19th-century Norway reconnect with its heritage. (While you're here, consider making a reservation and choosing a table for a *smörgåsbord* dinner tonight.) Leave the hotel lobby (from the door opposite to the one you entered), and head up to St. Olaf's Church (300 yards, described next). To continue this stroll, take King Bele's Way (described later) up the fjord.

St. Olaf's Church

This distinctive wooden church was built in 1897. Construction was started by Margaret Sophia Kvikne, the wife of Knut Kvikne

(of the Kviknes Hotel family; her portrait is in the rear of the nave), but she died in 1894, before the church was finished. This devout Englishwoman wanted a church in Balestrand where English services were held...and to this day, bells ring to announce services by British clergy. St. Olaf, who brought Christianity to Norway in the 11th century, was the country's patron saint in Catholic times. The church was built in a "Neo-stave" style, with lots of light from its windows and an altar painting inspired by the famous *Risen Christ* statue in Copenhagen's Cathedral of Our Lady. Here, Christ is flanked by fields of daisies (called "priests' collars" in Norwegian) and peace lilies. From the door of the church, enjoy a good view of the island in the fjord.

Cost and Hours: Free, open daily, services in English every Sun from late May through August.

Golden House (Det Gylne Hus)

This golden-colored house facing the ferry landing was built as a general store in 1928. Today it houses an art installation called "Golden Memories" and a quirky museum created by local watercolorist and historian Bjørg Bjøberg, and her husband, Arthur Adamson.

Cost and Hours: Free entry to the ground floor, 25 NOK for the second floor and the glass dome; optional private one-hour tour costs 50 NOK/person and includes all floors—

minimum 5 people, maximum 9; May-Aug daily 10:00-22:00, shorter hours late April and Sept, closed in winter; mobile 91 56 28 42, www.detgylnehus.no.

Visiting the Golden House: On the ground floor you'll find Bjørg's gallery, with her watercolors celebrating the beauty of Norway, and Arthur's paintings, celebrating the beauty of women. Upstairs is the Pilgrimage Balestrand room, focusing on their local nature pilgrimage program, along with an exhibit of historical knickknacks, contributed by locals wanting to preserve treasures from their families' past. You'll see a medicine cabinet stocked with old-fashioned pills, an antiquated tourist map, lots of skis, and WWII-era mementos. A wheel in the wall once powered a crane that could winch up goods from the fjord below (back when this store was actually on the waterfront). While there are no written English explanations, Bjørg is happy to explain things.

Unable to contain her creative spirit, Bjørg has paired an eccentric wonderland experience with her private tour of the Golden House's hidden rooms. The tour includes a 30-minute movie (at 17:00 and 18:00), either about her art and local nature, or about Balestrand in winter. Bjørg and Arthur also run the recommended on-site restaurant, Pilgrim. Diners have free access to the glass dome on top of the building, with a telescope and lovely views.

Strolling King Bele's Way up the Fjord

For a delightful walk (or bike ride), head west out of town up the "old road"—once the main road from the harbor—for about a mile. It follows the fjord's edge, passing numerous "villas" from the late 1800s. At the time, this Swiss style was popular with some locals, who hoped to introduce a dose of Romanticism into Norwegian architecture. Look for the dragons' heads (copied from Viking-age stave churches) decorating the gables. Along the walk, you'll pass a swimming area, a campground, and two burial mounds from the Viking age, marked by a ponderous statue of the Viking King Bele. Check out the wooden shelters for the mailboxes; some give the elevation (*m.o.h.* stands for "meters over *havet*"—the sea)—not too high, are they? The walk is described in the *Outdoor Activities in Balestrand* brochure (free at the TI or your hotel).

Aquarium

The tiny aquarium gives you a good look at marine life in the Sognefjord. For descriptions, borrow the English booklet at the front desk. While not thrilling, the well-explained place is a decent rainy-day option. A 15-minute slideshow starts at the top and bottom of each hour. The last room is filled with wood carvings depicting traditional everyday life in the fjordside village of Munken. The fish-filled tanks on the dock outside are also worth a look.

Cost and Hours: 70 NOK, daily 9:00-19:00, closed mid-Sept-April, tel. 57 69 13 03.

Biking

You can cycle around town, or go farther by circling the scenic Esefjord (north of town, en route to the ferry landing at Dragsvik—about 6 miles each way). Or pedal west up Sognefjord along the scenic King Bele's Way (described earlier). The roads here are relatively flat. Rental bikes are available at the TI and through Kviknes Hotel.

Kayak and Boat Tours

If you're looking for a recreational—and educational—kayak trip on the fjord, **Gone Paddling** offers a three-hour tour with an experienced guide (790 NOK, includes lunch, mobile 91 53 81 33, www.gonepaddling.no).

Balestrand Fjord Adventure specializes in Zodiac-type boat tours on the Sognefjord. Passengers wear full-body weather suits, life vests, and goggles. Join their daily round-trip cruise departing at 13:00 (650 NOK, 1.5 hours) or take the more extensive Nærøyfjord tour (1,300 NOK, 2.5 hours, 3/week, mobile 47 85 53 23, www.balestrandadventure.no).

NEAR BALESTRAND

These two side-trips are possible only if you've got the better part of a day in Balestrand. With a car, you can see Hopperstad Stave Church on the drive to Bergen.

▲▲Hopperstad Stave Church (Hopperstad Stavkyrkje) in Vik

The most accessible stave church in the area—and perhaps the most scenically situated in all of Norway—is located just a 20-minute express-boat ride across the Sognefjord, in the town of Vik. Hopperstad Stave Church boasts a breathtaking exterior, with several tiers of dragon heads overlooking rolling fields between fjord cliffs. The interior is notable for its emptiness. Instead of being crammed full of later additions, the church is blissfully uncluttered, as it was when it was built in the mid-12th century. (For more on stave churches, see page 201.)

Cost and Hours: 70 NOK; daily 10:00-17:00, mid-June-mid-Aug from 9:00, closed Oct-mid-May; good 30-NOK color booklet in English, tel. 57 69 52 70, www.stavechurch.com/hopperstad.

Tours: Attendants will give you a free tour at your request, provided they're not too busy. (Ask where the medieval graffiti is, and they'll grab their flashlight and show you.)

Getting There: Pedestrians can ride the express passenger boat between Balestrand and Vik (89 NOK each way). The only way to get to the church and back in one day is to take the 7:50 departure from Balestrand, then return on the 11:30 departure from Vik, arriving back in Balestrand at 11:50—just in time to join a 12:00 glacier excursion (described on the next page). Because schedules can change, be sure to double-check these times at the TI or www.norled.no under "Expressboat." The church is a 20-minute walk up the valley from Vik's harbor. From the boat landing, walk up the main street from the harbor about 200 yards (past the TI, a grocery store, and hotel). Take a right at the sign for *Hopperstad Stavkyrkje,* walk 10 minutes, and you'll see the church perched on a small hill in the distance.

Since cars can't go on the express boat, **drivers** must go around the small Esefjord to the town of Dragsvik, then catch the ferry across the Sognefjord to Vangsnes (a 20-minute drive from Vik and the church).

Visiting the Church: Originally built around 1140 and retaining most of its original wood, Hopperstad was thoroughly re-

stored and taken back to basics in the 1880s by renowned architect Peter Blix. Unlike the famous stave church at Urnes (described later), which has an interior that has been rejiggered by centuries of engineers and filled with altars and pews, the Hopperstad church looks close to the way it did when it was built. You'll see only

a few added features, including the beautifully painted canopy that once covered a side altar (probably dating from around 1300), and a tombstone from 1738. There are just a few colorful illustrations and some very scant medieval "graffiti" carvings and runic inscriptions.

Notice the intact chancel screen (the only one surviving in Norway), which separates the altar area from the congregation. As with the iconostasis (panel of icons) in today's Orthodox faith, this screen gave priests privacy to do the spiritual heavy lifting. Because Hopperstad's interior lacks the typical adornments, you can really grasp the fundamentally vertical nature of stave church architecture, leading your gaze to the heavens. Follow that impulse and look up to appreciate the Viking-ship rafters. Imagine the comfort this ceiling brought the church's original parishioners, whose seafaring ancestors had once sought refuge under overturned boats. For a unique angle on this graceful structure, lay your camera on the floor and shoot the ceiling.

▲Excursion to Fjærland and the Jostedal Glacier

From Balestrand, cruise up the Fjærlandsfjord to visit the Norwegian Glacier Museum in Fjærland and to see a receding tongue of the Jostedal Glacier (Jostedalbreen). Half-day (765 NOK) and full-day (800 NOK) excursions are sold by Balestrand's TI or onboard the boat. Reservations are smart (tours offered daily June-Aug only, tel. 57 63 14 00, www.visitflam.com and follow links for "Fjærlandsfjord").

While the museum and the glacier's tongue are underwhelming, it's a pleasant excursion with a dreamy fjord cruise (1.5 hours each way). To take the all-day trip, catch the 8:00 ferry; for the shorter trip, hop on the 12:00 boat. Either way, you can return on the 15:20 boat, getting you back to Balestrand at 16:50 (just in time to catch the fast boat back to Bergen). Both tours offer the same fjord ride, museum visit, and trip to the glacier. The all-day version, however, gives you a second glacier viewing point and about 2.5 hours to hang out in the town of Fjærland. (This sleepy village, famous for its secondhand book shops, is about as exciting as Walter Mondale, the former US vice president whose ancestors came from here.)

The ferry ride (no stops, no narration) is just a scenic glide with the gulls. Bring a picnic, as there's almost no food sold onboard, and some bread to toss to the gulls (they do acrobatics to catch whatever you loft into the air). You'll be met at the ferry dock (labeled *Mundal*) by a bus—and your guide, who reads a script about the glacier as you drive up the valley for about 15 minutes. You'll stop for an hour at the **Norwegian Glacier Museum** (Norsk Bremuseum). After watching an 18-minute aerial tour of the dramatic Jostedal Glacier in the theater, you'll learn how glaciers were formed, experiment with your own hunk of glacier, weigh evidence of the woolly mammoth's existence in Norway, and learn about the effect of global climate change on the fjords (way overpriced at 125 NOK, included in excursion price, daily June-Aug 9:00-19:00, April-May and Sept-Oct 10:00-16:00, closed Nov-March, tel. 57 69 32 88, www.bre.museum.no). From the museum, the bus runs you up to a café near a lake, at a spot that gives you a good look at the Bøyabreen, a tongue of the Jostedal Glacier. Marvel at how far the glacier has retreated—10 years ago, the visit was more dramatic. With global warming, glacier excursions like this become more sad than majestic. I wonder how long they'll even be able to bill this as a "glacier visit."

Considering that the fjord trip is the highlight of this journey, you could save time and money by just riding the ferry up and back (8:00-11:25). At 475 NOK for the round-trip boat ride, it's much cheaper than the tour.

Note that if you're into glaciers, a nearby arm of the Jostedal, called the **Nigard Glacier,** is a more dramatic and boots-on experience (described later, under "Sights on the Lustrafjord"). It's easy for drivers to reach; see "Orientation to Balestrand," earlier, for car-rental info.

Sleeping in Balestrand

$$$$ Kviknes Hotel is the classy grande dame of Balestrand, dominating the town and packed with tour groups. The pictur-

esque wooden hotel—and five generations of the Kvikne family—have welcomed tourists to Balestrand since the late 19th century. The hotel has two parts: a new wing, and the historic wooden section, with 25 older, classic rooms, and no elevator. All rooms come with balconies. The elegant Old World public spaces in the old section make you want to just sit there and sip tea all afternoon (family rooms, closed Oct-April, tel. 57 69 42 00, www.kviknes.no, booking@kviknes.no). Part of the Kviknes ritual is gorging on the *store koldt bord* buffet dinner—open to nonguests, and a nice way to soak in the hotel's old-time elegance without splurging on an overnight (see "Eating in Balestrand," later; cheaper if you stay at the hotel for 2 or more nights).

$$$ Balestrand Hotel, family-run by Unni-Marie Kvikne, her California-born husband Eric Palmer, and their three children, is your best fjordside home. Open mid-May through early September, this cozy, welcoming place has 30 well-appointed, comfortable, quiet rooms; a large, modern common area with lots of English paperbacks; laundry service, balconies (in some rooms), and outdoor benches for soaking in the scenery. The waterfront yard has inviting lounge chairs and a mesmerizing view. When reserving, let them know your arrival time, and they'll pick you up at the harborfront (5-minute walk from dock, past St. Olaf's Church—or free pick-up, tel. 57 69 11 38, www.balestrand.com, info@balestrand.com).

$ Thuegården offers five clean, bright, modern doubles with kitchenettes, conveniently located near the ferry dock and just up the street from the Co-op grocery store. Some rooms have balconies and some come with a fjord view (discount if staying more than 3 nights, no breakfast, office inside ground-floor hair salon, tel. 57 69 15 95, mobile 97 19 92 63, www.thuegaarden.com, thuegaarden@gmail.com).

¢-$$ Kringsjå Balestrand Hostel, a camp school for sixth-graders, rents beds and rooms to budget travelers from mid-June to mid-August. Three-quarters of their 58 beds are in doubles. All the rooms have private bathrooms and most have view balconies (private and family rooms, includes sheets and towels, game room, tel. 57 69 13 03, www.kringsja.no, kringsja@kringsja.no).

¢ **Sjøtun Camping** rents the cheapest beds around in their 11 rustic huts (sheets extra, no breakfast, a mile west of town, mobile 95 06 72 61, www.sjotun.com, camping@sjotun.com).

Eating in Balestrand

Balestrand's dining options are limited, but good.

$$$$ Kviknes Hotel offers a splendid, spendy *store koldt bord* buffet dinner in a massive yet stately old dining room. For a memorable fjordside *smörgåsbord* experience, it doesn't get any better than this. Don't rush. Consider taking a preview tour—surveying the reindeer meat, lingonberries, and fjord-caught seafood—before you dive in, so you can budget your stomach space. Get a new plate with each course and save room for dessert. Each dish is labeled in English (575 NOK/person, May-

Sept daily 18:30-21:00, closed Oct-April). They also offer a four-course, locally sourced dinner for 695 NOK. After dinner, head into the rich lounge to pick up your cup of coffee or tea (included), which you'll sip sitting on classy old-fashioned furniture and basking in fjord views. For tips on enjoying this feast, see page 715.

$$$ Pilgrim, inside the Golden House at the harbor, dishes up Norwegian home cooking and a variety of salads. Sit outside or inside, in a dining area built to resemble a traditional Norwegian kitchen. The restaurant upstairs shows off part of owner Bjørg's antique collection (Mon-Sat 16:00-21:00, closed Sun and all of Sept-mid-May, mobile 91 56 28 42).

$$ Gekken's is an informal summer restaurant serving good-value meat, fish, and vegetarian dishes, along with burgers, fish-and-chips, and other fried fare. Sit in the simply decorated interior, or out on the shaded little terrace. Geir Arne "Gekken" Bale can trace his family's roots back 400 years in Balestrand. He has filled his walls with fascinating historic photos and paintings, making his dining hall an art gallery of sorts (May-Aug daily 12:00-22:00, closed Sept-April, above and behind the TI from the harbor, tel. 57 69 14 14).

$ The Viking Ship, the hot-dog stand facing the harbor, is proudly run by Carola. A bratwurst missionary from Germany, she claims it took her years to get Norwegians to accept the tastier bratwurst over their beloved *pølser* weenies. Eat at her picnic tables or across the street on the harbor park (fine sausages, fish-and-chips, May-Sept daily 11:00-20:00, closed Oct-April).

Picnic: The delightful waterfront park next to the aquarium has benches and million-dollar fjord views. The Co-op and Joker **supermarkets** at the harbor have basic grocery supplies, including bread, meats, cheeses, and drinks; the Co-op is bigger and has a wider selection (both open generally Mon-Fri 8:00-20:00, shorter hours on Sat, closed Sun). **$ Mü's Bakery** offers a healthy assortment of sandwiches and fresh-baked goodies (Mon-Sat 9:30-18:00, Sun until 15:00, closed mid-Sept-early May, just inside the aquarium entrance).

Balestrand Connections

Because Balestrand is separated from the Lustrafjord by the long Fjærlandsfjord, most Balestrand connections involve a boat trip.

BY BOAT

Express Passenger Boat: The easiest way to reach Balestrand is on the handy express boat, which connects to **Bergen, Vik** (near Hopperstad Stave Church), **Aurland,** and **Flåm** (see sidebar for schedules). Note that you can also use this boat to join the Nutshell trip in Flåm. From here, continue on the Nutshell boat down the Nærøyfjord to Gudvangen, where you'll join the crowd onward to Voss, then Bergen or Oslo. As you're making schedule and sightseeing decisions, consider that the Balestrand-Flåm boat skips the Nærøyfjord, the most dramatic arm of the Sognefjord.

Car Ferry: Balestrand's main car-ferry dock is at the village of **Dragsvik,** a six-mile, 15-minute drive around the adorable little Eselfjord. From Dragsvik, a car ferry makes the short crossing east to **Hella** (a 30-minute drive from Sogndal and the Lustrafjord), then crosses the Sognefjord south to **Vangsnes** (a 20-minute drive to Hopperstad Stave Church and onward to Bergen). The ferry goes at least once per hour (2/hour in peak times, fewer boats Sun, 94 NOK for car and driver).

Note that you can also drive through Sogndal to catch the **Kaupanger-Gudvangen** or **Mannheller-Fodnes** ferries (described under "Lustrafjord Connections," near the end of this chapter).

BY BUS

A local bus links Balestrand to **Sogndal** (5/day Mon-Fri, 3/day Sat-Sun, 1.5 hours, includes ride on Dragsvik-Hella ferry, get details at TI).

Express Boat Between Bergen and the Sognefjord

The made-for-tourists express boat makes it a snap to connect Bergen with Balestrand and other Sognefjord towns (for foot passengers only—no cars). In summer, the boat links Bergen, Vik, Balestrand, Aurland, and Flåm. You can also use this boat to connect towns on the Sognefjord, such as zipping from quiet Balestrand to busy Flåm, in the heart of the Nutshell action (reservations are smart—call 51 86 87 00 or visit www.norled.no and select "Expressboat"; discounts for students and seniors, tickets also sold on boat and at TI). The following times were good as of press time—confirm them locally.

Between Bergen and the Sognefjord: The boat trip between Bergen and **Balestrand** takes four hours (600 NOK, departs Bergen May-Sept daily at 8:00 and 16:30, Oct-April Sun-Fri at 16:30, Sat at 14:15; departs Balestrand May-Sept Mon-Sat at 7:00 and 16:55, some Sun at 11:30 and 16:55, Oct-April Mon-Sat at 7:50, Sun at 16:25). In summer, the 8:00 boat from Bergen continues to Flåm.

Between Flåm and Balestrand: Going by boat between Flåm and Balestrand with the Norled ferry takes about 1.5 hours (285 NOK, departs Flåm May-Sept daily at 15:30, stops at Aurland, arrives in Balestrand at 16:55; departs Balestrand daily at 11:50 arriving Flåm at 13:25; no express boats between Flåm and Balestrand Oct-April). Another option is the Visitflam express-ferry, which also stops at Leikanger, Undredal, and Aurland (275 NOK, only runs June-mid-Aug, takes 2 hours, departs Flåm Mon-Fri at 6:00, departs Balestrand at 8:30, no boats Sat-Sun, tel. 57 63 14 00, www.visitflam.com). In peak season book ahead for any of the Flåm-Balestrand ferries.

From Oslo to Balestrand via the Nutshell: This variation on the standard Norway in a Nutshell route is called "Sognefjord in a Nutshell" (Oslo-Myrdal-Flåm-Balestrand-Bergen). From Oslo, you can take an early train to Flåm (no later than the 8:25 train as part of the Norway in a Nutshell route), then catch the 15:30 express boat to Balestrand. After your visit, you can continue on the express boat to Bergen, or return to the Nutshell route by taking the express boat to Flåm, and transferring to the next boat to Gudvangen.

The Lustrafjord

This arm of the Sognefjord is rugged country—only 2 percent of the land is fit to build on or farm. The Lustrafjord is ringed with tiny villages where farmers sell cherries and giant raspberries. A few interesting attractions lie along the Lustrafjord: the village

Dale Church at Luster; the impressive Nigard Glacier (a 45-minute drive up a valley); the postcard-pretty village of Solvorn; and, across the fjord, Norway's oldest stave church at Urnes. While a bit trickier to explore by public transportation, this beautiful region is easy by car, but still feels remote. There are no ATMs between Lom and Gaupne—that's how remote this region is.

SUGGESTED ROUTE FOR DRIVERS

The Lustrafjord can be seen either coming from the north (over the Sognefjell pass from the Jotunheimen region—see next chapter) or from the south (from Balestrand or the Norway in a Nutshell route—see previous chapter). Note that public buses between Lom and Sogndal follow this same route (see "Lustrafjord Connections," later).

Here's what you'll see if you're driving from the north (if you're coming from the south, read this section backward): Descending from Sognefjell, you'll hit the fjord at the village of Skjolden (decent TI in big community center, mobile 99 23 15 00). Follow Route 55 along the west bank of the fjord. In the town of Luster, consider visiting the beautifully decorated Dale Church. Farther along, near the hamlet of Nes, you'll have views across the fjord of the towering Feigumfoss waterfall. Drops and dribbles come from miles around for this 650-foot tumble. Soon Route 55 veers along an inlet to the town of Gaupne, where you can choose to detour about an hour to the Nigard Glacier (up Route 604). After Gaupne, Route 55 enters a tunnel and cuts inland, emerging at a long, fjord-like lake at the town of Hafslo. Just beyond is the turnoff for Solvorn, a town with the ferry across to Urnes and its stave church. Route 55 continues to Sogndal, where you can choose to turn off for the Kaupanger and Mannheller ferries across the Sognefjord, or continue on Route 55 to Hella and the boat across to either Dragsvik (near Balestrand) or Vangsnes (across the Sognefjord, near Vik and Hopperstad Stave Church).

Route Timings: If you're approaching from Lom in the Gudbrandsdal Valley, figure about 1.5 hours over Sognefjell to the start of the Lustrafjord at Skjolden, then another 30 minutes to Gaupne (with the optional glacier detour: 2 hours to see it, 4 hours to hike on it). From Gaupne, figure 20 minutes to Solvorn or 30 minutes to Sogndal. Solvorn to Sogndal is about 25 minutes. Sogndal to Hella, and its boat to Balestrand, takes about one hour. These estimated times are conservative, but they don't include photo stops.

Sights on the Lustrafjord

These attractions are listed as you'll reach them driving from north to south along the fjordside Route 55. If you're sleeping in this area, you could visit all four sights in a single day (but it'd be a busy, somewhat rushed day). If you're just passing through, Dale Church and Solvorn are easy, but the other two involve major detours—choose one or skip them both.

▲Dale Church (Dale Kyrkje) in Luster

The namesake town of Luster, on the west bank of the Lustrafjord, boasts a unique 13th-century Gothic church. In a land of wood-

en stave churches, this stone church, with its richly decorated interior, is worth a quick stop as you pass through town.

Cost and Hours: Free entry but donation requested, daily 10:00-20:00 but often closed for services and off-season, good posted English info inside, 5-NOK English brochure, just off the main road—look for red steeple, WC in graveyard, fresh goodies at bakery across the street.

Visiting the Church: The soapstone core of the church dates from about 1250, but the wooden bell tower and entry porch were likely built around 1600. As you enter, on the left you'll see a tall, elevated platform with seating, surrounded by a wooden grill. Nicknamed a "birdcage" for the feathery fashions worn by the ladies of the time, this high-profile pew—three steps higher than the pulpit—was built in the late 17th century by a wealthy parishioner. The beautifully painted pulpit, decorated with faded images of the four evangelists, dates from the 13th century. In the chancel (altar area), restorers have

uncovered frescoes from three different time periods: the 14th, 16th, and 17th centuries. Most of the ones you see here were likely created around the year 1500. The crucifix high over the pews, carved around 1200, predates the church, as does the old bench (with lots of runic carvings)—making them more than eight centuries old.

▲▲Jostedal's Nigard Glacier

The Nigard Glacier (Nigardsbreen) is the most accessible branch of mainland Europe's largest glacier (the Jostedalsbreen, 185 square

miles). Hiking to or on the Nigard offers Norway's best easy opportunity for a hands-on glacier experience. It's a 45-minute detour from the Lustrafjord up Jostedal Valley. Visiting a glacier is a quintessential Norwegian experience, bringing you face-to-face with the majesty of nature. If you can spare the time, it's worth the detour (even if you don't do a guided hike). But if glaciers don't give you tingles and you're feeling pressed, skip it.

Getting There: It's straightforward for **drivers.** When the main Route 55 along the Lustrafjord reaches Gaupne, turn onto Route 604, which you'll follow for 25 miles up the Jostedal Valley to the Breheimsenteret Glacier Information Center. Access to the glacier itself is down the toll road past the information center.

From mid-June through August, a **Glacier Bus** connects the Nigard Glacier to various home-base towns around the region (leaves Sogndal at 8:35 and 13:45, arrives at the glacier around 10:00 and 15:00, morning bus passes through Solvorn en route; departs glacier at 12:35 and 17:00, arrives back in Sogndal around 14:25 and 18:35; buses or boats from other towns, including Flåm and Aurland, may coordinate to meet this bus in Sogndal—ask at TI; combo-tickets include various glacier visits and hikes; for complete timetable, see www.visitnorway.no).

Visiting the Glacier: The architecturally striking Breheimsenteret Glacier Information Center services both Breheimen and Jostedalsbreen national parks. Drop by to confirm your glacier plans; you can also book excursions here. The center features a relaxing 15-minute film with highlights of the region, along with interactive glacier-related exhibits that explain these giant, slow-moving rivers of ice. The center also has a restaurant and gift shop (daily mid-June-mid-Aug 9:00-18:00, May-mid-June and mid-Aug-Sept 10:00-17:00, closed Oct-April, tel. 57 68 32 50, www.jostedal.comjostedal.com).

The best quick visit is to walk to, but not on, the glacier. (If you want to walk *on* it, see "Hikes on the Glacier," next.) From the information center, a 40-NOK toll road continues two miles to a lake facing the actual tongue of the glacier. About 75 years ago, the glacier reached all the way to today's parking lot. (It's named for the ninth farm—*ni gard*—where it finally stopped, after crushing eight farms higher up the valley.) From the lot, you can hike all the way to the edge of today's glacier (about 45 minutes each way); or, to save about 20 minutes of walking, take a special boat to a spot that's a 20-minute hike from the glacier (40 NOK one-way, 60 NOK round-trip, 10-minute boat trip, 4/hour, mid-June-mid-Sept daily 10:00-18:00).

The walk is uneven but well-marked—follow the red *T*'s and take your time. You'll hike on stone polished smooth by the glacier, and scramble over and around boulders big and small that were deposited by it. The path takes you right up to the face of the Nigardsbreen. Respect the glacier. It's a powerful river of ice, and fatal accidents do happen. If you want to walk on the glacier, see below.

Hikes on the Glacier: Don't attempt to walk on top of the glacier by yourself. The Breheimsenteret Glacier Information Center offers guided family-friendly walks that include about one hour on the ice (300 NOK, 150 NOK for kids, cash only, minimum age 6, I'd rate the walks PG-13 myself, about 4/day, generally between 11:30 and 15:00, no need to reserve—just call glacier center to find out time and show up). Leave the information

center one hour before your tour, then meet the group on the ice, where you'll pay and receive your clamp-on crampons. One hour roped up with your group gives you the essential experience. You'll find yourself marveling at how well your crampons work on the 5,000-year-old-ice. Even if it's hot, wear long pants, a jacket, and your sturdiest shoes. (Think ahead. It's awkward to empty your bladder after you're roped up.)

Longer, more challenging, and much more expensive hikes get you higher views, more exercise, and real crampons (starting at 660 NOK, includes boots; mid-May-mid-Sept daily at 10:15 and 11:45, 4 hours including 2.5 hours on the ice; 2-hour hike offered at 13:00; book by phone the day before—tel. 57 68 32 50, arrive at the information center 45 minutes early to pay for tickets and pick up your gear). If you're adventurous, ask about even longer hikes and glacier kayaking. While it's legal to go on the glacier on your own, it's dangerous and crazy to do so without crampons.

▲▲Solvorn

On the west bank of the Lustrafjord, 10 miles northeast of Sogndal, idyllic Solvorn is a sleepy little Victorian town with colorful wooden sheds lining its waterfront.

My favorite town on the Lustrafjord is tidy and quaint, well away from the bustle of the Nutshell action. Its tiny ferry crosses the fjord regularly to Urnes and its famous stave church. While not worth going far out of your way for, Solvorn is a mellow and surprisingly appealing place to kill some time waiting for the ferry...or just munching a picnic while looking across the fjord. A pensive stroll or photo shoot through the village's back lanes is a joy (look for plaques that explain historic buildings in English). Best of all, Solvorn also has a pair of excellent accommodations: a splurge (Walaker Hotel) and a budget place (Eplet Bed & Apple), described later under "Sleeping on the Lustrafjord."

Getting There: Solvorn is a steep five-minute **drive** down a switchback road from the main Route 55. The main road into town leads right to the Urnes ferry (see next page) and dead-ends into a handy parking lot (free, 2-hour posted—but unmonitored—limit). It's a 30-minute drive or bus trip into Sogndal, where you can transfer to other **buses** (2-4 buses/day between Solvorn and Sogndal, including the Glacier Bus to the Nigard Glacier—described earlier).

▲▲Urnes Stave Church

The hamlet of Urnes (sometimes spelled "Ornes") has Norway's oldest surviving stave church, dating from 1129. While not easy

to reach (it's across the Lustrafjord from other attractions), it's worth the scenic ferry ride. The exterior is smaller and simpler than most stave churches, but its interior—modified in fits and starts over the centuries—is uniquely eclectic. For more on stave churches, see page 201. If you want to pack along a bike (rentable in Solvorn), see "Bring a Bike?" at the end of this listing.

Cost and Hours: 90 NOK, includes 20-minute English tour (generally departs at :40 past the hour to coincide with ferry arrival); May-Sept daily 10:30-17:45, closed off-season, tel. 57 68 39 56, www.stavechurch.com.

MORE SOGNEFJORD

Getting There: Urnes is perched on the east bank of the Lustrafjord (across the fjord from Route 55 and Solvorn). Ferries generally depart Solvorn at the top of the hour and Urnes at 30 minutes past the hour (40 NOK one-way passenger fare, 110 NOK one-way for car and driver, no round-trip discount, 15-minute ride, mobile 91 72 17 19, www.lustrabaatane.no). You can either drive or walk onto the boat—but, since you can't drive all the way up to the church, you might as well leave your car in Solvorn. Once across, it's about a five-minute uphill walk to the main road and parking lot (where drivers must leave their cars; parking lot at the church only for disabled visitors). From here, it's a steep 15-minute walk up a switchback road to the church (follow signs for *Urnes*).

Planning Your Time: Don't dawdle on your way up to the church, as the tour is scheduled to depart at :40 past most hours, about 25 minutes after the ferry arrives (giving most visitors just enough time to make it up the hill to the church; last tour at 16:40). The first boat of the day departs Solvorn at 10:00 and the last boat at 16:50; the last boat back to Solvorn departs Urnes at 18:00. Confirm these times locally, especially the "last boat" times, and keep an eye on your watch to avoid getting stranded in Urnes.

Eating: A little café/restaurant is at the farm called Urnes Gard, across from the church (same hours as church, homemade apple cakes, tel. 57 68 39 44).

Visiting the Church: Most visitors to the church take the included 20-minute tour (scheduled to begin soon after the ferry arrives—described earlier). Here are some highlights:

Buy your ticket in the white house across from the church. Visit the little museum here after you see the church, so you don't miss the tour.

Many changes were made to the exterior to modernize the church after the Reformation (the colonnaded gallery was replaced,

the bell tower was added, and modern square windows were cut into the walls). Go around the left side of the church, toward the cemetery. This is the third church on this spot, but the carved doorway embedded in the wall here was inherited from the second church. Notice the two mysterious beasts—a warm-blooded predator (standing) and a cold-blooded dragon—weaving and twisting around each other, one entwining the other. Yet, as they bite each other on the neck, it's impossible to tell which one is "winning"...

perhaps symbolizing the everlasting struggle of human existence. The door you see in the middle, however, has a very different message: the harmony of symmetrical figure-eights, an appropriately calming theme for those entering the church.

Now go around to the real entry door (with a wrought-iron lock and handle probably dating from the first church) and head inside. While it feels ancient and creaky, a lot of what you see in here is actually "new" compared to the 12th-century core of the church. The exquisitely carved, voluptuous, column-topping capitals are remarkably well-preserved originals. The interior was initially stark (no pews) and dark—lit not by windows (which were added much later), but by candles laid on the floor in the shape of a cross. Looking straight ahead, you see a cross with Mary on the left (where the women stood) and John the Baptist on the right (with the men). When they finally added seating, they kept things segregated: Notice the pews carved with hearts for women, crowns for men.

When a 17th-century wealthy family wanted to build a special pew for themselves, they simply sawed off some of the pinecone-topped columns to make way for it. When the church began to lean, it was reinforced with the clumsy, off-center X-shaped supports. Churchgoers learned their lesson, and never cut anything again.

The ceiling, added in the late 17th century, prevents visitors from enjoying the Viking-ship roof beams. But all of these additions have stories to tell. Experts can read various cultural influences into the church decorations, including Irish (some of the carvings) and Romanesque (the rounded arches).

Bring a Bike? To give your Lustrafjord excursion an added dimension, take a bike on the ferry to Urnes (free passage, rentable for 300 NOK/day with helmets from Eplet Bed & Apple hostel in Solvorn, where you can park your car for free). From the stave church, bike the super-scenic fjordside road nine miles—with almost no traffic—to the big Feigumfossen waterfall, and back).

Sleeping on the Lustrafjord

These accommodations are along the Lustrafjord, listed from north to south.

IN NES
$$ Nes Gard Farmhouse B&B rents 15 homey rooms, offering lots of comfort in a grand 19th-century farmhouse (includes breakfast, three-course dinner extra, discount for staying multiple days, rooms in main building more traditional, family apartment, bike rental, mobile 95 23 26 94, www.nesgard.no, post@nesgard.no, Månum family—Mari and Asbjørn).

MORE SOGNEFJORD

¢ **Viki Fjord Camping** has great fjordside huts—many directly on the water, with views and balconies—located directly across from the Feigumfossen waterfall (no breakfast, sheets extra, tel. 57 68 64 20, mobile 99 53 97 30, www.vikicamping.no, post@vikicamping.no, Berit and Svein).

IN SOLVORN

For more on this delightful little fjordside town—my favorite home base on the Lustrafjord—see the description earlier in this chapter. While it lacks the handy boat connections of Flåm, Aurland, or Balestrand, that's part of Solvorn's charm.

$$$$ Walaker Hotel, a former inn and coach station, has been run by the Walaker family since 1690 (that's a lot of pressure on ninth-generation owner Ole Henrik). The hotel, set right on the Lustrafjord (with a garden perfect for relaxing and, if necessary, even convalescing), is open May through September. In the main house, the halls and living rooms are filled with tradition. Notice the patriotic hymns on the piano. The 22 rooms are divided into two types: nicely appointed standard rooms in the modern annex; or recently renovated "historic" rooms with all the modern conveniences in two different old buildings: rooms with Old World elegance in the main house, and brightly painted rooms with countryside charm in the Tingstova house next door (sea kayak rentals, tel. 57 68 20 80, www.walaker.com, hotel@walaker.com). They serve excellent four-course dinners (625 NOK plus drinks, nightly at 19:30, savor your dessert with fjordside setting on the balcony). Their impressive gallery of Norwegian art is in a restored, historic farmhouse out back (free for guests; Ole Henrik leads one-hour tours of the collection, peppered with some family history, nightly after dinner).

¢ **Eplet Bed & Apple** is my kind of hostel: innovative and friendly. It's creatively run by Trond and Agnethe, whose entrepreneurial spirit and positive attitude attract enjoyable guests. With welcoming public spaces and 22 beds in seven rooms (all with views, some with decks), this place is worth considering even if you don't normally sleep at hostels (open mid-April-Sept only, private rooms, no breakfast, no elevator, pay laundry, kitchen, tel. 41 64 94 69, www.eplet.net, post@eplet.net). It's about 300 yards uphill from the boat dock—look for the white house with a giant red apple painted on it. It's surrounded by a raspberry-and-apple farm (they make and sell tasty juices from both). The hostel provides free loaner bikes for guests and rents them to nonguests for 300 NOK/day (helmets available).

Eating in Solvorn: The **$$$ Linahagen Kafé,** next door to Walaker Hotel, serves good meals (June-Aug Mon-Fri 12:00-

18:00, Sat until 16:00, Sun 13:00-18:00, closed Sept-May, run by Tordis and her family).

IN SOGNDAL

Sogndal is the only sizeable town in this region. While it lacks the charm of Solvorn and Balestrand, it's big enough to have a busy shopping street and a helpful **TI** (daily 9:30-23:00, inside the MIX minimart at Parkvegen 5, mobile 41 78 13 00).

¢ **Sogndal Youth Hostel** rents good, cheap beds (private rooms, June-mid-Aug only, closed 10:00-17:00, at fork in the road as you enter town, tel. 57 62 75 75, www.hihostels.no/sogndal, sogndal@hihostels.no).

Lustrafjord Connections

Sogndal is the transit hub for the Lustrafjord region.

FROM SOGNDAL BY BUS

Buses go to **Lom** over the Sognefjell pass (2/day late June-Aug only, road closed off-season, 3.5 hours, 1/day off-season, goes around the pass, 5 hours, change in Skei), **Solvorn** (3/day, fewer Sat-Sun, 30 minutes), **Balestrand** (5/day Mon-Fri, 3/day Sat-Sun, 1.5 hours, includes ride on Hella-Dragsvik ferry), **Nigard Glacier** (Glacier Bus runs 2/day mid-June-Aug only, see listing earlier for times). Most buses run less (or not at all) on weekends—check the latest at www.kringom.no.

BY BOAT

Car ferry reservations are generally not necessary except for the boat to Gudvangen, and on many short rides, aren't even possible (confirm schedules at www.kringom.no). From near Sogndal, various boats fan out to towns around the Sognefjord. Most leave from two towns at the southern end of the Lustrafjord: **Kaupanger** (a 15-minute drive from Sogndal) and **Mannheller** (a 5-minute drive beyond Kaupanger, 20 minutes from Sogndal).

From Kaupanger: While Kaupanger is little more than a ferry landing, the small stave-type church at the edge of town merits a look. Boats go from Kaupanger all the way down the gorgeous Nærøyfjord to **Gudvangen,** which is on the Norway in a Nutshell route (where you catch the bus to Voss). Taking this leisurely boat allows you to see the best part of the Nutshell fjord scenery (the Nærøyfjord), but misses the other half of that cruise (Aurlandsfjord). From June through August, boats leave Kaupanger daily at 9:00 and 15:00 (July-mid-Aug also at 12:00 and 18:00) for the nearly 3-hour trip; check in 15 minutes before departure (car and driver-750 NOK, adult passenger-350 NOK; reserve at least one day in advance—or longer in July-Aug; tel. 57 62 74 00, www. fjord2.com). Prices are high because this route is mainly taken by tourists, not locals. Verify schedules and prices online. Boats also connect Kaupanger to **Lærdal**, but the crossing from Mannheller to Fodnes is easier (described next).

From Mannheller: Ferries frequently make the speedy 15-minute crossing to **Fodnes** (74 NOK for a car and driver, 3/ hour, no reservations possible). From Fodnes, drive through the five-mile-long tunnel to Lærdal and the main E-16 highway (near Borgund Stave Church, the long tunnel to Aurland, and the scenic overland road to the Stegastein fjord viewpoint—all described in the previous chapter).

To Balestrand: To reach Balestrand from the Lustrafjord, you'll take a short ferry trip (Hella-Dragsvik). For information on the car ferries to and from Balestrand, see "Balestrand Connections," earlier.

Scenic Drives from the Sognefjord

If you'll be doing a lot of driving, buy a good local map. The 1:335,000-scale *Sør-Norge nord* map by Cappelens Kart is excellent (available at local TIs and bookstores).

▲▲From the Lustrafjord to Aurland

The drive to the pleasant fjordside town of Aurland (see previous chapter) takes you either through the world's longest car tunnel,

or over an incredible mountain pass. If you aren't going as far as Lom and Jotunheimen, consider taking the pass, as the scenery here rivals the famous Sognefjell pass drive.

From Sogndal, drive 20 minutes to the Mannheller-Fodnes ferry (described earlier, under "Lustrafjord Connections"), float across the Sognefjord, then drive from Fodnes to Lærdal. From Lærdal, you have two options to Aurland: The speedy route is on E-16 through the 15-mile-long **tunnel** from Lærdal, or the Aurlandsvegen **"Snow Road"** over the pass.

The tunnel is free, and impressively nonchalant—it's signed as if it were just another of Norway's countless tunnels. But driving it is a bizarre experience: A few miles in, as you find yourself trying not to be hypnotized by the monotony, it suddenly dawns on you what it means to be driving under a mountain for 15 miles. To keep people awake, three rest chambers, each illuminated by a differently colored light, break up the drive visually. Stop and get out—if no cars are coming, test the acoustics from the center.

The second, immeasurably more scenic route is a breathtaking one-hour, 30-mile drive that winds over a pass into Aurland, cresting at over 4,000 feet and offering classic aerial fjord views (it's worth the messy pants). From the Mannheller-Fodnes ferry, take the first road to the right (to Erdal), then leave E-68 at Erdal (just west of Lærdal) for the Aurlandsvegen. This road, while well-maintained, is open only in summer, and narrow and dangerous during snowstorms (which can hit with a moment's notice, even in warm weather). Even in good weather, parts of the road can be a white-knuckle adventure, especially when meeting oncoming vehicles on the tiny, exposed hairpin turns. You'll enjoy vast and terrifying views of lakes, snowfields, and remote mountain huts and farmsteads on what feels like the top of Norway. As you begin the 12-hairpin zigzag descent to Aurland, you'll reach the "7"-shaped **Stegastein viewpoint**—well worth a stop. The "Snow Road" and viewpoint are both described on page 310.

▲From the Lustrafjord to Bergen, via Nærøyfjord and Gudvangen

Car ferries take tourists between Kaupanger and the Nutshell town of Gudvangen through an arm and elbow of the Sognefjord, including the staggering Nærøyfjord (for details on the ferry, see "Lustrafjord Connections," earlier). From Gudvangen, it's a 90-mile drive to Bergen via Voss (figure about one hour to Voss, then about an hour and a half into Bergen). This follows essentially the same route as the Norway in a Nutshell (Gudvangen-Voss bus, Voss-Bergen train) route. For additional commentary on the journey, see page 304.

Get off the ferry in Gudvangen and drive up the Nærøy valley past a river. You'll see the two giant falls and then go uphill through a tunnel. After the tunnel, look for a sign marked *Stalheim* and turn right. Stop for a break at the touristy Stalheim Hotel. Then follow signs marked *Stalheimskleiva*. This incredible road doggedly worms its way downhill back into the depths of the valley. My brakes started overheating in a few minutes. Take it easy. As you wind down, you can view the falls from several turnouts.

The road rejoins E-16. You retrace your route through the tunnel and then continue into a mellower beauty, past lakes and farms, toward Voss. Just before you reach Voss itself, watch the right side of the road for Tvindefossen, a waterfall with a handy campground/

WC/kiosk picnic area that's worth a stop. Highway E-16 takes you through Voss and into Bergen. If you plan to visit Edvard Grieg's Home and the nearby Fantoft Stave Church, now is the ideal time, since you'll be driving near them—and they're a headache to reach from downtown. Both are worth a detour if you're not rushed (see the Bergen chapter).

▲▲From Balestrand to Bergen, via Vik

If you're based in Balestrand and driving to Bergen, you have two options: Take the Dragsvik-Hella ferry, drive an hour to Kaupanger (via Sogndal), and drive the route just described; or, take the following slower, twistier, more remote, and more scenic route, with a stop at the beautiful Hopperstad Stave Church. This route is slightly longer, with more time on mountain roads and less time on the boat. Figure 15 minutes from Vangsnes to Vik, then about 1.5 hours to Voss, then another 1.5 hours into Bergen.

From Vangsnes, head into Vik on the main Route 13. In Vik, follow signs from the main road to Hopperstad Stave Church (described earlier in this chapter). Then backtrack to Route 13 and follow it south, to Voss. You'll soon begin a series of switchbacks that wind you up and out of the valley. The best views are from the Storesvingen Fjellstove restaurant (on the left). Soon after, you'll crest the ridge, go through a tunnel, and find yourself on top of  the world, in a desolate and harshly scenic landscape of scrubby mountaintops, snow banks, lakes, and no trees, scattered with vacation cabins. After cruising atop the plateau for a while, the road twists its way down (next to a waterfall) into a very steep valley, which it meanders through the rest of the way to Voss. This is an hour-long, middle-of-nowhere journey, with few road signs—you might feel lost, but keep driving toward Voss. When Route 13 dead-ends into E-16, turn right (toward Voss and Bergen) and re-enter civilization. From here, the route follows the same roads as in the Lustrafjord-Bergen drive described earlier (including the Tvindefossen waterfall).

GUDBRANDSDAL VALLEY & JOTUNHEIMEN MOUNTAINS

Norway in a Nutshell is a great day trip, but with more time and a car, consider a scenic meander from Oslo to Bergen. You'll arc up the Gudbrandsdal Valley and over the Jotunheimen Mountains, then travel along the Lustrafjord.

After an introductory stop in Lillehammer, with its fine folk museum, you might spend the night in a log-and-sod farmstead-turned-hotel, tucked in a quiet valley under Norway's highest peaks. Next, Norway's highest pass takes you on an exhilarating roller-coaster ride through the heart of the myth-inspiring Jotunheimen, bristling with Norway's biggest mountains. Then the road hairpins down into fjord country (see previous chapter).

PLANNING YOUR TIME

While you could spend five or six days in this area on a three-week Scandinavian rampage, this slice of the region is worth three days. By car, I'd spend them like this:

Day 1: Leave Oslo early, and spend midday at Lillehammer's Maihaugen Open-Air Folk Museum for a tour and picnic. Drive up the Gudbrandsdal Valley, stopping at the stave church in Lom. Stay overnight in the Jotunheimen countryside.

Day 2: Drive the Sognefjell road over the mountains, then down along the Lustrafjord, stopping to visit the Dale Church and the Nigard Glacier (see previous

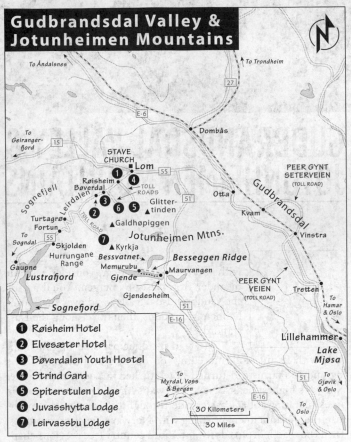

Gudbrandsdal Valley & Jotunheimen Mountains

To Åndalsnes
To Trondheim
27
E-6
To Geiranger-fjord
15
Dombås
STAVE CHURCH
Lom
55
Røisheim
Bøverdal
TOLL ROADS
Sognefjell
Leirdalen
Glitter-tinden
51
Otta
PEER GYNT SETERVEIEN (TOLL ROAD)
Gudbrandsdal
Kvam
Turtagrø
Fortun
TOLL ROAD
Galdhøpiggen
Jotunheimen Mtns.
Vinstra
To Sogndal
55
Skjolden
Hurrungane Range
Kyrkja
Bessvatnet
Besseggen Ridge
Gaupne
Memurubu
Maurvangen
PEER GYNT VEIEN (TOLL ROAD)
Tretten
Lustrafjord
Gjende
Gjendesheim
To Hamar & Oslo
Sognefjord
51
E-16
Lillehammer
Lake Mjøsa

❶ Røisheim Hotel
❷ Elvesæter Hotel
❸ Bøverdalen Youth Hostel
❹ Strind Gard
❺ Spiterstulen Lodge
❻ Juvasshytta Lodge
❼ Leirvassbu Lodge

To Myrdal, Voss & Bergen
51
To Gjøvik & Oslo
E-16
To Oslo
30 Kilometers
30 Miles

chapter). Sleep in your choice of fjord towns, such as Solvorn, Balestrand, or Aurland (all described in previous chapters).

Day 3: Cruise the Aurland and/or Nærøy fjords and try to visit another stave church or two (such as Urnes, Hopperstad, or Borgund—all described in previous chapters) before carrying on to Bergen.

This plan can be condensed into two days if you skip the Nigard Glacier side-trip.

Lillehammer and the Gudbrandsdal Valley

The Gudbrandsdal Valley is the tradition-steeped country of Peer Gynt, the Norwegian Huck Finn. This romantic valley of time-worn hills, log cabins, and velvet farms has connected northern and southern Norway since ancient times. While not as striking as other parts of the Norwegian countryside, Gudbrandsdal offers a suitable first taste of the natural wonders that crescendo farther north and west (in Jotunheimen and the Sognefjord). Throughout this region, the government subsidizes small farms to keep the countryside populated and healthy. (These subsidies would not be permitted if Norway were a member of the European Union.)

Orientation to Lillehammer

The de facto capital of Gudbrandsdal, Lillehammer, is a pleasant winter and summer resort town of 27,000. While famous for its brush with Olympic greatness (as host of the 1994 Winter Olympiad), Lillehammer is a bit disappointing—worthwhile only for its excellent Maihaugen Open-Air Folk Museum, or to break up the long drive between Oslo and the Jotunheimen region. If you do wind up here, Lillehammer has happy, old, woody pedestrian zones (Gågata and Storgata).

Tourist Information: Lillehammer's TI is inside the train station (Mon-Fri 8:00-18:00, Sat-Sun 10:00-16:00; shorter hours and closed Sun in off-season; Jernbanetorget 2, tel. 61 28 98 00, www.lillehammer.com).

Sights in Lillehammer

Lillehammer's two most worthwhile sights are up the hill behind the center of town. It's a fairly steep 15-minute walk from the train station to either sight and a 10-minute, mostly level walk between the two (follow the busy main road that connects them). Because the walk from the station is uphill (and not very well signed), consider catching the bus from in front of the train station (bus #003 or #002 to Olympics Museum, 2/hour; bus #006 to Maihaugen, 1/hour; 37 NOK one-way for either bus).

▲▲Maihaugen Open-Air Folk Museum
(Maihaugen Friluftsmuseet)

This idyllic park, full of old farmhouses and pickled slices of folk culture, provides a good introduction to what you'll see as you drive

GUDBRANDSDAL

through the Gudbrandsdal Valley. Anders Sandvig, a "visionary dentist," started the collection in 1887. You'll divide your time between the fine indoor museum at the entrance and the sprawling exterior exhibits.

Upon arrival, ask about special events, crafts, or musical performances. A TV monitor shows what's going on in the park. Summer is busy with crafts in action and people re-enacting life in the past, à la Colonial Williamsburg. There are no tours, so it's up to you to initiate conversations with the "residents." Off-season it's pretty dead, with no live crafts and most buildings locked up.

Cost and Hours: 170 NOK in summer, 130 NOK off-season; 25 percent off when combined with Olympics Museum; June-Aug daily 10:00-17:00; Sept-May Tue-Sun 11:00-16:00, closed Mon; paid parking, scant English descriptions—consider purchasing the English guidebook; tel. 61 28 89 00, www.maihaugen.no.

Visiting the Museum: The outdoor section, with 200 buildings from the Gudbrandsdal region, is divided into three areas:

the "Rural Collection," with old sod-roof log houses and a stave church; the "Town Collection," with reconstructed bits of old-time Lillehammer; and the "Residential Area," with 20th-century houses that look like most homes in today's Norway. The time trip can be jarring: In the 1980s house, a bubble-gum-chewing girl enthuses about her new, "wireless" TV remote and plays ABBA tunes from a cassette-tape player.

The museum's excellent "We Won the Land" exhibit (at the entry) sweeps you through Norwegian history from the Ice Age to the Space Age. The Gudbrandsdal art section shows village life at its best. And you can walk through Dr. Sandvig's old dental office and the original shops of various crafts- and tradespeople.

Though the museum welcomes picnickers and has a simple cafeteria, Lillehammer's town center (a 15-minute walk below the museum), with lots of fun eateries, is better for lunch (see the next page).

Norwegian Olympics Museum
(Norges Olympiske Museum)

This cute museum is housed in the huge Olympic ice-hockey arena, Håkon Hall. With brief English explanations, an emphasis on Norwegians and Swedes, and an endearingly gung-ho Olympic spirit, it's worth a visit on a rainy day or for sports fans. The ground-floor exhibit traces the ancient history of the Olympics, then devotes one wall panel to each of the summer and winter Olympiads of the modern era (with special treatment for the 1952 Oslo games). Upstairs, walk the entire concourse, circling the arena seating while reviewing the highlights (and lowlights) of the 1994 games (remember Tonya Harding?). While you're up there, check out the gallery of great Norwegian athletes and the giant egg used in the Lillehammer opening ceremony.

Cost and Hours: 130 NOK, 25 percent off when combined with Maihaugen Museum; June-Aug daily 10:00-17:00; Sept-May Tue-Sun 11:00-16:00, closed Mon; tel. 61 25 21 00, https://eng.ol.museum.no.

Nearby: On the hillside above Håkon Hall (a 30-minute hike or quick drive) are two ski jumps that host more Olympics sights, including a ski lift, the ski jump tower, and a bobsled ride (www.olympiaparken.no). In the summer, ski jumpers practice on the jumps, which are sprayed with water.

Sleeping and Eating in the Gudbrandsdal Valley

I prefer sleeping in the more scenic and Norwegian-feeling Jotunheimen area (described later). But if you're sleeping here, Lillehammer and the surrounding valley offer several good options. My choices for Lillehammer are near the train station; the accommodations in Kvam provide a convenient stopping point in the valley.

IN LILLEHAMMER

Sleeping: True to its name, **$$ Mølla Hotell** is situated in an old mill along the little stream running through Lillehammer. The 58 rooms blend Old World charm with modern touches. It's more cutesy-cozy and less businesslike than other Lillehammer hotels in this price range (elevator, a block below Gågata at Elvegata 12, tel. 61 05 70 80, www.mollahotell.no, post@mollahotell.no).

$$ First Hotel Breiseth is a business-class hotel with 89 rooms in a handy location directly across from the train station (free parking, Jernbanegaten 1, tel. 61 24 77 77, www.firsthotels.no/breiseth, breiseth@firsthotels.no).

¢ **Vandrerhjem Stasjonen,** Lillehammer's youth hostel, is upstairs inside the train station. With 100 beds in 33 institutional but new-feeling rooms—including 21 almost hotel-like doubles—it's a winner (elevator, Jernbanetorget 2, tel. 61 26 00 24, www.stasjonen.no, lillehammer@hihostels.no).

Eating: Good restaurants are scattered around the city center, but for the widest selection, head to where the main pedestrian drag (Gågata) crosses the little stream running downhill through town. Poke a block or two up and down **Elvegata,** which stretches along the river and hosts a wide range of tempting eateries—from pubs (both rowdy and upscale) to pizza and cheap sandwich stands.

IN KVAM

This is a popular vacation valley for Norwegians, and you'll find loads of reasonable small hotels and campgrounds with huts for those who aren't quite campers (*hytter* means "cottages" or "cabins," *rom* is "private room," and *ledig* means "vacancy"). These huts normally cost about 400-600 NOK, depending on size and amenities, and can hold from four to six people. Although they are simple, you'll have a kitchenette and access to a good WC and shower. When available, sheets rent for around 60 NOK per person. Here are a couple of listings in the town of Kvam, located midway between Lillehammer and Lom.

$$ Vertshuset Sinclair has a quirky Scottish-Norwegian ambience. The 15 fine rooms are in old-fashioned motel wings. The motel was named after a Scotsman who led a band of adventurers into this valley, attempting to set up their own Scottish kingdom. They failed. All were kilt (family deals, tel. 61 29 54 50, www.vertshuset-sinclair.no, post@vertshuset-sinclair.no). The motel's **$$ cafeteria,** in the main building, is handy for a quick and filling bite on the road between Lillehammer and Lom (long hours daily).

¢ Kirketeigen Ungdomssenter ("Church Youth Center"), behind the town church, welcomes travelers year-round. They have camping spots, small cabins without water, cabins with kitchen and bath, plus simple four-bed rooms in the main building (sheets and blankets extra, tel. 61 21 60 90, www.kirketeigen.no, post@kirketeigen.no).

Jotunheimen Mountains

Norway's Jotunheimen ("Giants' Home") Mountains feature the country's highest peaks and some of its best hikes and drives. This national park stretches from the fjords to the glaciers. You can play roller-coaster with mountain passes, take rugged hikes, wind up scenic toll roads, get up close to a giant stave church...and sleep in a time-passed rural valley. The gateway to the mountains is the unassuming town of Lom.

Lom

Pleasant Lom—the main town between Lillehammer and Sogndal—feels like a modern ski resort village. It's home to one of Norway's most impressive stave churches. While Lom has little else to offer, the church causes the closest thing to a tour-bus traffic jam this neck of the Norwegian woods will ever see.

Orientation to Lom

Park by the stave church—you'll see its dark spire just over the bridge. The church shares a parking lot with a gift shop/church museum and some public WCs. Across the street is the TI, in the sod-roofed building that also houses the Norwegian Mountain Museum. If you're heading over the mountains, Lom's bank (at the Kommune building) has the last ATM until Gaupne.

Tourist Information: Lom's TI, a good source of information for hikes and drives in the Jotunheimen Mountains, is just across the river in Lom's Co-op Mega grocery store (Mon-Sat 9:00-21:00, Sun 10:00-18:00; office closed Sept-mid-June but info available by phone or email; tel. 61 21 29 90, http://visitjotunheimen.no, info@visitjotunheimen.no).

Sights in Lom

▲▲Lom Stave Church (Lom Stavkyrkje)

Despite extensive renovations, Lom's church (from 1158) remains a striking example of a Nordic stave church. For more on these distinctive medieval churches, see page 201.

Cost and Hours: Church-60 NOK, daily mid-June-mid-Aug 9:00-19:00 (until 17:00 last half of Aug), mid-May-mid-June and Sept 10:00-16:00, closed in winter and during funerals; museum-10 NOK, same hours as church in summer, shorter hours in off-season, closed Sun in winter; tel. 40 43 84 86, www.lomstavechurch.no.

Tours: Try to tag along with a guided tour of the church—or, if it's not too busy, a docent can give

GUDBRANDSDAL

you a quick private tour (included in ticket). Even outside of opening times—including winter—small groups can arrange a tour (60 NOK/person, 600-NOK minimum, call 97 07 53 97 in summer or 61 21 73 00 in winter).

Visiting the Church: Buy your ticket and go inside to take in the humble **interior** (still used by locals for services—notice the posted hymnal numbers). Men sat on the right, women on the left, and prisoners sat with the sheriff in the caged area in the rear. Standing in the middle of the nave, look overhead to see the earliest surviving parts of the church, such as the circle of X-shaped St. Andrew crosses and the Romanesque arches above them. High above the door (impossible to see without a flashlight—ask a docent to show you) is an old painting of a dragon- or lion-like creature—likely an old Viking symbol, possibly drawn here to smooth the forced conversion local pagans made to Christianity. When King Olav II (later to become St. Olav) swept through this valley in 1021, he gave locals an option: convert or be burned out of house and home.

On the white town flag, notice the spoon—a symbol of Lom. Because of its position nestled in the mountains, Lom gets less rainfall than other towns, so large spoons were traditionally used to spread water over the fields. The apse (behind the altar) was added in 1240, when trendy new Gothic cathedrals made an apse a must-have accessory for churches across Europe. Lepers came to the grilled window in the apse for a blessing. When the Reformation hit in 1536, the old paintings were whitewashed over. The church has changed over the years: Transepts, pews, and windows were added in the 17th century. And the circa-1720 paintings were done by a local priest's son.

Drop into the **gift shop/church museum** in the big black building in the parking lot. Its one-room exhibit celebrates 1,000 years of the stave church—interesting if you follow the loaner English descriptions. Inside you'll find a pair of beautiful model churches, headstones and other artifacts, and the only surviving stave-church dragon-head "steeple." In the display case near the early-1900s organ, find the little pencil-size stick carved with runes, dating from around 1350. It's actually a love letter from a would-be suitor. The woman rejected him, but she saved them both from embarrassment by hiding the stick under the church floorboards beneath a pew...where it was found in 1973. (Docents inside the church like to show off a replica of this stick.)

Before or after your church visit, explore the tidy, thought-provoking **graveyard** surrounding the church. Also, check out the precarious-looking little footbridge over the waterfall (the best view is from the modern road bridge into town).

Norwegian Mountain Museum
(Norsk Fjellmuseum)

This worthwhile museum traces the history of the people who have lived off the land in the Jotunheimen Mountains from the Stone Age to today (and also serves as a national park office). It is one of the better museums in fjord country, with well-presented displays and plenty of actual artifacts. The exhibit, "Over the Ice: Discoveries from the Ice Show the Way," explores prehistoric human and animal migrations in the surrounding mountains based on recent archaeological finds, including a 1,300-year-old ski.

Cost and Hours: 80 NOK; daily 9:00-16:00, July-mid-Aug until 19:00, generally closed in off-season; in the sod-roofed building across the road from the Lom Stave Church parking lot, tel. 61 21 16 00, http://fjell.museum.no.

Sleeping near Lom

Lom itself has a handful of hotels, but the most appealing way to overnight in this area is at a rural rest stop in the countryside. All of these are on Route 55 south of Lom, toward Sognefjord—first is Strind Gard, then Bøverdalen, Røisheim, and finally Elvesæter (all within 20 minutes of Lom).

$$$$ Røisheim, in a marvelously remote mountain setting, is an extremely expensive storybook hotel composed of a cluster of centuries-old, sod-roofed log farmhouses. Its posh and generous living rooms are filled with antiques. Each of the 20 rooms (in 14 different buildings) is rustic but elegant, with fun "barrel bathtubs" and four-poster or canopy beds. Some rooms are in old, wooden farm buildings—*stabburs*—with low ceilings and heavy beams. The deluxe rooms are larger, with king beds and fireplaces. Call ahead so they'll be prepared for your arrival (open May-Sept; packed lunch, and an over-the-top four-course traditional dinner served at 19:30; 10 miles south of Lom on Route 55, tel. 61 21 20 31, www. roisheim.no, booking@roisheim.no).

$$ Elvesæter Hotel has its own share of Old World romance, but is bigger, cheaper, and more modest. Delightful public spaces bunny-hop through its traditional shell, while its 200 beds sprawl through nine buildings. The Elvesæter family has done a great job of retaining the historic character of their medieval farm, even though the place is big enough to handle large tour groups. The renovated "superior" rooms are new-feeling, but have sterile modern furniture; the older, cheaper "standard" rooms are well-worn but more characteristic (open May-Sept, family rooms, good three-course dinners, swimming pool, farther up Route 55, just past Bøverdal, tel. 61 21 12 10, www.topofnorway.no, elveseter@ topofnorway.no). Even if you're not staying here, stop by to wander through the public spaces and pick up a flier explaining the towering Sagasøyla (Saga Column). It was started in 1926 to celebrate the Norwegian constitution, and was to stand in front of Oslo's Parliament Building—but the project stalled after World War II (thanks to the artist's affinity for things German and membership in Norway's fascist party). It was eventually finished and erected here in 1992.

¢ **Bøverdalen Youth Hostel** offers cheap-but-comfortable beds and a far more rugged clientele—real hikers rather than car hikers. While a bit institutional, it's well-priced and well-run (open late May-Sept, sheets extra, breakfast extra, hot meals, self-serve café, tel. 61 21 20 64, www.hihostels.no, boverdalen@hihostels.no, Anna Berit). It's in the center of the little community of Bøverdal (store, campground, and toll road up to Galdhøpiggen area).

¢ **Strind Gard** is your very rustic option if you can't spring for Røisheim or Elvesæter, but still want the countryside-farm experience. This 150-year-old farmhouse, situated by a soothing waterfall, rents two rooms and one apartment, plus four sod-roofed log huts. The catch: Many of the buildings have no running water, so you'll use the shared facilities at the main building. While not everyone's cup of tea, this place will appeal to romantics who always wanted to sleep in a humble log cabin in the Norwegian mountains—it's downright idyllic for those who like to rough it (sheets and towels extra, no breakfast, low ceilings, farm smells, valley views, 2 miles south of Lom on Route 55, tel. 61 21 12 37, www.strind-gard.no, post@strind-gard.no, Anne Jorunn and Trond Dalsegg).

Drives and Hikes in the Jotunheimen Mountains

Route 55, which runs between Lom and the Sognefjord to the south, is the sightseeing spine of this region. From this main (and already scenic) drag, other roads spin upward into the mountains—offering even better views and exciting drives and hikes. Many of these get you up close to Norway's highest mountain, Galdhøpiggen (8,100 feet). I've listed these attractions from north to south, as you'll reach them driving from Lom to the Sognefjord; except for the first, they all branch off from Route 55. Another great high-mountain experience nearby—the hike to the Nigard Glacier near Lustrafjord—is covered in the previous chapter.

Remember that the Norwegian Mountain Museum in Lom acts as a national park office, offering excellent maps and advice for drivers and hikers—a stop here is obligatory if you're planning a jaunt into the mountains.

Besseggen

This trail offers an incredible opportunity to walk between two lakes separated by a narrow ridge and a 1,000-foot cliff. It's one of Norway's most beloved hikes, which can make it crowded in the summer. To get to the trailhead, drivers detour down Route 51 after Otta south to Maurvangen. Turn right to Gjendesheim to park your car. From Gjendesheim, catch the boat to Memurubu, where the path starts at the boat dock. Hike along the ridge—with a blue lake (Bessvatnet) on one side and a green lake (Gjende) on the other—and keep your balance. The six-hour trail loops back to Gjendesheim. Because the boat runs sporadically, time your visit to catch one (150 NOK for 20-minute ride, 3 morning departures daily, check schedules at www.gjende.no, mobile 91 30 67 44). This is a thrilling but potentially hazardous hike, and it's a major detour: Gjendesheim is about 1.5 hours and 50 miles from Lom.

Spiterstulen

From Røisheim, this 11-mile toll road (80 NOK) takes you from Route 55 to the Spiterstulen mountain hotel/lodge in about 30 minutes (3,600 feet). This is the best destination for serious all-day hikes to Norway's two mightiest mountains, Glittertinden and Galdhøpiggen (a 5-hour hike up and a 3-hour hike down, doable without a guide). Or consider a guided, two-hour glacier walk (tel. 61 21 94 00, www.spiterstulen.no).

Juvasshytta

This toll road takes you (in about 40 minutes) to the highest you can drive and the closest you can get to Galdhøpiggen (6,050 feet) by car. The road starts in Bøverdal, and costs 85 NOK; at the end of it, daily, guided, six-hour hikes go across the glacier to the summit and back (200 NOK, late June-late Sept daily at 10:00, July-mid-Aug also daily at 11:30, check in 30 minutes before, strict age limit—no kids under age 7, 4 miles each way, easy ascent but can be dangerous without a guide, hiking boots required—possible to rent from nearby ski resort). You can sleep in the recently updated **$$ Juvasshytta lodge** (includes breakfast, dinner optional, open June-Sept, tel. 61 21 15 50, www.juvasshytta.no).

Leirvassbu

This 11-mile, 50-NOK toll road (about 30 minutes one-way from Bøverkinnhalsen, south of Elvesæter) is most scenic for car hikers. It takes you to a lodge at 4,600 feet with great views and easy walks. A serious (5-hour round-trip) hike goes to the lone peak, Kyrkja—"The Cathedral," which looms like a sanded-down mini-Matterhorn on the horizon (6,660 feet).

▲▲Sognefjell Drive to the Sognefjord

Norway's highest pass (at 4,600 feet, the highest road in northern Europe) is a thrilling drive through a cancan line of mountains, from Jotunheimen's Bøverdal Valley to the Lustrafjord (an arm of the Sognefjord). Centuries ago, the farmers of Gudbrandsdal took their horse caravans over this difficult mountain pass on treks to Bergen. Today, the road (Route 55) is still narrow, windy, and otherworldly (and usually closed mid-Oct-May).

As you begin to ascend just beyond Elvesæter, notice the viewpoint on the left for the Leirdalen Valley—capped at the end with the Kyrkja peak (described earlier). Next you'll twist up into a lake-filled valley, then through a mild canyon with grand waterfalls. Before long, as you corkscrew up more switchbacks, you're above the tree line, enjoying a "top of the world" feeling. The best views (to the south) are of the cut-glass range called Hurrungane ("Noisy Children"). The 10 hairpin turns between Turtagrø and Fortun are exciting. Be sure to stop, get out, look around, and enjoy the lavish views. Treat each turn as if it were your last.

Just before you descend to the fjord, the terrain changes, and you reach a pullout on the right, next to a hilltop viewpoint—offering your first glimpse of the fjord. The Lustrafjord village of Skjolden is just around the bend (and down several more switchbacks). Entering Skjolden, continue following Route 55, which now traces the west bank of the Lustrafjord. For more on the sights from here on out, turn to page 334.

Gudbrandsdal and Jotunheimen Connections

BY TRAIN AND BUS

Cars are better, but if you're without wheels, here are your options: Trains run from **Oslo to Lillehammer** (almost hourly, 2.5 hours, just 2 hours from Oslo airport) and **Lillehammer to Otta** (6/day, 1.5 hours). Buses meet some trains (confirm schedule at the train station in Oslo) for travelers heading from **Otta to Lom** (2/day, 1 hour) and onward from **Lom to Sogndal** (2/day late June-Aug only, road closed off-season, 3.5 hours).

ROUTE TIPS FOR DRIVERS

Use low gears and lots of patience both up (to keep the engine cool) and down (to save your brakes). Uphill traffic gets the right-of-way, but drivers, up or down, dive for the nearest fat part of the road whenever they meet. Ask backseat drivers not to scream until you've actually been hit or have left the road.

It's 2.5 hours from Oslo to Lillehammer and 3 hours after that to Lom.

From Oslo to Lillehammer: Wind out of Oslo following signs for *E-6* (not to *Drammen*, but for *Stockholm* and then to *Trondheim*). In a few minutes, you're in the wide-open pastoral countryside of eastern Norway. Norway's Constitution Hall—Eidsvoll Manor—is a five-minute detour off E-6, several miles south of Eidsvoll in Eidsvoll Verk (described on page 268; follow the signs to *Eidsvoll Bygningen*). Then E-6 takes you along Norway's largest lake (Mjøsa), through the town of Hamar, and past more lake scenery into Lillehammer. Signs direct you uphill from downtown Lillehammer to the Maihaugen Open-Air Folk Museum.

From Lillehammer to Jotunheimen: From Lillehammer, signs to *E-6/Trondheim* take you north, up the bucolic valley of

Gudbrandsdal (en route to Otta and Lom), with fine but unremarkable scenery. Along the way, a pair of toll-road side-trips (Gynt Veien and Peer Gynt Seterveien) loop off the E-6 road. While they sound romantic, they're basically windy, curvy dirt roads over high, desolate heath and scrub-brush plateaus with fine mountain views. They're scenic, but pale in comparison with the Sognefjell road between Lom and the Lustrafjord (described earlier). At Otta, exit for Lom. Halfway to Lom, on the left, look for the long suspension bridge spanning the milky-blue river—a good opportunity to stretch your legs, and a scenic spot to enjoy a picnic.

GUDBRANDSDAL

BERGEN

Bergen is permanently salted with robust cobbles and a rich sea-trading heritage. Norway's capital in the 13th century, Bergen's wealth and importance came thanks to its membership in the heavyweight medieval trading club of merchant cities called the Hanseatic League. Bergen still wears her rich maritime heritage proudly—nowhere more scenically than the colorful wooden warehouses that make up the picture-perfect Bryggen district along the harbor.

Protected from the open sea by a lone sheltering island, Bergen is a place of refuge from heavy winds for the giant working boats that serve the North Sea oil rigs. (Much of Norway's current affluence is funded by the oil it drills just offshore.) Bergen is also one of the most popular cruise-ship ports in northern Europe, hosting about 300 ships a year and up to five ships a day in peak season. Each morning is rush hour, as cruisers hike past the fortress and into town.

Bergen gets an average of 80 inches of rain annually (compared to 30 inches in Oslo). A good year has 60 days of sunshine. The natives aren't apologetic about their famously lousy weather. In fact, they seem to wear it as a badge of pride. "Well, that's Bergen," they'll say matter-of-factly as they wring out their raincoats. When I complained about an all-day downpour, one resident cheerfully informed me, "There's no such thing as bad weather—just inappropriate clothing"...a local mantra that rhymes in Norwegian.

With about 275,000 people, Bergen has big-city parking problems and high prices, but visitors sticking to the old center find it charming. Enjoy Bergen's salty market, then stroll the easy-on-foot old quarter, with cute lanes of delicate old wooden houses.

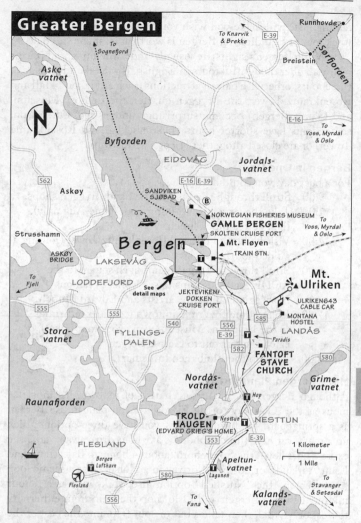

From downtown Bergen, a funicular zips you up a little mountain for a bird's-eye view of this sailors' town. A short foray into the countryside takes you to a variety of nearby experiences: a dramatic cable-car ride to a mountaintop perch (Ulriken643); an evocative stave church (Fantoft); and the home of Norway's most beloved composer, Edvard Grieg, at Troldhaugen.

PLANNING YOUR TIME

Bergen can be enjoyed even on the tail end of a day's scenic train ride from Oslo before returning on the overnight train. But that teasing taste will make you wish you had more time. On a three-week tour of Scandinavia, Bergen is worth at least one full day.

While Bergen's sights are visually underwhelming and pricey, nearly all offer thoughtful tours in English. If you take advantage of these tours, otherwise barren attractions (such as Håkon's Hall and Rosenkrantz Tower, the Bryggen quarter, the Leprosy Museum, and Gamle Bergen) become surprisingly interesting. Off-season, some sights have shorter hours (Håkon's Hall and Rosenkrantz Tower) or are closed altogether (Leprosy Museum).

Bergen in One Day

For a busy day, you could do this:

 9:00   Stroll through the Fish Market and Bryggen shops.

11:00   Take the Bryggen Walking Tour (June-Aug only), then grab a quick lunch.

14:00   Visit Håkon's Hall and Rosenkrantz Tower (joining a guided tour).

15:00   Stroll through Torgallmenningen square to the KODE Art Museums to see works by famous Norwegian landscape artists and Edvard Munch.

17:00   Enjoy some free time in town (consider returning to the Bryggens Museum using your tour ticket), or catch the bus out to Gamle Bergen.

18:00   Ride up the Fløibanen funicular.

More Bergen Planning Tips

Although Bergen has plenty of charms of its own, it's most famous as the "Gateway to the Fjords." If you plan to use Bergen as a springboard for fjord country, you have three options: Pick up a rental car here (fjord wonder is a 3-hour drive away); take the express boat down the Sognefjord (about 4 hours to Balestrand and Flåm/Aurland); or do the "Norway in a Nutshell" as a scenic loop from Bergen. The "Nutshell" option also works well as a detour midway between Bergen and Oslo (hop the train from either city to Voss or Myrdal, then take a bus or spur train into the best of the Sognefjord; scenic ferry rides depart from there). While there are a million ways to enjoy the fjords, first-timers should start with this region (covered thoroughly in the Norway in a Nutshell and More on the Sognefjord chapters).

Also note that Bergen, a geographic dead-end, is actually an efficient place to begin or end your Scandinavian tour. Consider flying into Bergen and out of another city, such as Helsinki (or vice versa).

Orientation to Bergen

Bergen clusters around its harbor—nearly everything listed in this chapter is within a few minutes' walk. The busy Torget (the square

with the Fish Market) is at the head of the harbor. As you face the sea from here, Bergen's TI is at the left end of the Fish Market. The town's historic Hanseatic Quarter, Bryggen (BRUHY-gun), lines the harbor on the right. Express boats to the Sognefjord (Balestrand and Flåm) dock at the harbor on the left.

Charming cobbled streets surround the harbor and climb the encircling hills. Bergen's popular Fløibanen funicular climbs high above the city to the top of Mount Fløyen for the best view of the town. Surveying the surrounding islands and inlets, it's clear why this city is known as the "Gateway to the Fjords."

TOURIST INFORMATION

The centrally located TI is upstairs in the long, skinny, modern, Torghallen market building, next to the Fish Market (daily June-Aug 8:30-22:00, May and Sept 9:00-20:00; Oct-April Mon-Sat 9:00-16:00, closed Sun; free Wi-Fi, handy budget eateries downstairs and in Fish Market; tel. 55 55 20 00, www.visitbergen.com).

The TI covers Bergen and western Norway, provides information and tickets for tours, has a fjord information desk, books rooms, will exchange currency, and maintains a very handy events board listing today's and tomorrow's slate of tours, concerts, and other events. Pick up this year's edition of the free *Bergen Guide* (also likely at your hotel), which has a fine map and lists sights, hours, and special events. This booklet can answer most of your questions.

Bergen Card: You have to work hard to make this greedy little card pay off (240 NOK/24 hours, 310 NOK/48 hours, 380 NOK/72 hours, sold at TI and Montana Family & Youth Hostel). It gives you free use of the city's tram and buses, half off the Fløibanen funicular, free admission to most museums (but not the Hanseatic Museum; aquarium included only in winter), and discounts on some events and sights such as Edvard Grieg's Home.

ARRIVAL IN BERGEN

By Train or Bus: Bergen's train and bus stations are on Strømgaten, facing a park-rimmed lake. The small, manageable train station has an office open long hours for booking all your travel in Norway—you can get your Nutshell reservations here (Mon-Fri 6:45-19:15, Sat-Sun 7:30-16:00). There are pay baggage lockers (daily 6:00-23:30), pay toilets, a newsstand, a sandwich shop, and a coffee shop. (To get to the bus station, follow the covered walkway behind the Narvesen newsstand via the Storsenter shopping mall.) Taxis wait to the right (with the tracks at your back); a tram stop is to your left, just around the corner. From the train station, it's a 10-minute walk to the TI: Cross the street (Strømgaten) in front of the station and take Marken, a cobbled street that eventually turns into a modern retail street. Continue walking in the same direction until you reach the water.

By Plane: Bergen's sleek and modern Flesland Airport is 12 miles south of the city center (airport code: BGO, tel. 67 03 15 55, www.avinor.no/bergen). The airport **bus** runs between the airport and downtown Bergen, stopping at the Radisson Blu Royal Hotel in Bryggen, the harborfront area near the TI (if you ask), the Radisson Blu Hotel Norge (in the modern part of town at Ole Bulls Plass), and the bus station (about 120 NOK, pay driver, 6/hour at peak times, fewer in slow times, 30-minute ride). **Taxis** take up to four people and cost about 400 NOK for the 20-minute ride (depending on time of day).

The cheapest option is to take the Bybanen **tram** (departs every 5-10 minutes, 45-minute trip, schedule at www.skyss.no) to the end of the line at Byparken. But keep in mind that this stop—on Kaigaten, between Bergen's little lake and Ole Bulls Plass—is several blocks from most of my recommended hotels. For tram ticket details, see "Getting Around Bergen," later.

By Car: Driving is a headache in Bergen; avoid it if you can. Approaching town on E-16 (from Voss and the Sognefjord area), follow signs for *Sentrum,* which spits you out near the big, modern bus station and parking garage. Parking is difficult and costly—ask your hotelier for tips. Note that all drivers entering Bergen must pay a 19-NOK toll (45-NOK during rush hour). There are no toll-collection gates, since the system is automated. Assuming they bill you, it'll just show up on your credit card (which they access through your rental-car company). For details, ask your rental company or see www.bomringenbergen.no.

By Cruise Ship: Bergen is easy for cruise passengers, regardless of which of the city's two ports your ship uses. A taxi into downtown from either port costs about 150-170 NOK.

The **Skolten** cruise port is just past the fortress on the main harborfront road. Arriving here, simply walk into town (stroll with the harbor on your right, figure about 10 minutes to Bryggen, plus five more minutes to the Fish Market and TI). After about five minutes, you'll pass the fortress—the starting point for my self-guided walk. Hop-on, hop-off buses also pick up passengers at the port (though in this compact town, I'd just walk).

The **Jekteviken/Dokken** cruise port is in an industrial zone to the south, a bit farther out (about a 20-minute walk). To discourage passengers from walking through all the containers, the port operates a convenient and free **shuttle bus** that zips you into town. It drops you off along Rasmus Meyers Allé in front of the KODE Art Museums, facing the cute man-made lake called Lille Lungegårds-vannet. From here, it's an easy 10-minute walk to the TI and Fish Market: Walk with the lake on your right, pass through the park (with the pavilion) and head up the pedestrian mall called Ole Bulls Plass, and turn right (at the bluish slab) up the broad square called Torgallmenningen. Note that my self-guided Bergen walk conveniently ends near the shuttle-bus stop.

For more in-depth cruising information, pick up my *Rick Steves Scandinavian & Northern European Cruise Ports* guidebook.

HELPFUL HINTS

Museum Tours: Many of Bergen's sights are hard to appreciate without a guide. Fortunately, several offer wonderful and intimate guided tours. Make the most of the following sights by taking advantage of their tours: Håkon's Hall and Rosenkrantz Tower, Bryggens Museum, Hanseatic Museum, Leprosy Museum, Gamle Bergen, and Edvard Grieg's Home.

Crowd Control: In high season, cruise-ship passengers mob the waterfront between 10:00 and 15:00; to avoid the crush, consider visiting an outlying sight during this time, such as Gamle Bergen or Edvard Grieg's Home.

Laundry: Drop your laundry off at **Hygienisk Vask & Rens,** and pick it up clean the next day (no self-service, Mon-Fri 8:30-16:30, closed Sat-Sun, Halfdan Kjerulfsgate 8, tel. 55 31 77 41).

GETTING AROUND BERGEN

Most in-town sights can easily be reached by foot; only the aquarium, the Norwegian Fisheries Museum, and Gamle Bergen (and farther-flung sights such as the Fantoft Stave Church, Edvard Grieg's Home at Troldhaugen, and the Ulriken643 cable car) are more than a 10-minute walk from the TI.

By Bus: City buses cost 60 NOK per ride (pay driver in cash), or 37 NOK per ride if you buy a single-ride ticket from a machine or convenience stores such as Narvesen, 7-Eleven, Rimi, and Deli de Luca. The best buses for a Bergen joyride are #6 (north along the coast) and #11 (into the hills).

By Tram: Bergen's light-rail line (Bybanen) is a convenient way to visit Edvard Grieg's Home and the Fantoft Stave Church, or to get to Flesland Airport. The tram begins next to Byparken (on Kaigaten, between Bergen's little lake and Ole Bulls Plass), then heads to the train station and continues south, ending at the airport. Buy your 37-NOK ticket from the machine before boarding (to use a US credit card, you'll need your PIN, also accepts coins). You can also buy single-ride tickets at Narvesen, 7-Eleven, Rimi, and Deli de Luca stores—you'll get a gray *minikort* pass. Validate the pass when you board by holding it next to the card reader (watch how other passengers do it). Ride it about 20 minutes to the Paradis stop for **Fantoft** Stave Church (don't get off at the "Fantoft" stop, which is farther from the church); or continue to the next stop, Hop, to hike to **Troldhaugen.**

By Ferry: The *Beffen,* a little orange ferry, chugs across the harbor (Vågen) every half-hour, from the dock a block south of the Bryggens Museum to the dock—directly opposite the fortress—a block from the Nykirken church (25 NOK, Mon-Fri 7:30-16:00, plus Sat May-Aug 11:00-16:00, fewer on Sun, 4-minute ride). Another *Beffen* ferry runs from the right side of the Fish Market (as you face the water) to the Norwegian Fisheries Museum (for details, see the Hanseatic Museum listing under "Sights in Bergen"). The *Vågen* "Akvariet" ferry runs from the left side of the Fish Market every half-hour to a dock near the aquarium (see the Aquarium listing under "Sights in Bergen"). All of these "poor man's cruises" offer good harbor views.

By Taxi: For a taxi, which can be pricey, call 07000 or 08000.

Tours in Bergen

▲▲▲Bryggen Walking Tour

This tour of the historic Hanseatic district is one of Bergen's best activities. Local guides take visitors on an excellent 1.5-hour walk

in English through 900 years of Bergen history via the old Hanseatic town (20 minutes in Bryggens Museum, 20-minute visit to the medieval Hanseatic Assembly Rooms (Schøtstuene), 20-minute walk through Bryggen, and 20 minutes in Hanseatic Museum). Tours leave from the Bryggens Museum (next to the Radisson Blu Royal Hotel). When you consider that the price includes entry tickets to all three sights, the tour more than pays for itself (150 NOK, June-Aug daily at 11:00 and 12:00, maximum 30 in group, no tours Sept-May, tel. 55

30 80 30, post@bymuseet.no). While the museum visits are a bit rushed, your tour ticket allows you to re-enter the museums for the rest of the day. The 11:00 tour can sell out, especially in July; to be safe, you can call, email, or drop by ahead of time to reserve a spot.

Local Guide

Sue Lindelid is a British expat who has spent more than 25 years showing visitors around Bergen (1,200 NOK/2-hour tour, 1,600 NOK/3-hour tour; mobile 90 78 59 52, suelin@hotmail.no).

▲Bus Tours

The TI sells tickets for various bus tours, including a 2.5-hour Grieg Lunch Concert tour that goes to Edvard Grieg's Home at Troldhaugen—a handy way to reach that distant sight (250 NOK, 50-NOK discount with Bergen Card, includes 30-minute concert but not lunch, May-Sept daily at 11:30, departs from TI). Buses are comfy, with big views and a fine recorded commentary. There are also several full-day tour options from Bergen, including bus/boat tours to nearby Hardanger and Sogne fjords. The TI is packed with brochures describing all the excursions.

Hop-On, Hop-Off Buses

City Sightseeing links most of Bergen's major sights and also stops at the Skolten cruise port, but doesn't go to the Fantoft Stave Church, Troldhaugen, or Ulriken643 cable car. If your sightseeing plans don't extend beyond the walkable core of Bergen, skip this (275 NOK/24 hours, early May-late Sept 9:00-16:00, every 30 minutes, also stops in front of Fish Market, mobile 97 78 18 88, www.citysightseeing.no/bergen).

Inflatable Boat Tour

After a scenic cruise along the Bergen harborfront, you'll zip out into the open fjord past islands and rocky skerries aboard a fast and breezy Fjord Tours rigid inflatable boat (RIB). Before heading out you'll don a survival suit and goggles for the thrilling high-speed part of the journey. Tours last 50 minutes and depart from near the round Narvesen kiosk on the Bryggen side of the Fish Market. Get tickets at the TI (595 NOK, meet at dock at 13:10, 1 tour/day, www.fjordtours.com).

Tourist Train

The tacky little "Bergen Express" train departs from in front of the Hanseatic Museum for a 55-minute loop around town (200 NOK, 1/hour daily June-Aug 10:00-18:00, less frequent off-season, headphone English commentary).

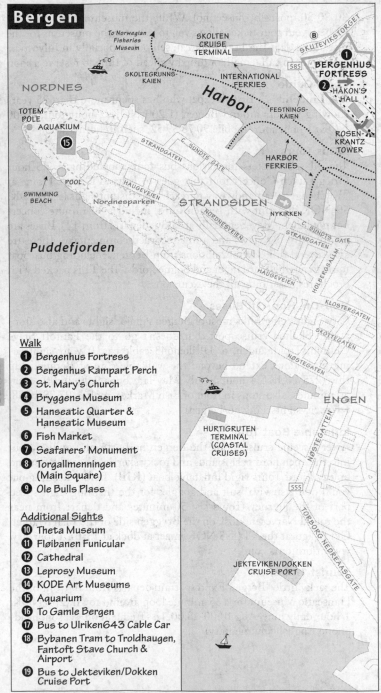

Bergen

Walk

1. Bergenhus Fortress
2. Bergenhus Rampart Perch
3. St. Mary's Church
4. Bryggens Museum
5. Hanseatic Quarter & Hanseatic Museum
6. Fish Market
7. Seafarers' Monument
8. Torgallmenningen (Main Square)
9. Ole Bulls Plass

Additional Sights

10. Theta Museum
11. Fløibanen Funicular
12. Cathedral
13. Leprosy Museum
14. KODE Art Museums
15. Aquarium
16. To Gamle Bergen
17. Bus to Ulriken643 Cable Car
18. Bybanen Tram to Troldhaugen, Fantoft Stave Church & Airport
19. Bus to Jekteviken/Dokken Cruise Port

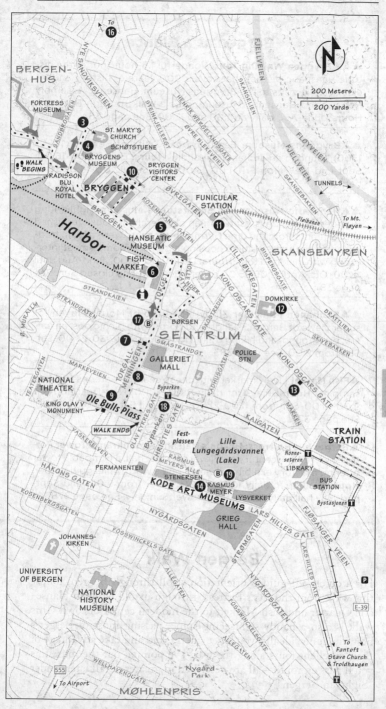

To **16**

BERGEN-HUS

FORTRESS MUSEUM

3 ST. MARY'S CHURCH

SCHØTSTUENE

4 BRYGGENS MUSEUM

WALK BEGINS

RADISSON BLU ROYAL HOTEL

10 BRYGGEN VISITORS' CENTER

BRYGGEN

ØVREGATEN

FUNICULAR STATION

Fløibanen

To Mt. Fløyen

Harbor

5 HANSEATIC MUSEUM

11

SKANSEMYREN

6 FISH MARKET

STRANDKAIEN

STRANDGATEN

TORGET

Domkirke **12**

17 B

BØRSEN

SENTRUM

7

SMÅSTRANDGT.

GALLERIET MALL

POLICE STN.

8

NATIONAL THEATER

9 Ole Bulls Plass

KING OLAV MONUMENT

18 T

Byparken

13

WALK ENDS

Festplassen

Lille Lungegårdsvannet (Lake)

TRAIN STATION

LIBRARY

19 B

STENERSEN

14 RASMUS MEYER

KODE ART MUSEUMS

LYSVERKET

BUS STATION

Bystasjonen T

GRIEG HALL

PERMANENTEN

JOHANNES-KIRKEN

UNIVERSITY OF BERGEN

NATIONAL HISTORY MUSEUM

E-39

P

To Fanteft Stave Church & Troldhaugen

555 To Airport

Nygård Park

MØHLENPRIS

BERGEN

Bergen at a Glance

▲▲▲**Bryggen Walking Tour** Wonderful 1.5-hour tour of the historic Hanseatic district that covers 900 years of history and includes short visits to the Bryggens Museum, Hanseatic Assembly Rooms, and Hanseatic Museum, plus a walk through Bryggen. **Hours:** June-Aug daily at 11:00 and 12:00. See page 364.

▲▲**Bryggens Museum** Featuring early bits of Bergen (1050-1500), found in an archaeological dig. **Hours:** Daily 10:00-16:00; Sept-mid-May Mon-Fri 11:00-15:00, Sat-Sun 12:00-16:00. See page 380.

▲▲**Hanseatic Museum and Schøtstuene** Museum highlighting Bryggen's glory days, featuring an old merchant house furnished with artifacts from the time German merchants were tops in trading and a separate building housing assembly rooms—most interesting with included tour. **Hours:** Daily 9:00-17:00, June-Aug until 18:00, Oct-April 11:00-15:00 except Schøtstuene closed Sun. See page 381.

▲▲**Fløibanen Funicular** Zippy lift to top of Mount Fløyen for super views of Bergen, islands, and fjords, with picnic ops, an eatery, playground, and hiking trails. **Hours:** Mon-Fri 7:30-23:00, Sat-Sun from 8:00. See page 383.

▲**Fish Market** Lively market with cheap seafood eateries and free samples. **Hours:** May-Oct daily 8:00-23:00; Nov-Dec Mon-Sat 9:00-21:00, Sun from 11:00-21:00; Jan-April Sat only 9:00-15:00. See page 374.

▲**Bergenhus Fortress: Håkon's Hall and Rosenkrantz Tower** Fortress with a 13th-century medieval banquet hall, a climbable tower offering a history exhibit and views, and a worthwhile guided tour. **Hours:** Hall open daily 10:00-16:00, tower from 9:00; mid-Sept-mid-May hall daily 12:00-15:00, tower Sun only. See page 378.

Bergen Walk

For a quick self-guided orientation stroll through Bergen, follow this walk from the city's fortress, through its old wooden Hanseatic Quarter and Fish Market, to the modern center of town. This walk is also a handy sightseeing spine, passing most of Bergen's best museums; ideally, you'll get sidetracked and take advantage of their excellent tours along the way. I've pointed out the museums you'll pass en route—all are described in greater detail later, under "Sights in Bergen."

▲**KODE Art Museums** Collection spread among four neighboring lakeside buildings: KODE 4 (international and Norwegian artists), KODE 3 (Norwegian artists, including Munch), KODE 2 (contemporary art), and KODE 1 (decorative arts). **Hours:** Daily 11:00-17:00 (KODE 3 10:00-18:00), closed Mon mid-Sept–mid-May. See page 385.

▲**St. Mary's Church** Bergen's oldest church, dating to the 12th century. **Hours:** Mon-Fri 9:00-16:00, closed mid-Sept–May. See page 383.

▲**Aquarium** Well-presented sea life, with a walk-through "shark tunnel" and feeding times at the top of most hours in summer. **Hours:** Daily May-Aug 9:00-18:00, shorter hours off-season. See page 386.

▲**Gamle Bergen (Old Bergen)** Quaint gathering of 50 homes and shops dating from 18th-20th century, with guided tours of museum interiors at the top of the hour. **Hours:** Daily 9:00-16:00, closed Sept–mid-May. See page 386.

Near Bergen
▲▲**Edvard Grieg's Home, Troldhaugen** Home of Norway's greatest composer, with artifacts, tours, and concerts. **Hours:** Daily 9:00-18:00, Oct-April 10:00-16:00. See page 389.

▲**Ulriken643 Cable Car** A quick ride up to the summit of Ulriken, Bergen's tallest mountain, with nonstop views, a restaurant, and hiking trails. **Hours:** Daily 9:00-21:00, off-season until 17:00. See page 388.

BERGEN

• *Begin where Bergen did, at its historic fortress. From the harborfront road, 50 yards before the stone tower with the water on your left, veer up the ramp behind the low stone wall on the right, through a gate, and into the fortress complex. Stand before the stony skyscraper.*

❶ Bergenhus Fortress
In the 13th century, Bergen became the Kingdom of Norway's first real capital. (Until then, kings would circulate, staying on royal farms.) This fortress—built in the 1240s and worth ▲—was a garrison, with a tower for the king's residence (Rosenkrantz Tower) and a large hall for his banquets (Håkon's Hall).

Rosenkrantz Tower, the keep of the 13th-century castle, was expanded in the 16th century by the Danish-Norwegian king, who wanted to exercise a little control over the German merchants who dominated his town. He was tired of the Germans making all the money without paying taxes. This tower—with its cannon trained not on external threats but toward Bryggen—while expensive, paid for itself many times over as Germans got the message and paid their taxes.

• *Step through the gate (20 yards to the right of the tower) marked 1728 and into the courtyard of the Bergenhus Fortress. In front of you stands Håkon's Hall with its stepped gable. Tours for both the hall and the tower leave from the building to the right of Håkon's Hall.*

Pop into the museum lobby to enjoy a free exhibit about the massive 1944 explosion of the German ammunition ship in the harbor. For the best view of Håkon's Hall, walk through the gate and around the building to the left. Stand on the rampart between the hall and the harbor.

Håkon's Hall is the largest secular medieval building in Norway. When the pope sent a cardinal to perform Håkon's coronation there was no suitable building in Norway for such a VIP. King Håkon fixed that by having this impressive banqueting hall built in the mid-1200s. When Norway's capital moved to Oslo in 1299, the hall was abandoned and eventually used for grain storage. For a century it had no roof. In the Romantic 19th century, it was appreciated and restored. It's essentially a giant, grand reception hall used today as it was eight centuries ago: for banquets.

• *Continue walking along the rampart (climbing some steps and going about 100 yards past Håkon's Hall) to the far end of Bergenhus Fortress where you find a statue of a king and a fine harbor view.*

❷ Bergenhus Rampart Perch and Statue of King Håkon VII

The cannon on the ramparts here illustrates how the fort protected this strategic harbor. The port is busy with both cruise ships and supply ships for the nearby North Sea oil rigs. Long before this modern commerce, this is where the cod fishermen of the north met the traders of Europe. Travelers in the 12th century described how there were so many trading vessels here "you could cross the harbor without getting your feet wet." Beyond the ships is an island protecting Bergen from the open sea.

Look left and right at the dangerous edge with no railing. If someone were to fall and get hurt here and then try to sue, the Norwegian judge's verdict would be: stupidity—case dismissed. Around you are Bergen's "seven mountains." One day each summer locals race to climb each of these in rapid succession, accomplishing the feat in less than 12 hours.

The statue is of the beloved King Håkon VII (1872-1957),

grandfather of today's king. While exiled in London during World War II, King Håkon kept up Norwegian spirits through radio broadcasts. The first king of modern Norway (after the country won its independence from Sweden in 1905), he was a Danish prince married to Queen Victoria's granddaughter—a savvy monarch who knew how to play the royalty game.

A few steps behind the statue (just right of tree-lined lane) is the site of Bergen's first cathedral, built in 1070. A hedge grows where its walls once stood. The statue of Mary marks the place of the altar, its pedestal etched with a list of 13th-century kings of Norway crowned and buried here.

These castle grounds (notice the natural amphitheater on the left) host cultural events and music festivals; Elton John, Paul McCartney, and Kygo have all packed this outdoor venue in recent years.

Continuing around Håkon's Hall, follow the linden tree-lined lane. On the left, a massive concrete structure disguised by ivy looms as if evil. It was a German bunker built during the Nazi occupation—easier now to ignore than dismantle.

Twenty yards ahead on the right is a rare set of free public toilets. Notice they come with blue lights to discourage heroin junkies from using these WCs as a place to shoot up. The blue lights make it hard to see veins.

• *You've now returned to the tower and circled the castle grounds. Before leaving, consider taking a guided tour of the hall and tower. Head back down the ramp, out to the main road, and continue with the harbor on your right. (After a block, history buffs could follow* Bergenhus *signs, up the street to the left, to the free and fascinating* **Fortress Museum**—*with its collection of Norwegian military history and Nazi occupation exhibits.) Proceed one more block along the harbor until you reach the open, parklike space on your left. Walk 100 yards (just past the handy Rema 1000 supermarket) to the top of this park where you'll see...*

❸ St. Mary's Church (Mariakirken)

Dating from the 12th century, this is Bergen's oldest preserved building. This stately church of the Hanseatic merchants has a dour stone interior, but it's enlivened by a colorful, highly decorated pulpit.

In the park below the church, find the statue of Snorri Sturlason. In the 1200s, this Icelandic scribe and scholar wrote down the Viking sagas. Thanks to him, we have a better understanding of this Nordic era. A few steps to the right, look through the window of the big modern building at an archaeological site showing the oldest remains of Bergen—stubs of the 12th-century trading town's streets tumbling to the harbor before land reclamation pushed the harbor farther out.

• *The window is just a sneak peek at the excellent ❹ Bryggens Museum, which provides helpful historical context for the Hanseatic Quarter we're about to visit. The museum's outstanding **Bryggen Walking Tour** is your best bet for seeing this area (June-Aug daily at 11:00 and 12:00; see "Tours in Bergen," earlier). Continue down to the busy harborfront. On the left is the most photographed sight in town, the Bryggen quarter. To get your bearings, first read the "Bryggen's History" sidebar; if it's nice out, cross the street to the wharf and look back for a fine overview of this area. (Or, in the rain, huddle under an awning.)*

❺ Bergen's Hanseatic Quarter (Bryggen)

Bergen's fragile wooden old town is its iconic front door. The long "tenements" (rows of warehouses) hide atmospheric lanes that creak and groan with history.

Remember that while we think of Bergen as "Norwegian," Bryggen was German—the territory of *Deutsch*-speaking merchants and traders. (The most popular surname in Bergen is the German name Hanson—"son of Hans.") From the front of Bryggen, look back at the Rosenkrantz Tower. The little red holes at its top mark where cannons once pointed at the German quarter, installed by Norwegian royalty who wanted a slice of all that taxable trade revenue. Their threat was countered by German grain—without which the Norwegians would've starved.

Notice that the first six houses are perfectly straight; they were built in the 1980s to block the view of a modern hotel behind. The more ramshackle stretch of 11 houses beyond date from the early 1700s. Each front hides a long line of five to ten businesses.

• *To wander into the heart of this woody medieval quarter, head down Bredsgården, the lane a couple of doors before the shop sign featuring the anatomically correct unicorn. We'll make a loop to the right: down this lane nearly all the way, under a passage into a square (with a well, a vibrant outdoor restaurant, and a big wooden cod), and then back to the harbor down a parallel lane. Read the information below, then explore, stopping at the big wooden cod.*

Bit by bit, Bryggen is being restored using medieval techniques and materials. As you explore, you may stumble upon a rebuilding project in action.

Strolling through Bryggen, you feel swallowed up by history. Long rows of planky buildings (medieval-style double tenements)  lean haphazardly across narrow alleys. The last Hanseatic merchant moved out centuries ago, but this is still a place of (touristy) commerce. You'll find artists' galleries, T-shirt boutiques, leather workshops, atmospheric restaurants, fishing tackle shops, sweaters, sweaters, sweaters...and trolls.

Look up at the winch-and-pulley systems on the buildings. These connected ground-floor workrooms with top-floor storerooms. Notice that the overhanging storerooms upstairs were supported by timbers with an elbow created by a tree trunk and its root—considered the strongest way to make a right angle in construction back then. Turning right at the top of the lane, you enter a lively cobbled square. On the far side is that big wooden fish.

The wooden cod (next to a well) is a reminder that the economic foundation of Bergen—the biggest city in Scandinavia until 1650 and the biggest city in Norway until 1830—was this fish. The stone building behind the carved cod was one of the fireproof cookhouses serving a line of buildings that stretched to the harbor. Today it's the Hetland Gallery, filled with the entertaining work of a popular local artist famous for fun caricatures of the city. Facing the same square is the Bryggen visitors center, worth peeking into.

• *Enjoy the center and the shops. Then return downhill to the harborfront, turn left, and continue the walk.*

Half of Bryggen (the brick-and-stone stretch to your left between the old wooden facades and the head of the bay) was torn down around 1900. Today the stately buildings that replaced it—far less atmospheric than Bryggen's original wooden core—are filled with tacky trinket shops and touristy splurge restaurants. They do make a nice architectural cancan of pointy gables, each with its date of construction indicated near the top.

Head to the lone wooden red house at the end of the row, which houses the **Hanseatic Museum.** The man who owned this building recognized the value of the city's heritage and kept its 18th-century interior intact. Once considered a nutcase, today he's celebrated as a visionary, as his decision has left visitors with a fine example of an old merchant house that they can tour. This highly

BERGEN

recommended museum is your best chance to get a peek inside one of those old wooden tenements.

• *The Fish Market is just across the street. Before enjoying that, we'll circle a few blocks inland and around to the right.*

The red-brick building (with frilly white trim, stepped gable, and a Starbucks) is the old meat market. It was built in 1877, after the importance of hygiene was recognized and the meat was moved inside from today's Fish Market. At the intersection just beyond, look left (uphill past the meat market) to see the Fløibanen station. Ahead, on the right, is an unusually classy McDonald's in a 1710 building that was originally a bakery.

Across the street, Anne Madam Restaurant is a celebration of white and fishy cuisine—very Norwegian, with a few Norwegian meat dishes thrown in. Notice the Los Tacos restaurant next door; Norwegians love Tex-Mex food, and "Taco Friday" has become a tradition for many. A few steps uphill, the tiny red shack flying the Norwegian flags is the popular, recommended 3-Kroneren hot-dog stand. Review the many sausage options.

At the McDonald's, wander the length of the cute lane of 200-year-old buildings. Called Hollendergaten, its name comes from a time when the king organized foreign communities of traders into various neighborhoods; this was where the Dutch lived. The curving street marks the former harborfront—these buildings were originally right on the water.

Hooking left, you reach the end of Hollendergaten. Turn right back toward the harborfront. Ahead is the grand stone Børsen building (now Matbørsen, a collection of trendy restaurants), once the stock exchange. Step inside to enjoy its 1920s Art Deco-style murals celebrating Bergen's fishing heritage.

• *Now, cross the street and immerse yourself in Bergen's beloved Fish Market.*

❻ Fish Market (Fisketorget)

A fish market has thrived here since the 1500s, when fishermen rowed in with their catch and haggled with hungry residents.

While it's now become a food circus of eateries selling fishy treats to tourists—no local would come here to actually buy fish—this famous market is still worth ▲, offering lots of smelly photo fun and free morsels to taste (May-Oct daily 8:00-23:00, but vendors may close earlier if they're not busy;

Nov-Dec Mon-Sat 9:00-21:00, Sun from 11:00; Jan-April Sat only 9:00-15:00).

Many stands sell premade smoked-salmon *(laks)* sandwiches, fish soup, and other snacks ideal for a light lunch (confirm prices before ordering). To try Norwegian jerky, pick up a bag of dried cod snacks *(tørrfisk)*. The red meat is minke (pronounced mink-ee) whale, caught off the coast of northern Norway. Norwegians, notorious for their whaling, defend it as a traditional livelihood for many of their people. They remind us that they only harvest the minke whale, which is not on an endangered list. In recent years, Norway has assigned itself a quota of nearly 1,000 minke whales a year, with the actual catch coming to a bit over half of that.

• *Watch your wallet: If you're going to get pickpocketed in Bergen, it'll likely be here. When done exploring, with your back to the market, hike a block to the right (note the pointy church spire in the distance and the big blocky stone monument dead ahead) into the modern part of town and a huge wide square. Pause at the intersection just before crossing into the square, about 20 yards before the blocky monument. Look left to see Mount Ulriken with its TV tower. A cable car called Ulriken643 takes you to its 2,110-foot summit. (Shuttle buses leave from this corner, at the top and bottom of the hour, to its station; for summit details, see page 388.) Now, walk up to that big square monument and meet some Vikings.*

❼ Seafarers' Monument

Nicknamed "the cube of goat cheese" for its shape, this 1950 monument celebrates Bergen's contact with the sea and remembers

those who worked on it and died in it. Study the faces: All social classes are represented. The statues relate to the scenes depicted in the reliefs above. Each side represents a century (start with the Vikings and work clockwise): 10th century—Vikings, with a totem pole in the panel above recalling the pre-Columbian Norwegian discovery of America; 18th century—equipping Europe's ships; 19th century—whaling; 20th century—shipping and war. For the 21st century, see the real people—a cross-section of today's Norway—sitting at the statue's base. Major department stores (Galleriet, Xhibition, and Telegrafen) are all nearby.

• *The monument marks the start of Bergen's main square...*

❽ Torgallmenningen

Allmenningen means "for all the people." Torg means "square."

Bryggen's History

Pretty as Bryggen is today, it has a rough-and-tumble history. A horrific plague decimated the population and economy of Norway in 1350, killing about half of its people. A decade later, German merchants arrived and established a Hanseatic trading post, bringing order to that rustic society. For the next four centuries, the port of Bergen was essentially German territory.

Bergen's old German trading center was called "the German wharf" until World War II (and is now just called "the wharf," or "Bryggen"). From 1370 to 1754, German merchants controlled Bergen's trade. In 1550, it was a Germanic city of 1,000 workaholic merchants—surrounded and supported by some 5,000 Norwegians.

The German merchants were very strict and lived in a harsh, all-male world (except for Norwegian prostitutes). This wasn't a military occupation, but a mutually beneficial economic partnership. The Norwegian cod fishermen of the far north shipped their dried cod to Bergen, where the Hanseatic merchants marketed it to Europe. Norwegian cod provided much of Europe with food (a source of easy-to-preserve protein) and cod oil (which lit the lamps until about 1850).

While the city dates from 1070, little survives from before the last big fire in 1702. In its earlier heyday, Bergen was one of the largest wooden cities in Europe. Congested wooden buildings, combined with lots of small fires (to provide heat and light in this cold and dark corner of Europe), spelled disaster for Bergen. Over the centuries, the city suffered countless fires, including 10 devastating ones. Back then, it wasn't a question of *if* there would be a fire, but *when* there would be a fire—with major blazes every 20 or so years. Each time the warehouses burned, the merchants would toss the refuse into the bay and rebuild. Gradually,

And, while this is the city's main gathering place, it was actually created as a firebreak. The residents of this wood-built city knew fires were inevitable. The street plan was designed with breaks, or open spaces like this square, to help contain the destruction. In 1916, it succeeded in stopping a fire, which is why it has a more modern feel today.

Walk the length of the square to the angled slab of blue stone (quarried in Brazil) at the far end. This is a monument to King Olav V, who died in 1991, and a popular meeting point: Locals like to say, "Meet you at the Blue Stone." It marks the center of a parklike swath known as...

the land crept out, and so did the buildings. (Looking at the Hanseatic Quarter from the harborfront, you can see how the buildings have settled. The foundations, composed of debris from the many fires, settle as they rot.)

After 1702, the city rebuilt using more stone and brick, and suffered fewer fires. But this one small wooden quarter was built after the fire, in the early 1700s. To prevent future blazes, the Germans forbade all fires and candles for light or warmth except in isolated and carefully guarded communal houses behind each tenement. It was in these communal houses that apprentices studied, people dried out their soggy clothes, hot food was cooked, and the men drank and partied. When there was a big banquet, one man always stayed sober—a kind of designated fire watchman.

Flash forward to the 20th century. One of the biggest explosions of World War II occurred in Bergen's harbor on April 20, 1944. An ammunition ship loaded with 120 tons of dynamite blew up just in front of the fortress. The blast leveled entire neighborhoods on either side of the harbor (notice the ugly 1950s construction opposite the fortress) and did serious damage to Håkon's Hall and Rosenkrantz Tower. How big was the blast? There's a hut called "the anchor cabin" a couple of miles away in the mountains. That's where the ship's anchor landed. The blast is considered to be accidental, despite the fact that April 20 happened to be Hitler's 55th birthday and the ship blew up about 100 yards away from the Nazi commander's headquarters (in the fortress).

After World War II, Bryggen was again slated for destruction. Most of the locals wanted it gone—it reminded them of the Germans who had occupied Norway for the miserable war years. Then excavators discovered rune stones indicating that the area predated the Germans. This boosted Bryggen's approval rating, and the quarter was saved. Today this picturesque and historic zone is the undisputed tourist highlight of Bergen.

BERGEN

❾ Ole Bulls Plass

This drag leads from the National Theater (above on right) to a little lake (below on left).

Detour a few steps up for a better look at the **National Theater,** built in Art Nouveau style in 1909. Founded by violinist Ole Bull in 1850, this was the first theater to host plays in the Norwegian language. After 450 years of Danish and Swedish rule, 19th-century Norway enjoyed a cultural awakening, and Bergen became an artistic power. Ole Bull collaborated with the playwright Henrik Ibsen. Ibsen commissioned Edvard Grieg to compose the music for his play *Peer Gynt*. These three lions of Norwegian culture all lived and worked right here in Bergen.

Head downhill on the square to a delightful fountain featuring a **statue of Ole Bull** in the shadow of trees. Ole Bull was an 1800s version of Elvis. A pop idol and heartthrob in his day, Ole Bull's bath water was bottled and sold by hotels, and women fainted when they heard him play violin. Living up to his name, he fathered over 40 children. Speaking of children, I love to hang out here watching families frolic in the pond, oblivious to the waterfall troll (see the statue with the harp below Ole Bull). According to legend, the troll bestows musical talent on anyone—like old Ole—who gives him a gift (he likes meat).

From here, the park spills farther downhill to a cast-iron pavilion given to the city by Germans in 1889, and on to the little man-made lake (Lille Lungegårdsvannet), which is circled by an enjoyable path. This green zone is considered a park and is cared for by the local parks department.

• *If you're up for a lakeside stroll, now's your chance. Also notice that alongside the lake (to the right as you face it from here) is a row of buildings housing the enjoyable* **KODE Art Museums.** *And to the left of the lake are some fine residential streets (including the picturesque, cobbled Marken); within a few minutes' walk is the* **Leprosy Museum** *and the* **cathedral.**

Sights in Bergen

Several museums listed here—including the Bryggens Museum, Håkon's Hall, Rosenkrantz Tower, Leprosy Museum, and Gamle Bergen—are part of the Bergen City Museum (Bymuseet) organization. If you buy a ticket to any of them, you'll pay half-price at any of the others simply by showing your ticket.

▲Bergenhus Fortress: Håkon's Hall and Rosenkrantz Tower

The tower and hall, sitting boldly out of place on the harbor just beyond Bryggen, are reminders of Bergen's importance as the first permanent capital of Norway. Both sights feel vacant and don't really speak for themselves; the guided tours, which provide a serious introduction to Bergen's history, are essential for grasping their significance.

Cost and Hours: Hall and tower-120 NOK for both (or 80 NOK each), half-price with ticket to another Bergen City Museum; hall open daily 10:00-16:00, tower from 9:00; mid-Sept-mid-

May hall open daily 12:00-15:00, tower open Sun only; tel. 55 30 80 30, free WC.

Tours: 20 NOK extra for guided tour that includes both buildings (mid-June-Aug tours leave daily at 11:00, 14:00, and 15:00 from the building to the right of Håkon's Hall.

Håkon's Hall, dating from the 13th century, was built as a banqueting hall, and that's essentially what it still is today. It was

restored in the early 20th century, but was heavily damaged in World War II when a munitions ship exploded in the harbor, leaving nothing but the walls standing. In the 1950s it was restored again, with the grand wooden ceiling and roof modeled after the medieval roof on a church in northern Norway. Beneath the hall is a whitewashed cellar that is thought to have been used mainly for storage.

Rosenkrantz Tower, the keep of a 13th-century castle, is today a stack of barren rooms connected by tight spiral staircases,

with a good history exhibit on the top two floors and a commanding view from its rooftop. In the 16th century, the ruling Danish-Norwegian king enlarged the tower and trained its cannon on the German-merchant district, Bryggen, to remind the merchants of the importance of paying their taxes.

Fortress Museum (Bergenhus Festningmuseum)

This humble museum (which functioned as a prison during the Nazi occupation), set back a couple of blocks from the fortress, will interest historians with its thoughtful exhibits about military history, especially Bergen's WWII experience (look for the Norwegian Nazi flag). You'll learn about the resistance movement in Bergen (including its underground newspapers), the role of women in the Norwegian military, and Norwegian troops who have served with UN forces in overseas conflicts.

Cost and Hours: Free, Tue-Sun 11:00-17:00, ask to borrow a translation of the descriptions, just behind Thon Hotel Orion at Koengen, tel. 55 54 63 87.

BERGEN

The Hanseatic League, Blessed by Cod

Middlemen in trade, the clever German merchants of the Hanseatic League ruled the waves of northern Europe for 500 years (c. 1250-1750). These sea-traders first banded together in a Hanse, or merchant guild, to defend themselves against pirates. As they spread out from Germany, they established trading posts in foreign lands, cut deals with local leaders for trading rights, built boats and wharves, and organized armies to protect ships and ports.

By the 15th century, these merchants had organized more than a hundred cities into the Hanseatic League, a free-trade zone that stretched from London to Russia. The League ran a profitable triangle of trade: Fish from Scandinavia was exchanged for grain from the eastern Baltic and luxury goods from England and Flanders. Everyone benefited, and the German merchants—the middlemen—reaped the profits.

At its peak in the 15th century, the Hanseatic League was the dominant force—economic, military, and political—in northern Europe. This was an age when much of Europe was fragmented into petty kingdoms and dukedoms. Revenue-hungry kings and robber-baron lords levied chaotic and extortionist tolls and duties. Pirates plagued shipments. It was the Hanseatic League, rather than national governments, that brought the stability that allowed trade to flourish.

BERGEN

▲▲Bryggens Museum

This modern museum explains the 1950s archaeological dig to uncover the earliest bits of Bergen (1050-1500). Brief English explanations are posted. From September through May, when there is no tour, consider buying the good museum guidebook (25 NOK).

Cost and Hours: 80 NOK; in summer, entry included with Bryggen Walking Tour described earlier; daily 10:00-16:00; Sept-mid-May Mon-Fri 11:00-15:00, Sat-Sun 12:00-16:00; inexpensive cafeteria; in big, modern building just beyond the end of Bryggen and the Radisson Blu Royal Hotel, tel. 55 30 80 30, www.bymuseet.no.

Visiting the Museum: The manageable, well-presented permanent exhibit occupies the ground floor. First up are the foundations from original wooden tenements dating back to the 12th century (displayed right where they were excavated) and a giant chunk of the hull of a 100-foot-long, 13th-century ship that was found here. Next, an exhibit (roughly shaped like the long, wooden

Bergen's place in this Baltic economy was all about cod—a form of protein that could be dried, preserved, and shipped anywhere. Though cursed by a lack of natural resources, the city was blessed with a good harbor conveniently located between the rich fishing spots of northern Norway and the markets of Europe. Bergen's port shipped dried cod and fish oil southward and imported grain, cloth, beer, wine, and ceramics.

Bryggen was one of four principal Hanseatic trading posts (Kontors), along with London, Bruges, and Novgorod. It was the last Kontor opened (c. 1360), the least profitable, and the final one to close. Bryggen had warehouses, offices, and living quarters. Ships docked here were unloaded by counterpoise cranes. At its peak, as many as a thousand merchants, journeymen, and apprentices lived and worked here.

Bryggen was a self-contained German enclave within the city. The merchants came from Germany, worked a few years here, and retired back in the home country. They spoke German, wore German clothes, and attended their own churches. By law, they were forbidden to intermarry or fraternize with the Bergeners, except on business.

The Hanseatic League peaked around 1500, then slowly declined. Rising nation-states were jealous of the Germans merchants' power and wealth. The Reformation tore apart old alliances. Dutch and English traders broke the Hanseatic monopoly. Cities withdrew from the League and Kontors closed. In 1754, Bergen's Kontor was taken over by the Norwegians. When it closed its doors on December 31, 1899, a sea-trading era was over, but the city of Bergen had become rich...by the grace of cod.

double-tenements outside) shows off artifacts and explains lifestyles from medieval Bryggen. Behind that is a display of items you might have bought at the medieval market. You'll finish with exhibits about the church in Bergen, the town's role as a royal capital, and its status as a cultural capital. Upstairs are two floors of temporary exhibits.

▲▲Hanseatic Museum and Schøtstuene
(Det Hanseatiske Museum og Schøtstuene)

The **Hanseatic Museum** offers the best possible look inside the wooden houses that are Bergen's trademark. Its creaky old rooms—with hundred-year-old cod hanging from the ceiling—offer a time-tunnel experience back to Bryggen's glory days. It's located in an atmospheric old merchant house furnished with dried fish, antique ropes, an old oxtail (used for wringing spilled cod-liver oil back into the bucket), sagging steps, and cupboard beds from the early 1700s—one sporting what some claim is a medieval pinup girl. You'll explore two upstairs levels, fully furnished and with funhouse floors. The place still feels eerily lived-in; neatly sorted desks with tidy ledgers seem to be waiting for the next workday to begin.

Included with your admission are visits to the **Schøtstuene** (Hanseatic Assembly Rooms) and the Norwegian Fisheries Muse-

um (described later). The Schøtstuene assembly rooms are in a building near St. Mary's Church that's accessed behind Bryggen from Øvregaten. Here, Hanseatic merchants would cook hot meals and gather to feast, hold court, conduct ceremonies, be schooled, and get warm—fires were allowed in this building only because it was separate from the other (highly flammable) Bryggen offices.

Cost: 160 NOK ticket (sold May-mid-Sept) includes all three sights and shuttle bus to Fisheries Museum, 100 NOK Oct-April; 100 NOK after 15:45 for Hanseatic Museum only. (Bryggen Walking Tour entry does not include Fisheries Museum.)

Hours: Daily 9:00-18:00, May and Sept until 17:00, Oct-April 11:00-15:00 except Schøtstuene closed Sun; Finnegården 1a, tel.55 54 46 90, www.museumvest.no.

Tours: The Hanseatic Museum has scant English explanations—it's much better if you take the good, included 30-minute guided tour (3/day in English—call to confirm, June-mid-Sept only, times displayed on a monitor). Even if you tour the museum with the Bryggen Walking Tour, you're welcome to revisit (using the same ticket) and take this tour.

Norwegian Fisheries Museum: Just up the coast (along the water just north of Bryggen) is the Norwegian Fisheries Museum, an authentic wharfside warehouse with exhibits about life along and on the sea. Catch the free shuttle bus from the Hanseatic Museum (5-minute ride) or cruise 20 minutes aboard the *Beffen* ferry to the museum (130 NOK round-trip, June-Aug hourly 11:00-17:00, departs from the Bryggen side of the Fish Market).

Theta Museum

This small museum highlights Norway's resistance movement. You'll peek into the hidden world of a 10-person cell of courageous students, whose group—called Theta—housed other fighters and communicated with London during the Nazi occupation in World

War II. It's housed in Theta's former headquarters—a small upstairs room in a wooden Bryggen building.

Cost and Hours: 50 NOK, June-Aug Tue, Sat, and Sun 14:00-16:00, closed Mon, Wed-Fri, and Sept-May, Enhjørningsgården.

▲▲Fløibanen Funicular

Bergen's popular funicular climbs 1,000 feet in seven minutes to the top of Mount Fløyen for the best view of the town, surrounding islands, and fjords all the way to the west coast. The top is a popular picnic spot, perfect for enjoying the sunset. The **$$** Fløien Folkerestaurant, the white building at the top of the funicular, offers affordable self-service food all day in season. Behind the station, you'll find a playground and a fun giant troll photo op. The top is also the starting point for many peaceful hikes.

You'll buy your funicular ticket at the base of the Fløibanen (notice the photos in the entry hall of the construction of the funicular and its 1918 grand opening).

If you'll want to hike down from the top, ask for the *Fløyen Hiking Map* when you buy your ticket; you'll save 50 percent by purchasing only a one-way ticket up.

From the top, walk behind the station and follow the signs to the city center. The top half of the 30-minute hike is a gravelly lane through a forest with fine views. The bottom is a paved lane passing charming old wooden homes. It's a steep descent. To save your knees, you could ride the lift most of the way down and get off at the Promsgate stop to wander through the delightful cobbled and shiplap lanes (note that only the :00 and :30 departures stop at Promsgate).

Cost and Hours: 90 NOK round-trip, 45 NOK one-way, lines can be long if cruise ships are in town—buy tickets online to skip the line; Mon-Fri 7:30-23:00, Sat-Sun from 8:00, departures 4/hour—on the quarter-hour most of the day, runs continuously if busy; tel. 55 33 68 00, www.floyen.no.

▲St. Mary's Church (Mariakirken)

The oldest parish church and preserved building in Bergen dates to between 1130 and 1170, and is said to be one of the best-decorated

BERGEN

medieval churches in Norway. For many years, St. Mary's Church was known as the "German Church," as it was used by the German merchants of the Hanseatic League from 1408 to 1766. The last service in German was held in 1906. The stony interior is accented with a golden altarpiece, a Baroque pulpit of Dutch origin partly made from exotic materials (such as turtle skin), and artworks from various time periods.

Cost and Hours: 50 NOK, Mon-Fri 9:00-16:00, closed mid-Sept-May; 25-minute English guided tour (75 NOK, including church entry) runs June-Aug Mon-Fri at 15:30; http://bergendomkirke.no, tel. 55 59 71 75.

Cathedral (Domkirke)

Bergen's main church, dedicated to St. Olav (the patron saint of Norway), dates from 1301. The cathedral may be closed for renovation during your visit, but if it's open, drop in to enjoy its stoic, plain interior with stuccoed stone walls and a giant wooden pulpit. Sit in a hard, straight-backed pew and just try to doze off. Like so many old Norwegian structures, its roof makes you feel like you're huddled under an overturned Viking ship. The church is oddly lopsided, with just one side aisle. Before leaving, look up to see the gorgeous wood-carved organ over the main entrance. In the entryway, you'll see portraits of each bishop dating all the way back to the Reformation.

Cost and Hours: Free; Mon-Fri 10:00-16:00, Sun 9:30-13:00, closed Sat; shorter hours mid-Aug-mid-June.

Leprosy Museum (Lepramuseet)

Leprosy is also known as "Hansen's Disease" because in the 1870s a Bergen man named Armauer Hansen did groundbreaking work

in understanding the ailment. This unique museum is in St. Jørgens Hospital, a leprosarium that dates back to about 1700. Up until the 19th century, as much as 3 percent of Norway's population had leprosy. This hospital—once called "a graveyard for the living" (its last patient died in 1946)—has a meager exhibit in a thought-provoking dorm for the dying. It's most worthwhile if you read the translation of the exhibit (borrow a copy at the entry) or take the free tour (at the top of each hour). As you leave, if you're interested, ask if you can see the medicinal herb garden out back.

Cost and Hours: 80 NOK, half-price with ticket to another Bergen City Museum, daily 11:00-15:00, closed Sept-mid-May, between train station and Bryggen at Kong Oscars Gate 59, tel. 55 30 80 30, www.bymuseet.no.

▲KODE Art Museums

If you need to get out of the rain (and you enjoyed the National Gallery in Oslo), check out this collection, filling four neighboring buildings facing the lake along Rasmus Meyers Allé. The KODE 4 building, on the far left, has an eclectic cross-section of both international and Norwegian artists. The KODE 3 branch specializes in Norwegian artists and has an especially good Munch exhibit. The KODE 2 building has installations of contemporary art and a big bookstore on the first floor, while the KODE 1 building has decorative arts and silver crafts from Bergen. Small description sheets in English are in each room.

Cost and Hours: 100 NOK, daily 11:00-17:00 except KODE 3 10:00-18:00, closed Mon mid-Sept-mid-May, Rasmus Meyers Allé 3, tel. 53 00 97 04, www.kodebergen.no.

Visiting the Museums: Many visitors focus on **KODE 4** (from outside, enter through Door 4), featuring an easily digestible collection. Here are some of its highlights: The ground floor includes an extensive display of works by Nikolai Astrup (1880-1928), who depicts Norway's fjords with bright colors and Expressionistic flair. One flight up is a great collection titled *Bergen and the World, 1400-1900,* which depicts fascinating stories from Europe

and Norway. Another section has paintings by J. C. Dahl and his students, who captured the majesty of Norway's natural wonders (look for Adelsteen Normann's impressive, photorealistic view of Romsdalsfjord). "Norwegian Art 1840-1900" includes works by Christian Krohg, as well as some portraits by Harriet Backer and realistic scenes of everyday life by Frits Thaulow.

Up on the third floor, things get modern. The Tower Hall (Tårnsalen) features Norwegian modernism and a large exhibit of Bergen's avant-garde art (1966-1985), kicked off by "Group 66." The International Modernism section has four stars: Pablo Picasso (sketches, etchings, collages, and a few Cubist paintings), Paul Klee (the Swiss childlike painter), and the dynamic Norwegian duo of Edvard Munch and Ludvig Karisten. Rounding it out are a smattering of Surrealist, Abstract Expressionist, and Op Art pieces.

KODE 3 presents one of the finest collections of work by Edvard Munch, including such masterpieces as *Jealousy, Melancholy, Woman in Three Stages,* and *Evening on Karl Johan.* Also on hand is a fine collection from Norway's Golden Age (1880-1905), including highlights from the careers of romantic landscape painters Hans Gude and J. C. Dahl. And don't miss the iconic troll and folktale drawings and watercolors by Theodor Kittelsen.

KODE 2 focuses on contemporary art from 1980 to the present. **KODE 1** hosts temporary exhibitions and a permanent exhibition showcasing the rich legacy and craftsmanship of Bergen silversmiths.

▲Aquarium (Akvariet)

Small but fun, this aquarium claims to be the second-most-visited sight in Bergen. It's wonderfully laid out and explained in English. Check out the view from inside the "shark tunnel" in the tropical shark exhibit.

Cost and Hours: 270 NOK, kids-185 NOK, daily May-Aug 9:00-18:00, shorter hours off-season, feeding times at the top of most hours in summer, cheery cafeteria with light sandwiches, Nordnesbakken 4, tel. 55 55 71 71, www.akvariet.no.

Getting There: It's at the tip of the peninsula on the south end of the harbor—about a 20-minute walk or short ride on bus #11 from the city center. Or hop on the handy little *Vågen* "Akvariet" ferry that sails from the Fish Market to near the aquarium (50 NOK one-way, 80 NOK round-trip, show ferry ticket for 20 percent off aquarium admission, 2/hour, 10-minute ride, June-Aug 10:00-17:30, off-season until 16:00).

Nearby: The lovely park behind the aquarium has views of the sea and a popular swimming beach (described later, under "Activities in Bergen"). The totem pole erected here was a gift from Bergen's sister city in the US—Seattle.

▲Gamle Bergen (Old Bergen)

This Disney-cute gathering of 50-some 18th- through 20th-century homes and shops was founded in 1934 to save old buildings from destruction as Bergen modernized. Each of the buildings was moved from elsewhere in Bergen and reconstructed here. Together, they create a virtual town that offers a cobbled look at the old life. It's free to wander through the town and park to enjoy the facades of the historic buildings, but to get into the 20 or so museum buildings, you'll have to join a tour (departing on the hour 10:00-16:00).

Cost and Hours: 100 NOK, half-price with ticket to another Bergen City Museum, daily 9:00-16:00, closed Sept-mid-May, tel. 55 39 43 04, www.bymuseet.no.

Getting There: Take any bus heading west from Bryggen (such as #4, #5, or #6, direction: Lønborglien) to Gamle Bergen (stop: Gamle Bergen). You'll get off after the tunnel at a freeway pullout and walk 200 yards, following signs to the museum. Any bus heading back into town takes you to the center (buses come by every few minutes). With the easy bus connection, there's no reason to taxi.

ACTIVITIES IN BERGEN
▲Strolling
Bergen is a great town for wandering. Enjoy a little Norwegian paseo. On a balmy Norwegian summer evening, I'd stroll from the castle, along the harborfront, up the main square to Ole Bulls Plass, and around the lake.

For a slightly more strenuous yet rewarding walk, head up the zig-zagging road behind the Fløibanen funicular station to a city viewpoint in front of a white building with a lookout tower. The building was once a fire station (which explains the tower). The lake next to it used to be a reservoir. And the white houses past the lake were built by firemen on land given to them so that they could live close to the station. After enjoying the city views, you can either return to town the way you came, or follow Øvre Blekeveien down past the lake and white houses; then take any road to the left off Blekeveien back down to the harbor.

Shopping
Most shops are open Monday through Friday 9:00-17:00, Thursday until 19:00, Saturday 9:00-15:00, and closed Sunday. Many of the tourist shops at the harborfront strip along Bryggen are open daily—even during holidays—until 20:00 or 21:00. You'll see the same products offered at different prices, so shopping around can be a good idea.

Ting (Things) offers a fun alternative to troll shopping, with contemporary housewares and quirky gift ideas (daily 9:00-22:30, at Bryggen 13, a block past the Hanseatic Museum, tel. 55 21 54 80).

Nilssen på Bryggen, next to the Hanseatic Museum, is one of the oldest shops in Bergen. You'll find Norwegian yarn for knitting and modern-style Sandnes wool sweaters, along with souvenirs and hand-embroidered Christmas items (Mon-Sat 10:00-18:00, closed Sun, Bryggen 3, tel. 55 31 67 90).

Husfliden is a shop popular for its handmade goodies and reliably Norwegian sweaters (fine variety and quality but expensive, just off Torget, the market square, at Vågsallmenninge 3, tel. 55 54 47 40).

The Galleriet Mall, a shopping center on Torgallmenningen, holds six floors of shops, cafés, and restaurants. You'll find a pharmacy, photo shops, clothing, sporting goods, bookstores, mobile-phone shops, and a basement grocery store (Mon-Fri 9:00-21:00, Sat 9:00-18:00, closed Sun).

BERGEN

Swimming

Bergen has two seaside public swimming areas: one at the aquarium and the other in Gamle Bergen. Each is a great local scene on a hot sunny day. **Nordnes Sjøbad,** near the aquarium, offers swimmers an outdoor heated pool and a protected area of the sea (80 NOK, kids-35 NOK, mid-May-Aug Mon-Fri 7:00-19:00, Sat 9:00-14:00, Sun 10:00-14:00, Sat-Sun until 19:00 in good weather, closed off-season, Nordne-sparken 30, tel. 53 03 91 90). **Sandviken Sjøbad,** at Gamle Bergen, is free and open all summer. It comes with changing rooms, a roped-off bit of the bay (no pool), a high dive, and lots of sunbathing space.

SIGHTS NEAR BERGEN
▲Ulriken643 Cable Car

It's amazingly easy and quick to zip up six minutes to the 643-meter-high (that's 2,110 feet) summit of Ulriken, the tallest mountain near Bergen. Stepping out of the cable car, you enter a different world, with views stretching to the ocean. A chart clearly shows the many well-marked and easy hikes that fan out over the vast, rocky, grassy plateau above the tree line (circular walks of various lengths, a 40-minute hike down, and a 4-hour hike to the top of the Fløibanen funicular). For less exercise, you can simply sunbathe, crack open a picnic, or enjoy the Ulriken restaurant.

Cost and Hours: 110 NOK one-way, 170 NOK round-trip, 8/hour, daily 9:00-21:00, off-season until 17:00, tel. 53 64 36 43, www.ulriken643.no.

Getting There: It's about three miles southeast of Bergen. From the Fish Market, you can take a blue double-decker shuttle bus that includes the cost of the cable-car ride (270 NOK, ticket valid 24 hours, May-Sept daily 9:00-18:00, hourly, departs from the corner of Torgallmenningen and Strandgaten, buy ticket as you board or at TI). Alternatively, public buses #2 and #3 run from Småstrandgaten in the city center and stop 200 yards from the lift station.

▲▲Edvard Grieg's Home, Troldhaugen

Norway's greatest composer spent his last 22 summers here (1885-1907), soaking up inspirational fjord beauty and composing many

of his greatest works. Grieg fused simple Norwegian folk tunes with the bombast of Europe's Romantic style. In a dreamy Victorian setting, Grieg's "Hill of the Trolls" is pleasant for anyone and essential for diehard fans. You can visit his house on your own, but it's more enjoyable if you take the included 20-minute tour. The house and adjacent museum are full of memories and artifacts, including the composer's Steinway. The walls are festooned with photos of the musical and literary superstars of his generation. When the hugely popular Grieg died in 1907, 40,000 mourners attended his funeral. His little studio hut near the water makes you want to sit down and modulate.

Cost and Hours: 100 NOK, includes guided tour in English, daily 9:00-18:00, Oct-April 10:00-16:00, café, tel. 55 92 29 92, www.griegmuseum.no.

Grieg Lunch Concert: Troldhaugen offers a great guided tour/concert package that includes a shuttle bus from the Bergen TI to the doorstep of Grieg's home on the fjord (departs 11:00), an hour-long tour of the home, a half-hour concert (Grieg's greatest piano hits, at 13:00), and the ride back into town (you're back in the center by 14:25). Your guide will narrate the ride out of town as well as take you around Grieg's house (250 NOK, daily May-Sept). Lunch isn't included, but there is a café on site, or you could bring a sandwich along. You can skip the return bus ride and spend more time in Troldhaugen. While the tour rarely sells out, it's wise to drop by the TI earlier that day to reserve your spot.

Evening Concerts: Ask at the TI about piano performances in the concert hall at Grieg's home—a gorgeous venue with the fjord stretching out behind the big black grand piano (350 NOK, 300 NOK with Bergen Card, concerts roughly mid-June-Sept Sun at 18:00, free round-trip shuttle bus leaves TI at 16:30, show your concert ticket).

Getting to Troldhaugen: It's six miles south of Bergen. The Bybanen tram drops you a long 20-minute walk away from Troldhaugen. Catch the tram in the city center at its terminus near Byparken (between the lake and Ole Bulls Plass), ride it for about 25 minutes, and get off at the stop called Hop. Walk in the direction of Bergen (about 25 yards), cross at the crosswalk, and follow signs to Troldhaugen. Part of the way is on a pedestrian/bike path; you're halfway there when the path crosses over a busy highway. If you want to make the 13:00 lunchtime concert, leave Bergen at 12:00.

To avoid the long walk from the tram stop, consider the Grieg Lunch Concert package (described earlier). If you're driving into Bergen from the east (such as from the Sognefjord), you'll drive right by Troldhaugen on your way into town.

Fantoft Stave Church

This huge, preserved-in-tar stave church burned down in 1992. It was rebuilt and reopened in 1997, but it will never be the same (for more on stave churches, see page 201). Situated in a quiet forest next to a mysterious stone cross, this replica of a 12th-century wooden church is bigger, though no better, than others covered in this book. But it's worth a look if you're in the neighborhood, even after-hours, for its atmospheric setting.

Cost and Hours: 60 NOK, mid-May-mid-Sept daily 10:30-18:00, interior closed off-season, no English information, tel. 55 28 07 10, www.fantoftstavkirke.com.

Getting There: It's three miles south of Bergen on E-39 in Paradis. Take the Bybanen tram (from Byparken, between the lake and Ole Bulls Plass) or bus #83 (from Torget, by the Fish Market) to the Paradis stop (not the "Fantoft" stop). From Paradis, walk uphill to the parking lot on the left, and find the steep foot-path to the church.

BERGEN NIGHTSPOTS

With the high latitude, Bergen stays light until 23:00 in the summer. On warm evenings, people are out enjoying the soft light and the mellow scene.

For a selection of cool nightspots, visit the **Pingvinen** and **Café Opera** (both described in "Eating in Bergen," later) and explore the neighboring streets.

For something a little funkier, **Skostredet** ("Shoe Street," recalling the days when cobblers set up shop here) is emerging as the hip, bohemian-chic area. You'll sort through cafés, pubs, and retro shops. There's an American-style Rock and Roll '59er Diner. And

Folk og Røvere ("People and Robbers") is an unpretentious bar with cheap beer (nightly until late, Skostredet 12).

For candlelit elegance, enjoy a drink at the historic **Dyvekes Wine Cellar.** Named for the mistress of King Christian II of Denmark (her portrait is on the signboard hanging above the door), the atmosphere of the ground-floor bar and the cellar downstairs is hard to beat (daily from 15:00, 80-90 NOK for wine by glass, beer on tap, Hollendergaten 7).

For live music, try **Madam Felle Nightclub** (on the Bryggen strip), which usually has musicians on the weekends (sometimes without a cover). And if you're really drunk at 3:00 in the morning and need a spicy hotdog, the **3-Kroneren** *pølse* stand is open.

Sleeping in Bergen

Busy with business travelers and popular with tourists, Bergen can be jammed any time of year. Even with this crush, proud and pricey hotels may be willing to make deals. You might save a bundle by checking the websites of the bigger hotels for their best prices. Otherwise, Bergen has some fine budget alternatives to normal hotels that can save you money.

HOTELS

$$$$ Hotel Havnekontoret, with 116 rooms and the best location in town, fills a grand old shipping headquarters dating from the 1920s. It's an especially fine value on weekends and in the summer, for those who eat the included dinner. While part of a chain, it has a friendly spirit. Guests are welcome to climb its historic tower (with a magnificent view) or enjoy its free sauna and exercise room downstairs. If you aren't interested in fancy dining, the room price includes virtually all your food—a fine breakfast, self-service waffles in the afternoon, fruit and coffee all day, and a light dinner buffet each evening. If you take advantage of them, these edible extras are easily worth 600 NOK per day per couple, making the cost of this fancy hotel little more than a hostel (facing the harbor across the street from the Radisson Blu Royal Hotel at Slottsgaten 1, tel. 55 60 11 00, www.choicehotels.no, cc.havnekontoret@choice.no).

$$$$ Hotel Park Bergen is classy, comfortable, and in a fine residential neighborhood a 15-minute uphill walk from the town center (10 minutes from the train station). It's tinseled in Old World, lived-in charm, yet comes with all of today's amenities. The 35 rooms are split between two buildings, with 22 in the classy old-fashioned hotel and 13 in the modern annex across the street. They also offer eight fully furnished apartments (Harald Hårfagres Gate 35, tel. 55 54 44 00, www.hotelpark.no, booking@hotelpark.no).

$$$$ Thon Hotel Rosenkrantz, with 129 rooms and an

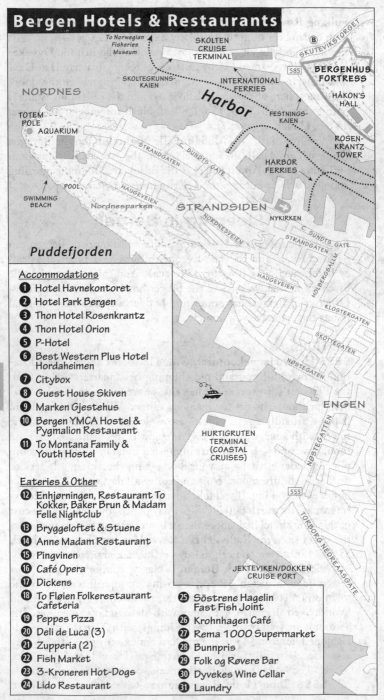

Bergen Hotels & Restaurants

To Norwegian Fisheries Museum

SKOLTEN CRUISE TERMINAL

SKUTEVIKSTORGET

B

SKOLTEGRUNNS-KAIEN

INTERNATIONAL FERRIES

585

BERGENHUS FORTRESS

NORDNES

Harbor

HÅKON'S HALL

TOTEM POLE

AQUARIUM

FESTNINGS-KAIEN

ROSEN-KRANTZ TOWER

STRANDGATEN

C. SUNDTS GATE

HARBOR FERRIES

POOL

HAUGEVEIEN

SWIMMING BEACH

Nordnesparken

STRANDSIDEN

NYKIRKEN

C. SUNDTS GATE

NORDNESVEIEN

STRANDGATEN

Puddefjorden

HAUGEVEIEN

HOLBERGSALLM.

KLOSTERGATEN

SKOTTEGATEN

NØSTEGATEN

ENGEN

HURTIGRUTEN TERMINAL (COASTAL CRUISES)

NØSTEGATEN

555

TORBORG NEDREAASGATE

JEKTEVIKEN/DOKKEN CRUISE PORT

Accommodations

1. Hotel Havnekontoret
2. Hotel Park Bergen
3. Thon Hotel Rosenkrantz
4. Thon Hotel Orion
5. P-Hotel
6. Best Western Plus Hotel Hordaheimen
7. Citybox
8. Guest House Skiven
9. Marken Gjestehus
10. Bergen YMCA Hostel & Pygmalion Restaurant
11. To Montana Family & Youth Hostel

Eateries & Other

12. Enhjørningen, Restaurant To Kokker, Baker Brun & Madam Felle Nightclub
13. Bryggeloftet & Stuene
14. Anne Madam Restaurant
15. Pingvinen
16. Café Opera
17. Dickens
18. To Fløien Folkerestaurant Cafeteria
19. Peppes Pizza
20. Deli de Luca (3)
21. Zupperia (2)
22. Fish Market
23. 3-Kroneren Hot-Dogs
24. Lido Restaurant
25. Söstrene Hagelin Fast Fish Joint
26. Krohnhagen Café
27. Rema 1000 Supermarket
28. Bunnpris
29. Folk og Røvere Bar
30. Dyvekes Wine Cellar
31. Laundry

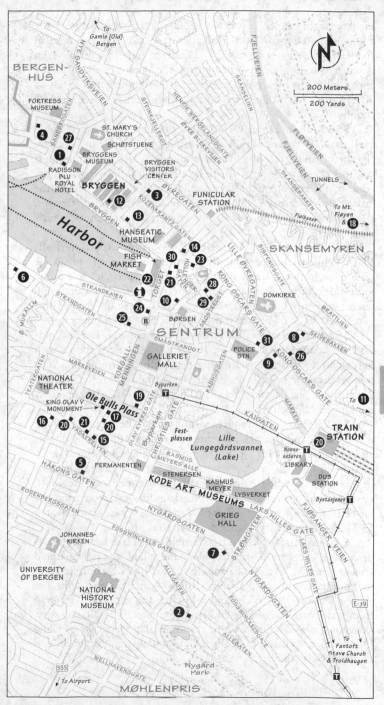

included light dinner, is one block behind Bryggen, between the Bryggens Museum and the Fløibanen funicular station—right in the heart of Bergen's appealing old quarter. Ask for a double even if you're traveling alone—they go for the same price as a single, and you'll get a bigger bed (elevator, Rosenkrantzgaten 7, tel. 55 30 14 00, www.thonhotels.comno/rosenkrantz, rosenkrantz@ thonhotels.no).

$$$$ Thon Hotel Orion, beyond Bryggen near Håkon's Hall, has 219 rooms with a light dinner included. But be aware that many rooms face the fortress grounds, which sometimes host summer evening concerts. If you love music ask for a room on the concert side and enjoy the show; otherwise ask for a room on the quiet side and bring earplugs—or stay somewhere else (elevator, Bradbenken 3, tel. 55 30 87 00, www.thonhotels.com, orion@ olafthon.no).

$$$ P-Hotel has 114 basic rooms just up from Ole Bulls Plass. While it's not particularly charming and some rooms come with noise from the street and a ground-floor disco, it's in a prime location. Ask for a room facing the courtyard in the renovated wing (credit card only, box breakfast in your room, elevator, Vestre Torggate 9, tel. 80 04 68 35, www.p-hotels.no, bergen@p-hotels.no).

$$$ Best Western Plus Hotel Hordaheimen is Bergen's oldest hotel, dating back to 1918. It has 88 well-priced rooms with hardwood floors and a welcoming decor. The charming breakfast room is decorated with vintage Kinsarvik wood furniture, giving it a traditional feel (elevator, tel. 55 33 50 00, www.hordaheimen.no, booking@hordaheimen.no).

$$ Citybox is a unique, no-nonsense hotel concept: plain, white, clean, and practical. It rents 122 rooms online or by phone, and provides you with a confirmation number. Check-in is automated—just punch in your number and get your ticket. The call-in reception is staffed 24 hours daily (family room, no breakfast, elevator, rooftop terrace, self-service laundry, just away from the bustle in a mostly residential part of town at Nygårdsgaten 31, tel. 55 31 25 00, www.citybox.no, post@citybox.no).

$ Guest House Skiven is a humble little place beautifully situated on a steep, traffic-free cobbled lane called "the most painted street in Bergen." Alf and Elizabeth Heskja (who live upstairs) rent four bright, nonsmoking doubles. Rooms have their own sinks, but share a shower, two WCs, and a kitchen (no breakfast, 4 blocks from train station, at Skivebakken 17, mobile 90 05 30 30, www. skiven.no, rs@skiven.no). From the train station, go down Kong Oscars Gate, uphill on D. Krohns Gate, and up the stairs at the end of the block on the left.

DORMS AND HOSTELS

¢-$$ **Marken Gjestehus** is a quiet, tidy, and conveniently posi-
tioned 100-bed place between the station and the harborfront. Its
rooms, while spartan, are modern and cheery. Prices can rise with
demand, especially in summer (private rooms available, breakfast
extra, elevator, open all year but with limited reception hours,
fourth floor at Kong Oscars Gate 45, tel. 55 31 44 04, http://
marken.publish.visbook.com, post@marken-gjestehus.com).

¢-$$ **Bergen YMCA Hostel,** located two blocks from the
Fish Market, is the best location for the price, and its rooms are
nicely maintained (private rooms available, family room with private bathroom and kitchen, breakfast extra, roof terrace, fully open
June-Aug, Nedre Korskirkeallmenningen 4, tel. 55 60 60 55, www.
bergenhostel.com, booking@bergenhostel.com).

**Away from the Center: ¢-$ Montana Family & Youth Hos-
tel (IYHF),** while one of Europe's best, is high-priced for a hostel
and way out of town. Still, the bus connections (#12, 20 minutes
from the center) and the facilities—modern rooms, classy living
room, no curfew, huge free parking lot, and members' kitchen—are
excellent (private rooms available, 30 Johan Blytts Vei, tel. 55 20 80
70, www.montana.no, bergen.montana@hihostels.no).

Eating in Bergen

Bergen has numerous choices: restaurants with rustic, woody atmosphere, candlelight, and steep prices; trendy pubs and cafés that
offer good-value meals; cafeterias, chain restaurants, and ethnic
eateries with less ambience where you can get quality food at lower
prices; and takeaway sandwich shops, bakeries, and cafés for a light
bite.

You can always get a glass or pitcher of water at no charge, and
fancy places give you free seconds on potatoes—just ask. Remember, if you get your food to go, it's
taxed at a lower rate and you'll save
12 percent.

SPLURGES AT BRYGGEN

You'll pay a premium to eat at these
restaurants, but you'll have a memorable meal in a pleasant setting. If
they appear to be beyond your budget, remember that you can fill up
on potatoes and drink tap water
to dine for exactly the price of the
dinner plate.

$$$$ Enhjørningen Restaurant ("The Unicorn") is *the* place in Bergen for fish. With thickly painted walls and no right angles, this dressy-yet-old-time wooden interior wins my "Bryggen Atmosphere" award. The dishes, while not hearty, are close to gourmet and beautifully presented (main dishes, multicourse meals, nightly 16:00-23:00, reservations smart, #29 on Bryggen harborfront—look for anatomically correct unicorn on the old wharf facade and dip into the alley and up the stairs, tel. 55 30 69 50, www.enhjorningen.no).

$$$$ Restaurant To Kokker, down the alley from Enhjørningen (and with the same owners), serves more meat and game. The prices and quality are equivalent, but even though it's also in an elegant old wooden building, I like The Unicorn's atmosphere much better (main dishes, multicourse meals, Mon-Sat 18:00-23:00, closed Sun, tel. 55 30 69 55).

$$$ Bryggeloftet & Stuene Restaurant, in a brick building just before the wooden stretch of Bryggen, is a vast eatery serving seafood, vegetarian, and traditional meals. To dine memorably yet affordably, this is your best Bryggen bet. Upstairs feels more elegant and less touristy than the main floor—if there's a line downstairs, just head on up (lunches, dinners, Mon-Sat 11:00-23:30, Sun from 13:00, try reserving a view window upstairs—no reservations for outside seating, #11 on Bryggen harborfront, tel. 55 30 20 70).

NEAR THE FISH MARKET

$$ Pygmalion Restaurant has a happy salsa vibe, with local art on the walls and a fun, healthy international menu. It's run with creativity and passion by Sissel. Her burgers are a hit, and there are always good vegetarian options, hearty salads, and pancakes (wraps, burgers, main plates, Mon-Sat 11:00-22:00, Sun 12:00-23:00, two blocks inland from the Fish Market at Nedre Korskirkealmenning 4, tel. 55 31 32 60).

$$ Anne Madam Restaurant serves up well-priced Norwegian-inspired dishes in a laid-back atmosphere. It's close to the Fish Market and a good choice if you are up for some seafood, though they also serve traditional Norwegian meat dishes (sandwiches, burgers, main dishes, Sun-Thu 11:00-23:00, Fri-Sat until late, Kong Oscars Gate 2a, tel. 46 52 06 62).

CHARACTERISTIC PLACES NEAR OLE BULLS PLASS

Bergen's "in" cafés are stylish, cozy, small, and open very late. Around the cinema on Neumannsgate, there are numerous ethnic restaurants, including Italian, Middle Eastern, and Chinese.

$$$ Pingvinen ("The Penguin") is a homey place in a charming neighborhood, serving traditional Norwegian home cooking to an enthusiastic local clientele. The pub has only indoor seating, with a long row of stools at the bar and five charming, living-room-cozy tables—a great setup for solo diners. After the kitchen closes, the place stays open very late as a pub. For Norwegian fare in an untouristy atmosphere, this is a good, affordable option. Their seasonal menu (reindeer in the fall, whale in the spring) is listed on the board (nightly until 22:00, Vaskerelven 14 near the National Theater, tel. 55 60 46 46).

$$$ Café Opera, with a playful-slacker vibe and chessboards for the regulars, is the hip budget choice for its loyal, youthful following. With two floors of seating and tables out front across from the theater, it's a winner (light sandwiches until 16:00, daily 10:00-23:30, Engen 18, tel. 55 23 03 15).

$$$ Dickens is a lively, checkerboard-tiled, turn-of-the-century-feeling place. The window tables in the atrium are great for people-watching, as is the fine outdoor terrace, but you'll pay higher prices for the view (lunch and dinner, daily 11:00-23:00, Kong Olav V's Plass 4, tel. 55 36 31 30).

ATOP MOUNT FLØYEN, AT THE TOP OF THE FUNICULAR

$$ Fløien Folkerestaurant Cafeteria offers meals indoors and out with a panoramic view. It's self-service, with 60-NOK sandwiches and a 139-NOK soup buffet (daily 10:00-22:00, Sept-April Sat-Sun only 12:00-17:00, tel. 55 33 69 99).

GOOD CHAIN RESTAURANTS

You'll find these chain restaurant in Bergen and throughout Norway. All are open long hours daily. In good weather, enjoy a takeout meal with sun-worshipping locals in Bergen's parks.

$$$ Peppes Pizza on Ole Bulls Plass has cold beer and good pizzas—consider the Thai Chicken, with satay-marinated chicken, pineapple, peanuts, and coriander (Mon-Wed 11:00-23:00, Thu-Sat until 24:00, Sun 12:00-23:00, seating inside or takeaway, Olav Kyrres Gate 11, tel. 22 22 55 55).

$ Baker Brun makes 75-100-NOK sandwiches, including wonderful shrimp baguettes, and pastries such as *skillingsboller*—cinnamon rolls—warm out of the oven for 29 NOK. Their shop at Bryggen is a prime spot for a simple, inexpensive bite (open from 7:00, a little later Sat-Sun, seating inside or takeaway).

$ Deli de Luca is a cut above other takeaway joints, adding sushi, noodle dishes, and calzones to the normal lineup of sandwiches. While a bit more expensive than the others, the variety and quality are appealing (open daily 24 hours, branches in train station and near Ole Bulls Plass at Torggaten 5, branch with indoor seating on corner of Engen and Vaskerelven, tel. 55 23 11 47).

$$$ Zupperia is a lively, popular chain that offers burgers, salads, Norwegian fare, and Asian dishes; their Thai soup is a local favorite. For a lighter (and cheaper) meal, order off the lunch menu any time of day (Sun-Wed 12:00-22:00, Thu-Sat until 23:30). Branches are across from the Fish Market at Torget 13 and near the National Theater at Vaskerelven 12).

BUDGET BETS NEAR THE FISH MARKET

The Fish Market has lots of stalls bursting with salmon sandwiches, fresh shrimp, fish-and-chips, and fish cakes. For a tasty, memorable, and inexpensive Bergen meal, assemble a seafood picnic here (ask for prices first; May-Oct daily 8:00-23:00, vendors may close early if they're not busy; Nov-Dec Mon-Sat 9:00-21:00, Sun from 11:00; Jan-April Sat only 9:00-15:00). Also be sure to peruse the places next door on the ground floor of the TI building, Torghallen.

$ 3-Kroneren, your classic hot-dog stand, sells a wide variety of sausages (including reindeer). The well-described English menu makes it easy to order your choice of artery-clogging guilty pleasures (tiny, medium, and jumbo weenies; open daily from 11:00 until 5:00 in the morning—you'll see the little hot-dog shack a block up Kong Oscars Gate from the harbor, Kenneth is the boss). Each dog comes with a free little glass of fruit punch.

$$$ Lido Restaurant offers a varied menu with great harbor and market views and a museum's worth of old-town photos on the walls. Lunch, served until 17:00, includes open-face sandwiches and small plates (Mon-Sat 11:00-22:00, Sun until 23:00; second floor at Torgallmenningen 1a, tel. 55 32 59 12).

$ Söstrene Hagelin Fast Fish Joint is an easygoing eatery that's cheerier than its offerings—a pale extravaganza of Norway's white cuisine. It's all fish here: fish soup, fish burgers, fish balls, fish cakes, fish wraps, and even fish pudding (Mon-Fri 9:00-19:00, Sat 10:00-17:00, closed Sun, Strandgaten 3, tel. 55 90 20 13).

$ Krohnhagen Café, a humble community center next to a retirement home, is run by the church and partly staffed by volunteers. While it's designed to give Bergen's poor (and the retired) an inviting place to enjoy, everyone's welcome (it's a favorite of local guides). The dining area is bright and spacious, the staff friendly, and the menu is simple yet tasty (salad and dinner buffets, soup, waffles, cheap sandwiches, Mon-Fri 11:00-16:00, closed Sat-Sun, Wi-Fi, Kong Oscars Gate 54, tel. 45 22 07 95).

PICNICS AND GROCERIES

While you'll be tempted to drop into 7-Eleven-type stores, you'll pay for the convenience. Pick up your groceries for half the price at a real supermarket. The **Rema 1000 supermarket,** just across from the Bryggens Museum and St. Mary's Church, is particularly handy (Mon-Fri 7:00-23:00, Sat 8:00-21:00, closed Sun). For groceries on a Sunday, check out **Bunnpris**—just a short walk inland from the Fish Market, across the street from Korskirken church (Mon-Fri 8:00-22:00, Sat from 9:00, Sun from 10:00, Nedre Korskirkeallmenningen 3a).

Bergen Connections

Bergen is conveniently connected to **Oslo** by plane and train (trains depart Bergen daily at 7:57, 11:59, 15:50, and 22:59—but no night train on Sat, arrive at Oslo seven scenic hours later, additional departures in summer and fall, confirm times at station, 50-NOK seat reservation with second-class rail pass required—but free with first-class rail pass, book well in advance if traveling mid-July-Aug and look for cheaper "minipris" tickets at www.nsb.no). From Bergen, you can take the Norway in a Nutshell train/bus/ferry route; for information, see the Norway in a Nutshell chapter. Train info: Tel. 61 05 19 10, and then 9 for English.

To get to **Stockholm** or **Copenhagen,** you'll go via Oslo (see "Oslo Connections" on page 288). Before buying a ticket for a long train trip from Bergen, look into cheap flights.

By Express Boat to Balestrand and Flåm (on Sognefjord): A handy express boat links Bergen with Balestrand (4 hours) and Flåm (5.5 hours). For details, see page 332.

By Bus to Kristiansand: If you're heading to Denmark on the ferry from Kristiansand, catch the Nor-Way express bus (departing Bergen daily at 9:00, www.nor-way.no). After a one-hour layover in Stavanger, take the bus at 14:45, arriving at 18:35 in Kristiansand in time for the evening ferry to Denmark (for boat details, see page 415).

By Boat to Denmark: Fjordline runs a boat from Bergen to Hirtshals, Denmark (18 hours; departs daily at 13:30; boat from Hirtshals departs daily at 20:00; seat in reclining chair around 1,750 NOK, tel. 81 53 35 00, www.fjordline.com).

By Boat to the Arctic: Hurtigruten coastal cruises depart nearly daily (June-Oct at 20:00, Nov-May at 22:30) for the seven-day trip north up the scenic west coast to Kirkenes on the Russian border.

This route was started in 1893 as a postal and cargo delivery service along the west coast of Norway. Although no longer delivering mail, their ships still fly the Norwegian postal flag by special permission and deliver people, cars, and cargo from Bergen to Kirkenes. A lifeline for remote areas, the ships call at 34 fishing villages and cities.

For the seven-day trip to Kirkenes, allow from $1,600 and up per person based on double occupancy (includes three meals per day, taxes, and port charges). Prices vary greatly depending on the season (highest June-July), cabin, and type of ship. Their fleet includes those with a bit of brass built in the 1960s, but most of the ships in service were built in the mid-1990s and later. Shorter voyages are possible (including even just a day trip to one of the villages along the route). Cabins should be booked well in advance. Ship services include a 24-hour cafeteria, a launderette on newer boats, and optional port excursions. Check online for senior and off-season (Oct-March) specials at www.hurtigruten.us.

Call Hurtigruten in New York (US tel. 866-552-0371) or in Norway (tel. 81 00 30 30). For most travelers, the ride makes a great one-way trip, but a flight back south is a logical last leg (rather than returning to Bergen by boat—a 12-day round-trip).

Route Tips for Drivers: For tips on connecting Bergen to Denmark via the Setesdal Valley and the Kristiansand ferry, see the South Norway chapter.

SOUTH NORWAY

Stavanger • Setesdal Valley • Kristiansand

South Norway is not about must-see sights or jaw-dropping scenery—it's simply pleasant and pretty. Spend a day in the harborside town of Stavanger. Delve into the oil industry at the surprisingly interesting Norwegian Petroleum Museum. Peruse the Stavanger Cathedral, window-shop in the old town, cruise the harbor, or hoof it up Pulpit Rock for a fine view. A series of time-forgotten towns stretch across the Setesdal Valley, with sod-roofed cottages and locals who practice fiddles and harmonicas, rose painting, whittling, and gold- and silver-work.

PLANNING YOUR TIME

The main draw in this part of Norway is the famous Pulpit Rock hike; poking around Stavanger, a pleasant port city and the springboard for reaching Pulpit Rock, helps round out your time here. The hike takes the better part of a day, requiring at least one overnight. Several cruises also call at Stavanger.

The Setesdal Valley—covered at the end of this chapter—is for people with ample time, a car, and a desire to explore a scenic corner of Norway. Since it's not "on the way" to much of anything (except dreary Kristiansand and the ferry to Denmark), it only makes the cut for Norway completists.

Stavanger

This burg of about 125,000 is a mildly charming (if unspectacular) waterfront city with streets that are lined with unpretentious shiplap cottages that echo its perennial ties to the sea. Stavanger feels more cosmopolitan than most small Norwegian cities, thanks in part to its oil industry—which brings multinational workers (and their money) into the city. Known as Norway's festival city, Stavanger hosts several lively events, including jazz in May (www.maijazz. no), Scandinavia's biggest food festival in July (www.gladmat.no), and chamber music in August (www.icmf.no).

From a sightseeing perspective, Stavanger barely has enough to fill a day: The Norwegian Petroleum Museum is the only big-time sight in town, Gamle Stavanger (the "old town") offers pleasant wandering on cobbled lanes, and the city's fine cathedral is worth a peek. For most visitors, the main reason to come to Stavanger is to use it as a launch pad for side-tripping to the famous, iconic Pulpit Rock: an eerily flat-topped rock thrusting 2,000 feet above the fjord, offering an eagle's-eye view deep into the Lysefjord.

Orientation to Stavanger

Stavanger is most interesting around its harbor, where you'll find the Maritime Museum, lots of shops and restaurants (particularly around the market plaza and along Kirkegata, which connects the cathedral to the Petroleum Museum), the indoor fish market, and a produce market (closed Sun). The artificial Lake Breiavatnet—bordered by Kongsgaten on the east and Olav V's Gate on the west—separates the train and bus stations from the harbor.

TOURIST INFORMATION

The centrally located TI can help with day trips, including logistics for reaching Pulpit Rock and other scenic hikes (June-Aug daily 8:00-18:00; Sept-May Mon-Fri 9:00-16:00, Sat until 14:00, closed Sun; free Wi-Fi, Strandkaien 61, tel. 51 85 92 00, www. regionstavanger.com).

SOUTH NORWAY

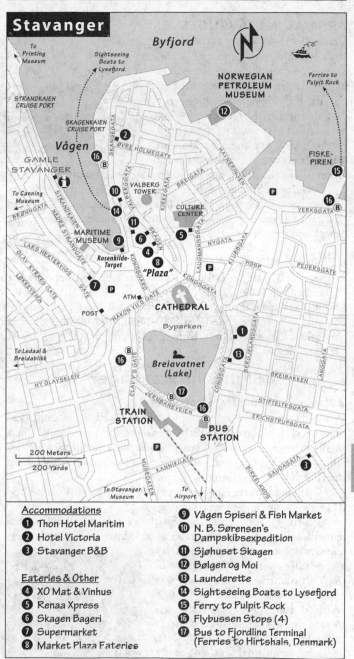

Accommodations
1 Thon Hotel Maritim
2 Hotel Victoria
3 Stavanger B&B

Eateries & Other
4 XO Mat & Vinhus
5 Renaa Xpress
6 Skagen Bageri
7 Supermarket
8 Market Plaza Eateries
9 Vågen Spiseri & Fish Market
10 N. B. Sørensen's Dampskibsexpedition
11 Sjøhuset Skagen
12 Bølgen og Moi
13 Launderette
14 Sightseeing Boats to Lysefjord
15 Ferry to Pulpit Rock
16 Flybussen Stops (4)
17 Bus to Fjordline Terminal (Ferries to Hirtshals, Denmark)

ARRIVAL IN STAVANGER

Cruise liners dock right at the Vågen harbor in the very center of town. Some tie up on the west side of the harbor (called Strandkaien) next to the TI, and others put in along the east side (called Skagenkaien)—but both are an easy walk to the central market plaza. Stavanger's **train and bus stations** are a five-minute walk around Lake Breiavatnet to the inner harbor and cathedral.

Stavanger's **Sola Airport** is about nine miles outside the city (airport code: SVG, tel. 67 03 10 00, www.avinor.no). The airport bus, called Flybussen, connects to the train and bus stations, city center, and ferry terminal (see www.flybussen.no).

HELPFUL HINTS

Money: ATMs are on buildings facing the harbor, opposite the cathedral.

Laundry: Renseriet offers expensive drop-off service and affordable self-service (Mon-Fri 8:30-16:30, Thu until 19:00, Sat 9:00-15:00, closed Sun, Kongsgata 40, tel. 51 89 56 53, www.renseriet.as).

Sights in Stavanger

▲Stavanger Cathedral (Domkirke)

While it's hardly the most impressive cathedral in Scandinavia, Stavanger's top church—which overlooks the town center on a small ridge—has a harmonious interior and a few intriguing details worth lingering over. Good English information throughout the church brings meaning to the place.

Cost and Hours: 30 NOK, open daily 11:00-16:00, tel. 51 84 04 00, www.stavangerdomkirke.no.

Visiting the Church: St. Swithun's Cathedral (its official name) was originally built in 1125 in a Norman style, with basket-handle Romanesque arches. After a fire badly damaged the church in the 13th century, a new chancel was added in the pointy-arched Gothic style. You can't miss where the architecture changes about three-quarters of the way up the aisle. On the left, behind the baptismal font, notice the ivy-lined railing on the stone staircase; this pattern is part of the city's coat of arms. And nearby, ap-

preciate the colorful, richly detailed "gristle Baroque"-style pulpit (from 1658). Notice that the whole thing is resting on Samson's stoic shoulders—even as he faces down a lion.

Stroll the church, perusing its several fine "epitaphs" (tomb markers), which are paintings in ornately decorated frames. Go on a scavenger hunt for two unique features; both are on the second columns from the back of the church. On the right, at the top facing away from the nave, notice the stone carvings of Norse mythological figures: Odin on the left, and a wolf-like beast on the right. Although the medieval Norwegians were Christians, they weren't ready to entirely abandon all of their pagan traditions. On the opposite column, circle around the base and look at ankle level, facing away from the altar. Here you see a grotesque sculpture that looks like a fish head with human hands. Notice that its head has been worn down. One interpretation is that early worshippers would ritualistically put their foot on top of it, as if to push the evil back to the underworld. Mysteriously, both of these features are one-offs—you won't find anything like them on any other column in the church.

▲▲Norwegian Petroleum Museum (Norsk Oljemuseum)

This entertaining, informative museum—dedicated to the discovery of oil in Norway's North Sea in 1969 and the industry built up around it—offers an unapologetic look at the country's biggest moneymaker. With half of Western Europe's oil reserves, the formerly poor agricultural nation of Norway is the Arabia of the North, and a world-class player. It's ranked third among the world's top oil exporters, producing 1.6 million barrels a day.

SOUTH NORWAY

Cost and Hours: 120 NOK; daily 10:00-19:00; Sept-May Mon-Sat 10:00- 16:00, Sun until 18:00; tel. 51 93 93 00, www. norskolje.museum.no. The small museum shop sells various petroleum-based products. The museum's Bølgen og Moi restaurant, which has an inviting terrace over the water, serves lunch and dinner; see "Eating in Stavanger," later.

Visiting the Museum: The exhibit describes how oil was formed, how it's found and produced, and what it's used for. You'll see models of oil rigs, actual drill bits, see-through cylinders that you can rotate to investigate different types of crude, and lots of explanations (in English) about various aspects of oil. Interactive exhibits cover everything from the "History of the Earth" (4.5 billion years displayed on a large overhead globe, showing how our planet has changed—stay for the blast that killed the dinosaurs), to day-to-day life on an offshore platform, to petroleum products in our lives (though the peanut-butter-and-petroleum-jelly sandwich is a bit much). Kids enjoy climbing on the model drilling platform, trying out the emergency escape chute at the platform outside, and playing with many other hands-on exhibits.

Several included movies delve into specific aspects of oil: The main movie, *Oljeunge (Oil Kid),* stars a fictional character who was born in 1969—the year Norway discovered oil—and shows how that discovery changed Norwegian society over the last 50 years. Other movies (in the cylindrical structures outside) highlight intrepid North Sea divers and the construction of an oil platform. Each film runs in English at least twice hourly.

Even the museum's architecture was designed to echo the foundations of the oil industry—bedrock (the stone building), slate and chalk deposits in the sea (slate floor of the main hall), and the rigs (cylindrical platforms). While the museum has its fair share of propaganda, it also has several good exhibits on the environmental toll of drilling and consuming oil.

Gamle Stavanger

Stavanger's "old town" centers on Øvre Strandgate, on the west side of the harbor. Wander the narrow, winding, cobbled back lanes, with tidy wooden houses, oasis gardens, and flower-bedecked entranceways. Peek into a workshop or gallery to find ceramics, glass, jewelry, and more. Many shops are open roughly daily 10:00-17:00, coinciding with the arrival of cruise ships (which loom ominously right next to this otherwise tranquil zone).

Museum Stavanger (M.U.S.T.)

This "museum" is actually 10 different museums scattered around town (covered by individual tickets or a single combo-ticket, most closed Mon off-season, for details see www.museumstavanger.no). The various branches include the **Stavanger Museum,** featuring the history of the city and a zoological exhibit (Muségate 16); the **Maritime Museum** (Sjøfartsmuseum), near the bottom end of Vågen harbor (Nedre Strandgate 17-19); the **Norwegian Canning Museum** (Norsk Hermetikkmuseum—the *brisling,* or herring, is smoked the first Sunday of every month—Øvre Strandgate 88A); **Ledaal,** a royal residence and manor house (Eiganesveien 45); and **Breidablikk,** a wooden villa from the late 1800s (Eiganesveien 40A).

DAY TRIPS TO LYSEFJORD AND PULPIT ROCK

The nearby Lysefjord is an easy day trip. Those with more time (and strong legs) can hike to the top of 2,000-foot-high Pulpit Rock (Preikestolen). Its dramatic 270-square-foot natural platform gives you a fantastic view of the fjord and surrounding mountains. The TI has brochures for several boat tour companies and sells tickets.

Boat Tour of Lysefjord

Rødne Clipper Fjord Sightseeing offers three-hour round-trip excursions from Stavanger to Lysefjord (including a view of Pulpit Rock—but no stops). Conveniently, their boats depart from the main Vågen harbor in the heart of town (east side of the harbor, in front of Skansegata, along Skagenkaien; 490 NOK; May-Sept daily at 10:00 and 14:00, also at 12:00 July-Aug; April and Oct daily at 11:00; Jan-Feb and Nov-Dec Wed-Sun at 11:00; tel. 51 89 52 70, www.rodne.no). A different company, **Norled,** also runs similar trips, as well as slower journeys up the Lysefjord on a "tourist car ferry" (www.norled.no).

Ferry and Bus to Pulpit Rock (Preikestolen)

Hiking up to the top of Pulpit Rock is a popular outing that will take the better part of a day; plan on at least four hours of hiking (two hours up, two hours down), plus time to linger at the top for photos, plus round-trip travel from Stavanger (about an hour each way by a ferry-and-bus combination)—eight hours minimum should do it. The trailhead is easily reached in summer by public transit or tour package.

Two different companies sell ferry-and-bus packages to the trailhead from Stavanger. Ferries leave from the Fiskepiren boat terminal to Tau; buses (labeled *Preikestolen*) meet the incoming ferries and head to the Preikestolen Fjellstue lodge and Preikestolhytta hostel, both near the trailhead. Be sure to time your hike so that you don't miss the last bus leaving the trailhead for the ferry (confirm time when booking your ticket). These trips generally go daily from mid-May through mid-September; weekends-only in April, early May, and late September; and not at all from October to March (when the ferry stops running). Confirm schedules with the TI or the individual companies: **Tide Reiser** (320 NOK, best options for an all-day round-trip are weekdays at 8:40 or 9:20 or Sat-Sun at 9:00, return bus from trailhead corresponds with ferry to Stavanger, tel. 55 23 88 87, www.tidereiser.com) and **Boreal** (190 NOK for the bus plus 112 NOK for the ferry round-trip—you'll buy the ferry ticket separately, best options depart at 8:40 or 9:20, last bus from trailhead to ferry leaves at 21:15, tel. 51 74 02 40, www.pulpitrock.no).

Rødne Clipper Fjord Sightseeing (listed earlier) runs a handy trip that begins with a scenic Lysefjord cruise (2.5 hours), then drops you off at Oanes to catch the bus to the Pulpit Rock hut trailhead; from there you can do the four-hour round-trip trek to Pulpit Rock and back; afterwards, you catch the bus to Tau for the ferry return to Stavanger. It's similar to the options described above, but adds a scenic fjord cruise at the start (780 NOK plus 56 NOK for return ferry to Stavanger, May-Sept daily at 10:00, also July-Aug at 12:00, tel. 51 89 52 70, www.rodne.no).

Hiking to Pulpit Rock

At just over 4.5 miles round-trip, with an elevation gain of about 1,100 feet, this hike takes four hours total—longer if the trail is very crowded. The hike is fairly stren-uous and includes scrambling over sometimes tricky, rocky terrain. Bring food and plenty of water, pack extra clothes as the weather is changeable, and wear sturdy hiking shoes or boots. Start early or you'll be sharing the trail with dogs on long leashes, toddlers navigating boulders, and the unprepared Bermuda-shorts crowd in flip-flops.

The trail starts by the big sign at the entrance to the main parking lot. From there the path climbs steadily through forest at first and eventually into open, rocky terrain. Along the way, you can thank Nepalese Sherpas—who were hired to improve sections of the route—for their fine stonework on the trail.

The farther and higher you go, the more rocky and spectacular the scenery becomes. Whenever the trail disappears onto bare rock, look for the red T's painted on stones or posts marking the route. As you near Pulpit Rock, the path tiptoes along the cliff's edge with airy views out to the Lysefjord that can only be topped by those from the rock itself.

Before you head back, scramble up the mountainside behind the rock for that iconic, tourist-brochure scene of the people-speckled Pulpit Rock soaring out over the fjord 2,000 feet below.

Sleeping at the Pulpit Rock Trailhead

The Pulpit Rock trail is usually very crowded during the middle of the day, even in bad weather. I prefer to spend the night at the trailhead, and get an early start on the trail the next morning. If you don't have a car, you can still get here from Stavanger by using one of the ferry-and-bus options listed above.

$$$$ Preikestolen Fjellstue is a modern building with 27 bright, simple, functional rooms and a **$$$** restaurant with a lovely lake view (includes breakfast, free parking). Below the Fjellstue and closer to the lake, the rustic, grass-roofed **$ Preikestolhytta** hostel has rooms that sleep 2-4 and bathrooms down the hall (includes breakfast). Both are run by the Norwegian Trekking Association (tel. 51 74 20 74, www.preikestolenfjellstue.no—use Norwegian site to book rooms, post@preikestolenfjellstue.no).

Guided Hike to Pulpit Rock

Outdoorlife Norway offers guided tours for individuals or small groups. They'll pick you up at your hotel and even provide hiking poles. Check out their "Preikestolen Off the Beaten Track Hike" (1,290 NOK, April-Sept) or "Preikestolen Sunrise Hike" (1,290 NOK, April-Oct, mobile 97 65 87 04, www.outdoorlifenorway. com, booking@outdoorlifenorway.com).

Sleeping in Stavanger

$$$ Thon Hotel Maritim, with 140 rooms, is two blocks from the train station near the artificial Lake Breiavatnet. It can be a good deal for a big business-class hotel (elevator, Kongsgaten 32, tel. 51 85 05 00, www.thonhotels.no/maritim, maritim@olavthon.no).

$$$ Hotel Victoria has 107 business-class rooms over a stately, high-ceilinged lobby facing the Skagenkaien embankment right on the harbor (elevator, Skansegata 1, tel. 51 86 70 00, www. victoria-hotel.no, victoria@victoria-hotel.no).

$ Stavanger B&B is Stavanger's best budget option. This large red house among a sea of white houses has tidy, tiny rooms. The lodgings are basic, verging on institutional—not cozy or doily— but they're affordable and friendly. The shared toilet is down the hall; 14 rooms have their own showers, while eight share showers down the hall. Waffles, coffee, and friendly chatter are served up every evening at 21:00 (10-minute uphill walk behind train station in residential neighborhood, Vikedalsgate 1A, tel. 51 56 25 00, www.stavangerbedandbreakfast.no, post@sbb.no). If you let them know in advance, they may be able to pick you up or drop you off at the boat dock or train station.

Eating in Stavanger

CASUAL DINING

$$$ XO Mat & Vinhus, in an elegant setting, serves up big portions of traditional Norwegian food and pricier contemporary fare (Mon-Wed 14:30-23:30, Thu 11:00-23:00, Fri-Sat 11:30 until late, closed Sun, a block behind main drag along harbor at Skagen 10 ved Prostebakken, mobile 91 00 03 07).

$$ Renaa Xpress, popular with the locals, is inside Stavanger's library and cultural center. It's a cozy café where bakers make their own bread and pastries. In addition to a variety of sandwiches, salads, and soups, they also offer sourdough pizza after 13:00

(Mon-Thu 10:00-22:00, Fri-Sat until 24:00, Sun 12:00-22:00, Sølvberggata 2, mobile 94 00 93 48).

$ Skagen Bageri, in a lovely, leaning wooden building dating to the 1700s, serves baked goods and traditional open-face sandwiches at reasonable prices in a cozy, rustic-elegant setting (Mon-Fri 8:00-15:00, Sat until 16:00, closed Sun; in the blue-and-white building a block off the harborfront at Skagen 18; tel. 51 89 51 71).

Meny is a large supermarket with a good selection and a fine deli for super picnic shopping (Mon-Fri 7:00-20:00, Sat 9:00-18:00, closed Sun, in Straen Senteret shopping mall, Lars Hertervigs Gate 6, tel. 51 50 50 10).

Market Plaza Eateries: The busy square between the cathedral and the harbor is packed with reliable Norwegian chain restaurants. If you're a fan of **Deli de Luca, Dolly Dimple's,** or **Dickens Pub,** you'll find them within a few steps of here.

DINING ALONG THE HARBOR WITH A VIEW

The harborside street of Skansegata is lined with lively restaurants and pubs, and most serve food. Here are a few options:

$$$$ Vågen Spiseri, in the same building as the fish market, serves tasty seafood dishes based on the catch of the day (affordable lunch specials, Mon-Wed 11:00-21:00, Thu-Sat until 24:00, closed Sun, Strandkaien 37, tel. 51 52 73 50, www.fisketorget-stavanger.no).

$$$$ N. B. Sørensen's Dampskibsexpedition consists of a lively pub on the first floor (pasta, fish, meat, and vegetarian dishes; Mon-Wed 16:00-24:00, Sat 11:00-late, Sun 13:00-23:00) and a fine-dining restaurant on the second floor, with tablecloths, view tables overlooking the harbor, and a pricey menu (Mon-Sat 18:00-23:00, closed Sun, Skagenkaien 26, tel. 51 84 38 20, www. herlige-stavanger.no). The restaurant is named after an 1800s company that shipped from this building, among other things, Norwegians heading to the US. Passengers and cargo waited on the first floor, and the manager's office was upstairs. The place is filled with emigrant-era memorabilia.

$$$$ Sjøhuset Skagen, with a woodsy interior, invites diners to its historic building for lunch or dinner. The building, from the late 1700s, once housed a trading company. Today, you can choose from local seafood specialties with an ethnic flair, as well as plenty of meat options (Mon-Sat 11:30-24:00, Sun from 13:00, Skagenkaien 16, tel. 51 89 51 80, https://skagenrestaurant.no/en).

$$$$ Bølgen og Moi, the restaurant at the Petroleum Museum, has fantastic views over the harbor (good lunch specials, lunch daily 11:00-16:00; dinner Tue-Sat 18:00-20:00—reservations recommended; Kjeringholmen 748, tel. 51 93 93 53, www. bolgenogmoi.no).

Stavanger Connections

From Stavanger by Train to: Kristiansand (6/day, 3 hours), **Oslo** (5/day, 8 hours, overnight possible).

By Bus to Bergen: Kystbussen operates buses between Stavanger and Bergen (hourly, 5.5 hours, tel. 52 70 35 26, http://kystbussen.no).

By Boat to Denmark: Fjordline ferries sail overnight from Stavanger to Hirtshals, Denmark (11 hours, www.fjordline.com).

The Setesdal Valley

Welcome to the remote, and therefore very traditional, Setesdal Valley. Probably Norway's most authentic cranny, the valley is a mellow montage of sod-roofed water mills, ancient churches, derelict farmhouses, yellowed recipes, and gentle scenery. The Setesdal Valley isn't "on the way" to anything (except the ferry crossing from Kristiansand to Hirtshals, in Denmark). But that's sort of the point. Come here only if you have ample time, and really want to commune with time-passed, rural Norway.

The famous Setesdal filigree echoes the rhythmical designs of the Viking era and Middle Ages. Each town has a weekly rotating series of hikes and activities for the regular, stay-put-for-a-week visitor. The upper valley is dead in the summer but enjoys a bustling winter.

The Setesdal Valley joined the modern age with the construction of the valley highway in the 1950s. All along the valley you'll see the unique two-story storage sheds called *stabburs* (the top floor was used for storing clothes; the bottom, food) and many sod roofs. Even the bus stops have rooftops the local goats love to munch.

In the high country, just over the Sessvatn summit (3,000 feet), you'll see herds of goats and summer farms. If you see an *ekte geitost* sign, that means genuine, homemade goat cheese is for sale. (It's sold cheaper and in more manageable sizes in grocery stores.) To some, it looks like a decade's accumulation of earwax. I think it's delicious. Remember, *ekte* means all-goat—really strong. The more popular and easier-to-eat version is a mix of cow and goat cheese.

Without a car, the Setesdal Valley is not worth the trouble. There are no trains in the valley, bus schedules are as sparse as the

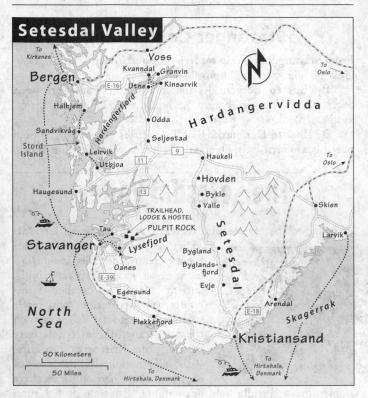

Setesdal Valley

population, and the sights are best for joyriding. But if you're in Bergen with a car, and want to get to Denmark, this route is more interesting than repeating Oslo.

For more information on the Setesdal Valley, see www.setesdal.com.

Sights in the Setesdal Valley

I've described these roadside sights from north to south, most logically connected on a 10-hour drive from Bergen to Kristiansand.

From Bergen, drive about two hours to catch the 9:00 Kvanndal-Utne ferry to give yourself plenty of time (www.norled.no). To reach **Kvanndal,** take Route E-16 toward Voss and Oslo (signs for *Nestune, Landås, Nattland*); then, after a long tunnel, leave the Voss road and take Route 7 heading for Norheimsund, and then Kvanndal. This road, treacherous for the famed beauty of the Hardanger Fjord it hugs as well as for its skinniness, is faster and safer if you beat the traffic.

The Kvanndal ferry drops you in **Utne,** where a lovely road takes you south along the Hardanger Fjord. At the fjord's end, just past the huge zinc-and-copper industrial plant, you'll hit the industrial town of **Odda** (TI on market square at Torget 2-4, tel. 53 65 40 05, www.visitodda.com). Odda brags that Kaiser Wilhelm came here a lot, but he's dead and I'd drive right through. If you want to visit the tongue of a glacier, drive to Buer and hike an hour to Buerbreen.

From Odda, drive into the land of boulders. The many mighty waterfalls that line the road seem to have hurled huge rocks (with rooted trees) into the rivers and fields. Stop at the giant **double waterfall** called Låtefossen (on the left, pullout on the right, drive slowly through it if you need a car wash).

Continue over Røldalsfjellet and follow E-134 into the valley below, where the old town of **Røldal** is trying to develop some tourism (drive on by—its old church isn't worth the stop). Lakes are like frosted mirrors, making desolate huts come in pairs. Farther along on the Hardangervidda plateau is **Haukeliseter**—a group of sod-roofed buildings filled with cultural clichés and tour groups, offering light food in a lakeside setting.

At the Haukeli transportation junction, turn south on Route 9 and wind up to **Sessvatn** at 3,000 feet (toward Hovden). Enter the upper Setesdal Valley. From here, you'll follow the Otra River downhill for 140 miles south to the major port town of Kristiansand. Skip the secondary routes.

A ski resort at the top of the Setesdal Valley (2,500 feet), **Hovden** is barren in the summer and painfully in need of charm. Still, it makes a good home base if you want to explore the area (TI tel. 37 93 93 70, www.hovden.com). Hovden has boat rental (at Hegni Center, south edge of town, tel. 37 93 93 70); a swimming pool (Hovden Badeland, tel. 37 93 93 93, www.badeland.com); the free Museum of Iron Production (Jernvinnemuseum—learn about iron production from the late Iron Age with the aid of drawings, exhibits, and recorded narration in English from a "Viking," about 100 yards behind the Hegni Center); and plenty of choices for hikes and mountain biking. Good walks offer you a chance to see reindeer, moose, arctic fox, and wabbits—so they say. Berry picking is popular in late August, when small, sweet blueberries are in season. A sporadically running chairlift sometimes takes sightseers to the top of a nearby peak, with great views in clear weather; bikers can ride the trails downhill. Hunting season starts in late August for reindeer (only in higher elevations) and later in the fall for grouse and moose *(elg)*. In fact, the TI offers a 2.5-hour "moose safari"— a late-night drive through Setesdal's back roads with a stop for moose-meat soup.

For an affordable place to sleep or eat in Hovden, consider the big, old ski chalet called ¢ **Hovden Fjellstoge.** Check out the mural in the balcony overlooking the lobby—an artistic rendition of this area's history. Behind the mural is a frightening taxidermy collection (tel. 37 93 95 43, www.hovdenfjellstoge.no).

Leaving Hovden, you enter the most scenic stretch of the drive. Nine miles south of Hovden is a two-mile side-trip to a 400-foot-high rock-pile dam, called **Dammar Vatnedalsvatn,** with great view and an impressive rockery. Sit out of the wind a few rows down the rock pile and ponder the vastness of Norwegian wood.

Farther south, the most interesting folk museum and church in Setesdal are in the teeny town of **Bykle.** The 17th-century church has two balconies—one for men and one for women (www.setesdalsmuseet.no).

On the east side of the main road (at the *Grasbrokke* sign) is an old water mill (1630). A few minutes farther south, at the sign for *Sanden Såre Camping,* exit onto a little road to stretch your legs at another old water mill with a fragile, rotten-log sluice.

In Flateland, the **Setesdal Museum** (Rygnestadtunet) offers more of what you saw at Bykle; unless you're a glutton for culture, I wouldn't do both (www.setesdalsmuseet.no). Past Flateland at **Honnevje** is a nice picnic and WC stop, with a dock along the water for swimming...for hot-weather days or polar bears.

Valle is Setesdal's prettiest village (but don't tell Bykle). In the center, you'll find fine silver- and gold-work, homemade crafts next to the TI (tel. 37 93 75 29), and occasional *lefse* cooking demonstrations. The fine suspension bridge attracts kids of any age (b-b-b-b-bounce), and anyone interested in a great view over the river to strange mountains that look like polished, petrified mudslides. European rock climbers, tired of the over-climbed Alps, often entertain spectators with their sport. Is anyone climbing? To sleep in Valle, consider the basic **Valle Motell** (www.valle-motell.no).

South of Valle, the area has a lot more logging (and is less scenic). In **Nomeland,** the Sylvartun silversmith shop, whose owner Hallvard Bjørgum is also a renowned Hardanger fiddle player, sells Setesdal silver in a 17th-century, grass-roofed log cabin next to the main road.

Farther south, the road traces first the west and then the east shore of the long and scenic freshwater Byglandsfjord to **Grendi,** where the Ardal Church (1827) has a rune stone in its yard. Three hundred yards south of the church is a 900-year-old oak tree.

A huge town by Setesdal standards (3,500 people), **Evje** is famous for its gems and mines. Fancy stones fill the shops here. Rock hounds find the nearby mines fun; for a small fee, you can hunt for gems (TI tel. 37 93 14 00). The **Setesdal Mineral Park** is on the main road, two miles south of town (www.mineralparken.no).

From Evje, it's about an hour's drive to this region's transportation hub, **Kristiansand.**

NEAR THE SETESDAL VALLEY: KRISTIANSAND

The "capital of the south," Kristiansand has 85,000 inhabitants, a pleasant Renaissance grid-plan layout (Posebyen), a famous zoo with Norway's biggest amusement park, a daily bus to Bergen, lots of big boats going to Denmark, and a TI (Rådhusgata 18, tel. 38 12 13 14, www.visitkrs.no). It's the closest thing to a beach resort in Norway. Markensgate is the bustling pedestrian market street—an enjoyable place for good browsing, shopping, eating, and people-watching. Stroll along the Strand Promenaden (marina) to Christiansholm Fortress. The otherwise uninteresting harbor area has a cluster of wooden buildings called **Fiskebasaren** ("Fish Bazaar")—with an indoor fish market (only open during the day) and numerous restaurants offering a nice dinner atmosphere.

Sleeping in Kristiansand: You may need to sleep here to break up your Setesdal journey. Hotels are expensive and nondescript; consider the **$$$$ Rica Hotel Norge** (Dronningensgate 5, tel. 38 17 40 00, www.hotel-norge.no) or the **$$$$ Thon Hotel Wergeland** (ask for quiet room, Kirkegate 15, tel. 38 17 20 40, www.thonhotels.no/wergeland).

Kristiansand Connections: Trains connect to **Stavanger** (6/day, 3 hours) and **Oslo** (5/day, 4.5 hours). Kristiansand is also a hub for the three-hour **ferry to Hirtshals, Denmark,** operated by two companies: Color Line (2/day year-round, more in summer, www.colorline.com) and Fjordline (1-2/day in summer, none in winter, www.fjordline.com). You can either drive on or walk on.

SWEDEN

SWEDEN

Sverige

Scandinavia's heartland, Sweden is far bigger than Denmark and far flatter than Norway. This family-friendly land is home to Ikea, Volvo, ABBA, and long summer vacations at red-painted, white-trimmed summer cottages. Its capital, Stockholm, is Scandinavia's grandest city.

While it's still the capital of blond, Sweden is now also home to a growing immigrant population. Sweden is committed to its peoples' safety and security, and proud of its success in creating a society with one of the lowest poverty rates in the world. Yet Sweden has thrown in its lot with the European Union, and locals debate whether to open their economy even further.

Until 1996, Swedes automatically became members of the Lutheran Church at birth if one parent was Lutheran, and up until the year 2000, Sweden was a Lutheran state, with the Church of Sweden as its official religion. That's now changed: Swedes can choose to join (or not join) the church, and although the culture is nominally Lutheran, few people attend services regularly. While church is handy for Christmas, Easter, marriages, and burials, most Swedes are more likely to find religion in nature, hiking in the vast forests or fishing in one of the thousands of lakes or rivers.

Sweden is almost 80 percent wilderness, and modern legislation incorporates an ancient right of public access called *allemansrätten*, which guarantees the right for anyone to move freely through Sweden's natural scenery without asking landowners for permission, as long as they behave responsibly. In summer, Swedes take advantage of the long days and warm evenings for festivals such as Midsummer (in late June) and crayfish parties *(kräftskiva)* in August and September. Many Swedes have a summer cottage—or know someone

who does—where they spend countless hours swimming, soaking up the sun, and devouring boxes of juicy strawberries.

While Denmark and Norway look westward to Britain and the Atlantic, Sweden has always faced east, across the Baltic Sea. As Vikings, Norwegians went west to Iceland, Greenland, and America; Danes headed south to England, France, and the Mediterranean; and Swedes went east into Russia. (The word "Russia" has Viking roots.) In the early Middle Ages, Swedes founded the Russian cities of Nizhny Novgorod and Kiev, and even served as royal guards in Constantinople (modern-day Istanbul). During the later Middle Ages, German settlers and traders strongly influenced Sweden's culture and language. By the 17th century, Sweden was a major European power, with one of the largest naval fleets in Europe and an empire extending around the Baltic, including Finland, Estonia, Latvia, and parts of Poland, Russia, and Germany. But by the early 19th century, Sweden's war-weary empire had shrunk. The country's current borders date from 1809.

During a massive wave of emigration from the 1860s to World

Sweden Almanac

Official Name: Konungariket Sverige—the Kingdom of Sweden—or simply Sweden

Population: Sweden's 9.9 million people (about 57 per square mile) are mostly ethnically Swedish. Foreign-born and first-generation immigrants account for about 17 percent of the population and are primarily from Finland, Poland, and the Middle East. Sweden is also home to about 20,000 indigenous Sami people. Swedish is the dominant language, with most speaking English as well. While immigrants bring various religions with them, ethnic Swedes who go to church tend to be Lutheran. For background on everything in Swedish society from religion to the Sami people, see www.sweden.se.

Latitude and Longitude: 62°N and 15°E, similar latitude to Canada's Northwest Territories.

Area: 174,000 square miles (a little bigger than California).

Geography: A chain of mountains divides Sweden from Norway on the Scandinavian Peninsula. Sweden's mostly forested landscape is flanked to the east by the Baltic Sea, which contributes to the temperate climate. Sweden also encompasses several islands, of which Gotland and Öland are the largest.

Biggest City: Sweden's capital city, Stockholm, has a population of 897,000, with more than two million in the metropolitan area. Göteborg (526,000) and Malmö (307,000) are the next-largest cities.

Economy: Sweden has a $498 billion gross domestic product and a per capita GDP of $49,800—similar to Switzerland's. Manufacturing, telecommunications, automobiles, and processed foods rank among its top industries, along with timber, hydropower, and

War II, about a quarter of Sweden's people left for the Promised Land—America. Many emigrants were farmers from the southern region of Småland. The House of Emigrants museum in Växjö tells their story (see the Southeast Sweden chapter), as do the movies *The Emigrants* and *The New Land,* based on the books of Vilhelm Moberg.

The 20th century was good to Sweden. While other European countries were embroiled in two world wars, neutral Sweden grew stronger, finding equilibrium between the extremes of communism and the free market. In the postwar years, Sweden adopted its famous "middle way," an economic model that balanced the needs of the democratic state and the private business sector.

The Swedish model worked very well for a while, providing a booming economy and robust social services for all. But the flip side of those ambitious programs is one of the highest tax levels in the world. After a recession hit in the early 1990s, some started to iron ore. The Swedish economy is one of the strongest in Europe, helped by its competitive high-tech businesses—and by the government's generally conservative fiscal policies. Some 71 percent of Swedish workers belong to a labor union.

Currency: 8 Swedish kronor (SEK) = about $1.

Government: King Carl XVI Gustav is the ceremonial head of Sweden's constitutional monarchy. Elected every four years, the 349-member Swedish Parliament (Riksdag) is currently led by Prime Minister Stefan Löfven of the Social Democratic Party (elected in October 2014). *The Economist* magazine—which considered factors such as participation, impact of people on their government, and transparency—ranks Sweden by far the world's most democratic country (followed by the other Scandinavian countries and the Netherlands, with North Korea coming in last).

Flag: The Swedish flag is blue with a yellow Scandinavian cross. The colors are derived from the Swedish coat of arms, with yellow symbolizing the generosity of the people and blue representing vigilance, truth, loyalty, perseverance, and justice.

The Average Swede: He or she is 41 years old, has 1.88 children, and will live to be 82.

criticize the middle way as unworkable. But Sweden's economy improved in the late 1990s and early 2000s, buoyed by a strong lineup of successful multinational companies. Volvo (now Chinese-owned but Sweden-based), Scania (trucks and machinery), Ikea, H&M (clothing), and Ericsson (the telecommunications giant) led the way in manufacturing, design, and technology.

The global economic downturn of 2008-2009 had its impact on Sweden's export-driven economy: Unemployment ticked upward (although it remains enviably low compared to other countries), its famously generous welfare systems felt the pressure, and its Saab car manufacturer filed for bankruptcy protection. But Sweden has rebounded since the crisis, and the country's fortunes have outpaced those of the European Union—Sweden's main export market.

Historically Sweden has had an open-door policy when it comes to accepting immigrants (the country's immigration laws are

SWEDEN

the most generous in Europe). Since the 1960s, Sweden (like Denmark and Norway) has accepted many immigrants and refugees from southeastern Europe, the Middle East, and elsewhere. This praiseworthy humanitarian policy has dramatically—and sometimes painfully—diversi-fied a formerly homogenous country. Many of the service-industry workers you will meet have come to Sweden from elsewhere.

More recently, with refugees flooding in from Syria and Iraq, Swedish social services have been tested as never before. The politics of immigration have become more complex and intense, as Swedes debate the costs (real and societal) of maintaining a culture that wants to be blind to class differences and ethnic divisions.

Though most Swedes speak English, and communication is rarely an issue, a few Swedish words are helpful and appreciated. "Hello" is *"Hej"* (hey) and "Good-bye" is *"Hej då"* (hey doh). "Thank you" is *"Tack"* (tack), which can also double for "please." For a longer list of Swedish survival phrases, see the following page.

Swedish Survival Phrases

Swedish pronunciation (especially the vowel sounds) can be tricky for Americans to say, and there's quite a bit of variation across the country; listen closely to locals and imitate, or ask for help. The most difficult Swedish sound is *sj*, which sounds roughly like a guttural "*h*w" (made in your throat); however, like many sounds, this is pronounced differently in various regions—for example, Stockholmers might say it more like "shw."

English	Swedish	Pronunciation
Hello. (formal)	*Goddag!*	goh-**dah**
Hi. / Bye. (informal)	*Hej. / Hej då.*	hey / hey doh
Do you speak English?	*Talar du engelska?*	**tah**-lar doo **eng**-ehl-skah
Yes. / No.	*Ja. / Nej.*	yaw / nay
Please.	*Snälla. / Tack.**	**snehl**-lah / tack
Thank you (very much).	*Tack (så mycket).*	tack (soh **mee**-keh)
You're welcome.	*Ingen orsak.*	**eeng**-ehn **oor**-sahk
Can I help you?	*Kan jag hjälpa dig?*	kahn yaw **jehl**-pah day
Excuse me.	*Ursäkta.*	**oor**-sehk-tah
(Very) good.	*(Mycket) bra.*	(**mee**-keh) brah
Goodbye.	*Adjö.*	ah-**yew**
zero / one / two	*noll / en / två*	nohl / ehn / tvoh
three / four	*tre / fyra*	treh / **fee**-rah
five / six	*fem / sex*	fehm / sehks
seven / eight	*sju / åtta*	*h*woo / **oh**-tah
nine / ten	*nio / tio*	**nee**-oh / **tee**-oh
hundred	*hundra*	**hoon**-drah
thousand	*tusen*	**too**-sehn
How much?	*Hur mycket?*	hewr **mee**-keh
local currency: (Swedish) kronor	*(Svenska) kronor*	(svehn-**skeh**) **kroh**-nor
Where is...?	*Var finns...?*	var feens
the toilet	*...toaletten*	toh-ah-**leh**-tehn
men	*man*	mahn
women	*kvinna*	**kvee**-nah
water / coffee	*vatten / kaffe*	**vah**-tehn / **kah**-feh
beer / wine	*öl / vin*	url / veen
Cheers!	*Skål!*	skohl
The bill, please.	*Kan jag få notan, tack.*	kahn yaw foh **noh**-tahn tack

*Swedish has various ways to say "please," depending on the context. The simplest is *snälla,* but Swedes sometimes use the word *tack* (thank you) the way we use "please."

STOCKHOLM

If I had to call one European city home, it might be Stockholm. One-third water, one-third parks, one-third city, on the sea, surrounded by woods, bubbling with energy and history, Sweden's stunning capital is green, clean, and underrated.

The city is built on a string of islands connected by bridges. Its location midway along the Baltic Sea, behind the natural fortification of its archipelago, made it a fine port, vital to the economy and security of the Swedish peninsula. In the 1500s, Stockholm became a political center when Gustav Vasa established the monarchy (1523). A century later, the expansionist King Gustavus Adolphus made it an influential European capital. The Industrial Revolution brought factories and a flood of farmers from the countryside. In the 20th century, the fuming smokestacks were replaced with steel-and-glass Modernist buildings housing high-tech workers and an expanding service sector.

Today, with more than two million people in the greater metropolitan area (one in five Swedes), Stockholm is Sweden's largest city, as well as its cultural, educational, and media center. It's also the country's most ethnically diverse city. Despite its size, Stockholm is committed to limiting its environmental footprint. Development is strictly monitored, and cars must pay a toll to enter the city. If there's a downside to Stockholm, it's that the city feels wealthy (even its Mac-toting hipsters), sometimes snobby, and a bit sure of itself. Stockholm rivals Oslo in expense, and beats it in pretense.

For the visitor, Stockholm offers both old and new. Crawl through Europe's best-preserved old warship and relax on a scenic harbor boat tour. Browse the cobbles and antique shops of the lantern-lit Old Town. Take a trip back in time at Skansen, Europe's first and best open-air folk museum. Marvel at Stockholm's glittering City Hall, slick shopping malls, and art museums. (Even "also ran" museums in this city rank high on the European scale.) Explore the funky vibrancy of the design-forward Södermalm district.

While progressive and sleek, Stockholm respects its heritage. In summer, military bands parade daily through the heart of town to the Royal Palace, announcing the Changing of the Guard and turning even the most dignified tourist into a scampering kid.

With extra time, consider one or more Stockholm side-trips, including the nearby royal residence, Drottningholm Palace; the cute town of Sigtuna; or the university town of Uppsala, with its grand cathedral, Linnaeus Garden and Museum, and Iron Age mounds (see the Near Stockholm chapter). Stockholm is also an ideal home base for cruising to island destinations in the city's archipelago (see Stockholm's Archipelago chapter).

PLANNING YOUR TIME

On a two- to three-week trip through Scandinavia, Stockholm is worth at least two days. For the busiest and best two- to three-day plan, I'd suggest this:

Day 1

10:00	See the *Vasa* warship (movie and tour).
12:00	Tour the Skansen open-air museum and grab lunch there.
14:30	Walk or ride tram #7 to the Swedish History Museum.
16:30	Ride tram #7 to Nybroplan and follow my self-guided walk through the modern city from Kungsträdgården.
18:00	Dinner at one of my recommended waterfront restaurants, or take a harbor dinner cruise.

Day 2

10:00	Ride one of the city orientation bus tours (either the hop-on, hop-off or the 1.25-hour bus tour from the Royal Opera House), or take the City Hall tour and climb its tower.
12:15	Catch the Changing of the Guard at the palace (13:15 on Sun).
13:00	Lunch on Stortorget.

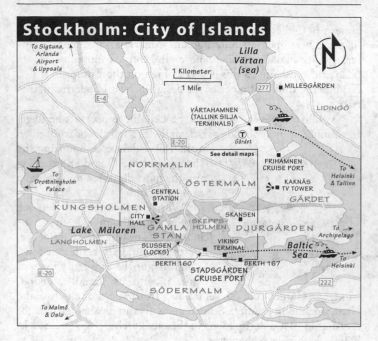

Stockholm: City of Islands

14:00   Tour the Royal Armory (if it's reopened from its renovation; if time and budget allow, also consider the Nobel Museum and/or Royal Palace sights), and follow my Old Town self-guided walk.

18:30   Explore Södermalm for dinner—it's just across the locks from Gamla Stan—or take the Royal Canal boat tour (confirm last sailing time).

Day 3

With an extra day, add a cruise through the scenic island archipelago (easy to do from Stockholm), visit the royal palace at Drottningholm, take a side-trip to charming Sigtuna or Uppsala (see next two chapters), or spend more time in Stockholm (there's plenty left to do and experience).

Orientation to Stockholm

Greater Stockholm's two million residents live on 14 islands woven together by 54 bridges. Visitors need only concern themselves with these districts, most of which are islands:

Norrmalm is downtown, with hotels and shopping areas, and the combined train and bus station. **Östermalm,** to the east, is more residential.

Kungsholmen, the mostly suburban island across from Norrmalm, is home to City Hall and inviting lakefront eateries.

Gamla Stan is the Old Town island of winding, lantern-lit streets, antique shops, and classy cafés clustered around the Royal Palace. The adjacent **Riddarholmen** is similarly atmospheric, but much sleepier. The locks between Lake Mälaren (to the west) and the Baltic Sea (to the east) are at a junction called **Slussen,** just south of Gamla Stan on the way to Södermalm.

Skeppsholmen is the small, central, traffic-free park/island with the Museum of Modern Art and two fine youth hostels.

Djurgården is the park-island—Stockholm's wonderful green playground, with many of the city's top sights (bike rentals just over bridge as you enter island).

Södermalm, just south of the other districts, is sometimes called "Stockholm's Brooklyn"—it's young and creative. Apart from fine views and some good eateries, this residential island may be of less interest to those on a quick visit.

TOURIST INFORMATION

Stockholm's helpful city-run TI—called **Visit Stockholm**—has two branches. The main office is downtown in the Kulturhuset, facing Sergels Torg (Mon-Fri 9:00-19:00—until 18:00 off-season, Sat until 16:00, Sun 10:00-16:00, Sergels Torg 3, T-bana: T-Centralen, tel. 08/5082-8508, www.visitstockholm.com). There's also a branch at the airport, in Terminal 5, where most international flights arrive (long hours daily, tel. 08/797-6000).

Around town, you'll also see the green *i* logo of **Stockholm Info,** run by a for-profit agency. While less helpful than the official TI, they hand out maps and brochures, and may be able to answer basic questions (locations include the train station's main hall and Gamla Stan). They sell the pricey **City Pass** that covers transportation and a limited number of museums (www.stockholminfo.com).

Stockholm Pass: This pass covers entry to 60 Stockholm sights (including Skansen and the Royal Palace) as well as unlimited City Sightseeing hop-on, hop-off bus/boat tours. It's available in one-day and multiday versions, with an optional Travelcard transit add-on. Prices range from 600 SEK to 1300 SEK (www.stockholmpass.com).

ARRIVAL IN STOCKHOLM
By Train or Bus

Stockholm's adjacent stations for trains (Centralstation) and buses (Cityterminalen), at the southwestern edge of Norrmalm, are a hive of services (including an unofficial Stockholm Info "TI"), eateries, shops, exchange desks, and people on the move. From the train station, the bus station is up the escalators from the main hall and through a glassy atrium (lined with sales desks for bus companies and cruise lines). Those sailing to Estonia or Finland with Tallink Silja (Värtahamnen port) or Viking (Stadsgården port) can catch a shuttle bus from the bus terminal (www. flygbussarna.se). Underground is the T-Centralen subway (T-bana) station—probably the easiest way to reach your hotel. Taxi stands are outside.

The best way to connect the city and its airport is via the Arlanda Express shuttle train, which leaves from tracks 1 and 2 (follow *Arlanda Express/airport train* signs through the station; see below).

By Plane
Arlanda Airport
Stockholm's Arlanda Airport is 28 miles north of town (airport code: ARN, tel. 08/797-6000, www.arlanda.se).

Getting Between the Airport and Downtown: The Arlanda Express **train** is the fastest way to zip between the airport and the central train station. Traveling most of the way at 125 mph, it gets you downtown in just 20 minutes—but it's not cheap (280 SEK one-way, 540 SEK round-trip, free for kids under 17 with adult, covered by rail pass; generally 4-6/hour; tel. 0771/720-200, www. arlandaexpress.com). Buy your ticket either at the window near the track or from a ticket machine, or pay an extra 100 SEK to buy it on board. It's worth checking the website for advance-purchase discounts and two-for-one weekend specials.

Airport shuttle buses (Flygbussarna) run between the airport and Stockholm's train/bus stations (119 SEK, 6/hour, 45 minutes, may take longer at rush hour; buy tickets online—cheapest, from station kiosks, or from 7-Eleven and Pressbyrån convenience stores at the airport and train/bus station, www.flygbussarna.se).

Taxis between the airport and the city center take 30-40 minutes (about 675 SEK, but look for price posted on side of cab). Establish the price first. Most taxis prefer credit cards.

The **cheapest airport connection** is to take bus #583 from the airport to Märsta, then switch to the *pendeltåg* #36 (suburban train, 4-5/hour), which goes to Stockholm's central train station (86 SEK, 1 hour total journey time).

Skavsta Airport
Some discount airlines use Skavsta Airport, about 60 miles south of Stockholm (code: NYO, www.skavsta.se). Flygbussarna shuttle buses connect to the city (159 SEK, cheaper online, 1-2/hour, 80 minutes—but allow extra time for traffic, www.flygbussarna.se).

By Boat

For details on arriving in Stockholm by cruise ship, see "Stockholm Connections" at the end of this chapter. For information on ferries from Stockholm to Tallinn and Helsinki, see the "Connections" sections in those chapters.

By Car

Only a Swedish meatball would drive a car in Stockholm. Park it in one of the park-and-ride lots that ring the city and use public transit instead (see lot map at www.visitstockholm.com). Those sailing to Finland or Estonia should ask about long-term parking at the terminal when reserving tickets; to minimize the risk of theft and vandalism, pay extra for the most secure parking garage.

HELPFUL HINTS

Theft Alert: Even in Stockholm, when there are crowds, there are pickpockets (such as at the Royal Palace during the Changing of the Guard). Too-young-to-arrest teens—many from other countries—are hard for local police to control.

Pharmacy: The **C. W. Scheele** 24-hour pharmacy is near the train station at Klarabergsgatan 64 (tel. 08/454-8130).

English Bookstore: The aptly named **English Bookshop** sells a variety of reading materials (including Swedish-interest books) in English (Mon-Fri 11:00-18:30, Sat until 16:00, Sun 12:00-16:00, in the Södermalm district at Södermannag 22, tel. 08/790-5510).

Laundry: Tvättomaten is a rare find—the only self-service independent launderette in Stockholm (48-hour full-service available; open Mon-Fri 8:30-18:30—until 17:00 in July-mid-Aug, Sat 9:30-13:00, closed Sun; across from Gustav Vasa church, Västmannagatan 61 on Odenplan, T-bana: Odenplan, tel. 08/346-480, www.tvattomaten.se).

Museum Admission: Entry to many of Stockholm's fine state-owned museums swings from free (when left-leaning parties control the reins of government) to fee (when center-right parties are in charge). Ask locally for the latest.

GETTING AROUND STOCKHOLM
By Public Transit

Stockholm's fine but pricey public transport network (Stockholm Transport, officially Storstockholms Lokaltrafik—but signed as *SL*) includes subway (Tunnelbana, called "T-bana") and bus systems, and a single handy tram from the commercial center to the sights at Djurgården. It's a spread-out city, so most visitors will need public transport at some point (transit info tel. 08/600-1000, www.sl.se/english). The subway is easy to figure out, but many sights are better served by bus. The main lines are listed on the back of the official city map. A more detailed system map is available free from subway ticket windows, SL Centers (info desks) in main stations, and TIs.

Tickets: A single ride for subway, tram, or bus costs 43 SEK (up to 1.25 hours, including transfers); a 24-hour pass is 120 SEK, while a 72-hour pass is 240 SEK. Tickets are sold on the tram (with an extra surcharge), but not on buses. All SL ticket-sellers are clearly marked with a blue flag with the *SL* logo.

Locals and savvy tourists carry a blue **SL-Access card,** which you can buy for 20 SEK at ticket agents, subway and commuter rail stations, and SL Centers. To use the card, just touch it against the blue pad to enter the T-bana turnstile or when boarding a bus or tram. You can add value to the card at station machines or with a ticket agent.

It's still possible to buy single-journey **paper tickets** (at Pressbyrån convenience stores inside almost every T-bana station, at self-service machines, and at some transit-ticket offices)—but it's not worth the hassle.

Transit App: SL also has an easy-to-use ticketing app (search "SL-Stockholm" in app stores) that you can tie to a bank card (works with US cards). Buy tickets as you need them on your phone, which you'll then hold to a scanner to enter the T-bana turnstile (or show to a bus/tram driver).

By Harbor Shuttle Ferry

In summer, city ferries let you make a fun, practical, and scenic shortcut across the harbor to Djurgården Island. Boat #82 leaves from the southeast end of Gamla Stan, stops near the Museum of Modern Art on Skeppsholmen, then docks near the Gröna Lund amusement park on Djurgården; boat #80 departs from Nybroplan for Djurgården (43 SEK, covered by public-transit passes, 3-4/hour May-late Sept, 10-minute trip, www.sl.se). The private ferry *Emelie* makes the journey from Nybroplan to Djurgården, landing near the ABBA Museum, then goes on to cruise berth 167 (60 SEK, buy ticket onboard—credit cards only and SL app not valid, hourly, April-Sept roughly Mon-Fri 7:50-18:20, Sat-Sun 9:50-17:50, tel. 08/731-0025, www.ressel.se). While buses and trams run between the same points more frequently, the ferry option gets you out onto the water and can be faster—and certainly more scenic—than overland connections. The hop-on, hop-off boat tour (see "Tours in Stockholm," next) also connects many of these stops.

By Taxi

Stockholm is a good taxi town—provided you find a reputable cab that charges fair rates. Taxis are unregulated, so companies can charge whatever they like. Before hopping in a taxi, look carefully at the big yellow label that should be displayed prominently on the outside of the car (usually in the rear door window). The big number, on the right, shows the "highest unit price" *(högsta järnförpriset)* for a 10-kilometer ride that lasts 15 minutes; this number should be between 290 and 390 SEK—if it's higher, move on. (You're not obligated to take the first cab in line.) Most cabs charge a drop fee of about 45 SEK. Taxis with inflated rates tend to congregate at touristy places like the Vasa Museum or in Gamla Stan. I've been ripped off enough by cabs here to know: Take only "Taxi Stockholm" cabs with the phone number (08/150-000) printed on the door. (Other reportedly honest companies include Taxi Kurir, tel. 08/300-000, and Taxi 020, tel. 08/850-400 or 020-20-20-20.) Your hotel, restaurant, or museum can call a cab, which will generally arrive within minutes (no extra charge—the meter starts when you hop in).

Tours in Stockholm

The sightseeing company **Strömma** has a lock on most city tours, whether by bus, by boat, or on foot. Their website (www.stromma. se) details the entire program, or you can call for more information (08/1200-4000). Tours can be paid for online, or simply as you board.

BY BUS

Hop-On, Hop-Off Bus Tour

Three hop-on, hop-off buses make a 1.5-hour circuit of the city, orienting riders with a recorded commentary and linking all the essential places from Skansen to City Hall; when cruises are in town, they also stop at both cruise ports (Stadsgården and Frihamnen). **Hop-On Hop-Off**'s green buses and **City Sightseeing**'s red buses both cooperate with Strömma (300 SEK/24 hours, ticket covers both buses; May-Sept 2-3/hour daily 10:00-16:00, fewer off-season, none mid-Jan-mid-Feb, www.stromma.se). **Red Buses** offers a similar hop-on, hop-off itinerary in open-top buses for the same price (3/hour, www.redbuses.se). All offer free Wi-Fi.

Quickie Orientation Bus Tour

Several different city bus tours leave from the Royal Opera House on Gustav Adolfs Torg. Strömma's Stockholm Panorama tour provides a good overview—but, as it's the same price as the 24-hour hop-on, hop-off ticket, I'd take this tour only if you want a quick

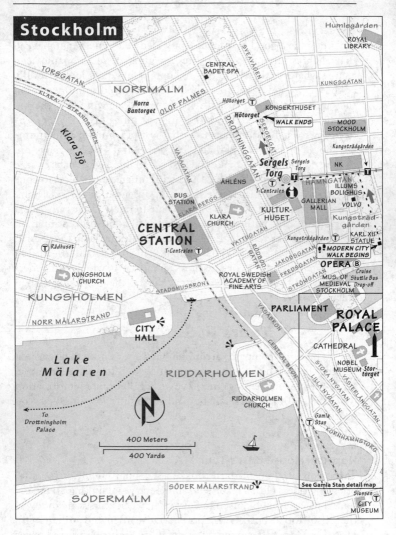

Stockholm

Humlegården

ROYAL LIBRARY

TORSGATAN

KLARA - STRANDLEDEN

NORRMALM

Norra Bantorget

OLOF PALMES

KUNGSGATAN

CENTRAL-BADET SPA

SVEAVÄGEN

Hötorget Ⓣ

Hötorget ◄WALK ENDS

KONSERTHUSET

MOOD STOCKHOLM

Kungsträdgården

DROTTNINGGATAN

VASAGATAN

Sergels Torg

Sergels Torg

NK Ⓣ

ÅHLÉNS

BUS STATION

KLARA BERGS

T-Centralen Ⓣ

HAMNGATAN

ILLUMS BOLIGHUS

GALLERIAN MALL

VOLVO

KLARA CHURCH

KULTUR-HUSET

Kungsträd-gården

Klara Sjö

CENTRAL STATION

VATTUGATAN

T-Centralen Ⓣ

RÖDBODGATAN

Kungsträdgården Ⓣ

KARL XII STATUE

Ⓣ Rådhuset

JAKOBSGATAN

◆ MODERN CITY WALK BEGINS

OPERA Ⓑ

KUNGSHOLM CHURCH

ROYAL SWEDISH ACADEMY OF FINE ARTS

FREDSGATAN

STRÖMGATAN

MUS. OF MEDIEVAL STOCKHOLM

Cruise Shuttle Bus Drop-off

KUNGSHOLMEN

STADSHUSBRON

VASABRON

PARLIAMENT

ROYAL PALACE

NORR MÄLARSTRAND

CENTRALBRON

CATHEDRAL

CITY HALL

NOBEL MUSEUM

Stor-torget

STORA NYGATAN

VÄSTERLÅNGGATAN

Lake Mälaren

RIDDARHOLMEN

RIDDARHOLMEN CHURCH

LILLA NYGATAN

Gamla Stan Ⓣ

KÖRNHAMNSTORG

To Drottningholm Palace

N

400 Meters

400 Yards

SÖDER MÄLARSTRAND

See Gamla Stan detail map

SÖDERMALM

Slussen Ⓣ

CITY MUSEUM

and efficient loop with no unnecessary stops (300 SEK, 4-6/day, fewer Oct-May, 1.25 hours).

BY BOAT

▲City Boat Tours

For a good floating look at Stockholm and a pleasant break, consider a sightseeing cruise. These boat tours are pleasant at the end of the day, when the light is warm and the sights and museums are closed. The handiest are the Strömma/Stockholm Sightseeing boats, which leave from Strömkajen, in front of the Grand Hotel, and stop at Nybroplan five minutes later. The **Royal Canal Tour** is short and informative (200 SEK, 50 minutes, departs at :30 past

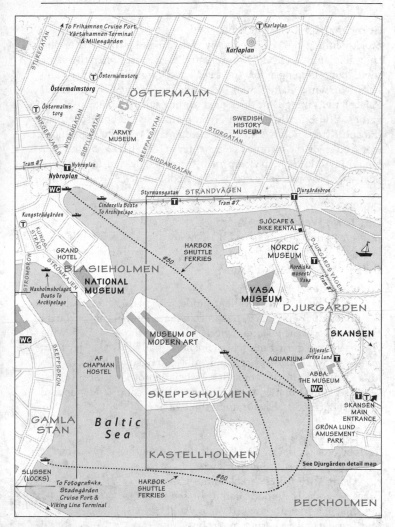

each hour May-Aug 10:30-18:30, less frequent off-season, none Jan-March). The nearly two-hour **Under the Bridges Tour** goes through two locks and under 15 bridges (260 SEK, departures on the hour May-mid-Sept). The **Historic Canal Tour** leaves from the Stadshusbron dock at City Hall (200 SEK, 50 minutes, departs at :30 past the hour June-Aug). You'll circle Kungsholmen island while learning about Stockholm's history from the early Industrial Age to modern times.

Hop-On, Hop-Off Boat Tour

Stockholm is a city surrounded by water, making this boat option enjoyable and practical. Strömma and Red Buses offer the same small loop, stopping at key spots such as Djurgården (Skansen and Vasa Museum), Gamla Stan (near Slussen and again near Royal Palace), the Viking Line dock next to the cruise terminal at Stadsgården, cruise berth 167, and Nybroplan. Use the boat strictly as transport from Point A to Point B, or make the whole one-hour loop and enjoy the recorded commentary (180 SEK/24 hours, 2-3/hour May-mid-Sept, pick up map for schedule and locations of boat stops, www.stromma.se or www.redbuses.se).

ON FOOT

Old Town Walk

Strömma offers a 1.25-hour Old Town walk (180 SEK, July-Aug only at 13:30, departs from ticket booth at north end of Gustav Adolfs Torg, www.stromma.se).

Local Guides

Håkan Frändén is an excellent guide who brings Stockholm to life (mobile 070-531-3379, hakan.franden@hotmail.com). **Marita Bergman** is a teacher and a licensed guide who enjoys showing visitors around during her school breaks (1,650 SEK/half-day tour, mobile 073-511-9154, bergman57.mb@gmail.com). You can also hire a private guide through the Association of Qualified Tourist Guides of Stockholm (www.guidestockholm.com). The standard rate is about 1,650 SEK for up to three hours.

BY BIKE

To tour Stockholm on two wheels, you can either use one of the city's shared bikes or rent your own.

Using City Bikes: Stockholm's City Bikes program is a good option for seeing this bike-friendly town. While you'll find similar bike-sharing programs all over Europe, Stockholm's is the most usable and helpful for travelers. It's easy, the bikes are great, and the city lends itself to joyriding.

Purchase a 165-SEK, three-day City Bike card at the TI, at the SL Center (transit info office) at Sergels Torg, or at many hotels and hostels. The card allows you to grab a bike from one of more than 140 City Bike racks around town. You must return it within three hours (to any rack), but if you want to keep riding, just check out another bike. You can do this over and over for three days (available April-Oct only, www.citybikes.se).

The downside: Unless you have a lock, you can't park your bike as you sightsee. You'll need to return it to a station and get another when you're ready to go—which sounds easy enough, but in practice stations can be full (without an empty port in which to leave a bike) or have no bikes available. To overcome this problem, download City Bike's fun, easy, and free app (search "City Bikes by Clear Channel"), which identifies the nearest racks and bikes.

Renting a Bike: You can also rent bikes (and boats) at the **Sjöcafét** café, next to Djurgårdsbron bridge near the Vasa Museum. It's ideally situated as a springboard for a pleasant bike ride around the parklike Djurgården island—use their free and excellent bike map/guide. For details, see the Djurgårdsbron section under "Sights in Stockholm," later.

Walks in Stockholm

This section includes two different self-guided walks to introduce you to Stockholm, both old (Gamla Stan) and new (the modern city).

▲▲GAMLA STAN WALK

Gamla Stan, Stockholm's historic island old town, is charming, photogenic, and full of antique shops, street lanterns, painted ceilings, and surprises. Until the 1600s, all of Stockholm fit in Gamla Stan. Stockholm traded with other northern ports such as Amsterdam, Lübeck, and Tallinn. German culture influenced art, building styles, and even the language, turning Old Norse into modern Swedish. With its narrow alleys and stairways, Gamla Stan mixes poorly with cars and modern economies. Today, it's been given over to the Royal Palace and to the tourists, who throng Gamla Stan's main drag, Västerlånggatan, seemingly unaware that most of Stockholm's best attractions are elsewhere. While you could just happily wander, this quick walk gives meaning to Stockholm's Old Town.

• *Our walk begins along the harborfront. Start at the base of Slottsbacken (the Palace Hill esplanade) leading up to the...*

Royal Palace: Along the water, check out the ❶ **statue of King Gustav III** gazing at the palace, which was built in the 1700s on the site of Stockholm's first castle (for more about the palace, see the description later in this chapter, under "Sights in Stockholm"). Gustav turned Stockholm from a dowdy Scandinavian port into a sophisticated European capital, modeled on French culture. Gustav loved the arts, and he founded the Royal Dramatic Theater and the Royal Opera in Stockholm. Ironically, he was assassinated by a

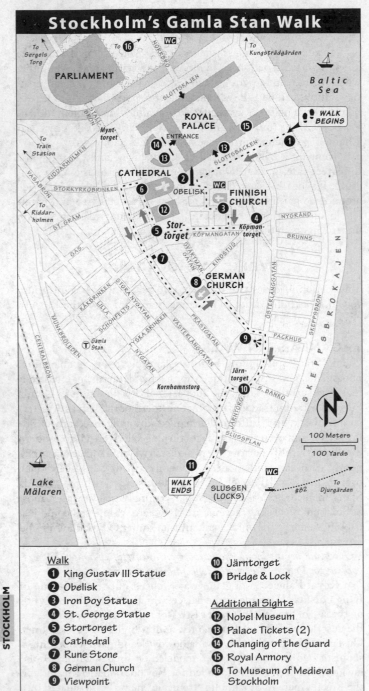

Stockholm's Gamla Stan Walk

Walk
1. King Gustav III Statue
2. Obelisk
3. Iron Boy Statue
4. St. George Statue
5. Stortorget
6. Cathedral
7. Rune Stone
8. German Church
9. Viewpoint
10. Järntorget
11. Bridge & Lock

Additional Sights
12. Nobel Museum
13. Palace Tickets (2)
14. Changing of the Guard
15. Royal Armory
16. To Museum of Medieval Stockholm

discontented nobleman, who shot Gustav in the back at a masquerade ball at the Royal Opera House in 1792 (inspiring Verdi's opera *Un Ballo in Maschera*).

Walk up the broad, cobbled boulevard alongside the palace to the crest of the hill. Stop, look back, and scan the harbor. The grand building across the water is the National Museum, which is often mistaken for the palace. Beyond that, in the distance, is the fine row of buildings on Strandvägen street. Until the 1850s, this area was home to peasant shacks, but as Stockholm entered its grand stage, it

was cleaned up and replaced by fine apartments, including some of the city's smartest addresses. A blocky gray TV tower stands tall in the distance. Turn to the palace facade on your left (finished in 1754, replacing one that burned in 1697). The niches are filled with Swedish bigwigs (literally) from the mid-18th century.

As you crest the hill, you're facing the ❷ **obelisk** that honors Stockholm's merchant class for its support in a 1788 war against Russia. In front of the obelisk are tour buses (their drivers worried about parking cops) and a pit used for *boules*. The royal family took a liking to the French game during a Mediterranean vacation, and it's quite popular around town today.

Behind the obelisk stands Storkyrkan, Stockholm's cathedral (which we'll visit later on this walk). From this angle you can see its Baroque facade, which was added to better match the newer palace. Opposite the boules court and palace is the Finnish church (Finska Kyrkan, the deep orange building), which originated as the royal tennis hall. When the Protestant Reformation hit in 1527, church services could at last be said in the peoples' languages rather than Latin. Suddenly, each merchant community needed its own church. Finns worshipped here, the Germans built their own church (coming up on this walk), and the Swedes got the cathedral.

Stroll up the lane to the right of the Finnish church into the shady churchyard, where you'll find the fist-sized ❸ *Iron Boy,* the tiniest public statue (out of about 600 statues) in Stockholm. Swedish grannies knit caps for him in the winter. Local legend says the statue honors the orphans who had to transfer cargo from sea ships to lake ships before Stockholm's locks were built. Some people rub his head for good luck (which the orphans didn't have). Others, perhaps needy when it comes to this gift, rub his head for wisdom. The artist says it's simply a self-portrait of himself as a child, sitting on his bed and gazing at the moon.

• *Exit through either of the churchyard gates, turn left onto Trädgårdsgatan, then bear right with the lane until you pop out at...*

Köpmangatan: Take a moment to explore this street from one end to the other. With its cobbles and traditional pastel facades, this is a quintessential Gamla Stan lane—and one of the oldest in town. The mellow yellow houses are predominantly from the 18th century; the reddish facades are mostly 17th century. Once merchants' homes, today these are popular with antique dealers and refined specialty shops. Back when there was comfort living within a city's walls, Gamla Stan streets like this were densely populated.

If you head left, you'll emerge on Köpmantorget square, with the breathtaking ❹ **statue of St. George** slaying the dragon, with a maiden representing Stockholm (about 10 steps to the right) looking on with thanks and admiration. If you go right, you'll reach old Stockholm's main square, our next stop.

❺ **Stortorget:** Colorful old buildings topped with gables line this square—Stockholm's oldest. In 1400, this was the heart

of medieval Stockholm (pop. 6,000). Here at the town well, many tangled lanes intersected, making it the natural center for trading. Today Stortorget is home to lots of tourists—including a steady storm of cruise groups following the numbered Ping-Pong paddle of their guides on four-hour blitz tours of the city (300 ships call here between June and September). The square also hosts concerts, occasional demonstrators, and—in winter—Christmas shoppers at an outdoor market.

The grand building on the right is the old stock exchange, now home to the noble **Nobel Museum** (described under "Sights in Stockholm"), although it may move by the time you visit. On the immediate left is the social-services agency **Stockholms Stadsmission** (offering the cheapest and best lunch around at the recommended Grillska Huset). If you peek into the adjacent bakery, you'll get a fine look at the richly decorated ceilings characteristic of Gamla Stan in the 17th century—the exotic flowers and animals implied that the people who lived or worked here were worldly. You'll also spy some tempting marzipan cakes (a local favorite) and *kanelbullar* (cinnamon buns). There's a cheap sandwich counter in the back and lots of picnic benches in the square.

The town well is still a popular meeting point. This square long held the town's pillory. Scan the fine old facades. The site of the **Stockholm Bloodbath** of 1520, this square has a notorious history. During a Danish power grab, many of Stockholm's movers and shakers who had challenged Danish rule—Swedish aristocracy, leading merchants, and priests—were rounded up, brought here, and beheaded. Rivers of blood were said to have flowed through the streets. Legend holds that the 80 or so white stones in the fine red facade across the square symbolize the victims. (One victim's son escaped, went into hiding, and resurfaced to lead a Swedish revolt against the Danish rulers. Three years later, the Swedes elected that rebel, Gustav Vasa, as their first king. He went on to usher in a great period in the country's history—the Swedish Renaissance.)

• *At the far end of the square (under the finest gables), turn right and follow Trångsund toward the cathedral.*

❻ **Cathedral** (Storkyrkan): Just before the yellow-brick church, you'll see my personal phone booth (Rikstelefon) and the gate to

the churchyard—guarded by statues of Caution and Hope. Enter the church—Stockholm's oldest, from the 13th century (60 SEK, daily 9:00-16:00). Signs explain special events, as this church is busy with tours and services in summer.

When buying your ticket, pick up the free, worthwhile English-language flier. Exploring the cathedral's interior, you'll find many styles, ranging from medieval to modern. The front of the nave is paved with centuries-old **tombstones.** The tombstone of the Swedish reformer Olaus Petri is appropriately simple and appropriately located—under the finely carved and gilded pulpit on the left side of the nave. A witness to the Stockholm Bloodbath, Petri was nearly executed himself. He went on to befriend Gustav Vasa and guide him in Lutheranizing Sweden (and turning this cathedral from Catholic to Protestant).

Opposite the pulpit, find the **bronze plaque** in the pillar. It recalls the 1925 Swedish-led ecumenical meeting of Christian leaders that encouraged all churches to renew their efforts on behalf of peace and justice, especially given the horrific toll of World War I.

Next, the best seats in the house: the carved wood **royal boxes,** dating from 1684. This has been a royal wedding church throughout the ages. It was here, in June 2010, that Crown Princess Victoria, heir to the throne, married Daniel Westling (her personal trainer) with much pomp and ceremony.

The fine 17th-century **altar** is made of silver and ebony. Above it, the silver Christ stands like a conquering general evoking the 1650s, an era of Swedish military might.

Next to the altar is a wondrous 1489 statue, carved from oak and elk horn, of **St. George** slaying the dragon (we saw a copy of it outside a few minutes ago). To some, this symbolizes the Swedes overcoming the evil Danes (commemorating a military victory in 1471). In a broader sense, it's an inspiration to take up the struggle against even non-Danish evil. Regardless, it must be the gnarliest dragon's head in all of Europe.

Return to the back of the church to find the exit. Before leaving, just to the left of the door, notice the **painting** that depicts Stockholm in the early 1500s, showing a walled city filling today's Gamla Stan. It's a 1630 copy of the 1535 original. The church, with its black spire, dominated the town back then. The strange sun and sky predicted big changes in Sweden—and as a matter of fact, that's what happened. Gustav Vasa brought on huge reforms in religion and beyond. (The doors just to the left and right of the painting lead to a free WC.)

Heading outside, you'll emerge into the kid-friendly churchyard, which was once the cemetery.

• *With your back to the church's front door, go right. At the next corner, turn left (on Storkyrkobrinken), then left again on...*

Prästgatan: Enjoy a quiet wander down this peaceful 15th-century "Priests' Lane." Västerlånggatan, the touristy drag, parallels this lane one block over. (While we'll skip it now, you can walk back up it from the end point of this walk.) As you stroll Prästgatan, look for bits of its past: hoists poking out horizontally from gables (merchants used these to lift goods into their attics), tie bolts (iron bars necessary to bind the timber beams of tall buildings together), small coal or wood hatches (for fuel delivery back in the good old days), and flaming gold phoenixes under red-crown medallions (telling firefighters which houses paid insurance and could be saved in case of fire—for example, #46). Like other Scandinavian citics, Stockholm was plagued by fire until it was finally decreed that only stone, stucco, and brick construction (like you see here) would be allowed in the town center.

After a few blocks (at Kåkbrinken), a cannon barrel on the corner (look down) guards a Viking-age ❼ **rune stone.** In case you can't read the old Nordic script, it says: "Torsten and Frogun erected this stone in memory of their son."

· *Continue one block further down Prästgatan to Tyska Brinken and turn left. Look up to see the powerful brick steeple of the...*

❽ **German Church** (Tyska Kyrkan): The church's carillon has played four times a day since 1666. Think of the days when German merchants worked here. Today, Germans come to Sweden not to run the economy, but to enjoy its pristine nature (which is progressively harder to find in their own crowded homeland). Sweden formally became a Lutheran country even before the northern part of Germany—making this the very first German Lutheran church (free to enter).

· *Wander through the churchyard (past a cute church café) and out the back. Exit right onto Svartmangatan and follow it to the right, ending at an iron railing overlooking Österlånggatan.*

❾ **Viewpoint:** From this perch, survey the street below to the left and right. Notice how it curves. This marks the old shoreline. In medieval times, piers stretched out like fingers into the harbor. Gradually, as land was reclaimed and developed, these piers were extended, becoming lanes leading to piers farther away. Behind you is a cute shop where elves can actually be seen making elves.

· *Walk right to Österlånggatan, and continue on to...*

❿ **Järntorget:** A customs square in medieval times, this was the home of Sweden's first bank back in 1680 (the yellow building with the bars on the windows). The Co-op Nära supermarket on this square offers picnic fixings. From here, Västerlånggatan—the eating, shopping, and commercial pedestrian mall of Gamla Stan—leads back across the island. You'll be there in a minute, but first finish this walk.

· *Continue from the square (opposite where you entered) down Järntorgsgatan until you emerge (suddenly) into traffic hell. For now, things are a bit of a mess because of an enormous redevelopment project that will eventually turn this area into a green people-zone. Let's continue ahead, crossing over the busy street to reach a viewpoint window (cut into the construction wall that lines the bridge).*

⓫ **Bridge Overlooking Slussen:** This area is called Slussen, named for the locks between the salt water of the Baltic Sea (to your left) and the fresh water of the huge **Lake Mälaren** (to your right). In fact, Stockholm exists because this is where Lake Mälaren meets the sea. Traders would sail their goods from far inland to this point, where they'd meet merchants who would ship the goods south to Europe. In the 13th century, the new kingdom of Sweden needed revenue, and began levying duty taxes on all the iron, copper, and furs shipped through here.

From the bridge, you may notice a current in the water, indicating that the weir has been lowered and water is spilling from Lake Mälaren (about two feet above sea level) into the sea. Today, the locks are nicknamed "the divorce lock" because this is where captains and first mates learn to communicate under pressure and in the public eye.

Opposite Gamla Stan is the island of **Södermalm**—bohemian, youthful, artsy, and casual—with its popular Katarina viewing platform (see "Stockholm's Best Views" sidebar, later). Moored on the saltwater side are cruise ships, which bring thousands of visitors into town each day during the season. Many of these boats are bound for Finland. The towering white syringe is the Gröna Lund amusement park's free-fall ride. The revolving *Djurgården Färjan* sign, along the embankment to your left, marks the ferry that zips from here directly to Gröna Lund and Djurgården.

• *Our walk is finished, but feel free to linger longer in Gamla Stan— day or night, it's a lively place to enjoy.* **Västerlånggatan,** *Gamla Stan's main commercial drag, is a touristy festival of distractions that keeps most visitors from seeing the historic charms of the Old Town—which you just did. Now you're free to window-shop and eat (see "Shopping in Stockholm" and "Eating in Stockholm," later). Or, if it's late, find some live music (see "Nightlife and Entertainment in Stockholm").*

For more sightseeing, consider the other sights in **Gamla Stan** *or at the* **Royal Palace** *(all described under "Sights in Stockholm"). Or backtrack to Västerlånggatan (always going straight), to reach the parliament building and cross the water back over onto Norrmalm (where the street becomes Drottninggatan). This pedestrian street leads back into Stockholm's modern town.*

Yet another option is to walk 15 minutes to **Kungsträdgården,** *the starting point of my "Stockholm's Modern City" self-guided walk. Either walk along the embankment and take the diagonal bridge directly across to the square, or walk back through the middle of Gamla Stan, take the stately walkway past the Swedish Parliament building, then turn right when you cross the bridge.*

STOCKHOLM'S MODERN CITY WALK

On this walk, we'll use the park called Kungsträdgården as a springboard to explore the modern center of Stockholm—a commercial zone that puts the focus not on old kings and mementos of

Fika: Sweden's Coffee Break

Swedes drink more coffee per capita than just about any other country in the world. The Swedish coffee break—or *fika*—is a ritual. *Fika* is to Sweden what teatime is to Britain. The typical *fika* is a morning or afternoon break in the workday, but can happen any time, any day. It's the perfect opportunity (and excuse) for tourists to take a break as well.

Fika fare is coffee with a snack—something sweet or savory. Your best bet is a *kanelbulle,* a Swedish cinnamon bun, although some prefer *parserbulle,* a bun filled with vanilla cream. These can be found nearly everywhere coffee is sold, including just about any café or *konditori* (bakery) in Stockholm. A coffee and a cinnamon bun in a café will cost you about 40 SEK. (Most cafés will give you a coffee refill for free.) But at Pressbyrån, the Swedish convenience stores found all over town, you can satisfy your *fika* fix for 25 SEK by getting a coffee and bun to go. Grab a park bench or waterside perch, relax, and enjoy.

superpower days, but on shopping. For the route, see the "Stockholm" map.

• *Find the statue of King Karl XII, facing the waterfront at the harbor end of the park.*

Kungsträdgården: Centuries ago, this "King's Garden" was the private kitchen garden of the king, where he grew his cabbage

salad. Today, this downtown people-watching center, worth ▲, is considered Stockholm's living room, symbolizing the Swedes' freedom-loving spirit. While the name implies that the garden is a private royal domain, the giant clump of elm trees just behind the statue reminds locals that it's the people who rule now. In the 1970s, demonstrators chained themselves to these trees to stop the building of an underground train station here. They prevailed, and today, locals enjoy the peaceful, breezy ambience of a teahouse instead.

Farther on, watch for the AstroTurf zone with "latte dads" and their kids, and enjoy a summer concert at the bandstand. There's always something going on. High above is a handy reference point—the revolving NK clock.

Kungsträdgården—surrounded by the harborfront and tour boats, the Royal Opera House, and shopping opportunities (including a welcoming Volvo showroom near the top-left side of the square, showing off the latest in Swedish car design)—is *the* place to feel Stockholm's pulse (but always ask first: *"Kan jag kanna på din puls?"*).

The garden also plays host to huge parties. The Taste of Stockholm festival runs for a week in early June, when restaurateurs show off and bands entertain all day. Beer flows liberally—a rare public spectacle in Sweden.

• *Stroll through Kungsträdgården, past the fountain and the Volvo store, and up to Hamngatan street. From here, we'll turn left and walk the length of the NK department store (across the street) as we wade through...*

Stockholm's Urban Shopping Zone (Hamngatan): In just a couple of blocks, we'll pass some major landmarks of Swedish consumerism. First, anchoring the corner at the top of Kungsträdgården, is the gigantic **Illums Bolighus** design shop. (You can enter from the square and stroll all the way through it, popping out at Hamngatan on the far end.) This is a Danish institution, making its play for Swedish customers with this prime location. Across the street, notice the giant gold *NK* marking the **Nordiska Kompaniet** department store (locals joke that the NK stands for "no kronor left"). It's located in an elegant early-20th-century building that dominates the top end of Kungsträdgården. If it feels like an old-time American department store, that's because its architect was inspired by grand stores he'd seen in the US (circa 1910).

Another block down, on the left, is the sleeker, more modern **Gallerian mall.** Among this two-story world of shops, upstairs you'll find a Clas Ohlson hardware and electronics shop (most Stockholmers have a cabin that's always in need of a little DIY repair). And there are plenty of affordable little lunch bars and classy cafés for your *fika* (Swedish coffee-and-bun break). You may notice that American influence (frozen yogurt and other trendy food chains) is challenging the notion of the traditional *fika*.

• *High-end shoppers should consider heading into the streets behind NK, with exclusive designer boutiques and the chichi Mood Stockholm mall (see "Shopping in Stockholm," later). Otherwise, just beyond the huge Gallerian mall, you'll emerge into Sergels Torg. (Note that the handy tram #7 goes from here directly to Skansen and the other important sights on Djurgården; departures every few minutes.)*

Sergels Torg and Kulturhuset: Sergels Torg square, worth ▲, dominates the heart of modern Stockholm with its stark 1960s-era functionalist architecture. The glassy tower in the middle of the fountain plaza is ugly in daylight but glows at night, symbolic of Sweden's haunting northern lights.

Kulturhuset, the hulking, low-slung, glassy building overlooking the square, is Stockholm's "culture center"—a public space for everyone in Stockholm. In this lively cultural zone, there are libraries, theater, a space for kids, chessboards, fun shops, fine art cinema, art exhibits, and a music venue (tel. 08/5062-0200, http://kulturhusetstadsteatern.se).

I like to take the elevator to the top of the Kulturhuset and explore each level by riding the escalator back down to the ground floor. On the rooftop, the recommended Cafeteria Panorama has cheap meals and a salad bar with terrific city views.

Back at ground level outside, stand in front of the Kulturhuset (across from the fountain) and survey the expansive square nick-named "Plattan" (the platter). Everything around you dates from the 1960s and 1970s, when this formerly run-down area was re-invented as an urban "space of the future." In the 1970s, with no nearby residences, the desolate Plattan became the domain of junk-ies. Now the city is actively revitalizing it, and the Plattan is be-coming a people-friendly heart of the commercial town.

DesignTorget (enter from the lower level of Kulturhuset) showcases practical items for everyday use from established and emerging designers. Nearby are the major boutiques and depart-ment stores, including, across the way, H&M and Åhléns.

Sergelgatan, a thriving pedestrian and commercial street, leads past the five uniform white towers you see beyond the foun-tain. These office towers, so modern in the 1960s, have gone from seeming hopelessly out-of-date to being considered "retro," and are now quite popular with young professionals.

• *Walk up Sergelgatan past the towers, enjoying the public art and peo-ple-watching, to the market at Hötorget.*

Hötorget: "Hötorget" means "Hay Market," but today its stalls feed people rather than horses. The adjacent indoor market,

Hötorgshallen, is fun and fragrant. It dates from 1914 when, for hygienic reasons, the city forbade selling fish and meat outdoors. Carl Milles' statue of *Orpheus Emerging from the Underworld* (with seven sad Muses) stands in front of the city concert hall (which hosts the annual Nobel Prize award ceremony). The concert house, from 1926, is Swedish Art Deco (a.k.a. "Swedish Grace"). The lobby (open through much of the summer) still evokes Stockholm's

Roaring Twenties. If the door's open, you're welcome to look in for free.

Popping into the Hötorget T-bana station provides a fun glimpse at local urban design. Stockholm's subway system was inaugurated in the 1950s, and many stations are modern art installations in themselves.

• *Our walk ends here. For more shopping and an enjoyable pedestrian boulevard leading back into the Old Town, cut down a block to Drottninggatan and turn left. This busy drag leads straight out of the commercial district, passes the parliament, then becomes the main street of Gamla Stan.*

Sights in Stockholm

GAMLA STAN (OLD TOWN)

The best of this island is covered in my "Gamla Stan" self-guided walk, earlier. But here are a few ways to extend your time in the Old Town.

On Stortorget
▲Nobel Museum (Nobelmuseet)

Opened in 2001 for the 100-year anniversary of the Nobel Prize, this wonderful little museum tells the story of the world's most prestigious prize. Pricey but high-tech and eloquent, it fills the grand old stock exchange building that dominates Gamla Stan's main square, Stortorget. By the time you visit, the museum may have relocated to a new building on Blasieholmen—inquire locally.

Cost and Hours: 120 SEK, free Tue after 17:00; daily 9:00-20:00; Sept-May Tue-Fri 11:00-17:00, Tue until 20:00, Sat-Sun 10:00-18:00, closed Mon; audioguide-20 SEK, free 40-minute orientation tours in English—check website for times, tel. 08/5348-1800, www.nobelmuseum.se.

Background: Stockholm-born Alfred Nobel was a great inventor, with more than 300 patents. His most famous invention: dynamite. Living in the late 1800s, Nobel was a man of his age. It was a time of great optimism, wild ideas, and grand projects. His dynamite enabled entire nations to blast their way into the modern age with canals, railroads, and tunnels. It made warfare much more destructive. And it also made Alfred Nobel a very wealthy man. Wanting to leave a legacy that celebrated and supported people with great ideas, Alfred used his fortune to fund the Nobel Prize. Every year since 1901, laureates have been honored in the fields of physics, chemistry, medicine, literature, economic sciences, and peacemaking.

Visiting the Museum: Inside, portraits of all 700-plus prize-winners hang from the ceiling—shuffling around the room like shirts at the dry cleaner's (miss your favorite, and he or she will come around again in six hours). Behind the ticket desk are monitors that represent the six Nobel Prize categories, each honoring the most recent laureate in that category.

Flanking the main hall beyond that—where touchscreens organized by decade invite you to learn more about the laureates of your choice—two rooms run a continuous video montage of quick programs (on one side, films celebrating the creative milieus that encouraged Nobel laureates past and present; on the other side, short films about their various paths to success).

To the right of the ticket desk, find "The Gallery," with a surprisingly captivating collection of items that various laureates have cited as important to their creative process, from scientific equipment to inspirational knickknacks. The randomness of the items offers a fascinating and humanizing insight into the great minds of our time.

The Viennese-style Bistro Nobel is the place to get creative with your coffee...and sample the famous Nobel ice cream. All Nobel laureates who visit the museum are asked to sign the bottom of a chair in the café. Turn yours over and see who warmed your chair. And don't miss the lockable hangers, to protect your fancy, furry winter coat. The Swedish Academy, which awards the Nobel Prize for literature each year, is upstairs.

Royal Palace Complex (Kungliga Slottet)

Although the royal family beds down at Drottningholm (see next chapter), this complex in Gamla Stan is still the official royal residence. The palace, designed in Italian Baroque style, was completed in 1754 after a fire wiped out the previous palace—a much more characteristic medieval/Renaissance complex. This blocky Baroque replacement, which houses various museums, is big and (frankly) pretty dull. See the "Gamla Stan Walk" map to sort out the various entrances.

Planning Your Time: Visiting the several sights in and near the palace could fill a day, but Stockholm has far better attractions elsewhere. Prioritize.

Visitors in a rush should see the Changing of the Guard, enter the (free) Royal Armory—if it's open when you visit, and skip the rest. Information booths in the semicircular courtyard (at the top, where the guard changes) and just inside the east entry give out a

Stockholm at a Glance

▲▲▲Skansen Europe's first and best open-air folk museum, with more than 150 old homes, churches, shops, and schools. **Hours:** Park-opens daily at 10:00, closes at 22:00 late June-Aug and progressively earlier the rest of the year; historical buildings-generally 11:00-17:00, late June-Aug some until 19:00, most closed in winter. See page 462.

▲▲▲Vasa Museum Ill-fated 17th-century warship dredged from the sea floor, now the showpiece of an interesting museum. **Hours:** Daily 8:30-18:00; Sept-May 10:00-17:00 except Wed until 20:00. See page 464.

▲▲Military Parade and Changing of the Guard Punchy pomp starting near Nybroplan and finishing at Royal Palace outer courtyard. **Hours:** Late April-Aug daily, Sept-late April Wed and Sat-Sun only, start time varies with season but always at midday. See page 450.

▲▲Royal Armory A fine collection of ceremonial medieval royal armor, historic and modern royal garments, and carriages, in the Royal Palace (most of museum may be closed for renovation when you visit). **Hours:** Daily May-June 11:00-17:00, July-Aug 10:00-18:00; Sept-April Tue-Sun 11:00-17:00, Thu until 20:00, closed Mon. See page 451.

▲▲City Hall Gilt mosaic architectural jewel of Stockholm and site of Nobel Prize banquet, with tower offering the city's best views. **Hours:** Required tours daily generally June-Aug every 30 minutes 9:30-15:30, fewer off-season. See page 454.

▲▲Swedish History Museum Collection of artifacts spanning Sweden's entire history, highlighted by fascinating Viking exhibit and Gold Room. **Hours:** Daily 10:00-17:00; Sept-May closed Mon and open Wed until 20:00. See page 458.

▲Nordic Museum Danish Renaissance palace design and five fascinating centuries of traditional Swedish lifestyles. **Hours:** Daily 9:00-18:00; Sept-May 10:00-17:00 except Wed until 20:00. See page 466.

list of the day's guided tours and an explanatory brochure/map that marks the entrances to the different sights. The main entrance to the Royal Palace (including the apartments, chapel, and treasury) faces the long, angled square and obelisk (but you can cut through the palace's interior courtyard to get there).

The Royal Palace ticket includes four museums. Of these, the

▲**Nobel Museum** Star-studded tribute to some of the world's most accomplished scientists, artists, economists, and politicians. **Hours:** Daily 9:00-20:00; Sept-May Tue-Fri 11:00-17:00, Tue until 20:00, Sat-Sun 10:00-18:00, closed Mon. See page 446.

▲**Royal Palace Museums** Complex of Swedish royal museums, the two best of which are the Royal Apartments and Royal Treasury. **Hours:** Daily 10:00-17:00, July-Aug from 9:00; Oct-April until 16:00 and closed Mon. See page 451.

▲**Kungsträdgården** Stockholm's lively central square, with life-size chess games, concerts, and perpetual action. See page 442.

▲**Sergels Torg** Modern square with underground mall. See page 444.

▲**ABBA: The Museum** A super-commercial and wildly-popular-with-ABBA-fans experience. **Hours:** Daily 9:00-19:00; Sept-May daily 10:00-18:00 except Wed until 19:00. See page 468.

▲**Thielska Galleriet** Enchanting waterside mansion with works of Scandinavian artists Larsson, Zorn, and Munch. **Hours:** Tue-Sun 12:00-17:00, closed Mon. See page 470.

▲**Fotografiska** Fun photography museum focusing on contemporary and international work, with eye-popping views from its top-floor café. **Hours:** Daily 9:00-23:00, later on weekends. See page 471.

▲**Millesgården** Dramatic cliffside museum and grounds featuring works of Sweden's greatest sculptor, Carl Milles. **Hours:** Daily 11:00-17:00 except closed Mon Oct-April. See page 472.

▲**Museum of Medieval Stockholm** Underground museum shows off parts of town wall King Gustav Vasa built in 1530s. **Hours:** Tue-Sun 12:00-17:00, Wed until 19:00, closed Mon. See page 453.

Royal Apartments are not much as far as palace rooms go but still worthwhile; the Royal Treasury is worth a look; the Museum of Three Crowns gets you down into the medieval cellars to learn about the more interesting earlier castle; and Gustav III's Museum of Antiquities is skippable. The chapel is nice enough (and it's free to enter).

Tours: In peak season, the main Royal Palace offers a full slate of English tours covering the different sights (included in admission)—allowing you to systematically cover nearly the entire complex. If you're paying the hefty price for a ticket, you might as well join at least one of the tours—otherwise, you'll struggle to appreciate the place. Some tours are infrequent, so be sure to confirm times when you purchase your admission (for more on tours, see the individual listings below).

Expect Changes: Since the palace is used for state functions, it's sometimes closed to tourists. And, as the exterior is undergoing a 20-year renovation, don't be surprised if parts are covered in scaffolding. Most of the Royal Armory is closed for renovation, while the Royal Coin Cabinet has closed and will reopen in a new location in Östermalm in a few years.

▲▲Military Parade and Changing of the Guard

Starting from the Army Museum (two blocks from Nybroplan at Riddargatan 13), Stockholm's daily military parade marches

over Norrbro bridge, in front of the parliament building, and up to the Royal Palace's outer courtyard, where the band plays and the guard changes. Smaller contingents of guards spiral in from other parts of the palace complex, eventually convening in the same place.

The performance is fresh and spirited, because the soldiers are visiting Stockholm just like you—and it's a chance for young soldiers from all over Sweden in every branch of the service to show their stuff in the big city. Pick your place at the palace courtyard, where the band arrives at about 12:15 (13:15 on Sun). The best spot to stand is along the wall in the inner courtyard, near the palace information and ticket office. There are columns with wide pedestals for easy perching, as well as benches that people stand on to view the ceremony (arrive early). Generally, after the barking and goose-stepping formalities, the band shows off for an impressive 30-minute marching concert.

Marching Band and Parade: Departs from Army Museum late April-Aug Mon-Sat at 11:45, Sun at 12:45 (11:35 and 12:35, respectively, if departing from Cavalry Barracks); Sept-Oct Wed and Sat at 11:45,

Sun at 12:45; off-season departs from Mynttorget Wed and Sat at 12:09, Sun at 13:09. Royal appointments can disrupt the schedule; confirm times at TI. In summer, you might also catch the mounted guards (they don't appear on a regular schedule).

Royal Guards Ceremony at the Palace: Mon-Sat at 12:15, Sun at 13:15, about 40 minutes, in front of the Royal Palace. You can get details at www.forsvarsmakten.se (click on "Activities").

▲▲Royal Armory (Livrustkammaren)

The oldest museum in Sweden is both more and less than an armory. Rather than dusty piles of swords and muskets, it focuses on royal clothing: impressive ceremonial armor (never used in battle) and other fashion through the ages (including a room of kidswear), plus a fine collection of coaches. It's an engaging slice of royal life. Everything is displayed under sturdy brick vaults, beautifully lit, and well-described in English and by a good audioguide. The museum has undertaken a major renovation that closed the main exhibit halls, but the lower level, with a good display of royal coaches, remains open.

Cost and Hours: Free; daily May-June 11:00-17:00, July-Aug 10:00-18:00; Sept-April Tue-Sun 11:00-17:00, Thu until 20:00, closed Mon; audioguide-40 SEK, information sheets in English available in most rooms; entrance at bottom of Slottsbacken at base of palace, tel. 08/402-3010, www.livrustkammaren.se.

▲Royal Palace

The Royal Palace consists of a chapel (free) and four museums. Compared to many grand European palaces, it's underwhelming and flooded with cruise-excursion groups who don't realize that Stockholm's best sightseeing is elsewhere.

Cost and Hours: 160-SEK combo-ticket covers all four museums, includes guided tours; daily 10:00-17:00, July-Aug from 9:00; Oct-April until 16:00 and closed Mon; tel. 08/402-6130, www.royalcourt.se.

Orientation: I've listed the museums in order of sightseeing worthiness. But if you want to see them all with minimal backtracking, follow this plan: Begin at the entrance on Slottsbacken. Head up to the chapel for a peek, then descend to the treasury. Tour the Royal Apartments, exiting at the far side of the building—where you can head straight into the Museum of Three Crowns. Exiting there, you'll find the final sight (Museum of Antiquities) to your right.

Royal Apartments: The stately palace exterior encloses 608 rooms (one more than Britain's Buckingham Palace) of glittering 18th-century Baroque and Rococo decor. Guided 45-minute tours in English run twice daily (at 10:30 and 13:30).

Clearly the palace of Scandinavia's superpower, it's steeped in royal history. You'll enter the grand main hall (cheapskates can get a free look at this first room before reaching the ticket checkpoint), then walk the long halls through four sections. On the main level are the Hall of State (with an exhibit of fancy state awards) and the lavish Bernadotte Apartments (some fine Rococo interiors and portraits of the Bernadotte dynasty); upstairs you'll find the State Apartments (with rooms dating to the 1690s—darker halls, faded tapestries, and a wannabe hall of mirrors) and the Guest Apartments (with less lavish quarters, where visiting heads of state still crash).

Royal Treasury (Skattkammaren): Refreshingly compact compared to the sprawling apartments, the treasury gives you a good, up-close look at Sweden's crown jewels. It's particularly worthwhile with an English guided tour (daily at 11:30) or the included audioguide (which covers basically the same information).

Climbing down into the super-secure vault, you'll see 12 cases filled with fancy crowns, scepters, jeweled robes, the silver baptismal font of Karl XI, and plenty of glittering gold. The first room holds the crowns of princes and princesses, while the second shows off the more serious regalia of kings and queens. For more than a century, these crowns have gone unworn: The last Swedish coronation was Oskar II's in 1873; in 1907 his son and successor—out of deference for the constitution (and living in a Europe that was deep in the throes of modernism)—declined to wear the crown, so he was "enthroned" rather than "coronated." The crowns still belong to the monarchs and are present in the room on special occasions—but they are symbols rather than accessories.

Museum of Three Crowns (Museum Tre Kronor): This museum shows off bits of the palace from before a devastating 1697 fire (guided tours in English offered at 11:30). The models, illustrations, and artifacts are displayed in vaulted medieval cellars that are far more evocative than the run-of-the-mill interior of today's palace. But while the stroll through the cellars is atmospheric, it's basically just more old stuff, interesting only to real history buffs.

Royal Chapel: If you don't want to spring for a ticket, but would like a little taste of palace opulence, climb the stairs inside the main entrance for a peek into the chapel. It's standard-issue royal Baroque: colorful ceiling painting, bubbly altars, and a giant organ.

Gustav III's Museum of Antiquities (Gustav III's Antikmuseum): In the 1700s, Gustav III traveled through Italy and brought home an impressive gallery of classical Roman statues. These are displayed exactly as they were in the 1790s. This was a huge deal for those who had never been out of Sweden.

▲Royal Coin Cabinet (Kungliga Myntkabinettet)

More than your typical royal coin collection, this is the best money museum I've seen in Europe. But it's being relocated (to a space at the Swedish History Museum), and won't be displaying its coins and banknotes again for a few years. For the latest, consult the museum website (www.myntkabinettet.se).

More Gamla Stan Sights

These first two sights sit on the Gamla Stan islet of Helgeandsholmen (just north of the Royal Palace), which is dominated by the Swedish Parliament building. Also at the edge of Gamla Stan is the stately island of Riddarholmen.

Parliament (Riksdag)

For a firsthand look at Sweden's government, tour the parliament buildings. Guides enjoy a chance to teach a little Swedish poli-sci along the standard tour of the building and its art. It's also possible to watch the parliament in session.

Cost and Hours: Free one-hour tours go in English late June-mid-Aug, usually 4/day Mon-Fri (when parliament is not in session). The rest of the year tours run 1/day Sat-Sun only; you're also welcome to join Swedish citizens in the viewing gallery (free); enter at Riksgatan 3a, call 08/786-4862 from 9:00 to 11:00 to confirm tour times, www.riksdagen.se.

▲Museum of Medieval Stockholm (Medeltidsmuseet)

This modern, well-presented museum offers a look at medieval Stockholm. When the government was digging a parking garage near the parliament building in the 1970s, workers uncovered a major archaeological find: parts of the town wall that King Gustav Vasa built in the 1530s, as well as a churchyard. This underground museum preserves these discoveries and explains how Stockholm grew from a medieval village to a major city, with a focus on its interactions with fellow Hanseatic League trading cities. Lots of artifacts, models, life-size dioramas, and sound and lighting effects—all displayed in a vast subterranean space—help bring the story to life.

The museum does a particularly good job of profiling individuals who lived in medieval Stockholm; their personal stories vividly set the context of the history. You'll also see the preserved remains of a small cannon-ship from the 1520s and a reconstructed main market square from 13th-century Stockholm.

Cost and Hours: Free, Tue-Sun 12:00-17:00, Wed until 19:00, closed Mon, free English guided tours July-Aug Tue-Sun at 14:00, audioguide-20 SEK, enter museum from park in front of parliament—down below as you cross the bridge, tel. 08/5083-1790, www.medeltidsmuseet.stockholm.se.

Nearby: The museum sits in **Strömparterren** park. With its café and Carl Milles statue of the *Sun Singer* greeting the day, it's a pleasant place for a sightseeing break (pay WC in park, free WC in museum).

Riddarholmen

Literally the "Knights Isle," Riddarholmen is the quiet and stately far side of Gamla Stan, with a historic church, private palaces, and

a famous view. The knights referred to in its name were the nobles who built their palaces on this little island to be near the Royal Palace, just across the way. The island, cut off from the rest of Gamla Stan by a noisy highway, is pretty lifeless, with impersonal government agencies filling its old mansions. Still, a visit is worthwhile for a peek at its church and to enjoy the famous view of City Hall and Lake Mälaren from its far end.

A statue of Birger Jarl (considered the man who founded Stockholm in 1252) marks the main square. Surrounding it are 17th-century private palaces of old noble families (now government buildings). And towering high above is the spire of the Riddarholmen Church. Established in the 13th century as a Franciscan church, this has been the burial place of nearly every Swedish royal since the early 1600s. If you're looking for a Swedish Westminster Abbey, this is it (50 SEK, daily 10:00-17:00, Oct-Nov until 16:00). An inviting, shady café at the far end of the island is where people (and photographers) gather for Riddarholmen's iconic Stockholm view.

DOWNTOWN STOCKHOLM

I've organized these sights and activities in the urban core of Stockholm by island and/or neighborhood.

On Kungsholmen, West of Norrmalm
▲▲City Hall (Stadshuset)

The Stadshuset is an impressive mix of eight million red bricks, 19 million chips of gilt mosaic, and lots of Stockholm pride. While churches dominate cities in southern Europe, in Scandinavian capitals, City Halls seem to be the most impressive buildings, celebrating humanism and the ideal of people working together in community. Built in 1923, this is still a functioning City Hall. The members of the city council—101 men and women representing the 850,000 citizens of Stockholm—are hobby legislators with

regular day jobs. That's why they meet in the evening once a week. One of Europe's finest public buildings, the site of the annual Nobel Prize banquet, and a favorite spot for weddings (they do two per hour on Saturday afternoons, when some parts of the complex may be closed), City Hall is particularly enjoyable and worthwhile for its entertaining and required 50-minute tour.

Cost and Hours: 110 SEK; English tours offered daily, generally June-Aug every 30 minutes 9:30-15:30, fewer off-season; schedule can change due to special events—call to confirm; 300 yards behind the central train station—about a 15-minute walk from either the station or Gamla Stan, bus #3 or #50, cafeteria open to public at lunch Mon-Fri; tel. 08/5082-9058, www.stockholm.se/stadshuset.

Visiting City Hall: On the tour, you'll see the building's sumptuous National Romantic-style interior (similar to Britain's Arts and Crafts style), celebrating Swedish architecture and craftwork, and created almost entirely with Swedish materials. Highlights include the so-called Blue Hall (the Italian piazza-inspired, brick-lined courtyard that was originally intended to be painted blue—hence the name—where the 1,300-plate Nobel banquet takes place); the City Council Chamber (with a gorgeously painted wood-beamed ceiling that resembles a Viking longhouse—or maybe an overturned Viking boat); the Gallery of the Prince (lined with frescoes executed by Prince Eugene of Sweden); and the glittering, gilded, Neo-Byzantine-style (and aptly named) Golden Hall, where the Nobel recipients cut a rug after the banquet.

In this over-the-top space, a glimmering mosaic Queen of Lake Mälaren oversees the proceedings with a welcoming but watchful

eye, as East (see Istanbul's Hagia Sophia and the elephant, on the right) and West (notice the Eiffel Tower, Statue of Liberty, and skyscrapers with the American flag, on the left) meet here in Stockholm. Above the door across the hall is Sweden's patron saint, Erik, who seems to have lost his head (due to some sloppy mosaic planning). On the tour, you'll find out exactly how many centimeters each Nobel banquet attendee gets at the table, why the building's plans were altered at the last minute to make the tower exactly one meter taller, where the prince got the inspiration for his scenic frescoes, and how the Swedes reacted when they first saw that Golden Hall (hint: they weren't pleased).

▲City Hall Tower

This 348-foot-tall tower rewards those who make the climb with the classic Stockholm view: The old church spires on the atmospheric islands of Gamla Stan pose together, with the rest of the green and watery city spread-eagle around them.

Cost and Hours: 50 SEK, daily 9:15-17:15, May and Sept until 15:55, closed Oct-April.

Crowd-Beating Tips: Only 30 people at a time are allowed up into the tower, every 40 minutes throughout the day. To ascend, you'll need a timed-entry ticket, available only in person at the tower ticket office on the same day. It can be a long wait for the next available time, and tickets can sell out by mid-afternoon. If you're touring City Hall, come to the tower ticket window first to see when space is available. Ideally an appointment will coincide with the end of your tour.

Visiting the Tower: A total of 365 steps lead to the top of the tower, but you can ride an elevator partway up—leaving you only 159 easy steps to the top.

First you'll climb up through the brick structure, emerging at an atmospheric hall filled with models of busts and statues that adorn City Hall and a huge, 25-foot-tall statue of St. Erik. The patron saint of Stockholm, Erik was supposed to be hoisted by cranes up through the middle of the tower to stand at its top. But plans changed, big Erik is forever parked halfway up the structure, and the tower's top is open for visitors to gather and enjoy the view.

From Erik, you'll twist gradually up ramps and a few steps at a time through the narrow, labyrinthine brick halls with peek-a-boo views of the city. Finally you'll emerge into the wooden section of the tower, where a spiral staircase brings you up to the roof terrace. Enjoy the view from there, but also take some time to look around at the building's features. Smaller statues of Erik, Klara, Maria Magdalena, and Nikolaus, all patron saints, face their respective parishes. Look up: You're in the company of the tower's nine bells. And if you listen carefully, you might hear departure-hall announcements wafting all the way up from the central train station.

▲National Museum of Fine Arts (Nationalmuseum)

Though mediocre by European standards, this 200-year-old museum is small, central, and user-friendly. An extensive renovation may cause it to be closed when you visit—check ahead. Highlights include several canvases by Rembrandt and Rubens, a fine group of Impressionist works, and a sizeable collection of Russian icons. Seek out the exquisite paintings by the Swedish artists Anders Zorn, Ernst Josephson, and Carl Larsson. An excellent audioguide describes the top works.

Cost and Hours: 100 SEK, can be more with special exhibits, audioguide-30 SEK; museum may be closed for renovation, confirm times on website; likely Wed-Sun 11:00-17:00, until later Tue and Thu, closed Mon; Södra Blasieholmshamnen, T-bana: Kungsträdgården, tel. 08/5195-4310, www.nationalmuseum.se.

Museum Highlights: The Stockholm-born **Carl Larsson** (1853-1919) became very popular as the Swedish Norman Rockwell, chronicling the everyday family life of his own wife and brood of kids. His two vast, 900-square-foot murals celebrate Swedish history and are worth a close look. *The Return of the King* shows Gustav Vasa astride a white horse. After escaping the Stockholm Bloodbath and leading Sweden's revolt, he drove out the Danes and was elected Sweden's first king (1523). Now he marches his victorious troops across a drawbridge, as Stockholm's burghers bow and welcome him home. In *The Midwinter Sacrifice*, it's solstice eve, and Vikings are gathered at the pagan temple at Gamla Uppsala. Musicians blow the *lur* horns, a priest in white raises the ceremonial hammer of Thor, and another priest in red (with his back to us) holds a sacrificial knife. The Viking king arrives on his golden sled, rises from his throne, strips naked, gazes to the heavens, and prepares to sacrifice himself to the gods of winter, so that spring will return to feed his starving people.

The museum also dedicates space to **design**, spanning the 1500s up to present day. Of the more recent examples, the collection includes gracefully engraved glass from the 1920s, works from the Stockholm Exhibition of 1930, industrial design of the 1940s, Scandinavian Design movement of the 1950s, plastic chairs from the 1960s, modern furniture from the 1980s, and the Swedish new simplicity from the 1990s.

On Blasieholmen and Skeppsholmen

The peninsula of Blasieholmen pokes out from downtown Stockholm, and is tethered to the island of Skeppsholmen by a narrow bridge (with great views and adorned with glittering golden crowns). While not connected to the city by T-bana or tram, you can reach this area on bus #65 or the harbor shuttle ferry. Skeppsholmen offers a peaceful break from the bustling city, with glorious views of Gamla Stan on one side and Djurgården on the other.

Museum of Modern Art (Moderna Museet)

This bright, cheery gallery on Skeppsholmen island is as far out as can be. For serious art lovers, it warrants ▲▲. The impressive permanent collection includes modernist all-stars such as Picasso, Braque, Dalí, Matisse, Munch, Kokoschka, and Dix; lots of goofy Dada art (including a copy of Duchamp's urinal); Pollock, Twombly, Bacon, and other postmodernists; and plenty of excellent contemporary stuff as well (don't miss the beloved Rauschenberg *Goat with Tire*). Swedish artists of the 20th and 21st centuries are also featured. The curators draw from this  substantial well of masterpieces to assemble changing exhibits.

The museum's fine collection of modern and contemporary sculpture is installed on the leafy grounds of Skeppsholmen island—perfect for a stroll even when the museum is closed. The building also houses the Architecture and Design Center, with changing exhibits (www.arkdes.se).

Cost and Hours: Free but sometimes a fee for special exhibits; download the excellent, free audioguide to enhance your visit; open Tue and Fri 10:00-20:00, Wed-Thu and Sat-Sun until 18:00, closed Mon; fine bookstore, good shop, and harborview café; T-bana: Kungsträdgården plus 10-minute walk, or take bus #65; tel. 08/5202-3500, www.modernamuseet.se.

Östermalm

What this ritzy residential area lacks in museums or sights, it makes up for in posh style. Explore its stately streets, dine in its destination restaurants, and be sure to explore the delightful, upscale Saluhall food market right on Östermalmstorg (see "Eating in Stockholm," later). Östermalm's harborfront is hemmed in by the pleasant park called Nybroplan; from here, ferries lead to various parts of the city and beyond (as this is the jumping-off point for cruises into Stockholm's archipelago). If connecting to the sights in Djurgården, consider doing Östermalm by foot.

▲▲Swedish History Museum (Historiska Museet)

The displays and artifacts in this excellent museum cover all of Swedish history, but the highlights are its fascinating Viking exhibit and impressive Gold Room. Also worth a look are sections on Scandinavian prehistory, medieval church art, and a well-realized

Stockholm's Best Views

For a bird's-eye perspective on this wonderful urban mix of water, parks, concrete, and people, consider these viewpoints.

City Hall Tower: Top of the tower comes with the classic city view (see listing earlier).

Katarina: This viewing platform—offering fine views over the steeples of Gamla Stan—rises up from Slussen (the busy transit zone between Gamla Stan and Södermalm). The elevator making this an easy destination may be under renovation during your visit, in which case, you'll have to huff your way up. You can get to the platform via pedestrian bridge from Mosebacke Torg, up above in Södermalm. In good summer weather, you'll have to wade through the swanky tables of Eriks restaurant to reach the (free and public) viewpoint.

Himlen: Rising above Södermalm's main drag, the Skrapan skyscraper has a free elevator to the 25th-floor restaurant, called Himlen. While they're hoping you'll buy a meal (200-SEK starters, 350-SEK main courses) or nurse a 150-SEK cocktail in the lounge, it's generally fine to take a discreet peek at the 360-degree views—just march in the door at #78 and ride the elevator up to 25 (daily 14:00-late, Götgatan 78, tel. 08/660-6068, www.restauranghimlen.se).

Kaknäs Tower: This bold, concrete, 500-foot-tall TV tower—looming above the eastern part of the city, and visible from just about everywhere—was once the tallest building in Scandinavia (55 SEK, Mon-Sat 9:00-22:00, Sun until 19:00, shorter hours off-season, restaurant on 28th floor, east of downtown—bus #69 from Nybroplan or Sergels Torg to Kaknästornet Södra stop, tel. 08/667-2105, www.kaknastornet.se).

display about the Danish invasion of 1361—the battle of Gotland—in which 1,800 ill-equipped Swedish farmers lost their lives.

Cost and Hours: Free, daily 10:00-17:00; Sept-May closed Mon and open Wed until 20:00; a few blocks north of the Djurgården bridge at Narvavägen 13, bus #67 stops out front, tel. 08/5195-5562, www.historiska.se.

Tours: Audioguide-30 SEK. Daily guided tours are offered in summer (at 12:00 and 13:00), and kids' activities are available in an inner courtyard until 16:00.

Visiting the Museum: The featured exhibit (on the ground floor), titled simply **"Vikings,"** probes the many stories and myths about these people. Were they peaceful traders and farmers—or brutal robbers and pillagers? The focus is on everyday activities, religious beliefs, and family life in the years from 800 to 1050—the Viking Age.

A reconstruction of a Viking village gives a view of early trading communities, but most people lived by farming, hunting, and fishing. Exhibits feature grave goods, combs of horn and bone, gaming pieces, and brooches. A rare find is a wooden chest filled with tools and scrap metal, believed to have belonged to a blacksmith/carpenter.

A fine section of "picture stones" relate the stories of the Norse gods, and amulets shaped like little hammers demonstrate the importance of the god Thor. The small group of Vikings who did venture abroad to trade (and to pillage) returned to Scandinavia with new customs—including Christianity.

The **"Gold Room"** (in the basement) dazzles viewers with about 115 pounds of gold: spiral hair ornaments from 1500 B.C.; gold collars worn by fifth-century aristocrats; hoards of coins from Roman and Arab empires; once-buried treasure troves of jewelry and votive objects; and medieval jewel-encrusted reliquaries.

In all, the museum has about 3,000 finely crafted gold objects—largely thanks to Swedish legislation that has protected antiquities since the 17th century.

Waterside Walk

Enjoy Stockholm's ever-expanding shoreline promenades. Tracing the downtown shoreline while dodging in-line skaters and ice-cream trolleys (rather than cars and buses), you can walk from Slussen across Gamla Stan, all the way to the good ship *Vasa* in Djurgården. Perhaps the best stretch is along the waterfront Strandvägen street (from Nybroplan past weather-beaten old boats and fancy facades to Djurgården). As you stroll, keep in mind that there's free fishing in central Stockholm, and the harbor waters are restocked every spring with thousands of new fish. Locals tell of one lucky lad who pulled in an 80-pound salmon. The waterside lanes are extremely bike-friendly here and throughout Stockholm.

DJURGÅRDEN

Four hundred years ago, Djurgården was the king's hunting ground (the name means "Animal Garden"). You'll see the royal gate to the island immediately after the bridge that connects it to the main-

land. Now this entire lush island is Stockholm's fun center, protected as a national park. It still has a smattering of animal life among its biking paths, picnicking families, art galleries, various amusements, and museums, which are some of the best in Scandinavia.

Orientation: Of the three great sights on the island, the Vasa and Nordic museums are neighbors, and Skansen is a 10-minute walk away (or hop on any bus or tram—they come every couple of minutes). Several lesser or special-interest attractions (from the ABBA museum to an amusement park) are also nearby.

To get around more easily, consider **renting a bike** as you enter the island. You can get one at Sjöcaféet, a café just over the Djurgårdsbron bridge; they also rent boats (bikes-80 SEK/hour, 275 SEK/day; canoes-150 SEK/hour, kayaks-125 SEK/hour; open daily 9:00-21:00, closed off-season and in bad weather; handy city cycle maps, tel. 08/660-5757, www.sjocafeet.se).

In the concrete building upstairs from the café, you'll find a **Djurgården visitors center,** with free maps, island bike routes, brochures, and information about the day's events (daily in summer 8:00-20:00, shorter hours off-season).

Getting There: Take tram #7 from Sergels Torg (the stop is right under the highway overpass) or Nybroplan (in front of the gilded theater building) and get off at one of these stops: Nordic Museum (use also for Vasa Museum), Liljevalc Gröna Lund (for ABBA museum), or Skansen. In summer, you can take a city ferry from the southeast end of Gamla Stan or from Nybroplan (see "Getting Around Stockholm," earlier). Walkers enjoy the harborside Strandvägen promenade, which leads from Nybroplan directly to the island (described under "Waterside Walk," earlier).

Major Museums on Djurgården

▲▲▲Skansen

Founded in 1891, Skansen was the first in what became a Europe-wide movement to preserve traditional architecture in open-air museums. It's a huge park gathering more than 150 historic buildings (homes, churches, shops, and schoolhouses) transplanted from all corners of Sweden. Other languages have borrowed the Swedish term "Skansen" (which originally meant "the Fort") to describe an "open-air museum." Today, tourists enjoy exploring this Swedish-culture-on-a-lazy-Susan, seeing folk crafts in action and wonderfully furnished old interiors. Kids love Skansen, where they can ride a life-size wooden *Dala*-horse and stare down a hedgehog, visit Lill-Skansen (a children's zoo), and take a mini-train or pony ride. This is an enjoyable place to visit on summer days, when it's lively with families and tourists.

Cost and Hours: 180 SEK, kids-60 SEK, less off-season; park opens daily at 10:00, closes at 22:00 late June-Aug and progressively earlier the rest of the year; historical buildings generally open 11:00-17:00, late June-Aug some until 19:00, most closed in winter. Check their excellent online calendar for what's happening during your visit (www.skansen.se) or call 08/442-8000.

Music: Skansen does great music in summer. There's fiddling, folk dancing, and public dancing to live bands on Friday and Saturday nights. Confirm performance times before you go.

Visiting Skansen: Skansen isn't designed as a one-way loop; it's a sprawling network of lanes and buildings, yours to explore. For the full story, invest in the museum guidebook (sold at the info booth just after the entrance). With the book, you'll understand each building you duck into and even learn about the Nordic animals awaiting you in the zoo. While you're at the info booth, check the live crafts schedule to make a smart Skansen plan (the scale model displayed at the entrance will give you an idea of the park's size—and the need for a plan). Guides throughout the park are happy to answer your questions—but only if you ask them. The old houses come alive when you take the initiative to get information.

From the entrance, go up the stairs and bear left to find the escalator, and ride it up to **"The Town Quarter"** (Stadskvarteren), where shoemakers, potters, and glassblowers are busy doing their traditional thing (daily 10:00-17:00) in a re-created Old World Stockholm. Continuing deeper into the park—past the bakery, spice shop/grocery, hardware store, and a cute little courtyard café—you'll reach the central square, **Bollnästorget** (signed as "Central Skansen" but labeled on English maps as "Market Street"), with handy food stands. The rest of Sweden spreads out from here. Northern Swedish culture and architecture is in the north (top of park map), and southern Sweden's in the south (bottom of map). Various homesteads—each clustered protectively around an inner courtyard—are scattered around the complex.

Poke around. Follow signs—or your instincts. It's worth stepping into the old, red-wood Seglora Church (just past Bollnästorget), which aches with atmosphere under painted beams. The park has two zoos: Lill-Skansen is a children's petting zoo. Beyond the big brick spa tower and carnival rides sprawls the Scandinavian Animals section, with bears, wolves, moose ("elk"), seals, reindeer (near the Sami camp), and other animals.

Eating at Skansen: The park has ample eating options to suit every budget. The most memorable—and affordable—meals are at the small folk food court on the main square, **Bollnästorget.** Here, among the duck-filled lakes, frolicking families, and peacenik local toddlers who don't bump on the bumper cars, kiosks dish up "Sami slow food" (smoked reindeer), waffles, hot dogs, and more. There are lots of picnic benches—Skansen encourages **picnicking.** (A small grocery store is tucked away across the street and a bit to the left of the main entrance.)

For a sit-down meal, the old-time **$$$ Stora Gungan Krog,** right at the top of the escalator in the craftsmen's quarter, is a cozy inn (indoor or outdoor lunches— meat, fish, or veggie—with a salad-and-cracker bar). Another snug spot is **$$ Gubbhyllan,** on the ground floor and fine porch of an old house (at base of escalator, just past main entrance). For a less atmospheric choice, consider one of three restaurants that share a modern building facing the grandstand (just up the hill inside the main entrance), all with nice views over the city: the simple **$$$ Skansen Terrassen** cafeteria; **$$$ Tre Byttor Taverne,** with 18th-century pub ambience; and, upstairs, the fussy **$$$$ Solliden** restaurant, with a dated blue-and-white dining hall facing a wall of windows; the main reason to eat here is the big *smörgåsbord* lunch (served 12:00-16:00).

Aquarium: The "aquarium"—featuring lemurs, meerkats, baboons, Gila monsters, giant anacondas, rattlesnakes, geckos, crocodiles, colorful tree frogs, and small sharks...but almost no fish—is located within Skansen, but is not covered by your Skansen ticket. Only animal lovers find it worth the steep admission price (120 SEK, July-Aug daily 10:00-19:00, closes earlier rest of year, tel. 08/660-1082, www.skansen-akvariet.se).

▲▲▲Vasa Museum (Vasamuseet)

Stockholm turned a titanic flop into one of Europe's great sightseeing attractions. The glamorous but unseaworthy warship *Vasa*—top-heavy with an extra cannon deck—sank 40 minutes into her 1628 maiden voyage when a breeze caught the sails and blew her over. After 333 years at the bottom of Stockholm's harbor, she rose again from the deep with the help of marine archaeologists. Rediscovered in 1956 and raised in 1961, this Edsel of the sea  is today the best-preserved ship of its age anywhere—housed since 1990 in a brilliant museum. The masts perched atop the roof—best seen from a distance—show the actual height of the ship.

Cost and Hours: 130 SEK, includes film and tour; daily 8:30-18:00; Sept-May 10:00-17:00 except Wed until 20:00; WCs on level 3, good café, Galärvarvet, Djurgården, tel. 08/5195-5810, www.vasamuseet.se.

Getting There: The *Vasa* is on the waterfront immediately behind the stately brick Nordic Museum (facing the museum,  walk around to the right) and a 10-minute walk from Skansen. From downtown, take tram #7.

Crowd-Beating Tips: There are two lines for tickets: on the right, for machines that take PIN-enabled credit cards; and on the left, for other cards or cash. The museum can have very long lines, but they generally move quickly—you likely won't wait more than 15-20 minutes.

If crowds are a concern, get here either right when it opens, or after about 16:00 (but note that the last tour starts at 16:30).

Tours: The free 25-minute **tour** is worthwhile. Because each guide is given license to cover whatever he or she likes, no two tours are alike—if you're fascinated by the place, consider taking two different tours to pick up new details. In summer, English tours run on the hour and half-hour (last tour at 16:30); off-season (Sept-May) tours go 3/day Mon-Fri, hourly Sat-Sun (last tour at 15:30). Listen for the loudspeaker announcement, or check at the info desk for the next tour. Alternatively, you can access the **audioguide** by logging onto the museum's Wi-Fi (www.vasamuseet.se/audioguide).

Film: The excellent 17-minute film digitally re-creates *Vasa*-era Stockholm (and the colorfully painted ship itself), dramatizes its sinking, and documents the modern-day excavation and preservation of the vessel. It generally runs three times per hour; virtually all showings are either in English or with English subtitles.

Visiting the Museum: For a thorough visit, plan on spending at least an hour and a half—watch the film, take a guided tour, and linger over the exhibits (this works in any order). After buying your ticket, head inside. Sort out your film and tour options at the information desk to your right.

Upon entry, you're prow-to-prow with the great ship. The *Vasa*, while not quite the biggest ship in the world when launched in 1628, had the most firepower, with two fearsome decks of cannons. The 500 carved wooden statues draping the ship— once painted in bright colors—are all symbolic of the king's power. The 10-foot lion on the magnificent prow is a reminder that Europe considered the Swedish King Gustavus Adolphus the "Lion from the North." With this great ship, Sweden was preparing to establish its empire and become more engaged in European power politics. Specifically, the Swedes (who already controlled much of today's Finland and Estonia) wanted to push south to dominate the whole of the Baltic Sea, in order to challenge their powerful rival, Poland.

Designed by a Dutch shipbuilder, the *Vasa* had 72 guns of the same size and type (a rarity on mix-and-match warships of the age), allowing maximum efficiency in reloading—since there was no need to keep track of different ammunition. Unfortunately, the king's unbending demands to build the ship high (172 feet tall) but skinny made it extremely unstable; no amount of ballast could weigh the ship down enough to prevent it from tipping.

Now explore the **exhibits,** which are situated on six levels around the grand hall, circling the ship itself. All displays are well

STOCKHOLM

described in English. You'll learn about the ship's rules (bread can't be older than eight years), why it sank (stale bread?), how it's preserved (the ship, not the bread), and so on. Best of all is the chance to do slow laps around the magnificent vessel at different levels. Now painstakingly restored, 98 percent of the *Vasa*'s wood is original (modern bits are the brighter and smoother planks).

On **level 4** (the entrance level), right next to the ship, you'll see a 1:10 scale model of the *Vasa* in its prime—vividly painted and fully rigged with sails. Farther along, models show how the *Vasa* was salvaged; a colorful children's section re-creates the time period; and a 10-minute multimedia show explains why the *Vasa* sank (alternating between English and Swedish showings). Heading behind the ship, you'll enjoy a great view of the sculpture-slathered stern of the *Vasa*. The facing wall features full-size replicas of the carvings, demonstrating how the ship was originally colorfully painted.

Several engaging displays are on **level 5.** "Life On Board" lets you walk through the gun deck and study cutaway models of the hive of activity that hummed below decks (handy, since you can't enter the actual ship). Artifacts—including fragments of clothing actually worn by the sailors—were salvaged along with the ship. "Battle!" is a small exhibit of cannons and an explanation of naval warfare.

Level 6 features "The Sailing Ship," with models demonstrating how the *Vasa* and similar vessels actually sailed. You'll see the (very scant) remains of some of the *Vasa*'s actual riggings and sails. **Level 7** gives you even higher views over the ship.

Don't miss **level 2**—all the way at the bottom (ride the handy industrial-size elevator)—with some of the most interesting exhibits. "The Ship" explains how this massive and majestic vessel was brought into being using wood from tranquil Swedish forests. Tucked under the ship's prow is a laboratory where today's scientists continue with their preservation efforts. The "Objects" exhibit shows off actual items found in the shipwreck, while "Face to Face" introduces you to some of those who perished when the *Vasa* sunk—with faces that were re-created from skeletal remains. Nearby, you'll see some of the skeletons found in the shipwreck. Those remains have been extensively analyzed, revealing remarkable details about the ages, diets, and general health of the victims.

As you exit, you'll pass a hall of (generally excellent) temporary exhibits.

▲Nordic Museum (Nordiska Museet)

Built to look like a Danish Renaissance palace, this museum offers a fascinating peek at 500 years of traditional Swedish lifestyles. The exhibits insightfully place everyday items into their social/

historical context in ways that help you really grasp various chapters of Sweden's past. It's arguably more informative than Skansen. Take time to let the excellent, included audioguide enliven the exhibits.

Cost and Hours: 120 SEK, free Wed Sept-May after 17:00; open daily 9:00-18:00, Sept-May 10:00-17:00 except Wed until 20:00; Djurgårdsvägen 6-16, at Djurgårdsbron, tram #7 from downtown, tel. 08/5195-4770, www.nordiskamuseet.se.

Visiting the Museum: Entering the museum's main hall, you'll be face-to-face with Carl Milles' huge painted-wood statue of Gus-

tav Vasa, father of modern Sweden. The rest of this floor is usually devoted to temporary exhibits.

Highlights of the permanent collection are on the top two floors. Head up the stairs, or take the elevator just to the left of Gustav. Begin on floor 4 and work your way down.

On **floor 4,** four different exhibits ring the grand atrium. The **"Homes and Interiors"** section displays 400 years of home furnishings, both as individual artifacts and as part of room dioramas. As you travel through this parade of furniture—from dark, heavily draped historical rooms to modern living rooms, and from rustic countryside cottages to aristocratic state bedrooms—you'll learn the subtle meaning behind everyday furniture that we take for granted. For example, the advent of television didn't just change entertainment—it gave people a reason to gather each evening in the living room, which, in turn, became a more-used (and less formal) part of people's homes. You'll learn about the Swedish designers who, in the 1930s, eschewed stiff-backed traditional chairs in favor of sleek perches that merged ergonomics and looks—giving birth to functionalism.

Also on this floor, the **"Folk Art"** section shows off colorfully painted furniture and wood carvings; vibrant traditional costumes; and rustic Bible-story illustrations that adorned the walls of peasants' homes. The **"Sápmi"** exhibit tells the fascinating and often overlooked story of the indigenous Sami people (formerly called "Lapps"), who lived in the northern reaches of Norway, Sweden,

Finland, and Russia centuries before Europeans created those modern nations. On display are shoes, ceremonial knives, colorful hats and clothing, and other features of Sami culture. You'll learn how their nomadic lifestyle—following their herds of grazing reindeer—allowed them to survive so far north, and how the Sami (who still number around 20,000) have had an impact on greater Swedish society. Finally, tucked behind the stairwell, the "Small Things" collection shows off timepieces, ceramics, and tobacco pipes, among other items.

Floor 3 has several smaller exhibits. The most interesting are "Table Settings" (with carefully set tables from the 16th century until about 1950, representing customs and traditions around gathering to share food and drink—from an elegant tea party to a rowdy pub) and "Traditions" (showing and describing each old-time celebration of the Swedish year—from Christmas to Midsummer—as well as funerals, confirmations, and other life events). Also on display: 300 years of Swedish attire (including a fun video showing how complicated and time-consuming it was for a woman to dress in the 18th century); jewelry and textile exhibits; a dollhouse and toy collection; and a photo exhibition pulled from the museum's archive.

▲ABBA: The Museum

The Swedish pop group ABBA was, for a time, a bigger business than Volvo. Since bursting on the scene in 1974 by winning the Eurovision Song Contest with "Waterloo," and serenading Sweden's newly minted queen with "Dancing Queen" in 1976, they've sold more than 380 million records, and the musical based on their many hits, *Mamma Mia!*, has been enjoyed by 50 million people. It was only a matter of time before Stockholm opened an ABBA museum, which is conveniently located just across the street from Skansen and next to Gröna Lund amusement park. Like everything ABBA, it is aggressively for-profit and slickly promoted, with the steepest ticket price in town. True to its subject, it's bombastic, glitzy, and highly interactive. If you like ABBA, it's lots of fun; if you love ABBA, it's ▲▲▲ nirvana.

Cost and Hours: 250 SEK—credit cards only, 595 SEK family ticket covers two adults and up to four kids; daily 9:00-19:00, Sept-May 10:00-18:00 except Wed until 19:00, Djurgårdsvägen 68, bus #44 or tram #7 to Liljevalc Gröna Lund stop, tel. 08/1213-2860, www.abbathemuseum.com.

Tours: ABBA aficionados will happily fork over 20 SEK extra for the intimate audioguide, in which Agnetha, Benny, Björn, and Anni-Frid share their memories, in their own words.

Getting In: Only 75 people are let in every 15 minutes with timed-entry tickets. The museum strongly encourages getting tickets in advance from their website or at the TI. In fact, they'll charge you 20 SEK extra per ticket to buy in person (but computer terminals are standing by if you want to "prebook" on the spot). It can be crowded on summer weekends, in which case you may have to wait for a later time.

Visiting the Museum: The museum is high-tech, with plenty of actual ABBA artifacts, re-creations of rooms where the group did its composing and recording (including their famous "Polar Studio" and their rustic archipelago cottage), a room full of gold and platinum records, plenty of high-waisted sequined pantsuits, and lots of high-energy video screens.

Included in the ticket is a "digital key" that lets you take advantage of several interactive stations. For example, you can record a music video karaoke-style as a fifth member of the group—with virtual ABBA members dancing around you—and share your musical debut via the museum's website. A small wing features the Swedish Music Hall of Fame, but apart from that, it's all ABBA.

Waterfront Sights

While the tram zips sightseers between the Vasa Museum and Skansen, it's a short, enjoyable, and very scenic walk along the waterfront—a delight on a nice day. You'll see food stands, boats bobbing in the harbor, and sunbathing Swedes.

You'll also pass several sights, listed here in the order you'll reach them (from the Djurgårdsbron bridge): **Junibacken** is a fairy-tale house based on the writings of Astrid Lindgren, who created *Pippi Longstocking*. While oriented toward Swedish kids, American children may enjoy it, too (www.junibacken.se). The pier directly in front of the Vasa Museum is actually part of the **Maritime Museum** (Sjöhistoriska), where historic ships are moored (typically big icebreakers from the Arctic, and sometimes military boats). About halfway along the waterfront is the **Museum of Spirits** (see next listing), offering a weird but welcome break from heavier sightseeing. Finally, you'll reach **Vikingaliv,** a small myth-busting museum about the Vikings that uses interactive displays to present them as colonizers and traders more than looters and warriors (you won't find a horned helmet in the place). A low-tech, hokey 10-minute ride tells "Ragnfrid's Saga" (the fictional story of the long-suffering wife of a voyaging husband; www.vikingaliv.se).

Museum of Spirits (Spiritmuseum)

The museum's highly conceptual permanent exhibit considers the role of alcohol—and specifically, flavored vodkas—in Swedish society. While Sweden got a reputation for its "loose morals" in the 1970s (mostly surrounding sex and nudity), at the same time it was extremely puritanical when it came to alcohol; the government actively tried to get Swedes to stop drinking (hence the liquor-store system and sky-high alcohol taxes that still exist). In the exhibit's season-themed rooms, you'll be able to smell different types of fla-vored liquors (orange in the spring, elderflower in the summer, and so on); upstairs, you can ace a virtual pub quiz, recline (or nap) in the boozy drunk-simulator room, and step into a garishly lit, buzz-ing room that simulates a hangover. The temporary exhibits here are also quite good.

Cost and Hours: 120 SEK, 250-SEK ticket adds a taster kit of flavored vodkas; Mon 10:00-17:00, Tue-Sat until 19:00, Sun 12:00-17:00, shorter hours off-season; summertime beer pier opens for dining and 17 types of draft beer, Djurgårdsvägen 38, tel. 08/1213-1300, www.spritmuseum.se.

Other Djurgården Sights
Gröna Lund Amusement Park
Stockholm's venerable and lowbrow Tivoli-type amusement park still packs in the local families and teens on cheap dates. It's a busy venue for local pop concerts.

Cost and Hours: 115 SEK to enter (free over 65 or under 7), then buy ride pass or coupons; daily late April-late Sept 12:00-23:00, closed off-season, www.gronalund.com.

▲Thielska Galleriet
If you liked the Larsson and Zorn art in the National Gallery, and/or if you're a Munch fan, this charming mansion on the water at the far end of the Djurgården park is worth the trip. The building was designed in the early 20th century for banker and art patron Ernest Thiel as a residence, but with skylight galleries to accommodate his extensive collection, which has hung here ever since.

Cost and Hours: 130 SEK, Tue-Sun 12:00-17:00, closed Mon, bus #69 (not #69K) from downtown, tel. 08/662-5884, www. thielska-galleriet.se.

▲Biking the Garden Island
In all of Stockholm, Djurgården is the most natural place to enjoy a bike ride. There's a good and reasonably priced bike-rental place just over the bridge as you enter the island (Sjöcaféet; see beginning of Djurgården section, earlier), and a world of parklike paths and lanes with harbor vistas to enjoy.

Ask for a free map and route tips when you rent your bike. Fig-ure about an hour to pedal around Djurgården's waterfront perimeter; it's mostly flat, but with some short, steeper stretches that take you up and over the middle of the island. Those who venture beyond the Skansen park find themselves nearly all alone in the lush and evocative environs.

At the summit of the island you'll come upon Rosendal's Garden, with a bakery and café. You can sit in the greenhouse or in the delightful orchard or flower garden, where locals come to pick a bouquet and pay by the weight. (The garden is fertilized by the horse pies from adjacent Skansen.) Just beyond is the **Rosendals Slott,** the cute mini-palace of Karl Johans XIV, founder of the Bernadotte dynasty. This palace, in the so-called Karl Johans style ("Empire style"), went together in prefabricated sections in the 1820s. The story is told on a board in front, and a 9-ton porphyry vase graces the backyard.

A garden café at the eastern tip of the island offers a scenic break midway through your pedal. For a longer ride, you can cross the canal to the Ladugårdsgärdet peninsula ("Gärdet" for short), a swanky, wooded residential district just to the north.

SÖDERMALM

Just south of Gamla Stan, the Södermalm district is the real-life antidote to the upscale areas where most visitors spend their time. While it has few tourist sights (aside from the Fotografiska museum, and the Stockholm City Museum, which may be closed for renovation when you visit), Södermalm offers fine views and fun places to eat (for recommendations and more on this area, see "Södermalm Streets and Eats," later). Towering over Södermalm's main road is the Skrapan building, with the Himlen view terrace on its 25th floor (see "Stockholm's Best Views" sidebar, earlier).

▲Fotografiska (Photography Museum)

This museum, in a renovated 1906 industrial building right on the Stadsgården embankment, is fun and appealing. The focus is on contemporary and international photography, exhibited in well-curated, thematic displays that change several times a year. It's a complete destination, with a top-floor café giving drop-dead views over the city (open until 21:00 in summer), a people-watching terrace café on the embankment, and a browse-worthy store.

Cost and Hours: 135 SEK—credit cards only, daily 9:00-23:00, later on weekends, at Stadsgårdshamnen 22 (a 10-minute walk from Slussen; hop-on, hop-off boats stop here), tel. 08/5090-0500, www.fotografiska.eu.

ON THE OUTSKIRTS

The home and garden of Carl Milles, Sweden's greatest sculptor, is less than an hour from the city center. For sights farther outside

Stockholm (all reachable by public transportation), see the next chapter.

▲Millesgården

The villa and garden of Carl Milles is a veritable forest of statues by Sweden's greatest sculptor. Millesgården is dramatically situated on a bluff overlooking the harbor in Stockholm's upper-class suburb of Lidingö. While the art is engaging and enjoyable, even the curators have little to say about it from an interpretive point of view—so your visit is basically without guidance. But in Milles' house, which dates from the 1920s, you can see his north-lit studio and get a sense of his creative genius.

Carl Milles spent much of his career teaching at the Cranbrook Academy of Art in Michigan. But he's buried here at his villa, where he lived and worked for 20 years, lovingly designing this sculpture garden for the public. Milles wanted his art to be displayed on pedestals...to be seen "as if silhouettes against the sky." His subjects—often Greek mythological figures such as Pegasus or Poseidon—stand out as if the sky were a blank paper. Yet unlike silhouettes, Milles' images can be enjoyed from many angles. And Milles liked to enliven his sculptures by incorporating water features into his figures. *Hand of God*, perhaps his most famous work, gives insight into Milles' belief that when the artist created, he was—in a way—divinely inspired.

Cost and Hours: 150 SEK; daily 11:00-17:00 except closed Mon Oct-April; English booklet explains the art, restaurant and café, tel. 08/446-7590, www.millesgarden.se.

Getting There: Catch the T-bana to Ropsten, then take bus #207 to within a five-minute walk of the museum; several other #200-series buses get you close enough to walk (allow about 45 minutes total each way).

Shopping in Stockholm

Sweden offers a world of shopping temptations. Smaller stores are open weekdays 10:00-18:00, Saturdays until 17:00, and Sundays 11:00-16:00. Some of the bigger stores (such as NK, H&M, and Åhléns) are open later on Saturdays and Sundays.

Fun Chain Stores

These chains have multiple branches around town; the most convenient are marked on the "Stockholm Hotels & Restaurants" map.

DesignTorget, dedicated to contemporary Swedish design, receives a commission for selling the unique works of local designers (generally Mon-Fri 10:00-19:00, Sat until 18:00, Sun 11:00-17:00, big branch underneath Sergels Torg—enter from basement level of Kulturhuset, other branches are at Nybrogatan 23 and at the airport, www.designtorget.se).

Systembolaget is Sweden's state-run liquor store chain. A sample of each bottle of wine or liquor sits in a display case. A card in front explains how it tastes and suggests menu pairings. Look for the item number and order at the counter. Branches are in Hötorget underneath the movie theater complex, in Norrmalm at Vasagatan 21, and just up from Östermalmstorgat Nybrogatan 47 (Mon-Wed 10:00-18:00, Thu-Fri until 19:00, Sat until 15:00, closed Sun, www.systembolaget.se).

Gudrun Sjödén is named for its fashion-designer founder, whose life's work has been creating cheery, functional clothing for Swedish women. Some might sniff at her sensible but colorful designs (some inspired by her summer garden), but they're free-spirited in a Pippi Longstocking sort of way (think aubergine and sunflower). You'll love it or hate it—all around town (at Regeringsgatan 30, Götgatan 44, and Stora Nygatan 33, daily 10:00-19:00, Sat until 17:00, Sun 12:00-16:00, www.gudrunsjoden.com).

Hamngatan

The main shopping zone between Kungsträdgården and Sergels Torg (described in "Stockholm's Modern City Walk," earlier) has plenty of huge department stores. At the top of Kungsträdgården, **Illums Bolighus** is a Danish design shop. Across the street, **Nordiska Kompaniet** (NK) is elegant and stately; the Swedish design (downstairs) and kitchenware sections are particularly impressive. The classy **Gallerian** mall is just up the street from NK and stretches seductively nearly to Sergels Torg. The **Åhléns** store, kitty-corner across Sergels Torg, is less expensive than NK and has two cafeterias and a supermarket. Affordable clothing chain **H&M** has a store right across the street. Tucked behind Åhléns is **Kartbutiken,** a handy map-and-guidebook shop that covers all of Sweden, Scandinavia, and beyond (daily, at Mäster Samuelsgatan 54).

Mood Stockholm

The city's most exclusive mall is a downtown block filled with big-name Swedish and international designers, plus a pricey food court and restaurants. The upscale decor and mellow music give it a Beverly Hills vibe (Mon-Fri 10:00-20:00, Sat until 18:00, Sun 11:00-17:00, Regeringsgatan 48). The mall anchors a ritzy, pedestrianized shopping zone; for more exclusive shops, browse the nearby streets Jakobsbergsgatan and Biblioteksgatan.

Södermalm

When Swedes want the latest items by local designers, they skip the downtown malls and head for funky Södermalm. **Götgatan,** the main drag that leads from Slussen up to this neighborhood, is a particularly good choice, with shop after shop of mostly Swedish designers. Boutiques along here—some of them one-offs, others belonging to Swedish chains—include Weekday (known for denim), Filippa K (high-end attire), and Tiogruppen (colorful bags and fabrics). More intrepid shoppers will want to explore the area south of **Folkungagatan**—"SoFo," where scores of fun stores feature new and vintage clothing, housewares, and jewelry in the streets surrounding Nytorget.

Nybrogatan

This short and pleasant traffic-free street, which connects Östermalmstorg with the Nybroplan waterfront, is lined with small branches of interesting design shops, including Nordiska Galleriet (eye-catching modern furniture, at #11). It also has shoe and handbag stores, and an enticing cheese shop and bakery.

Flea Markets

For a *smörgåsbord* of Scanjunk, visit the **Loppmarknaden,** northern Europe's biggest flea market, at Vårberg Center (free entry weekdays and Sat-Sun after 15:00, 10-15 ISK on weekends—when it's busiest; Mon-Fri 11:00-18:00; Sat 10:30-16:00, Sun from 11:00; T-bana: Vårberg, tel. 08/710-0060, www.loppmarknaden.se). Hötorget, the produce market, also hosts a Sunday flea market in summer (see "Eating in Stockholm," later).

Nightlife and Entertainment in Stockholm

Bars and Music in Gamla Stan

The street called Stora Nygatan, with several lively bars, has perhaps the most accessible and reliable place for live jazz in town: Stampen. Several pubs here offer live Irish traditional music sessions or bluegrass several times each week; they tend to share musicians, who sometimes gather at one of these pubs for impromptu jam sessions (ask around, or stroll this street with your ears peeled). While it may seem odd to listen to Irish or bluegrass music in Stockholm, these venues are extremely popular with locals.

Stampen is two venues under one roof: a stone-vaulted cellar below (called Geronimo's FGT) and a fun-loving saloon-like jazz and R&B bar upstairs (check out the old instruments and antiques hanging from the ceiling). There's live music every night that Stampen is open (cover Fri-Sat only; Tue-Fri and Sun 17:00-late, Sat from 14:00, closed Mon, Stora Gråmunkegränd 7, tel. 08/205-793, www.stampen.se). Geronimo's, downstairs, is more of a nightclub/ concert venue with a menu inspired by the American Southwest (Tue-Sun 17:00 until late, enter at Stora Nygatan 5). For locations, see the "Gamla Stan Hotels & Restaurants" map.

Several other lively spots are within a couple of blocks of Stampen on Stora Nygatan. Your options include **Wirströms Pub** (live blues bands play in crowded cellar Mon-Sat 21:00-24:00, no cover; daily 11:00-late, Stora Nygatan 13, www.wirstromspub.se); **O'Connells Irish Pub** (a lively expat sports bar with music—usually Tue-Sat at 21:00; Mon-Sat 11:00-late, Sun from 12:00, Stora Nygatan 21, www.oconnells.se); and **The Liffey** (classic Irish pub with 150-180-SEK pub grub, live music Wed-Sun from 21:30; daily 12:00-late, Stora Nygatan 40-42, www.theliffey.se).

Icebar Stockholm

If you just want to put on a heavy coat and gloves and drink a fancy vodka in a modern-day igloo, consider the fun, if touristy, Icebar Stockholm. Everything's ice— shipped down from Sweden's far north. The bar, the glasses, even the tip jar are made of ice. You get your choice of vodka drinks and 45 minutes to enjoy the scene (online booking-199 SEK, drop-ins-210 SEK—on weekends drop-ins only allowed after 21:45, additional  drinks-95 SEK, reservations smart; daily 11:15-24:00, Sept-May from 15:00; in the Nordic C Hotel adjacent to the main train station's Arlanda Express platform at Vasaplan 4, tel. 08/5056-3520, www.icebarstockholm.se). If you go too early, it can be really dead—you'll be all alone. At busy times, people are let in all at once every 45 minutes. That means there's a long line for drinks, and the place goes from being very crowded to almost empty as people gradually melt away. While there are ice bars all over Europe now, this was the second one to open (after the Ice Hotel in Lapland). And it really is pretty cool...a steady 23°F.

Cinema

In Sweden, international movies are shown in their original language with Swedish subtitles. Swedish theaters sometimes charge more for longer films, and tickets come with assigned seats (drop by to choose seats and buy a ticket, box offices generally open 11:00-22:00 daily). The Hötorget and Drottninggatan neighborhoods have many theaters.

Swedish Massage, Spa, and Sauna

To treat yourself to a Swedish spa experience—maybe with an authentic "Swedish massage"—head for the elegant circa-1900 **CentralBadet Spa.** It's along downtown's main strolling street, Drottninggatan, tucked back inside a tranquil and inviting garden courtyard. Admission includes entry to an extensive gym, "bubblepool," sauna, steam room, "herbal/crystal sauna," and an elegant Art Nouveau pool. Most areas are mixed-gender, with men and women together, but some areas are reserved for women. If you won't make it to Finland, enjoy a sauna here (for more on this steamy experience, see the "Sauna" sidebar in the Helsinki chapter). Bring your towel into the sauna—not for modesty, but for hygiene (to separate your body from the bench). The steam room is mixed; bring two towels (one for modesty and the other to sit on). The pool is more for floating than for jumping and splashing. The leafy courtyard restaurant is a relaxing place to enjoy affordable, healthy, and light meals (220 SEK, 320 SEK on Sat, towels and robes available for rent; slippers required—20 SEK to buy, 10 SEK to rent; Mon-Fri 7:00-20:30; Sat 8:00-19:30, Sun until 17:30; ages 18 and up, Drottninggatan 88, 10 minutes up from Sergels Torg, tel. 08/5452-1300, reservation tel. 08/218-821, www.centralbadet. se).

Sleeping in Stockholm

Between business travelers and the tourist trade, occupancy for Stockholm's hotels is healthy but unpredictable, and most hotels' rates vary from day to day with demand.

Consider hostels here—Stockholm's are among Europe's best, offering good beds in simple but interesting places. Each has helpful English-speaking staff, pleasant family rooms, and good facilities.

NEAR THE TRAIN STATION

$$$$ Freys Hotel is a Scan-mod, four-star place, with 127 compact, smartly designed rooms. It's well-situated for train travelers, located on a dead-end pedestrian street across from the central station. While big, it works hard to be friendly and welcoming. Its cool, candlelit breakfast room becomes a bar in the evening, popular for its selection of Belgian microbrews (air-con, Bryggargatan 12, tel. 08/5062-1300, www.freyshotels.com, freys@freyshotels. com).

$$$$ Scandic No. 53 injects modernity into a classic old building a few blocks from the station. The 274 rooms are small and functional (no desk or chair in standard rooms) but comfortable. Everything surrounds a stylish, glassy atrium boasting a lounge/

Sleep Code

Hotels are classified based on the average price of a typical en suite double room with breakfast in high season.

$$$$	**Splurge:** Most rooms over 2,000 SEK
$$$	**Pricier:** 1,500-2,000 SEK
$$	**Moderate:** 1,000-1,500 SEK
$	**Budget:** 500-1,500 SEK
¢	**Hostel/Backpacker:** Under 500 SEK
RS%	**Rick Steves discount**

Unless otherwise noted, credit cards are accepted, and free Wi-Fi is available. Comparison-shop by checking prices at several hotels (on each hotel's own website, on a booking site, or by email). For the best deal, *always book directly with the hotel.* Ask for a discount if paying in cash; if the listing includes **RS%,** request a Rick Steves discount.

restaurant (live music until 24:00 most weekends), and a peaceful outdoor courtyard (air-con, elevator, Kungsgatan 53, tel. 08/5173-6500, www.scandichotels.com, no53@scandichotels.com.

$$ Queen's Hotel enjoys a great location at the quiet top end of Stockholm's main pedestrian shopping street (about a 10-minute walk from the train station, or 25 minutes from Gamla Stan). The 59 rooms are well worn, but they're generally spacious and have big windows—and it's reasonably priced. Rooms facing the courtyard are quieter (RS%—if booking online enter rate code "RICKS," elevator, Drottninggatan 71A, tel. 08/249-460, www.queenshotel. se, info@queenshotel.se).

$$ Hotel Bema, a bit farther from the center, is a humble place that rents 12 fine rooms for some of the best prices in town (breakfast served at nearby café, reception open Mon-Fri 8:30-17:00, Sat-Sun 9:00-15:00, bus #65 from station to Upplandsgatan 13—near the top of the Drottninggatan pedestrian street, or walk about 15 minutes from the train station—exit toward *Vasagatan* and head straight up that street, tel. 08/232-675, www.hotelbema. se, info@hotelbema.se).

¢ City Backpackers, with 140 beds a quarter-mile from the station, is youthful but classy (sheets extra, breakfast extra, pay laundry, tours, sauna; Upplandsgatan 2A, tel. 08/206-920, www. citybackpackers.se, info@citybackpackers.se).

¢ City Lodge Hostel, on a quiet side street just a block from the central station, has 68 beds, a convivial lounge, and a kitchen with free cooking staples (sheets and towels extra, breakfast extra, no curfew, Klara Norra Kyrkogata 15, tel. 08/226-630, www. citylodge.se, info@citylodge.se).

¢-$$ Generator Stockholm, a big and lively hostel, has 244

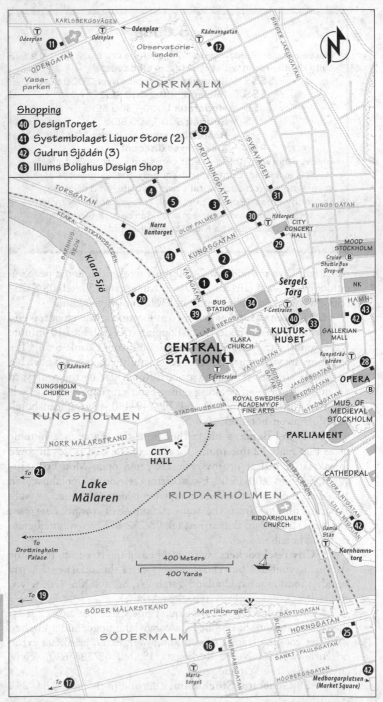

STOCKHOLM

Shopping
40 DesignTorget
41 Systembolaget Liquor Store (2)
42 Gudrun Sjödén (3)
43 Illums Bolighus Design Shop

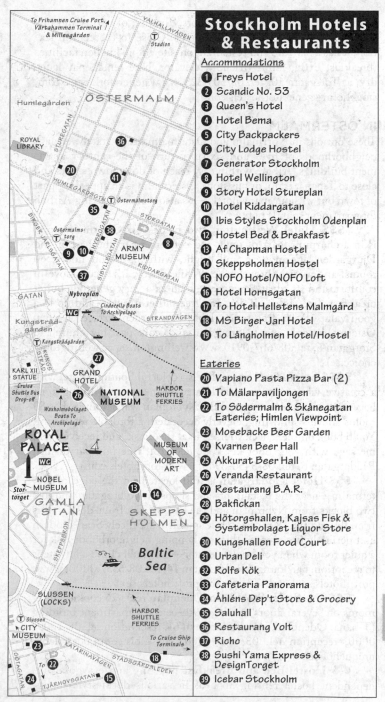

Stockholm Hotels & Restaurants

Accommodations

1. Freys Hotel
2. Scandic No. 53
3. Queen's Hotel
4. Hotel Bema
5. City Backpackers
6. City Lodge Hostel
7. Generator Stockholm
8. Hotel Wellington
9. Story Hotel Stureplan
10. Hotel Riddargatan
11. Ibis Styles Stockholm Odenplan
12. Hostel Bed & Breakfast
13. Af Chapman Hostel
14. Skeppsholmen Hostel
15. NOFO Hotel/NOFO Loft
16. Hotel Hornsgatan
17. To Hotel Hellstens Malmgård
18. MS Birger Jarl Hotel
19. To Långholmen Hotel/Hostel

Eateries

20. Vapiano Pasta Pizza Bar (2)
21. To Mälarpaviljongen
22. To Södermalm & Skånegatan Eateries; Himlen Viewpoint
23. Mosebacke Beer Garden
24. Kvarnen Beer Hall
25. Akkurat Beer Hall
26. Veranda Restaurant
27. Restaurang B.A.R.
28. Bakfickan
29. Hötorgshallen, Kajsas Fisk & Systembolaget Liquor Store
30. Kungshallen Food Court
31. Urban Deli
32. Rolfs Kök
33. Cafeteria Panorama
34. Åhléns Dep't Store & Grocery
35. Saluhall
36. Restaurang Volt
37. Richo
38. Sushi Yama Express & DesignTorget
39. Icebar Stockholm

STOCKHOLM

Scan-basic rooms spread across floors. The mix of dorms and private rooms all have private bathrooms. Close to the central station, it has a bar/café and restaurant on-site but no kitchen facilities (breakfast extra, family-friendly, elevator, bike rental, pay laundry; at Torsgatan 10, tel. 08/505-323, www.generatorhostels.com, stockholm@generatorhostels.com).

IN ÖSTERMALM

These options in Norrmalm and Östermalm are in stately, elegant neighborhoods of five- and six-story turn-of-the-century apartment buildings. All are within easy reach of downtown sights and close to T-bana, tram, or bus stops. Östermalm is an appealing part of town but without many hotels—it's also worth checking Airbnb for apartment rentals here.

$$$$ Hotel Wellington, two blocks off Östermalmstorg, is in a charming part of town and convenient to the harbor and Djurgården. It's modern and bright, with hardwood floors, 60 rooms, and a friendly welcome. While pricey, it's a cut above in comfort, and its great amenities—such as a very generous buffet breakfast, free coffee all day, and free buffet dinner—add up to a good value (RS%, free sauna, lobby bar, garden terrace, T-bana: Östermalmstorg, exit to Storgatan and walk past big church to Storgatan 6; tel. 08/667-0910, www.wellington.se, cc.wellington@choice.se).

$$$$ Story Hotel Stureplan is a colorful boutique hotel with a creative vibe. Conveniently located near a trendy dining zone between Östermalmstorg and the Nybroplan waterfront, it has 83 rooms above a sprawling, cleverly decorated, affordable restaurant. You'll book online, check yourself in at the kiosk, and receive a text message with your door key code (elevator, free minibar drinks, Riddargatan 6, tel. 08/5450-3940, www.storyhotels.com).

$$$ Hotel Riddargatan is well located on the edge of Östermalm—near the restaurants and shops on Nybrogatan and just two blocks from Nybroplan and the harbor. The front-desk staff is friendly, and the 78 rooms, while smallish, are nicely Scan-modern and perfectly functional. This is a hopping neighborhood: Ask for a quiet room when you book (elevator—but you'll climb a few steps to reception, bar/lounge, Riddargatan 14, tel. 08/5557-3000, www.profilhotels.se, hotelriddargatan@profilhotels.se).

$$$ Ibis Styles Stockholm Odenplan rents 76 cookie-cutter rooms on several floors of a late-19th-century apartment building (T-bana: Odenplan, Västmannagatan 61, reservation tel. 08/1209-0000, reception tel. 08/1209-0300, www.ibis.com, odenplan@uniquehotels.se).

¢-$ Hostel Bed and Breakfast is a tiny and easygoing independent hostel renting 36 beds in various dorm-style rooms.

Many families stay here (sheets and towels extra, laundry, across the street from T-bana: Rådmansgatan—use Stadsbibliotek exit, just off Sveavägen at Rehnsgatan 21, tel. 08/152-838, www. hostelbedandbreakfast.com, info@hostelbedandbreakfast.com).

IN GAMLA STAN

These options are in the midst of sightseeing, and a short bus or taxi ride from the train station. For locations, see the "Gamla Stan Hotels & Restaurants" map.

$$$$ Lady Hamilton Hotel, classic and romantic, is shoehorned into Gamla Stan on a quiet street a block below the cathedral and Royal Palace. The centuries-old building has 34 small but plush and colorfully decorated rooms. Each is named for a Swedish flower and is filled with antiques (elevator, Storkyrkobrinken 5, tel. 08/5064-0100, www.ladyhamiltonhotel.se, info@ladyhamiltonhotel.se).

$$$ Scandic Gamla Stan offers Old World elegance in the heart of Gamla Stan (a 5-minute walk from Gamla Stan T-bana station). Its 52 nicely decorated, smallish rooms have cheery wallpaper and hardwood floors (elevator, sauna, Nygatan 25, tel. 08/723-7250, www.scandichotels.com, gamlastan@scandichotels.com).

¢-$$ Castle House Inn is an Ikea-modern hostel/hotel situated in an ancient building that's located in an untrampled part of Gamla Stan, just a few steps off the harbor. The 53 whitewashed rooms are a mix of singles, mixed dorms, standard doubles, and family-friendly quads (breakfast extra, elevator, check-in 15:00-21:30, Brunnsgränd 4, tel. 08/551-5526, www.castlehouse.se, info@castlehouse.se.

ON SKEPPSHOLMEN

This relaxing island—while surrounded by Stockholm—feels a world apart, both in terms of its peacefulness and its somewhat less-convenient transportation connections (you'll rely on bus #65, the harbor shuttle ferry, or your feet—it's about a 20-minute walk from the train station). For locations, see the "Stockholm Hotels & Restaurants" map.

¢-$ Af Chapman Hostel, a permanently moored 100-year-old schooner, is Europe's most famous youth hostel and has provided a berth for the backpacking crowd for years. Renovated from keel to stern, the old salt offers 120 bunks in four- to six-bed rooms. Reception is at the Skeppsholmen Hostel (next, same contact info).

¢-$ Skeppsholmen Hostel is just ashore from the *Af Chapman* (private rooms, breakfast extra, 24-hour reception, tel. 08/463-2266, chapman@stfturist.se).

ON OR NEAR SÖDERMALM

Södermalm is residential and hip, with Stockholm's best café and bar scene. You'll need to take the bus or T-bana to get here from the train station, making it less than convenient for those with limited time.

$$$ NOFO Hotel/$$ NOFO Loft is a hybrid hotel/hostel located in a 19th-century building that faces a big courtyard in the heart of Södermalm. The 48 luxe hotel rooms are decorated with individual flair; the 26 simple hostel rooms are under the eaves, with bathrooms down the hall (breakfast extra in hostel; T-bana: Medborgarplatsen or bus #53 from train station to Tjärhovsplan, then a 5-minute walk to Tjärhovsgatan 11; tel. 08/5031-1200, www.nofohotel.se, info@nofo.se).

$$$ Hotel Hornsgatan is a tidy, welcoming, nicely decorated B&B upstairs in an old townhouse facing a busy but elegant-feeling boulevard. Four of the 17 small rooms have private baths; the others share five modern bathrooms. Thoughtfully run by Clara and Scott, this is a good value for the location (elevator, reception staffed until 22:00—make arrangements if arriving late, Hornsgatan 66B, T-bana: Mariatorget plus a short walk, 15-minute walk from Slussen/Gamla Stan, tel. 08/658-2901, www.hotelhornsgatan.se, info@hotelhornsgatan.se).

$$$ Hotel Hellstens Malmgård is an eclectic collage of 50 rooms crammed with antiques in a circa-1770 mansion. No two rooms are alike, but all have modern baths and quirky touches such as porcelain stoves or four-poster beds. Unwind in its secluded cobblestone courtyard, and you may forget what century you're in (elevator, T-bana: Zinkensdamm, then a 5-minute walk to Brännkyrkagatan 110; tel. 08/4650-5800, www.hellstensmalmgard.se, hotel@hellstensmalmgard.se).

$ The **MS Birger Jarl Hotel** is a floating hotel with 130 cabins, varying from small simple rooms to superior cabins with private baths (family rooms, Wi-Fi in public spaces, on Stadsgårdskajen in Slussen, tel. 08/6841-0130, www.msbirgerjarl.se, family@msbirgerjarl.se).

¢-$$$$ Långholmen Hotel/Hostel is on Långholmen, a small island off Södermalm that was transformed in the 1980s from Stockholm's main prison into a lovely park. Rooms are converted cells in the old prison building. You can choose between **¢** hostel-style and **$$$$** hotel-standard rooms at many different price levels (sheets and breakfast extra in hostel; hotel rooms include breakfast; family rooms, laundry room, kitchen, cafeteria, free parking, swimming beach and jogging paths nearby; T-bana: Hornstull, walk 10 minutes down and cross small bridge to Långholmen island, then follow hotel signs 5 minutes farther; tel. 08/720-8500, www.langholmen.com, hotel@langholmen.com).

Eating in Stockholm

To save money, eat your main meal at lunch, when cafés and restaurants have daily specials called *dagens rätt* (generally Mon-Fri only). Most museums have handy cafés with lunch deals and often with fine views. Convenience stores stock surprisingly fresh takeaway food. As anywhere, department stores and malls are eager to feed shoppers and can be a good, efficient choice. If you want culturally appropriate fast food, stop by a local hot dog stand. Picnics are a great option—especially for dinner, when restaurant prices are highest. There are plenty of parklike, harborside spots to give your cheap picnic some class. I've also listed a few splurges—destination restaurants that offer a good sample of modern Swedish cooking.

IN GAMLA STAN

Most restaurants in Gamla Stan serve a weekday lunch special. Choose from Swedish, Asian, or Italian cuisine. Several popular

places are right on the main square (Stortorget) and near the cathedral. Järntorget, at the far end, is another fun tables-in-the-square scene. Touristy places line Västerlånggatan. You'll find more romantic spots hiding on side lanes, such as the stretch of Österlånggatan that hides below Köpmantorget square (where St. George is slaying the dragon). I've listed my favorites below (for locations, see "Gamla Stan Hotels & Restaurants" map).

$$ Grillska Huset is a cheap and handy cafeteria run by Stockholms Stadsmission, a charitable organization helping the poor. It's grandly situated right on the old square, with indoor and outdoor seating (tranquil garden up the stairs and out back), fine daily specials, a hearty salad bar, and a staff committed to helping others. You can feed the hungry (that's you) and help house the homeless at the same time (daily 10:00-21:00 except Sun-Mon until 20:00, Stortorget 3, tel. 08/787-8605). They also have a fine little bakery *(brödbutik)* with lots of tempting cakes and pastries (closed Sun).

$$$$ Kryp In, a small, cozy restaurant (the name means "hide away") tucked into a peaceful lane, has a stylish hardwood and candlelit interior, great sidewalk seating, and an open kitchen letting you in on Vladimir's artistry. If you dine well in Stockholm once (or twice), I'd do it here. It's gourmet without pretense. They serve delicious, modern Swedish cuisine with a 455-SEK three-course dinner. In the good-weather months, they serve weekend

Restaurant Price Code

I've assigned each eatery a price category, based on the average cost of a typical main course. Drinks, desserts, and splurge items (steak and seafood) can raise the price considerably.

$$$$ **Splurge:** Most main courses over 200 SEK
$$$ **Pricier:** 150-200 SEK
$$ **Moderate:** 100-150 SEK
$ **Budget:** Under 100 SEK

In Sweden, a hot dog stand or other takeout spot is **$**; a sit-down café is **$$**; a casual but more upscale restaurant is **$$$**; and a swanky splurge is **$$$$**.

lunches, with specials starting at 120 SEK. Reserve ahead for dinner (275-290-SEK plates, daily 17:00-23:00, lunch Sat-Sun 12:00-16:00, a block off Stortorget at Prästgatan 17, tel. 08/208-841, www.restaurangkrypin.se).

$$ Vapiano Pasta Pizza Bar, a bright, high-energy, family-oriented eatery, issues you a smart card as you enter. Circulate to the different stations, ordering up whatever you like as they swipe your card. Portions are huge and easily splittable. As you leave, your card indicates the bill. Add flavor by picking a leaf of basil or rosemary from the potted plant on your table. Tables are often shared, making this a great place for solo travelers (daily 11:00-24:00, next to entrance to Gamla Stan T-bana station, Munkbrogatan 8, tel. 08/222-940). They also have locations on Östermalm (facing Humlegården park at Sturegatan 12) and Norrmalm (between the train station and Kungsholmen at Kungsbron 15)—for these locations, see the "Stockholm Hotels & Restaurants" map.

$$ Hermitage Restaurant is a faded, hippie-feeling joint that serves a decent vegetarian buffet in a communal dining setting (Mon-Fri 11:00-21:00, Sat-Sun from 12:00, Stora Nygatan 11, tel. 08/411-9500).

Picnic Supplies in Gamla Stan: The handy and affordable **Coop Nära** minimarket is strategically located on Järntorget, at the Slussen end of Gamla Stan; the **Munkbrohallen** supermarket downstairs in the Gamla Stan T-bana station is also very picnic-friendly (both long hours daily).

DINING ON THE WATER

In Gamla Stan: Sprawling along the harbor embankment, **$$$$ Mister French** faces a gorgeous Stockholm panorama—the main reason to eat here. The entire place opens up to the outdoors in good weather: Choose between the stylish bar (simple bar food), the full restaurant (French cuisine), or—my favorite—the lounge

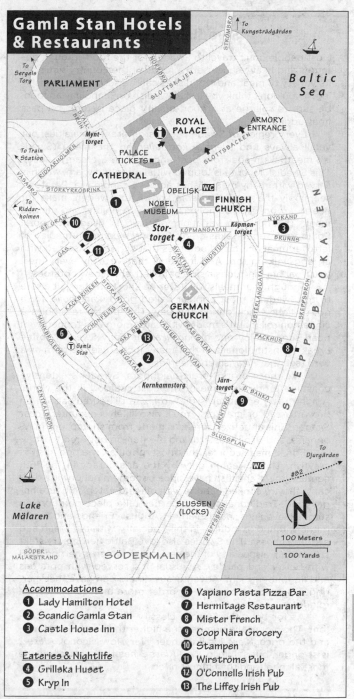

Gamla Stan Hotels & Restaurants

To Sergels Torg

PARLIAMENT

To Train Station

To Riddar-holmen

RIDDARHOLMEN

VASABRO

MYNTGATAN

Mynt-torget

STORKYRKOBRINK

ST GRAM

GÅS

KÅCKBRINKEN

STORA NYGATAN

SCHÖNFELTS

LILLA

MUNKBROLEDEN

CENTRALBRON

Gamla Stan

TYSKA BRINKEN

NYGATAN

Kornhamnstorg

CATHEDRAL

PALACE TICKETS

NOBEL MUSEUM

Stor-torget

SVARTMAN-GATAN

GERMAN CHURCH

VÄSTERLÅNGGATAN

KÖPMANGATAN

KINDSTUG

PRÄSTGATAN

Köpman-torget

NYGRÄND

BRUNNS

ÖSTERLÅNGGATAN

PACKHUS

Järn-torget

JÄRNTORG

SLUSSPLAN

SLUSSEN (LOCKS)

SKEPPSBRON

G. BANKO

O. BANKO

SKEPPSBROKAJEN

SÖDER MÄLARSTRAND

SÖDERMALM

Lake Mälaren

To Kungsträdgården

STRÖMBRO

SLOTTSKAJEN

NORRBRO

ROYAL PALACE

ARMORY ENTRANCE

SLOTTSBACKEN

OBELISK **WC**

FINNISH CHURCH

Baltic Sea

BYÅL BRON

To Djurgården

#82

WC

100 Meters

100 Yards

Accommodations

1. Lady Hamilton Hotel
2. Scandic Gamla Stan
3. Castle House Inn

Eateries & Nightlife

4. Grillska Huset
5. Kryp In
6. Vapiano Pasta Pizza Bar
7. Hermitage Restaurant
8. Mister French
9. Coop Nära Grocery
10. Stampen
11. Wirströms Pub
12. O'Connells Irish Pub
13. The Liffey Irish Pub

STOCKHOLM

Swedish Cuisine

Most people don't travel to Sweden for the food. Though potatoes and heavy sauces are a focus of the country's cuisine, its variety of meat and fish dishes can be surprisingly satisfying. If you don't think you'll like Swedish or Scandinavian food, be sure to splurge at a good-quality place before you pass final judgment.

Every region of Sweden serves different specialties, but you'll always find *svenska köttbullar* on the menu (Swedish meatballs made from beef and pork in a creamy sauce). This Swedish favorite is topped with lingonberry jam, which is served with many meat dishes across Scandinavia. Potatoes, seemingly the only vegetable known to Sweden, make for hearty *kroppkakor* dumplings filled with onions and minced meat. The northern variation, *pitepalt*, is filled with pork. Southern Sweden takes credit for *pytt i panna*, a medley of leftover meat and diced potatoes that's fried and served with an egg yolk on top. And it seems that virtually every meal you'll eat here includes a side of boiled, small new potatoes.

Though your meals will never be short on starch, be sure to try Sweden's most popular baked good, *kanelbulle*, for a not-so-light snack during the day. This pastry resembles a cinnamon roll, but it's made with cardamom and topped with pearl sugar. Enjoy one during *fika*, the daily Swedish coffee break so institutionalized that many locals use the term as a verb (see the *"Fika"* sidebar, earlier).

Like those of its Nordic neighbors, Sweden's extensive coastline produces some of the best seafood in the world. A light, tasty appetizer is *gravad lax*, a dill-cured salmon on brown bread or crackers. You'll also likely encounter *Toast Skagen*. This appetizer-spread is made from shrimp, dill, mayonnaise, and Dijon mustard, and is eaten on buttered toast.

For a main course, the most popular seafood dish is crayfish. Though eaten only by the aristocracy in the 16th century, these shellfish have since become a nationwide delicacy; they're cooked in brine with dill and eaten cold as a finger food. Traditional crayfish parties take place outdoors on summer evenings, particularly in August. Friends and family gather around to indulge in this specialty with rye bread and a strong cheese. The Swedes also love Baltic herring; try *stekt strömming*, a specialty of the east coast, which is herring fried with butter and parsley. As usual, it's served with potatoes and lingonberry jam. Adventurous diners can have their herring pickled or fermented—or order more unusual dishes like reindeer.

As for beer, the Swedes classify theirs by alcohol content. The higher the number, the higher the alcohol content— and the price. *Klass 1* is light beer—very low-alcohol. *Klass 2* is stronger, but still mild. And *Klass 3* has the most body, the most alcohol, and the highest price.

with comfy sofas (daily 11:30-24:00, smart to reserve ahead in good weather, Tullhus 2, tel. 08/202-095, www.mrfrench.se).

In Kungsholmen, Behind City Hall: On a balmy summer's eve, **$$$ Mälarpaviljongen** is a dreamy spot with hundreds of locals enjoying the perfect lakefront scene, as twinkling glasses of rosé shine like convivial lanterns. From City Hall, walk 15 minutes along Lake Mälaren (a treat in itself) to find a hundred casual outdoor tables floating on pontoons and scattered among the trees on shore. When it's cool, they have heaters and blankets (open in good weather April-Sept daily 11:00-late, easy lakeside walk or T-bana to Fridhemsplan plus a 5-minute walk to Nörr Mälarstrand 63, no reservations, tel. 08/650-8701).

In Djurgården: Just over the Djurgårdsbron bridge, **$$-$$$ Sjöcaféet** is beautifully situated and greedily soaking up the afternoon sun, filling a woody terrace stretching along the harbor. In summer, this is a fine place for a meal or just a drink before or after your Skansen or *Vasa* visit. They have affordable lunch plates (Mon-Fri 11:00-13:00 only); after 14:00, you'll pay a bit more (order at the bar, daily 8:00-20:00, often later in summer, closed off-season, bike and boat rentals, tel. 08/661-4488). For the location of this and the next restaurant, see the "Stockholm's Djurgården" map.

$$$$ Oaxen Slip Bistro, a trendy harborfront place 200 yards below the main Skansen gate, serves creative Nordic cuisine with sturdy local ingredients in a sleek interior or on its delightfully woody terrace. Overlooking a canal in what feels like an old shipyard, and filled with in-the-know locals, this place is a real treat. Reservations are smart (daily 12:00-14:00 & 17:00-21:30, Beckholmsvägen 26, tel. 08/5515-3105, www.oaxen.com).

Dinner Cruises on Lake Mälaren: The big sightseeing company Strömma sells a variety of lunch and dinner cruises that allow you to enjoy the delightful waterways of Stockholm and the archipelago while you eat. Options include shorter dinner cruises to Drottningholm Palace (2.5 hours round-trip), longer ones to the outer archipelago (up to 5 hours), and *smörgåsbord* cruises around Lake Mälaren. For details and booking (and other options, including a shrimp cruise and a jazz cruise), check www.stromma.se.

SÖDERMALM STREETS AND EATS

This quickly gentrifying district, just south of Gamla Stan (steeply uphill from Slussen), has some of Stockholm's most enticing food options—especially for beer lovers. It's a bit less swanky, and therefore more affordable, than some of the city's more touristy neighborhoods. Combine dinner here with a stroll through a side of Stockholm many visitors miss. The most interesting areas to explore are along Götgatan and the zone south of Folkungagatan street—nicknamed "SoFo."

Götgatan and Medborgarplatsen

The neighborhood's liveliest street is Götgatan, which leads from Slussen steeply up into the heart of Södermalm. Here, mixed between the boutiques, you'll find cafés tempting you to join Swedish *fika* (coffee break), plus plenty of other eateries. Even if you don't dine in Södermalm, it's worth a stroll here just for the window-shopping fun.

At the top of the street, you'll pop out into the big square called Medborgarplatsen (you can also ride the T-bana right to this square). This neighborhood hangout is a great scene, with almost no tourists and lots of options—especially for Swedish fast food. Outdoor restaurant and café tables fill the square, which is fronted by a big food hall. The recommended Kvarnen beer hall is just around the corner (see later).

$$ Melanders Fisk, inside the Söderhallarna food hall, offers table service inside or takeaway from their deli counter—but come in good weather and you can enjoy your meal outside on the square. *Skagenröra*, shrimp with mayo on toast or filling a baked potato, is the signature dish—and dear to the Swedish heart. There's also a wine bar that stays open until 22:00 (food served Mon-Sat from 11:00 until at least 15:00, some nights as late as 20:00, Medborgarplatsen 3, tel. 08/644-4040).

Skånegatan and Nytorget

A bit farther south, these cross-streets make another good spot to browse among fun and enticing restaurants, particularly for ethnic cuisine.

$$$ Urban Deli Nytorget is half fancy artisanal delicatessen—with all manner of ingredients—and half white-subway-tile-trendy eatery, with indoor and outdoor tables filled with Stockholmers eating well. If it's busy—as it often is—they'll scrawl your name at the bottom of the long butcher-paper waiting list (no reservations). If it's full, you can grab a place at the bar and eat there—or shop in the attached upscale grocery (lots of creative boxed meals and salads to go) and picnic in the park across the street (daily 7:00-23:00, at the far end of Skånegatan at Nytorget 4, tel. 08/5990-9180). Another branch is near Hörtorget at Sveavägen 44 (see the "Stockholm Hotels & Restaurants" map).

$$$ Kohphangan, with an almost laughably over-the-top island atmosphere that belies its surprisingly good Thai food, has been a hit for 20 years. (Thailand is to Swedes what Mexico is to Americans—the sunny "south of the border" playground.) The ambience? Mix a shipwreck, Bob Marley, and a Christmas tree and you've got it (Mon-Fri 16:00-24:00, Sat-Sun from 12:00, Skånegatan 57, tel. 08/642-5040).

$$ Gossip is a mellow, unpretentious hole-in-the-wall serving Bangladeshi street food (Mon-Fri 11:00-23:00, Sat-Sun from 13:00, Skånegatan 71, tel. 08/640-6901).

Beer and Pub Grub in Södermalm

Södermalm cultivates the most interesting beer scene in this beer-crazy city.

Beer Garden with a View: $$ Mosebacke, perched high above town, is a gravelly beer garden with a grand harbor view. The beer garden (open only on warm summer evenings) prides itself on its beer rather than its basic grub (read: bar snacks). It's a good place to mix with a relaxed young crowd. As each of the beer kiosks has its own specialties, survey all of them before making your choice (some open from 11:00, others later; a block inland from the top of the Katarina viewing platform, look for the triumphal arch at Mosebacke Torg 3, tel. 08/556-09890, www.sodrateatern.com). The adjacent restaurant serves fine **$$$$** plates.

Classic Swedish Beer Halls: Two different but equally traditional Södermalm beer halls serve well-executed, hearty Swedish grub in big, high-ceilinged, orange-tiled spaces with rustic wooden tables.

$$$ Kvarnen ("The Mill") is a reliable choice with a 1908 ambience. As it's the home bar for the supporters of a football club, it can be rough. Pick a classic Swedish dish from their fun and easy menu (Mon-Fri 11:00-late, Sat-Sun from 12:00, Tjärhovsgatan 4, tel. 08/643-0380).

$$$$ Pelikan, an old-school beer hall, is less sloppy and has nicer food, including meatballs as big as golf balls. It's a bit deeper into Södermalm (Mon-Thu 16:00-24:00, Fri-Sun from 12:00, Blekingegatan 40, tel. 08/5560-9290).

Trendier "Craft Beer" Pub: $$$ Akkurat has a staggering variety of microbrews—both Swedish and international (on tap and bottled)—as well as whisky. It's great if you wish you were in England with a bunch of Swedes (short pub-grub menu, daily 15:00-24:00 except Fri from 11:00 and Sun from 18:00, Hornsgatan 18, tel. 08/644-0015).

IN NORRMALM
At or near the Grand Hotel

$$$$ Royal Smörgåsbord: To stuff yourself with all the traditional Swedish specialties (a dozen kinds of herring, salmon, reindeer, meatballs, lingonberries, and shrimp, followed by a fine table of cheeses and desserts) with a super harbor view, consider splurging at the Grand Hotel's dressy **Veranda Restaurant.** While very touristy, this is considered the finest *smörgåsbord* in town. The Grand Hotel, where royal guests and Nobel Prize winners stay, faces the harbor across from the palace. Pick up their English flier for a good explanation of the proper way to enjoy this grand buffet (and read about *smörgåsbords* in the Practicalities chapter). Reservations are often necessary (545 SEK in evening, less at lunch, drinks extra, open nightly 18:00-22:00, also open for lunch Sat-Sun 13:00-16:00 year-round and Mon-Fri 12:00-15:00 in May-Sept, no shorts after 18:00, Södra Blasieholmshamnen 8, tel. 08/679-3586, www.grandhotel.se).

$$$$ Restaurang B.A.R. has a noisy, fun energy, with diners surveying meat and fish at the ice-filled counter, talking things over with the chef, and then choosing a slab or filet. Prices are on the board, and everything's grilled (Mon-Fri 11:30-14:00 & 17:00 until late, Sat 16:00-late, closed Sun, behind the Grand Hotel at Blasieholmsgatan 4, tel. 08/611-5335). They also have a nice (short and lower-priced) takeaway menu.

At the Royal Opera House

The Operakällaren, one of Stockholm's most exclusive restaurants, runs a little "hip pocket" restaurant on the side called **$$$ Bakfickan,** specializing in traditional Swedish quality cooking at reasonable prices. It's ideal for someone eating out alone, or for anyone wanting an early dinner. Choose from two different daily specials or order from their regular menu. Sit inside—at tiny private side tables or at the big counter with the locals—or, in good weather, grab a table on the sidewalk, facing a cheery red church (Mon-Thu 11:30-22:00, Fri-Sat until 23:00, Sun 12:00-17:00, on the inland side of Royal Opera House, tel. 08/676-5809).

At or near Hötorget

Hötorget ("Hay Market"), a vibrant outdoor produce market just two blocks from Sergels Torg, is a fun place to picnic-shop. The outdoor market closes at 18:00, and many merchants put their unsold produce on the push list (earlier closing and more desperate merchants on Sat).

Hötorgshallen, next to Hötorget (in the basement under the modern cinema complex), is a colorful indoor food market with an old-fashioned bustle, plenty of exotic and ethnic edibles, and—in the tradition of food markets all over Europe—some great little eateries (Mon-Fri 10:00-18:00, Sat until 16:00, closed Sun). The best is **$$ Kajsas Fisk,** hiding behind the fish stalls. They serve delicious fish soup to little Olivers who can hardly believe they're getting...more. For 110 SEK, you get a big bowl of hearty soup, a simple salad, bread and crackers—plus one soup refill. Their *stekt strömming* (traditional fried herring and potato dish) is a favorite

(Mon-Thu 11:00-18:00, Fri until 19:00, Sat until 16:00, closed Sun, Hötorgshallen 3, tel. 08/207-262). There's a great kebab and falafel place a few stalls away.

$ Kungshallen, an 800-seat indoor food court across the square from Hötorget, has more than a dozen basic eateries. What it lacks in ambience it makes up for in variety, quick service, and generally lower prices. The main floor has sit-down places, while the basement is a shopping-mall-style array of fast-food counters, including Chinese, sushi, pizza, Greek, and Mexican (daily 11:00-22:00).

Just a few blocks away is a branch of **Urban Deli** (at Sveavägen 44), a good takeaway option described earlier under "Skånegatan and Nytorget."

On or near Drottninggatan

The pleasant, pedestrianized shopping street called Drottninggatan, which runs from the train station area up into Stockholm's suburbs, is a fine place to find a forgettable meal but with memorable people-watching. Several interchangeable eateries with sidewalk tables line the street (and don't miss the delightful, leafy park courtyard of Centralbadet, at #88, with several outdoor cafés). None merits a special detour, except the next listing.

$$$$ Rolfs Kök, a vibrant neighborhood favorite, is worth the pleasant five-minute stroll up from the end of Drottninggatan. The long bar up front fades into an open kitchen hemmed in with happy diners at counters, and tight tables fill the rest of the space before spilling out onto the sidewalk. Trendy, casual, and inviting, this bistro features international fare with a focus on Swedish classics and a good wine list. Reservations are smart (Mon-Fri 11:30-24:00, Sat-Sun from 17:00, Tegnérgatan 41, tel. 08/101-696, www.rolfskok.se).

Near Sergels Torg

Kulturhuset: Handy for a simple meal with great city views, **$$ Cafeteria Panorama** offers cheap eats and a salad bar, inside and outside seating, and jaw-dropping vistas (90-SEK lunch specials with salad bar, Mon-Fri 11:00-19:00, Sat until 18:00, Sun until 17:00).

The many modern shopping malls and department stores around Sergels Torg all have appealing, if pricey, eateries catering to the needs of hungry local shoppers. **Åhléns** department store has a Hemköp supermarket in the basement (daily until 21:00) and two restaurants upstairs with 80-110-SEK daily lunch specials (Mon-Fri 11:00-19:30, Sat until 18:30, Sun until 17:30).

IN ÖSTERMALM

$$$ Saluhall, on Östermalmstorg (near recommended Hotel Wellington), is a great old-time indoor market dating from 1888. Depending on when you visit, the hall may be operating from an adjacent temporary market—or it may be completely refurbished, from top to bottom. Either way, you'll find top-quality artisanal producers and a variety of sit-down and takeout eateries. While it's nowhere near "cheap," it's one of the most pleasant market halls I've seen, oozing with upscale yet traditional Swedish class. Inside

you'll find Middle Eastern fare, sushi, classic Scandinavian open-face sandwiches, seafood salads, healthy wraps, cheese counters, designer chocolates, gourmet coffee stands, and a pair of classic old sit-down eateries (Elmqvist and Tysta Mari). This is your chance to pull up a stool at a lunch counter next to well-heeled Swedes (Mon-Fri 9:30-19:00, Sat until 16:00, closed Sun).

$$$$ Restaurang Volt is a destination restaurant for those looking to splurge on "New Nordic" cooking: fresh, locally sourced ingredients fused into bold new recipes with fundamentally Swedish flavors. Owners Fredrik Johnsson and Peter Andersson fill their minimalist black dining room with just 31 seats, so reservations are essential (no a la carte, choose from 4- or 6-course tasting menus, Tue-Sat 18:00-24:00, closed Sun-Mon, Kommendörsgatan 16, tel. 08/662-3400, www.restaurangvolt.se).

$$$$ Riche, a Parisian-style brasserie just a few steps off Nybroplan at Östermalm's waterfront, is a high-energy place with a youthful sophistication. They serve up pricey but nicely executed Swedish and international dishes in their winter garden, bright dining room, and white-tile-and-wine-glass-chandeliered bar (Mon-Fri 7:30-24:00, Sat-Sun from 11:00, Birger Jarlsgatan 4, tel. 08/5450-3560).

$$ Sushi Yama Express is a quick and tasty option for takeaway sushi, sashimi, and rolls (Mon-Fri 10:00-20:00, closed Sat-Sun, at Nybrogatan 18, tel. 08/202-031).

Stockholm Connections

BY BUS

Swebus is the largest operator of long-distance buses, which can be cheaper than trains (tel. 0771/21-8218, www.swebus.se); Nettbuss also has lots of routes (www.nettbuss.se). Some bus companies offer discounts with advance purchase.

From Stockholm by Bus to: Copenhagen (about 3/day with change in Malmö, 9.5 hours, longer for overnight trips), **Oslo** (3/day, 8 hours), **Kalmar** (3/day, fewer on weekends, 6 hours).

BY TRAIN

The easiest and cheapest way to book train tickets is online at www.sj.se. Simply select your journey, pay with a credit card, and print out your ticket. You can also buy or print tickets at the station, using a self-service kiosk (bring your purchase confirmation code). If you need help, tickets are sold at a desk at bigger stations, but this can come with long lines and a surcharge. For timetables and prices, check online, call 0771/757-575, or use self-service ticket kiosks.

As with airline tickets and hotel rooms, Swedish train ticket prices vary with demand. The cheapest are advance-purchase, non-changeable, and nonrefundable.

For rail-pass holders, seat reservations are required on express (such as the "SJ high-speed" class) and overnight trains, and they're recommended on some longer routes (to Oslo, for example). If you have a rail pass, make your seat reservation at a ticket window in a train station, by phone (at the number above), or online.

From Stockholm by Train to: Uppsala (4/hour, 40 minutes; also possible on slower suburban *pendeltåg*—2/hour, 55 minutes, covered by local transit pass plus small supplement), **Växjö** (almost hourly, 3.5 hours, change in Alvesta, reservations required), **Kalmar** (almost hourly, 4.5-5 hours, transfer in Alvesta, reservations required), **Copenhagen** (almost hourly, 5-6 hours on high-speed train, some with a transfer at Lund or Hässleholm, reservations required; overnight train requires a change in Malmö or Lund; all trains stop at Copenhagen airport before terminating at the central train station).

By Train to Oslo: The speedy X2000 train zips from downtown Copenhagen to downtown Oslo in about 5.5 hours, runs several times daily, and requires reservations (160 NOK in first class, 65 NOK in second class; first class often comes with a hot meal, fruit bowl, and unlimited coffee). Note that through 2020, construction on this line will likely interrupt service, in which case you'll take the slower SJ InterCity train (recommended 35-NOK reservation in either class). There may also be (slower) connections possible with a change in Göteborg.

BY OVERNIGHT BOAT

Ferry boat companies run shuttle buses from the train station to coincide with each departure; check for details when you buy your ticket. When comparing prices between boats and planes, remember that the boat fare includes a night's lodging.

From Stockholm to: Helsinki and **Tallinn** (daily/nightly boats, 16 hours, see Helsinki and Tallinn chapters), **Turku** (daily/nightly boats, 11-12 hours). The St. Peter Line connects Stockholm to **St. Petersburg,** but the trip takes two nights—you'll sail the first night to Tallinn, then a second night to St. Petersburg; returning, you'll sail the first night to Helsinki, and the second night to Stockholm (www.stpeterline.com). Note: To visit Russia, American and Canadian citizens need a visa (arrange weeks in advance); for details on the visa requirement and the company, see "Connecting Helsinki and St. Petersburg" at the end of the Helsinki chapter.

BY CRUISE SHIP

For many more details on Stockholm's ports, and other cruise destinations, pick up my *Rick Steves Scandinavian & Northern European Cruise Ports* guidebook.

Stockholm has two cruise ports: the more central **Stadsgården,** used mainly by ships that are just passing through, is in Södermalm; **Frihamnen,** used primarily by ships beginning or ending a cruise in Stockholm, is three miles northeast of the city center.

Getting Downtown: Most cruise lines offer a convenient **shuttle bus** (about 120 SEK round-trip) that drops you in downtown Stockholm (likely near the Opera House). From there it's an easy walk or public bus/tram ride to the sights. **Taxis** from each port are also available (depending on your destination, figure 165-220 SEK from Stadsgården and 200-300 SEK from Frihamnen). Other options, including a hop-on, hop-off bus or boat from Stadsgården or the public bus from Frihamnen, are explained later.

Port Details: TI kiosks (with bus tickets, city guides, and maps) open at both ports when ships arrive.

Stadsgården is a long embankment, with cruises arriving at areas that flank the busy Viking Line Terminal (used by boats to Helsinki). The nearest transportation hub (with bus and T-bana stops) is Slussen, which sits beneath the bridge connecting the Old Town/Gamla Stan and the Södermalm neighborhood. Berth 160 is an easy 15-minute **walk** to Slussen; berth 167 is farther out but still walkable (about 30 minutes to Slussen).

From Stadsgården, a good option is the handy **hop-on, hop-off harbor boat** tour, which stops near both berths and connects to worthwhile downtown areas for a reasonable price (tickets often discounted from cruise port). **Taxis** and **hop-on, hop-off tour buses** are also available (for details on all these options, see "Tours in Stockholm," earlier).

Frihamnen is a sprawling port zone used by cruise liners as well as overnight boats to St. Petersburg (boats to Tallinn, Helsinki, and Riga go from nearby Värtahamnen). Cruises typically use one of three berths—634, 638, or 650. Berth 638 is the main dock and has a dedicated terminal building (with a TI desk and gift shops). Along the main harborfront road you'll find a TI kiosk; hop-on, hop-off bus tours (for details see "Tours in Stockholm," earlier); and a public **bus** stop—a good option. Bus #76 zips you to several major sights, including Djurgårdsbron, Nybroplan, Kungsträdgården, Räntmästartrappan, and Slussen (4-7/hour Mon-Fri, 3-4/hour Sat-Sun). **Bus #1** cuts across the top of Östermalm and Norrmalm to the train station (every 5-8 minutes daily). You can't buy bus tickets on board—get one at the TI inside the terminal, at the booth near the bus stop, from the ticket machine at the bus stop, or use the handy SL ticketing app (called "SL-Stockholm"; see "Getting Around Stockholm," earlier).

BY PLANE

For information on arriving at Stockholm's airports, see "Arrival in Stockholm," earlier in this chapter.

NEAR STOCKHOLM

Drottningholm Palace • Sigtuna • Uppsala

At Stockholm's doorstep is a variety of fine side-trip options—all within an hour of the capital. Drottningholm Palace, on the city's outskirts, was the summer residence—and most opulent castle—of the Swedish royal family, and has a uniquely well-preserved Baroque theater, to boot. The adorable town of Sigtuna is a cutesy, cobbled escape from the big city, studded with history and rune stones. Uppsala is Sweden's answer to Oxford, offering stately university facilities and museums, the home and garden of scientist Carl Linnaeus, as well as a grand cathedral and the enigmatic burial mounds of Gamla Uppsala on the outskirts of town. Note that another side-trip option is to visit a few of the islands in Stockholm's archipelago (described in the next chapter).

Drottningholm Palace

The queen's 17th-century summer castle and current royal residence has been called "Sweden's Versailles." While that's a bit of a stretch, taken as a whole the Drottningholm Palace complex (Drottningholms Slott) is worth ▲▲. It's enjoyable to explore the place where the Swedish royals bunk and to stroll their expansive gardens. Even more worthwhile is touring the Baroque-era theater on the grounds (itself rated ▲▲), which preserves 18th-century stage sets and rare special-effects machinery. If you've seen plenty of palaces, skip the interior but enjoy the grounds and theater tour. You can likely squeeze everything in with half a day here, or linger for an entire day.

GETTING THERE

Drottningholm is an easy boat or subway-plus-bus ride from downtown Stockholm. Consider approaching by water (as the royals traditionally did) and then returning by bus and subway (as a commoner). If your heart is set on touring the palace interior, check the website before you go: It can close unexpectedly for various events.

Boats depart regularly from the Klara Malarstrand pier just across from City Hall for the relaxing hour-long trip (160 SEK one-way, 210 SEK round-trip, on the hour daily, likely additional departures at :30 past the hour on weekends or any day in July-Aug, fewer departures Sept-April, tel. 08/1200-4000, www.stromma.se). The pier is a five-minute walk from the central train station (on Vasagatan, walk toward the water, staying to the right and crossing a plaza under the freeway to reach the pier). It's worth reserving a spot in advance on weekends, or if your day plan requires a particular departure.

It's faster (30-45 minutes total) to take **public transit:** Ride the T-bana about 20 minutes to Brommaplan, where you can catch any #300-series bus for the five-minute ride to Drottningholm (as you leave the Brommaplan station, check monitors to see which bus is leaving next—usually from platform A, E, or F).

BACKGROUND

"Drottningholm" means "Queen's Island." When the original castle mysteriously burned down in 1661 immediately after a visit

from Queen Hedvig Eleonora, she (quite conveniently) had already commissioned plans for a bigger, better palace.

Built over 40 years—with various rooms redecorated by centuries of later monarchs—Drottningholm has the air of overcompensating for an inferiority complex. While rarely absolute rulers, Sweden's royals long struggled with stubborn parliaments. Perhaps this made the propaganda value of the palace decor even more important. Touring the palace, you'll see art that makes the point that Sweden's royalty is divine and belongs with the gods. Portraits and prominently displayed gifts from fellow monarchs attempt to legitimize the royal family by connecting the Swedish blue bloods with Roman emperors, medieval kings, and Europe's great royal

families. The portraits you'll see of France's Louis XVI and Russia's Catherine the Great are reminders that Sweden's royalty was related to or tightly networked with the European dynasties.

Of course, today's monarchs are figureheads ruled by a constitution. The royal family makes a point to be as accessible and as "normal" as royalty can be. King Carl XVI Gustaf (b. 1946)—whose main job is handing out Nobel Prizes once a year—is a car nut who talks openly about his dyslexia. He was the first Swedish king not to be crowned "by the grace of God." At his 1976 wedding to the popular Queen Silvia, ABBA serenaded his bride with "Dancing Queen." Their daughter Crown Princess Victoria is heir to the throne (she studied political science at Yale, interned with Sweden's European Union delegation, and married her personal trainer, Daniel Westling, in 2010). The king and queen still live in one wing of Drottningholm, while other members of the royal family attempt to live more "normal" lives elsewhere.

SIGHTS AT DROTTNINGHOLM
Drottningholm Palace

While not the finest palace interior in Europe (or even in Scandinavia), Drottningholm offers a chance to stroll through a place where a monarch still lives. You'll see two floors of lavish rooms, where Sweden's royalty did their best to live in the style of Europe's divine monarchs.

Cost and Hours: 130 SEK, combo-ticket with Chinese Pavilion-190 SEK; May-Sept daily 10:00-16:30, April until 15:30, rest of year open weekends only—see website for hours, closed last two weeks of Dec.

Information: Tel. 08/402-6280, www.kungahuset.se.

Tours: You can explore the palace on your own, but with sparse posted explanations and no audioguide, it's worth the 30 SEK extra for the 30-minute English guided tour. Tours are offered daily, usually at 10:00, 12:00, 14:00, and 16:00 (fewer tours Oct-May). Alternatively, you could buy the inexpensive palace guidebook.

Services: The gift shop/café at the entrance to the grounds (near the boat dock and bus stop) acts as a visitors center; Drottningholm's only WCs are in the adjacent building. A handy Pressbyrån convenience store is also nearby (snacks, drinks, and transit tickets), and taxis are usually standing by.

Visiting Drottningholm Palace: Ascend the grand staircase (decorated with faux marble and relief-illusion paintings) and buy your ticket on the first floor. Entering the staterooms on the **first floor,** admire the craftsmanship of the walls, with gold leaf shimmering on expertly tooled leather. Then pass through the Green Cabinet and hook right into Hedvig Eleonora's State Bed Chambers. The richly colored Baroque decor here, with gold embellishments, is representative of what the entire interior once looked like. Hedvig Eleonora was a "dowager queen," meaning that she was the widow of a king—her husband, King Karl X, died young at age 24—after they had been married just six years. Looking around the room, you'll see symbolism of this tragic separation. For example, in the ceiling painting, Hedvig Eleonora rides a cloud, with hands joined below her—suggesting that she will be reunited with her beloved in heaven.

This room was also the residence of a later monarch, Gustav III. That's why it looks like (and was) more of a theater than a place for sleeping. In the style of the French monarchs, this is where the ceremonial tucking-in and dressing of the king would take place.

Backtrack into the golden room, then continue down the other hallway. You'll pass through a room of royal portraits with very consistent characteristics: pale skin with red cheeks; a high forehead with gray hair (suggesting wisdom); and big eyes (windows to the soul). At the end of the hall is a grand library, which once held some 7,000 books. The small adjoining room is filled by a large model of a temple in Pompeii; Gustav III—who ordered this built—was fascinated by archaeology, and still today, there's a museum of antiquities named for him at the Royal Palace in Stockholm.

On the **second floor,** as you enter the first room, notice the faux doors, painted on the walls to create symmetry, and the hidden doors for servants (who would scurry—unseen and unheard—through the walls to attend to the royal family). In the Blue Drawing Room is a bust of the then-king's cousin, Catherine the Great. This Russian monarch gave him—in the next room, the Chinese Drawing Room—the (made-in-Russia) faux "Chinese" stove. This dates from a time when exotic imports from China (tea, silk, ivory, Kung Pao chicken) were exciting and new. (Around the same time, in the mid-18th century, the royals built the Chinese Pavilion on Drottningholm's grounds.) The Gobelins tapestries in this room were also a gift, from France's King Louis XVI. In the next room, the darker Oskar Room, are more tapestries—these a gift from England's King Charles I. (Sensing a trend?) You'll pass through Karl XI's Gallery (overlooking the grand staircase)—which is still used for royal functions—and into the largest room on this floor, the Hall of State. The site of royal weddings and receptions, this room boasts life-size paintings of very important Swedes in golden frames and a bombastically painted ceiling.

Drottningholm Palace Park

Like so many European "summer palaces," the Drottningholm grounds are graced with sprawling gardens that are a pretty place to stroll on a fine day. Directly behind the palace is the strictly geometrical Baroque Garden, with angular hedges, tidy rows of trees, fountains, and outdoor "rooms" at the far end. It adjoins the more naturalistic English Garden, which Gustav III was determined to have after seeing one of the landscape gardens belonging to his cousin Catherine the Great. (It was  Gustav, too, who speckled the grounds with marble statues.) At the far end of the grounds is the Chinese Pavilion, containing a fine Rococo interior with chinoiserie.

Drottningholm Court Theater

This 18th-century theater (Drottningholms Slottsteater) has miraculously survived the ages—complete with its instruments, original stage sets, and hand-operated sound-effects machines for wind, thunder, and clouds. The required guided tour is short (30 minutes), entertaining, and informative—I found it more enjoyable than the palace tour.

Cost and Hours: 100 SEK for 30-minute guided tour—buy tickets in the theater shop next door, English tours about hourly May-Aug 11:00-16:30, Sept 12:00-15:30—these are first and last tour times, limited tours possible on weekends in April and Oct-Dec, no tours Jan-March.

Information: Tel. 08/759-0406, www.dtm.se.

Performances: Check their schedule for the rare opportunity to see perfectly authentic operas (about 25 performances each summer). Tickets for this popular time-travel musical and theatrical experience cost 300-1,000 SEK and go on sale each March; purchase online (www.ticktmaster.se), at the theater shop, or by phone (from the US, call +46-77-170-7070; see theater website for details).

Background: A Swedish king built the theater in the mid-1700s to pacify his Prussian wife, who was appalled by the provincialism of Sweden's performing arts. This is one of two such historic theaters remaining in Europe (the other is in the Czech town of Český Krumlov). Their son, King Gustav III, loved the theater (some say more than he loved ruling Sweden): Besides ordering Stockholm's Royal Opera to be built, he also wrote, directed, and acted in several theatrical presentations (including the first-ever production in Swedish instead of French, the usual court language). He even died in a theater, assassinated at a masquerade ball in the very opera house he had built. When he died, so too did this flourishing of culture: The theater became a warehouse for storing royal bric-a-brac. The stage stayed dark until the mid-1940s, when opera and plays were once again performed here.

Visiting the Theater: On the tour, you'll see the bedrooms where famous actors and conductors would sleep while performing here, then enter the theater itself, lit only with (now simulated) candles. You'll see the extremely deep stage (with scenery peeking in from the edges), the royal boxes where the king and queen entered, and doors and curtains that were painted onto walls to achieve perfect symmetry.

It's fascinating to think that the system of pulleys, trap doors, and actors floating in from the sky isn't so different from the techniques employed on stages today. Because the mechanisms are fragile, they aren't demonstrated on the tour, but you can watch a video demonstration in the theater shop next door.

Sigtuna

Sigtuna, the oldest town in Sweden (established in the 970s), is the country's cutest town as well. Worth ▲, it sits sugary sweet on Lake Mälaren, about 30 miles inland from Stockholm (reachable by train/bus or sightseeing boat). A visit here affords a relaxed look at an open-air folk museum of a town, with ruined churches, ancient rune stones, and a lane of 18th-century buildings—all with English info posts. It also offers plenty of shopping and eating options in a parklike lakeside setting. If you're looking for stereotypical Sweden and a break from the big city, Sigtuna is a fun side-trip.

Getting There: By **public transport** from Stockholm, it's a one-hour trip. Take the *pendeltåg* suburban train from Stockholm to Märsta and then change to bus #570 or #575. You can buy all four train and bus tickets needed for a round-trip journey in Stockholm— just scan the ticket for each leg at the sensor before boarding each train or bus (but be alert that you can accidentally validate all at once if you stack them and scan the one on top).

Guided two-hour **sightseeing cruises** run to Sigtuna in summer (375 SEK round-trip, Wed-Sun morning departures from Stockholm's Stadshusbron dock, www.stromma.se). If traveling by **car** to Uppsala or Oslo, Sigtuna is a short detour.

Tourist Information: The helpful TI is on the main street and eager to equip you with a town map (daily 10:00-17:00, Storagatan 33, tel. 08/5948-0650, http://destinationsigtuna.se/en/).

Sights in Sigtuna

Main Street: Storagatan

Sigtuna's main street provides the town's spine. Along it, besides the TI, you'll find the Town Hall from 1744, with a nicely preserved interior (free, June-Aug daily 12:00-16:00), and the Sigtuna History Museum, with archaeological finds from the Viking culture here (may be closed for renovation). As you stroll the street, read the historical signs posted along the way and poke into shops and cafés. The most charming place for lunch, a snack, or a drink is Tant Brun ("Auntie Brown's") Café, tucked away just around the corner from the TI in a super-characteristic 17th-century home with a cozy garden.

Churches

Before the Reformation came along, Sigtuna was an important political and religious center, and the site of the country's archbishopric. Along with powerful monastic communities, the town had seven churches. When the Reformation hit, that was the end of the monasteries, and there was a need for only one church—the Gothic Mariakyrkan. It survived, and the rest fell into ruins. Mariakyrkan, or Mary's Church, built by the Dominicans in the 13th century, is decorated with pre-Reformation murals and is worth a look (free, daily 9.00-17:00).

The stony remains of St. Olaf's Church stand in the Mary's Church cemetery. This 12th-century ruin is evocative, with stout vaults and towering walls that served the community as a place of last refuge when under attack.

Rune Stones

Sigtuna is dotted with a dozen rune stones. Literally "word stones," these memorial stones are carved with messages in an Iron Age runic language. Sigtuna has more of these than any other Swedish town. Those here generally have a cross, indicating that they are from the Christian era (11th century). Each is described in English. I like Anund's stone, which says, "Anund had this stone erected in memory of himself in his lifetime." His rune carver showed a glimpse of personality and that perhaps Anund had no friends. (It worked. Now he's in an American guidebook, and 10 centuries later, he's still remembered.)

Uppsala

Uppsala, Sweden's fourth-largest city, is a rather small town with a big history. A few blocks in front of its train station, an inviting commercial center bustles around the main square and along a scenic riverfront. Towering across the river are its historic cathedral and a venerable university. For visitors, the university features a rare 17th-century anatomical theater, an exhibit of its prestigious academic accomplishments, and a library with literary treasures on display. Uppsala is home to the father of modern botany, Carl Linnaeus, whose garden and house—now a museum—make for a fascinating visit. And, just outside town stands Gamla Uppsala, the site of a series of majestic burial mounds where Sweden buried its royalty back in the 6th century. While Gamla Uppsala is a short bus ride away, everything else is within delightful walking distance. If you're not traveling anywhere else in Sweden other than Stockholm, Uppsala (less than an hour away) makes a pleasant day

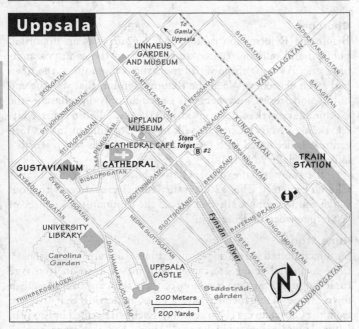

trip. While buzzing during the school year, this university town is sleepy during summer vacations.

GETTING THERE

Take the train from Stockholm's central station (5/hour, 40 minutes, 85 SEK; also possible on slower suburban *pendeltåg*—2/hour, 55 minutes, covered by local transit pass plus small supplement). Since the Uppsala station has lockers and is in the same direction from Stockholm as the airport, you could combine a quick visit here with an early arrival or late departure.

Orientation to Uppsala

TOURIST INFORMATION

The helpful TI, across the street from the train station, has the informative *What's On Uppsala* magazine, which includes the best map of the center and a list of sights (Mon-Fri 10:00-17:00, Sat until 15:00, Sun July-Aug only 11:00-15:00, Kungsgatan 59, tel. 018/727-4800, www.destinationuppsala.se).

ARRIVAL IN UPPSALA

From the train station (pay lockers), cross the busy street and find the TI on the right (pick up the *What's On* magazine). Walk two blocks to Kungsängsgatan, turn right, and walk to the main square,

Stora Torget. The spires of the cathedral mark two of the top three sights (the cathedral itself and the adjacent university buildings). The Linnaeus Garden and Museum is a few blocks up the river, and the bus to Gamla Uppsala is a couple of blocks away.

Sights in Uppsala

▲▲Uppsala Cathedral (Uppsala Domkyrkan)

One of Scandinavia's largest, most historic cathedrals feels as vital as it does impressive. While the building was completed in 1435, the spires and interior decorations are from the late 19th century. The cathedral—with a fine Gothic interior, the relics of St. Erik, memories of countless Swedish coronations, and the tomb of King Gustav Vasa—is well worth a visit.

Cost and Hours: Free, daily 8:00-18:00; free guided English tours go 1-2 times/day in season (mid-June–mid-Aug Mon-Sat at 11:00 and 14:00, Sun at 15:00), or pick up brochure in gift shop; tel. 018/187-177, www.uppsaladomkyrka.se.

Visiting the Cathedral: Grab a seat in a pew and take in the graceful Gothic lines of the longest nave in Scandinavia (130 yards). The gorgeously carved, gold-slathered Baroque pulpit is a reminder of the Protestant (post-Reformation) focus on preaching the word of God in the people's language. Look high above in the choir area to enjoy fine murals, restored in the 1970s. For ages, pilgrims have come here to see the relics of St. Erik. All around you are important side chapels, tombs, and memorials (each with an English description).

Near the entrance is the tomb and memorial to scientist Carl Linnaeus, the father of modern botany, who spent his career at the university here (for more on him, see the Linnaeus Garden and Museum listing, later).

In the chapel at the far east end of the church is the tomb of King Gustav Vasa and his family. This chapel was originally dedicated to the Virgin Mary. But Gustav Vasa brought the Reformation to Sweden in 1527 and usurped this prized space for his own tomb. In good Swedish style, the decision was affirmed by a vote in parliament, and bam—the country was Lutheran. (A few years later, England's King Henry VIII tried a similar religious revolution—and had a much tougher time.) Notice that in the tomb sculpture, Gustav is shown flanked by two wives—his first wife died after suffering a fall; his second wife bore him 10 children. High above are murals of Gustav's illustrious life.

Speaking of Mary, notice the modern statue of a common-rather-than-regal Protestant Mary outside the chapel looking in. This eerily lifelike statue from 2005, called *Mary (The Return)*, captures Jesus' mother wearing a scarf and timeless garb. In keeping with the Protestant spirit here, this new version of Mary is shown not as an exalted queen, but as an everywoman, saddened by the loss of her child and seeking solace—or answers—in the church.

Cathedral Treasury: By the gift shop, you can pay to ride the elevator up to the treasury collection. Here (with the help of a loaner flashlight and English translations), you'll find medieval textiles (tapestries and vestments), swords and crowns found in Gustav's grave, and the Nobel Peace Prize won by Nathan Söderblom, an early-20th-century archbishop here (40 SEK, daily 10:00-17:00, until 16:00 off-season). In this same narthex area, notice the debit-card machine for offerings.

Eating: The **$$ Cathedral Café** (a few steps to the right as you exit the cathedral) is charming, reasonable, and handy—and your money supports the city's mission of helping the local homeless population (lunch specials, Mon-Fri 10:00-16:30, Sat-Sun 11:00-16:00). Or, survey the many eateries on or near the main square or along the river below the cathedral.

UNIVERSITY AND NEARBY

Scandinavia's first university was founded in Uppsala in 1477. Two famous grads are Carl Linnaeus (the famous botanist) and Anders Celsius (the scientist who developed the temperature scale that bears his name). The campus is scattered around the cathedral part of town, and two university buildings are particularly interesting and welcoming to visitors: the Gustavianum and the library.

▲▲Gustavianum

Facing the cathedral is the university's oldest surviving building, with a bulbous dome that doubles as a sundial (notice the gold numbers). Today it houses a well-presented museum that features an anatomical theater, a cabinet filled with miniature curiosities, and Celsius' thermometer. The collection is curiously engaging for the glimpse it gives into the mindset of 17th-century Europe.

Cost and Hours: 50 SEK, Tue-Sun 10:00-16:00, Sept-May from 11:00, closed Mon year-round, Akademigatan 3, tel. 018/471-7571, www.gustavianum.uu.se.

Visiting the Gustavianum: Ride the elevator (near the gift shop/ticket desk) up to the fourth floor. Then, see the exhibits as you walk back down.

Up top is a collection of **Viking artifacts** discovered at Valsgärde, a prehistoric site near Uppsala used for burials for more than 700 years. Archaeologists have uncovered 15 boat graves here (dating from A.D. 600-1050—roughly one per generation), providing insight on the Viking Age. The recovered artifacts on display here show fine Viking workmanship and a society more refined than many might expect.

Next you'll find the **anatomical theater** (accessible from the fourth and third floors). This theater's only show was human dissection. In the mid-1600s, as the enlightened ideas of the Renaissance swept far into the north of Europe, scholars began to consider dissection of the human body the ultimate scientific education. Corpses of hanged criminals were carefully sliced and diced here, under a dome in an almost temple-like atmosphere, demonstrating the lofty heights to which science had risen in society. Imagine 200 students standing tall all around and leaning in to peer intently at the teacher's scalpel. Notice the plaster death masks of the dissected in a case at the entry.

On the second floor is a fascinating exhibit on the **history of the university.** The Physics Chamber features a collection of instruments from the 18th and 19th centuries that were used by university teachers. The Augsburg Art Cabinet takes center stage here with a dizzying array of nearly 1,000 minuscule works of art and other tidbits held in an ornately decorated oak cabinet. Built in the 1620s for a bigwig who wanted to impress his friends, the cabinet once held the items now shown in the display cases surrounding it. Find the interactive video screen, where you can control a virtual tour of the collection. Just beyond the cabinet is a thermometer that once belonged to Celsius (in his handwriting, notice how 0 and 100 were originally flip-flopped, with water boiling at 0 degrees Celsius rather than 100).

On the first floor is the university's **classical antiquities collection** from the Mediterranean. These ancient Greek and Roman artifacts and Egyptian sarcophagi were used to bring classical culture and art to students unable to travel abroad.

▲University Library (Universitetsbiblioteket)

Uppsala University's library, housed in a 19th-century building called the Carolina Rediviva, is a block uphill from the cathedral and Gustavianum. Off the entry hall (to the right) is a small but exquisite exhibit of treasured old books. Well-displayed and well-described in English, the carefully selected collection is surprisingly captivating.

Cost and Hours: Free, daily 9:00-18:00, Dag Hammarskjölds väg 1, tel. 018/471-1000, www.ub.uu.se.

Visiting the Library: With precious items like Mozart scores in the composer's own hand, margin notes by Copernicus in a 13th-century astronomy book, and a map of Mexico City dating from 1555, the display cases here feel like the Treasures room at the British Library.

The most valuable item is the **Silver Bible,** a translation from Greek of the four Gospels into the now-extinct Gothic language. Written in Ravenna in the 6th century, Sweden's single most precious book is so named for its silver-ink writing on purple-colored calfskin vellum. Booty from a 1648 Swedish victory in Prague, it ended up at Uppsala University in 1669.

Another rarity is the **Carta Marina,** the first more-or-less accurate map of Scandinavia, printed in Venice in 1539 from nine woodblocks. Compare this 16th-century understanding of the region with your own travels.

▲Linnaeus Garden and Museum (Linnéträdgården)

Carl Linnaeus, famous for creating the formal system for naming different species of plants and animals, spent his career in Uppsala as a professor. This home, office, greenhouse, and garden is the ultimate Linnaeus sight, providing a vivid look at this amazing scientist and his work.

Cost and Hours: 80 SEK for museum and garden; museum open daily 11:00-17:00 except closed Mon in May, Mon-Thu in Sept, and Oct-April; garden open until 20:00; daily 45-minute English tour at 14:30; after 17:00, when the museum closes, the garden becomes a free public space—enter on Svartbäcksgatan at #27; tel. 018/471-2874, www.linnaeus.uu.se.

Visiting the Garden and Museum: While Linnaeus (whose noble name was Carl von Linné) was professor of medicine and botany at the University of Uppsala, he lived and studied here. From 1743 until 1778, he ran this botanical garden and lived on site to study the plant action—day and night, year-round—of about 3,000 different species. When he moved in, the university's department of medicine and botany moved in as well.

It was in this garden (the first in Sweden, originally set up in 1655) that Linnaeus developed a way to classify the plant kingdom. Wandering the garden where the most famous of all botanists did his work, you can pop into the orangery, built so temperate plants could survive the Nordic winters.

The museum, in Linnaeus' home (which he shared with his wife and seven children), is filled with the family's personal possessions and his professional gear. You'll see his insect cabinet, herbs cabinet, desk, botany tools, and notes. An included audioguide helps bring the exhibit to life.

More Sights near the University

Uppsala has a range of lesser sights, all within walking distance of the cathedral. The **Uppland Museum** (Upplandsmuseet), a regional history museum with prehistoric bits and folk-art scraps, is on the river by the waterfall, near the TI (free, Tue-Sun 12:00-17:00, closed Mon). Uphill from the university library is the 16th-century **Uppsala Castle,** which houses an art museum and runs slice-of-castle-life tours (inquire at TI, tel. 018/727-2485).

ON THE OUTSKIRTS
▲Gamla Uppsala

This pleasant, scenic site on the outskirts of town gives historians goose bumps. Gamla Uppsala—literally, "Old Uppsala"—includes  nine large royal burial mounds circled by a walking path. Fifteen hundred years ago, when the Baltic Sea was higher and it was easy to sail all the way to Uppsala, the pagan Swedish kings had their capital here. Old Uppsala is where the Swedish kingdoms came together and a nation coalesced.

Cost and Hours: The **mounds** are free and always open. The **museum** is 80 SEK and open daily 11:00-17:00 (shorter hours Sept-March—generally 12:00-16:00 and closed Tue, Wed, and Fri). In summer your museum admission includes a 40-minute guided English tour of the mounds (July-Aug daily at 12:30 and 15:30, tel. 018/239-312, www.raa.se/gamlauppsala). The **church** is free and open daily 9:00-18:00, Sept-March until 16:00 (tiny church museum across the lane is free and open Sat-Sun only 12:00-15:00).

Getting There: A direct city bus stops right at the site. From the Uppsala train station, go to the bus stop on the town square (Stora Torget, 2 blocks away) and take bus #2, marked *Gamla Uppsala,* to the last stop—Kungshögarna (35 SEK if bought on board—credit cards only, otherwise buy ticket at Pressbyrån kiosk on the square; 2-4/hour, 15-minute trip). All the Gamla Uppsala sights are within 200 yards of each other, making it an easy visit.

Eating: Gamla Uppsala is great for picnics, or you can drop by the rustic and half-timbered **$** Odinsborg café, which serves sandwiches, mead, and daily specials (daily 10:00-18:00, tel. 018/323-525).

Visiting Gamla Uppsala: The highlight of a visit is to climb the evocative mounds, which you're welcome to wander. Also at the site is a small but interesting museum and a 12th-century church.

The Mounds: The focus of ritual and religious activities from the 6th through 13th centuries, the mounds are made meaningful with the help of English info boards posted around.

Imagine the scene over a thousand years ago, when the democratic tradition of this country helped bring the many small Swedish kingdoms together into one nation. A *ting* was a political assembly where people dealt with the issues of the day. Communities would gather here at the rock that marked their place, and then the leader, standing atop the flat mound (nearest today's café), would address the crowd as if in a natural amphitheater. It was here that Sweden became Christianized a thousand years ago. In 1989 Pope John Paul II gave a Mass right here to celebrate the triumph of Christianity over paganism in Sweden. (These days, this is a pretty secular society and relatively few Swedes go to church.)

Museum: Gamla Uppsala's museum gives a good overview of early Swedish history and displays items found in the mounds. While humble, it is instructive, with plenty of excavated artifacts.

Church: Likely standing upon a pagan holy site, the church dates from the 12th century and was the residence of the first Swedish archbishop. An 11th-century rune stone is embedded in the external wall. In the entryway, an iron-clad oak trunk with seven locks on it served as the church treasury back in the 12th century. In the nave, a few Catholic frescoes, whitewashed over in the 16th century with the Reformation, have been restored.

STOCKHOLM'S ARCHIPELAGO

Vaxholm • Grinda • Svartsö • Sandhamm

Some of Europe's most scenic islands stretch 80 miles out into the Baltic Sea from Stockholm. If you're cruising to (or from) Finland, you'll get a good look at this island beauty. If you have more time and want to immerse yourself in all that simple Swedish nature, consider spending a day or two island-hopping.

The Swedish word for "island" is simply *ö*, but the local name for this area is Skärgården—literally, "garden of skerries," which are unforested rocks sticking up from the sea. That stone is granite, carved out and deposited by glaciers. The archipelago closer to Stockholm is rockier, with bigger islands and more trees. Farther out (such as at Sandhamn), the glaciers lingered longer, slowly grinding the granite into sand and creating smaller islands.

Locals claim there are more than 30,000 of these islands, and as land here is rising slowly, more pop out every year. Some 150 are inhabited year-round, and about 100 have ferry service. There's an unwritten law of public access in the archipelago: Technically you're allowed to pitch your tent anywhere for up to two nights, provided the owner of the property can't see you from his or her house. It's polite to ask first and essential to act responsibly.

With thousands of islands to choose from, every Swede seems to have a favorite. This chapter covers four very different island destinations that offer an overview of the archipelago. Vaxholm, the gateway to the archipelago, comes with an imposing fortress, a charming fishermen's harbor, and the easiest connections to Stockholm. Rustic Grinda feels like—and used to be—a Swedish summer camp. Sparsely populated Svartsö is another fine back-to-nature experience. And swanky Sandhamn thrills the sailboat set,

ARCHIPELAGO

with a lively yacht harbor, a scenic setting at the far edge of the archipelago, and (true to its name) sandy beaches.

The flat-out best way to experience the magic of the archipelago is simply stretching out comfortably on the rooftop deck of your ferry. The journey truly is the destination. Enjoy the charm of lovingly painted cottages as you glide by, sitting in the sun on delicate pairs of lounge chairs that are positioned to catch just the right view, with the steady rhythm of the ferries lacing this world together, and people savoring quality time with each other and nature.

PLANNING YOUR TIME

On a Tour: For the best quick look, consider one of the many half- or full-day package boat trips from downtown Stockholm to the archipelago. **Strömma** runs several options, including the three-hour Archipelago Tour (2-4/day, 280 SEK), or the all-day Thousand Island Cruise (departs daily in summer at 9:30, 1,235 SEK, includes lunch and dinner; tel. 08/1200-4000, www.stromma.se).

On Your Own: For more flexibility, freedom, and a better dose of the local vacation scene, do it on your own. Any one of the islands in this chapter is easily doable as a single-day side-trip from Stockholm. And, because all boats to and from Stockholm pass through Vaxholm, it's easy to tack on that town to any other one. For general information about the archipelago, see www.visitskargarden.se.

For a very busy all-day itinerary that takes in the two most enjoyable island destinations (Grinda and Sandhamn), consider this plan: 8:00—Set sail from Stockholm; 9:30—Arrive in Grinda for a quick walk around the island; 10:50—Catch the boat to Sandhamn; 11:45—Arrive in Sandhamn, have lunch, and enjoy the town; 17:00—Catch the boat to Stockholm (maybe have dinner on board); 19:05—Arrive back in Stockholm. Or you could craft a route tailored to your interests: For example, for a back-to-nature experience, try Stockholm-Grinda-Svartsö-Stockholm. For an urban mix of towns, consider Stockholm-Vaxholm-Sandhamn-Stockholm.

Overnighting on an island really lets you get away from it all and enjoy the island ambience. I've listed a few accommodations, but note that midrange options are few; most tend to be either pricey and top-end or very rustic (rented cottages with minimal plumbing).

Don't struggle too hard with the "which island?" decision. The

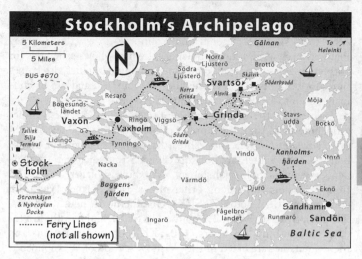

Stockholm's Archipelago

5 Kilometers

5 Miles

BUS #670

Gälnan

To Helsinki

Norra Ljusterö

Södra Ljusterö

Brottö

Skälvik

Söderboudd

Svartsö

Alsvik

Resarö

Norra Grinda

Möja

Bogesunds-landet

Ringö

Viggsö

Grinda

Stavs-udda

Bockö

Vaxön

Vaxholm

Södra Grinda

Tallink Silja Terminal

Lidingö

Tynningö

Vindö

Kanholms-fjärden

Storö

Stock-holm

Nacka

Värmdö

Djurö

Eknö

Stromkäjen & Nybroplan Docks

Baggens-fjärden

Fågelbro-landet

Runmarö

Sandhamn

Sandön

Ingarö

Baltic Sea

------- Ferry Lines
(not all shown)

ARCHIPELAGO

main thing is to get well beyond Vaxholm, where the scenery gets more striking. I'd sail an hour or two past Vaxholm, have a short stop on an island, then stop in Vaxholm on the way home. The real joy is the view from your ferry.

GETTING AROUND THE ARCHIPELAGO

A few archipelago destinations (including Vaxholm) are accessible overland, thanks to modern bridges. For other islands, you'll take

a boat. Two major companies run public ferries from downtown Stockholm to the archipelago: the bigger Waxholmsbolaget and the smaller Cinderella Båtarna.

Tickets: Regular tickets are sold on board. Simply walk on, and at your convenience, stop by the desk to buy your ticket before you disembark (or wait for them to come around and sell you one). Waxholmsbolaget offers a deal that's worthwhile if you're traveling with a small group or doing a lot of island-hopping. You can save 25 percent by buying a 1,000-SEK ticket credit for 750 SEK (sold only on land; use the splittable credit to buy tickets on the boat). If you're staying in the archipelago for a few days and want to island-hop, consider the Island Hopping Pass, a five-day, all-inclusive pass (445 SEK, plus a 20-SEK smartcard fee). Buy the card at the Waxholmsbolaget office.

Note that tickets and passes for the Waxholmsbolaget ferries are not valid on Cinderella Båtarna boats (and vice versa).

Schedules: Check both companies' schedules when planning your itinerary; you might have to mix and match to make your itinerary work. The most user-friendly option is to use the "Journey Planner" on www.waxholmsbolaget.se, which shows schedules for both companies. A single, confusing schedule booklet also mixes times for both lines. Ferry schedules are complex, and can be confusing even to locals, especially outside of peak season.

Note that the departures mentioned below are for summer (mid-June–mid-Aug); the number of boats declines off-season.

Waxholmsbolaget: Their ships depart from in front of Stockholm's Grand Hotel, at the stop called Stromkäjen (tel. 08/686-2465, www.waxholmsbolaget.se). Waxholmsbolaget boats run from Stockholm to, among other places, these islands: **Vaxholm** (at least hourly, 1.5 hours, 79 SEK), **Grinda** (nearly hourly, 2 hours, 95 SEK), **Svartsö** (3/day, 2.5 hours, 116 SEK), and **Sandhamn** (1/day, Sat-Sun only, 3.5 hours, 150 SEK). These destinations and their timetables are listed in the "Visitor" section of Waxholmsbolaget's website.

Cinderella Båtarna: These ships (operated by Strömma) focus their coverage on the most popular destinations. They're generally faster, make fewer stops, are more comfortable, and are a little pricier than their rivals (boats leave from near Stockholm's Nybroplan, along Strandvägen, tel. 08/1200-4045, www.stromma.se/stockholm/cinderellabatarna). Cinderella boats sail frequently (4/day Mon-Thu, 5/day Fri-Sun) from Stockholm to **Vaxholm** (50 minutes, 115 SEK) and **Grinda** (1.5 hours, 145 SEK). After Grinda, the line splits, going either to **Sandhamn** (from Stockholm: 1/day Mon-Thu, 2/day Fri-Sun, 2.5 hours, 165 SEK), or Finnhamn, with a stop en route at **Svartsö** (from Stockholm: 2/day, 2.5 hours, 165 SEK). These fares are for peak season (mid-June–mid-Aug); Cinderella's fares are slightly cheaper off-season.

On Board: When you board, tell the conductor which island you're going to. Boats don't land at all of the smaller islands unless passengers have requested a stop. Hang on to your ticket, as you'll have to show it to disembark. Some boats have luggage-storage areas (ask when you board).

You can usually access the outdoor deck; if you can't get to the front deck (where the boats load and unload), head to the back. Or nab a window seat inside. For the best seat, with less sun and nicer views, I'd go POSH: Port Out, Starboard Home (on the left side leaving Stockholm, on the right side coming back). As you sail, a monitor on board shows the position of your boat as it motors through the islands.

Food: You can usually buy food on board, ranging from simple fare at snack bars to elegant sea-view dinners at fancy restaurants. If your boat has a top-deck restaurant and you want to combine your cruise with dinner, make a reservation as soon as you board.

Once you have a table, it's yours for the whole trip, so you can simply claim your seat and enjoy the ride, circling back later to eat. You can also try calling ahead to reserve a table for a specific cruise (for Waxholmsbolaget, call 08/600-1000; for Cinderella, call 08/1200-4045).

HELPFUL HINTS

ARCHIPELAGO

Tourist Information: Stockholm's city-run TI, called **Visit Stockholm,** has a free map of the archipelago, which gives a great overview and introduction to the area (downtown in the Kulturhuset, see hours and contact info in Stockholm chapter, under "Orientation to Stockholm").

Opening Times: Any opening hours I list in this chapter are reliable only for peak season (mid-June–mid-Aug). During the rest of the tourist year ("shoulder season"—late May, early June, late Aug, and Sept), hours are flexible and completely weather-dependent; more services tend to be open on weekends than weekdays. Outside the short summer season, many places close down entirely.

Money: Bring cash. The only ATMs are in Vaxholm; farther out, you'll wish you'd stocked up on cash in Stockholm, though most vendors do accept credit cards.

Signal for Stop: At the boat landings or jetties on small islands, you'll notice a small signal tower (called a semaphore) that's used to let a passing boat know you want to be picked up. Pull the cord to spin the white disc and make it visible to the ship. Be sure to put it back before boarding the boat. At night, you signal with light—locals just use their mobile phones.

Weather: The weather on the islands is often better than in Stockholm. For island forecasts, check Götland's (the big island far to the south) instead of Stockholm's. A good local website for weather forecasts (in English) is www.yr.no.

Local Drink: A popular drink here is *punsch,* a sweet fruit liqueur. Stately old buildings sometimes have *punsch–verandas,* little glassed-in upstairs porches where people traditionally would imbibe and chat.

Vaxholm

The self-proclaimed "gateway to the archipelago," Vaxholm is more developed and less charming than the other islands. Connected by bridge to Stockholm, it's practically a suburb, and not the place to commune with Swedish nature. But it also has an illustrious history as the anchor of Stockholm's naval defense network, and it couldn't be easier to reach (constant buses and boats from Stockholm). While Vaxholm isn't the rustic archipelago you might be looking for, you're almost certain to pass through here at some point on your trip. If you have some extra time, hop off the boat for a visit.

Getting There: Boats constantly shuttle between Stockholm's waterfront and Vaxholm (see "Getting Around the Archipelago," earlier). **Bus** #670 runs regularly from the Tekniska Högskolan T-bana stop in northern Stockholm to the center of Vaxholm (4/hour Mon-Fri, 3/hour Sat-Sun, 40 minutes, 43 SEK one-way, buy ticket in Pressbyrån convenience store across the street from station). Unless you're on a tight budget, I'd take the boat for the scenery.

Orientation to Vaxholm

Vaxholm, with about 5,000 people, is on the island of Vaxön, connected to the mainland (and Stockholm) by a series of bridges. Everything of interest is within a five-minute walk of the boat dock.

TOURIST INFORMATION

Vaxholm's good TI is well-stocked with brochures about Vaxholm itself, Stockholm, and the archipelago, and can help you with boat schedules (Mon-Fri 10:00-18:00, Sat-Sun until 16:00, shorter hours off-season; in the Town Hall building on Rådhustorget, tel. 08/5413-1480, www.vaxholm.se).

ARRIVAL IN VAXHOLM

Ferries stop at Vaxholm's south harbor (Söderhamnen). The **bus** from Stockholm arrives and departs at the bus stop called Söderhamnsplan, a few steps from the boats. To get your bearings, follow my Vaxholm Walk. Luggage lockers are in the Waxholmsbolaget building on the waterfront. The handy electronic departure board (*Nästa Avgang* means "next departure") near the ticket office shows when boats are leaving. For more help, confirm your plans with the person at the ticket office.

Vaxholm Walk

This 30-minute, self-guided, two-part loop will take you to the most characteristic corners of Vaxholm. Begin at the boat dock—you can even start reading as you approach.

Waterfront: Dominating Vaxholm's waterfront is the big Art Nouveau Waxholms Hotell, dating from the early 20th century.

Across the strait to the right is Vaxholm's stout fortress, a reminder of this town's strategic importance over the centuries.

With your back to the water, turn left and walk with the big hotel on your right-hand side. Notice the Waxholmsbolaget office building. Inside you can buy tickets, confirm boat schedules, or stow your bag in a locker. After the hamburger-and-hot-dog stand, you'll reach a roundabout. Just to your left is the stop for bus #670, connecting Vaxholm to Stockholm. Beyond that, a wooden walkway follows the seafront to the town's private boat harbor (Västerhamnen, or "west harbor"), where you can count sailboats and rent a bike.

But for now, continue straight up Vaxholm's appealing, shop-lined main street, Hamngatan. After one long block (notice the handy Co op/Konsum grocery store across the street), turn right up Rådhusgatan (following signs to *Rådhustorget*) to reach the town's main square. The TI is inside the big, yellow Town Hall building on your left. Continue kitty-corner across the square (toward the granite slope) and head downhill on a street leading to the...

Fishermen's Quarter: This Norrhamnen ("north harbor") is ringed by former fishermen's homes. Walk out to the dock and survey the charming wooden

cottages. In the mid-19th century, Stockholmers considered Vaxholm's herring, called *strömming,* top-quality. Caught fresh here, the herring could be rowed into the city in just eight hours and eaten immediately, while herring caught farther out on the archipelago, which had to be preserved in salt, lost its flavor.

As you look out to sea, you'll see a pale green building protruding on the left. This is the charming Hembygdsgården homestead museum, with a pleasant indoor-outdoor café. It's worth heading to this little point (even if the museum is closed, as it often is): As you face the water, go left about one block, then turn right down the gravel lane called Trädgårdsgatan (also marked for *Hembygds-gården*).

Continuing down Trädgårdsgatan lane, you'll run right into the **Hembygdsgården homestead.** The big house features an endearing museum showing the simple, traditional fisherman's lifestyle (pop in if it's open; free but donation requested). Next door is a fine recommended café serving sweets and light meals with idyllic outdoor seating (both in front of and behind the museum—look around for your favorite perch, taking the wind direction into consideration). This is the best spot in town for coffee or lunch. From here, look across the inlet at the tiny beach (where we're heading next).

Backtrack to the fishermen's harbor, then continue straight uphill on Fiskaregatan road, and take the first left up the tiny gravel lane marked *Vallgatan.* This part of the walk takes you back in time, as you wander among old-fashioned wooden homes. At the end of the lane, head left. When you reach the water, go right along a path leading to a thriving little **sandy beach.** In good weather, this offers a fun chance to commune with Swedes at play. (In bad weather, it's hard to imagine anyone swimming or sunning here.)

When you're done relaxing, take the wooden stairs up to the top of the rock and **Battery Park** (Batteripark)—where giant artillery helped Vaxholm flex its defensive muscles in the late 19th century. As you crest the rock and enjoy the sea views, notice (on your right) the surviving semicircular tracks from those old artillery guns. With a range of 10 kilometers, the recoil from these powerful cannons could shatter glass in nearby houses. Before testing them, they'd play a bugle call to warn locals to stow away their valuables. More artifacts of these defenses are dug into the rock.

To head back to civilization, turn right before the embedded bunker (crossing more gun tracks and passing more fortifications on your left). As you leave the militarized zone, take a left at the fork, and the road will take you down to the embankment—just around the corner from where the boat docks, and our starting point. From along this stretch of embankment, you can catch a boat across the water to Vaxholm Fortress.

Sights in Vaxholm

Vaxholm Fortress and Museum
(Vaxholms Kastell/Vaxholms Fästnings Museum)

Vaxholm's only real attraction is the fortification just across the strait. While the town feels sleepy today, for centuries it was a crucial link in Sweden's nautical defense because it presided over the most convenient passage between Stockholm and the outer archipelago (and, beyond that, the Baltic Sea, Finland, and Russia). The name "Vaxholm" means "Island of the Signal Fire," emphasizing the burg's strategic importance. In 1548, King Gustav Vasa decided to pin his chances on this location, ordering the construction of a fortress here and literally filling in other waterways, effectively making this the only way into or out of Stockholm...which it remained for 450 years. A village sprang up across the waterway to supply the fortress, and Vaxholm was born. The town's defenses successfully held off at least two major invasions (Christian IV of Denmark in 1612, and Peter the Great of Russia in 1719). Vaxholm's might gave Sweden's kings the peace of mind they needed to expand their capital to outlying islands—which means that the pint-size powerhouse of Vaxholm is largely to thank for Stockholm's island-hopping cityscape.

Cost and Hours: 80 SEK, July-Aug daily 11:00-17:00, June daily 12:00-16:00, May and Sept Sat-Sun from 12:00, closed off-season, tel. 08/1200-4870, www.vaxholmsfastning.se.

Getting There: A ferry shuttles visitors back and forth from Vaxholm (40 SEK round-trip, every 20 minutes when museum is open, catch the boat just around the corner and toward the fortress from where the big ferries put in). Once on the island, hike into the castle's inner courtyard and look to the left to find the museum entrance.

Visiting the Fortress: The current, "new" fortress dates from the mid-19th century, when an older castle was torn down and replaced with this imposing granite behemoth. During the 30 years it took to complete the fortress, the tools of warfare changed. Both defensively and offensively, the new fortress was obsolete before it was even completed. The thick walls were no match for the invention of shells (rather than cannonballs), and the high hatches used for attacking tall sailing vessels were useless against new, low-lying, *Monitor*-style attack boats.

Today, the fortress welcomes guests to wander its tough little island and visit its museum. Presented chronologically on two floors (starting upstairs), the modern exhibit traces the military history of this fortress and of Sweden in general. It uses lots of models and mannequins, along with actual weaponry and artifacts, to tell the story right up to the 21st century. There's no English posted, but you can pick up good English translations as you enter. It's as interesting as a museum about Swedish military history can be.

Sleeping and Eating in Vaxholm

Since Vaxholm is so close to Stockholm, there's little reason to sleep here. But in a pinch, Waxholms is the only hotel in town.

Sleeping: $$$ Waxholms Hotell's stately Art Nouveau facade dominates the town's waterfront. Inside are 42 pleasant rooms with classy old-fashioned furnishings (loud music some nights in summer—ask what's on and request a quiet room if necessary, Hamngatan 2, tel. 08/5413-0150, www.waxholmshotell.se, info@waxholmshotell.se). The hotel has a grill restaurant outside in summer and a fancy dining room inside.

Eating: Vaxholm's most tempting eatery, **$ Hembygdsgården ("Homestead Garden") Café** serves "summer lunches" (salads and sandwiches) and homemade sweets, with delightful outdoor seating around the Homestead Museum in Vaxholm's characteristic fishermen's quarter. Anette's lingonberry muffins are a treat (daily May-mid-Sept, closed off-season, tel. 08/5413-1980).

$ Boulangerie Waxholm is the perfect place for a *fika* break (coffee and sweets), but also serves sandwiches, salads, and hot dishes. From the south harbor (Söderhamnen), walk to the roundabout and turn left; you'll find it at the end of the block (Mon-Thu 6:30-18:30, Fri until 19:00, Sat-Sun from 8:00, tel. 08/5413-1872).

Grinda

The rustic, traffic-free isle of Grinda—half retreat, half resort—combines back-to-nature archipelago remoteness with easy proximity to Stockholm. The island is a tasteful gaggle of hotel buildings idyllically situated amid Swedish nature—walking paths, beaches, trees, and slabs of glacier-carved granite sloping into the sea. Since Grinda is a nature preserve (owned by the Stockholm Archipelago Foundation, or Skärgårdsstiftelsen), only a few families actually live here. There's no real town. But in the summer, Grinda becomes a magnet for day-tripping urbanites, which can make it quite crowded. Adding to its appeal is the nostalgia it holds for many Stockholmers, who fondly recall when this was a summer camp island. In a way, with red and-white cottages bunny-hopping up its gentle hills and a stately old inn anchoring its center, it retains that vibe today.

Orientation to Grinda

Grinda is small and easy to manage. It's a little wider than a mile in each direction; you can walk from end to end in a half-hour. Its main settlement—the historic **Wärdshus building** (a busy hub of tourist activities including a restaurant, bar, Wi-Fi, and conference facilities), hotel, and related amenities—sit next to its harbor, where private yachts and sailboats put in. Everything on the island is owned and operated by the same company; fortunately, it does a tasteful job of managing the place to keep the island's relaxing personality intact.

Major points of interest are well-signposted in Swedish: *Södra Bryggan* (south dock), *Norra Bryggan* (north dock), *Värdshus* (hotel at the heart of the island), *Gästhamn* (guest harbor); *Affär* (general store); *stuga/stugby* (cottage/s); *Grindastigen* (nature trail); and *Tält-plats* (campground).

TOURIST INFORMATION

The red cottage marked *Expedition/Lilla Längan* greets arriving visitors just up the hill from the Södra Grinda ferry dock. The staff answers questions, and the cottage serves as a small shop, a place to rent kayaks or saunas, and a reception desk for the island's cottages and hostel (open daily in season; Wärdshus general info tel. 08/5424-9491, www.grinda.se).

ARRIVAL IN GRINDA

Public ferries use one of two docks, at opposite ends of the island: Most use Södra Grinda to the south (nearest the hostel and cottages), while a few use Norra Grinda to the north (closer to the campground). From either of these, it's about a 10- to 15-minute walk to the action.

Sights in Grinda

Grinda is made to order for strolling through the woods, taking a dip, picnicking, and communing with Swedish nature. Watch the boats bob in the harbor and work on your Baltic tan. You can simply stick to the gravel trails connecting the island's buildings, or for more nature, take the Grindastigen trail, which loops to the far end of the island and back in less than an hour (signposted from near the Wärdshus).

You can also rent a kayak or rent the private little sauna hut bobbing in the harbor. There's no bike rental here—and the island is a bit too small to keep a serious biker busy—but you could bring one on the boat from Stockholm.

As you stroll, you might spot a few haggard-looking tents through the trees. The right to pitch a tent here was established by the Swedish government during World War II, to give the downtrodden a cheap place to sleep. Those permissions are still valid, inherited, bought, and sold, which means that Grinda has a thriving community of tent-dwelling locals who camp out here all summer long (April-Oct). While some may be the descendants of those original hobos, these days they choose this lifestyle and live as strange little barnacles attached to Grinda. Once each summer they have a progressive tent-crawl bender before heading to the Wärdshus to blow a week's food budget on a fancy meal.

The island just across from the Södra Grinda dock (to the right) is Viggsö, where the members of ABBA have summer cottages and wrote many of their biggest hits.

Sleeping in Grinda

You have various options, in increasing order of rustic charm: hotel, hostel, and cottages. You can reserve any of these through the Wärdshus (tel. 08/5424-9491, www.grinda.se, info@grinda.se).

Grinda is busiest in the summer, when tourists fill its hotel; in spring and fall, it mostly hosts conferences. If sleeping at the hostel or cottages, arrange arrival details (you'll probably pick up your keys at the *Expedition/Lilla Längan* shed near the dock). The hostel and cottages charge extra for bed linens. If you have a tent, you can pitch it at the basic campsite near the north jetty for a small fee.

$$$$ Grinda Hotel rents 30 rooms (each named for a local bird or fish) in four buildings just above the Wärdshus. These are modern, comfortable, and made for relaxing, intentionally lacking distractions such as TVs or phones (cheaper if you skip breakfast; if dining at the restaurant, the "Wärdshus package" will save you a few kronor).

$ The 27 **cottages**—most near the Södra Grinda ferry dock—are rentable, offering a rustic retreat (kitchenettes but no running water, shared bathroom facilities outside). From mid-June to mid-August, these come with a one-week minimum and cost more.

¢ **Grinda Hostel** (Van-drarhem) is the place to sleep if you wish you'd gone to Swedish summer camp as a kid. The 44 bunks are in simple two- and four-bed cottages, surrounding a pair of fire pits (great shared kitchen/dining hall). A small pebbly beach and a basic sauna are nearby.

Eating in Grinda

All your options (aside from bringing your own picnic from Stockholm) are run by the hotel, with choices in each price range.

$$$$ Grinda Wärdshus, the inn at the center of the complex, has a good restaurant that combines rural island charm with fine food. You can choose between traditional Swedish meals and contemporary international dishes. Servings are small but thoughtfully designed to be delicious. Eat in the woody dining room or on the terrace out front (late June-Aug daily 12:00-24:00; weekends only—and some Fri—in off-season).

$$$ Grindas Framficka ("Grinda's Front Pocket") is a pleasant bistro that serves up basic but tasty food (seafood, salads, and pizza) right along the guest harbor. Order at the counter, then choose a table, or wait to be seated for a more formal atmosphere (early June-mid-Aug daily 11:00-22:00, otherwise sporadically open in good weather—especially weekends).

The **general store and café** (Lanthandel) just below the Wärdshus is the place to rustle up some picnic fixings. You'll also find coffee, ice cream, "one-time grills" for a disposable barbecue, and kayak rentals (open long hours daily early June-mid-Aug, Fri-Sun only in shoulder season).

Svartsö

The remote and lesser-known isle of Svartsö (svert-show, literally "Black Island"), a short hop beyond Grinda, is the "Back Door" option of the bunch. Unlike Grinda, Svartsö is home to a real community; islanders have their own school and library. But with only 80 year-round residents, the old generation had to specialize. Each person learned a skill to fill a niche in the community—one guy was a carpenter, the next was a plumber, the next was an electrician, and so on. While the island is less trampled than the others in this chapter (just one hotel and a great restaurant), it is reasonably well-served by ferries. Svartsö feels remote and potentially even boring for those who aren't wowed by simply strolling through meadows. But it's ideal for those who want to slow down and immerse themselves in nature.

Svartsö hosts the school for this part of the archipelago. Because Swedish law guarantees the right to education, even kids living on remote islands are transported to class. A school boat trundles from island to island each morning to collect kids headed for the school on Svartsö. If the weather is bad, a hovercraft retrieves them. If it's really bad, and all of the snow days have been used up, a helicopter takes the kids to school.

Orientation to Svartsö: The island, about five miles long and a half-mile wide, has four docks. The main one, at the southwestern tip, is called Alsvik (with the general store and restaurant). Halfway up is Skälvik, at the northeastern end is Söderboudd, and at the northwestern end is Norra Bryggan. Most boats stop at Alsvik, but if you want to go to a different dock, you can request a stop (ask the conductor on board, or use the semaphore signal at the dock).

At the **Alsvik dock,** the great little general store, called Svartsö Lanthandel, sells anything you could need and acts as the town TI, post office, pharmacy, and liquor store (daily mid-May-mid-Aug, more sporadic off-season but open year-round, tel. 08/5424-7325). You can rent bikes here; in busy times, call ahead to reserve (50 SEK/hour, 125 SEK/day). The little café on the dock sells drinks and light food, and rents **$** cottages (bunk beds, shared outdoor toilets, tel. 08/5424-7110).

The island has a few paved lanes and almost no traffic. Residents own three-wheeled utility motorbikes for hauling things to and from the ferry landing. The interior consists of little more than trees. With an hour or so, you can bike across the island and back, enjoying the mellow landscape and chatting with the friendly big-city people who've found their perfect escape.

Eating in Svartsö: If you leave the Alsvik dock to the right and walk five minutes up the hill, you'll find the excellent **$$-$$$$ Svartsö Krog** restaurant. Run by Henrik, this place specializes in well-constructed, ingredient-driven dishes with local herbs and vegetables grown on the island and seafood caught by the local fishermen. Choose one of the three eating zones (each with the same menu): outside, upscale dining room, or original pub interior (an Old West-feeling tavern). Try the cod or "Svartsö-kebab" with homemade pita bread if available (daily lunch specials, 3- and 4-course fixed-price dinner menus, good wine and beer selection; lunch and dinner daily June-Aug; May and Sept dinner Fri-Sun, lunch Sat-Sun; closed Oct-April; tel. 08/5424-7255).

Sleeping in Svartsö: Away from the crowds, **$ Svartsö Skärgårdshotel och Vandrarhem** is a five-minute uphill walk from the Norra Bryggan dock (served by both Waxholmsbolaget and Cinderella Båtarna). The rooms are basic and include breakfast (bike rental available, 15-minute ride to Alsvik harbor and Svartsö Krog restaurant, open year-round, tel. 08/5424-7400, www.svartsonorra.se, info@svartsonorra.se).

Sandhamn

Out on the distant fringe of the archipelago—the last stop before Finland—sits the proud village of Sandhamn (on the island of Sandön). Literally "Sand Harbor," this is where the glacier got hung up and kept on churning away, grinding stone into sand. The town has a long history as an important and posh place. In 1897, the Royal Swedish Sailing Society built its clubhouse here, putting Sandhamn on the map as the yachting center of the Baltic—Sweden's answer to Nantucket. It remains an extremely popular stop for boaters—from wealthy yachties to sailboat racers—as well as visitors simply seeking a break from the big city.

The island of Sandön feels stranded on the edge of the archipelago, rather than immersed in it. Sandhamn is on its sheltered side. Though it's far from Stockholm, Sandhamn is very popular. During the peak of summer (mid-June through late August), it's extremely crowded. Expect to stand in line, and call ahead for restaurant reservations. But even during these times, the Old Town is relatively peaceful and pleasant to explore. If the weather's decent, shoulder season is delightful (though it can be busy on weekends).

Orientation to Sandhamn

You'll find two halves to Sandhamn: In the shadow of that still-standing iconic yacht clubhouse is a ritzy resort/party zone throbbing with big-money nautical types. But just a few steps away, around the harbor, is an idyllic time-warp Old Town of colorfully painted shiplap cottages tucked between tranquil pine groves. While most tourists come here for the resort, the quieter part of Sandhamn holds the real appeal.

Sandhamn has a summer-only **TI** (open June-mid-Aug) in the harbor area (www.destinationsandhamn.se.)

Sandhamn Walk

To get your bearings from the ferry dock, take this self-guided walk. Begin by facing out to sea.

As you look out to the little point across from the dock, notice the big yellow building. In the 18th century, this was built

as the **pilot house.** Because the archipelago is so treacherous to navigate—with its tens of thousands of islands and skerries, not to mention untold numbers of hidden underwater rocks—locals don't trust outsiders to bring their boats here. So passing ships unfamiliar with these waters were required to pick up a local captain (or "pilot") to take them safely all the way to Stockholm. The tradition continues today. The orange boats marked *pilot,* moored below the house, ferry loaner captains to oncoming ships. And, since this is the point of entry into Sweden, foreign ships can also be processed by customs here.

The little red shed just in front of the pilot house is home to a humble **town museum** that's open sporadically in the summer, featuring exhibits on Sandhamn's history and some seafaring tales.

Just above the barn, look for the yellow building with the blue letters spelling **Sandhamns Värdshus.** This traditional inn, built in the late 17th century, housed sailors while they waited here to set out to sea. During that time, Stockholm had few exports, so ships that brought and unloaded cargo there came to Sandhamn to load up their holds with its abundant sand as ballast. Today the inn still serves good food (see "Eating in Sandhamn," later).

Stretching to the left of the inn are the quaint storefronts of most of Sandhamn's **eateries** (those that aren't affiliated with the big hotel)—bakery, deli, and grocery store, all of them humble but just right for a simple bite or picnic shopping. Local merchants enjoy a pleasantly symbiotic relationship. Rather than try to compete with each other, they attempt to complement what the next shop sells—each one finding just the right niche.

The area stretching beyond these storefronts is Sandhamn's **Old Town**—a maze of wooden cottages that's an absolute delight to explore (and easily the best activity in town). Only 50 of Sandhamn's homes (of around 450) are occupied by year-rounders. The rest are summer cottages of wealthy Stockholmers, or bunkhouses for seasonal workers in the tourist industry. Most locals live at the farthest-flung (and therefore least desirable) locations. Imagine the impact of 100,000 annual visitors on this little town.

Where the jetty meets the island, notice (on the right) the old-fashioned telephone box with the fancy *Rikstelefon* logo. Just

to the right of the phone box, you can see the town's bulletin board, where locals post their classified ads. To the left at the base of the dock is Sandhamns Kiosk, a newsstand selling local and international publications (as well as candy and *mjukglass*—soft-serve ice cream). A bit farther to the left, the giant red building with the turret on top is the **yacht clubhouse** that put Sandhamn on the map, and still entertains the upper crust today with a hotel, several restaurants, spa, minigolf course, outdoor pool, and more. You'll see its proud SSS-plus-crown logo (standing for Svenska Segelsällskapet—Swedish Sailing Society) all over town. In the 1970s, the building was owned by a notorious mobster who made meth in the basement, then smuggled it out beneath the dock to sailboats moored in the harbor.

Look for the "Bluewater Oasis" **water station** in front of the yacht clubhouse. Due to Sandhamn's low groundwater level, and the enormous increase in visitors during summer months, local authorities impose water rationing part of the year. To provide more water, a filtration system was installed that purifies water direct from the Baltic Sea. It's totally drinkable, and a good place to fill up your water bottle.

Spinning a bit farther to the left, back to where you started, survey the island across the strait (Lökholmen). Just above the trees, notice the copper dome of an **observatory** that was built by this island's eccentric German oil-magnate owner in the early

ARCHIPELAGO

20th century. He also built a small castle (not quite visible from here) for his kids to play in.

To stroll to another fine viewpoint, walk into town and turn left along the water. After about 50 yards, a sign on the right points up a narrow lane to *Posten*. This unassuming gravel path is actually one of Sandhamn's most important streets, with the post office, police department (which handles only paperwork—real crimes are deferred to the Stockholm PD), and doctor (who visits town every second Wednesday). While Sandhamn feels remote, it's served—like other archipelago communities—by a crack emergency-response network that can dispatch a medical boat or, in extreme cases, a helicopter. With top-notch hospitals in Stockholm just a 10-minute chopper ride away, locals figure that if you have an emergency here, you might just make it to the doctor faster than if you're trying to make it through congested city streets in an ambulance. At the end of this lane, notice the giant hill of the town's namesake sand.

Continuing along the main tree-lined harborfront strip, you can't miss the signs directing yachters to the *toalett* (toilet) and *sopor* (garbage dump). Then you'll pass the Sandhamns Guiderna office, a **travel agency** where you can rent bikes, kayaks, and fishing gear (tel. 08/640-8040). Just after that is the barn for the volunteer fire department (Brandstation). With all the wooden buildings in town, fire is a concern—one reason why Sandhamn restricts camping (and campfires).

Go beneath the skyway connecting the big red hotel to its modern annex. Then veer uphill (right) at the *Badstranden Trouville* sign, looking down at the minigolf course. After you crest the top of the hill, on the left is a big, flat expanse of rock nicknamed Dansberget ("Dancing Rock") because it once hosted community dances with a live orchestra. Walk out to enjoy fine **views** of the Baltic Sea—from here, boaters can set sail for Finland, Estonia, and  St. Petersburg, Russia. Looking out to the horizon, notice the three lighthouse towers poking up from the sea, used to guide ships to this gateway to the archipelago. The finish line for big boat races stretches across this gap (from the little house on the point to your left). In summer, this already busy town gets even more jammed with visitors, thanks to the frequent sailing races that end here. The biggest annual competition is the Götlandrunt, a round-trip from here to the island of Götland. In 2009, Sandhamn was proud to be one of just 10 checkpoints on the Volvo Ocean Race, a nine-month race around the world that called mostly at bigger cities (such as Boston, Singapore, and Rio).

Our walk is finished. You can head back into town. Or, to hit the beach, continue another 15 minutes to Trouville beach (explained next).

Sights in Sandhamn

Beaches (Stränder)

True to its name, Sandön ("Sandy Island") has some of the archipelago's rare sandy beaches. The closest, and local favorite, is the no-name beach tucked in a cove just behind the Old Town (walk through the community from the main boat dock, then follow the cove around to the little sandy stretch).

The most popular—which can be quite crowded in summer—is Trouville beach, at the opposite end of the island from Sandhamn (about a 20-minute walk). To find it, walk behind the big red hotel and take the right, uphill fork (marked with the low-profile *Badstranden Trouville* sign) to the "Dancing Rock," then proceed along the road. Take a left at the fork by the tennis courts, then walk about 10 minutes through a mysterious-feeling forest (sometimes filled with lingonberries and blueberries), until you reach a little settlement of red cottages. Take a right at the fork (look up for the *Till Stranden* sign), and then, soon after, follow the middle fork (along the plank walks) right to the beach zone: two swathes of sand marked off by rocks, stretching toward Finland.

Kvarnberget

Just inside the Old Town you'll find this little hilltop with a beautiful view of the sea. From the Sandhamns Värdshus B&B, take the path leading to the left and follow it straight past the old wooden houses until you see the hill. You can simply walk up the hill to enjoy the view, or pack a picnic (beware of seagulls hovering overhead, eager to steal your lunch).

Sleeping in Sandhamn

Sandhamn has a pair of very expensive top-end hotels, a basic but comfortable B&B, and little else. If you're sleeping on Sandhamn, the B&B is the best choice.

$$$$ Sands Hotell is a stylish splurge sitting proudly at the top of town. While oriented mostly to conferences and private parties, its 19 luxurious rooms also welcome commoners in the summer (elevator, spa, tel. 08/5715-3020, www.sandshotell.se, info@sandshotell.se).

$$$$ Sandhamns Seglarhotellet rents 79 nautical-themed rooms in a modern annex behind the old yacht club building (where you'll find the reception). The rooms are fine, but the prices are sky-high (loud music from disco inside the clubhouse—light sleepers should ask for a quieter back room, great gym and pool area, tel. 08/5745-0400, www.sandhamn.com, reception@sandhamn.com).

$ Sandhamns Värdshus B&B rents five rustic but tasteful, classically Swedish rooms in an old mission house buried deep in the colorful Old Town. To melt into Sandhamn and get away from the yachties, sleep here (mostly twins, all rooms share WC and shower, tiny cottage with its own bathroom for same price, includes breakfast, reception is at the restaurant—see next, tel. 08/5715-3051, www.sandhamns-vardshus.se, info@sandhamns-vardshus.se). The rooms are above a reception hall that is rented out for events, but after 22:00, quiet time kicks in.

Eating in Sandhamn

IN THE OLD TOWN

Sandhamn's most appealing eateries are along the Old Town side of the harbor.

$$-$$$$ Sandhamns Värdshus, right on the water, is the town's best eatery. They serve traditional Swedish food in three separate dining zones (which mostly share the same menu, but each also has its own specials): out on an inviting deck overlooking the water; upstairs in a salty dining room with views; or downstairs in a simple pub (daily lunch and dinner nearly year-round, lunch specials, tel. 08/5715-3051).

To grab a bite or assemble a picnic, browse through these smaller eateries: **$ Monrads Deli,** behind the yacht club, is a bright, innovative shop where you can buy sandwiches and salads, a wide array of meats for grilling, cheeses, cold cuts, drinks, fresh produce, and other high-quality picnic fixings (long hours daily in summer, mobile 0709-650-300).

In the opposite direction, **Westerbergs Livsmedel** grocery store has basic supplies (sporadic hours daily). **$$ Dykarbaren Café** serves lunches and dinners with indoor and outdoor seating (daily mid-June-mid-Aug, Wed-Sun only in shoulder season, closed off-season; tel. 08/5715-3554). **$ Ankaret** has a little market for takeaway and outdoor seating, serving smoked fish and shrimp, sandwiches, and ice cream. Just around the corner (uphill from the harbor and behind the Värdshus), **$ Sandhamns Bageriet** is a popular early-morning venue serving coffee, sweet rolls, and sandwiches (daily in summer, Sat-Sun only late-Aug-Sept).

AMONG THE YACHTIES

$-$$$$ Sandhamn Seglarhotell has several eateries, open to guests and nonguests. Out on the dock, about 100 yards to the right, is the posh Sea Club Poolbar and Grill, an American-style restaurant with outdoor tables surrounding a swimming pool (hamburgers and salads, open summer in good weather only). Upstairs in the building's main ballroom is an eatery serving good but pricey Swedish and international food (traditional daily lunch special). The restaurant enjoys fine sea views and has a bar/dance hall zone (with loud music until late, nearly nightly in summer). Down on the ground floor is a pub/nightclub (tel. 08/5745-0421).

ARCHIPELAGO

SOUTHEAST SWEDEN

Växjö • Glass Country • Kalmar • Öland Island

The sights in Sweden's southeastern province of Småland are a worthy runner-up to big-city Stockholm. More Americans came from this densely forested area than any other part of Scandinavia, and the House of Emigrants in Växjö tells the story well. Between Växjö and Kalmar is Glass Country, a 70-mile stretch of forest sparkling with glassworks that welcome guests to tour and shop. Historic Kalmar has a rare Old World ambience and the most magnificent medieval castle in Scandinavia. From Kalmar, you can cross one of Europe's longest bridges to hike through the limestone bedrock of the beachy island of Öland.

PLANNING YOUR TIME

While I'm not so hot on the Swedish countryside (OK, blame my Norwegian heritage), you can't see only Stockholm and say you've seen Sweden. Växjö and Kalmar give you the best possible dose of small-town Sweden. (I find Lund and Malmö, both popular side-trips from Copenhagen, relatively dull. And I'm not old or sedate enough to find a sleepy boat trip along the much-loved Göta Canal appealing.)

If you have the time and a car, the sights described in this section are an interesting way to spend a couple of days.

Without a car, or if you're short on time, I'd skip this area in favor of taking the direct, high-speed train from Copenhagen to Stockholm. Those with more time could spend a night in either Växjö or Kalmar, which can be reached by train.

By Car

Drivers can spend three days getting from Copenhagen to Stockholm this way:

Day 1: Leave Copenhagen after breakfast; drive over the bridge to Sweden and on to Växjö, touring Växjö's House of Emigrants; drive into Glass Country and tour one of the glassworks (I'd choose little Transjö Hytta or the Glass Factory) as well as the papermaking mill at Lessebo; arrive in Kalmar in time for dinner.

Day 2: Spend the day in Kalmar touring the castle and Kalmar County Museum, and browsing its people-friendly streets; if you're restless, cross the bridge for a joyride on the island of Öland, especially its south end.

Day 3: Start early for the five-hour drive north along the coast to Stockholm; break in Västervik, then stop in Söderköping for a picnic lunch and walk along the Göta Canal; continue driving north to Stockholm, arriving in time for dinner.

By Public Transit

Växjö and Kalmar are easy to visit by train. Without a car, I'd skip Glass Country and Öland, but if you wouldn't, take the bus (from

Växjö to Kosta Boda glassworks, and from Kalmar to Öland; see "Växjö Connections," later).

Växjö

A pleasant, sleepy town of almost 85,000, Växjö (locals say VEK-hwuh; Stockholmers pronounce it VEK-shuh) is in the center of Småland. An important trading town for centuries, its name loosely means "where the road meets the lake." Coming in by train or car, you'd think it might mean "buried in a vast forest." Today an enjoyable three-mile path encircles that lake, and a farmers market enlivens the otherwise quiet main square on Wednesday and Saturday mornings.

My favorite activity in Växjö is to simply enjoy browsing through quintessential, small-town Sweden without a tourist in sight. While there isn't much heavy-duty sightseeing in Växjö, it does have a trio of worthwhile attractions: the earnest House of Emigrants, chronicling the plight of Swedes who fled to North America; the Smålands Museum, offering a convenient look at the region's famous glass without a trip to Glass Country; and the cathedral, decorated with fine modern glass sculptures.

In 1996, Växjö set itself the goal of becoming a fossil-fuel-free city by the year 2050. Now a single biomass power plant provides nearly all the community's heat and hot water, half of its energy comes from renewable sources, and carbon dioxide emissions are down considerably. Växjö earned the title "Greenest City in Europe" when it received the EU's first award for sustainable development in 2007.

Orientation to Växjö

Växjö's town center is compact and pedestrian-friendly; the train station, main square, and two important museums are all within two blocks of each other. Blocks here are short; everything I mention is within about a 15-minute walk of everything else. Tourists are so rare that a polite English-speaking visitor will find locals generous, warm, and helpful.

For a delightful three- or four-hour stopover, I'd do this loop from the station: Cross the tracks on the overpass to tour the glass and history museums (Smålands Museum and House of Emigrants). A block away is the lovely lake (encircled by a path), next to a pretty park and the cathedral. A block in front of the cathedral is the town square, Stortorget (with the TI); from there stretches the main commercial drag, Storgatan. Browse this orderly street before heading back to the station.

ARRIVAL IN VÄXJÖ

Växjö's modern train station has snack stands and coin-op lockers (an ATM is a block away to the right as you leave). Pick up a city map at the information desk. The station faces the heart of town; walk a few steps straight ahead, and you'll be in the pedestrian shopping zone. Everything in town is in front of you except the two main museums, which are behind the station; to reach these, cross the tracks using the pedestrian overpass. Drivers will find several parking lots near the station.

TOURIST INFORMATION

The **TI** is inside the municipal building facing the main town square, about a 10-minute walk from the train station. With your back to the station, go right two blocks to Kungsgatan, then left to the town square, a block away (June-Aug Mon-Fri 10:00-18:00, Sat until 14:00, closed Sun; shorter hours off-season; pick up Glass Country map and brochures here, Kronobergsgatan 6B, tel. 0470/733-280, www.vaxjoco.se).

Sights in Växjö

Växjö's attractions cluster around the north end of its pleasant lake and the surrounding park. The glass and history museums are on the hill just behind the train station (the pedestrian overpass takes you there).

Smålands Museum/Swedish Glass Museum
(Sveriges Glasmuseum)

This instructive museum, while humble, celebrates the region of Småland and its glassmaking tradition. On the ground floor, the "Six Centuries of Swedish Glass" exhibit traces the history of the product that still powers the local economy. Upstairs you'll find more on glass, along with displays on the region's prehistory, and a look at Kronoberg County (which includes Växjö) in the 19th century. This is a handy place to learn a bit about glass if you're not headed deeper into Glass Country. Who knew that the person who designed the original Coca-Cola bottle in 1915 was a Swede?

Cost and Hours: 90-SEK combo-ticket includes House of Emigrants; June-Aug daily 10:00-17:00, shorter hours and closed

Mon off-season; **$** café with light meals, Södra Järnvägsgatan 2, tel. 0470/704-200, www.smalandsmuseum.se.

▲House of Emigrants (Utvandrarnas Hus)

If you have Swedish roots, this tidy museum is exciting. Even if you don't, it's an interesting stop for anyone with immigrant ancestors. While modest, the well-presented, inspiring "Dream of America" exhibit captures the experiences of the more than one million Swedes who sought refuge in North America in the late 19th and early 20th centuries.

Cost and Hours: Same ticket and hours as Swedish Glass Museum; 50 yards down the hill behind the glass museum, Vilhelm Mobergs Gata 4, tel. 0470/20120, www.smalandsmuseum.se.

Visiting the Museum: As economic woes wracked Sweden from the 1850s to the 1920s, the country was caught up in an "American Fever." Nearly 1.3 million mostly poor Swedes endured long voyages and culture shock to seek prosperity and freedom in the American promised land. In that period, one in six Swedes went to live in the US. So many left the country that Swedish authorities were forced to rethink their social policies and to institute reforms.

The "Dream of America" exhibit focuses on various aspects of the immigrant experience. One display vividly recounts how 3.8 million new arrivals from around the world entered the US through Manhattan's Castle Garden processing center between 1886 and 1890. Firsthand accounts recall the entry procedure, including medical evaluations and an uncomfortable eye exam.

Swedes were compelled to emigrate in part because of the potato—a staple food in 19th-century Sweden. With dependable (or so everyone thought) nourishment, a peacetime king, and mandatory smallpox vaccinations, the mortality rate had been dropping even among ordinary Swedes. With good (or at least better) times, families got bigger. But as the sad model of a poor village demonstrates, when potato crops failed (especially from catastrophic freezes in 1867 and 1868), it wasn't possible to feed those extra mouths, and many Swedes were forced to leave.

They formed enclaves across North America: on farms and prairies, from New York to Texas, from Maine to Seattle—and, of course, in Chicago's "Swede Town" (the world's second-biggest Swedish town in 1900). The life-size *Snusgatan* re-creates the main street in a Swedish neighborhood—called "Snoose Boulevard," for

Swedish snuff. Other displays trace immigrant lifestyles, religion, treatment in the press, women's experiences, and the Swedish cultural societies that preserved the traditions of the Old World in the New. Rounding out the exhibit, homage is paid to prominent Swedish-Americans, including Charles Lindbergh and the second man on the moon, Buzz Aldrin.

Don't miss the display about the *Titanic*, which takes pains to point out that—after Americans—Swedes were the second-largest group to perish on that ill-fated vessel. On view are a few items that went to the bottom of the Atlantic with one of those Swedes.

The Moberg Room celebrates local writer Vilhelm Moberg (1898-1973), who put the Swedish immigrant experience on the map with his four-novel series *The Emigrants*. (These books—and two Max von Sydow/Liv Ullmann films based on them, *The Emigrants* and *The New Land*—are essential pretrip reading and viewing for Swedish-Americans.) Here you'll see a replica of Moberg's "writer's hut," his actual desk, and some original manuscripts.

Växjö Town Park (Växjö Stadspark)

Directly downhill from the House of Emigrants, you'll reach the big lake called **Växjösjön.** This is a fine place to relax with a picnic or go for a stroll. The pleasant three-mile park path around the lake takes you from manicured flower gardens through forested areas. The top part of the lake borders the inviting Linnéparken next to the cathedral (both described next).

A 10-minute walk around the top of the lake from the House of Emigrants is the town's modern **swimming hall** (*Simhall*, 80-SEK base price includes sauna; extra fee to tan, use the exercise room, or rent a towel or locker; family ticket available, call or check online for open-swim hours, tel. 0470/41204, www.medley.se/vaxjosimhall).

Växjö Cathedral (Växjö Domkyrka)

Växjö's striking orange church, with its distinctive double-needle steeple, features fine sacred art—in glass, of course. Its austere, bright-white interior is enlivened by gorgeous, colorful, and highly symbolic glass sculptures.

Cost and Hours: Free entry, daily 9:00-18:00.

Visiting the Cathedral: Near the entrance, pick up the brochure offering a detailed and evangelical self-guided tour. Near the back-left

corner, the *Tree of Life and Knowledge* is a
fantastically detailed candelabra. On one
side, find Adam and Eve reaching for a
very tempting apple with the clever snake
egging them on from below. On the other
side, Jesus and Mary welcome the faith-
ful with arms outstretched. In similar
opposition, the snake's tempting apple is
suspended across from a bunch of grapes
(symbolizing the wine of the Eucharist).
At the front of the church, the modern
stone altar stands before a glass-decorated
triptych, itself a subtle interplay of light
and dark. Explore the other pieces of glass
art around the church, and take in its trio
of pipe organs.

Linnaeus Park (Linnéparken)

This peaceful park beside the cathedral is dedicated to the great
Swedish botanist Carl von Linné (a.k.a. Carolus Linnaeus). It has
an arboretum, lots of well-categorized perennials, a cactus garden,
and a children's playground.

▲Strolling Storgatan

Växjö's main pedestrian shopping boulevard offers a fun way to cap
your visit. From the main square (with the TI), Storgatan stretches
several blocks west. Walk the entire length of the street to observe
small-town Sweden without any tourists. (You could make the
popular Askelyckan bakery and café, at #24, your goal.) Imagine
growing up or raising a family here: safe but boring, friendly but
traditional, pleasant but predictable. The community seems super-
content and super-conformist; it's very blond, with hints of multi-
ethnicity. Feel the order and the quiet, like there's Valium in the
air. Sweden is among the most highly taxed, affluent, and satisfied (and least church-going) societies in the world. This region
lost more to emigration than any other, and it's thought-provoking
to consider what impact that had on the character of those who
remained behind (and their descendants).

Sleeping in Växjö

If you're parking a car in Växjö, be sure to use the pay-and-display
meters. Parking is free from 18:00 until 9:00 the next morning.

$$$ PM & Vänner Hotel, with 74 stylish rooms, has a restful
in-the-know vibe. Extras include free loaner bikes, a gym, and a
pool, which shares the rooftop with an appealing bar/terrace (el-

evator, sauna, pay parking, centrally located at Västergatan 10, tel. 0470/759-700, www.pmhotel.se, reservations@pmhotel.se).

$$ Elite Stadshotell is a big, modern, business-class hotel with all the comforts in its 163 rooms. It's conveniently set on the town's main square and close to everything (loaner bikes, about a block from the train station at Kungsgatan 6, tel. 0470/13400, www.elite.se, info.vaxjo@elite.se).

$ Hotell Värend is friendly, comfortable, and inexpensive. It has 24 worn but workable rooms at the edge of a residential neighborhood six blocks from the train station along Kungsgatan (elevator, free parking, a block beyond N. Esplanaden at Kungsgatan 27, tel. 0470/776-700, mobile 076-769-0700, www.hotellvarend.se, info@hotellvarend.se).

$$ Hotel Esplanad offers 26 comfortable, fresh rooms, all with private bath (free parking, N. Esplanaden #21A, tel. 0470/22580, www.hotellesplanad.com, info@hotellesplanad.com). From the train station, walk five blocks up Klostergatan and turn left on N. Esplanaden.

¢ Hostel: Växjö's fine **Vandrarhem Evedal Hostel** (an old resort hotel) is near a lake three miles north of town (breakfast extra, sheets extra, confirm reception hours before you arrive, tel. 0470/63070, www.vaxjovandrarhem.se, info@vaxjovandrarhem. se). From Växjö's train station, catch bus #7 (about hourly, 15 minutes).

Eating in Växjö

The restaurant scene is picking up in sleepy Växjö, with a few memorable spots in the center. If you're looking to save money, or if it's a Sunday—when other restaurants are closed—visit one of downtown Växjö's many Asian restaurants or kebab-and-pizza shops.

$$$$ PM & Vänner is a trendy eatery where a younger crowd stands in line to see and be seen. They have good international cuisine with Swedish flair, a mod black-and-white interior, and nice outdoor tables on the pedestrian mall. Their menu changes to feature seasonal and local ingredients (Mon-Sat 11:30-23:00, closed Sun, Storgatan 22 at corner of Västergatan, tel. 0470/759-711).

$$$$ Izakaya Moshi serves flavorful Japanese-style small plates (sushi, dumplings, salads, grilled fish, and meats) in an airy and light space. Choose from the long communal table, a cozy booth, or terrace seating when weather allows. Reservations are smart (Tue-Sat 17:00-21:00, closed Sun-Mon, immediately adjacent to the Smålands Museum at Södra Järnvägsgatan 2, tel. 0470/786-830, http://izakayamoshi.se).

$$$ Kafe De Luxe, about a block from the station, is a hip and funky hangout with live music many nights. They serve lunches and dinners daily—from burgers to *tarte flambée*—in a cozy Old World interior or under a happy tent outside (credit cards only, daily 11:30-24:00, Sandgärdsgatan 19, tel. 0470/740-409).

$$ Umami Monkey bills itself as having the "hippest burgers south of the North Pole"—and they just might be right. Their brioche-bun burgers pop with international flavors and come with great crispy fries (credit cards only, Mon-Fri 11:00-24:00, Sat from 12:00, closed Sun, Storgatan 18, tel. 0470/739-000).

$ Askelyckan Bakery Café, with an inviting terrace under a tree by a fountain on the city's main commercial drag, is a delightful place for a drink, cake, or light lunch on a sunny day (cakes, pastries, salads and sandwiches at lunch, daily 9:00-18:30, Storgatan 25, tel. 0470/12311).

Groceries: Visit the **ICA supermarket** at the corner of Sandgärdsgatan and Klostergatan, one block from the train station (long hours daily).

Växjö Connections

From Växjö by Bus to: Kosta (2-4/day, 1 hour, bus #218 from Växjö bus station; for schedules see www.lanstrafikenkron.se/en).

By Train to: Copenhagen (hourly, 2.5 hours), **Stockholm** (hourly, 3.5 hours, change in Alvesta, reservations required), **Kalmar** (hourly, 60-70 minutes). See the "Stockholm Connections" section in the Stockholm chapter for information on taking trains in Sweden.

Glass Country

Filling the remote-feeling woods between Växjö and Kalmar with busy glassmaking workshops, Sweden's famous Glasriket ("Kingdom of Crystal") is worth ▲▲ for those with a car. There's something deeply pleasing about a visit to a glassworks *(glasbruk):* Even at the bigger places—and especially at the smaller ones—you'll feel genuine artistic energy at work, as skilled craftspeople persuade glowing globs of molten glass to take shape.

The rich natural environment of this area, with inviting forests and lakes all around, has been fundamental to the glassworks (they needed a lot of wood to keep those fires going) and the region's other product, paper (small papermaking mills relied on plentiful water to wash cotton fiber to create paper pulp).

Visiting a glassworks is usually free and typically has two parts: a sales shop, which sells pieces produced on-site (and might have an exhibition of attractive pieces by local artists); and the hot shop, or *hytta*, where glassblowers are hard at work. At most glass-works, it's possible to walk through the hot shop—close enough to feel the heat from the glowing furnaces (arrive before the midafternoon quitting time). Taking a guided tour of at least one hot shop is a must to really understand the whole process. (For starters, read the "Glassmaking in Sweden" sidebar.)

The glassworks listed here are a representative mix of the dozen or so you can visit in Glass Country, ranging from charming artistic workshops to big corporate factories. On the corporate side, Kosta Boda dominates; its flagship complex is the biggest of all the glassworks. But there are many smaller, independent producers, where you can get a more intimate view of the process.

Besides the tradition of hand-crafted glass, the region sustains the only surviving hand papermaking workshop in all of Scandinavia, in the town of Lessebo. It's well worth a visit.

For a complete change of pace, check out the local moose population (you can visit them at the Moose and Farm Animal Park just outside Kosta).

Information: The *Glasriket/Kingdom of Crystal* magazine (available at any TI) and the region's official website (www.glasriket.se) describe the many glassworks that welcome the public. Most are open Mon-Fri 10:00-18:00, Sat until 16:00, and Sun 12:00-16:00—but there's plenty of seasonal variability. Check ahead to be sure the shop you want to visit will be open. The 100-SEK **Glasriket Pass** is worthwhile only if you're visiting several hot shops and doing some serious shopping (10 percent discount at certain shops once you've spent 700 SEK).

PLANNING YOUR TIME

Though you can take a bus from Växjö to Kosta (see "Växjö Connections"), the glassworks are realistically best reached with a car. Train travelers should instead take a careful look at the glass exhibit in Växjö's Smålands Museum, and then go straight to Kalmar.

By Car

With a car, the drive from Växjö to Kalmar is a 70-mile joy—light traffic with endless forest-and-lake scenery punctuated by numerous glassworks. The driving time between Växjö and Kosta is 45 minutes; it's another 45 minutes between Kosta and Kalmar.

Looking at a map, you'll notice the glassworks are scattered around the center of the region. While it would take the better part of a day to visit them all, distances are relatively short and roads are good. Still, it's smart to be selective. On a tight schedule, I'd visit the Glass Factory and Transjö Hytta, possibly Kosta and Bergdala, and the Lessebo paper mill, skipping the rest.

If you're visiting Glass Country en route from Växjö to Kal-

SOUTHEAST SWEDEN

Glassmaking in Sweden

In the mid-16th century, King Gustav Vasa decided he wanted more fine glass to decorate his palace, so he invited German glassmakers to train his subjects, and the trend took off. It's no surprise that glassmaking caught on here in Sweden. The resources needed for glass are abundant: vast forests to fire the ovens, and lakes with an endless supply of sand. By the difficult 19th century—when a sixth of Sweden's population emigrated to North America—the iron mills had closed, leaving behind unemployed workers who were highly skilled at working with materials at high temperatures. Glassmaking was their salvation, and by the early 1900s, this region had more than 100 glassworks.

While glassmaking was important throughout Sweden, it was in the dense forest between Växjö and Kalmar that it took hold the strongest, and lasted the longest. When other materials became cheaper than glass (for example, paper cartons instead of glass bottles), the industry was hit hard, and it dried up in other parts of Sweden. But here in Glass Country, workers refocused their efforts: They still make some everyday items, but their emphasis is on high-quality art pieces that command top kronor. An Ikea wine glass made in China costs 10 SEK, while a handmade Swedish one might cost 150 SEK—but consumers interested in quality are willing to pay that premium.

The glassmaking process is fascinating—and hasn't changed much over the centuries. If you visit a hot shop, you'll see both everyday tableware and art pieces being created. "Mass-produced" tableware—such as wine glasses—is created by small teams of glassblowers who use an assembly-line system to produce a uniform product. Art-glass pieces, however, are never the same. The region has a passel of big-name designers, each with his or her own aesthetic and all considered local celebrities.

Either way, the process is the same. First, a worker places the

mar, consider this driving plan: Head southeast from Växjö on highway 25, following signs for *Kalmar*. To visit Bergdala, turn off after Hovmantorp; to skip it, head straight to Lessebo (and its paper mill). In Lessebo, turn north for Kosta and tour the big Kosta glassworks there. Then, detour slightly east to Orrefors and Orranäs Bruk, or head south on highway 28, watching for signs to *Transjö* for the best of the smaller, artsy glassworks. Pick up highway 25 again, where you'll soon see signs for the village of Boda

glassblowing rod into the furnace (notice the foot pedals used to open and close the doors) and grabs a blob of molten glass. Glassblowers have to move quickly—before the glass hardens too much—but deliberately, to avoid shattering the medium or burning their colleagues. After rolling the glass out on a heat-resistant graphite table to give it the desired shape, they blow into the end of the rod to open a space inside. If creating a mass-produced item, they generally stick it into a mold to ensure the correct dimensions. Other appendages are added; for example, if it's a wineglass with a stem and foot, separate pieces of glass are stretched out to the appropriate shape and attached.

For this entire process, the glass is at about 2,100 degrees Fahrenheit. If it gets too hot, glassblowers cool it down with water or air; if the glass needs to be reheated, they use a blowtorch or poke it momentarily back into the furnace. Finally, the area where the glass was attached to the rod is cut with an industrial diamond, broken off, and ground and polished smooth. When the piece is finished, it's set in a special oven to cool gradually.

At the workday's end, the raw materials for the next day's glass are dumped into giant, custom-made clay pots and placed in the ovens. Overnight, these will gradually melt down to the molten medium the glassblowers will need the next morning.

The last stop is quality control. Only the best pieces are deemed "first quality" (*1:A Sortering*)—you'll pay a premium for these flawless items. Some items, deemed "second quality" (*2:A Sortering*), have minor imperfections that bring the price down substantially. When shopping, pay close attention to these labels; if you don't need your glass perfect, you can save by looking for second quality.

and its Glass Factory museum. From there, make a beeline east to Kalmar.

Sights in Glass Country

These attractions are tied together by the driving plan described above. Don't forget the historic paper mill, and the Moose and Farm Animal Park, described after the glassworks.

GLASSWORKS (GLASBRUKS)

These are listed in the order you'll reach them, from Växjö to Kalmar. Note that many workshops take a lunch break sometime between 11:00 and 12:00, and stop work entirely after about 15:00 or 15:30. Hours are always subject to change at the smaller glassworks, but they welcome a phone call to confirm open times. It's not uncommon for glassblowers to take vacation in July-Aug (along with the rest of Sweden).

▲Bergdala Glassworks (Bergdalahyttan)

The small, independent Bergdala glassworks, in a village of the same name, has an enjoyably artsy hot shop. Its well-stocked shop is full of its affordable trademark blue-rimmed glassware, and the engaging "museum" around back shows off a different sampling of local artists every year.

Cost and Hours: Free, gallery/shop open daily July-Aug 10:00-18:00 except Sat-Sun until 17:00, shorter hours off-season; glassblowing Mon-Fri 7:00-15:30 (lunch break 11:00-12:00); off highway #25 near Hovmantorp, tel. 0478/31650, http://bergdala-glastekniska-museum.se.

▲▲Kosta Boda

About an hour east of Växjö, the village of Kosta boasts the oldest of the *glasbruks,* dating back to 1742. Today, the Kosta Boda campus includes a modern outlet mall, a factory store, a fancy new art hotel...and, of course, the glassworks.

The highlight here is watching the **glassworks** in action. Visitors are welcomed to the hot-shop floor, where a team of glassblowers rotates through a carefully choreographed routine: grabbing a glob of molten glass on the blow pipe, rolling it on a steel table into a general shape, then turning and blowing the piece into its final form. You can visit the glassworks and its gallery on your own, but it's worth calling or emailing ahead to reserve a spot on a 30-minute English tour.

In the surprisingly modest **exhibition gallery,** each piece is identified with a photo and brief bio (in English) of its designer, which personalizes the art (often offered for sale).

Cost and Hours: Glassworks-free, usually open Mon-Fri 9:00-15:30 (lunch break 10:30-11:30), Sat-Sun 10:00-16:00; gallery-Mon-Fri 10:00-17:00, Sat-Sun until 16:00; www.kostaboda.se.

Tours: 100 SEK, usually 3/day in English, but best to arrange ahead by phone (tel. 0478/34529) or email (info@kostaboda.se).

Shopping: In the Kosta **factory outlet shop,** crystal "seconds" (with tiny bubbles or sets that don't quite match) and discontinued pieces are sold at good prices. This is duty-free shopping, and they'll happily mail your purchases home (Mon-Fri 10:00-18:00, Sat-Sun until 17:00). Don't confuse this with the big outlet mall across the street.

Sleeping and Eating: I ate well at the **cafeteria** inside the outlet mall, which features thrifty lunch specials. Nearby is the pricey **$$$$ Kosta Boda Art Hotel,** designed to impress. Everything's decorated to the hilt with (of course) artistic glass, created in the hot shop across the street. With Växjö and Kalmar so close, there's little reason to sleep here (tel. 0478/34830, www. kostabodaarthotel.se). But if you have a few extra minutes, poke around this over-the-top, world-of-glass complex, which includes a "glass bar," a mind-bending indoor swimming pool, and a restaurant where, on most evenings, you can watch an actual glassblower at work while you dine.

▲▲Transjö Hytta

Set up in an old converted farm 10 minutes south of Kosta, this tiny, friendly glassworks creates high-quality fine-art pieces. From the

main shop, a canal-like pond (enlivened with colorful glass art baubles) leads back to the hopping hot shop. Transjö—started by a pair of highly regarded glass designers—employs up-and-coming artists as apprentices, and their youthful vigor is infectious. You can feel the art oozing out of the ovens. The hot shop closes from July through December, but even if you don't catch the artists in action here, the setting is charming.

The gift shop out front sells a fine selection of one-of-a-kind glass art and limited-run production items made on-site (the *elevarbete*/apprentice works are cheaper). The shop keeps routine hours, but if you find it closed, dial the phone numbers posted on the door and someone will let you in.

Cost and Hours: Free, shop usually open early June-mid-Sept daily 9:00-17:00; hot shop hours irregular, closed July-Dec, smart to call or email ahead; tel. 0478/50700, www.transjohytta.com, info@transjohytta.com. To find it, look for *Transjö* signs just south of Kosta.

SOUTHEAST SWEDEN

Orrefors and Orranäs Bruk

The town of Orrefors once had a glassworks with its own proud history, but glass is no longer commercially produced there. Formerly a premier art brand, Orrefors exists now only as a stepchild of Kosta Boda, and is mostly machine-made abroad. With its glassworks shuttered, Orrefors became a ghost town.

But concerned locals are blowing life back into Orrefors. Starting with an **open-air hot shop** that's already operating in a park near the old shop, their project will unfold in stages over several years, with the ultimate goal of reintroducing art-glass production to the town (to be sold under the name Orranäs Bruk).

Meanwhile, the town's dazzling **glass museum** continues to display its historic art pieces chronologically (from early-20th-century pieces with Art Nouveau flair through works from the 1940s).

Cost and Hours: Hot shop and glass museum July-Aug only; for the most current details, consult www.glasriket.se.

▲Glass Factory

Just off highway 25, in the little village of Boda, is a new enterprise, on the site of the former Boda glass production workshop. When glass producers fell on hard times in the 1980s and 1990s, many shops either folded or consolidated. When Boda closed, the municipality came together to buy its glass archive, an amazing record of artistic achievement that's now on display in the Glass Factory museum. There's also a great hot shop with regular demonstrations, a gallery of more modern Boda glass, and an affordable shop that sells glasswork from all over Scandinavia.

Cost and Hours: 60 SEK, late April-early Sept Mon-Fri 10:00-18:00, Sat-Sun 11:00-17:00; off-season Wed-Sun 11:00-17:00; in Boda at Storgotan 5, well-signed off highway 25, tel. 0471/249-360, www.theglassfactory.se.

OTHER ATTRACTIONS

▲▲Lessebo Handmade Paper Mill (Handpappersbruket)

The town of Lessebo has a 300-year-old paper mill (tucked next to a giant modern one) that's well worth a visit for its guided tour. Making handmade paper using strictly traditional methods (the newest piece of machinery is from the 1920s), Lessebo is a study in the way things used to be: Cotton fibers are soaked until they become pulp, packed into a frame, pressed, dried, glazed, and hand-torn into the perfect size and shape.

This paper has long been coveted throughout Sweden for special purposes: top-of-the-line stationery (for wedding invitations), impossible-to-forge embossed document paper (for certificates or important examinations), and long-lasting archival use (the cotton fibers ensure the paper will stay pristine for decades).

You can visit the excellent gift shop on your own (watercolor paper, stationery, and cards), but to see papermaking in action, plan to join one of the fascinating 45-minute English tours. It's a rare opportunity to witness a centuries-old craft up close and personal.

Cost and Hours: Shop-June-Aug Mon-Fri 9:00-17:00, closed Sat-Sun, off-season closes at 16:00 and for lunch 12:00-13:00; 95-SEK guided tours depart 5/day in summer—check website for current times; look for black-and-white *Handpappersbruk* sign just after the Kosta turnoff, Storgatan 79, tel. 0478/47691, www. lessebopapper.se.

Grönåsen Moose and Farm Animal Park (Grönåsen Älg- & Lantdjurspark)

This offbeat attraction, just outside Kosta, demonstrates the love-hate relationship Swedes feel toward their moose population. A  third of a million of these giant, majestic beasts live in Sweden. They're popular with hunters but unpopular with drivers. At this attraction, you'll walk through the moose-happy gift shop before taking a mile-long stroll around the perimeter of a pen holding live moose. Periodic museum exhibits—life-size dioramas with stuffed moose (including one plastered to the hood of a car)—round out the attraction. You can even buy moose sausage to grill on-site. Sure it's a hokey roadside stop, and will hardly be a hit with animal-rights activists, but for many the park is an enjoyable stop.

Cost and Hours: 90 SEK, daily June-Aug 10:00-18:00, shorter hours April-May and Sept-Nov, closed off-season, just outside Kosta on the road to Orrefors, tel. 0478/50770, www.gronasen.se.

Eating in Glass Country

You'll find plenty of simple eateries designed for day-trippers. For example, the cafeteria in the outlet mall at the big Kosta complex is the perfect place for fast and cheap, Ikea-style Swedish grub.

If you'd like to linger over a more serious dinner, consider joining one of the special *hyttsill* **dinners** at various glass workshops. Traditionally, a hot shop's fires made it a popular place to convene after hours on frigid winter nights. People would huddle around the ovens and be entertained by wandering minstrel-type entertainers called *luffar*. The food was nothing special (*hyttsill* literally means "hot-shop herring," usually served with crispy pork, potatoes, and other stick-to-your-ribs fare), but it was a nice opportunity for a convivial rural community to get together. Today modern glassworks carry on the tradition, inviting tourists on several nights through the summer. They usually have live music and glassblowers working while you dine (figure around 400 SEK per person; for more information, see www.glasriket.se).

Kalmar

Kalmar feels like it used to be of strategic importance. In its heyday—back when the Sweden/Denmark border was just a few miles to the south—they called Kalmar Castle the "Key to Sweden." But today Denmark is distant, and Kalmar is a bustling small city of 64,000 (with 9,000 students in its university and maritime academy). Kalmar's salty old center, classic castle, and busy waterfront give it a wistful sailor's charm.

History students may remember Kalmar as the place where the treaty establishing the 1397 Kalmar Union was signed. This "three crowns" treaty united Norway, Sweden, and Denmark against their common enemy: German Hanseatic traders. It created a huge kingdom, dominated by Denmark, that lasted a bit more than a hundred years. But when the Swede Gustav Vasa came to power in 1523, Kalmar was rescued from the Danes, the union was dissolved...and even the European Union hasn't been able to reunify the Scandinavian Peninsula since.

Kalmar town was originally next to the castle. But that put the townsfolk directly in the line of attack whenever the castle was besieged. So, after a huge fire in 1647, they relocated the town on Kvarnholmen, an adjacent, easier-to-defend island. There it was encircled by giant 17th-century earthworks and bastions, parts of which still survive.

The town center of Kvarnholmen, the charming Old Town, the castle, and the nearby vacation island of Öland are all enjoyable to explore, making Kalmar Sweden's most appealing stop after Stockholm. Its tourist season is boom-or-bust, busiest from mid-June through mid-August.

Orientation to Kalmar

Kalmar is easily walkable and fun by bike. The mostly pedestrianized core of the town is on the island of Kvarnholmen, walled and with a grid street plan. The Old Town district is between Kvarnholmen and Kalmar Castle, which is on a little island of its own (a 10-minute walk from Kvarnholmen). The train station and TI sit on the edge of Kvarnholmen.

Additional islands make up Kalmar (including charming Ängö and mod Varvsholmen), but most visitors stick to Kvarnholmen, the Old Town, and the castle. If your time is limited, your top priorities should be a town walk, the castle, and the public beach just beyond the castle.

TOURIST INFORMATION

The TI is in the big, modern building next to the marina (summer Mon-Fri 9:00-18:00, Sat until 14:00, Sun closed; shorter hours off-season; Ölandskajen 9, tel. 0480/417-700, www.kalmar.com).

Ask about live music and entertainment; for example, there are often free concerts on Larmtorget, in Kvarnholmen, on Tue and Thu in the summer.

Biking: Many hotels have loaner or rental bikes for guests. Kalmar Cykeluthyrning (across from TI, closed Sun) rents bikes for 120 SEK per day (tel. 0480/010-600); Ölands Cykeluthyrning, with a convenient office right in the train station, has bikes for 140 SEK per day (handy one-way rentals with locations in Borgholm and Mörbylánga on Öland, daily late June-Aug 9:00-19:00, tel. 070/667-6280, www.olandscykeluthyrning.se). Consider riding the ferry from the harbor to the island of Öland (55 SEK—credit cards only, about hourly, 30 minutes, www.ressel.se), then renting a bike—Öland is made to order for a Swedish country bike ride. (Note you cannot ride a bike over the Öland Bridge.)

ARRIVAL IN KALMAR

Arriving at the combined train and bus station couldn't be easier (train ticket office open Mon-Fri 6:30-18:00, Sat until 15:00, Sun 10:30-17:00; lockers available). As you walk out the front door, the town center (Kvarnholmen) is dead ahead. The TI is 100 yards to your right, across the busy street on the harbor. Kalmar Castle and the Old Town are behind you (follow the tracks to your left until the first crosswalk, then follow the big tree-lined boulevard to the castle; with more time, take my scenic "Back-Streets Walk" to the castle, later).

Sights in Kalmar

▲▲ KALMAR CASTLE (KALMAR SLOTT)

This moated castle is one of Europe's great medieval experiences. The imposing exterior, anchored by stout watchtowers and cuddled by a lush park, houses a Renaissance palace interior. Built in the 12th century, the

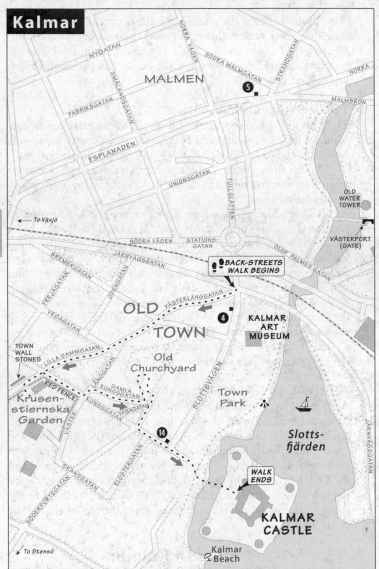

castle was enlarged and further fortified by the great King Gustav Vasa (r. 1523-1560) and lived in by two of his sons, Erik XIV and Johan III. In the 1570s, Johan III redecorated the castle in the trendy Renaissance style, giving it its present shape. Kalmar Castle remained a royal hub until 1658, when the Swedish frontier shifted south and the castle lost its strategic importance. Kalmar Castle was neglected, then used as a prison, distillery, and granary. Finally, in the mid-19th century, a newfound respect for history led to

KATT-RUMPAN

KVARNHOLMEN

ÄNGÖ BRON BRIDGE

To Varvsholmen, Ängö, Öland Bridge & 6 KLAPPHUS

WALK ENDS

BEACH

KANALGATAN

SÖDRA KANALGATAN

STRÖMGATAN

FISKAREGATAN

NORRA LÄNGGATAN

STORGATAN

CATHEDRAL

Stor-torget 1

KALMAR COUNTY MUSEUM

MARITIME MUSEUM

KVARNHOLMEN WALK BEGINS

STORGATAN

11

TOWN HALL

SÖDRA LÄNGGATAN

3 KALMAR-SALEN

Larm-torget

Lilla Torget

TULLHUSET

2

12

7

RAMPARTS

ÖLANDSGATAN

SÖDRA VALLGATAN

LARMGATAN

ÖLANDSKAJEN

Baltic Sea

P

SKEPPSBROGATAN

8

13 BARONEN SHOPPING MALL

9

Pedestrian & Bike Ferry to Öland

15 BUS & TRAIN STATION

100 Meters

100 Yards

ÖLANDSKAJEN

15

10

Harbor

N

MARITIME ACADEMY

Eateries & Other
7 Källaren Kronan
8 Gröna Stugan
9 Bryggan
10 Grill Brygghuset
11 Kullzénska Caféet
12 Ernesto Restaurante
13 Supermarket
14 Söderport
15 Bike Rental (2)

Accommodations
1 Calmar Stadshotell
2 Frimurare Hotellet
3 Kalmar Sjömanshem Vandrarhem
4 Slottshotellet
5 Hotell Hilda
6 To Hotell Svanen

SOUTHEAST SWEDEN

the castle's renovation. Today, it's a vibrant sight giggling with kids' activities, park-like ramparts, and well-described historic rooms.

Cost and Hours: 135 SEK, daily late June-Aug 10:00-18:00, May-late June and Sept-Oct until 16:00; Nov-Dec Sat-Sun only 10:00-16:00, café and restaurant, tel. 0480/451-490, www.kalmarslott.se.

Tours: Catch the one-hour English tour to hear about the goofy medieval antics of Sweden's kings (included in admission, 3/day late June-mid-Aug—check website for current times).

Visiting the Castle: There's no designated route for visitors, but I've proposed one in the little tour below. Be sure to pick up and use the castle map to help you follow my route (castle rooms are not numbered except on the map—so the room numbers below refer to that handout). Otherwise, just read my tour in advance and then ramble, reading plaques as you go. There are good English descriptions throughout.

Approaching the castle, you'll cross a wooden drawbridge. Peering into the grassy, filled-in moat, look for sunbathers, who

enjoy soaking up rays while the ramparts protect them from cool winds. To play "king of the castle," scramble along these outer ramparts.

In the central **courtyard** is the canopied Dolphin Well, a fine work of Renaissance craftsmanship.

Access to most of the rooms is from the main courtyard, but we'll use the entrance just to the right of the gift shop (unceremoniously labeled *Toalett*).

Once inside, turn right to find the **Governor's Quarters** (Room 10) with a model of the early castle. Notice the bulky medieval shape of the towers, before they were capped by fancy Renaissance cupolas; and the Old Town that once huddled in the not-protective-enough shadow of the castle.

In the adjoining **Dungeon** (Room 9), you can peer down into the pit where unfortunate prisoners were held. The room was later converted into a kitchen (notice the big fireplace), and the pit became a handy place to dump kitchen waste.

Now go through the labyrinth of rooms to the right that show daily life at the castle: a reconstruction of the castle kitchen (Room 12), an excellent set of models showing the evolution of the building from medieval castle to Renaissance palace (Room 17), and an impressive copy of Erik XIV's 1561 coronation robe (Room 14, where there's also a complete rundown of the Vasa kings). In the next room (13) are similarly resplendent reproductions of royal gowns.

Now backtrack to where we entered, and climb the **Queen's Staircase** (Room 6), up steps made of Catholic gravestones. While this simply might have been an economical way to recycle building materials, some speculate that it was a symbolic move in support of King Gustav Vasa's Reformation, after the king broke with the pope in a Henry VIII-style power struggle.

At the top of the stairs, go left through the wooden door into the **Queen's Bedroom** (Room 23). The ornate 1625 Danish bed (captured from the Danes after a battle) is the only surviving original piece of furniture in the castle. The faces decorating the bed have had their noses chopped off, as superstitious castle-dwellers believed that potentially troublesome spirits settled in the noses. This bed could easily be disassembled ("like an Ikea bed," as my guide put it) and moved from place to place—handy for medieval kings and queens, who were forever traveling throughout their realm. Smaller servants' quarters adjoin this room.

Proceed into the **Checkered Hall** (Room 24). Examine the intricately inlaid wall panels, which make use of 17 different types of wood—each a slightly different hue. Appreciate the faded Renaissance frescoes throughout the palace.

Continue into the **dining room** (a.k.a. Gray Hall—Room 25) for the frescoes of Samson and Delilah high on the wall. The table is set for an Easter feast (based on a detailed account by a German visitor to one particular Easter meal held here). For this holiday event, the whole family was in town—including Gustav Vasa's two sons, Erik XIV and Johan III. Erik's wife, Katarzyna Jagiellonka, was a Polish Catholic (their marriage united Sweden, Poland, and Lithuania into a grand empire); for her, Easter meant an end to Lenten abstinences. Notice the diverse savories on the table, including fish patties with egg, elaborate pies, and chopped pike in the shape of pears. The giant birds are for decoration, not for eating. Logically, forks (which resembled the devil's pitchfork) were not used—just spoons, knives, and hands.

The door in the far corner with the faded sun above it leads to the **King's Chamber** (Room 26). Notice the elaborate lock on the door, installed by King Erik XIV because of constant squabbles about succession. The hunting scenes inside have been restored a bit too colorfully, but the picture of Hercules over the left window is original—likely painted by Erik himself. Examine more of the inlaid panels. To see the king's toilet, peek into the little room to the left of the fireplace, with a fine castle illustration embedded in its hidden door (if closed, ask a museum wench to open it). Also in here was a secret escape hatch the king could use in case of trouble. Perhaps King Erik XIV was right to be so paranoid; he eventually died under mysterious circumstances, perhaps poisoned by his brother Johan III, who succeeded him as king.

Backtrack through the dining room and continue into the **Golden Hall** (Room 27), with its gorgeously carved (and painstakingly restored) gilded ceiling. The entire ceiling is suspended

from the true ceiling by chains. If you visually trace the lines of the ceiling, the room seems crooked—but it's actually an optical illusion to disguise the fact that it's not perfectly square. Ponder the portraits of the royal family: Gustav Vasa, one of his wives, sons Erik XIV and Johan III, and Johan's son Sigismund. Imagine the reality-show-level dysfunction that carbonated the social scene here back then.

Peek into **Agda's Chamber** (Room 28), the bedroom of Erik's consort. The replica furniture re-creates how it looked when the king's kept woman lived here. Later, the same room was used for a different type of captivity: as a prison cell for female inmates.

Cut across to the top of the King's Staircase (also made of gravestones like the Queen's Staircase, and topped by a pair of lions). The big door leads to the grand **Green Hall** (Room 31), once used for banquets and now for concerts.

At the end of this hall, the **chapel** (Room 32) is one of Sweden's most popular wedding venues (up to four ceremonies each

Saturday). As reflected by the language of the posted Bible quotations, the sexes sat separately: men, on the warmer right side, were more literate and could read Latin; women, on the cooler left side, read Swedish. The fancy pews at the front were reserved for the king and queen.

Going through the door to the right of the altar, you'll enter a stairwell (Room 33), above which hangs a model ship, donated by a thankful sailor who survived a storm. In the next room (34) is Anita, a taxidermic horse who served with the Swedish military (until 1937).

The rest of the castle complex includes the vast **Burnt Hall** (Room 36), where in summer you'll likely find an interesting special art exhibit.

▲THE OLD TOWN

The original Kalmar town burned (in 1647) and is long gone. But the cute, garden-filled residential zone that now fills the parklike space between the castle and the modern town center is worth a look.

It's a toy village of colorfully painted wooden homes, tidy yards, and perfect picket fences. Locals still call it the Old Town

(Gamla Stan), even though almost everything here is newer
than the buildings on Kvarnholmen, now the heart of town.

Back-Streets Walk to the Castle

Consider a slight detour strolling through the Old Town on

your way from the train station to the castle (the walk is marked on
the "Kalmar" map). Begin where the pleasant, tree-shaded Slotts-
vägen boulevard intersects with little Västerlånggatan, the cobbled
street angling to the right.

Västerlånggatan: Wandering down this quaint lane, enjoy
the time-passed cottages as you peek over fences into private gardens. You'll pass behind the grand mansion (now the recommended **Slottshotellet**) that belonged to the prestigious Jeansson family,
who donated the parkland near the castle to the town.

Continue through the first intersection, following the path
through the middle of the grassy park. As you cross the road on the
far side of the park, you'll pass two lines of stones, a small surviving
remnant of Kalmar's town wall (on the right).

Krusenstiernska Gården: Watch on the left for the entrance
to this relaxed, kid-friendly garden, with its breezy café selling
traditional homemade cakes. Poke inside to discover a manicured
world of charming plantings clustered around a well, and peek
into time-warp workshops. On summer evenings, this garden is
a venue for top Swedish comedy acts, which pack the place (park
free, daily 11:00-18:00 in summer, shorter hours on weekends and
off-season).

From the garden, backtrack to the street and follow the red
fence to the right. Where the fence ends, jog left and squeeze between the yellow and red houses.

Gamla Kungsgatan and the Old Churchyard: Immerse
yourself in this Swedish village world of charming cottages and
flower-filled window boxes. At the bottom of the lane, on the left,
watch for the Old Churchyard (Gamla Kyrkogården), dating from
the 13th century and scattered with headstones. It's virtually all
that remains of the original Old Town. Look for the monument
topped by a statue of a man carrying a boy (St. Christopher, patron
of traders and seafarers). Circling this slab, you'll see the floor plan
of the original cathedral, an image looking down the cathedral's
nave, and a rendering of the town before it was destroyed. The cathedral tower—which had partially survived the 1647 fire—was
torn down in 1678 by the Swedes themselves, who wanted to en-

sure that their enemies (the Danes) couldn't use the tower to launch an attack on the castle.

About 50 yards farther into the yard, the stone slab on the pedestal (marked *Kalmarunionen 600 ar*) commemorates the 600th anniversary of the 1397 Kalmar Union, which united the Nordic states. On June 14, 1997, the contemporary leaders of those same nations—Sweden, Norway, Denmark, Finland, and Iceland—came here to honor that union. You can see their signatures etched in the stone.

Exit the churchyard the way you came in, turn right on the paved street, and take the first left (down Kungsgatan) to the main boulevard. You'll be facing the town park and the castle; on your left is the appealing, recommended Söderportcafé (with an inviting terrace and an economical buffet-lunch deal).

Town Park (Stadsparken): Unfurling along the waterfront between the castle and the city, this beautifully landscaped arboretum-style garden is Kalmar's playground. While thoughtfully planned, it's also rugged, with surprises around each corner. Locals brag that their region is a "banana belt" that enjoys a milder climate than most of Sweden; some of the plants here grow nowhere else in the country. This diversity of foliage, and the many sculptures and monuments, make the park a delight to explore. The modern art museum stands in an appropriately modern building in the center of the park.

▲Kalmar Beach (Kalmarsundsbadet)

Kalmar's best beach is at the edge of the Old Town, just beyond the castle. On a hot summer day, this is a festive and happy slice of Swedish life—well worth a stroll even if you're not "going to the beach." With snack stands, showers, sand castles, wheelchair beach access, and views of the castle and the island of Öland, the beach has put Kalmar on the fun-in-the-sun map. It's quite popular with RVers and the yachting crowd. And if you enjoy people-watching, it's a combination Swedish beauty pageant/tattoo show. For some extra views and kid-leaping action, be sure to walk to the end of the long pier.

The beach stretches a mile south. Beyond it is the charming little seafront community of **Stensö,** with its own pocket-size harbor and charming fishing cottages.

▲KVARNHOLMEN TOWN CENTER

Today, downtown Kalmar is on the island of Kvarnholmen. Get your bearings with the following walk, which basically just cuts straight through the length of town. Then dig into its museums.

Kvarnholmen Self-Guided Walk

Most action centers on the lively, restaurant-and-café-lined square called **Larmtorget,** a few steps uphill from the train station. This is the most inviting square in town for outdoor dining—scout your options for dinner later tonight. It's also the nightlife center of town, especially on Tuesday and Thursday evenings in summer, when there are often free concerts. The many cafés bordering the square are a reminder that this is a college town, with lots of students; and a tourist town, with lots of vacationing Swedes. The fountain depicts David standing triumphantly over the slain Goliath—a thinly veiled allusion to King Gustav Vasa, who defeated the Danes (the fountain's reliefs depict his arrival in Kalmar in 1520).

The area just to the north, up Larmgatan, is a charming old quarter with the historic Västerport gate and a restored old water tower. The tower, dating from 1900, was turned into a modern apartment building, winning an award for the architect who successfully maintained the tower's historic design.

But for now, we'll stroll straight through town on the main pedestrian shopping street, **Storgatan** (with Ben & Jerry's on the corner). Kvarnholmen is a planned Renaissance town, laid out on a regular grid plan (after the devastating 1647 fire consumed the Old Town). While a 1960s push to "modernize" stripped away much of the Old World character, surviving historic buildings and the lack of traffic on most of its central streets make Kvarnholmen a delightful place to stroll.

The first major cross-street, Kaggensgatan, leads (to the right, past a fine row of 17th-century stone houses) down to the harbor; a block to the left, on the right (at #26), is the landmark and recommended Kullzénska Caféet, whose owners refused to let this charming 18th-century merchant's house be torn down to make way for "progress." (It remains a good place for *fika* in a genteel setting.)

Continue window-shopping your way down Storgatan. On the right just after #20, admire the building marked *1667,* with the cannonballs decorating the doorway. This was the home of a war profiteer—a lucrative business in this military-minded town (now an inviting gift shop with local products, teas, chocolates, and cheese).

Storgatan leads to the town's main square, **Stortorget.** Built in the 17th century in a grand style befitting a European power, the "big square" tries a little too hard to show off—today it feels too big and too quiet (locals prefer hanging out on the cozier Larmtorget).

The **cathedral** *(domkyrkan)* dominating the square is the biggest and (some say) finest Baroque church in Sweden. Its interior,

which contains a gigantic 17th-century pulpit and bells from the earlier town cathedral, has been elegantly restored to its original glory. Its architect was inspired by the great Renaissance churches of Rome. The interior is all very high-church (for such a Lutheran country), with a fine Baroque altar, carved tombstones used for flooring, and homogeneous white walls (free, Mon-Fri 8:00-20:00, Sat-Sun from 9:00, shorter hours off-season, free noon "Lunch Music" organ concerts daily in summer—check the program on the board left of the entrance). Facing the cathedral is the decorated facade of the **Town Hall** *(rådhuset).*

From here, go straight through the square and stroll down Storgatan. Notice the fine old houses, all lovingly cared for. At the end of town, the area beyond Östra Vallgatan (the old eastern wall of the city) has a pleasant **park** and small **swimming beach.** You may notice dads out with their babies—most Scandinavians get over a year of paid leave for the mom and dad to split as they like. (They're nicknamed "Latte Dads," and cafés complain that they clog their floor space with too many carriages.)

Head across the street and down the stairs toward the playground (to the left) to find, on a little pier in the water, the last remaining *klapphus*—laundry building—in Kalmar (and Scandinavia). In the mid-1800s, four of these small, wooden structures with

floating floors stood here at the seaside. Washers would stand in barrels inset around the central laundry pool for a better working position. Today the *klapphus* is still occasionally used for washing rugs and carpets. The Baltic seawater is considered good for carpet health.

Across the water is the island neighborhood of Varvsholmen, which once housed an eyesore shipyard but has been converted into a futuristic residential development. To the left of Varvsholmen is the sleepy island neighborhood of Ängö, traditionally home to sailors and fishermen, now one of Kalmar's most desirable residential areas. To the right stretches the Öland Bridge. When built in 1972 to connect Öland with the mainland, it was Europe's longest bridge.

• *Your walk is finished. Hooking around to the right, you first reach the former city bathhouse (in a 1909 Art Nouveau building), which faces the tiny Maritime History Museum (described later). A block beyond that, the waterfront is dominated by giant red-brick buildings—steam mills once used to grind flour. Today this complex houses the fascinating Kalmar County Museum, described next.*

▲▲Kalmar County Museum (Kalmar Läns Museum)

This museum is worth a visit for its excellent exhibit on the royal ship *Kronan,* a shipwrecked 17th-century warship that still sits on the bottom of the Baltic just off the island of Öland. Soggy bits and rusted pieces, well-described in English, give visitors a here's-the-buried-treasure thrill. It's a more intimate look at life at sea than Stockholm's grander Vasa Museum, though this exhibit lacks the boat's actual hull. (The amateur marine archaeologist Anders Franzén was instrumental in locating and salvaging both ships.)

Cost and Hours: 120 SEK, daily 10:00-17:00, off-season until 16:00, included 45-minute English tours daily in season at 13:00; kid-friendly café on floor 4, Skeppsbrogatan 51, tel. 0480/451-300 www.kalmarlansmuseum.se.

Visiting the Museum: While the museum has plenty of exhibits, your visit will focus mostly on the third floor with the *Kronan* shipwreck artifacts.

Beyond the entry, the first floor has temporary exhibits and shows off the cannons recovered from the *Kronan* wreckage. In those days, cannons were so valuable they were prized the way a Rolls Royce would be today, so each one has its own story (described in English). In the years following the ship's sinking, these cannons were the only artifacts considered worth recovering.

From the first floor, I'd skip the temporary exhibits on Floor 2 and head directly to Floor 3, which displays salvage from the ***Kronan.*** Twice the size of Stockholm's famous *Vasa,* this warship was a floating palace and the most heavily armed vessel in the world. But it exploded and sank about three miles beyond the island of Öland in 1676. The painted wall at the elevator shows the dramatic event: The *Kronan*'s admiral misjudged conditions and harnessed too much wind, causing the vessel to tip and its gun ports to fill with water. As the ship began to list into the water, a fallen lantern ignited explosives in the hold, and...BLAM! The ship went right down. Its Danish and Dutch foes—who hadn't fired a shot—happily watched it sink into the deep. Of the 850 people on board, only about 40 were rescued. The wreck's whereabouts were forgotten until 1980, when it was rediscovered by the same oceanographer who found the *Vasa*.

Head into the exhibit, where you'll view a model of the ship-wreck site (press the button for a short English explanation). You'll see a cross-section of the mighty vessel and a recovered carving of the potbellied Swedish king (one of many such carvings that decorated the ship). The small theater plays a 15-minute film about the ship (English subtitles).

The replica of the middle gun deck leads to the exhibit's most interesting section, which explains everyday life on board. The 850 sailors who manned the ship (about the population of a midsized town of that age) represented all walks of life, "all in the same boat." Engaging illustrations, eyewitness accounts, and actual salvage items bring the story to life. You'll see guns, musical instruments, a medicine chest, dishes, and clothing—items that emphasize the nautical lifestyles of the simple, common people who worked and perished on the ship. A treasure chest contains coins from all around the known world at the time, each one carefully identified.

The final exhibit (with another short film) reminds us that the *Kronan* still rests on the sea floor, awaiting funding to be raised to the surface. You'll see a replica of the diving bell used in 1680 to retrieve the cannons, and the modern diving bell from very early explorations of the site. Today a dedicated crew of scientists and enthusiasts—including, at times, Sweden's King Carl XVI Gustav—continue to dive to recover bits and pieces.

For extra credit, head up to Floor 4 for its exhibit on **Jenny Nyström,** an early-1900s Kalmar artist who gained fame for her cute Christmas illustrations featuring elves and pixies. You'll see some of her children's books and textbooks, as well as some less commercial, more artistic portraits (with a touch of Art Nouveau flair). Ponder Nyström's status as a proto-feminist icon: She was one of the first female artists to support her family by selling her paintings.

Kalmar Maritime Museum (Kalmar Sjöfartsmuseum)

This humble, dusty little exhibit sits a long block beyond the Kalmar County Museum. It's a jumble of photos of vessels, model boats, charts, and other seafaring bric-a-brac that traces the nautical story of Kalmar up to modern times. The collection is displayed in four rooms of a former apartment, shuffled between beautiful porcelain stoves left behind by a previous owner. (These were display models for his stove retail business.) While it's explained by an English booklet (that you can borrow or buy), the volunteers love to talk and are eager to show you around.

Cost and Hours: 50 SEK, daily mid-June-Aug 11:00-16:00, off-season Sun only 12:00-16:00, Södra Långgatan 81, tel. 0480/15875, www.kalmarsjofartsmuseum.se.

Sleeping in Kalmar

IN KVARNHOLMEN TOWN CENTER

$$$ Calmar Stadshotell is a 132-room fancy hotel filling its 1907 historic shell right on Kalmar's main square, Stortorget (elevator, Stortorget 14, tel. 0480/496-900, www.profilhotels.se, calmarstadshotell@profilhotels.se).

$$ Frimurare Hotellet, in a grand old building overlooking inviting Larmtorget square, is just steps from the train station.

Warmly run, the place has soul and a disarmingly friendly staff. Rich public areas, wide-plank hardwood floors, and chandeliers give it a 19th-century elegance. Guests can help themselves to coffee, tea, juice, and other refreshments in the lounge anytime. The 35 rooms provide modern comfort amid period decor. Because it's squeezed between a café-packed square and a park that's popular for concerts, it can come with some noise (RS%, elevator, free sauna, a few loaner bikes free for Rick Steves readers, 50 yards in front of train station, Larmtorget 2, tel. 0480/15230, www.frimurarehotellet.se, info@frimurarehotellet.se).

$ Kalmar Sjömanshem Vandrarhem, a charming green house built in 1910 for sailors and now used for student housing, opens to travelers in the summer (mid-June-mid-Aug only). While its 13 rooms are very simple and bathrooms are down the hall, it has an inviting TV lounge, handy guest kitchen, and a peaceful garden behind a white picket fence facing the harbor (family rooms, sheets and towels extra, no breakfast, plenty of nearby pay parking, Ölandsgatan 45, tel. 0480/10810, www.kalmarsjomanshem.se, info@kalmarsjomanshem.se).

OUTSIDE THE TOWN CENTER

$$$ Slottshotellet ("Castle Hotel") is an enticing splurge in the atmospheric Old Town. It's the nicely upgraded but still homey former mansion of a local big shot. The 70 rooms—some in the mansion, others sprinkled throughout nearby buildings—sit across a leafy boulevard from Kalmar's Town Park, just up the street from the castle (Slottsvägen 7, tel. 0480/88260, www.slottshotellet.se, info@slottshotellet.se).

$$ Hotell Hilda has 12 good rooms in an updated old house, located in a modern residential zone just over the canal from the town center (elevator, limited free parking—reserve a spot when you book, Esplanaden 33, tel. 0480/54700, www.hotellhilda.se, info@hotellhilda.se). The ground-floor Kallskänken café, which doubles as the reception, serves good salads and sandwiches (Mon-Sat 8:00-21:00, Sun 10:00-20:00; if checking in outside of these times, email for the door code).

¢-$$ Hotell Svanen, a 15-minute walk or short bus ride from the center in the Ängö neighborhood, has a mix of nicer hotel rooms with private bath, cheaper rooms with shower down the hall, and hostel beds (no more than six beds per room). Services include laundry and kitchen facilities, a TV room, a sauna, and rental bikes and canoes. While it's a bit institutional, you can't argue with the value (family rooms, sheets extra in hostel rooms, breakfast extra; reception daily 7:30-21:00, elevator, Rappegatan 1, tel. 0480/25560, www.hotellsvanen.se, info@hotellsvanen.se). You'll see a blue-and-white hotel sign and a hostel symbol at the edge of town on Ängöleden street, a mile from the train station. Catch bus #405 at the station to Ängöleden (2-3/hour, 5 minutes), or take a taxi for about 70 SEK.

Eating in Kalmar

Kalmar has a surprising number of good dining options for a small city. For lunch, look for a *dagens rätt* (daily special), which gets you a main dish, salad, bread, and usually coffee or a soft drink.

IN KVARNHOLMEN TOWN CENTER
$$$ Källaren Kronan, open only for dinner, is a candlelit cellar restaurant with romantic tables under low stone arches. They serve old-time Swedish dishes, including elk, as well as modern cuisine (nightly 18:00-23:00, Ölandsgatan 7, tel. 0480/411-400).

$$$$ Gröna Stugan ("The Green Cottage") has a great location just off the harbor. Enjoy the eclectic menu (burgers, short ribs, grilled arctic char) on their patio deck or in the light and bright dining room. Reservations are smart (lunch Mon-Fri 11:30-14:00, dinner Mon-Sat 17:00-22:00, closed Sun, Larmgatan 1, tel. 0480/15858, www.gronastuganikalmar.se).

$$$ Bryggan sits inside the Baronen shopping mall, but it's poised over the harbor with view tables inside and deck seating over the water. They serve typical bistro fare, including burgers and fish-and-chips (Mon-Sat 10:00-19:00, Sat until 16:00, Sun 11:00-16:00, tel. 0480/363-626).

$$ Grill Brygghuset, open only in summer, seems made to order for visiting yachters. Casual and right on the dock, it grills everything, serving traditional and modern dishes with local ingredients (mid-June-mid-Aug Tue-Sun from 17:00, closed Mon, at the marina near the TI and train station at Ölandskajen 9, tel. 073-354-0333).

$$ Kullzénska Caféet, a cozy, antique-filled eatery in a historic 18th-century house, is great for a *fika* break. They serve sandwiches and homemade pastries, but locals adore the always-fresh berry cobblers (with vanilla sauce or ice cream). While it has street seating, the dining rooms upstairs are what it's all about (Mon-Fri 10:00-18:30, Sat-Sun 12:00-16:00, on the second floor at Kaggensgatan 26, at the corner of Norra Långgatan, tel. 0480/28882).

$$ Ernesto Restaurante is driven by Ernesto, who came here from Naples 30 years ago. This local favorite for pasta and pizza has a high-energy feel with good indoor and outdoor seating (most menu items available for takeout, great selection of Italian wines, daily from 16:00, Södra Långgatan 5, tel. 0480/24100).

Supermarket: The **Co-op** has everything you need for a good picnic, including a salad bar (daily 6:00-23:00, in the Baronen shopping mall at the harbor, on Skeppsbrogatan).

NEAR THE CASTLE

The castle lawn cries out for a picnic (buy one at the Co-op supermarket before your visit). Or you can grab a bite in the café inside the castle itself. Otherwise, consider:

$$$$ Söderport, just across the street from the castle, offers an all-you-can-eat buffet, as well as a regular menu; the dining room is pleasantly spacious but the outdoor patio has castle views (daily 11:30-15:00 & 17:00-22:00, Slottsvägen 1, tel. 0480/12501). There's live music Wed-Sat evenings.

Kalmar Connections

From Kalmar by Train to: Växjö (hourly, 60-70 minutes), **Copenhagen** and its airport (hourly, 4 hours, some transfer in Alvesta), **Stockholm** (almost hourly, 4.5-5 hours, transfer in Alvesta, reservations required; some prefer the slower but more scenic coastal route via Linköping).

By Bus to Stockholm: The bus to Stockholm is much cheaper but slower than the train (3/day, fewer on weekends, 6 hours).

ROUTE TIPS FOR DRIVERS

Kalmar to Copenhagen: See "Route Tips for Drivers" at the end of the Near Copenhagen chapter.

Kalmar to Stockholm (230 miles, 5 hours): Leaving Kalmar, follow *E-22 Lindsdal* and *Nörrköping* signs. Sweden did a cheap widening job, paving the shoulders of the old two-lane road to get

3.8 lanes. Fortunately, traffic is polite and sparse. There's little to see, so stock the pantry, set the compass on north, and home in on Stockholm. Make two pleasant stops along the way: Västervik and the Göta Canal.

Västervik is 90 miles north of Kalmar, with an 18th-century core of wooden houses (3 miles off the highway, *Centrum* signs lead you to the harbor). Park on the waterfront near the great little smoked-fish market (Mon-Sat).

Sweden's famous **Göta Canal** consists of 190 miles of canals that cut the country in half, with 58 locks *(slussen)* that work up to a summit of 300 feet. It was built 150 years ago at a low ebb in the country's self-esteem—with more than seven million 12-hour man-days (60,000 men working about 22 years)—to show her industrial might. Today it's a lazy three- or four-day tour, which shows Sweden's zest for good living.

Take just a peek at the Göta Canal over lunch, in the medieval town of **Söderköping:** Stay on E-22 past where you'd think you'd exit for the town center, then turn right at the *Kanalbåtarna/Slussen.* Look for the *Kanal P* signs leading to a handy canalside parking lot. From there, walk along the canal into the action. The TI on Söderköping's Rådhustorget (a square about a block off the canal) has good town and Stockholm maps, a walking brochure, and canal information (www.ostergotland.info). On the canal is the Kanalbutiquen, a yachters' laundry, shower, shop, and WC, with idyllic picnic grounds just above the lock. From the lock, stairs lead up to the Utsiktsplats pavilion (commanding view).

From Söderköping, E-22 takes you to Nörrköping. Follow *E-4* signs through Nörrköping, past a handy rest stop, and into Stockholm. The *Centrum* is clearly marked.

Öland Island

The island of Öland—90 miles long and only 8 miles wide—is a pleasant resort known for its windmills, wildflowers, dry-stacked limestone walls, happy birdwatchers, prehistoric sights, roadside produce stands on the honor system, and Swede-filled beaches. This castaway island, with only about 25,000 permanent residents, attracts some 2.5 million visitors annually. It's a top summer vacation destination for Swedes—even the king and queen have their summer home here. Because of its relatively low rents, better weather, and easy bridge access to the mainland, Öland is also a popular bedroom community for Kalmar. If you've got a car, good weather, and some time to spare—and if the place isn't choked with summer crowds—Öland is a fine destination, especially if you don't rush it. (For a basic map of Öland, see the "Southeast Sweden" map at the beginning of this chapter.)

Dubbed the "Island of Sun and Wind," Öland enjoys a steady sea breeze and an even warmer climate than already mild Kalmar (remember, "warm" is relative in Sweden). And, because its top layer of soil was scraped off by receding glaciers, it has a completely different landscape than the pines-and-lakes feel of mainland Sweden. The island's chalky limestone plain, rich soil, and lush vegetation make it feel almost more Midwestern US than Baltic (Öland is one of Sweden's premier agricultural zones). Visitors are pleasantly surprised by the island's colorful spring wildflowers and bright sunshine, which works its magic on both holidaymakers and artists.

Centuries ago, the entire island was the king's private hunting ground. Because local famers were not allowed to fell trees (and there are fewer here than on the mainland), they made their simple houses from limestone. The island's 34 limestone churches, which were also used for defense, have few windows. Limestone walls demarcate property and contained grazing livestock.

When built in 1972, the **Öland Bridge** from Kalmar to the island was Europe's longest (3.7 miles). The channel between Kalmar and Öland is filled with underwater rocks, making passage here extremely treacherous—but ideal for the Vikings' flat-bottomed boats. (In fact, "Kalmar" comes from the phrase "stones in water.") The little town of Färjestaden, near the island end of the bridge, was once the "ferry town" where everyone came and went; today it sits sad and neglected.

GETTING THERE

The island is most worthwhile if you have a car and at least four extra hours to explore. **Drivers** simply head north from Kalmar a few minutes on highway 137 to the Öland Bridge. Once across, highway 136 is the island's main north-south artery. **Buses** regularly connect Kalmar with the town of Borgholm (56 SEK, nearly hourly in summer, 50-60 minutes) and, with less frequency, to other Öland destinations (check www.klt.se). **Bikers** with adequate time enjoy biking to and around Öland, but note that you're not allowed to ride your bike on the bridge; instead, take the ferry that carries bikers across from Kalmar to Öland (55 SEK, about hourly, 30 minutes, www.ressel.se). To plan a bike trip, consult with Ölands Cykeluthyrning, who will rent you a bike in either Kalmar, Borgholm, or Mörbylånga and let you return it at a different location (shops in Kalmar and on the island in Borgholm and Mörbylånga, tel. 076-103-9879, www.olandscykeluthyrning.se).

Sights on Öland

Visitors can (and do) spend days exploring this giant island's pleasures. But on a quick visit of a few hours, you'll want to narrow your focus. Your basic choices are center/north Öland (developed and resorty, with royal sights, and more services—and traffic) or south Öland (rugged, remote, and scenic, with tilting windmills, charming cottages, and a giant limestone plain dominating its middle; demands more time). I've outlined a few basic ideas for each area below, but these are just the beginning—there's much more to discover on Öland.

Regardless if you go north or south, make your first stop just after crossing the bridge at Öland's mid-island **TI** in Färjestaden—follow signs off the bridge for *turistbyrä* (Träffpunkt Öland 102, tel. 0485/88800, www.olandsturist.se; there's also a branch on the main street in Borgholm). Friendly staff can help you plan a reasonable agenda for the amount of time you have.

CENTRAL/NORTH ÖLAND

For a quick spin to the island, stick with the strip of Öland just north of the bridge. As you drive north along highway 136, keep an eye out for some of Öland's characteristic, old-fashioned windmills. Occasional stone churches dot the landscape (including the one in Räpplinge—just off the main road—where the royals worship when in town).

The island's main town is **Borgholm** (BOY-holm), about a 30-minute drive north of the bridge. Borgholm itself isn't much to see, unless you enjoy watching Swedes at play. It's got a smattering of turn-of-the-century wooden villas, erected here after the royal palace was built nearby. Notice that many of these have a humble shack in the garden: Locals would move into these cottages so they could rent the main villas to vacationing Stockholmers in the summer and make a killing. The traffic-free main drag, Storgatan, is lined with tacky tourist shops and ice-cream parlors (Ölandsglass, at #10, is tops). There's also a handy **TI** right on the town's main street.

A pair of interesting sights sits on the hill just above Borgholm (to reach them, you can either drive or hike—get details at TI). **Borgholm Castle** (Borgholms Slott), which looks like Kalmar Castle with its top blown off, broods on the bluff above town, as if to remind visitors of the island's onetime strategic function. Its hard-fought history has left it as the empty shell you see today—impressive, but not worth the entry fee (www.borgholmsslott.se).

From near the castle, you can hike down to a more recent and appealing royal sight, the current royal summer residence, **Solliden Palace** (Sollidens Slott). It was built in 1906 in an Italianate style after physicians to Queen Victoria suggested the milder Öland climate might ease her ill health. The palace interior is off-limits, but its sprawling, gorgeously landscaped garden is open to us common-ers. Divided into Italian

(geometrical and regimented), English (wild), and Dutch (flowers) sections, the Solliden garden complex is well worth a wander (105 SEK, daily 11:00-18:00, last entry at 17:00, closed off-season, on-site café, tel. 0485/15356, www.sollidensslott.se).

SOUTH ÖLAND

A 60-mile loop south of the bridge will give you a good dose of the island's more remote, windy rural charm. Head south on highway 136 to experience the savannah-like limestone plain, old grave-yards, and mysterious prehistoric monuments. Just before the town of Karlevi you'll notice the beautifully preserved stone mill to your right, the **Karlevi Stenkvarn.** While its weathervane shows the year 1791, no one is really sure how old it is (it's a Dutch-type mill that was common in the 19th century). Island farmers milled flour here until the mid-1950s.

Near here, you have a few choices for getting a closer look at the limestone plain: Either take the road (heading east) that starts near the town of Resmo, or drive on a little farther to the turnoff just past N. Bårby. This open, agricultural landscape (quite unlike the forested mainland) was first farmed during the Stone Age, and still shows evidence of how the land was divided among farmers in medieval days.

Gettlinge Gravfält (off the road about 10 miles up from the south tip, just south of Smedby) is a wonderfully situated, boat-shaped, Iron Age graveyard littered with monoliths and overseen by a couple of creaky old windmills. It offers a commanding view of the windy and mostly treeless island.

Farther south is the **Eketorp Prehistoric Fort** (Eketorps Borg), a reconstructed fifth-century stone fort that, as Iron Age

forts go, is fairly interesting. Several evocative huts and buildings are de-signed in what someone imagined was the style back then, and the huge rock fort is surrounded by runty Linderöd pigs, a native breed that was common in Sweden 1,500 years ago. A sign reads: "For your convenience and pleasure, don't leave your children alone with the ani-mals" (120 SEK, daily mid-June–mid-Aug 10:30–18:00, closed off-season, tel. 0485/662-000, www.eketorp.se). It's near the southern tip of the island, on the eastern side: When you approach Grön-högen on the main road from the north, look for signs on the left.

You can push on even farther to the very southern tip of the island, home to Sweden's tallest lighthouse, the **Ottenby Nature Center** (exhibits on the nature and culture of the island), and the **Ottenby Bird Observatory,** where ornithologists monitor migra-tory birds that pass through this major flyway (guided tours avail-able, see www.birdlife.se).

FINLAND

FINLAND

Suomi

Finland is a fun, fascinating, sadly overlooked corner of Europe. Its small population fills a sprawling, rocky, forested land that shares a long border with Russia. The Finns have often been overshadowed by their powerful neighbors, the Swedes and the Russians. And yet, they've persevered magnificently, with good humor, a zest for architecture and design, a deep love of saunas, and an understandable pride in things that are uniquely Finnish.

For much of their history, the Finns embraced a simple agrarian and fishing lifestyle. They built not cities, but villages—easy pickings for their more ambitious neighbors. From medieval times to 1809, Finland was part of Sweden, and Finland today still has a sizeable Swedish-speaking minority, bilingual street signs, and close cultural ties to Sweden.

In 1809, Sweden lost Finland to Russia. Under the next century of relatively benign Russian rule, the "Grand Duchy of Finland" began to industrialize, and Helsinki grew into a fine and elegant city. Still, at the beginning of the 1900s, the rest of Finland was mostly dirt-poor and agricultural, and its people were eagerly emigrating to northern Minnesota. (Read Toivo Pekkanen's *My Childhood* to learn about the life of a Finnish peasant in the early 1900s.)

Finland and the Baltic States won their independence from Russia in 1917, then fought brief but vicious civil wars against their pro-Russian domestic factions. Finland then enjoyed two decades of prosperity...until the secret Nazi-Soviet pact of August 1939 assigned it to the Soviet sphere of influence. When the Red Army invaded, white-camouflaged Finnish ski troops won the Winter War against the Soviet Union (1939-1940). They  then held off the Soviets in what's called the Continuation War from 1941 until 1944, when the exhausted and outgunned Finns agreed to a ceasefire.

After World War II, Finland was made to suffer for having allied itself for a time with Nazi Germany and for having fought against one of the Allied Powers. As reparations, the Finns ceded Karelia (eastern Finland) and part of Lapland to the USSR, accepted a Soviet naval base on Finnish territory, and paid huge sums to the Soviet government.

In the ensuing Cold War era, Finland maintained a position of friendly neutrality toward its powerful neighbor to the east. Still, Finland's bold, trendsetting modern design and architecture blossomed, and it built up successful timber, paper, and electronics industries. All through the Cold War, Finland teetered between the West and the Soviet Union, trying to be part of Western Europe's strong economy while making nice with the Soviets.

The collapse of the Soviet Union has done to Finland what a good long sauna might do to you. When Moscow's menace vanished, so did about 20 percent of Finland's trade. After a few years of adjustment, Finland bounced back strongly, joining the European Union and adopting the euro currency. In earlier years, Finns would move to Sweden (where they are still the biggest immigrant group), looking for better jobs. But now Finland is among the most technologically advanced countries in Europe, and its talented young people are more likely to seek their fortunes at home. Headquarters of the giant telecommunications company Nokia, Finland ranks near the top European nations in the number of Internet users per capita.

We think of Finland as Scandinavian, but it's more accurate to

Finland Almanac

Official Name: Republic of Finland.

Population: Finland is home to 5.5 million people (42 per square mile). The majority are Finnish in descent (93 percent). Other ethnicities include Swedish (6 percent), Russian, Estonian, Roma, and Sami (less than 1 percent each). The official languages are Finnish, spoken by 90 percent, and Swedish, spoken by 5 percent. Small minorities speak Sami and Russian. Finland is about 72 percent Lutheran, 2 percent Orthodox, 2 percent other Christian, and 24 percent unaffiliated.

Latitude and Longitude: 64°N and 26°E, similar latitude to Nome, Alaska.

Area: 130,500 square miles (about the size of Washington state and Oregon combined).

Geography: Finland is bordered by Russia to the east, Sweden and Norway to the north, the Baltic Sea to the west, and Estonia (across the Gulf of Finland) to the south. Much of Finland is flat and covered with forests, with the Lapland region extending north of the Arctic Circle. Finland is home to thousands of lakes and encompasses nearly as many islands: It has 187,800 lakes and 179,500 islands (the last time I counted).

Biggest City: Helsinki is the capital of Finland and has a population of 616,000; 1.4 million people—about one in four Finns—live in the Helsinki urban area.

Economy: Finland's gross domestic product is $195 billion and its per-capita GDP is $37,600. Manufacturing, timber, engineering, electronics, and telecommunications are its chief industries.

Currency: €1 (euro) = about $1.20.

Government: Finland has both a president, responsible for foreign policy, and a prime minister, who—along with the 200-member Parliament (Eduskunta)—is responsible for domestic legislation. The current president—Sauli Niinistö—is the first conservative head of state in Finland in five decades. Prime Minister Juha Sipila heads a center-right coalition government made up of the Centre Party, the Blue Reform Party, and the National Coalition Party.

Flag: White with a blue Scandinavian cross, representing winter snow and lakes.

The Average Finn: He or she is 42 years old, has 1.75 children, will live to be 80, and drinks a lot of *kahvi*—the nation leads the world in per-capita coffee consumption nearly every year.

call it "Nordic." Technically, the Scandinavian countries are Denmark, Sweden, and Norway—all constitutional monarchies with closely related languages. Add Iceland, Finland, and maybe Estonia—all republics that are former Danish or Swedish colonies—and you have the "Nordic countries." Finland has been a pioneer of gender equality: In 1906, Finnish women were the first in Europe to vote. The country's president from 2000 to 2012 was a woman, and today, about 40 percent of the Finnish parliament is female.

Finnish is a difficult-to-learn language whose only relatives in Europe are Estonian (close) and Hungarian (distant). Finland is officially bilingual, and about 1 in 20 residents speaks Swedish as a first language. You'll notice that Helsinki is called *Helsingfors* in Swedish. Helsinki's street signs list places in both Finnish and Swedish. Nearly every educated young person speaks effortless English—the language barrier is just a speed bump. But to get you started, I've included a selection of Finnish survival phrases on the following page.

The only essential word needed for a quick visit is *kiitos* (KEE-tohs)—that's "thank you," and locals love to hear it. *Hei* (hey) means "hi" and *hei hei* (hey hey) means "goodbye." *Kippis* (KIHP-pihs) is what you say before you down a shot of Finnish vodka or cloudberry liqueur *(lakka)*.

Finnish Survival Phrases

In Finnish, the emphasis always goes on the first syllable. Double vowels (e.g., *ää* or *ii*) sound similar to single vowels, but are held a bit longer. The letter *y* sounds like the German *ü* (purse your lips and say "oh"). In the phonetics, ī sounds like the long *i* in "light," and bolded syllables are stressed.

English	Finnish	Pronunciation
Good morning. (formal)	Hyvää huomenta.	**hew**-vaah **hwoh**-mehn-tah
Good day. (formal)	Hyvää päivää.	**hew**-vaah **pī**-vaah
Good evening. (formal)	Hyvää iltaa.	**hew**-vaah **eel**-taah
Hi. / Bye. (informal)	Hei. / Hei-hei.	hey / hey-hey
Do you speak English?	Puhutko englantia?	**poo**-hoot-koh **ehn**-glahn-tee-yah
Yes. / No.	Kyllä. / Ei.	**kewl**-lah / ay
Please.	Ole hyvä.	**oh**-leh **hew**-vah
Thank you (very much).	Kiitos (paljon).	**kee**-tohs (**pahl**-yohn)
You're welcome.	Kiitos. / Ei kestä.	**kee**-tohs / ay **kehs**-tah
Can I help you?	Voinko auttaa?	**voin**-koh **owt**-taah
Excuse me.	Anteeksi.	**ahn**-teek-see
(Very) good.	(Oikein) hyvä.	(**oy**-kayn) **hew**-vah
Goodbye.	Näkemiin.	**nah**-keh-meen
zero / one / two	nolla / yksi / kaksi	**noh**-lah / **ewk**-see / **kahk**-see
three / four	kolme / neljä	**kohl**-meh / **nehl**-yah
five / six	viisi / kuusi	**vee**-see / **koo**-see
seven / eight	seitsemän / kahdeksan	**sayt**-seh-mahn / **kah**-dehk-sahn
nine / ten	yhdeksän / kymmenen	**ew**-dehk-sahn / **kewm**-meh-nehn
hundred	sata	**sah**-tah
thousand	tuhat	**too**-haht
How much?	Paljonko?	**pahl**-yohn-koh
local currency: euro	euro	**ay**-oo-roh
Where is...?	Missä on...?	**mee**-sah ohn
...the toilet	...WC	**vay**-say
men	miehet	**mee**-ay-heht
women	naiset	**nī**-seht
water / coffee	vesi / kahvi	**veh**-see / **kah**-vee
beer / wine	olut / viini	**oh**-luht / **vee**-nee
Cheers!	Kippis!	**kip**-pis
The bill, please.	Saisinko laskun, kiitos.	**sī**-seen-koh **lahs**-kuhn **kee**-tohs

HELSINKI

The Finnish capital (Europe's youngest) feels like an outpost of both the Nordic and European worlds—it's the northernmost capital of the EU, and a short train ride from Russia. Yet against all odds, this quirky metropolis thrives, pleasing locals and tickling tourists. While it lacks the cutesy cobbles of Copenhagen, the dramatic setting of Stockholm, or the futuristic vibe of Oslo, Helsinki holds its own among Nordic capitals with its endearing Finnish personality. It's a spruce-and-stone wonderland of stunning 19th- to 21st-century architecture, with a bustling harborfront market, a lively main boulevard, fine museums, a sophisticated design culture, dueling cathedrals (Lutheran and Orthodox), a quirky east-meets-west mélange of cultures...and a welcoming Finnish spirit to tie it all together.

Gusting winds swirl crying seagulls against a perfectly azure sky scattered with cotton-ball clouds. Rock bands and folk-dancing troupes enliven the Esplanade from the stage in front of Café Kappeli, sunny days lure coffee sippers out onto the sidewalks, and joyous festivals fill the summer (when the sky is still bright after midnight). And in this capital of a country renowned for design, window-shopping the Design District can turn browsers into buyers. You'll see home decor, clever kitchen gadgets, eye-grabbing prints, delicately handmade jewelry, and unique clothes with a Finnish accent.

While budget flights affordably connect Helsinki to the other

Scandinavian capitals (and beyond), for many travelers, the next best thing to being in Helsinki is getting there on Europe's most enjoyable overnight boat. The trip from Stockholm starts with dramatic archipelago scenery, a setting sun, and a royal *smörgåsbord* dinner. Dance until you drop and sauna until you drip. Budget travel rarely feels this hedonistic. Sixteen hours after you depart, it's "Hello Helsinki." You can also cross—much more quickly—by boat to or from Tallinn, Estonia. For details on these options, see "Helsinki Connections," near the end of this chapter.

PLANNING YOUR TIME

On a three-week trip through Scandinavia, Helsinki is worth at least the time between two successive nights on the overnight boat—about seven hours. To do the city justice, two days is ideal. (Wear layers; Helsinki can be windy and cold.)

For a quick one-day visit, start with the 1.75-hour "Helsinki Panorama" orientation bus tour (see later, under "Tours in Helsinki"). Then take my self-guided walking tour through the compact city center from the harbor—enjoying Helsinki's ruddy harborfront market and getting goose bumps in the churches—ending at the underground Temppeliaukio Church.

With more time, explore the Design District, dive into Finnish culture in the open-air folk museum, or take a walk in Kaivopuisto Park. If the weather's good, head for Suomenlinna, the island fortress where Helsinki was born. If it's bad, go for a sauna. Enjoy a cup of coffee at the landmark Café Kappeli before sailing away.

Orientation to Helsinki

Helsinki (pop. 616,000) has a compact core. The city's natural gateway is its main harbor, where ships from Stockholm and Tallinn dock. At the top of the harbor is Market Square (Kauppatori), an outdoor food and souvenir bazaar. Nearby are two towering, can't-miss-them landmarks: the white Lutheran Cathedral and the red-brick Orthodox Cathedral.

Helsinki's grand pedestrian boulevard, the Esplanade, begins right at Market Square, heads up past the TI, and ends after a few blocks in the central shopping district. At the top end of the Esplanade, the broad, traffic-filled Mannerheimintie avenue veers north through town past the train and bus stations on its way to many of Helsinki's museums and architectural landmarks. For a

Helsinki History

Helsinki is the only European capital with no medieval past. Although it was founded in the 16th century by the Swedes in hopes of countering Tallinn as a strategic Baltic port, it stayed a village until the 18th century. Then, in 1746, Sweden built a huge fortress on an island outside its harbor, and Helsinki boomed as it supplied the fortress. After taking over Finland in 1809, the Russians decided to move Finland's capital and university closer to St. Petersburg—from Turku to Helsinki. They hired a young German architect, Carl Ludvig Engel, to design new public buildings for Helsinki and told him to use St. Petersburg as a model. This is why the oldest parts of Helsinki (around Market Square and Senate Square) feel so Russian—stone buildings in yellow and blue pastels with white trim and columns. Hollywood used Helsinki for the films *Gorky Park* and *Dr. Zhivago,* because filming in Russia was not possible during the Cold War.

Though the city was part of the Russian Empire in the 19th century, most of its residents still spoke Swedish, which was the language of business and culture. In the mid-1800s, Finland began to industrialize. The Swedish upper class in Helsinki expanded the city, bringing in the railroad and surrounding the old Russian-inspired core with neighborhoods of four- and five-story apartment buildings, including some Art Nouveau masterpieces. Meanwhile, Finns moved from the countryside to Helsinki to take jobs as industrial laborers. The Finnish language slowly acquired equal status with Swedish, and eventually Finnish speakers became the majority in Helsinki (though Swedish remains an official language).

Since downtown Helsinki didn't exist until the 1800s, it was more conscientiously designed and laid out than other European capitals. With its many architectural overleafs and fine Neoclassical and Art Nouveau buildings, Helsinki often turns guests into students of urban design and planning. Good neighborhoods for architecture buffs to explore are Katajanokka, Kruununhaka, and Eira.

All of this makes Helsinki sound like a very dry place. It's not. Despite its sometimes severe cityscape and chilly northern latitude, splashes of creativity and color hide around every corner. With a shorter (and, admittedly, less riveting) history than this book's other big cities, it helps to approach Helsinki as a city of today. Ogle its fine architecture, and delve into the boutiques of the Design District for some of Scandinavia's most eye-pleasing fashion and home decor. As you browse, remember that for the past several decades, global trends—from Marimekko's patterned fabrics to Nokia's pioneering mobile phones to the Angry Birds gaming empire—have been born right here in Helsinki.

HELSINKI

do-it-yourself orientation to town along this route, follow my self-guided walk on page 585. The "Helsinki Tram Tour" (see page 595) also provides a good drive-by introduction to some sights, and takes you into outlying neighborhoods that most tourists miss.

Linguistic Orientation: Finnish is completely different from the Scandinavian languages of Norwegian, Danish, and Swedish. That can make navigating a bit tricky. Place names ending in *-katu* are streets, *-tie* is "road" or "way," and *-tori* or *-aukio* means "square." Complicating matters, Finland's bilingual status means that most street names, tram stops, and map labels appear in both Finnish and Swedish. The two names often look completely different (for example, the South Harbor—where many overnight boats arrive—is called Eteläsatama in Finnish and Södra Hamnen in Swedish; the train station is Rautatieasema in Finnish, Järnvägsstationen in Swedish). The Swedish names can be a little easier to interpret than the Finnish ones. In any event, I've rarely met a Finn who doesn't speak excellent English.

TOURIST INFORMATION

The friendly, energetic **main TI,** just off the harbor, offers great service and excellent materials on the city. It's located a half-block inland from Market Square, at the beginning of the Esplanade, at the corner with Unioninkatu (mid-May-mid-Sept Mon-Sat 9:00-18:00, Sun until 16:00, off-season Mon-Fri 9:00-18:00, Sat-Sun 10:00-16:00, tel. 09/3101-3300, www.visithelsinki.fi). Pick up a public-transit map and a detailed pamphlet on the Suomenlinna Fortress. If you want a sightseeing Helsinki Card, you can buy it here (at the on-site Strömma desk; see below).

The tiny **train station TI,** a one-person booth in the main hall, provides many of the same services and publications. There's also a regional tourist information desk at Helsinki airport (open daily year-round).

Strömma/Sightseeing Helsinki: This private service, located within the main TI, sells the Helsinki Card (described next), ferry tickets, and sightseeing tours by bus and boat. They operate the TI branch in the train station and small, summer-only sightseeing kiosks on the Esplanade and by the harbor (all branches open Mon-Sat 9:00-16:30, Sun until 16:00, tel. 09/2288-1600, www.stromma.fi).

Helsinki Card: If you plan to visit a lot of museums in Helsinki, this card can be a good deal. The card includes free entry to nearly 30 museums, fortresses, and other major sights; free use of buses, trams, and the ferry to Suomenlinna; and 24-hour access to a hop-on, hop-off bus (€46/24 hours, multiday passes available; sold online and at all Strömma locations including at main TI,

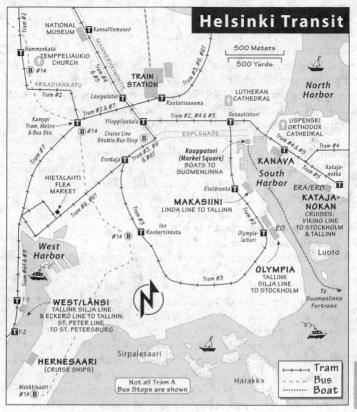

most hotels, and both Viking Line and Tallink Silja ferry terminals, www.helsinkicard.com).

For a cheaper alternative, you could buy a public-transit day ticket (see "Getting Around Helsinki," later), take my self-guided walk, visit the free and low-cost churches (Temppeliaukio Church, Lutheran Cathedral, Uspenski Orthodox Cathedral, and Kamppi Chapel), and stop by the free Helsinki City Museum.

ARRIVAL IN HELSINKI

By Boat: For details on taking the overnight boat from Stockholm to Helsinki, or the boat across the Gulf of Finland from Tallinn to Helsinki, see "Helsinki Connections" near the end of this chapter.

Helsinki's main South Harbor (Eteläsatama) has four terminals; for locations, see the adjacent map and the color map in the front of this book. The Olympia and Makasiini Terminals are on the south side of the main harbor. The Olympia Terminal hosts Tallink Silja boats, while the Makasiini Terminal is mostly for fast boats to Tallinn. The Katajanokan Terminal, on the north side of the harbor, is used primarily by Viking Line boats. Trams stop near all the South Harbor terminals (tram #5 near Katajanokan, trams #2/#3 near Olympia).

Large ferries to/from Tallinn and St. Peter Line boats to St. Petersburg use West Terminals 1 and 2 (Länsiterminaali 1/2). You can get to downtown Helsinki's central train station on trams #9 and #6T (leave from right outside the terminals, zips you to the train station downtown) or by taxi (about €15-20).

By Cruise Ship: Cruises arrive at both West Harbor and South Harbor; for details, see the end of this chapter.

By Train and Bus: The train station, an architectural landmark, is near the top of the Esplanade, a 15-minute walk from Market Square. Local buses leave from both sides of the building, trams stop out front, and the Metro runs underneath. The long-distance bus station is two blocks (or one tram stop) away, on the other side of Mannerheimintie, at the Kamppi shopping mall; the ticket office and machines are on the ground floor, with bus platforms below.

By Plane: Helsinki Airport (Helsinki-Vantaa) is about 10 miles north of the city (airport code: HEL, www.helsinki-vantaa. fi). Local trains I and P run from the airport to the central rail station in about 30 minutes (€5.50, access tracks from the corridor between Terminals 1 and 2; buy ticket from machines on platform—credit card only, or from conductor onboard—credit card or cash). A Finnair bus also runs to the city center (€6.30, 3/hour, 35-minute trip, www.finnair.com; stops at some downtown hotels on request; return buses leave for airport from platform 30 at Elielinaukio on west side of train station) or public bus #615 (€5.50, buy from HSL transit company ticket machine or pay driver, not covered by transit tickets or Helsinki Card, 3-6/hour, 45-minute trip, also stops at Hakaniemi; return buses leave for airport from platform 3 at Rautatientori on east side of train station). Or take the Yellow Line door-to-door shared van service (€20 for 1-2 people, €30 for 3-4 people, €40 for 5-6 people, tel. 010-00700 or toll tel. 0600-555-555, can book online at www.yellowline.fi). An ordinary taxi from the airport runs about €45.

HELPFUL HINTS

Time: Finland and Estonia are one hour ahead of Sweden and the rest of Scandinavia.

Money: Finland's currency is the euro. ATM machines are labeled *Otto*.

Telephones: Finland's phone system generally uses area codes, but some national or mobile numbers (starting with 010 or 020) must be dialed in full when you're calling from anywhere in the country.

Wi-Fi: Helsinki has free Wi-Fi all along the Esplanade and throughout the city center; look for the "Helsinki City Open" network.

Pharmacy: The **Erottajan pharmacy** *(apteekki)* is conveniently located on the basement level of Stockmann department store (similar hours as store, Mannerheimintie 1, tel. 09/622-9930).

Laundry: Also in the Stockmann department store, **Sol** (seventh floor) has reasonably priced drop-off/pickup service (open same hours as store—9:00-21:00, closes earlier Sat-Sun, Aleksanterinkatu 52, tel. 040-779-7222).

Bike Rental: Helsinki's **HSL** transit company has 140 bike stations located throughout the city. To use a bike, buy a pass and register online; you'll then receive an ID and PIN for picking up your bike from any bike station. Passes are sold by the day and the week, and include up to 30 minutes of riding time per bike—but you can keep it and pay more for a longer ride. Convenient bike station locations include Kamppi shopping center, Market Square, the train station, and near the Esplanade (24-hour pass–€5, one-week pass–€10; for bike station maps and more info, see www.hsl.fi/en/citybikes).

Best View: The **Torni Tower's Ateljee Bar** offers a free panorama view. Ride the elevator from the lobby of the venerable Torni Hotel (built in 1931) to the 12th floor, where you can browse around the perch or sit down for a pricey drink (Sun-Thu 14:00-24:00, Fri-Sat from 12:00, Yrjönkatu 26, tel. 020-123-4604).

Meet the Finns: With **Cozy Finland**'s "Meet the Finns" program, you can match your hobbies with a local—and suddenly, you're searching out classic comics at the flea market with a new Finnish friend. Their most popular service involves arranging dinner at a local host's home (around €60); contact Cozy Finland for exact prices (www.cosyfinland.com).

What's With the Slot Machines? Finns just have a love affair with lotteries and petty gambling. You'll see coin-operated games of chance everywhere, including restaurants, supermarkets, and the train station.

GETTING AROUND HELSINKI

In compact Helsinki, you can get by without using much public transportation, but it can save steps.

By Bus and Tram: With the public-transit route map (available at the TI, also viewable on the Helsinki Region Transport

website—www.hsl.fi) and a little
mental elbow grease, the buses and
trams are easy. The single Metro line
is also part of the system, but not
useful for most visitors.) and a little
mental elbow grease, the buses and
trams are easy. The single Metro line
is also part of the system, but not useful for most visitors.

Single tickets are good for an hour of travel (€3.20 from driver, €2.90 at ticket machines at a few larger bus and tram stops).
A day ticket (€9/24 hours of unlimited travel, issued on a plastic
card you'll touch against the card reader when entering the bus or
tram) pays for itself if you take four or more rides; longer versions
are also available (7-day maximum). Day tickets can be bought at
the ubiquitous yellow-and-blue R-Kiosks (convenience stores), as
well as at TIs, the train station, Metro stations, ticket machines
at a handful of stops, and on some ferries, but not from drivers.
The Helsinki Card also covers public transportation. All of these
tickets and cards are only valid within the city of Helsinki, not the
suburbs; for example, you pay extra for the public bus to the airport.
The HSL mobile ticket app (HSL Mobiililippu) is a convenient
way to buy single tickets and day passes on your smartphone (see
www.hsl.fi/en).

Tours in Helsinki

The big company Strömma (also called Sightseeing Helsinki) has
a near monopoly on city tours, whether by bus, boat, or foot. For
a fun, cheap tour, use my self-guided "Helsinki Tram Tour" (described later and rated ▲▲) to pass by most of the town's major
sights in an hour.

▲▲▲Orientation Bus Tours
These 1.75-hour "Helsinki Panorama" bus tours give an ideal city
overview with a look at all of the important buildings, from the
Olympic Stadium to Embassy Row. You stay on the bus the entire
time, except for a 10-minute stop or two (when possible, they try
to stop at the Sibelius Monument and/or Temppeliaukio Church).
You'll learn strange facts, such as how Finns took down the highest
steeple in town during World War II so that Soviet bombers flying
in from Estonia couldn't see their target. Tours get booked up, so
it's wise to reserve in advance online or ask your hotelier to help
(€32, free with Helsinki Card, daily May-Aug at 11:00 and 13:30,
rest of year at 11:00 with 13:30 departures Fri-Sat only, departs

Helsinki at a Glance

▲▲▲**Temppeliaukio Church** Awe-inspiring, copper-topped 1969 "Church in the Rock." **Hours:** June-Sept Mon-Sat 10:00-17:45, Sun 11:45-17:45; closes one hour earlier off-season. See page 605.

▲▲**Uspenski Orthodox Cathedral** Orthodoxy's most prodigious display outside of Eastern Europe. **Hours:** Tue-Fri 9:30-16:00, Sat 10:00-15:00, Sun 12:00-15:00, closed Mon. See page 599.

▲▲**Lutheran Cathedral** Green-domed, 19th-century Neoclassical masterpiece. **Hours:** Daily 9:00-18:00, June-early Aug until 24:00. See page 599.

▲▲**Suomenlinna Fortress** Helsinki's harbor island, sprinkled with picnic spots, museums, and military history. **Hours:** Museum daily 10:00-18:00, Oct-April 10:30-16:30. See page 607.

▲▲**Seurasaari Open-Air Folk Museum** Island museum with 100 historic buildings from Finland's farthest corners. **Hours:** June-Aug daily 11:00-17:00; shorter hours May and Sept, buildings closed rest of the year. See page 611.

▲**Ateneum, The National Gallery of Finland** Largest collection of art in Finland, including local favorites plus works by Cézanne, Chagall, Gauguin, and Van Gogh. **Hours:** Tue and Fri 10:00-18:00, Wed-Thu 9:00-20:00, Sat-Sun 10:00-17:00, closed Mon. See page 600.

▲**National Museum of Finland** The scoop on Finland, featuring folk costumes, an armory, czars, and thrones; the prehistory and 20th-century exhibits are best. **Hours:** Tue-Sun 11:00-18:00, closed Mon. See page 604.

▲**Design Museum** A chronological look at Finland's impressive design pedigree, plus cutting-edge temporary exhibits. **Hours:** Daily 11:00-18:00; Sept-May Wed-Sun 11:00-18:00, Tue until 20:00, closed Mon. See page 606.

HELSINKI

from Esplanade—intersection with Fabianinkatu, tel. 09/2288-1600, www.stromma.fi, sales@stromma.fi).

Bus Tours Departing from South Harbor: Conveniently, the Helsinki Panorama bus tours pick up cruise-ship passengers from Katajanokan Terminal at 10:30 (but not during July), and from Olympia Terminal at 10:45 (tours end at the Esplanade—not back at the docks).

Hop-On, Hop-Off Bus Tours

If you'd enjoy the tour described earlier, but want the chance to hop on and off at will, consider **City Sightseeing Helsinki** (operated by Strömma), with a 1.5-hour loop that connects downtown Helsinki, several outlying sights—including the Sibelius Monument and Olympic Stadium—as well as the Olympia cruise terminal (on cruise-ship days, the bus generally stops at Hernesaari and West Harbor's Melkki quay—confirm in advance). Buses run every 30-45 minutes and make 15 stops (€28, €41 combo-ticket also includes harbor tour—see next, all tickets good for 24 hours, May-Sept daily 10:00-16:00, www.stromma.fi). A different company, **Sightseeing City Tour** (also red buses), offers a similar route for similar prices, but has fewer departures (www.citytour.fi).

Harbor Tours

Three boat companies compete for your attention along Market Square, offering snoozy cruises around the harbor and its islands roughly hourly from 10:00 to 18:00 in summer (typically 1.5 hours for €20-24; www.royalline.net, www.ihalines.fi, www.stromma.fi). The narration is slow-moving—often recorded and in as many as four languages. I'd call it an expensive nap. Taking the ferry out to Suomenlinna and back gets you onto the water for much less money (€5 round-trip, covered by day transit ticket or Helsinki Card). If you do take a harbor cruise, here's how the competing companies differ: **Helsinki Sightseeing/Strömma** (yellow-and-white boats) offers the best and priciest route, going through a narrow channel in the east to reach sights that the other cruises miss. The other companies focus on the harbor itself and Suomenlinna fortress; of these, **Royal Line** (green-and-white boats) has the best food service on board, while **IHA** (blue-and-white boats) is more likely to have a live guide (half their boats have live guides, the others have recorded commentary).

SpåraKoff Pub Tram

In summer, this antique red tram makes a 45-minute loop through the city while its passengers get looped on the beer for sale on board (€11 to ride, €6 beer, May-Sept Mon-Sat 14:00-20:00, no trams Sun, leaves at the top of the hour from the Mikonkatu stop—in front of the Fennia building, across from train-station tower, www.koff.fi/sparakoff).

Local Guides

Helsinki Sightseeing can arrange a private guide (book at least three days in advance, €208/2 hours, tel. 09/2288-1222, sales@stromma.fi). **Christina Snellman** is a good, licensed guide (mobile 050-527-4741, chrisder@pp.inet.fi). **Archtour** offers local guides who specialize in Helsinki's architecture (tel. 09/477-7300, www. archtours.com).

Helsinki Walk

This self-guided walk—worth ▲▲▲—offers a convenient spine for your Helsinki sightseeing. I've divided the walk into two parts: On a quick visit, focus on Part 1 (which takes about an hour). To dig deeper into the city's architectural landmarks—and reach some of its museums—continue with Part 2 (which adds another 45 minutes). Note that several points of interest on this walk are described in more detail under "Sights in Helsinki."

PART 1: THE HARBORFRONT, SENATE SQUARE, AND ESPLANADE

• *Start at the obelisk in the center of the harborfront market.*

❶ Market Square (Kauppatori)

This is the **Czarina's Stone,** with its double-headed eagle of imperial Russia. It was the first public monument in Helsinki, designed by Carl Ludvig Engel and erected in 1835 to celebrate the visit by Czar Nicholas I and Czarina Alexandra. Step over the chain and climb to the top step for a clockwise spin-tour:

Begin by facing the **harbor.** The big, red Viking ship and white Silja ship are each floating hotels for those making the 40-hour

Stockholm-Helsinki round-trip. Farther back, a giant Ferris wheel spins over the harbor (SkyWheel Helsinki, €12, www.skywheel.fi). Now pan to the right. The brick-and-tan building along the harborfront is the Old Market Hall, with some enticing, more upscale options than the basic grub at the outdoor market (for a rundown on both options, see "Eating in Helsinki," later). Between here and there, a number of harbor cruise boats vie for your business.

Farther to the right, the trees mark the beginning of Helsinki's grand promenade, the Esplanade. Hiding in the leaves is the venerable iron-and-glass Café Kappeli. The yellow building across from the trees is the TI. From there, a string of Neoclassical buildings lines the harbor. The blue-and-white City Hall was designed by Engel in 1833 as the town's first hotel, built to house the czar and czarina. The Lutheran Cathedral is hidden from view behind this building. Next, after the short peach-colored building, is the Swedish Embassy (flying the blue-and-yellow Swedish flag

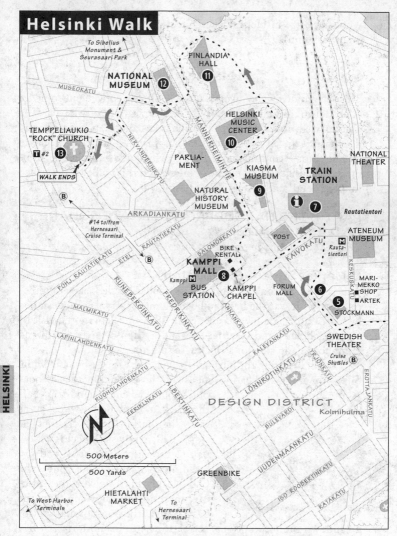

Helsinki Walk

To Sibelius
Monument &
Seurasaari Park

FINLANDIA
HALL **11**

**NATIONAL
MUSEUM** **12**

MUSEOKATU

HELSINKI
MUSIC
CENTER **10**

TEMPPELIAUKIO
"ROCK" CHURCH

T #2 **13**

WALK ENDS

PARLIA-
MENT

MANNERHEIMINTIE

KIASMA
MUSEUM **9**

TRAIN
STATION

NATIONAL
THEATER

NERVANDERINKATU

ARKADIANKATU

RAUTATIEKATU

NATURAL
HISTORY
MUSEUM

#14 to/from
Hernesaari
Cruise Terminal

B

POST

Rautatientori

7

ATENEUM
MUSEUM

M Rauta-
tientori

KESKUSKATU

POHJ. RAUTATIEKATU

ETELÄ.

RUNEBERGINKATU

SALOMONKATU

BIKE
RENTAL

B

**KAMPPI
MALL** **8**

Kamppi M

BUS
STATION

KAMPPI
CHAPEL

FORUM
MALL

KAIVOKATU

MARI-
MEKKO
SHOP

ARTEK

STOCKMANN **5**

6

FREDRIKINKATU

MALMIKATU

LAPINLAHDENKATU

ANNANKATU

KALEVANKATU

SWEDISH
THEATER

*Cruise
Shuttles* B

YRJÖNKATU

LÖNNROTINKATU

RUOHOLAHDENKATU

EERIKINKATU

ALBERTINKATU

DESIGN DISTRICT
Kolmikulma

BULEVARDI

UUDENMAANKATU

EROTTAJANKATU

N

500 Meters

500 Yards

GREENBIKE

To West Harbor
Terminals

HIETALAHTI
MARKET

To
Hernesaari
Terminal

ISO ROOBERTINKATU

RATAKATU

HELSINKI

and designed to look like Stockholm's Royal Palace). Then comes
the Supreme Court and, tucked back in the far corner, Finland's
Presidential Palace. Finally, standing proud, and reminding Helsinki of the Russian behemoth to its east, is the Uspenski Orthodox
Cathedral.

Explore the colorful **outdoor market**—part souvenirs and
crafts, part fruit and veggies, part fish and snacks. Sniff the stacks
of trivets, made from cross-sections of juniper twigs—an ideal, fragrant, easy-to-pack gift for the folks back home (they smell even
nicer when you set something hot on them).

· *Done exploring? Walk to the corner of the square next to City Hall,*

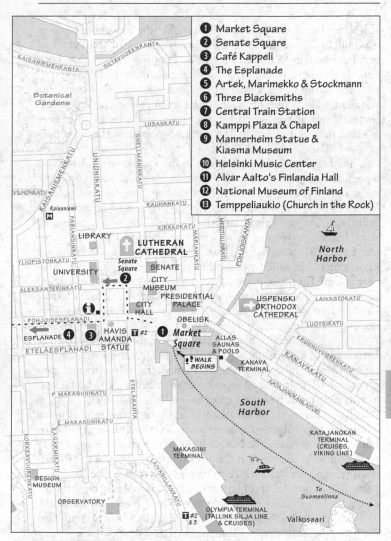

1. Market Square
2. Senate Square
3. Café Kappeli
4. The Esplanade
5. Artek, Marimekko & Stockmann
6. Three Blacksmiths
7. Central Train Station
8. Kamppi Plaza & Chapel
9. Mannerheim Statue & Kiasma Museum
10. Helsinki Music Center
11. Alvar Aalto's Finlandia Hall
12. National Museum of Finland
13. Temppeliaukio (Church in the Rock)

and turn right up Sofiankatu street (City Hall has huge public WCs in the basement, and free exhibits on Helsinki history). Near the end of the block, you'll pop out right in the middle of...

❷ Senate Square (Senaatintori)

This was once a simple town square with a church and City Hall—but its original buildings were burned when Russians invaded in 1808. Later, after Finland became a grand duchy of the Russian Empire, the czar sent in architect Carl Ludvig Engel (a German who had lived and worked in St. Petersburg) to give the place some Neo-class. The result: the finest Neoclassical square in Europe.

Engel represents the paradox of Helsinki: The city as we know it was built by Russia, but with an imported European architect, in a very intentionally "European" style. So Helsinki is, in a sense, both entirely Russian...and not Russian in the slightest.

The statue in the center of the square honors **Russian Czar Alexander II.** While he wasn't popular in Russia (he was assassinated), he was well-liked by the Finns. That's because he gave Finland more autonomy in 1863 and never pushed the Russification of Finland.

The huge **staircase** leading up to the **Lutheran Cathedral** is a popular meeting (and tanning) spot in Helsinki. Head up those stairs and survey Senate Square from the top. Scan the square from left to right. First, 90 degrees to your left is the yellow **Senate building** (now the prime minister's office). The small, blue-gray stone building with the slanted mansard roof in the far-left corner, from 1757, is one of just two pre-Russian-conquest buildings remaining in Helsinki (it's now the home of the Helsinki City Museum). **Café Engel** (opposite the cathedral at Aleksanterinkatu 26) is a fine place for a light lunch or cake and coffee. The café's winter lighting seems especially designed to boost the spirits of daylight-deprived Northerners.

Facing the Senate directly across the square is its twin, the **University of Helsinki**'s main building (36,000 students, 60 percent female). Symbolically (and physically), the university and government buildings are connected via the cathedral, and both use it as a starting point for grand ceremonies.

Tucked alongside the cathedral, a line of once-grand Russian administration buildings now house the **National Library of Finland.** In czarist times, the National Library received a copy of every book printed in the Russian Empire. With all the chaos Russia suffered throughout the 20th century, a good percentage of its Slavic texts were destroyed. But Helsinki, which enjoyed relative stability, claims to have the finest collection of Slavic books in the world. This purpose-built Neoclassical building, its facade lined with Corinthian columns, is one of Engels' finest and worth a look.

If you'd like to visit the **cathedral interior,** now's your chance; the entrance is tucked around the left side as you face the towering dome (see page 599 for a description).

• *When you're ready, head back down the stairs and angle right through the square, continuing straight down Unioninkatu.*

Along **Unioninkatu,** do a little window-shopping; this is the first of many streets we'll see lined with made-in-Finland shops (though these are more touristy than the norm). In addition to the jewelry shops and clothes boutiques, look for the Schröder sporting goods store (on the left, at #23), which shows off its famous selection of popular Finnish-made Rapala fishing lures—ideal for the fisher folk on your gift list.

At the end of this street (TI on the right), cross over the tram tracks to reach the fountain called *Havis Amanda*. Designed by Ville Vallgren and unveiled here in 1908, the fountain has become the symbol of Helsinki, the city known as the "Daughter of the Baltic"—graduating students decorate her with a school cap. The voluptuous figure, modeled after the artist's Parisian mistress, was a bit too racy for the conservative town, and Vallgren had trouble getting paid. But as artists often do, Vallgren had the last laugh: For more than a hundred years now, the city budget office across the street has seen only her backside.

• *Now turn toward the Esplanade's grassy median, with the delightful...*

❸ Café Kappeli

If you've got some time, dip into this old-fashioned, gazebo-like oasis of coffee, pastry, and relaxation (get what you like at the bar inside and sit anywhere). In the 19th century, this was a popular hangout for local intellectuals and artists. Today the café offers romantic tourists waiting for their ship a great cup-of-coffee memory. The bandstand in front hosts nearly daily music and dance performances in summer.

• *Beyond Café Kappeli stretches...*

❹ The Esplanade (Esplanaden)

Helsinki's top shopping boulevard sandwiches a park in the middle (another Engel design from the 1830s). The grandiose street designations—*esplanadi* and *bulevardi*—while fitting today, would have been purely aspirational in rustic little 1830s Helsinki.

The north side (on the right) is interesting for window-shopping, people-watching, and sun-worshipping. In fact, after the first block, shoppers may want to leave the park and cross over to that side of the street to browse (see page 612).

But the rest of you should stay in the park, the green heart of the city. As you stroll, admire the mature linden trees and imagine this elegant promenade in the old days. The Esplanade was laid out in 1826 to connect the old city of the late 18th century—the established power center—with the new parts of town, where impressive new stone houses in a neo-Renaissance style were being built by the 1870s.

Notice the ornately decorated **Hotel Kämp** (on the right at #29). This city landmark is typical of the elegant hotels, shops, and restaurants that began springing up in the late 19th century as the Esplanade became famous as a place to be seen. Today, the street's exclusive air is maintained by enterprises such as **Galleria Esplanad** (entrance at #31), a high-end fashion mall with big-name Finnish and international stores, and the recommended **Strindberg Café,** one of many tony spots along the Esplanade to nurse a drink.

At the very top of the Esplanade, the park dead-ends at the **Swedish Theater.** Built under Russian rule to cater to Swedish residents of a Finnish city, this building encapsulates Helsinki's complex cultural mix. (The theater's recommended Teatterin deli and bar are handy for a drink or meal out in the park.)

Right across from the theater, at #39, is the huge **Academic Bookstore** (Akateeminen Kirjakauppa), designed by Modernist architect Alvar Aalto, with an extensive map and travel section, periodicals, English books, and the pricey Café Aalto (with ageless Aalto furniture; see the next stop) on the back mezzanine level.

• *At the end of the Esplanade, on the right, you'll reach a pedestrianized street with several landmarks of Finnish shopping and design...*

❺ Artek, Marimekko, and Stockmann

Around the corner from the Academic Bookstore is **Artek,** founded in 1935 by Alvar Aalto to showcase his practical, modern designs for furniture and housewares. And at the far corner is perhaps Finland's most famous export: **Marimekko,** the fabric designer whose bold and colorful patterns adorn everything from purses to shower curtains (more Marimekko branches are within a block of here). The other side of the street is dominated by Finland's answer to Harrods or Macy's: **Stockmann,** the biggest, best, and oldest department store in town (with a great gourmet supermarket in the basement).

• *Just beyond Stockmann is Helsinki's main intersection, where the Esplanade and Mannerheimintie meet. Turn right on Mannerheimintie. At the far side of Stockmann, you'll see a landmark statue, the...*

❻ Three Blacksmiths

While there's no universally accepted meaning for this statue (from 1932), most say it celebrates human labor and cooperation and shows the solid character of the Finnish people. On the base, note the rare, surviving bullet damage from World War II. The Soviet

Union used that war as an opportunity to invade Finland—which it had lost just 20 years prior—to try to reclaim their buffer zone. In a two-part war (the "Winter War," then the "Continuation War"), Finland held fast and emerged with its freedom—and relatively little damage.

Stockmann's entrance on Aleksanterinkatu, facing the *Three Blacksmiths*, is one of the city's most popular meeting points. Everyone in Finland knows exactly what it means when you say: "Let's meet under the Stockmann's clock." Tram #3 makes a stop around the corner from the clock, on Mannerheimintie. Across the street from the clock, the Old Student Hall is decorated with legendary Finnish heroes.

• *For a shortcut to our next stop, duck through the passage (marked* City-Käytävä*) directly across the street from Stockmann's clock. This will take you through a bustling commercial zone. You'll enter—and continue straight through—the City Center shopping mall. Emerging on the far side, you're face-to-face with four granite giants guarding the...*

❼ Central Train Station (Rautatieasema)

This Helsinki landmark was designed by Eliel Saarinen (see sidebar). The strange, huge figures on the facade, carrying illuminated globes, seem to have stepped right out of a Nordic myth. Duck into the main hall and the Eliel Restaurant inside to catch the building's early 20th-century ambience.

With your back to the train station, look to the left; diagonally across the square is the **Ateneum**, Finland's national gallery of art. It faces the **Finnish National Theater** (not visible from here)—founded to promote Finnish-speaking theater in the years Finland was dominated by Russian and Swedish speakers.

• *We've worked our way through the central part of town. Now, if you're ready to explore some more interesting buildings and monuments, continue with...*

PART 2: HELSINKI'S ICONIC ARCHITECTURE

The rest of this walk follows the boulevard called Mannerheimintie, which serves as a showcase for much of Helsinki's signature architecture; this walk also helps you reach some of the city's farther-flung sights. (Details on many of these appear later, under "Sights in Helsinki.")

• *With your back to the station, turn right and follow the tram tracks (along Kaivokatu street) back out to Mannerheimintie. Cross the street and tracks, and continue straight ahead, toward what looks like a giant wooden bowl. You'll pop out in front of the Kamppi shopping mall, at...*

HELSINKI

❽ Kamppi Plaza (Narinkkatori) and Kamppi Chapel (Kampin Kappeli)

This plaza is a Helsinki hub—both for transportation (with a Metro stop and bus station nearby) and for shopping (with the towering Kamppi Center shopping mall). Turn your attention to the round, wooden structure at the corner of the plaza nearest the Esplanade. This is one of Helsinki's most surprising bits of architecture: the **Kamppi Chapel.** Enter through the black building just to the right, and enjoy a moment or three of total serenity. (For more on the chapel, see page 601.)

• *Leaving the chapel, cut through the middle of the big plaza, with the shopping mall on your left and the low-lying yellow building on your right. Veer right through the gap at the end of the square, and in a minute you'll see (across the busy street) an equestrian statue. Cross over to it.*

❾ Carl Gustaf Mannerheim and the Kiasma Museum of Contemporary Art (Nykytaiteen Museo Kiasma)

The busy street is named for the Finnish war hero Carl Gustaf Mannerheim, who led anti-Russian forces in the newly independent Finland's 1918 "Civil War." Later, during the "Winter War" of 1939-1940, Mannerheim and his fellow Finns put up a stiff resistance to a massive Soviet invasion. While the Baltic States—across the Gulf of Finland—were quickly "liberated" by the Red Army, dooming them to decades under the Soviet system, the Finns managed to refuse this assistance. Mannerheim became Finland's first postwar president, and thanks to his efforts (and those of countless others), Finland was allowed to chart its own democratic, capitalist course after the war. (Even so, Finland remained officially neutral through the Cold War, providing both East and West a political buffer zone.)

Mannerheim is standing in front of the glassy home of the **Kiasma Museum,** with changing exhibits of contemporary art. A bit farther along and across the street from Kiasma stands the Finnish **Parliament,** with its stoic row of Neoclassical columns.

From Mannerheim and Kiasma, head down into the grassy, sloping park. At the lowest point, watch out—you're crossing a busy **bicycle highway** that cuts right through the middle of the city center. Look left under the tunnel to see how a disused rail line has been turned into a subterranean pedalers' paradise.

• *The glassy building dominating the end of the park is the...*

Two Men Who Remade Helsinki

Eliel Saarinen (1873-1950)

At the turn of the 20th century, architect Eliel Saarinen burst on the scene by pioneering the Finnish National Romantic style. Inspired by peasant and medieval architectural traditions, his work was fundamental in creating a distinct—and modern—Finnish identity. The château-esque National Museum of Finland, designed by Saarinen and his two partners after winning a 1902 architectural competition, was his first major success (see page 604). Two years later, Saarinen won the contract to construct the Helsinki train station (completed in 1919). Its design marks a transition into the Art Nouveau style of the early 1900s. The landmark station—characterized by massive male sculptures flanking its entrance, ornate glass and metalwork, and a soaring clock tower—welcomes over 300,000 travelers each day.

In the early 1920s, Saarinen and his family emigrated to the US where his son, Eero, would become the architect of such iconic projects as the Gateway Arch in St. Louis and the main terminal at Dulles International Airport near Washington, DC.

Alvar Aalto (1898-1976)

Alvar Aalto was a celebrated Finnish architect and designer working in the Modernist tradition; his buildings used abstract forms and innovative materials without sacrificing functionality. Finlandia Hall in Helsinki is undoubtedly Aalto's most famous structure, but that's just the beginning. A Finnish Frank Lloyd Wright, Aalto concerned himself with nearly every aspect of design, from furniture to light fixtures. Perhaps most notable of these creations was his sinuous Savoy Vase, a masterpiece of simplicity and sophistication that is emblematic of the Aalto style. His designs became so popular that in 1935 he and his wife opened Artek, a company that manufactures and sells his furniture, lamps, and textiles to this day (see page 613).

HELSINKI

⑩ Helsinki Music Center (Musiikkitalo)

Completed in 2011, this structure is even bigger than it looks: two-thirds of it is underground, and the entire complex houses seven separate venues. It's decorated, inside and out, with bold art (such as the gigantic pike on tiptoes that stands in the middle of the park). As you approach the bottom of the building, step into the atrium and look up to ogle the shimmering silver sculpture. While you're there, consider stopping by the ticket desk (on the lower floor, closed Sun) to ask about performances while you're in town

(the season is Sept-April). Upstairs is a music store. The interior features a lot of pine and birch accents, which warm up the space and improve the (Japanese-designed) acoustics. It didn't take long for the Music Center to become an integral part of the city's cultural life; in the first season of performances, some 400,000 people attended events here (for English tours of the facility, see "Sights in Helsinki," later).

Back outside, circle around the back side of the Music Center. Follow the straight, flat promenade that runs alongside a grassy park used for special events.

• *Crossing the street, you'll see (on the left) perhaps the most important work of Finnish architecture...*

⑪ Alvar Aalto's Finlandia Hall (Finlandia-Talo)

This big, white building can be a bit difficult for casual observers to appreciate. To get the best view of it, walk through the long parking lot all the way to the far end, and look back. The building—entirely designed by Aalto, inside and out—opened in 1971 and immediately became a national icon. Notice how Aalto employs geometric shapes and sweeping lines to create a striking concert hall, seating up to 1,700 guests. Aalto designed the inclined roof to try to maximize the hall's

acoustics—imitating the echo chamber of an old-fashioned church tower—with marginal success.

The exterior is clad in thin white marble in what appears to be a basket-weave pattern. But this effect (while beautiful) is unintentional: Not long after the hall was finished, the marble panels began bending ever so slightly. So in 1999, they were replaced at great expense—and within 10 years' time they bowed out again.

HELSINKI

The city is now planning a third renovation, but this time is considering a material that can withstand the freeze/thaw cycles of a Helsinki winter.

Turn to face shimmering **Töölönlahti Bay** (not a lake, but an inlet of the Baltic Sea)—ringed by a popular walking and jogging track. From here, you can see more Helsinki landmarks: across the lake and a bit to the left, the white tower marks the Olympic Stadium that hosted the world in 1952. And to the right are the rides of Helsinki's old-time amusement park, Linnanmäki.

• *If you'd like to extend this walk, join the natives on the waterfront path (which offers even better views of Finlandia Hall). Otherwise, consider...*

More Helsinki Sights

To reach two more major sights, go up the stairs immediately to the right of Finlandia Hall, then continue all the way up to the main road. Directly across the street stands the fine ⓬ **National Museum of Finland,** which tells this country's story with lots of artifacts.

About a 10-minute walk behind the National Museum is the beautiful "Church in the Rock," ⓭ **Temppeliaukio.** Once inside, sit. Enjoy the music. It's a wonderful place to end this walk.

To continue on to the **Sibelius Monument,** located in a lovely park setting, take bus #24 (direction: Seurasaari) from nearby Arkadiankatu street. The same ticket is good for your return trip (within one hour), or ride it to the end of the line for the bridge to Seurasaari Island and Finland's open-air folk museum. From there, bus #24 returns to the top of the Esplanade.

All three of these sights are explained in more detail under "Sights in Helsinki."

Helsinki Tram Tour

Of Helsinki's many trams, two convenient routes seem made-to-order for a tourist's joyride. Follow the route below to ride tram #2 and then #3, together worth ▲▲.

If you buy a single ticket, it's good for an hour—just long enough for the entire circuit outlined below (€3.20 from driver, €2.90 from ticket machines at a few major stops). Better yet, using a day ticket (see "Getting Around Helsinki," earlier) or a Helsinki Card allows you to hop off to tour a sight, then catch a later tram (runs every 10 minutes).

While you can hop on anywhere, it's most convenient to start your tour at Market Square, by the TI.

❶ **Market Square:** Stand at the tram stop that is between the fountain and the market, and wait for one of the frequent #2 trams.

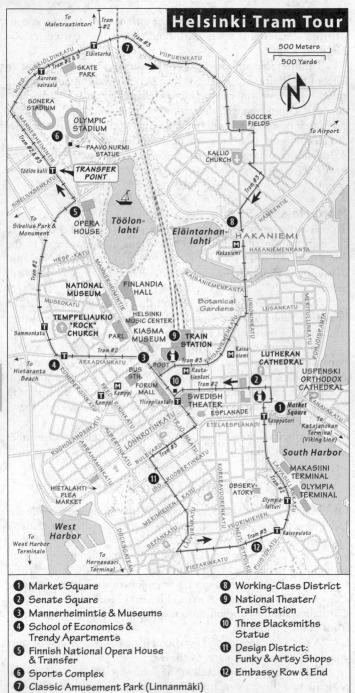

Helsinki Tram Tour

500 Meters
500 Yards

HELSINKI

1. Market Square
2. Senate Square
3. Mannerheimintie & Museums
4. School of Economics & Trendy Apartments
5. Finnish National Opera House & Transfer
6. Sports Complex
7. Classic Amusement Park (Linnanmäki)
8. Working-Class District
9. National Theater/ Train Station
10. Three Blacksmiths Statue
11. Design District: Funky & Artsy Shops
12. Embassy Row & End

Since the tracks split here briefly, it's hard to get on in the wrong direction; still, confirm that the front of the tram reads *Eläintarha* (not *Olympiaterminaali*).

❷ Senate Square: From Market Square, you'll first pass this proud square, with the gleaming white Lutheran Cathedral, a statue of Alexander II—Finland's favorite czar, and many of the oldest buildings in town. Then you'll head up Aleksanterinkatu street, Helsinki's Fifth Avenue-type main shopping drag (tram stop: Aleksanterinkatu).

❸ Mannerheimintie and Museums: A turn onto the broad Mannerheimintie boulevard will take you near the contemporary Kiasma Museum and, after turning onto Arkadiankatu street (with the imposing Parliament building on the corner), to the Finnish Museum of Natural History (known as LUOMUS—on your right), home to about eight million specimens ranging from spiders to dinosaurs (tram stop: Luonnontieteellinen museo).

❹ School of Economics and Trendy Apartments: After passing the yellow brick buildings of the School of Economics (on your left, note facade—Kauppakorkeakoulut stop), you'll enter a neighborhood with lots of desirable 1920s-era apartments. Young couples start out here, move to the suburbs when they have their kids, and return as empty-nesters. The Temppeliaukio Church (a.k.a. "Church in the Rock"), while out of sight, is just a block uphill from the next stop (Sammonkatu).

❺ Finnish National Opera House and Transfer: Built in 1993, the National Opera House is the white, sterile, shower-tile building on the right (tram stop: Ooppera). Now, get ready to hop out at the next stop—Töölön halli—to transfer to tram #3. If you're interested, this stop is a short walk from the Sibelius Monument and its pretty park (detour along a street called Sibeliuksenkatu). Otherwise, climb aboard tram #3 to continue our tour. (This is a terminus for tram #3, so it only goes one way from here.)

❻ Sports Complex: The white building with the skinny tower (in the distance on the right) marks the Olympic Stadium, used for the summer games in 1952. (Finland's most famous Olympian is long-distance runner Paavo Nurmi, the "Flying Finn," who won five gold medals early in the 20th century.) After the Auroran sairaala stop, you'll see skateboarders enjoying a park of their own (on the right).

❼ Classic Amusement Park: Linnanmäki, Helsinki's low-end, Tivoli-like amusement park is by far the most-visited sight in town (on the right, free admission to park, rides cost €4-6, open daily until late, tram stop: Alppila, www.linnanmaki.fi). Roller-coaster nuts enjoy its classics from the 1950s.

❽ Working-Class District: Next you'll enter an old working-class neighborhood. Its soccer fields (on your left) are frozen into

ice rinks for hockey in the winter. You'll pass the striking granite **Kallio Church** (Art Nouveau, on your right) and **Hakaniemi**
square, with a big indoor/outdoor market (on your left). Crossing
a saltwater inlet, you'll pass Helsinki's **Botanical Gardens** (on the
right).

❾ **National Theater and Train Station:** From here, you'll
head back toward the town center, where you'll reach a big square.
Fronting it is Finland's granite **National Theater,** in Art Nouveau
style, with a statue honoring Aleksis Kivi, the father of Finnish literature. On the left is the **Ateneum,** Finland's national art gallery.
Next, you'll pass the striking central **train station,** with its iconic
figures stoically holding lamps (designed by the great Finnish architect Eliel Saarinen).

❿ *Three Blacksmiths* **Statue:** After turning left on big, busy
Mannerheimintie, you'll pass the most famous statue in town, the
Three Blacksmiths (on your left), which honors hard work and cooperation. Towering above the smiths is the Stockmann department
store. Then (at the Ylioppilastalo stop), the round, white Swedish Theater marks the top of the town's graceful park—the Esplanade—which leads back down to the harbor (where you began this
tour). From here, you'll loop through the colorful and artsy Design
District.

⓫ **Design District—Funky and Artsy Shops:** The cemetery
of the church (which dates from 1827) on the right was cleaned
out to make a park. It's called the "Plague Park," recalling a circa-
1700 plague that killed more than half the population. Coming up,
funky small boutiques, cafés, and fun shops line the streets (stops:
Fredrikinkatu, Iso Roobertinkatu, and Viiskulma). After the Art
Deco brick church (on your right), the tram makes a hard left (at
the Eiran sairaala stop, for a hospital) and enters a district with Art
Nouveau buildings. Look down streets on the right for facades and
decorative turrets leading to the Baltic Sea.

⓬ **Embassy Row and the End of the Line:** After the Neitsytpolku stop, spy the Russian Embassy (on left), still sporting its
hammer and sickle; it was built to look like London's Buckingham Palace. Across the street is the Roman Catholic church, and
beyond that (on the right), a street marked "no entry" leads to a
fortified US Embassy. Returning to the harbor, you'll likely see
the huge Tallink Silja ship that leaves each evening for Stockholm.
Its terminal (the appropriately named Olympiaterminaali; also the
name of the tram stop) was built for the 1952 Olympics, which inundated Helsinki with visitors. The #3 tram route ends here: your
choices are to transfer back to the #2 tram, which starts right here
(ride it two stops to get back to Market Square), or walk 15 minutes
back to Market Square. Along the way, you'll pass the cute brick
Old Market Hall (with several great little eateries).

Sights in Helsinki

NEAR THE SOUTH HARBOR

▲▲Uspenski Orthodox Cathedral (Uspenskin Katedraali)

This house of worship was built for the Russian military in 1868, at a time when Finland belonged to Russia (*Uspenski* is Russian for

the Assumption of Mary). It hovers above Market Square and faces the Lutheran Cathedral, just as Russian culture faces Europe.

Cost and Hours: Free; Tue-Fri 9:30-16:00, Sat 10:00-15:00, Sun 12:00-15:00, closed Mon, Pormestarinrinne 1 (about a 10-minute walk beyond the harborfront market).

Visiting the Cathedral: Before heading inside, view the exterior. The uppermost "onion dome" represents the sacred heart of Jesus, while the smaller ones represent his 12 apostles.

The rich imagery of the cathedral's interior is a stark contrast to the sober Lutheran Cathedral. While commonly called the "Russian church," the cathedral is actually Eastern Orthodox, answering to the patriarch in Constantinople (Istanbul). Today, the cathedral is the seat of the archdiocese of Helsinki, to which much of eastern Finland belongs.

The cathedral's Orthodox Mass is beautiful, with a standing congregation, candles, incense, icons in action, priests behind the iconostasis, and timeless vocal music. In the front left corner, find the icon featuring the Madonna and child, surrounded by rings and jewelry (under glass), given in thanks for prayers answered. Across from the icon, a white marble table holds memorial candles and a dish of wheat seeds, representing new life—the hope of resurrection—for the departed.

▲▲Lutheran Cathedral (Tuomiokirkkoseurakunta)

With its prominent green dome, gleaming white facade, and the 12 apostles overlooking the city and harbor, this church is Carl Ludvig Engel's masterpiece.

Cost and Hours: Free; daily 9:00-18:00, June-early Aug until 24:00, no visits during church services or special events; on Senate Square, www.helsinkicathedral.fi. In summer, free organ concerts are held on Sundays at 20:00.

Visiting the Cathedral: Enter the building around the left side.

HELSINKI

Finished in 1852, the interior is pure architectural truth. Open a pew gate and sit, surrounded by the saints of Protestantism, to savor Neoclassical nirvana. Physically, this church is perfectly Protestant—austere and unadorned—with the emphasis on preaching (prominent pulpit) and music (huge organ). Statuary is limited to the local Reformation big shots: Martin Luther, Philipp Melanchthon (Luther's sidekick), and the leading Finnish reformer, Mikael Agricola. A follower of Luther at Wittenberg, Agricola brought the Reformation to Finland. He also translated the Bible into Finnish and is considered the father of the modern Finnish language. Agricola's Bible is to Finland what the Luther Bible is to Germany and the King James Bible is to the English-speaking world.

Helsinki City Museum

This interesting museum, just off Senate Square in one of the city's oldest buildings, gives an accessible overview of the city's history and culture. On the ground floor, visitors use 3-D glasses to take a trip through time, viewing the many ways the city has changed over the years (professional photographers and Helsinki citizens contributed the images used for this "time machine"). A whiteboard animation cleverly condenses about 350 years of the city's history into four minutes (from 1550 and Swedish rule, through the decades of Russian domination, to Finland's declaration of independence in 1917). Exhibits on the second floor take you to a typical Helsinki home in the 1950s and a local bar from the 1970s, complete with vintage soundtracks. Kids can go to school in an old-fashioned classroom, try on costumes, or jump into a horse-drawn carriage.

There's a lot to study and explore here, and it's a great place for kids or on a rainy day. Most visitors won't need to linger, but everyone leaves with a better understanding of why residents choose to call Helsinki home.

Cost and Hours: Free, Mon-Fri 11:00-19:00, Sat-Sun until 17:00, Aleksanterinkatu 16, www.helsinkicitymuseum.fi.

BEYOND THE ESPLANADE

These sights are scattered in the zone west of the Esplanade, listed roughly in the order you'll reach them from the city center (and in the order they appear on my self-guided walk, earlier).

▲Ateneum

The Ateneum, Finland's national art gallery, has the country's oldest and largest art collection. Come here to see Finnish artists (mid-18th to 20th century) and a fine international collection, including works by Cézanne, Chagall, Gauguin, and Van Gogh. The museum also hosts good special exhibits of Finnish and international art.

Cost and Hours: €15, Tue and Fri 10:00-18:00, Wed-Thu 9:00-20:00, Sat-Sun 10:00-17:00, closed Mon, near train station at Kaivokatu 2, tel. 0294-500-401, www.ateneum.fi.

Visiting the Museum: The permanent collection is spread over several floors in the "Stories of Finnish Art" display. The paintings—hung gallery by gallery in thematic groupings such as landscape, people, symbolism, and urban life—illustrate the development of art in Finland from 1809 until the 1970s.

You can follow the chronological display if you have the time and interest, but to see the cream of the crop, head directly up two flights of the grand entry staircase to Room 13, where classics from Finland's Golden Age of painting occupy every inch of wall space. In the late 19th century, Finnish artists began absorbing Parisian influences. They moved their easels outside, loosened their brushwork and handling of paint, and chose distinctly Finnish people and landscapes as their subjects. You'll see an aging grandfather walking with a young boy, country women gathered outside a church, laborers burning vegetation, pristine forests and lakes, and quietly beautiful snow.

▲Kamppi Chapel (Kampin Kappeli)

Sitting unassumingly on the busy, commercial plaza in front of the Kamppi shopping mall/bus-station complex, this restful space was opened by the city of Helsinki in 2012 to give residents and visitors a place of serenity. The wooden structure, clad in spruce and with an oval footprint, encloses a 38-foot-tall, windowless cylinder of silence. Inside, indirect light seeps in around the edges of the ceiling, bathing the clean, curved, alder-wood paneling in warmth and tranquility. Does it resemble Noah's Ark? The inside of an egg? The architects intentionally left it vague—and open to each visitor's interpretation. Although it's a church, there are no services; it's open to anyone needing a reflective pause. Locals drop by between their shopping chores to sit in a pew and ponder their deity, wrestle with tough issues...or just get a break. In this peaceful spot, secular modern architecture and meditative spirituality converge beautifully.

Cost and Hours: Free, Mon-Fri 8:00-20:00, Sat-Sun 10:00-18:00, Simonkatu 7, enter through adjacent low-profile black building.

Kiasma Museum

Finland's museum of contemporary art, designed by American architect Steven Holl, hosts changing exhibitions of international art (there's no permanent collection). Ask at the TI or check online to find out what's showing.

Cost and Hours: €10, Tue and Sun 10:00-17:00, Wed-Fri until 20:30, Sat until 18:00, closed Mon, Mannerheiminaukio 2, near train station, tel. 0294-500-501, www.kiasma.fi.

Sauna

Finland's vaporized fountain of youth is the sauna—Scandinavia's answer to support hose and facelifts. A traditional sauna is a wood-paneled room with wooden benches and a blistering-hot wood-fired stove topped with rocks. Undress entirely before going in. Lay your towel on the bench, and sit or lie on it (for hygienic reasons). Ladle water from the bucket onto the rocks to make steam. Choose a higher bench for hotter temperatures. Let yourself work up a sweat, then, just before bursting, go outside to the shower for a Niagara of liquid ice. Suddenly your shower stall becomes a Cape Canaveral launch pad, as your body scatters to every corner of the universe. A moment later you're back together and can re-enter the steam room. Repeat as necessary. The famous birch branches are always available for slapping your skin. Finns claim this enhances circulation while emitting a refreshing birch aroma that opens your sinuses. For more on the history of saunas, see www.sauna.fi.

Your hostel, hotel, or cruise ship may have a sauna, which may be heated only at specific times. Some saunas are semipublic (separate men's and women's hours), while others are for private use (book a 45- to 60-minute time slot; to save money, split the cost with a group of friends, either mixed or same-sex).

Public saunas are a bit of a dying breed these days, because most Finns have private saunas in their homes or cabins. But the public sauna tradition has gotten a boost with the arrival of two new saunas in town: Allas (right off Market Square) and Löyly (on the Hernesaari peninsula).

For a good, traditional sauna with a local crowd, try the **Kotiharjun Sauna.** Pay €13 plus €3 for a towel (cash only), find a locker, strip (keep the key on your wrist), and head for the steam. Cooling off is nothing fancy—just a bank of cold showers. A woman in a fish-cleaner's apron will give you a wonderful full-body scrub with Brillo pad-like mitts (€9, only on Tue and Fri-Sat

Finnish Museum of Natural History (LUOMUS)

Run by the University of Helsinki, this museum has the largest collection of its kind in Finland. Its wide-ranging exhibits emphasize the biodiversity of Finland and the world (all with English descriptions).

Cost and Hours: €13, but free during the last three opening hours; June-Aug Tue-Sun 10:00-17:00; Sept-May Tue-Fri 9:00-16:00, Sat-Sun 10:00-16:00; closed Mon year-round; up the street behind the Parliament at Pohjoinen Rautatiekatu 13, www.luomus.fi.

16:00-19:00). Regulars relax with beers on the sidewalk just outside (open Tue-Sun 14:00-21:30, closed Mon, last entry 1.5 hours before closing; men—ground floor, women—upstairs; 200 yards from Sörnäinen Metro stop, Harjutorinkatu 1, tel. 09/753-1535, www.kotiharjunsauna.fi).

The **Kulttuurisauna** sits in a little park along the Baltic—to cool off, take a dip in the sea. Designed and operated by a husband-and-wife, Finnish-Japanese, artist-and-architect team, it's both modern and traditional. This is a *savusauna* (smoke sauna, without a chimney)—and, while the room is ventilated before bathers arrive, the smoky atmosphere lingers (€15, towel rental-€4, all nude and gender-segregated, Wed-Sun 16:00-21:00, closed Mon-Tue, last entry at 20:00, just north of downtown at Hakaniemenranta 17, nearest tram/bus stop is Hakaniemi—about a 10-minute walk away, www.kulttuurisauna.fi).

The sophisticated **Löyly** sauna is situated on the Hernesaari peninsula, with its saunas and a restaurant open to the sea. The modern building is covered in wood slats—from inside the saunas it's like looking through Venetian blinds. There are separate dressing rooms and showers for men and women, but the saunas themselves are communal—everyone wears a bathing suit. It's possible to swim in the sea here, and in winter, there's a hole in the ice for hardy swimmers. The attached coffee bar/café/restaurant is fun even without a sauna; it spills out onto a big view veranda and up to a rooftop terrace (€19 covers 2 hours—includes towel, seat cover, soap, and shampoo; sauna generally open Mon-Wed 16:00-22:00, Thu 13:00-22:00, Fri-Sat 13:00-23:00, Sun 13:00-21:00; **$$** restaurant serves daily 11:00-22:00; Hernesaarenranta 4, tel. 09/6128-6550, www.loylyhelsinki.fi). It's smart to book ahead online.

Allas sits in the middle of the South Harbor action, at the edge of Market Square, with saunas that lead to a huge floating deck with three outdoor pools (fresh and sea water). Inside, there are three saunas: male, female, and mixed (€12, Mon-Fri 6:15-23:00, Sat-Sun from 8:00, café and bistro, Katajanokanlauturi 2a, www.allasseapool.fi).

HELSINKI

Helsinki Music Center (Musiikkitalo)

This modern facility provides a home for the performing arts in Helsinki. Containing seven different venues, its biggest draw may be the park and creative contemporary art that surrounds it. You can stop in anytime it's open to look around, and in summer, the main concert hall is open for free public viewing. Music lovers can also consider taking in a performance (season runs Sept-April), and architecture fans may want to take an English tour.

Cost and Hours: Building open Mon-Fri 8:00-22:00, Sat from 10:00, Sun 10:00-20:00; concert hall open July-Aug Mon-Sat

12:00-15:00; English tours offered most days in summer for €15, check website for schedule; Mannerheimintie 13A, tel. 020-707-0400, www.musiikkitalo.fi.

Finlandia Hall (Finlandia-Talo)

This 1,700-seat concert hall is Modernist designer/architect Alvar Aalto's most famous building in his native Finland. To see it from

its best angle, view it from the parking lot, on the side facing Töölönlahti Bay (not from Mannerheimintie street). Aalto was involved in every aspect of the building's design, right down to the door handles, and many fans see it as his most iconic work. Aalto devotees or newcomers should consider a guided tour to make sense of this distinctive structure. For more, see page 594 of my self-guided walk).

Cost and Hours: €15 for a tour, call ahead or visit website to check times; hall info point open Mon-Fri 9:00-19:00, closed Sat-Sun; Mannerheimintie 13e, tel. 09/40241, www.finlandiatalo.fi.

▲National Museum of Finland (Kansallismuseo)

This pleasant, easy-to-handle collection is in a grand building designed by three of this country's greatest architects—including Eliel Saarinen—in the early 1900s. The museum is

under renovation, with its exhibits gradually being reinstalled in phases. When completed, the galleries will chronologically trace the land of the Finns from prehistory to the 20th century. Highlights include Finland's largest permanent archaeological collection, the 1420 altarpiece dedicated to St. Birgitta (patron saint of Sweden—which owned Finland at the time), and a reconstructed early 1800s "smoke cabin" (sauna). While the renovation is underway, it's best to check the museum's website for current offerings.

Cost and Hours: €10, free on Fri 16:00-18:00; open Tue-Sun 11:00-18:00, closed Mon; Mannerheimintie 34, tel. 09/4050-9552, www.kansallismuseo.fi/en. The museum café has a tranquil outdoor courtyard. It's just a five-minute walk from Temppeliaukio Church (see next listing).

Visiting the Museum: Following the clear English-language descriptions (and perhaps checking with the front desk to hear about the progress of the renovation), visit each of the museum's four parts, in chronological order. First, the **Prehistory of Finland**

shows how Stone, Bronze, and Iron Age tribes in this area lived. You'll see lots of early stone tools (ax and arrow heads), pottery, human remains, and—at the end of the exhibit—Iron Age weapons and jewelry.

The Realm picks up the story with the Middle Ages, represented by the 14th-century St. Birgitta, a top saint. You'll pass through dimly lit halls of mostly wood-carved church art—from roughly hewn Catholic altarpieces to brightly painted, post-Reformation, Lutheran pulpits—then learn about Finland's time as part of Sweden (the introduction of the Renaissance). Continuing upstairs, you'll find out about the different social classes in historical Finland—the nobility, the peasants, the clergy, the rulers and monarchs, and the burghers (craftsmen and guild members). Look for a Rococo-period drawing room and—transitioning from Swedish to Russian rule—portraits of Russia's last czars around an impressive throne.

From there, temporary exhibits lead back to the main hall, where you can continue into **A Land and Its People.** In this display of Finnish peasant traditions, you'll see farming and fishing tools, a thought-provoking exhibit about the indigenous Sami people (distributed across the northern reaches of Finland, Sweden, Norway, and Russia), and a particularly fine collection of beautifully decorated tools used for spinning—folk art used to make folk art.

From the folk furniture, find the stairs back down to the ground floor and the **SF-1900** exhibit (that's Suomi/Finland from 1900), starting with the birth of modern Finland in 1917 and its 1918 civil war. A six-minute loop of archival footage shows you early-20th-century Finland. Touchscreen tables help tell the story of the fledgling nation, as do plenty of well-presented artifacts (including clothing, household items, vehicles, and a traditional outhouse).

▲▲▲Temppeliaukio Church

A modern example of great church architecture (from 1969), this "Church in the Rock" was blasted out of solid granite. Architect-brothers Timo and Tuomo Suomalainen won a competition to design the church, which they built within a year's time. Barren of decor except for a couple of simple crosses, the church is capped with a copper-and-skylight dome; it's normally filled with live or recorded music and awestruck

visitors. Grab a pew. Gawk upward at a 13-mile-long coil of copper ribbon. Look at the bull's-eye and ponder God. Forget your camera. Just sit in the middle, ignore the crowds, and be thankful for peace (under your feet is an air-raid shelter that can accommodate 6,000 people).

The church has excellent acoustics and is a popular concert venue; check at the TI for upcoming programs.

Cost and Hours: €3, generally Mon-Sat 10:00-17:45, Sun from 11:45, closes one hour earlier off-season—but because of frequent events and church services, it's good to confirm open times by listening to the recorded message at 09/2340-5940, Lutherinkatu 3, tel. 09/2340-6320, www.helsinginseurakunnat.fi.

Getting There: The church is at the top of a gentle hill in a residential neighborhood, about a 15-minute walk north of the bus station or a 10-minute walk from the National Museum (or take tram #2 to Sammonkatu stop).

▲Sibelius Monument

Six hundred stainless-steel pipes called "Love of Music"—built on solid rock, as is so much of Finland—shimmer in a park to honor Finland's greatest composer, Jean  Sibelius. It's a forest of pipe-organ pipes in a forest of trees. The artist, Eila Hiltunen, was forced to add a bust of the composer's face to silence critics of her otherwise abstract work. City orientation bus tours stop here for 10 minutes—long enough. The monument is a few blocks from the transfer point of the Helsinki Tram Tour outlined in this chapter (Töölön halli stop), and near the bus #24 line that also serves the Seurasaari Open-Air Folk Museum, described on page 611.

DESIGN DISTRICT

Exploring Helsinki's Design District is a sightseeing highlight for many visitors. A good starting point is the Design Museum, which sits just a few blocks southwest of the Esplanade. For more on the district, see "Shopping in Helsinki," later.

▲Design Museum

Design is integral to contemporary Finnish culture, and this fine museum—with a small but insightful permanent collection and well-presented temporary exhibits—offers a good overview (all in English). Worth ▲▲▲ to those who came to Finland just for the design, its interesting and clever installations will appeal to just about anybody.

Cost and Hours: €10; daily 11:00-18:00; Sept-May Wed-Sun

11:00-18:00, Tue until 20:00, closed Mon; excellent (if pricey) gift shop, Korkeavuorenkatu 23, www.designmuseum.fi.

Visiting the Museum: From the ticket desk on the ground floor, turn into the permanent exhibit, called **Utopia Now: The Story of Finnish Design.** The first gallery considers the process of design—the steps from inspiration to production—and presents iconic objects from the Golden Age of Finnish design of the 1950s (glass bowls by Alvar Aalto) as well as more recent innovations (the addictive Angry Birds video game; successive generations of Nokia mobile phones).

The "Icons of Design" gallery introduces viewers to the life stories of leading Finnish designers and the functional objects they've created (Aalto's iconic wooden stool, for example—a staple in classrooms around the world). The "Warehouse" collects items from different periods of the museum's collections, with a focus on "better things for everyday life," with everything from brightly colored but practical jerry cans for transporting fuel to a government-issued maternity box (a starter kit for new mothers, including clothes and sheets).

Digital applications throughout the galleries make your visit participatory: You can test how to control a Scorpion harvester (a staple of the Finnish forest industry), or you can animate a Marimekko pattern of your choosing on a wall-sized screen. A virtual headset lets you time travel to Finland's pavilion at the 1900 Paris World's Fair.

Upstairs and downstairs, you'll also find typically excellent **temporary exhibits** that allow individual Finnish designers to take center stage.

OUTER HELSINKI

A weeklong car trip up through the Finnish lakes and forests to Mikkeli and Savonlinna would be relaxing, but you can actually enjoy Finland's green-trees-and-blue-water scenery without leaving Helsinki. Here are three great ways to get out and go for a walk on a sunny summer day. If you have time, do at least one of them during your stay.

▲▲Suomenlinna Fortress

The island guarding Helsinki's harbor served as a strategic fortress for three countries: Finland, Sweden, and Russia. It's now a popu-

Suomenlinna Timeline

1748—Construction begins on the "Sweden Fortress" (Finland is part of Sweden's kingdom).

1788—The fort is a base during the Russo-Swedish War.

1808—During the Finnish War, the fortress surrenders to Russia—and remains a Russian naval base for the next 110 years.

1809—Finland becomes part of the Russian Empire.

1855—French and British navies bombard the fort during the Crimean War, inflicting heavy damage.

1917—Finland declares independence.

1918—The fort is annexed by Finland and renamed "Finland Fortress" (Suomenlinna).

1939—The fort serves as a base for the Finnish navy throughout World War II.

1973—The Finnish garrison moves out, the fort's administration is transferred to the Ministry of Education, and the fort is opened to the public.

lar park, with delightful paths, fine views, and a visitors center. On a sunny day, it's a wonderful place to stroll among hulking buildings with recreating Finns. The free Suomenlinna guidebooklet (stocked at the Helsinki TI, ferry terminal, and the visitors center) covers the island thoroughly. The island has one good museum (the Suomenlinna Museum, at Suomenlinna Centre—described later) and several skippable smaller museums, including a toy museum and several military museums (open summer only).

Getting There: Catch a ferry to Suomenlinna from Market Square. Walk past the high-priced excursion boats to the public HKL ferry (€5 round-trip, covered by day ticket and Helsinki Card, 15-minute trip, May-Aug 2-3/hour—generally at :00, :20, and :40 past the hour, but pick up schedule to confirm; Sept-April every 40-60 minutes). If you'll be taking at least two tram rides within 24 hours of visiting Suomenlinna, it pays to get a day ticket instead of a round-trip ticket. If your goal is the Suomenlinna Centre and the museum, the private JT Line "water bus" gets you closer to them than the public ferry (€7 round-trip, May-Sept 2/hour, departs from Market Square, tel. 09/534-806, www.jt-line.fi).

Visitor Information: The information desk at the Jetty Barracks, at the ferry landing, is open to visitors year-round (daily 10:00-18:00, Oct-April until 16:00), tel. 029-533-8410, www.suomenlinna.fi. Pick up the free island map/booklet here.

Tours: The one-hour English-language island tour departs from the Suomenlinna Centre (€11, free with Helsinki Card; June-Aug daily at 11:00, 12:30, and 14:30; Sept-May 1/day Sat-Sun only). The tour is fine if you're a military history buff, but it kind of misses the point of what's now essentially a giant playground for all ages.

Background: The fortress was built by the Swedes with French financial support in the mid-1700s to counter Russia's rise to power. (Russian Czar Peter the Great had built his new capital, St. Petersburg, on the Baltic and was eyeing the West.) Named Sveaborg ("Fortress of Sweden"), the fortress was Sweden's military pride and joy. With five miles of walls and hundreds of cannons, it was the second strongest fort of its kind in Europe after Gibraltar. Helsinki, a small community of 1,500 people before 1750, soon became a boomtown supporting this grand "Gibraltar of the North."

The fort, built by more than 10,000 workers, was a huge investment and stimulated lots of innovation. In the 1760s, it had the world's biggest and most modern dry dock. It served as a key naval base during a brief Russo-Swedish war from 1788 to 1790. But in 1808, the Russians took the "invincible" fort without a fight—by siege—as a huge and cheap military gift.

Today, Suomenlinna has 800 permanent residents, is home to Finland's Naval Academy, and is most appreciated by locals for its fine scenic strolls. The island is large—actually, it's six islands connected by bridges—and you and your imagination get free run of the fortifications and dungeon-like chambers. When it's time to eat, you'll find a half-dozen cafés and plenty of picnic opportunities.

Visiting Suomenlinna: Start your stroll of the island at the Jetty Barracks near the public ferry landing. A suggested visitors' route, marked with blue signs, runs from north to south across the fortress and will take you to all the key sights. You'll wander on cobbles past dilapidated shiplap cottages that evoke a more robust time for this once-strategic, now-leisurely island. The garrison church on your  left, which was Orthodox until its 20th-century conversion to Lutheranism, doubled as a lighthouse.

A five-minute walk from the ferry brings you to the **Suomenlinna Centre,** which houses the worthwhile Suomenlinna Museum. Inside the (free) lobby, you'll find an information desk, gift shop, café, and giant model of all six islands that make up Suomenlinna—handy for orientation. The exhibits themselves are well-presented but dryly explained: fragments of old walls, cannons, period clothing, model ships, and so on; the upstairs focuses on the site's transition from a fortress to a park. The main attraction is the fascinating 25-minute film that presents the island's complete history (€6.50 for museum and film, runs 2/hour, daily 10:00-18:00, Oct-April 10:30-16:30).

From the Suomenlinna Centre, cross the bridge—noticing the giant, rusted seaplane hall on the right, housing the Regatta Club, with a fun sailboat photo exhibition and shop. On the far side of the hall, peer into the gigantic dry dock.

Back on the main trail, climb five minutes uphill to the right into **Piper Park** (Piperin Puisto). Hike up past its elegant 19th-century café (with rocky view tables), and continue up and over the ramparts to a surreal swimming area. From here, follow the waterline—and the ramparts—to the south. You'll walk above bunkers burrowed underground, like gigantic molehills (or maybe Hobbit houses). Periodic ladders let you scramble down onto  the rocks. Imposing cannons, now used as playsets and photo-op props for kids, are still aimed ominously at the Gulf of Finland—in case, I imagine, of Russian invasion...or if they just get fed up with all of those cruise ships. Reaching the southern tip of the island, called King's Gate, peek out through the cannon holes. Then make your walk a loop by circling back to the Suomenlinna Centre and, beyond that, the ferry dock for the ride home.

Peninsula Promenade

For a breezy, salty seaside walk with island views, consider this promenade around the Kaivopuisto Park peninsula. Allow 1.5 hours at a leisurely pace. From Market Square, wander past the brick Old Market Hall and Tallink Silja terminal, and follow the shoreline pedestrian path. The first island you'll pass, Valkosaari, hosts the local yacht club—NJK—the oldest in Scandinavia, with the classy NJK restaurant. The next island, Luoto, is home to the posh Saaristo restaurant (with shuttle boat service). During a typical winter, the bay freezes (18 inches of ice is strong enough to allow cars to drive to the islands—in the past there was even a public bus route that extended to an island during winter). The fortress island of Suomenlinna is in the distance. The hill you're circling (on the right) is a swanky neighborhood and home to several embassies; ahead, the classic Ursula Café, with its fine harbor views, is good for a coffee break (at Ehrenströmintie 3).

Around the corner, the next island, Uunisaari, is a fun destination in summer, when a little ferry connects the mainland with its sandy beach—perfect for a picnic. The island's unique plant life (much studied by local students) is believed to have hitched a ride to Finland from Siberia on the boots of Russian soldiers.

The odd-looking pier nearby is a station for washing rugs (those are not picnic tables). Saltwater brightens the rag rugs traditionally made by local grandmas. While American men put on aprons and do the barbecue, Finnish men wash the carpets. After the scrub, the rugs are sent through big mechanical wringers and hung on nearby racks to dry in the wind. The posted map shows 11 such stations scattered around Helsinki. Buy an ice cream at the nearby stand and watch the action (best in the morning).

In the distance looms Helsinki's big West Harbor port, hosting hundreds of cruise ships a year. From here you can follow Neitsytpolku street back to the town center, keeping an eye out for fun Art Nouveau buildings.

▲▲Seurasaari Open-Air Folk Museum

Inspired by Stockholm's Skansen, also on a lovely island on the edge of town, this is a collection of 100 historic buildings from

every corner of Finland. It's wonderfully furnished and gives rushed visitors an opportunity to sample the far reaches of Finland without leaving the capital city—you can see the highlights here in about an hour (if you're not taking a tour, get the map or the helpful guidebook). But it's easy to stretch out your visit with a picnic or light lunch (snacks and cakes available in the Antti farmstead at the center of the park). Off-season, when the buildings are closed, the place is empty and not worth the trouble.

Cost and Hours: Free park entry, €9 to enter buildings; June-Aug daily 11:00-17:00; shorter hours May and Sept; buildings closed rest of year; tel. 09/4050-9660, www.seurasaari.fi.

Tours: One-hour English tours are free with entry ticket, offered mid-June–mid-Aug generally at 15:00 (confirm time on website).

Getting There: To reach the museum, ride bus #24 (from the top of the Esplanade, 2/hour, 25 minutes) to the last stop at Seurasaari (note departure times for your return) and walk across the quaint footbridge.

NEAR HELSINKI

Porvoo, the second-oldest town in Finland, has wooden architecture that dates from the Swedish colonial period. This coastal town can be reached from Helsinki by bus (one hour) or by summertime excursion boat from Market Square (3.5 hours; www.msjlruneberg.fi/cruises).

Turku, the historic capital of Finland, is a two-hour bus or train ride from Helsinki. Overall, Turku is a pale shadow of Helsinki, and there is little reason to make a special trip. It does have a handicraft museum in a cluster of wooden houses (the only part of town to survive a devastating fire in the early 1800s), an old castle, a fine Gothic cathedral (this was the first part of Finland to be Christianized, in the 12th century), and a market square. Viking and Tallink Silja boats sail from Turku to Stockholm every morning and evening, passing through the especially scenic Turku archipelago.

Naantali, a cute, commercial, well-preserved medieval town with a quaint harbor, is an easy 20-minute bus ride from Turku.

Shopping in Helsinki

Helsinki may be the top shopping town in the Nordic countries. Even in this region of creative design culture, Helsinki is a trendsetter; many Finnish designers are household names worldwide. The easiest place to get a taste of Finnish design is in the shops at the top of the Esplanade, but with a little more time, it's worth delving into the nearby Design District.

Opening Times: Most shops are open all day Monday through Friday (generally 10:00 or 11:00 until 17:00 or 18:00), and often have shorter hours on Saturday. Most are closed on Sundays. The exception is the shops on the Esplanade, which stay open later and keep Sunday hours.

THE ESPLANADE AND NEARBY

Helsinki's elegant main drag, the Esplanade, is a coffee-sipper's and window-shopper's delight. Practically every big name in Finnish design has a flagship store along or near this people-pleasing strip. Here are some worth dipping into:

Marimekko, the well-known Finnish fashion company, was founded in the early 1950s but really took off on the international stage in the 1960s, especially after Jackie Kennedy bought seven Marimekko dresses (and wore one of them on the cover of *Sports Illustrated*). You'll find the company's colorful, patterned scarves, clothes, purses, and fabrics in locations throughout central Helsinki, including right across from Stockmann department store (at Aleksanterinkatu 50, www.marimekko.com). Other nearby Marimekko branches include one specializing in children's items (at Mikonkatu 1), and stores in the Kamppi and Forum shopping centers.

These three shops are strung along the north side of the Esplanade: **Aarikka** (#27, www.aarikka.com) has affordable and casual handmade jewelry, tableware, and home decor, most of it made from colorful spheres of wood. **Iittala** (#23, www.iittala.com) is the flagship store of a longtime Finnish glassmaker. Popping into the shop, you'll see Alvar Aalto's signature wavy-mouthed vases, which haven't gone out of fashion since 1936; Oiva Toikka's iconic "dew drop"-patterned chalices and pedestal bowls from 1964; and an array of other decorative and functional glassware. **Kalevala** (at #25) has been selling finely crafted, handmade-in-Finland jewelry since 1937; some pieces are modern, while others are inspired by old Scandinavian and Sami themes (www.kalevalakoru.com).

Finlayson, on the south side of the Esplanade, is a venerable textile design company that's been around since 1820—but their sheets, towels, rugs, and curtains are fun and modern (#14, www.finlayson.fi).

The Esplanade is capped by the enormous, eight-floor **Stockmann** department store, arguably Scandinavia's most impressive (Mon-Fri 9:00-21:00, Sat until 18:00, Sun 12:00-18:00, great basement supermarket, Aleksanterinkatu 52B, www.stockmann.fi). Bookworms enjoy the impressive **Academic Bookstore** just downhill from Stockmann (#39, same hours as Stockmann). **Artek,** Alvar and Elissa Aalto's flagship store (across from Stockmann at Keskuskatu 1B, www.artek.fi), offers fine furniture and lighting by the leading Finnish design concern.

Fans of Tove Jansson's Moomin children's stories will enjoy the **Moomin Shop,** on the second floor of the Forum shopping mall at Mannerheimintie 20, across the busy tram-lined street from Stockmann (and with the same hours).

THE DESIGN DISTRICT

Helsinki's Design District is a several-block cluster of streets that's filled with design and antique shops, fashion stores highlighting local designers, and trendy restaurants. Explore this engaging zone to feel the creativity and uniqueness of Finnish design and urban culture. For a handy orientation to the options in this ever-changing area, visit www.designdistrict.fi (with themed walking maps) or pick up the Design District brochure from the TI.

While the Design District sprawls roughly southwest of the Esplanade nearly to the waterfront, the following zones are most worthy of exploration.

Kolmikulma Park and Nearby

Just a block south of the Esplanade's top end (down Erottajankatu), the park called Kolmikulma (Diana Park, with its spear-throwing statue centerpiece) is a handy epicenter of Design District liveliness.

Uudenmaankatu street (west from the park) has the highest concentration of shops, especially fashion boutiques of local designers such as **Ivana Helsinki** (#15, patterned casual dresses). You'll also find **Nounou** (at #2, modern, handmade glass pieces); the recommended **Café Bar No. 9; Astia Taivas** (#13, crammed with secondhand glassware); and, around the corner on Annankatu street, **Momono** (#12, well-selected examples of modern and vintage Finnish design).

Meanwhile, a block south, pedestrianized **Iso Roobertinkatu** has lots of cheap eateries; **Formverk** has fun home decor and kitchenware (on the corner at Annankatu 5).

Fredrikinkatu

This street, which crosses Uudenmaankatu two blocks west of the park, is one of the most engaging streets in town.

Start at the corner with Uudenmaankatu and work your way north to Bulevardi. Besides fashion boutiques, you'll discover **C. Hagelstam Antique Books** (#35, quaint and beautiful shop with vintage prints and books), **Kauniste** (#24, uniquely patterned fabrics and prints) and **Chez Marius** (#26, fun kitchen gadgets and cooking gear). This shop also marks the pleasant intersection with the tree- and tram-lined Bulevardi. **Day,** kitty-corner from the Chez Marius, has funky, quirky home decor and gifts (Bulevardi 11).

Continuing north along Fredrikinkatu, the next block has several home decor shops, including **Casuarina** (#30, with a spare, rustic, reclaimed aesthetic), and **Primavera Interiors** (#41, with a more artistic and funky style).

Browse your way two more blocks up Fredrikinkatu to the cross-street, **Eerikinkatu,** which also has lots of inviting little galleries and boutiques; two are at the same address (at Eerikinkatu 18): **DesiPeli,** with a variety of home decor, including some very cool, Marimekko-type fabrics; and **Napa & Paja,** a collective gallery of three jewelry designers, showcasing their beautiful, unique, delicate designs. They also stock casual handbags and books about Finland.

Near the Design Museum

The Design Museum anchors an appealing area of boutiques—and itself has a good shop with a wide range of Finnish design products (often related to current exhibits). A block south of the museum, on **Korkeavuorenkatu,** you'll find vintage shops, kitchenware, antiques, pop-up stores, fashion boutiques, hair salons, and cafés. In particular, keep an eye out for **Pore Helsinki** (at #3), with casual fashion and accessories; and **Fasaani** (a.k.a. Helsinki Secondhand, at #5) is crammed with affordable pre-owned home-decor items just like those in galleries around town—furniture, dishes, glassware, and more (closed Sun, Korkeavuorenkatu 5, www.fasaani.fi).

OTHER SHOPPING OPTIONS

Market Square: This harborfront square is packed not only with fishmongers and producers, but also with stands selling Finnish souvenirs and more refined crafts (roughly Mon-Fri 6:30-17:00, an hour later in summer, Sat until 16:00, only tourist stalls open on Sun 10:00-16:00).

Modern Shopping Malls: For less glamorous shopping needs, the **Kamppi** mall above and around the bus station is good. The **Forum** shopping center at Mannerheimintie 20 is filled with Euro fashion brands.

Flea Market: If you brake for garage sales, the outdoor **Hietalahti Market** is a 15-minute walk from the harbor or a short ride on tram #6 from Mannerheimintie to the Hietalahdentori stop (June-Aug Mon-Fri 9:00-19:00, Sat 8:00-16:00, Sun 10:00-16:00; less action, shorter hours, and closed Sun off-season). The adjacent red-brick indoor Hietalahti Market Hall houses food stands (described later, under "Eating in Helsinki").

Sleeping in Helsinki

I've listed a wide range of accommodations in Helsinki, from fancy, well-located big hotels, to modest but cozy smaller hotels, to some unusually comfortable hostels. (And remember that some of the cheapest beds in Helsinki are on the overnight boats to Stockholm.) The hotels listed here all have air-con and an elevator unless otherwise noted.

Every hotel in Helsinki employs dynamic pricing, with room rates fluctuating unpredictably with demand—you'll have to check hotel websites for exact rates (and any special deals) for your dates. Peak-season months (not surprisingly) are the better-weather months from May to September.

Sleep Code

Hotels are classified based on the average price of a typical en suite double room with breakfast in high season.

$$$$	**Splurge:** Most rooms over €225
$$$	**Pricier:** €175-225
$$	**Moderate:** €125-175
$	**Budget:** €75-125
¢	**Backpacker:** Under €75
RS%	**Rick Steves discount**

Unless otherwise noted, credit cards are accepted, hotel staff speak basic English, and free Wi-Fi is available. Comparison-shop by checking prices at several hotels (on each hotel's own website, on a booking site, or by email). For the best deal, *always book directly with the hotel.* Ask for a discount if paying in cash; if the listing includes **RS%**, request a Rick Steves discount.

HOTELS

$$$$ Hotel Haven, with 77 elegantly appointed, comfortable rooms and a lobby that artfully mingles class and rustic comfort, owns a convenient location with good access to the harbor and the Esplanade. "Standard" rooms face the back, with some street noise; quieter "style" rooms face the harbor (but with no views). It's worth a splurge, particularly if you can snare a deal (Unioninkatu 17, tel. 09/681-930, www.hotelhaven.fi).

$$$$ GLO Hotel Kluuvi, with 184 stylish rooms, has a spa-like quality that gives you an appreciation for one (expensive) way to survive a long, dark winter. This tempting if trendy splurge, perfectly situated just north of the Esplanade, is worth considering if you prize elegance and a central location—especially if you can get a good discount (Kluuvikatu 4, tel. 010-3444-400, www.glohotels.fi).

$$$ Hotel Rivoli Jardin has a handy location, tucked away in a courtyard just off the middle of the Esplanade. Warm and personal, it has an inviting lounge and 55 rooms with classic Finnish comfort and a few classy flourishes (Kasarmikatu 40, tel. 09/681-500, www.rivoli.fi, rivoli.jardin@rivoli.fi). They also rent apartments (one-week minimum).

$$$ Hotel Fabian, Hotel Haven's sister property a few blocks from the Esplanade, has 58 spacious and comfortable rooms with a black-and-white color scheme, nicely decorated public spaces, and a relaxing outdoor courtyard (Fabianinkatu 7, tel. 09/6128-2000, www.hotelfabian.fi, sales@hotelfabian.fi).

$$$ Hotel Katajanokka occupies a former prison building, built in 1888, but you wouldn't know it from the chic design of this appealing four-star hotel with 106 quiet rooms. The windows no longer have bars (thanks to the local fire code) and walls have been removed so that two or three cells make a room. Check out the two original cells in the restaurant (no air-con, gym, bike rental, by Vyökatu stop of tram #4 near the Viking cruise ship terminal, Merikasarminkatu 1A, tel. 09/686-450, www.hotelkatajanokka.fi, sales@hotelkatajanokka.fi).

$$$ Scandic Grand Marina is a huge 462-room, impersonal four-star hotel filling a big, brick warehouse building near the Viking cruise ship terminal (Katajanokanlaituri 7, tel. 09/16661, www.scandichotels.com/grandmarina, grandmarina@scandichotels.com).

$$$ GLO Hotel Art has a fine location convenient to the Design District, with 171 modern rooms behind a striking Art Nouveau facade that makes it feel like a stony medieval château has landed in the middle of Helsinki (Lönnrotinkatu 29, tel. 010-3444-100, www.glohotels.fi, art@glohotels.fi).

$$ Hotel Anna is plain, conscientiously run, and feels a bit tired. Its 64 rooms in the heart of the Design District are well-worn but help raise funds for the Finnish Free Church (it's actually attached to a church—ask to see the shortcut to the choir loft). For more air in the rooms, ask at the desk for a key to open the larger windows (RS%, no air-con, family rooms available, 4 blocks south of the top of the Esplanade—take tram #3 from train station to Iso Roobertinkatu, Annankatu 1, tel. 09/616-621, www.hotelanna.fi, info@hotelanna.fi).

$ Hotelli Finn is inexpensive and wonderfully central. Its 35 tidy rooms are stowed quietly on the sixth floor of an office building near the top of the Esplanade. It's short on amenities: tiny bathrooms, no breakfast (though a nearby bakery offers a buffet spread), and no real lobby or common space—but the price, location, and service are just right (Kalevankatu 3B, tel. 09/684-4360, www.hotellifinn.fi, info@hotellifinn.fi).

$ Essex Home is a good budget alternative. Sweet Seija Lappalainen rents 13 apartments (all with kitchenettes) scattered around the residential streets of the Katajanokka peninsula (expect lots of stairs, Luotsikatu 9A, mobile 040-516-2714, www.essexhome.fi, info@essexhome.fi). The two "Essex Studio" rooms are a bit farther out.

HOSTELS

Helsinki's hostels are unusually comfortable, and all ages are welcome with or without a hostel membership. Eurohostel and Academica are more like budget hotels than hostels.

¢ Eurohostel is 400 yards from the Viking ferry terminal and a 10-minute walk from Market Square. It's a modern hostel with

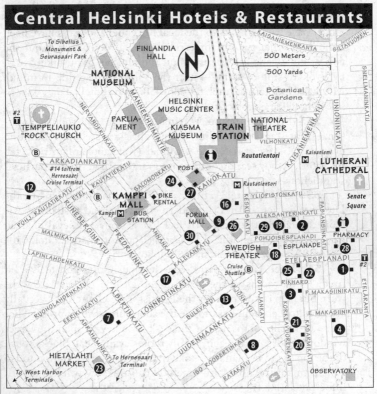

Central Helsinki Hotels & Restaurants

a restaurant and good budget-travel information. While generally fully booked in advance, they release no-show beds at 18:00 (private and family rooms available, free morning sauna, evening sauna—€7.50, Vyökatu stop for tram #4 is around the corner, Linnankatu 9, tel. 09/622-0470, www.eurohostel.eu/fi, eurohostel@eurohostel.fi).

¢ **Academica Summer Hostel** is a university dorm that's professionally run as a hostel from June through August. Finnish university students have it good—the rooms are hotel-quality with private baths and kitchenettes, though all doubles have twin beds. Guests can have a morning sauna and use the swimming pool for free (wired Internet access in rooms—but you can rent a Wi-Fi router from front desk for your stay, tram #2 to the Kauppakorkeakoulut stop, then walk 5 minutes to Hietaniemenkatu 14, tel. 09/1311-4334, www.hostelacademica.fi, hostel.academica@hyy.fi).

¢ **Hostel Diana Park** is a small, friendly, centrally located hostel on the third floor of a 19th-century apartment building in the heart of the happening Design District. This is a better place to stay than Eurohostel if you're looking to meet fellow travelers

Accommodations
1. Hotel Haven
2. GLO Hotel Kluuvi
3. Hotel Rivoli Jardin
4. Hotel Fabian
5. Hotel Katajanokka
6. Scandic Grand Marina
7. GLO Hotel Art
8. Hotel Anna
9. Hotelli Finn
10. Essex Home
11. Eurohostel
12. Academica Summer Hostel
13. Hostel Diana Park & Café Bar No. 9

Eateries & Other
14. Market Square
15. Old Market Hall
16. Zetor
17. Lappi Restaurant
18. Teatterin Deli, Bar & Grilli
19. Strindberg
20. Spis
21. Juuri
22. Emo Restaurant & Picnic
23. Hietalahti Market Hall
24. Lasipalatsi
25. Savoy Restaurant
26. Stockmann Dep't Store
27. S Market Grocery
28. Café Kappeli
29. Café Aalto (in Academic Bookstore)
30. Ateljee Bar (in Torni Tower)

HELSINKI

in the common room and don't mind lugging your bags up the stairs (private room available, no elevator, Uudenmaankatu 9, tel. 09/642-169, www.dianapark.fi, info@dianapark.fi).

Eating in Helsinki

Helsinki's many restaurants are smoke-free and a good value for lunch on weekdays. Finnish companies get a tax break if they distribute lunch coupons (worth €10) to their employees. It's no surprise that most downtown Helsinki restaurants offer weekday lunch specials that cost exactly the value of the coupon. These low prices evaporate in the evenings and all day Saturday and Sunday, when picnics and Middle Eastern kebab restaurants are the only budget options. Dinner reservations are smart at nicer restaurants.

FUN HARBORFRONT EATERIES

Stalls on Market Square: Helsinki's delightful and vibrant square is magnetic any time of day...but especially at lunchtime. This really is the most memorable, casual, quick-and-easy lunch place in town. A half-dozen orange tents (erected to shield diners from

Restaurant Price Code

I've assigned each eatery a price category, based on the average cost of a typical main course. Drinks, desserts, and splurge items (steak and seafood) can raise the price considerably.

$$$$ **Splurge:** Most main courses over €25
$$$ **Pricier:** €20-25
$$ **Moderate:** €15-20
$ **Budget:** Under €15

In Finland, a takeout spot is **$;** a sit-down café is **$$;** a casual but more upscale restaurant is **$$$;** and a swanky splurge is **$$$$.**

dive-bombing gulls) serve moose meatballs, smoked reindeer, and creamy salmon soup on paper plates until 18:00. It's not unusual for the Finnish president to stop by here with visiting dignitaries. There's a crêpe place, and at the far end—my favorites—several salmon grills (€11-13 for a good meal). The only real harborside dining in this part of town is picnicking. While these places provide picnic tables, you can also have your food foil-wrapped to go and grab benches right on the water down near Uspenski Orthodox Cathedral.

Old Market Hall (Vanha Kauppahalli): Just beyond the harborside market is a cute, red-brick, indoor market hall. It's beautifully renovated with rich woodwork, and quite tight inside (daily 8:00-18:00, not all stalls open on Sun). Today, along with produce stalls, it's a hit for its fun, inexpensive eateries. You'll find enticing coffee shops with tempting pastries; grilled, smoked, or pickled fish options; mounds of saffron-yellow paella; delectable open-face sandwiches; a handy chance to sample reindeer meat; and an array of ethnic eats, from Middle Eastern and Lebanese meals to Vietnamese banh mi sandwiches. In the market hall, **$ Soppakeittiö** ("Soup Kitchen") serves big bowls of filling, tasty seafood soup.

FINNISH-THEMED DINING

$$$ Zetor, a self-proclaimed "110 percent Finnish" restaurant, mercilessly lampoons Finnish rural culture and cuisine (while celebrating it deep down). Sit next to a cow-crossing sign at a tractor-turned-into-a-table, in a "Finnish Western" atmosphere. Main courses include reindeer, smoked perch pies, grilled liver, and less exotic fare. A bit touristy and tacky, this quirky place can be fun—and it gets loud after 20:00, when the dance floor gets going (daily 12:00-24:00, 200 yards north of Stockmann department store, across street from McDonald's at Mannerheimintie 3, tel. 010-766-4450).

$$$$ Lappi Restaurant is a fine place for tasty Lapp (Sami) cuisine, with an entertaining menu (including house-smoked fish, roasted elk, and reindeer shank). The snug, woody atmosphere will have you thinking you've traveled north and lashed your reindeer to the hitchin' post. Dinner reservations strongly recommended (Mon-Fri 16:00-22:30, Sat from 13:00, closed Sun, off Bulevardi at Annankatu 22, tel. 09/645-550, www.lappires.com).

VENERABLE ESPLANADE CAFÉS

Restaurants line the sunny north side of the Esplanade—offering creative lunch salads and light meals in their cafés (with fine sidewalk seating), plush sofas for cocktails in their bars, and fancy restaurant dining upstairs.

$$ The **Teatterin Deli** and **Teatterin Bar** are among several interconnected eateries attached to the landmark Swedish Theater. Order a sandwich or salad from the deli counter (facing the Academic Bookstore) to eat in or take away. The long cocktail bar that faces the Esplanade is a fun space for a drink and people-watching. Whether you order a meal or a drink, you're welcome to find a seat out on the leafy Esplanade terrace (deli counter open daily until 21:00, at the top of the Esplanade, Pohjoisesplanadi 2, tel. 09/6128-5000). The fancy **$$$$ Grilli** restaurant is also here.

$$$ Strindberg, near the corner of the Esplanade and Mikonkatu, oozes atmosphere and class. Downstairs is an elegant café with outdoor and indoor tables great for people-watching (sandwiches and salads). The upstairs cocktail lounge—with big sofas and bookshelves—has a den-like coziness that attracts an after-work crowd. Also upstairs, the inviting restaurant has huge main dishes with fish, meat, pasta, and vegetarian options; reserve in advance to get a window seat overlooking the Esplanade (restaurant open Mon-Sat 11:00-23:00, closed Sun; café open Mon-Sat 9:00-24:00, Sun 10:00-22:00, Pohjoisesplanadi 33, tel. 09/681-2030).

TRENDY EATERIES IN AND NEAR THE DESIGN DISTRICT

Several creative eateries clustered in the Design District, a short stroll south and west of the Esplanade, offer a fresh take on the cuisine of Finland, featuring seasonal ingredients and modern presentations (for more on "New Nordic" cuisine, see page 110).

$$$$ Spis is your best Helsinki bet for splurging on Finnish New Nordic. Reserve ahead for one of the prized tables in its tiny, peeling plaster, rustic-chic dining room (tasting menus only, Tue-Thu from 18:00, Fri-Sat from 17:30, last seating at 20:30, closed Sun-Mon, Kasarmikatu 26, mobile 045-305-1211, www.spis.fi).

$$$$ Juuri has a casual interior and a few outdoor tables. They serve a variety of "sapas"—small plates highlighting Finland's culinary bounty, such as herring, pike roe, and arctic char (Mon-Fri 11:30-14:30 & 17:00-23:00, Sat 12:00-23:00, Sun 16:00-23:00, Korkeavuorenkatu 27, tel. 09/635-732).

$$$ Emo Restaurant is a pleasantly unpretentious wine bar in a sleepy zone just a block off of the Esplanade. They serve up €10 small plates as well as à la carte choices—cassoulet, rack of pork, rainbow trout (lunch Tue-Fri 11:30-14:30; dinner Mon-Sat 17:00-24:00, closed Sun; Kasarmikatu 44, mobile 010-505-0900, www.emo-ravintola.fi).

Pub Grub: A simpler choice tucked between shops in the heart of the Design District, **$$ Café Bar No. 9** attracts a loyal local following, who enjoy digging into plates of unpretentious pub food (Uudenmaankatu 9, tel. 09/621-4059).

Market Hall: Hiding at the western edge of the Design District, the **$$ Hietalahti Market Hall** is a fun place to browse for a meal. Like the Old Market Hall along the South Harbor, this elegantly renovated (but less touristy) food hall is filled with an enticing array of vendors, with delightful seating upstairs (Mon-Thu 8:00-18:00, Fri-Sat until 22:00, Sun 10:00-16:00, www.hietalahdenkauppahalli.fi).

NEAR THE STATIONS

$$ Lasipalatsi, the renovated, rejuvenated 1930s Glass Palace, is on Mannerheimintie between the train and bus stations. The café—with a youthful terrace on the square out back—offers a self-service buffet (€11 lunch menu available all day); there are always €5 sandwiches and cakes (Mon-Sat 8:30-20:00, closed Sun). Upstairs there's a more expensive **$$$** restaurant that's a Helsinki classic, with bird's-eye city views (Mon-Fri 11:00-24:00, closed Sat-Sun, across from the old post office building at Mannerheimintie 22, tel. 09/612-6700).

DRESSY SPLURGE DINNERS

$$$$ Savoy Restaurant, where locals go for special occasions, is expensive, formal but friendly, and drenched in Alvar Aalto design. Everything in this eighth-floor view restaurant—from the chairs and lampshades to the doors—is 1937 original. The food is Continental with a Finnish touch. While the glassed-in terrace offers a great rooftop view, the elegant interior is where you'll experience a classic Finnish atmosphere. Reservations are advised for meals, but come up anytime for a drink, either inside or on the tight terrace (Mon-Fri 11:30-15:00 & 18:00-24:00, Sat 18:00-24:00, closed Sun, Eteläesplanadi 14, tel. 09/6128-5300, www.ravintolasavoy.fi).

PICNICS

In supermarkets, buy the semiflat bread (available dark or light) that Finns love—every slice is a heel. Finnish liquid yogurt is also a treat (sold in liter cartons). Karelian pasties, filled with rice or mashed potatoes, make a good snack. A beautiful, upscale supermarket is in the basement of the **Stockmann** department store—follow the *Delikatessen* signs downstairs (Mon-Fri until 21:00, Sat-Sun until 18:00, Aleksanterinkatu 52B). Two blocks north, **S Market** is a more workaday supermarket under the Sokos department store next to the train station (daily until 22:00).

Another option is **$ Picnic,** a casual chain offering fresh, made-to-go sandwiches, salads, and pastries. There's one just south of the midsection of the Esplanade (at Kasarmikatu 42), but you'll see them all around town, including in the Forum and Kamppi shopping centers (www.picnic.fi).

Helsinki Connections

BY BUS OR TRAIN

From Helsinki, it's easy to get to **Turku** (hourly, 2 hours by either bus or train) or **St. Petersburg, Russia** (see options later). For train info, visit www.vr.fi. For bus info in English, consult www.matkahuolto.fi.

BY OVERNIGHT BOAT BETWEEN STOCKHOLM AND HELSINKI

Two fine and fiercely competitive lines, Viking Line and Tallink Silja, connect the capitals of Sweden and Finland. Each line offers state-of-the-art, 2,700-bed ships with luxurious *smörgåsbord* meals, reasonable cabins, plenty of entertainment (discos, saunas, gambling), and enough duty-free shopping to sink a ship.

The fares are kept at a reasonable rate to encourage locals to sail to shop and drink tax-free. It's a huge operation. The boats are filled with about 45 percent Finns, 45 percent Swedes, and 10 percent cruisers from other countries. The average passenger spends as much on booze and tax-free items as on the boat fare. To maintain their tax-free status, the boats make a midnight stop in the Åland Islands—a self-governing, Swedish-speaking province of Finland that's exempt

HELSINKI

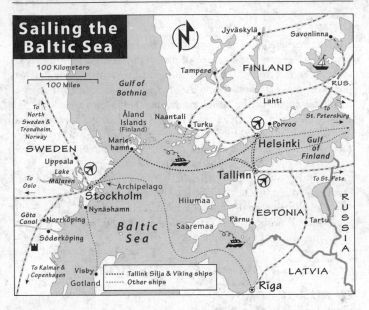

Sailing the Baltic Sea

from the European Union's value-added tax (VAT). See "Arrival in Helsinki" for terminal locations.

Of the two lines, Viking Line has the reputation as the party boat. Tallink Silja is considered more elegant. But both lines have their share of noisy passengers making duty-free booze runs.

Schedules and Tickets

Schedules: Both Viking Line (www.vikingline.fi) and Tallink Silja (www.tallinksilja.com) sail nightly between Stockholm and Helsinki year-round. Boats leave (from either port) between 16:30 and 17:30, and arrive the next morning around 10:00.

Cost: As with Scandinavian hotels, cruise fares vary by season, by day of the week, and by cabin class. Check both lines' websites to see the cabin options for your itinerary. Mid-June to mid-August is most crowded and expensive, as are Friday nights. In summer, one-way tickets start at about €88 and go up from there. Travelers with rail passes that include Sweden or Finland get 20 to 50 percent discounts on both lines (cabins extra). There can be discounts for early booking, seniors, and families.

Itinerary Options: "Round-trip" fares (across and back on **successive nights,** giving you access to your bedroom throughout the day) generally cost less than two one-way fares. The drawback is that you'll have only a few hours on land. But you may be able to get the round-trip fare on **nonsuccessive nights** if you book a hotel through the cruise line for the intervening night(s). If it fits your schedule, this can be a good deal.

HELSINKI

Reservations: For summer or weekend sailings, reserve well in advance. Book online with a credit card—you'll get a reservation number and pick up your boarding card at the port. You can also book by phone or in person: **Viking Line**'s customer service line is Finnish based: toll tel. 0600-41577. **Tallink Silja** has offices in Helsinki (near the Swedish Theater at Erottajankatu 19, tel. 09/18041) and in Stockholm (across from the train station at Klarabergsviadukten 72, Swedish tel. 08/440-5990). Any travel agent in Scandinavia can also sell you a ticket (with a small booking fee).

Terminals in Stockholm and Helsinki

Terminal buildings are well-organized, with cafés, lockers, and tourist information desks. Boats open 1.5 hours before departure, and you must be checked in 20 minutes before departure. Parking is available at terminals in both cities (but space is limited in Helsinki); ask for details when you reserve your ticket.

In Stockholm: Viking Line has its own terminal along the Stadsgården embankment on Södermalm. To get there, it's easiest to ride Viking Line's shuttle bus from Stockholm's bus station right to the terminal (55 SEK, departs according to boat schedule, www.flygbussarna.se). You can also ride public bus #53 (from the train station or Gamla Stan) or #71 (from the Opera House or Gamla Stan) to the Londonviadukten stop, then walk five minutes down to the terminal. A taxi from the train station will cost you around 200 SEK.

Tallink Silja's boats leave from the Värtahamnen port, about three miles northeast of the city center. It's simplest to catch the Tallink Silja shuttle bus from Stockholm's bus station (60 SEK, departs according to boat schedule). Or you can take public bus #76 from downtown (daily, direction: Ropsten, get off at Värtahamnen Färjeterminal stop). Figure about 300 SEK for a taxi from Gamla Stan, the train station, or other downtown areas.

For Stockholm public transport information, see www.sl.se.

In Helsinki: Both lines are perfectly central, on opposite sides of the main harbor, a 10-minute walk from the center. See the map on page 579.

Tips on Board

Meals: While ships have cheap, fast cafeterias as well as classy, romantic restaurants, they are famous for their *smörgåsbord* dinners (usually around €40-45; breakfast *smörgåsbord* €12-14). Dinner is self-serve in two sittings, one at about 17:30, the other around 20:00. (In summer, I'd have dinner at the first sitting—shortly after departure—and be on deck for sunset.) If you board without a *smörgåsbord* reservation, go to the restaurant and make one—window seats are highly sought after. (For more tips, see page 715.)

The price includes beer, wine, soft drinks, and coffee. Of course, you can also bring a picnic and eat it on deck, or eat at one of the ship's other restaurants.

Time Change: Finland is one hour ahead of Sweden. Sailing from Stockholm to Helsinki, operate on Swedish time until you're ready to go to bed, then reset your watch. Morning schedules are Finnish time, and vice versa when you return.

Money: For purchases, ships take credit cards, euros, and Swedish kronor. Ships have exchange desks, but not onboard ATMs; you'll find those in the terminals at each end.

Adding Other Destinations

Tallinn: The Estonian capital can be spliced into your Helsinki itinerary as a side-trip from Helsinki (or vice-versa), or as a triangle trip (Stockholm-Helsinki-Tallinn-Stockholm, must be booked as three one-ways). For details on the boats connecting Tallinn to Helsinki and to Stockholm, see "Tallinn Connections" on page 678.

Turku: Both Viking Line and Tallink Silja also sail from Stockholm to Turku in Finland, a shorter crossing (12 hours, departing daily at about 7:00-9:00 and 19:30-21:00). Turku, a "mini-Helsinki" with more medieval charm but less urban bustle, is two hours from Helsinki by bus or train. The cheaper boat fare saves you enough to pay for the train trip from Turku to Helsinki.

BY CRUISE SHIP

For more details on the following ports, and other cruise destinations, pick up my *Rick Steves Scandinavian & Northern European Cruise Ports* guidebook.

Cruises arrive in Helsinki at various ports circling two large harbors—West Harbor (Länsistama) and South Harbor (Eteläsatama). Each individual cruise berth is designated by a letter code (noted in this section, along with each terminal's name in both Finnish and Swedish). For a map, see www.portofhelsinki.fi.

Getting Downtown: In addition to the public transit and/or walking options outlined later, many cruise lines offer a **shuttle bus** (either complimentary or for a fee) into downtown (especially worth considering if you arrive at the farther-flung Hernesaari quays). This bus usually drops you off at the top end of the Esplanade, behind the Swedish Theater (at the intersection of Mannerheimintie and Bulevardi). Another option is to take a **hop-on, hop-off bus tour**; these meet arriving ships at Hernesaari, and are easy to find around the South Harbor (for details, see "Tours in Helsinki," earlier).

West Harbor (Länsistama)

This port is about two miles southwest of downtown. From any cruise port here, it's about a €15-20 taxi ride into town. An ambitious redevelopment project is underway to transform this area with green spaces, residences, recreational marinas, and a new tram line. You may see some of these improvements when you visit.

Hernesaari Quays: The primary cruise port for Helsinki sits on the eastern side of West Harbor, with two berths (LHB and LHC). There's a tiny-but-handy TI kiosk where you can pick up maps and brochures, buy a day ticket for public transit (€9, credit cards only), or use the free Wi-Fi. It's a five-minute walk to the stop for **bus #14,** which takes you downtown: Head through the parking lot, turn left at the street, take the next right, and look for the bus stop marked *Pajamäki/Smedjebacka* (3/hour). From here, ride bus #14 to Kamppi (a 10-minute walk from the train station area and the Esplanade) or continue to Kauppakorkeakoulut (near Temppeliaukio, the Church in the Rock—get off the bus, walk straight ahead one block, then turn right up Luthernikatu to find the church).

West Terminals 1 & 2 (Länsiterminaali): Directly in front of each terminal (with ATMs and other services) is a stop for trams #9 and #6T, which take you into town (6/hour, buy tickets with a credit card at bus-stop machine or from driver—cash only).

South Harbor (Eteläsatama)

This centrally located harbor fans out from Market Square and is an easy 15-minute walk to downtown (just stroll toward the white-and-green church dome). Ringing this harbor are several terminals for both cruises and overnight boats; two are most commonly used by cruise ships. Terminals have ATMs and other basic services.

Katajanokan Terminal: The harbor's northern embankment has two cruise berths (ERA and ERB). A third berth (EKL), used more by overnight boats than cruise ships, is closer to town. The Viking Line terminal in this area is across the street from the stop for **tram #5,** which zips you right into town (stops at City Hall, Senate Square, Lasipalatsi near the train station, and National Museum).

Olympia Terminal: Smaller cruise ships use this terminal (EO), along the southern embankment. Out front is a stop for **tram #2,** which takes you to Senate Square, and then goes on to the Sammonkatu stop near Temppeliaukio (the Church in the Rock).

The South Harbor berths that are closest to downtown (Kanava and Makasiini) are used mostly by overnight boats, though occasionally overflow cruise ships may end up there.

CONNECTING HELSINKI AND ST. PETERSBURG

Many visitors use Helsinki as a launch pad for a visit to St. Petersburg, Russia—just 240 miles east. For more details on St. Petersburg, consider my *Rick Steves Snapshot St. Petersburg, Helsinki & Tallinn.*

Visa Requirements: American and Canadian travelers to Russia need a visa, which must be arranged weeks in advance (you must submit your passport with your visa application, so plan ahead). For details and costs for obtaining a visa, see www.ricksteves.com/russianvisa.

Visa Exceptions: If you arrive in St. Petersburg **on a cruise,** the visa requirement is waived provided you contract with a local tour operator (or join one of your cruise line's excursions) for a guided visit around the city. But there is an exception that gives you time on your own in the city: If you go to St. Petersburg on a St. Peter Line ship (see below), then pay for a "shuttle service" from the dock into the city (typically €25 round-trip), you can stay up to 72 hours before returning with a St. Peter Line shuttle and boat. Although this is not a guided visit, it's treated as the "cruise exception" explained above.

By Land: You have two options. The **bus** is slower and cheaper (Matkahuolto runs one bus daily, 8-9 hours, about €25-30, www.matkahuolto.fi, arrives at Baltiisky Vokzal train station near the Baltiiskaya Metro stop; Lux Express also offers bus service, including overnight, see http://luxexpress.eu). The Allegro **train,** operated by Finnish Railways, is much faster (4/day, 3.5 hours, €45-110 depending on demand, www.vr.fi, book ahead online, arrives at Finlyandsky train station near Ploshchad Lenina Metro stop). There's also a daily overnight train to **Moscow.** Rail passes are not valid on the international trains to Russia.

By Sea: Many Baltic Sea **cruises** include a stop in St. Petersburg. But if you're traveling on your own, **St. Peter Line** can take you there from Helsinki. They sail there every other day, departing from Helsinki's West Harbor (from Terminal 1) at 18:00; 14 hours later, you reach St. Petersburg (where the ship turns around and, at 19:00, heads back to Helsinki). St. Peter Line also connects St. Petersburg to Tallinn about once weekly, then continues on to Stockholm. For details, see www.stpeterline.com; the Strömma/Sightseeing Helsinki desk at the TI also has information.

ESTONIA

ESTONIA

Eesti

A crossroads between Scandinavia and Central Europe, Estonia is shaped by its eclectic past and inspired by the prospect of an ever-brighter future. In the European Union, only three microstates (Cyprus, Luxembourg, and Malta) have a smaller population than Estonia. But like its fellow Baltic countries (Latvia and Lithuania), Estonia has an endearing enthusiasm for the things that make it unique—proving that you don't have to be big to have a clear cultural identity.

Estonians are related to the Finns and have a similar history—first Swedish domination, then Russian (1710-1918), and finally independence (after World War I). In 1940, Estonians were at least as affluent and as advanced as the Finns, but they could not preserve their independence from the USSR during World War II. As a result, Estonia sank into a nearly 50-year period of Soviet domination—and communist stagnation.

Since regaining its independence with the collapse of the Soviet Union, the country has made great strides. It joined the EU and NATO in 2004, adopted the euro currency in 2011, and today feels pretty much as "Western" as its Nordic neighbors.

EU membership seemed like a natural step to many Estonians; they already thought of themselves as part of the Nordic world. Language, history, religion, and twice-hourly ferry departures connect Finns and Estonians. Only 50 miles separate Helsinki and Tallinn, and Stockholm is just an overnight boat ride away. Finns visit Tallinn to eat, drink, and shop more cheaply than at home. While some Estonians resent that Tallinn becomes a Finnish nightclub on summer weekends, since the end of the Cold War most people on both sides are happy to have friendly new neighbors.

You'd be wrong to think of this "former USSR" country as backward. Thanks to visionary and aggressive development policies implemented soon after independence—including the designation of Internet access as a basic human right—Estonia is now a global trendsetter in technology. By 1998, every school in Estonia was already online. The country has some of the fastest broadband

Estonia Almanac

Official Name: Eesti Vabariik—the Republic of Estonia—or simply Estonia.

Population: Estonia is home to 1.3 million people (77 per square mile). Nearly seven in ten are of Estonian heritage, and about one-quarter are of Russian descent, with smaller minorities of Ukrainians, Belarusians, and Finns. About 70 percent speak the official language—Estonian—and nearly 30 percent speak Russian. The majority of Estonians are unaffiliated with any religion. About 10 percent are Lutheran and 16 percent are Orthodox.

Latitude and Longitude: 59°N and 26°E, similar latitude to Juneau, Alaska.

Area: 17,500 square miles, about the size of New Hampshire and Vermont combined.

Geography: Between Latvia and Russia, Estonia borders the Baltic Sea and Gulf of Finland. It includes more than 1,500 islands and islets, and has the highest number of meteorite craters per land area in the world.

Biggest City: The capital of Estonia, Tallinn, has 400,000 people (500,000 in the metropolitan area).

Economy: Estonia's transition to a free-market system included joining the World Trade Organization and the European Union. In recent years, it's had one of the highest per-capita income levels in Central Europe and boasts a per-capita GDP of $29,300. Its four major trading partners are Finland, Sweden, Russia, and Germany; the strengths of "E-stonia" are electronics and telecommunications.

Currency: €1 (euro) = about $1.20.

Government: Estonia is a parliamentary democracy, with a president elected by parliament and a prime minister. The 101-member parliament (Riigikogu) is elected by popular vote every four years.

Flag: The pre-1940 Estonian flag was restored in 1990. It has three equal horizontal bands with blue at the top, black in the middle, and white on the bottom. The blue represents Estonia's lakes and sea, and the loyalty and devotion of the country to its people. The black symbolizes the homeland's rich soil and the hardships the people have suffered. The white represents hope and happiness.

The Average Estonian: He or she is 42 years old and has 1.6 children. Among the quarter-million Estonians age 65 and older, about two-thirds of them are women. When she sings the national anthem, it has the same tune—but different words—as that of Finland.

Estonia

FINLAND
To St. Petersburg
RUSSIA
Turku
Helsinki
Gulf
of
Finland
To St. Petersburg
Tallinn
Sillamäe
Paldiski
Rakvere
Narva
Tapa
Kohtla-Järve
To St. Petersburg
To Stockholm
ESTONIA
Peipus
Kärdla
RUSSIA
Baltic Sea
Hiiumaa
Haapsalu
Viljandi
Saaremaa
Pärnu
Võrts-järv
Tartu
Kuressaare
Valka
Valga
Gulf of Rīga
To Rīga
LATVIA
100 Kilometers
100 Miles

speeds in the world, Estonians vote and file their taxes online, and the software for Skype—used by travelers worldwide to keep in touch—was invented right here. The multibillion-dollar windfall from Skype's 2005 sale to eBay kickstarted a whole new venture-capital industry that is still paying dividends today.

This little land has a long, jagged, hauntingly beautiful coastline, over 1,000 lakes, and more than 1,500 (mostly uninhabited) islands. About 50 percent of the landscape is forest, while marshlands and bogs cover another 20 percent.

Traditional folk music buoys the national spirit—especially at the Song Festival every five years, where a significant portion of the population convenes to pour out their souls in song. Some of Estonia's traditions may strike you as quirky. Estonians snack on nearly black rye bread slathered in garlic and bury their dead in evocative pine forests. And they're among the least religious people in the world.

Even as Estonia will always face West, across the Baltic, it also faces East, into the Russian hinterlands. One difficult legacy of the Soviet experience is Estonia's huge Russian population, a result of migration in those years. Twenty-five percent of Estonia's population is ethnically Russian, and many hold Russian passports.

After Russia vowed to "protect" Russian speakers in Ukraine and fostered a separatist revolt there, Estonians have wondered if something similar could happen here. To bridge what many see as divided loyalties, the Estonian government wants to better integrate its Russian minority, making it easier for them to acquire Estonian citizenship and addressing high unemployment in the border areas where many ethnic Russians live.

Most Estonians speak English—it's the first choice these days at school. Estonian is similar to Finnish and equally difficult; only a million people speak it worldwide. Two useful phrases to know are *"Tänan"* (TAH-nahn; "Thank you") and *"Terviseks!"* (TEHR-vee-sehks; "Cheers!"). If you'd like to learn a few more helpful words, see the Estonian survival phrases on the following page. The farther you go beyond the touristy zones, the more you see that Russian is still Estonia's second language. If you know some Russian, use it.

Estonian Survival Phrases

Estonian has a few unusual vowel sounds. The letter *ä* is pronounced "ah" as in "hat," but *a* without the umlaut sounds more like "aw" as in "hot." To make the sound *ö*, purse your lips and say "oh"; the letter *õ* is similar, but with the lips less pursed. Listen to locals and imitate. In the phonetics, *ī* sounds like the long *i* in "light," and bolded syllables are stressed.

English	Estonian	Pronunciation
Hello. (formal)	Tervist.	**tehr**-veest
Hi. / Bye. (informal)	Tere. / Nägemist.	**teh**-reh / **nah**-geh-meest
Do you speak English?	Kas te räägite inglise keelt?	kahs teh **raah**-gee-teh **een**-glee-seh kehlt
Yes. / No.	Jah. / Ei.	yah / ay
Please. / You're welcome.	Palun.	**pah**-luhn
Thank you (very much).	Tänan (väga).	**tah**-nahn (**vah**-gaw)
Can I help you?	Saan ma teid aidata?	saahn mah tayd **ī**-dah-tah
Excuse me.	Vabandust.	**vaw**-bahn-doost
(Very) good.	(Väga) hea.	(**vah**-gaw) **hey**-ah
Goodbye.	Hüvasti.	**hew**-vaw-stee
zero / one / two	null / üks / kaks	nuhl / ewks / kawks
three / four	kolm / neli	kohlm / **nay**-lee
five / six	viis / kuus	vees / koos
seven / eight	seitse / kaheksa	**sayt**-seh / **kaw**-hehk-sah
nine / ten	üheksa / kümme	**ew**-hehk-sah / **kew**-meh
hundred	sada	**saw**-daw
thousand	tuhat	**too**-hawt
How much?	Kui palju?	kwee **pawl**-yoo
Where is...?	Kus asub...?	koos ah-**soob**
...the toilet	...tualett	**too**-ah-leht
men	mees	mehs
women	naine	**nī**-neh
water / coffee	vesi / kohvi	**vay**-see / **koh**-vee
beer / wine	õlu / vein	**oh**-loo / vayn
Cheers!	Terviseks!	**tehr**-vee-sehks
The bill, please.	Arve, palun.	**ahr**-veh **pah**-luhn

TALLINN

Tallinn is a rewarding detour for those who want to spice up their Scandinavian travels with a Baltic twist. Among Nordic medieval cities, there's none nearly as well preserved as Tallinn. Its mostly intact city wall includes 26 watchtowers, each topped by a pointy red roof. Baroque and choral music ring out from its old Lutheran churches. I'd guess that Tallinn (with about 450,000 people) has more restaurants, cafés, and surprises per capita and square inch than any city in this book—and the fun is comparatively cheap. Yes, Tallinn's Nordic Lutheran culture and language connect it with Scandinavia, and two centuries of czarist Russian rule and 45 years as part of the Soviet Union left behind some Russian touches. But overlying all of that is the vibrancy of a free nation that's just a generation old. Estonian pride is in the air.

As a member of the Hanseatic League, the city of Tallinn was a medieval stronghold of the Baltic trading world. (For more on the Hanseatic League, see the sidebar on page 380.) In the 19th and early 20th centuries, Tallinn industrialized and expanded beyond its walls. Architects encircled the Old Town, putting up broad streets of public buildings, low Scandinavian-style apartment buildings, and single-family wooden houses. Estonia's brief period of independence ended in World War II, and after 1945, Soviet planners ringed the city with stands of now-crumbling concrete high-rises where many of Tallinn's Russian immigrants settled.

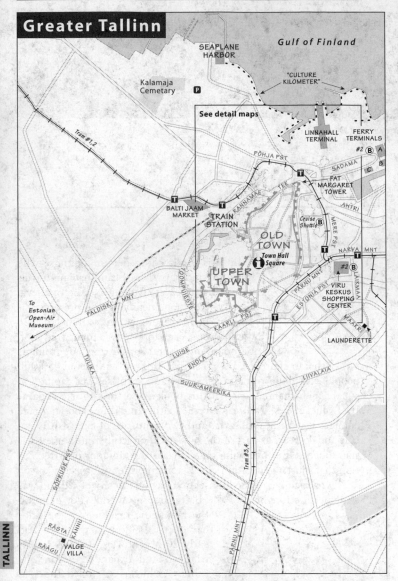

Greater Tallinn

Gulf of Finland

SEAPLANE HARBOR

"CULTURE KILOMETER"

Kalamaja Cemetery 🅿

See detail maps

LINNAHALL TERMINAL

FERRY TERMINALS

#2 🅱 Ⓐ

SADAMA

Ⓑ

Ⓒ

PÕHJA PST

Ⓣ

FAT MARGARET TOWER

AHTRI

Tram #1, 2

Ⓣ

Ⓣ

KANNAMÄE TEE

Cruise Shuttle 🅱

MERE PST

NARVA MNT

BALTI JAAM MARKET

TRAIN STATION

OLD TOWN

ⓘ Town Hall Square

Ⓣ

Ⓣ

UPPER TOWN

Cruise Shuttle

#2 🅱

PÄRNU MNT

VIRU KESKUS SHOPPING CENTER

KOMPUIESTE

ESTONIA PST

LAIKMAI

PALDISKI MNT

To Estonian Open-Air Museum

KAARLI PST

Ⓣ

MAAKRI

LAUNDERETTE

LUISE

ENDLA

SUUR-AMEERIKA

LIIVALAIA

TULIKA

TALLINN

Tram #3, 4

SÖPRUSE PST

RÄSTA

KANNU

VALGE VILLA

RAAGU

PÄRNU MNT

The post-communist chapter has been a success story. Since independence in 1991, Tallinn has westernized at an astounding rate. The Old Town has been scrubbed into a pristine Old World theme park—a fascinating package of pleasing towers, ramparts, facades, *striptiis* bars, churches, shops, and people-watching. Meanwhile, the nearby Rotermann Quarter is a Petri dish of architectural experimentation. Cruise ships have discovered Tallinn, and cruisers mob its cobbles at midday. Given its compact scale, Tallinn can be

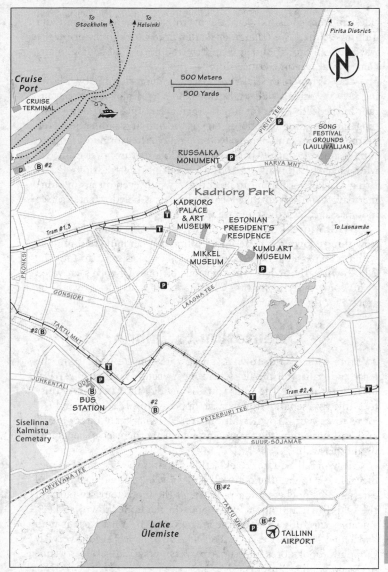

easily appreciated as a side-trip (from Helsinki, or from a cruise ship). But the city rewards those who spend the night. More time gives you the chance to explore some of the more colorful slices of life outside the Old Town walls.

PLANNING YOUR TIME

On a three-week tour of Scandinavia and the Baltic, Tallinn is certainly worth a day. Most people find it works best as a full-day side-trip from Helsinki. Or take overnights in both Helsinki and Tallinn—either as a triangular detour from Stockholm, or on the way between Stockholm and St. Petersburg. And, of course, many come to Tallinn on a cruise ship.

Day-Trippers or Cruisers: Hit the ground running by following my self-guided walk right from the port. Enjoy a nice restaurant in the Old Town for lunch. Then spend the afternoon shopping and browsing (or choose one of the outlying sights: Seaplane Harbor for boats and planes, Rotermann Quarter for new architecture, Estonian Open-Air Museum for folk culture, or Kumu Art Museum for Estonian art and a walk in nearby Kadriorg Park). Bring a jacket—Tallinn can be chilly or windy even on sunny summer days. And, given that locals call their cobbled streets "a free foot massage," sturdy shoes are smart, too.

With More Time: Start off with the self-guided walk, but slow things down a bit. Because Tallinn can be inundated midday with cruise passengers and day-trippers, it makes sense to tour the Old Town early or late, then get out of town when it's crowded to hit some outlying sights. Check concert schedules if you'll be around for the evening.

Orientation to Tallinn

Tallinn's walled Old Town is an easy 15-minute walk from the ferry and cruise terminals, where most visitors land (see "Arrival in Tallinn," later). The Old Town is divided into two parts (historically, two separate towns): the upper town (Toompea) and the lower town (with Town Hall Square). A remarkably intact medieval wall surrounds the two towns, which are themselves separated by another wall.

Town Hall Square (Raekoja Plats) marks the heart of the medieval lower town. The main TI is nearby, as are many sights and eateries. Pickpockets are a problem in the more touristy parts of the Old Town and at the viewpoints in the upper town, so keep valuables carefully stowed. The area around the Viru Keskus mall and Hotel Viru, just east of the Old Town, is useful for everyday shopping (bookstores and supermarkets), practical services (laundry), and public transport.

TOURIST INFORMATION

The hardworking and helpful TI is just a block off Town Hall Square (Mon-Fri 9:00-19:00, Sat-Sun until 17:00—stays open an hour later mid-June-Aug and closes an hour earlier Sept-April; Niguliste 2, tel. 645-7777, www.visittallinn.ee).

Tallinn Card: This card—sold at the TIs, airport, train station, travel agencies, ferry ports, and big hotels—gives you free use of public transport and entry to more than 40 museums and major sights (€25/24 hours, €37/48 hours, €45/72 hours, www.tallinncard.ee). A more expensive "Plus" version includes a hop-on, hop-off bus route.

ARRIVAL IN TALLINN

For advice on taking taxis, and more details on the public transportation and ticket options mentioned below, see "Getting Around Tallinn," later.

By Boat or Cruise Ship: Tallinn has three passenger/car-ferry terminals, A/B and D, a fourth one called Linnahall (used only by the fast Linda Line boat), and a dedicated cruise terminal. The side-by-side A/B Terminals are the closest to the Old Town; the cruise terminal is just to the north; D-Terminal is a 10-minute walk to the east (and the farthest from Old Town); the Linnahall Terminal is a 10-minute walk to the west. Each terminal offers baggage storage. Be sure to confirm which terminal your return boat will use.

If you have no luggage, you can **walk** 15 minutes to reach the center of town—just follow signs to the city center and set your

sights on the tallest spire in the distance (or follow my self-guided walk, later). (If you'd rather first visit the Seaplane Harbor, described on page 663, look for a red-gravel path—straight ahead as you leave the cruise port, marked *Kultuurikilomeeter*—which takes you there on a long, scenic, mostly seaside stroll.)

If you have bags, it's best to grab a **taxi**—otherwise your rolling suitcase will take a pounding on the Old Town's cobbled streets. The legitimate taxi fare to anywhere in or near the Old Town should be less than €10; before getting in a cab, ask for an estimate of the fare to weed out unscrupulous cabbies who might try to charge double or triple.

To get into town by bus, you have several options: Public **bus #2** goes from A-Terminal and D-Terminal directly to the A. Laikmaa stop just south of the Old Town—behind Hotel Viru and the Viru Keskus mall—then continues to the airport (2/hour, buy Üh-iskaart smartcard from R-Kiosk shops in terminals, or pay €2 for a ticket on board—cash only, exact change). Cruise lines sometimes offer a shuttle bus into town (to a spot near Hotel Viru), but—since it's so easy to walk into town—this isn't worth paying for.

By Plane: The convenient Tallinn airport (Tallinna Lennu-jaam), just three miles southeast of downtown, has a small info desk (airport code: TLL, www.tallinn-airport.ee, tel. 605-8888). A **taxi** to the Old Town should cost €8-10. Public **bus #2** runs about every 20 minutes from the lower entrance (floor 0) into town; the seventh stop, A. Laikmaa, is behind the Viru Keskus mall, a short walk from the Old Town (buy Ühiskaart smartcard from R-Kiosk store in terminal—or pay €2 for a single ticket on board; to reach the bus stop, follow bus signs down the escalator, go outside, and look left).

By Train and Bus: While Tallinn has a sleepy and cute little train station (called Balti Jaam), few tourists will need to use it. The station, a five-minute walk across a busy road from the Old Town (use the pedestrian underpass), is adjacent to the big, cheap Go Hotel Shnelli and the colorful Balti Jaam Market. Tallinn's long-distance bus station *(autobussijaam)* is midway between downtown and the airport, and served by bus #2 and trams #2 and #4.

HELPFUL HINTS

Money: Estonia uses the euro. You'll find ATMs (sometimes marked *Otto*) at locations around Tallinn.

Time: Estonia is one hour ahead of continental Europe, which means it's generally seven/ten hours ahead of the East/West Coasts of the US.

Telephones: In case of a medical emergency, dial 112. For police, dial 110. Most Estonian phone numbers are seven to eight digits with no area codes. Tallinn numbers begin with 6, and mobile phones (more expensive to call) begin with 5. (For more on dialing, see page 720.)

Wi-Fi: Public Wi-Fi is easy to find around Tallinn; look for the free "Tallinn WiFi" network.

Laundry: The Viru Keskus mall has a handy **Top Clean** laundry drop-off service downstairs (Mon-Fri 8:00-20:00, Sat from 10:00, closed Sun; underground facing bus stalls 1 and 2, tel. 610-1405, www.puhastuskeskus.ee). Otherwise, **Pesumaja Sol** offers self- or full-service; it's just beyond the Viru Keskus mall and Kaubamaja department store (just walkable from the Old Town, or take tram #2 or #4 to the Paberi stop, a few blocks away; Mon-Fri 7:00-20:00, Sat 8:00-16:00, closed Sun, Maakri 23, tel. 677-1551).

Travel Agency: Estravel, at the corner of Suur-Karja and Müürivähe, is handy and sells boat tickets for no extra fee (Mon-Fri 9:00-18:00, closed Sat-Sun, Suur-Karja 15, tel. 626-6233, www.estravel.ee).

Bike Rental: Head for **City Bike,** at the north end of the Old Town (€12/6 hours, €15/24 hours; electric bikes available; daily 10:00-18:00, Vene 33, mobile 511-1819, www.citybike.ee). They also do bike tours (see "Tours in Tallinn," later).

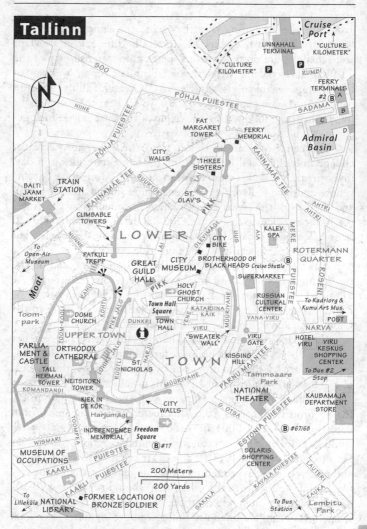

Parking: The Port of Tallinn has a cheap lot by D-Terminal (€6/day, www.portoftallinn.com). Old Town parking is very expensive; try parking in the lot underneath Freedom Square (Vabaduse väljak), at the southern edge of the Old Town, a short walk from the TI and Town Hall Square (€4/hour).

GETTING AROUND TALLINN

By Public Transportation: The Old Town and surrounding areas can be explored on foot, but use public transit to reach outlying sights (such as Kadriorg Park, Kumu Art Museum, or the Estonian Open-Air Museum). Tallinn has buses, trams, and trolley buses—

avoid mistakes by noting that they reuse the same numbers (bus #2, tram #2, and trolley bus #2 are totally different lines). Maps and schedules are posted at stops, or pick up a transit map at the TI (map also available at www.visittallinn.ee); for an overview of transit stops useful to visitors, see the "Greater Tallinn" map on page 636). As you approach a station, you'll hear the name of the impending stop, followed by the name of the next stop—don't get confused and hop off one stop too early.

You can buy a **single ticket** from the driver for €2 (exact change only). If you'll be taking more than three rides in a day, invest in an **Ühiskaart smartcard.** You can buy one for €2 at any yellow-and-blue R-Kiosk convenience store (found all over town), and then load it up with credit, which is deducted as you travel (€1.10 for any ride up to 1 hour, €3/24 hours, €5/72 hours, €6/120 hours). The card is shareable by multiple people for single rides, but you'll need separate cards for the multiride options.

Bus #2 (Moigu-Reisisadam) is helpful on arrival and departure, running every 20-30 minutes between the ferry port's A-Terminal and the airport. En route it stops at D-Terminal; at A. Laikmaa, next to the Viru Keskus mall (a short walk south of the Old Town); and at the long-distance bus station.

By Taxi: Taxis in Tallinn are handy, but because rates are not uniform, always confirm a ballpark fare before getting in. The safest way to catch a cab is to order one by phone (or ask a trusted local to call for you)—this is what Estonians usually do.

Tulika is the largest company, with predictable, fair prices (€3.85 drop charge plus €0.69/kilometer, €0.80/kilometer from 23:00-6:00, tel. 612-0001 or 1200, check latest prices at www.tulika.ee). **Tallink Takso** is another reputable option with similar fares (tel. 640-8921 or 1921). Cabbies are required to use the meter and give you a meter-printed receipt. Longer rides around the city (e.g., from the airport to the Old Town) should run around €8-10.

If you must catch a taxi off the street, go to a busy taxi stand where lots of cabs are lined up. Before you get in, take a close look at the yellow price list on the rear passenger-side door; the base fare should be no more than €5.50 and the per-kilometer charge no more than €1.10. If it's not, keep looking. Glance inside—a photo ID license should be attached to the middle of the dashboard. Rates must be posted by law, but are not capped or regulated, so the most common scam—unfortunately widespread and legal—is to list an inflated price on the yellow price sticker, and simply wait for a tourist to hop in without noticing. Singleton cabs lurking in tourist areas are usually fishing for suckers, as are cabbies who flag you down ("Taxi?")—give them a miss.

Tallinn at a Glance

Central Tallinn

▲▲▲**Tallinn's Old Town** Well-preserved medieval center with cobblestoned lanes, gabled houses, historic churches, and turreted city walls. See page 645.

▲▲**Russian Orthodox Cathedral** Accessible look at the Russian Orthodox faith, with a lavish interior. **Hours:** Daily 8:00-19:00, icon art in gift shop. See page 652.

▲**Tallinn City Museum** Interesting overview of Tallinn's past, from medieval times into the 20th century. **Hours:** Tue-Sun 10:30-18:00, closes earlier off-season, closed Mon year-round. See page 657.

▲**Museum of Estonian History** High-tech exhibits explain Estonia's engaging national narrative. **Hours:** May-Aug daily 10:00-18:00, same hours off-season except closed Wed. See page 656.

Outside of the Core

▲▲**Kumu Art Museum** The best of contemporary Estonian art displayed in a strikingly modern building. **Hours:** May-Sept Tue-Sun 11:00-18:00, Wed until 20:00, closed Mon; same hours off-season except closed Mon-Tue. See page 661.

▲▲**Seaplane Harbor** Impressive museum of boats and planes—including a WWII-era submarine—displayed in a cavernous old hangar along the waterfront. **Hours:** May-Sept daily 10:00-19:00; closes an hour earlier in off-season and closed Mon. See page 663.

▲**Kadriorg Park** Vast, strollable oasis with the palace gardens, Kumu Art Museum, and a palace built by Czar Peter the Great. See page 660.

▲**Estonian Open-Air Museum** Authentic farm and village buildings preserved in a forested parkland. **Hours:** Late April-Sept—park open daily 10:00-20:00, buildings open until 18:00; Oct-late April—park open daily 10:00-17:00 but many buildings closed. See page 666.

Tours in Tallinn

Bus and Walking Tour

This enjoyable, narrated 2.5-hour tour of Tallinn comes in two parts: first by bus for an overview of sights outside the Old Town, such as the Song Festival Grounds and Kadriorg Park, then on foot to sights within the Old Town (€30, pay driver, covered by Tallinn Card, in English; daily morning and early afternoon departures from ferry terminals and major hotels in city center; tel. 610-8616, www.traveltoestonia.com).

Local Guides

Mati Rumessen is a top-notch guide, especially for car tours inside or outside town (€35/hour driving or walking tours, price may vary with group size and length of tour, mobile 509-4661, www.tourservice.ee, matirumessen@gmail.com). Other fine guides are **Antonio Villacis** (rates negotiable, mobile 5662-9306, antonio.villacis@gmail.com) and **Miina Puusepp** (€20/hour, mobile 551-7028, miinapaul@gmail.com).

Tallinn Traveller Tours

These student-run tours show you the real city without the political and corporate correctness of official tourist agencies. Check www.traveller.ee to confirm details for their ever-changing lineup, and to reserve (or call mobile 5837-4800). They typically offer a two-hour **Old Town Walking Tour** and a **ghost walk** (each €15) and a **food tour** (€20), as well as **bike tours** and **minibus excursions** that get you into the Estonian countryside. All tours start from in front of the main TI.

Hop-On, Hop-Off Bus Tours

Tallinn City Tour offers three different one-hour bus tours—you can take all three (on the same day) for one price. Aside from a stop near Toompea Castle, the routes are entirely outside the Old Town, and the frequency is low (about every 60 minutes). But the tours do get you to outlying sights such as Kadriorg Park and the towering Russalka Monument. You can catch the bus at the port terminals and at Viru Square, near the Viru Turg clothing market (€21/24 hours, free with Tallinn Card, tel. 627-9080, www.citytour.ee). **CitySightseeing Tallinn** also runs three similar routes, with a similarly sparse frequency (€20 for all three lines, www.citysightseeing.ee).

City Bike Tours

City Bike offers a two-hour, nine-mile **Welcome to Tallinn** bike tour that takes you outside the city walls to Tallinn's more distant sights: Kadriorg Park, Song Festival Grounds, the beach at Pirita, and more (€19, 50 percent discount with Tallinn Card, daily at 11:00 year-round, departs from their office at Vene 33 in the Old Town). They can also arrange multiday, self-guided bike tours around Estonia (mobile 511-1819, www.citybike.ee).

Tallinn Walk

This self-guided walk, worth ▲▲▲, explores the "two towns" of Tallinn. The city once consisted of two feuding medieval towns separated by a wall. The upper town—on the hill, called Toompea—was the seat of government for Estonia. The lower town was an autonomous Hanseatic trading center filled with German, Danish, and Swedish merchants who hired Estonians to do their menial labor. Many of the Old Town's buildings are truly old, dating from the boom times of the 15th and 16th centuries. Decrepit before the 1991 fall of the Soviet Union, the Old Town has been entirely revitalized.

Two steep, narrow streets—the "Long Leg" and the "Short Leg"—connect the upper and the lower towns. This two-part walk goes up the short leg and down the long leg. Allow about two hours for the entire walk (not counting time to enter museums along the way).

PART 1: THE LOWER TOWN

• *The walk starts at Fat Margaret Tower—easy to reach from the port—where cruise ships and ferries from Helsinki arrive (just hike toward the tall tapering spire, go through a small park, and enter the Old Town through the archway by the squat Fat Margaret Tower. If you're coming*

from elsewhere in Tallinn, take tram #1 or #2 to the Linnahall stop, or just walk out to the Fat Margaret Tower from anywhere in the Old Town.

❶ Fat Margaret Tower

Fat Margaret Tower (Paks Margareeta) guarded the entry gate of the town in medieval times (the sea once came much closer than it does today). Besides being a defensive outpost, the tower was made big just to impress anyone (like you) coming to town from the harbor. The relief above the gate dates from the 16th century, during Hanseatic times, when Sweden took Estonia from the German Teutonic Knights. The origin of the tower's name is a bit of a mystery. Some say it was named for a huge cannon, but others think a cook called Margaret worked in the tower long ago.

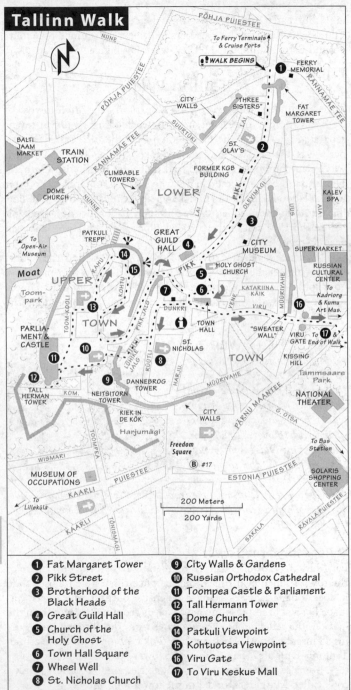

Tallinn Walk

N

PÕHJA PUIESTEE

To Ferry Terminals & Cruise Ports

🚩 **WALK BEGINS**

① FERRY MEMORIAL

NIINE

PÕHJA PUIESTEE

CITY WALLS

"THREE SISTERS"

FAT MARGARET TOWER

RANNAMÄE TEE

SUURTÜKI

ST. OLAV'S

②

BALTI JAAM MARKET

TRAIN STATION

RANNAMÄE TEE

CLIMBABLE TOWERS

FORMER KGB BUILDING

PIKK

OLEVIMÄGI

LAI

③

KALEV SPA

DOME CHURCH

NUNNE

LOWER

CITY MUSEUM

UUS

AIA

SUPERMARKET

To Open-Air Museum

PATKULI TREPP

GREAT GUILD HALL

④

PIKK

⑤ HOLY GHOST CHURCH

RUSSIAN CULTURAL CENTER

Moat

Toom-park

UPPER

RAHU

KOHTU

⑭

⑮

PIKK JALG

⑦

⑥

DUNKRI

KATARIINA KÄIK

MÜÜRIVAHE

YENE

VIRU

⑯

To Kadriorg & Kumu Art Mus.

TOOM-KOOLI

⑬

TOWN

TOWN HALL

ℹ

"SWEATER WALL"

VIRU & GATE

⑰ End of Walk

PARLIA-MENT & CASTLE

⑩

LÜHIKE JALG

KÜÜTI

ST. NICHOLAS

⑧

HARJU

TOWN

KISSING HILL

⑪

⑫

TALL HERMAN TOWER

KOM.

⑨

TOOMPEA

DANNEBROG TOWER

NEITSITORN TOWER

KIEK IN DE KÖK

Harjumägi

CITY WALLS

MÜÜRIVAHE

Tammsaare Park

NATIONAL THEATER

To Bus Station

WISMARI

Freedom Square

🅱 #17

PÄRNU MAANTEE

G. OTSA

MUSEUM OF OCCUPATIONS

PUIESTEE

ESTONIA PUIESTEE

SOLARIS SHOPPING CENTER

KAARLI

To Lilleküla

200 Meters

200 Yards

KAARLI

TÕNISMÄGI

SAKALA

RÄVALA PUIESTEE

TALLINN

① Fat Margaret Tower	⑨ City Walls & Gardens
② Pikk Street	⑩ Russian Orthodox Cathedral
③ Brotherhood of the Black Heads	⑪ Toompea Castle & Parliament
④ Great Guild Hall	⑫ Tall Hermann Tower
⑤ Church of the Holy Ghost	⑬ Dome Church
⑥ Town Hall Square	⑭ Patkuli Viewpoint
⑦ Wheel Well	⑮ Kohtuotsa Viewpoint
⑧ St. Nicholas Church	⑯ Viru Gate
	⑰ To Viru Keskus Mall

• *Once through the gate, head up Tallinn's main drag...*

❷ Pikk Street

Literally "Long Street," the medieval merchants' main drag leads from the harbor up into town. It's lined with interesting and historic buildings. Many were ware-houses, complete with cranes on the gables. Strolling here, you'll feel the economic power of those early German trading days.

One short block up the street on the right, the buildings nick-named **"Three Sisters"** (now a hotel/restaurant) are textbook examples of a merchant home/ware-house/office from the 15th-century Hanseatic Golden Age. The elabo-rately carved door near the corner evokes the wealth of Tallinn's mer-chant class—such detailed decoration would have come with a high price tag.

After another, longer block, you'll pass the Gothic **St. Olav's Church** (Oleviste Kirik, a Baptist church today), notable for what

was once the tallest spire in the land. That high spire helped approaching ships set their course—but it was also an effective lightning rod. Unfortunately, lightning strikes caused the church to burn to the ground three times.

If the name didn't tip you off that this was once a Lutheran church, then the stark, whitewashed interior guarantees it. Climbing 234 stairs up the tower rewards you with a great view. You can enter both the church and the tower around the back side (church-free entry, daily 10:00-18:00, July-Aug until 20:00; tower-€3, open April-Oct only).

While tourists see only a peaceful scene today, older locals strolling this street are reminded of dark times under Moscow's rule. The KGB used the tower at St. Olav's Church to block Finnish TV signals. The once-handsome building at **Pikk #59** (the second house after the church, on the right) was, before 1991, the sinister local headquarters of the KGB. "Creative interrogation methods" were used here. Locals well knew that the road of suffering started here, as Tallinn's troublemakers were sent to Siberian gulags. The ministry building was called the "tallest" building in town (because "when you're in the basement, you can already see Siberia"). Notice the bricked-up windows at foot level and the commemorative plaque (in Estonian only).

• *A few short blocks farther up Pikk (after the small park), on the left at #26, is the extremely ornate doorway of the...*

❸ Brotherhood of the Black Heads

Built in 1440, this house was used as a German merchants' club for nearly 500 years (until Hitler invited Estonian Germans back to their historical fatherland in the 1930s).

Before the 19th century, many Estonians lived as serfs on the rural estates of the German nobles who dominated the economy. In Tallinn, the German big shots were part of the Great Guild (which we'll see farther up the street), while the German little shots had to make do with the Brotherhood of the Black Heads. This guild, or business fraternity, was limited to single German men. In Hanseatic towns, when a fire or battle had to be fought, bachelors were deployed first, because they had no family. Because single men were considered unattached to the community, they had no opportunity for power in the Hanseatic social structure. When a Black Head member married a local woman, he automatically gained a vested interest in the town's economy and well-being. He could then join the more prestigious Great Guild, and with that status, a promising economic and political future often opened up.

Today the hall is a concert venue (and, while you can pay to tour its interior, I'd skip it—it's basically an empty shell). Its namesake "black head" is that of St. Maurice, an early Christian soldier-martyr, beheaded in the third century A.D. for his refusal to honor the Roman gods. Reliefs decorating the building recall Tallinn's Hanseatic glory days.

Keep going along Pikk street. Architecture fans enjoy several **fanciful facades** along here, including the boldly Art Nouveau #18 (on the left, reminiscent of the architectural bounty of fellow Baltic capital Rīga; appropriately enough, today this building houses one of Tallinn's leading-edge architectural firms) and the colorful, eclectic building across the street (with the pointy gable).

On the left, at #16, the famous and recommended **Maiasmokk** ("Sweet Tooth") coffee shop, in business since 1864, remains a fine spot for a coffee-and-pastry break.

• *Just ahead, pause at the big yellow building on the right (at #17).*

❹ Great Guild Hall (Suurgildi Hoone)

With its wide (and therefore highly taxed) front, the Great Guild Hall was the epitome of wealth. Remember, this was the home of the most prestigious of Tallinn's Hanseatic-era guilds. Today it houses the worthwhile **Museum of Estonian History,** offering a concise and engaging survey of this country's story (for details, see "Sights in Tallinn," later).

• *Across Pikk street from the Great Guild Hall is the...*

❺ Church of the Holy Ghost (Pühavaimu Kirik)

Sporting an outdoor clock from 1633, this pretty medieval church is worth a visit. (The plaque on the wall just behind the ticket desk is in Estonian and Russian, but not English; this dates from before 1991, when things were designed for "inner tourism"—within the USSR.) The church retains its 14th-century design. Sometimes flying from the back pillar, the old flag of Tallinn—the same as today's red-and-white Danish flag—recalls 13th-century Danish rule. (The name "Tallinn" means "Danish Town.") The Danes sold Tallinn to the German Teutonic Knights, who lost it to the Swedes, who lost it to the Russians. The windows are mostly from the 1990s (€1.50, Mon-Sat 9:00-18:00, closes earlier in winter, closed most of Sun to nonworshippers, Pühavaimu 2, tel. 646-4430, www.eelk.ee). The church hosts English-language Lutheran services Sundays at 13:00 (maybe earlier in summer).

• *If you were to go down the street to the left as you face the church, it's a three-minute walk to the **Tallinn City Museum** (described later, under "Sights in Tallinn").*

Leading alongside the church, tiny Saiakang lane (meaning "White Bread"—bread, cakes, and pies were long sold here) takes you to...

❻ Town Hall Square (Raekoja Plats)

A marketplace through the centuries, with a cancan of fine old buildings, this is the focal point of the Old Town. The square was the center of the autonomous lower town, a merchant city of Hanseatic traders. Once, it held criminals chained to pillories for public humiliation and knights showing off in chivalrous tournaments; today it's full of Scandinavians and Russians savoring cheap beer, children singing on the bandstand, and cruise-ship groups following the numbered paddles carried high by their well-scrubbed local guides.

At the passageway where you've entered the square, look left to find the **pharmacy** (Raeapteek) dating from 1422 and claiming to be Europe's oldest. With decor that goes back to medieval times, the still-operating pharmacy welcomes visitors with painted ceiling beams, English descriptions, and long-expired aspirin. Past the functioning counter is a room of display cases with historical exhibits (free entry, Mon-Sat 10:00-18:00, closed Sun).

The 15th-century **Town Hall** (Raekoda) dominates the square; it's open to visitors in the summer months, and climbing its tower earns you a commanding view (for details, see page 657).

Town Hall Square is ringed by inviting but touristy eateries. The TI is a block away (behind Town Hall).

• *Facing the Town Hall, head right up Dunkri street—lined with several more eateries—one long block to the ❼ wheel well, named for the "high-tech" wheel, a marvel that made fetching water easier.*

Turn left on Rataskaevu street (which soon becomes Rüütli) and walk two short blocks to...

❽ St. Nicholas Church (Niguliste Kirik)

This 13th-century Gothic church-turned-art-museum served the German merchants and knights who lived in this neighborhood 500

years ago. On March 9, 1944, while Tallinn was in German hands, Soviet forces bombed the city, and the church and surrounding area—once a charming district, dense with medieval buildings—were burned out; only the church was rebuilt.

The church's interior houses a fine collection of mostly Gothic-era ecclesiastical art (€6, Tue-Sun 10:00-17:00, closed Mon year-round—and Tue off-season; organ or choir concerts held most weekends).

You'll enter the church through the modern cellar, where you can see photos of the WWII destruction of the building (with its toppled steeple). Then make your way into the vast, open church

TALLINN

interior. Front and center is the collection's highlight: a retable (framed altarpiece) from 1481, by Herman Rode—an exquisite example of the northern Germanic late-Gothic style. Along with scenes from the life of St. Nicholas and an array of other saints, the altarpiece shows the skyline of Lübeck, Germany (Rode's hometown, and—like Tallinn—a Hanseatic trading city). The intricate symbolism is explained by a nearby touchscreen. Also look for another work by a Lübeck master, Bernt Notke's *Danse Macabre* ("Dance of Death"). Once nearly 100 feet long, the surviving fragment shows sinister skeletons approaching people from all walks of life. This common medieval theme reminds the viewer that life is fleeting, and no matter who we are, we'll all wind up in the same place.

• *As you face the church, if you were to turn left and walk downhill on Rüütli street, you'd soon pass near* **Freedom Square**—*for a taste of modern Tallinn (described on page 657).*

But for now, let's continue our walk into the upper town.

PART 2: THE UPPER TOWN (TOOMPEA)

• *At the corner opposite the church, climb uphill along the steep, cobbled, Lühike Jalg ("Short Leg Lane"), home to a few quality craft shops. At the top of the lane, pause at the arched gateway at #9. Notice the stone tower steps leading to the arched passage and a big oak door. This is one of two gates through the wall separating the two cities. This passage is still the ritual meeting point of the mayor and prime minister whenever there is an important agreement between town and country.*

Now continue through the main gateway and climb up until you emerge into a beautiful view terrace in front of the...

❾ City Walls and Gardens

This view terrace is known as the Danish King's Garden for the ruler who gave the land to the lower town in 1311. Tallinn is famous among Danes as the birthplace of their flag. According to legend, the Danes were losing a battle here, when suddenly, a white cross fell from heaven and landed in a pool of blood. The Danes were inspired and went on to win, and to this day, their flag is a white cross on a red background.

Once you pass through the opening in the wall (to the right), you've officially crossed from the lower to upper town. The imposing city wall once had 46 towers, of which 26 still stand. If you have interest and energy, you can climb some of the towers and ramparts (although we'll be reaching some dramatic viewpoints—overlooking different parts of town—later on this walk).

The easiest ascent is to simply scramble up the extremely steep and tight steps of the nearby **Dannebrog restaurant tower**—but you'll need to order an expensive drink to stay and enjoy the view.

To reach a higher vantage point you can pay €3 to enter the **Neitsitorn (Maiden) Tower** (at the far end of the garden terrace). It has a few skippable exhibits, an overpriced café, and great views—particularly from the top floor, where a full glass wall reveals a panoramic townscape (open Tue-Sat 11:00-18:00, closed Sun-Mon, shorter hours Oct-April).

For a genuine tower climb, though, cross into the upper town and follow the gravel path to the left to the **Kiek in de Kök.** This stout, round tower sits farther along the wall (with extremely tight, twisty, steep stone staircases inside). The fun-to-say name "Kiek in de Kök" is Low German for "Peek in the Kitchen"—so-called because the tower is situated to allow guards to literally peek into townspeople's homes. This tower is bigger than the Neitsitorn Tower, with more impressive exhibits—not a lot of real artifacts, but plenty of cannons, mannequins, model ships, movies, and models of the castle to give you a taste of Tallinn's medieval heyday (€6; extra for tour of tunnels below the tower).

• *When you're finished with the towers and ramparts, head uphill into the upper town to the big, onion-domed church, circling around to the far side (facing the pink palace) to find the entrance.*

❿ Russian Orthodox Cathedral

The Alexander Nevsky Cathedral—worth ▲▲—is a gorgeous building. But ever since the day it was built (in 1900), it has been a jab in the eye for Estonians. The church went up near the end of the two centuries when Estonia was part of the Russian Empire. And, as throughout Europe in the late 19th century, Tallinn's oppressed ethnic groups—the Estonians and the Germans—were caught up in national revival movements, celebrating their own culture, language, and history rather than their Russian overlords'.

So the Russians flexed their cultural muscle by building this church in this location, facing the traditional Estonian seat of power, and over the supposed grave of a legendary Estonian hero, Kalevipoeg. They also tore down a statue of Martin Luther to make room.

The church has been exquisitely renovated inside and out. Step inside for a sample of Russian Orthodoxy (church free and open daily 8:00-19:00, icon art in gift shop). It's OK to visit discreetly during services (daily at 9:00 and 18:00), when you'll hear priests singing the liturgy in a side chapel. Typical of Russian Orthodox churches, it has glittering icons (the highest concentration fills the big screen—called an iconostasis—that shields the altar from the congregation), no pews (worshippers stand through the service), and air that's heavy with incense. All of these features combine to create a mystical, otherworldly worship experience. Notice the many candles, each representing a prayer; if there's a request or a thank you in your heart, you're welcome to buy one at the desk by the door. Exploring this space, keep in mind that about 40 percent of Tallinn's population is ethnic Russian.

• *Across the street is the...*

⑪ Toompea Castle (Toompea Loss)

The pink palace is an 18th-century Russian addition onto the medieval Toompea Castle. Today, it's the Estonian Parliament (Riigigoku) building, flying the Estonian flag—the flag of both the first (1918-1940) and second (1991-present) Estonian republics. Notice the Estonian seal: three lions for three great battles in Estonian history, and oak leaves for strength and stubbornness. Ancient pagan Estonians, who believed spirits lived in oak trees, would walk through forests of oak to toughen up. (To this day, Estonian cemeteries are in forests. Keeping some of their pagan sensibilities, they believe the spirits of the departed live on in the trees.)

• *Facing the palace, go left through the gate into the park to see the...*

⑫ Tall Hermann Tower (Pikk Hermann)

This tallest tower of the castle wall is a powerful symbol here. For 50 years, while Estonian flags were hidden in cellars, the Soviet flag flew from Tall Hermann. As the USSR was unraveling, Estonians proudly and defiantly replaced the red Soviet flag here with their own black, white, and blue flag.

• *Backtrack to the square in front of the palace, passing the Russian church on your right. Climb Toom-Kooli street to the...*

⑬ Dome Church (Toomkirik)

Estonia is ostensibly Lutheran, but few Tallinners go to church. A recent Gallup Poll showed Estonia to be the least religious country in the European Union—only 14 percent of respondents identified religion as an important part of their daily lives. Most churches double as concert venues or museums, but this one is still used for worship. Officially St. Mary's Church—but popularly called the Dome Church—it's a perfect example of simple Northern European Gothic, built in the 13th century during Danish rule, then rebuilt after a 1684 fire. Once the church of Tallinn's wealthy German-speaking aristocracy, it's littered with more than a hundred coats of arms, carved by local masters as memorials to the deceased and inscribed with German tributes. The earliest dates from the 1600s, the latest from around 1900. For €5, you can climb 140 steps up the tower to enjoy the view (church entry free, daily 9:00-18:00, organ recitals Sat at 12:00, www.eelk.ee/tallinna.toom).

• *Leaving the church, turn left and hook around the back of the building. You'll pass the big, green, former noblemen's clubhouse on your right (at #1, vacated when many Germans left Estonia in the 1930s). Head down cobbled Rahukohtu lane (to the right of the yellow house with a peaked roof). Strolling the street, notice the embassy signs: Government offices and embassies have moved into these buildings and spruced up the neighborhood. Continue straight under the arch and belly up to the grand...*

⓮ Patkuli Viewpoint

Survey the scene. On the far left, the Neoclassical facade of the executive branch of Estonia's government overlooks a grand view.

Below you, a bit of the old moat remains. The *Group* sign marks Tallinn's tiny train station, and the clutter of stalls behind that is the rustic market. Out on the water, ferries shuttle to and from Helsinki (just 50 miles away). Beyond the lower town's medieval wall and towers stands the green spire of St. Olav's Church, once 98 feet taller and, locals claim, the world's tallest tower in 1492. Far in the distance is the 1,000-foot-tall TV tower, the site of a standoff between Soviet paratroopers and Estonian patriots in 1991 (see page 664).

During Soviet domination, Finnish TV was even more important, as it gave Estonians their only look at Western lifestyles. Imagine: In the 1980s, many locals had never seen a banana or a pineapple—except on TV. People still talk of the day that Finland broadcast the soft-porn movie *Emmanuelle*. A historic migration of Estonians purportedly flocked from the countryside to Tallinn to get within rabbit-ear's distance of Helsinki and see all that flesh onscreen. The refurbished TV tower is now open to visitors.

• Go back through the arch, turn immediately left down the narrow lane, turn right (onto Toom–Rüütli), take the first left, and pass through the trees to the...

⓯ Kohtuotsa Viewpoint

Scan the view from left to right. On the far left is St. Olav's Church, then the busy cruise port and the skinny white spire of the Church

of the Holy Ghost. The narrow gray spire farther to the right is the 16th-century Town Hall tower. On the far right is the tower of St. Nicholas Church. Below you, visually trace Pikk street, Tallinn's historic main drag, which winds through the Old Town, leading from Toompea Castle down the hill (from right to left), through the gate tower, past the Church of the Holy Ghost, behind St. Olav's, and out to the harbor. Less picturesque is the clutter of Soviet-era apartment blocks on the distant horizon, but these days they're being crowded out by modern high-rises. The nearest skyscraper (white) is Hotel Viru, in Soviet times the biggest hotel in the Baltics, and infamous as a clunky, dingy slumbermill. Locals joke that Hotel Viru was built from a new Soviet wonder material called "micro-concrete" (60 percent concrete, 40 percent microphones). Underneath the hotel is the modern Viru Keskus, a huge shopping mall and local transit center. To the left of Hotel Viru, between it and the ferry terminals, is the Rotermann Quarter, where old industrial buildings are being revamped into a new commercial zone.

• From the viewpoint, descend to the lower town. Go out and left down Kohtu, past the Finnish Embassy (on your left). Back at the Dome Church, turn left down Piiskopi ("Bishop's Street"). At the onion domes, turn left again and follow the old wall down Pikk Jalg ("Long Leg Lane") into the lower town (you'll pass a good handcrafts shop on the way). Go under the tower, then straight on

Pikk street, and after two doors turn right on Voorimehe, which leads into Town Hall Square.

⑯ Through Viru Gate

Cross through the square (left of the Town Hall's tower) and go downhill (passing the kitschy medieval Olde Hansa Restaurant, with its bonneted waitresses and merry men). Continue straight down Viru street toward Hotel Viru, the blocky white skyscraper in the distance. Viru street is old Tallinn's busiest and most touristy shopping street. Just past the strange and modern wood/glass/stone mall, Müürivahe street leads left along the old wall, called the "Sweater Wall." This is a colorful and tempting gauntlet of vendors selling knitwear (most is machine-made). Leading left, beyond the sweaters, the picturesque Katariina Käik is a lane with glassblowing, weaving, and pottery shops. Back on Viru street, pass the golden arches and walk through the medieval arches—Viru Gate—that mark the end of old Tallinn. Outside the gates, opposite Viru 23, above the flower stalls, is a small park on a piece of old bastion known as the Kissing Hill (come up here after dark and you'll find out why).

• *Our walk is done. If you want to find the real world, use the crosswalk to your right to reach the* **Viru Keskus Mall***, with its basement supermarket, ticket service, bookstore, and many bus and tram stops. If you still have energy, you can cross the busy street by the complex and explore the nearby Rotermann Quarter (see page 659).*

Sights in Tallinn

IN OR NEAR THE OLD TOWN

Central Tallinn has dozens of small museums, most suitable only for specialized tastes. The following are the ones I'd visit first.

▲Museum of Estonian History (Eesti Ajaloomuuseum)

The Great Guild Hall on Pikk street houses this museum with its modern, well-presented exhibits. The museum's "Estonia 101" approach—combining actual artifacts (from prehistory to today) and high-tech interactive exhibits—is geared toward educating first-time visitors about this obscure but endearing little country.

Cost and Hours: €6, daily 10:00-18:00, closed Wed off-season, tel. 696-8690, www.ajaloomuuseum.ee.

Visiting the Museum: The main event here displayed under the whitewashed vaults is the "Spirit of Survival" exhibit. It condenses 11,000 years of Estonian history with relative ease, while focusing on what it means to be an Estonian (Where did Estonians come from? What are their traditions?)—and outlining the important historical events that have shaped the Estonian cultural psyche (German crusaders, Danish domination, Reformation, multiple wars with Sweden, Russian occupation—to name a few). Steep steps lead down into the cellar, with an armory, ethnographic collection, items owned by historical figures, an exhibit about the Great Guild Hall itself, and a fun "time capsule" that lets you insert your face into videos illustrating episodes in local history.

Town Hall (Raekoda) and Tower

Tallinn's Town Hall opened in 1404 so the city's burgomasters would have a suitable place to meet. Now open to tourists as a museum (only in the summer), it has exhibits on the town's administration and history, along with an interesting bit on the story of limestone. The tower rewards those who climb its 155 steps with a wonderful city view.

Cost and Hours: Museum–€5, entrance through cellar, July-Aug Mon-Sat 10:00-16:00, closed Sun and Sept-June; audioguide–€4.75; tower–€3, June-Aug daily 11:00-18:00, closed rest of year; tel. 645-7900, www.tallinn.ee/raekoda.

▲Tallinn City Museum (Tallinna Linnamuuseum)

This humble but worthwhile museum, filling a 14th-century townhouse, features Tallinn history from 1200 to the 1950s. It's an excellent introduction to Tallinn's past, especially with the help of its good audioguide.

Cost and Hours: €4, includes audioguide, Tue-Sun 10:30-18:00, closes earlier off-season, closed Mon year-round, Vene 17, at corner of Pühavaimu, tel. 615-5180, www.linnamuuseum.ee.

Visiting the Museum: Begin your visit on the first floor, passing through exhibits about Tallinn's medieval past, with an emphasis on its trading days. The Hanseatic League maintained a monopoly in the North Baltic, safeguarding the economic interests of its 100 town-members—of which Tallinn and its Black Heads Guild were major players. You'll see exact replicas of their trading ships, made and donated to the church in gratitude after particularly safe and rewarding journeys, and a treasury room filled with precious objects of their merchant wealth. Another display draws attention to the roles Tallinn's townspeople played in support of the merchants and shippers (stonemason, blacksmith, cooper, shoemaker, etc.).

The highlight of the second floor is a model of circa-1825 Tallinn—looking much like it does today. The top floor is devoted to 20th-century life, with recreated rooms from the early 20th century and the Soviet period.

Freedom Square (Vabaduse Väljak)

Once a USSR-era parking lot at the southern tip of the Old Town, this fine public zone has been revamped by moving the cars un-

TALLINN

derground. It's now a glassy plaza that invites locals (and very few tourists) to linger. The recommended **Wabadus café,** with tables out on the square, is a popular hangout. The space, designed to host special events, feels miles away from the cutesy cobbles just a few steps away. But it's an easy opportunity to glimpse a contrast to the tourists' Tallinn.

The towering **cross** monument facing the square (marked *Eesti Vabadussõda 1918-1920*) honors the Estonian War of Independence. Shortly after the Bolshevik Revolution set a new course for Russia, the Estonians took advantage of the post-WWI reshuffling of Europe to rise up and create—for the first time ever—an independent Estonian state. The "cross of liberty" on top of the pillar represents a military decoration from that war (and every war since). The hill behind the cross has more monuments and fragments of past fortifications.

If you're interested in learning more about Estonia's history, it's an easy five-minute walk from this square to the next sight.

Museum of Occupations (Okupatsioonide Muuseum)

This compact museum tells the history of Estonia during the decades it was under oppressive rule—first by the Soviets (for one year), then by the Nazis (for three years), and then again by the USSR (for nearly 50 years). Visitors here are reminded of the struggles of small countries in the shadow of empires.

Cost and Hours: €6.50, daily 10:00-18:00, skip the amateurish €4 audioguide, Toompea 8, at corner of Kaarli Puiestee, tel. 668-0250, www.okupatsioon.ee.

Visiting the Museum: As you approach the entrance, you'll pass a series of sculptured suitcases, a visual reminder of people who fled the country—or were deported from it.

The displays are organized around seven TV monitors screening 30-minute **documentary films** (with dry commentary, archival footage, interviews, and English subtitles)—each focusing on a different time period. Surrounding each monitor is a display case crammed with artifacts of the era. The footage of the Singing Revolution is particularly stirring.

A few artifacts illustrate how the Soviets kept the Estonians in line. First you'll see a rustic boat that a desperate defector actually rowed across the Baltic Sea to the Swedish island of Gotland. Look for the unsettling surveillance peephole, which will make you want to carefully examine your hotel room tonight. Surrounded by a lot more of those symbolic suitcases, the large monument with a swastika and a red star is a reminder that Estonia was occupied by not one, but two different regimes in the 20th century. You'll also see vintage cars, phone boxes, and radios that give a flavor of that era. Somber prison doors evoke the countless lives lost to detention and deportation.

Near those prison doors, take the red-velvet staircase down to the **basement.** There, near the WCs, is a collection of Soviet-era statues of communist leaders—once they lorded over the people; now they're in the cellar guarding the toilets.

Nearby: One of Tallinn's most famous recent sights *can't* be seen in its original location, in front of the National Library (just south of the Museum of Occupations). Called simply **The Bronze Soldier,** this six-foot-tall statue of a Soviet solider marked the graves of Russians who died fighting to liberate Tallinn in 1944. In 2007, the Estonian government exhumed those graves and moved them—along with the statue—from this very central location to the Tallinn Military Cemetery, on the city's southern outskirts. Estonia's sizeable Russian minority balked at this move, and—through a series of protests and clashes—grabbed the world's attention. The Kremlin took note, furious protestors surrounded the Estonian embassy in Moscow for a week (essentially laying siege to the building), and mysterious "cyberattacks" from Russian computers crippled Estonian governmental websites. When the dust settled, The Bronze Soldier stayed in its new home—but Estonians of all stripes were confronted with a bitter reminder that even a generation after independence, tensions between ethnic Russians and ethnic Estonians have not been entirely resolved.

▲Rotermann Quarter (Rotermanni Kvartal)

Sprawling between Hotel Viru and the port, just east of the Old Town, this 19th-century industrial zone is being redeveloped into

shopping, office, and living space. Characteristic old brick shells are being topped with visually striking glass-and-steel additions. For those interested in the gentrification of an aging city, it's worth a quick stroll to see the cutting edge of old-meets-new Nordic architecture.

In recent years the area's former

grain elevators and salt-storage warehouses have been creatively repurposed as restaurants, cafés, boutiques, and offices. To take a look around, start at Hotel Viru, cross busy Narva Maantee and walk down Roseni street (at #7 you'll find the hard-to-resist Kalev chocolate shop), circling around to Stalkeri Käik street, with its many restaurants (see "Eating in Tallinn"). In summer months, food stalls and craft tables create an open-air market in the neighborhood's central space (Rotermanni Aatrium). Fans of 20th-century architecture will want to stop by the **Museum of Estonian Architecture,** which inhabits one of the historical salt-storage buildings (€6, Wed-Fri 11:00-18:00, Sat-Sun from 10:00, Ahtri 2, www.arhitektuurimuuseum.ee).

KADRIORG PARK AND THE KUMU MUSEUM
▲Kadriorg Park

This expansive seaside park, home to a summer royal residence and the Kumu Art Museum, is just a five-minute tram ride or a 25-minute walk from Hotel Viru.

After Russia took over Tallinn in 1710, Peter the Great built the cute, pint-sized Kadriorg Palace for Czarina Catherine (the palace's name means "Catherine's Valley"). Stately, peaceful, and crisscrossed by leafy paths, the park has a rose garden, duck-filled pond, playground and benches, and old czarist guardhouses harkening back to the days of Russian rule. It's a delightful place for a stroll or a picnic. If it's rainy, slip into one of the cafés in the park's art museums (described below).

Getting There: Reach the park on tram #1 or #3 (direction: Kadriorg; catch at any tram stop around the Old Town). Get off at the Kadriorg stop (the end of the line, where trams turn and head back into town), and walk 200 yards straight ahead and up Weizenbergi, the park's main avenue. Peter's summer palace is on the left; behind it, visit the formal garden (free). Across from the palace is the Mikkel Museum, and at the end of the avenue is the Kumu Art Museum, the park's most important sight. A taxi from Hotel Viru to this area should cost €8 or less. If you're returning from here directly to the port to catch your cruise ship, use tram #1—it stops at the Linnahall stop near the main cruise terminal.

Visiting Kadriorg Park: The palace's manicured **gardens** (free to enter) are a pure delight; on weekends, you'll likely see a steady parade of brides and grooms here, posing for wedding pictures. The summer palace itself is home to the **Kadriorg Art Museum** (Kadrioru Kunstimuuseum), with very modest Russian and Western European galleries (€6.50; Tue-Sun 10:00-18:00, Wed until 20:00, closed Mon year-round—off-season also closed Tue; Weizenbergi 37, tel. 606-6400, http://kadriorumuuseum.ekm.ee).

Across the road from the gardens, in the former kitchen building of the palace, is the **Mikkel Museum,** a fine little collection of Meissen porcelain (€5, same hours as Kadriorg Art Museum, http://mikkelimuuseum.ekm.ee).

The fenced-off expanse directly behind the garden is where you'll spot the local "White House" (although it's pink)—home of **Estonia's president.** Walk around to the far side to find its main entrance, with the seal of Estonia above the door, flagpoles flying both the Estonian and the EU flags, and stone-faced guards.

A five-minute walk beyond the presidential palace takes you to the Kumu Art Museum, described next. For a longer walk from here, the rugged park rolls down toward the sea.

▲▲Kumu Art Museum
(Kumu Kunstimuuseum)

This main branch of the Art Museum of Estonia brings the nation's best art together in a striking modern building designed by an international (well, at least Finnish) architect, Pekka Vapaavuori. The entire collection is accessible, well-presented, and engaging, with a particularly thought-provoking section on art from the Soviet period. The museum is well worth the trip for art lovers, or for anyone intrigued by the unique spirit of this tiny nation.

Cost and Hours: €8; Tue-Sun 11:00-18:00, Wed until 20:00, closed Mon year-round, off-season also closed Tue; audioguide-€4; trendy café, tel. 602-6000, http://kumu.ekm.ee.

Getting There: To reach the museum, follow the instructions for Kadriorg Park, explained earlier; Kumu is at the far end of the park. To get from the Old Town to Kumu directly (without walking through the park), take bus #67 or #68 (each runs every 10-15 minutes, #68 does not run on Sun); both leave from Teatri Väljak, on the far side of the pastel yellow theater, across from the Solaris shopping mall. Get off at the Kumu stop, then walk up the stairs and across the bridge.

Visiting the Museum: Just off the ticket lobby (on the second floor), the **great hall** has temporary exhibits; however, the permanent collection on the third and fourth floors is Kumu's main draw. While you can rent an audioguide, the laminated gallery guides in most rooms are enough to enjoy the collection. The maze-like layout on each floor presents the art chronologically.

The **third floor** displays classics of Estonian art from the early 18th century until the end of World War II. It starts with idyllic 18th-century portraits of local aristocrats of the Biedermeier era, a time when harmonious family life and clearly defined gender roles took precedence over all else. The exhibit then moves through 19th-century movements, including Romanticism (represented by some nice views of Tallinn, scenes of Estonian nature,

and idealized images of Estonian peasant women in folk costumes). Estonian artists were slow to adopt the art trends of the early 20th century, but in time Modernist styles took hold: Pointillism (linger over the lyrical landscapes of Konrad Mägi and the recently rediscovered works of Herbert Lukk), Cubism, and Expressionism. In the 1930s, the Pallas School provided a more traditional, back-to-nature response to the wilder artistic movements of the time. With the dawn of World War II, a period soon followed by two Soviet and one German occupation, Estonian artists faced extremely difficult and dramatic circumstances. The final canvases on this floor, from the war years, convey an unmistakable melancholy and grim intensity. In the corner, one very high-ceilinged room has a wall lined with dozens of expressive busts by sculptor Villu Jaanisoo.

The **fourth-floor exhibit,** called "Conflicts and Adaptations," is a fascinating survey of Estonian art from the Soviet era (1940-1991). Soviet officials understood the role of art purely as a means to convey the ideology of the Communist Party. Estonian art, the Soviets insisted, should actively promote the communist struggle, and in the strict canon now called **Socialist Realism.** Art's primary objective was to glorify labor and the state's role in distributing its fruits.

Despite these restrictions, Estonian art in this half-century took a wide range of approaches, from syrupy images of Soviet leadership, to stern portraits of Stalin, to glorifying canvases of miners, protesters, speechifiers, metalworkers, and tractor drivers. Though some Estonian artists flirted with social commentary and the avant-garde, a few ended up in Siberia as a result. But with the condemnation of Stalinism in 1956, artists began to attempt

bolder compositions and more contemporary forms of expression.

Nonetheless, the social function of art continued to take precedence over personal artistic statements throughout the Soviet era.

The rest of the museum is devoted to temporary exhibits, with contemporary art on the **fifth floor** (where there's a nice view back to the Old Town from the far gallery). Don't forget to admire the **architecture** of the building, which is partly dug into the limestone hill—the facade is limestone, too (for the big picture, look for the model of the building, just inside the main doors).

ALONG THE HARBORFRONT
▲▲Seaplane Harbor (Lennusadam)

One of Tallinn's most ambitious sights, this maritime museum fills a gigantic old hangar along the waterfront north of downtown

with everything from traditional wooden fishing boats to a submarine—all symbolic of the Estonian connection to the Baltic Sea. It has loads of hands-on activities for kids, and thrills anyone interested in the sea.

Cost and Hours: €14; daily 10:00-19:00, Oct-April Tue-Sun 10:00-18:00, closed Mon; last entry one hour before closing, Vesilennuki 6, tel. 620-0550, www.seaplaneharbour.com.

Getting There: It's along the waterfront, about a mile north of the Old Town. Plan on a long but doable **walk,** made more enjoyable if you follow the red-gravel "Culture Kilometer" (Kultuurikilomeeter) seaside path from near the cruise terminals. There's no handy tram or bus to the museum, but a one-way **taxi** from the town center shouldn't cost much more than €6. The **hop-on, hop-off buses** also stop here.

Visiting the Museum: The cavernous old **seaplane hangar** cleverly displays exhibits on three levels: the ground floor features items from below the sea (such as a salvaged 16th-century shipwreck; catwalks halfway up connect exhibits dealing with the sea surface (the impressive boat collection—from buoys to iceboats to the massive *Lembit* sub); and seaplanes are suspended overhead. The star of the show is the 195-foot-long *Lembit* submarine from 1937: Estonian-commissioned and British-built, this vessel saw fighting in World War II and later spent several decades in the service of the USSR's Red Fleet. You can climb down below decks to see how the sailors lived, peek through the periscope, and even stare down the torpedo tubes. A cool café on the top level (above the entrance) overlooks the entire space, which feels endless.

Outside, filling the old harbor, is the maritime museum's collection of **historic ships,** from old-fashioned tall ships to modern-day military boats. The highlight is the steam-powered icebreaker *Suur Tõll,* from 1914. Sometimes you can pay to go out on a brief trip on one of the sailboats (ask at the ticket desk when you enter).

OUTER TALLINN
▲Pirita Neighborhood
Several gently fascinating sights cluster in the Pirita neighborhood. If you have a car (or a local guide with a car), or have the time to lace things together with public transportation, this can be a fun way to escape the city and see some different facets of Estonia.

Getting There: It's easy to tie these sights together: You'll take the waterfront Pirita Tee highway north (passing behind the Song Festival Grounds, described on the next page) to Pirita, then turn right to cut through the forest to the TV tower. Buses #34A and #38 follow exactly this same route—departing from the underground bus platforms at Viru Keskus mall—and conveniently link all of the places listed here. The hop-on, hop-off bus also does a circuit that covers these sights.

Sights in Pirita: Coming from central Tallinn on Pirita Tee, you'll pass two starkly different memorials. First, as you skirt behind Kadriorg Park, watch on the left for the **Russalka Monument** (Russalka Mälestusmärk). An angel on a pedestal commemorates the 1893 sinking of the Russian warship *Russalka* ("Mermaid"). Farther along—after passing the Song Festival Grounds—look on the right for the towering **World War II Memorial** (Maarjamäe Memoriaal)—a 115-foot-tall obelisk erected to honor those who died defending the Soviet Union, and now the centerpiece of Estonia's war memorial.

Just after crossing the Pirita River and the little marina (with the yachting center built for the 1980 Olympics), watch on the right for the **ruins of St. Bridget's Convent** (Pirita Klooster; bus stop: Pirita). This early 15th-century convent, which housed both monks and nuns (in separate quarters, of course), was destroyed in 1577 by Ivan the Terrible. Its stones were quarried to build Baltic manor houses, but today you can pay a small fee to tour the evocative Gothic ruins (www.piritaklooster.ee).

Down along the water from here, **Pirita Beach** is one of the most popular in Tallinn. On a sunny summer day, Estonians are out enjoying sand, sun, and the Baltic Sea.

At the first traffic light after the convent ruins, turn right on Kloostrimetsa Tee, which cuts through a forest—and through the **Forest Cemetery** (Metsakalmistu), offering a poignant look at unique Estonian burial customs (bus stop: Metsakalmistu, then continue about 200 yards down the road, following *Teletorn* signs to the gate). Traditionally, Estonians bury the departed not in fields

Estonia's Singing Revolution

When you are a tiny nation lodged between two giants like Russia and Germany, simply surviving is a challenge. Having already endured 200 years of czarist Russian rule and the turmoil of World War I, little Estonia found itself annexed to the Soviet Union by the end of World War II. Their native culture was swept away: Russian replaced Estonian as the language in schools, and Russians and Ukrainians moved in, displacing Estonians. Moscow wouldn't even allow locals to wave their own flag.

But Estonians were determined to maintain their cultural identity. They had no weapons, but they created their own power by banding together and singing. Song has long been a cherished Estonian form of expression. As long ago as 1869 (during another era of Russian subjugation), Estonians gathered in massive choirs to sing and to celebrate their cultural uniqueness.

Finally, as the USSR began to crumble, the Estonians mobilized, using song to demand independence. In 1988, they

gathered—300,000 strong, a third of the population—at the Song Festival Grounds outside Tallinn. The next year, the people of Latvia, Lithuania, and Estonia held hands to make the "Baltic Chain," a human chain that stretched 360 miles from Tallinn to Vilnius in Lithuania.

This so-called Singing Revolution, peaceful and nonviolent, persisted for five years, and in the end, Estonians gained their freedom. It was a remarkable achievement: One million singing Estonians succeeded against 150 million Russian occupiers.

And the singing continues: Every five years, the Song Festival Grounds (built in 1959 and resembling an oversized Hollywood Bowl) welcome 25,000 singers and 100,000 spectators. The singers don traditional outfits and march to the festival site from Tallinn's Freedom Square. Overlooking the grounds from the cheap seats is a statue of Gustav Ernesaks, who directed the Estonian National Male Choir for 50 years through the darkest times of Soviet rule. He was a power in the drive for independence, and lived to see it happen. (To visit the grounds—free and open long hours even in nonfestival years, though there's not much to see—take a City Bike tour, or ride bus #1A, #5, #8, #34A, or #38 to the Lauluväljak stop).

While the Song Festival Grounds host big pop-music acts, too, it's a national monument for the role it played in Estonia's fight for independence. Watch the documentary film The Singing Revolution (www.singingrevolution.com) to draw inspiration from Estonia's valiant struggle for freedom.

or parks, but in forests—thanks to a deeply rooted belief that their spirit will live on in the trees. This particular cemetery is one of Estonia's best-known, and is the eternal resting place both of commoners and of VIPs—athletes, chess champions, musicians, writers, and politicians. Exploring here, find the "Hill of Celebrities" (Kuulsuste Küngas). Among the illustrious Estonians buried here is Konstantin Päts (1847-1956), the first president of independent Estonia, who later died in a Siberian mental institution. After freedom, his remains were located and moved here to be re-interred. Lydia Koidula (1843-1886, marked by a red stone) was Estonia's premier 19th-century poet and wrote the first play in Estonian.

Just past the Forest Cemetery, the **TV tower** (Teletorn)—with its antenna copping 1,000 feet tall—was built for the 1980 Moscow Olympics (the sailing regatta took place in Tallinn). You can ride up to the 550-foot-high observation deck for sweeping views over Estonia (and, on a clear day, all the way to Finland) and the endearing "Estonian Hall of Fame," celebrating Estonian contributions to the world (www.teletorn.ee).

In front of the tower, you'll see a monument to the brave Estonians who faced off against a potential Soviet counterattack. On August 19, 1991, a coup by generals in Moscow created confusion and panic across the USSR. The next day, on August 20—still celebrated today as Estonia's national holiday—the Declaration of Independence was signed. On August 21, Russian military forces moved to take this national broadcast tower and cut off Estonian communications. But two policemen and some radio operators cleverly prevented them from entering the tower's control station, by jamming the door and threatening to engage the fire-exhaust system. Eventually a ragtag gang of Estonian civilians showed up to defend the tower and stare down the troops. By late afternoon, it became clear that Boris Yeltsin had gained control in Moscow, and the Russian troops were told to stand down. Estonia had its tower—and a few weeks later, Russia recognized this little country's right to exist.

▲Estonian Open-Air Museum (Vabaõhumuuseum)

Influenced by their ties with Nordic countries, Estonians are enthusiastic advocates of open-air museums. For this one, they salvaged farm buildings, windmills, and an old church from rural

A Look at Lasnamäe

In its attempt to bring Estonia into the Soviet fold, Moscow moved tens of thousands of Russian workers into Tallinn, using the promise of new apartments as an incentive. Generations later, Tallinn still has a huge Russian minority (about 40 percent of the city's population) and three huge, charmless suburbs of ugly, Soviet-built apartments: Mustamäe, Õismäe, and Lasnamäe.

Today, about one of every two Tallinners lives in one of these Brezhnev-era suburbs of massive, cookie-cutter apartment blocks (many now privatized). About 80 percent of the residents who live in Lasnamäe are Russian-speaking. Some parts are poor, rough, and edgy, with blue lights in the public toilets so that junkies can't see their veins. Other sections are nicer, and by day, you can visit here without fear. You'll see carefully dressed young women, track-suited men, grass that needs mowing, cracked paving stones, grandmothers pushing strollers, and lots of new, boxy shops; a new Russian Orthodox cathedral (built with the support of Tallinn's mayor to curry favor with ethnic-Russian voters); and some modern city-owned "social apartment" buildings.

Forging Russians and Estonians into a single society, with the Estonian language dominant, was an optimistic goal after the fall of the Soviet Union. Ethnic Russians grumbled, but knew they probably had a brighter economic future in Estonia than in Russia. With a new generation of children learning both languages in school and most residents enjoying reasonable prosperity, peaceful ethnic coexistence (like between Swedes and Finns in Helsinki) may be achievable.

For a quick look at life in Lasnamäe, hop on bus #67 or #68 (each runs every 10-15 minutes); both leave from Teatri Väljak, on the far side of the pastel yellow theater from the Old Town, across from the Solaris shopping mall. Ride to the last stop (about 25 minutes).

TALLINN

areas and transported them to a parklike setting a few miles west of the Old Town. The goal: to both save and share their heritage. Attendants are posted in many houses, but to really visualize life in the old houses, download the free NUMU app before you visit (or rent an audioguide from ticket office). The park's Kolu Tavern serves traditional dishes. You can rent a bike (€3/hour) for a breezy roll to quiet, faraway spaces in the park.

Cost and Hours: Late April-Sept: €9, park open daily 10:00-20:00, historic buildings until 18:00; Oct-late April: €7, park open daily 10:00-17:00 but many buildings closed; tel. 654-9100, www.evm.ee.

Getting There: Take bus #21 or #21B from the train station or Freedom Square to the Rocca al Mare stop. Because buses back to Tallinn run infrequently, check the departure schedule as soon as you arrive, or ask staff how to find the Zoo stop, with more frequent service, a 15-minute walk away.

Lahemaa National Park (Lahemaa Rahvuspark)

This vast, flat, forested coastal preserve on the Gulf of Finland is only a one-hour drive east of Tallinn. While it is a popular tour destination and the nature is pristine, the park's charms are modest. I had a great guide, and it was a fascinating day out. But with an average guide, it could be a snore. Highlights include the thick forest (including cemeteries, because Estonians bury their dead in the woods), bog walks, rich berry and mushroom picking, rebuilt manor homes, and peaceful fishing villages surrounded by the evocative ruins of Soviet occupation. Tallinn Traveller Tours organizes day trips to the national park (see "Tours in Tallinn" near the beginning of the chapter). For hiking and cycling trail descriptions, check online (www.keskkonnaamet.ee) or stop at the park's visitor center when you arrive (open daily in summer, Mon-Fri off-season, tel. 329-5555).

Shopping in Tallinn

With so many cruisers inundating Tallinn, the Old Town is full of trinkets, but it is possible to find good-quality stuff. Wooden goods, like butter knives and juniper-wood trivets, are a good value. Marvel at the variety of booze on sale in Tallinn's liquor stores, popular with visiting Scandinavians. Tucked into the Old Town are many craft and artisan shops where prices are lower than in Nordic countries.

The **"Sweater Wall"** is a fun place to browse sweaters and woolens, though few are hand-knitted by grandmothers these days. Find the stalls under the wall on Müürivahe street (daily, near the corner of Viru street, described on page 656). From there, explore the picturesque **Katariina Käik,** a small alley between Müürivahe and Vene streets, which has several handicraft stores and workshops selling pieces that make nice souvenirs.

The cheery **Navitrolla Gallerii** is filled with work by the well-known Estonian artist who goes just by the name Navitrolla. His whimsical, animal-themed prints are vaguely reminiscent of *Where the Wild Things Are* (Mon-Fri 10:00-18:00, Sat until 17:00, Sun until 16:00, Sulevimägi 1, tel. 631-3716, www.navitrolla.ee).

The **Rahva Raamat** bookstore in the Viru Keskus mall (floors 3-4) has English-language literature on the main floor, and a huge wall of travel books upstairs (daily 9:00-21:00).

Estonian handicrafts focus on all kinds of knitted and felted clothing: colorful sweaters, scarves, hats, socks, and mittens. Linen is also widely sold. In the Old Town, you'll find good selections at the **Estonian Handicraft House** (Pikk 27) and **Eesti Käsitöö Kodu** (Vene 12).

Balti Jaam Market, Tallinn's bustling, newly restored market, is behind the train station. It's a great time-warp scene, fragrant

with dill, berries, onions, and mushrooms. You'll hear lots of Russian and find vendors selling everything from fresh produce and street food to children's clothes and gadgets. You could easily assemble a rustic picnic here. To find the market from the train station, just walk across the head of the train platforms (following *Jaama Turg* signs) and keep going (Mon-Sat 9:00-19:00, Sun until 17:00, better early).

For something tamer, the **Viru Turg outdoor market,** a block outside the Old Town's Viru Gate, has a lively, tourist-oriented collection of stalls selling mostly clothing, textiles, and flowers (daily, north of Viru street at Mere Puiestee 1).

Entertainment in Tallinn

Music

Tallinn has a dense schedule of classical music performances, especially during the annual Old Town Days, generally at the beginning of June (www.vanalinnapaevad.ee). Choral singing became a symbol of the struggle for Estonian independence after the first Estonian Song Festival in 1869 (still held every five years, including 2019).

Even outside of festival times, you'll find many performances in Tallinn's churches and concert halls, advertised on posters around town or at the TI. Tickets are usually available at the door or through the Piletilevi booth in the Viru Keskus mall (daily 9:00-

21:00, www.piletilevi.ee). Watch for performances by Hortus Musicus, one of Estonia's finest classical ensembles, or concerts featuring the work of Arvo Pärt, Veljo Tormis, or Erkki-Sven Tüür, who are among Estonia's best modern choral composers and arrangers. Estonian groups have put out a lot of good CDs; you'll find a good music shop on the top floor (A5) of the Kaubamaja department store (daily 9:00-21:00, behind Viru Keskus mall).

Swimming and Fitness

The indoor water park, fitness center, 50-meter pool, and hotel at the **Kalev Spa** have long attracted Finns who travel here on fitness packages. It's centrally located, between the Old Town and the modern shopping zone, but it may be closed for renovations when you visit; check the website for updated hours and pricing (swimsuit rental available, Aia 18, tel. 649-3370, www.kalevspa.ee).

Sleeping in Tallinn

Real hotel options are surprisingly sparse and expensive in the Old Town. You'll have more options and pay less if you're willing to stay a short walk or bus ride away, especially during the summer high-tourist season. Tallinn hotels employ dynamic pricing to establish a day rate entirely on demand, so the price you'll find on a hotel's website can vary dramatically from week to week, and even day to day.

IN AND NEAR THE OLD TOWN

$$$$ Baltic Hotel Imperial is a fine four-star hotel set in a lovely parklike spot under the Old Town wall. Its 32 rooms are modern and small; the public spaces have a spacious, professional ambience. Though it feels like a chain (and is), when it's discounted, it's the best Old Town, top-end value I've found (air-con, elevator, pay sauna, kids' playroom, Nunne 14, tel. 627-4800, www.imperial.ee, imperial@baltichotelgroup.com).

$$$$ My City Hotel fills a handsome 1950s building on the south edge of the Old Town with 68 nicely appointed rooms and a classy lobby lounge. Along with the Sõprus cinema across the street, it's done in the Stalinist Classical style—Soviet stars and sheaves of wheat still adorn the facade (air-con, elevator, pay sauna, Vana-Posti 11, tel. 622-0900, www.mycityhotel.ee, booking@mycityhotel.ee).

$$$ Rixwell Old Town Hotel sits at the tip of the Old Town, near Fat Margaret Tower and not far from the ferry terminals. Its 41 small, dated rooms are mostly doubles with twin beds and showers, and—as it faces a busy street—some could be noisy. But the price is right and the location convenient (discount if you skip breakfast,

Sleep Code

Hotels are classified based on the average price of a typical en suite double room with breakfast in high season.

$$$$	**Splurge:** Most rooms over €110
$$$	**Pricier:** €90-110
$$	**Moderate:** €70-90
$	**Budget:** €50-70
¢	**Backpacker:** Under €50
RS%	**Rick Steves discount**

Unless otherwise noted, credit cards are accepted, hotel staff speak basic English, and free Wi-Fi is available. Comparison-shop by checking prices at several hotels (on each hotel's own website, on a booking site, or by email). For the best deal, *always book directly with the hotel*. Ask for a discount if paying in cash; if the listing includes **RS%**, request a Rick Steves discount.

elevator, Lai 49, tel. 614-1300, www.meritonhotelsrixwell.com, reservations.oldtownhotel@meritonhotelsrixwell.com).

$$ Hotel Bern, tucked at the edge of the Old Town, is an endearing place with 50 businesslike rooms in a new brick building (air-con, elevator, Aia 10, tel. 680-6630, www.tallinnhotels.ee, bern@tallinnhotels.ee).

$$ St. Barbara Hotel, an affordable choice just outside the Old Town, fills a former hospital from 1904 just beyond the ring road from Freedom Square—about a 10-minute walk from Town Hall Square. This old building is filled with 53 modern, fairly simple rooms and an atmospheric beer cellar that gives the place a Germanic vibe (elevator, free parking, Roosikrantsi 2A—just take the pedestrian underpass from Freedom Square under the busy road, tel. 640-0040, www.stbarbara.ee, reservations@stbarbara.ee).

$$ Old Town Maestro's is a simple budget choice with 23 modern rooms tucked in the heart of the Old Town. While the prices are right, it comes with a catch: It sits along one of Tallinn's rowdiest nightlife streets, so try requesting a quieter courtyard room (elevator, Suur-Karja 10, tel. 626-2000, www.maestrohotel. ee, maestro@maestrohotel.ee).

$ Villa Hortensia rents six simple, creaky-floored rooms with kitchenettes above a sophisticated little café in a courtyard close to Town Hall Square. Named after the home of a group of down-and-outs in a famous Estonian novel, the hotel is creatively run by jewelry designer Jaan Pärn. It's a decent, inexpensive choice if you don't mind the ramshackle feeling and the fact that the rooms aren't serviced every day. Jaan's jewelry shop, up the stairs in the courtyard, serves as the reception (no breakfast, no elevator, 50

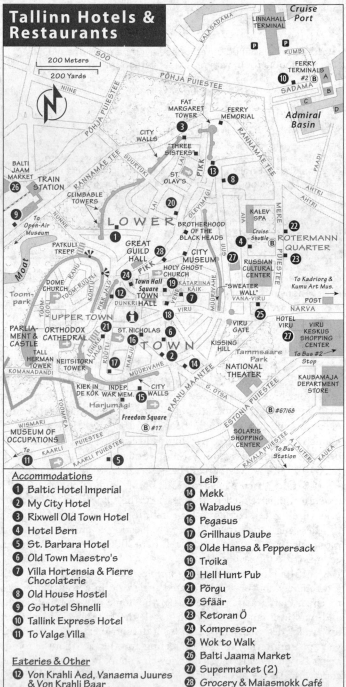

Tallinn Hotels & Restaurants

200 Meters

200 Yards

Accommodations

1. Baltic Hotel Imperial
2. My City Hotel
3. Rixwell Old Town Hotel
4. Hotel Bern
5. St. Barbara Hotel
6. Old Town Maestro's
7. Villa Hortensia & Pierre Chocolaterie
8. Old House Hostel
9. Go Hotel Shnelli
10. Tallink Express Hotel
11. To Valge Villa

Eateries & Other

12. Von Krahli Aed, Vanaema Juures & Von Krahli Baar
13. Leib
14. Mekk
15. Wabadus
16. Pegasus
17. Grillhaus Daube
18. Olde Hansa & Peppersack
19. Troika
20. Hell Hunt Pub
21. Põrgu
22. Sfäär
23. Retoran Ö
24. Kompressor
25. Wok to Walk
26. Balti Jaama Market
27. Supermarket (2)
28. Grocery & Maiasmokk Café

TALLINN

yards from the corner of Vene and Viru streets at Vene 6, look for *Masters' Courtyard* sign, mobile 504-6113, www.hoov.ee, jaan. parn@gmail.com).

¢ **Old House Hostel** is your cheap-and-basic option, split between two buildings on the edge of the Old Town and near the ferry terminals. There's street noise in many rooms, so bring earplugs (family rooms, breakfast extra, no lockout, shared shower and WC, kitchen facilities, unsecured free parking—reserve ahead, Uus 26, tel. 641-1464, www.oldhouse.ee, info@oldhouse.ee). They also rent apartments around the Old Town.

AWAY FROM THE OLD TOWN

Near the Train Station: $ **Go Hotel Shnelli,** a big, high-rise "efficiency hotel" adjacent to the sleepy little train station (a 5-minute walk from the Old Town in a neighborhood that feels slightly seedy at night), rents 137 Ikea-mod rooms. It fronts a noisy street, so request a quiet room in the back—these overlook the tracks, but no trains run at night (connecting family rooms, apartment, you can save a few euros if you skip breakfast, elevator, Toompuiestee 37, tel. 631-0100, www.gohotels.ee, reservations@gohotels.ee).

Near the Port: Given how compact Tallinn is (and how inexpensive honest taxis are), there's little reason to sleep near the ferry terminals—other than low prices. But if you're in a pinch, $$ **Tallink Express Hotel** is a few steps from the A/B Terminals, close to Linnahall Terminal, and a short walk from the Old Town. It's a modern, cheery Motel 6-type place with excellent prices and 166 comfortable, cookie-cutter rooms. The rooms can be stuffy in hot weather, as windows don't open very far and there's no air-conditioning (family rooms, elevator, free parking, Sadama 9, tel. 630-0808, www.tallinkhotels.com, expresshotel@tallink.ee).

In Lilleküla, Outside the Center: Lillcküla is a quiet, green, and peaceful residential area of single-family houses, small Soviet-era apartment blocks, and barking dogs. For a clearer understanding of Estonian life, stay here. You'll save money without sacrificing comfort. The downside: It's a 15-minute bus ride into the center.

$ **Valge Villa** ("White Villa") is a homey guesthouse set in a great garden. Run by Anne and Andres Vahtra and their family, who do everything right, they offer 10 spacious, wood-paneled, well-furnished rooms (family rooms, free parking, rental bikes, pay sauna, pay laundry; take bus #17 to Räägu stop, or trolley bus #2, #3, or #4 to Tedre stop; Kännu 26/2, between Rästa and Räägu streets—see map on page 672, tel. 654-2302, www.white-villa. com, villa@white-villa.com). I'd take a taxi here to check in (about €15 from the ferry port), and figure out the public-transit options later.

TALLINN

Eating in Tallinn

Tallinn's Old Town has a wide selection of mostly tourist-oriented eateries—don't expect bargains here. For a better value (and better food), roam at least a block or two off the main drags. Some restaurants have good-value lunch specials on weekdays (look for the words *päeva praad*). As a mark of quality, watch for restaurants with an *Astu Sisse!* label in the window; this Estonian equivalent of a Michelin star is awarded to just 50 restaurants each year. Tipping is not required, but if

you like the service, round your bill up by 5-10 percent when paying. Reserving ahead for dinner is a smart idea.

Authentic Estonian food is easy to find—a hearty mix of meat, potatoes, root vegetables, mushrooms, dill, garlic, bread, and soup. Pea soup is a local specialty. You usually get a few slices of bread as a free, automatic side dish. A typical pub snack is Estonian garlic bread *(küüslauguleivad)*—deep-fried strips of dark rye bread smothered in garlic and served with a dipping sauce. Estonia's Saku beer is good, cheap, and on tap at most eateries. Try the nutty, full-bodied Tume variety.

ESTONIAN CUISINE IN THE OLD TOWN

$$ Von Krahli Aed is an elegant, almost gourmet, health-food eatery calling itself "the embassy of pure food." While not vegetarian, it is passionate about serving organic, seasonal, modern Estonian cuisine in a woody, romantic setting. Take your pick from four dining options: under old beams, in the cellar, out front on the sidewalk, or out back on the garden terrace (daily 12:00-23:00, Rataskaevu 8, tel. 626-9088).

$$ Vanaema Juures ("Grandma's Place"), an eight-table cellar restaurant, serves homey, traditional Estonian meals, such as pork roast with sauerkraut and horseradish. This is a fine bet for local cuisine, and dinner reservations are strongly advised (daily 12:00-22:00, Rataskaevu 10, tel. 626-9080, www.vonkrahl.ee/vanaemajuures).

At **$$ Leib** ("Back Bread"), just outside the walls at the seaside end of the Old Town, you enter up steps into a fun garden under the medieval ramparts, and can sit indoors or out. The classy menu—built around a passion for Baltic ingredients (spring cabbage, beets, smoked trout, sturgeon)—changes with the seasons (daily 12:00-15:00 & 18:00-23:00, Uus 31, tel. 611-9026).

$$$$ Mekk is a small, fresh, upscale place, which has a name

Restaurant Price Code

I've assigned each eatery a price category, based on the average cost of a typical main course. Drinks, desserts, and splurge items (steak and seafood) can raise the price considerably.

$$$$	**Splurge:** Most main courses over €20
$$$	**Pricier:** €15-20
$$	**Moderate:** €10-15
$	**Budget:** Under €10

In Estonia, a takeout spot is **$**; a sit-down café is **$$**; a casual but more upscale restaurant is **$$$**; and a swanky splurge is **$$$$**.

that stands for "modern Estonian cuisine." While their dinner à la carte prices are high, they offer artful weekday lunch specials for just €7 (not available July-Aug), and a €40 four-course chef's menu at dinner (daily 11:00-23:00, Sun until 21:00, Suur-Karja 17, tel. 680-6688, www.mekk.ee).

Modern Cuisine on Freedom Square: The town meeting place since 1937, **$$ Wabadus,** facing the vast and modern square, turns its back on old Tallinn. This sleek, urbane café/restaurant serves coffee, cocktails, and international fare. Enjoy one of the terrace tables on the square if the weather's good (Mon-Thu 9:00-23:00, Fri-Sat 11:00-24:00, Sun 11:00-21:00, Vabaduse Väljak 10, tel. 601-6461).

NEAR ST. NICHOLAS CHURCH

$$$ Pegasus, tucked into three floors of a concrete and glass building, is the perfect antidote to the kitsch on Town Hall Square. The decor and the menu are Nordic-inspired, featuring flavorful soups, risottos, fish, and salads (daily 12:00-23:00, Harju 1, tel. 662-3013).

$$$ Grillhaus Daube dishes up grilled ribs, steaks, and fish in the relaxed, light-and-bright dining room of an 18th-century townhouse. Eat in front of the fireplace in bad weather, or out on the terrace in good (daily 12:00-23:00, just inside the walls off Freedom Square, Rüütli 11, tel. 645-5531).

TOURIST TRAPS ON AND NEAR TOWN HALL SQUARE

Tallinn's central square is a whirlpool of tacky tourism, where aggressive restaurant touts (some dressed as medieval wenches or giant *matryoshka* dolls) accost passersby to lure them in for a drink or meal. Surprisingly, some of these restaurants have good (if expensive) food.

"Medieval" Estonian Cuisine: Two well-run restaurants just below Town Hall Square specialize in re-creating medieval food (from the days before the arrival of the potato and tomato from the New World). They are each grotesquely touristy, complete with gift shops where you can buy your souvenir goblet. Sit inside to feel the atmosphere.

$$$ Olde Hansa, filling three creaky old floors and outdoor tables with tourists, candle wax, and scurrying medieval waitresses, has food far better than it has any right to be (daily 10:00-24:00; musicians circulate Tue-Sun after 18:00, a belch below Town Hall Square at Vana Turg 1, reserve in advance, tel. 627-9020, www. oldehansa.ee).

$$$ Peppersack, across the street, tries to compete in the same price range, and feels marginally less circus-like (Vana Turg 6, tel. 646-6800).

Russian Food: Right on Town Hall Square, with a folkloric-costumed waitstaff, **$$$ Troika** serves *bliny* (pancakes) and *pelmeni* (dumplings), and characteristic main dishes. Sit out on the square (reserve for dinner); in the more casual, Russian-village-themed tavern; or under a fine vault in the atmospheric cellar. A balalaika player usually strums and strolls in the evenings (daily 10:00-23:00, Raekoja Plats 15, tel. 627-6245, www.troika.ee).

PUBS IN THE OLD TOWN

Young Estonians eat well and affordably at pubs. In some pubs, you go to the bar to order and pay before finding a table.

$$ Hell Hunt Pub ("The Gentle Wolf") was the first Western-style pub to open after 1991, and its tasty food and microbrews on tap are still attracting a mixed expat and local crowd. You can make a meal from the great pub snacks plus a salad. Choose a table in its convivial, rustic-industrial interior or on the garden terrace across the street (daily 12:00-24:00, Pikk 39, tel. 681-8333).

$ Von Krahli Baar serves cheap, substantial Estonian grub—such as potato pancakes *(torud)* stuffed with mushrooms or shrimp—in a handsome stone building that doubles as a center for Estonia's alternative theater scene; there's also seating in the tiny courtyard where you enter. It started as the bar of the theater upstairs, then expanded to become a restaurant, so it has a young, avant-garde vibe (daily 10:00-24:00, Rataskaevu 10, a block uphill from Town Hall Square, near Wheel Well, tel. 626-9090).

$$ Põrgu ("Hell"), in a simple, uncluttered cellar, is serious about its beer. They have a wide variety of international and Estonian brews on tap—including some microbrews—and the usual range of bar snacks, salads, and main dishes (daily 12:00-24:00, Rüütli 4, tel. 644-0232).

TALLINN

IN THE ROTERMANN QUARTER

This modern, up-and-coming district (described on page 659), just across the busy road from Tallinn's Old Town, is well worth exploring for a jolt of cutting-edge architecture and hipster edginess. It's an antidote to the central area's ye-olde aura. As more and more buildings in this zone are being renovated, this is a fast-changing scene. But these two choices, in a long brick building facing the Old Town, are well-established and a good starting point.

$$$ Sfäär ("Sphere"), which combines an unpretentious bistro with a design shop, is a killing-two-birds look at the Rotermann Quarter. In this lively, cheery place, tables are tucked between locally designed clothes and home decor. The appealing menu features Estonian and international fare (Mon-Fri 8:00-22:00, Sat-Sun from 10:00, shop open Mon-Sat 12:00-21:00—restaurant and shop close Sun at 17:00, Mere Puiestee 6E, mobile 5699-2200).

$$$$ Retoran Ö (Swedish for "Island"), just a few doors down in the same building, is your Rotermann Quarter splurge. The dressy, trendy, retrofitted-warehouse interior feels a sophisticated world away from the Old Town's tourist traps. The seasonal menu highlights an Estonian approach to "New Nordic" cooking—small dishes carefully constructed with local ingredients. Reservations are smart (Mon-Sat 18:00-23:00, closed Sun, Mere Puiestee 6E—enter from the parking lot around back, tel. 661-6150, www.restoran-o.ee).

BUDGET EATERIES

$ Kompressor, a big, open-feeling beer hall, is in all the guidebooks for its cheap, huge, and filling pancakes—savory or sweet (daily 11:00-24:00, Rataskaevu 3, tel. 646-4210).

$ Wok to Walk, a clean and simple spot, offers tasty made-to-order stir-fries (daily 10:00-23:00, just off Viru Square at Vana Viru 14, tel. 444-3320).

Supermarkets: For picnic supplies, try the **Rimi minimart,** just a block off Town Hall Square (daily 8:00-22:00, Pikk 11); there's also a big **Rimi supermarket** just outside the Old Town at Aia 7, near the Viru Gate (daily 8:00-22:00). A larger, more upscale supermarket in the basement of the **Viru Keskus** mall (directly behind Hotel Viru) has inexpensive takeaway meals (daily 9:00-21:00).

BREAKFAST AND PASTRIES

The **$ Maiasmokk** ("Sweet Tooth") café and pastry shop, founded in 1864, is the grande dame of Tallinn cafés—ideal for dessert or breakfast. Even through the Soviet days, this was *the* place for a good pastry or a glass of herby Tallinn schnapps ("Vana Tallinn"). Point to what you want from the selection of classic local pastries at the counter, and sit down for breakfast or coffee on the other side of the shop. Everything's reasonable (Mon-Fri 8:00-21:00, Sat 9:00-21:00, Sun 9:00-20:00, Pikk 16, across from church with old clock, tel. 646-4079, www.kohvikmaiasmokke.ee). They also have a pricier full-menu café upstairs and a marzipan shop (separate entrance).

Pierre Chocolaterie at Vene 6 has scrumptious fresh pralines, sandwiches, and coffee in a courtyard filled with craft shops (also $ light meals, daily 8:30-late, tel. 641-8061).

Tallinn Connections

BY BUS OR TRAIN

The bus is usually the best way to travel by land from Tallinn (for domestic bus schedules, see www.tpilet.ee). The largest international operator, with the most departures, is Lux Express (tel. 680-0909, www.luxexpress.ee); there's also Ecolines (tel. 614-3600 or mobile 5637-7997, www.ecolines.net) and the spiffy Hansabuss (with onboard Wi-Fi, tel. 627-9080, www.hansabuss.ee). The bus station *(autobussijaam)* is at Lastekodu 46, a short taxi ride from the Old Town, or a few stops on trams #2 or #4 to the Autobussijaam stop (direction: Ülemiste). Not much English is spoken at the station; reserving online is recommended.

From Tallinn to: Rīga (12 buses/day, 4.5 hours, no train option; consider Tallinn Traveller Tours' "sightseeing shuttle" between these cities, a full-day, 12-hour journey with sightseeing stops en route—see "Tours in Tallinn," earlier), **Vilnius** (5 buses/day, plus 3/day overnight, 10 hours), **St. Petersburg** (buses daily, 6.5 hours; also possible by overnight cruise—about 1/week, 18.5 hours, www.stpeterline.com; for cruise details, see page 628), **Moscow** (take the overnight train—daily departures in late afternoon, 14.5-hour trip, check current timetables at www.gorail.ee—or fly). Americans and Canadians must generally obtain a visa to travel to Russia and need to plan long in advance (for more information on current visa requirements, see www.ricksteves.com/russianvisa, and confirm details at www.russianembassy.org or www.rusembassy.ca).

BY BOAT
Sailing Overnight Between Stockholm and Tallinn

Tallink Silja's overnight cruise ships between Stockholm and Tallinn leave each city in late afternoon or early evening and arrive in the other city midmorning. Ferry fares vary widely by the day and season; the highest rates are typically for Friday and Saturday nights and in summer from July to mid-August. Options range from four-person, sex-segregated dorm rooms to private cabins. The *smörgåsbord* dinner and buffet breakfast cost extra (book these meals and reserve a table when buying your ticket). Book online (www.tallinksilja.com); booking by phone or in person may come with an extra charge (US tel. 360/923-0125, Estonian tel. 640-9808).

Terminals: In **Stockholm,** Tallink Silja ships leave from the Värtahamnen harbor. To get there from downtown Stockholm, take the Tallink Silja shuttle bus from the train station (60 SEK, departs according to boat schedule), or take the T-bana (subway) to the Gärdet station, then walk 10 minutes to the harbor. Or take public bus #76 (direction: Ropsten), which takes you directly to the terminal (leaves from several downtown locations, including Kungsträdgården; get off at Värtahamnens stop). For Stockholm public transit information, see page 429 and www.sl.se. In **Tallinn,** Tallink Silja ships dock at D-Terminal (see "Arrival in Tallinn," earlier).

Speeding Between Helsinki and Tallinn

Four different companies—shown in the accompanying table—offer ferry trips between Helsinki and Tallinn. Fares run €20-55 one-way (evening departures from Helsinki and morning departures from Tallinn tend to be cheaper; student and senior discounts available). Their websites have all the latest information and prices. Advance reservations aren't essential, but usually save a little money, ensure your choice of departure, and provide peace of mind. If you travel round-trip on the same day, your ticket will cost barely more (and sometimes less) than a one-way fare, but you'll have just a few hours on shore. Prices differ only slightly from company to company—base your choice on the most convenient departure times and ferry terminal locations. Make sure you know which terminal your boat leaves from and how to get to it (for descriptions of Helsinki's terminals, see page 625; for Tallinn's, see "Arrival in Tallinn," earlier).

Unless you're bringing a car, the Linda and Viking lines are usually the most convenient, as their docks in Helsinki and Tallinn are easy to reach by foot or public transport. **Linda Line** uses 400-passenger, Australian-made catamarans that zip across the Gulf of Finland in just 1.75 hours several times each day. Boats leave from the Makasiini Terminal in Helsinki's South Harbor, just five minutes' walk from Market Square, and arrive in Tallinn at the Linnahall Terminal. Catamarans lack the spacious party atmosphere of larger boats, and can be slightly more expensive. Cancellations, which can occur in stormy conditions, rarely happen in summer; still, if you have a plane to catch, play it safe and take a regular ferry. **Viking Line** leaves from Helsinki's South Harbor, Katajanokan Terminal, and arrives at Tallinn's A-Terminal. Viking offers a more traditional experience on a big ferry with restaurants

Helsinki/Tallinn Connections

Company	Website	Terminal in Helsinki	Terminal in Tallinn
Tallink Silja	www.tallinksilja. com	Most from West Harbor Terminal 2	D
Linda Line (fast catamarans)	www.lindaline.ee	Makasiini	Linnahall
Eckerö Line	www.eckeroline.fi	West Harbor Terminal 1	A
Viking Line	www.vikingline.fi	Katajanokan	A

and shops (2/day, 2.5-hour crossing, generally a few euros less than Linda Line).

Tallink Silja and **Eckerö Line** leave from Helsinki's West Harbor (Länsistama), which you can reach on trams #7 and #6T (catch them in downtown Helsinki; the terminal is the end of the line). Most of Tallink Silja's sailings depart from Terminal 2 at West Harbor (but if you are booked on their Europa ferry, you'll depart from Terminal 1). At the other end of the journey, Tallink Silja uses Tallinn's D-Terminal—the farthest from the Old Town, making it a bit less convenient but still walkable. On the other hand, Tallink Silja's ferries are frequent and fast (6-7/day, 2-hour crossing for most departures, with some longer sailings). Eckerö Line has two to three sailings per day (2.5-hour crossing).

Slower boats—all except Linda Line—have *smörgåsbord* buffets. The slower the boat, the more likely it is to be filled with "four-legged Finns" crazy about cheap booze, slot machines, and karaoke.

TALLINN

SCANDINAVIA: PAST & PRESENT

On your trip, you'll see reminders everywhere of Scandinavia's long history. Eerie graves, carved rune stones, and horned helmets bring to mind *Lord of the Rings*-style warriors of old who worshipped Thor and Odin. You'll see the ships and weapons of their descendants—the Vikings—who terrorized Europe with their fierce, pagan culture. Evocative wooden-stave churches show how Christianity slowly seeped into the region.

You'll visit the harbors of these seafaring peoples and tour the stark castles of nobles who fought for control of Baltic trade. As modern nations emerged, absolute monarchs built luxurious palaces intended to rival Versailles. Today's streets and main squares are studded with statues and monuments honoring great kings and their battles, great patriots who lobbied for national independence, and great writers and musicians who enriched Scandinavian culture. Scandinavian museums are filled with paintings that capture the beauty of the landscape and celebrate its people. You'll hear bittersweet stories of the millions of 19th-century Scandinavians who left their homes for better lives in America. You'll learn about those who suffered under WWII Nazi occupation, and the heroes who organized resistance and sheltered Jewish people. And you'll experience the richness of Scandinavia today—its wealth, its liberal policies, and its global outlook.

Want to hear more of the Scandinavian story? Read on.

PREHISTORY AND HUNTERS WITH SPEARS (c. 8000 B.C.-A.D. 1)

Scandinavia became habitable when the glaciers receded at the end of the last ice age. Stone Age hunters moved north, chasing valuable deer, moose, and fish. Among these were the forebears of the Sami—or Laplanders—of northern Scandinavia, some of whom

continue to herd reindeer and live a nomadic lifestyle today. For more on the Sami, visit Oslo's National Historical Museum or Norwegian Folk Museum, or Stockholm's Nordic Museum. The early Scandinavians began farming (c. 4000 B.C.) and eventually developed tools and weapons made of bronze (c. 1800 B.C.). We know these people mainly by their graves—either burial mounds (as on the island of Öland, in southeast Sweden) or the heavy stone tombs called dolmens (as on Denmark's isle of Ærø).

IRON-AGE WARRIORS WITH HORNED HELMETS
(A.D. 1-800)

Isolated from the Continent and unconquered by the Romans, Scandinavia kept close to its prehistoric past. The 2,000-year-old Grauballe Man—whose corpse was preserved in a peat bog (and is now displayed at the Moesgård Museum just outside Aarhus, in Denmark's Jutland)—was a contemporary of Julius Caesar. But in his world, people spoke not Latin but a Germanic language, wore animal-horned helmets, and used ceremonial curvy-shaped *lur* horns. They forged iron implements decorated with the gods of their pagan religion (such as the Gundestrup Cauldron displayed in Copenhagen's National Museum). They commemorated heroic

deeds with large stones carved with the angular alphabet known as runes (see the rune stones at Copenhagen's National Museumand at Jelling, Denmark). One of their most sacred sites is at Gamla Uppsala near Stockholm, where mighty chieftains were buried along with their worldly possessions—weapons, jewels, dogs, horses, and even slaves. This distinct, pre-Christian Scandinavian culture thrived in the first centuries A.D. and continued even as the rest of Europe fell under the sway of Rome's Latin culture and, later, Christianity.

Though isolated, the Scandinavians made fleeting contact with Roman Europe, trading furs and amber (a petrified tree sap, used in jewelry) for crucial tool-making metals from the Continent. Eventually, the Scandinavians learned to extract their own bronze and iron. With better tools, they became productive farmers and shipbuilders. The population boomed due to a warmer climate and better nutrition. The Scandinavians were soon eyeing Europe and the North Atlantic as a source for new resources, and for potential expansion of their clans.

VIKINGS WITH SHIPS (800-1000)

Scandinavia's entrance onto the European stage was swift, dramatic, and unforgettable. On January 8, 793, a fleet of Scandinavian

pirates came ashore on the northeast coast of England and sacked the Lindisfarne monastery, slaughtering monks, burning buildings, and plundering sacred objects. Word spread like wildfire of brutal pirates who seemed to come from nowhere, looted and pillaged with extreme prejudice, then moved on. Their victims called them *Normanni, Dani, Rus,* or worse, but the name they gave themselves came from the inlets and bays *(vik)* where they lived: the Vikings.

For the next 200 years, hardy Viking sailors plundered and explored the coasts of northern Europe. Vikings from Norway primarily went west to the British Isles and settled Iceland, Greenland, and beyond; Swedes ventured east to the Baltic states, navigated the Russian rivers, and reached Constantinople; and Danes headed south (to England, France, Spain, and Italy).

The Vikings attacked in fleets of sleek, narrow, open-topped ships a hundred feet long, called *drakkars.* (See them for yourself at the Viking Ship Museums in Oslo, or in Roskilde, near Copenhagen.) Rigged with square sails and powered by dozens of men at the oars, they could attack at 15 miles an hour and land right on the beach, where they would pour out, brandishing their weapons.

Each Viking was decked out with a coat of mail, a small shield, and a helmet (though not one with horns, which by Viking times were merely ceremonial). Each warrior specialized in a particular kind of warfare: sword, spear, battle-ax, or bow-and-arrow. At the battle's crucial moment, the Vikings might send in their secret weapon—the so-called *berserkers.* These warriors attacked with a seemingly superhuman (and possibly drug-induced) frenzy, scaring the leotards off their enemies and giving us our English word "berserk."

Despite their reputation as ruthless pirates, most Vikings were settlers who established towns, married the locals, farmed the land, hunted in the forests, and traded with their neighbors. They spread Scandinavian culture and rune stones far and wide. In Northern France, the region of "Normandy" was settled by the "North-men." Eric the Red, a Norwegian Viking, was an early settler in Iceland,

and his son Leif Eriksson sailed as far as the coast of North America around A.D. 1000.

To the dismay of Roman Catholic bishops, while the rest of Europe became Christian, the Vikings held onto their pagan gods, many of whom were, like themselves, warriors: Odin, the king of the gods (who gave us our word for Wednesday), and Thor with his hammer, the god of war (and of Thursday). Believing in an afterlife, the Vikings buried their dead ceremonially along with their possessions. Some were interred beneath large mounds of dirt (such as the Gamla Uppsala burial mounds near Stockholm). Others were laid to rest in ships that were buried underground, or in graves marked with stones placed upright in the shape of a full-size ship.

By the year 1000, Scandinavian society was gradually changing—unifying, Christianizing, and assimilating into European culture. Scattered Nordic peoples coalesced into kingdoms, united under the banner of Christianity. In Norway, there was King (later "Saint") Olav II (c. 1020). Among the Svea people (Sweden), King Olof Skotkonung (c. 968-1020) unified and Christianized the land. The Danes were united by King Harald Bluetooth (c. 980), who commemorated Denmark's Christian conversion on a now-famous rune stone (located in Jelling)—although in reality, Bluetooth's "conversion" was a ploy to keep the German-Catholic bishops and missionaries at bay. Under Harald's grandson, King Canute, Denmark ruled a large empire that included parts of southern England (c. 1020). One of Canute's battles there inspired the nursery song "London Bridge Is Falling Down."

By 1100, the last pagans were gathering at Gamla Uppsala to put on their ceremonial horned helmets, worship the sun, bury fallen heroes, and retell the sagas of their ancestors. Viking culture blended into the European mainstream, but we still see traces of it today—in rune stones and burial sites; in surviving tools, weapons, and jewelry; and in the dragon-prowed designs found on Christian stave churches and even on contemporary Scandinavian coins.

MEDIEVAL CHRISTIANS, BICKERING NOBLES, AND GERMAN BUSINESSMEN (1000-1400)

In the Middle Ages, three separate (if loosely united) kingdoms emerged: Denmark, Sweden, and Norway. They were Christian and feudal, with land worked by peasants who owed allegiance to a petty noble sworn to the king. Towns sprang up, including what would become the main cities: Oslo (1048), Copenhagen (1165), and Stockholm (1255). Rulers began flying flags featuring a cross,

Typical Castle Architecture

Castles were fortified residences for medieval nobles. Castles come in all shapes and sizes, but knowing a few general terms will help you understand them.

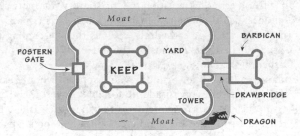

Barbican: A fortified gatehouse, sometimes a stand-alone building located outside the main walls.

Crenellation: A gap-toothed pattern of stones atop the parapet.

Drawbridge: A bridge that could be raised or lowered, using counterweights or a chain-and-winch.

Great Hall: The largest room in the castle, serving as throne room, conference center, and dining hall.

Hoardings (or Gallery): Wooden huts built onto the upper parts of the stone walls. They served as watch towers, living quarters, and fighting platforms.

The Keep (or Donjon): A high, strong stone tower in the center of the complex; the lord's home and refuge of last resort.

Loopholes (or Embrasures): Narrow wall slits through which soldiers could shoot arrows.

Machicolation: A stone ledge jutting out from the wall, with holes through which soldiers could drop rocks or boiling oil onto wall-scaling enemies below.

Moat: A ditch encircling the wall, sometimes filled with water.

Parapet: Outer railing of the wall walk.

Portcullis: An iron grille that could be lowered across the entrance.

Postern Gate: A small, unfortified side or rear entrance. In wartime, it became a "sally-port" used to launch surprise attacks, or as an escape route.

Towers: Square or round structures with crenellated tops or conical roofs serving as lookouts, chapels, living quarters, or the dungeon.

Turret: A small lookout tower rising from the top of the wall.

Wall Walk (or Allure): A pathway atop the wall where guards could patrol and where soldiers stood to fire at the enemy.

Yard (or Bailey): An open courtyard inside the castle walls.

which eventually became the main motif in each country's national flag.

Christianity dominated. Some of the region's oldest churches (especially in Norway) are wooden stave, made with vertical planks and ornamented with dragons and other semi-pagan figures to ward off evil and ease the transition to Christianity (for more about stave churches, see the Norway chapter). Devout Christians laid the cornerstones for huge cathedrals, such as the skyscraping Uppsala Cathedral in 1287, Aarhus Cathedral in 1201, and Stockholm Cathedral in 1306.

Finland entered the Scandinavian sphere when zealous Swedes launched a series of crusades to forcibly convert their pagan neighbors to the east, farm their lands, and fish in their lakes. They conquered and assimilated the region (c. 1200), making it a part of their own country for the next 600 years. Even today, Swedish is spoken on Finland's southern coast. Danish and German "warrior monks" fought a similar crusade against the loosely organized Estonian people, divvying up that region between themselves.

The many castles that dot Scandinavia attest to the civil warfare between nobles. A strong central government headed by a dominant king was still centuries away.

Sea trade between the Scandinavian neighbors boomed. The lucrative trade was controlled by enterprising German businessmen who organized Scandinavia's ports into a free-trade zone known as the Hanseatic League (c. 1200-1400). Under German direction, Scandinavia became a powerful player in overseas commerce with the Continent. Cities such as Bergen, Norway reaped big rewards under the Hanse (as evidenced by that city's fine Håkon's Hall). German settlers emigrated to Scandinavia, influencing the culture and language. By 1370, these German businessmen were so rich that they wielded more actual power than any Scandinavian king. It took a queen to break them.

DOMINANT DANES: WARS AND REFORMATION (1400-1600)

When Margrethe I of Denmark married the Norwegian king in 1363, Norway came under Danish control (where it would remain for the next 450 years). Denmark emerged as the region's main power. In 1397, Margrethe took on the Hanseatic League by uniting Norway, Denmark, and Sweden against the league with the Treaty of Kalmar. The German monopoly was broken, and Scandinavia gained control of its own wealth. But after Margrethe, the union faltered. For a century, Swedish nobles chafed and occasionally rebelled against Danish domination.

In 1520, Denmark invaded Sweden and—in the notorious Stockholm Bloodbath—massacred 80 rebellious Swedish nobles in the city's main square, Stortorget. Gustav Vasa rallied the enraged Swedes and drove out Denmark's King Christian (known as Christian II in Denmark and as Christian the Tyrant in Sweden). Vasa was crowned king of Sweden on June 6, 1523 (now Sweden's flag day). He centralized the Swedish government and Protestantized the country, seizing church property to form a strong nation-state. In many ways, this was the birth of modern Sweden (and the origin of the name for Wasa flatbread).

By the 1500s, all of Scandinavia had converted to Lutheran-style Protestantism. They'd been primed by the influence of German Hanseatic traders and preachers. And their kings jumped at the chance to confiscate former church property and authority.

For the next century, Denmark and Sweden—the region's two powerhouses—battled for control of the Baltic's lucrative trade routes, particularly for the Øresund, the crucial strait between Denmark and Sweden that connects the Baltic with the North Sea (and is now spanned by the modern Øresund Bridge). It was during this period that much of Estonia fell under control of the Swedish empire.

SWEDISH SUPERIORITY: ABSOLUTE MONARCHS (1600-1800)

By 1600, Denmark-Norway was still the region's superpower, but Sweden-Finland-Estonia was rising fast. Denmark's one-

eyed, high-living King Christian IV was spending centuries' worth of acquired wealth building lavish castles—including Rosenborg and Frederiksborg—and putting a Renaissance face on Copenhagen and Oslo (see page 76 and the sidebar on page 31). Meanwhile, his wars with Sweden and others were slowly sapping the country, emptying its coffers, and undermining Danish superiority. Christian IV even sold the Orkney and Shetland Islands to England to raise funds.

Sweden emerged under the inspired military leadership of King Gustavus Adolphus (1594-1632). The "Lion of the North" roared southward, conquering large chunks of Russia, Poland, Germany, and Denmark during the Thirty Years' War. The vast *Vasa* ship, which the king commissioned in 1628, trumpeted the optimism of the era—but sank ignominiously in the middle of Stockholm harbor on its maiden voyage (visit the unseaworthy vessel at the Vasa Museum in Stockholm).

Sweden's supreme moment came under Gustavus' great-grandson, Karl X Gustav (1622-1660). In 1657, Karl invaded Denmark through the back door—from the south. The winter was extremely cold, and the seas froze between several of Denmark's islands. In one of the most daring maneuvers in military history, Karl X Gustav led his armies across the ice between the islands—from Funen to Langeland to Lolland to Zealand—then sped toward Copenhagen. The astonished Danes surrendered, signing the humiliating Treaty of Roskilde (1658). The treaty gave Sweden a third of Danish territory, plus shared control of the Øresund Strait. Denmark would never again dominate, while Sweden became a major European power, with an imposing fleet and a Baltic empire that included Finland, Estonia, Latvia, and parts of Poland, Russia, and Germany.

In the 1660s, the kings of Denmark-Norway and Sweden-Finland-Estonia—following the trend set by Louis XIV in France—declared themselves to be absolute, divinely ordained monarchs. For the next 50 years, these kings scuffled with each other (and neighboring countries) for superiority in the Baltic. By 1720, the wars had drained both countries, at the very time that France and England were on the rise. Sweden ceded Estonia to the Russians, and Scandinavia sank back into relative obscurity.

For the rest of the 1700s, Denmark-Norway and Sweden-Finland mostly avoided war while trying to modernize and expand their economies. But the French Revolution (1789) and the Europe-wide wars that followed stirred up this relative peace, awakening a desire for democracy, ethnic recognition, and national independence.

PATRIOTS, ARTISTS, INDUSTRIALISTS, AND EMIGRANTS (1800s)

As Europe's monarchs ganged up on Revolutionary France under Napoleon, Scandinavia was forced to take sides. Through a series of complicated alliances, Denmark ended up backing the loser (France), while Sweden backed the winners (Britain and others). At war's end, Denmark was forced to cede Norway to Sweden in the 1814 Treaty of Kiel. Meanwhile, Sweden had just lost Finland to Russia in 1809. Thus began the nation-building process that, a century later, would result in the five independent countries we have today.

The wars also gave Sweden a new king—a French soldier who spoke not a word of Swedish, was not Scandinavian, and had not a drop of noble blood. But Jean-Baptiste Bernadotte, a career military man in Napoleon's army, was loved by Sweden's childless king, admired by Sweden's soldiers for his fighting prowess, and popular with the people for treating Swedish prisoners well during the wars. The bizarre choice of a French commoner was a surprise, but everyone said *oui-oui*, and Jean-Baptiste was crowned Sweden's King Karl Johan XIV (and Karl Johan III in Norway). During his reign (1818-1844), Bernadotte brought peace, prosperity, and fresh DNA, founding the royal dynasty that would produce the current monarchs of Sweden—and, by intermarriage, of Norway and Denmark.

The French Revolution (and Napoleon) spread the idea throughout Europe that people should embrace their ethnic roots and demand self-rule. Norwegians—having been ruled for centuries by Danes, and now Swedes—met at Eidsvoll Manor (outside Oslo), drafted a constitution with a parliament, elected a king, and demanded independence. Though the country was still too weak to make this a political reality, the date of May 17, 1814, has become the country's Fourth of July, celebrated today with plenty of flag-waving and folk costumes by Norwegians both in and out of Norway.

Culturally (if not politically), nationalism flourished, producing artists like J. C. Dahl, who captured the beauty of the Norwegian countryside and the simple dignity of its people. (You can see his works at Oslo's National Gallery.) Playwright Henrik Ibsen realistically portrayed the complexities of a changing Norwegian society. And composer Edvard Grieg used music to convey the majesty of the landscape near his home in Bergen (Troldhaugen).

In Denmark, nationalism inspired the German-speaking majority in the provinces of Schleswig and Holstein to call for autonomy (1848-1851). The region was finally taken by force from Denmark by Prussia (1864) and incorporated into the new state of Germany. The resulting nationwide sense of humiliation and self-critique actually spurred a cultural Golden Age. Philosopher Søren Kierkegaard captured the angst of an age when traditional certainties were crumbling. Storyteller Hans Christian Andersen (*The Ugly Duckling, The Emperor's New Clothes, The Little Mermaid,* and others) gained a Europe-wide reputation. And sculptor Bertel Thorvaldsen, who studied and worked in Rome, decorated Copenhagen with his realistic, Neoclassical statues (see them at the Cathedral of Our Lady and at Thorvaldsen's Museum).

Throughout the 1800s, Scandinavia was modernizing. The Industrial Revolution brought trains, factories, and larger cities. While some got rich, millions of poor farmers were forced to emigrate from Sweden, Norway, and Finland to America between 1850 and 1920, due to the changing economy, overpopulation, and famine. (The House of Emigrants museum in Växjö, Sweden tells their story.) As in other European countries, Scandinavia saw the steady advance of democracy, parliaments, labor unions, and constitutional monarchies. The 20th century would quicken that pace.

Also during this period, Norwegian polar explorers—including Fridtjof Nansen and Roald Amundsen—began pushing the boundaries of human knowledge by going where nobody had gone before, deep into the Arctic and Antarctic (for more, visit Oslo's Fram Museum).

INDEPENDENCE AND WORLD WARS (1900-1945)

In 1905—after five and a half centuries of Danish and Swedish rule—Norway finally was granted independence when it voted  overwhelmingly to break from Sweden. National pride ran high, as Oslo's own Roald Amundsen became the first person to reach the South Pole (in 1911). In 1919, Finland and Estonia—after centuries of Swedish and Russian rule— won their independence while Russia was distracted by the Bolshevik Revolution.

The Scandinavian nations remained neutral through World War I. But when Hitler's Nazi Germany began its European conquest in World War II, it was impossible for Scandinavians—try as they might—to remain uninvolved. While officially neutral, Sweden allowed Nazi troops "on leave" to march through. (Sweden's neutrality later provided a safe haven for Danish Jews and a refuge for the Danish and Norwegian resistance movements.)

Germany invaded Denmark and Norway on April 9, 1940, with Operation Weserübung. Scattered fighting at the Danish border was quickly put down, and Denmark capitulated and officially cooperated with the Nazis until 1943, when the Germans took over the government. Danish resistance groups harried the Nazis and provided intelligence to the Allies. In 1943, a German diplomat informed Copenhagen's rabbi that the Jews were about to be deported. Danish citizens quickly hid and eventually evacuated all but 500 of Denmark's Jews to neutral Sweden.

Norway's army held out a few weeks longer, allowing time for King Håkon VII to flee and organize a vital resistance movement (memorialized at Oslo's Norwegian Resistance Museum). Norway spent the war chafing under a Nazi puppet government headed by Vidkun Quisling, whose surname has become synonymous with "traitor."

Denmark, Sweden, and Norway came out of the war without the horrendous damage and loss of life suffered elsewhere in Europe—in part, probably, because Hitler wanted to turn the Scandinavian countries into model states. After all, these were the people Germany was trying to emulate: tall, blond, blue-eyed symbols of the Aryan race.

Finland and Estonia's fates were more complicated. During the war, the Finns valiantly battled Russian invaders, at one point allying with Hitler against the Russians. By war's end, Finland had fought both the Soviets and the Nazis. Estonia, meanwhile, was occupied first by the Soviets and later by the Nazis.

As postwar Europe was divvied up between the communist East and the democratic West, Estonia wound up in the Soviet sphere of influence. Finland avoided this fate through a compromise policy called "Finlandization." The Finns paid lip service to Soviet authority, censored their own media, acted as a buffer against military invasion from the West, rejected rebuilding money from the US (the Marshall Plan), and avoided treaties with the West. In return, Finland remained a self-ruling capitalist democracy and a firm part of the Nordic world. They imported raw materials from the Soviets, then shipped them back as manufactured products, in a mutually beneficial trade agreement.

Meanwhile, Norway and Denmark stood with the West, joining NATO and participating in the Marshall Plan. Sweden took a more neutral approach, and Swede Dag Hammarskjöld served as the UN's Secretary General from 1953 to 1961. Estonia was submerged into the Soviet Union as one of the 15 "republics" of the USSR, only regaining its independence with the breakup of the Soviet Union in 1991.

THE SOCIAL WELFARE STATE (1946-Present)

In the decades since World War II, the Scandinavian countries have made themselves quite wealthy following a mixed capitalist-

socialist model. In the late 1960s, Norway discovered oil in the North Sea, almost instantly transforming itself into a rich nation. Citizens across Scandinavia have come to take for granted cradle-to-grave security—health care, education, unemployment benefits, welfare, and so on—all financed with high taxes. In social policies, Scandinavia has often led the way in liberal attitudes toward sexuality, drug use, and gay rights. For more on current-day Scandinavia, see that chapter.

Immigration in the late 20th century brought many citizens from non-European nations. While adding diversity, it

Little Maria...or Metallica?

Scandinavia is viewed as one of the most liberal corners of Europe, so Americans are often surprised to learn there are government restrictions on what parents can name their children. Historically, parents in Denmark, Norway, Sweden, and Finland were required to choose their child's name from a published list of acceptable monikers. Any variations had to be approved by a government board. One intent of the rules was to prevent commoners from using royal names and to ban

names considered ridiculous, inappropriate, potentially harmful to the child, or just not Scandinavian enough. A Norwegian mom even spent two days in jail in the '90s for naming her son Gesher (it means "bridge" in Hebrew). But following a recent series of court rulings, Scandinavian countries are relaxing parts of their naming laws. Denmark has allowed some Legolases and Gandalfs, and in Sweden there's a girl named Metallica and a boy named Google.

Estonia took a different approach: In the 1930s it encouraged its citizens to change their Swedish-sounding names to the Estonian equivalents.

also threatened the homogenous fabric of a society whose roots have traditionally been white, Christian, European, democratic, and blond. Far-right parties gained support with anti-immigration platforms, but reaction to the July 2011 massacre in Norway weakened those movements, at least in the short term. In September 2013, however, a new right-wing government came to power in Norway, with the victorious Conservative Party forming a coalition with the anti-immigration Progress Party.

Today, Finland, Sweden, Denmark, and Estonia are all members of the European Union. Norway has stayed outside (a decision still hotly debated by Norwegians, though an association agreement gives the country most of the benefits of membership). While Finland and Estonia have embraced the euro, Norway, Sweden, and Denmark have preserved their own currencies (though Denmark's is pegged to the euro).

As the Scandinavian people forge into the 21st century, they are adamant about preserving their culture, traditions, and high standard of living while competing in a global economy.

PAST & PRESENT

PRACTICALITIES

This chapter covers the practical skills of European travel: how to get tourist information, pay for purchases, sightsee efficiently, find good-value accommodations, eat affordably but well, use technology wisely, and get between destinations smoothly. To round out your knowledge, check out "Resources from Rick Steves." For more information on these topics, see www.ricksteves.com/travel-tips.

Tourist Information

The Scandinavian Tourist Board's office in **the US** is a wealth of information on Norway, Denmark, Sweden, and Finland. Before your trip, download brochures and request any specifics you want (such as regional and city maps and festival schedules). Call 212/885-9700 or visit www.goscandinavia.com (info@goscandinavia.com). Estonia doesn't have a tourist office in the US, but you can check their website (www.visitestonia.com, tourism@eas.ee).

In Scandinavia, a good first stop in every town is generally the tourist information office (abbreviated **TI** in this book). Throughout Scandinavia, you'll find TIs are usually well-organized

PRACTICALITIES

and always have an English-speaking staff. TIs are good places to confirm sightseeing plans, pick up a city map, and get information on public transit, walking tours, special events, and nightlife. Prepare a list of questions and a proposed plan to double-check. Some TIs have information on the entire country or at least the region, so try to pick up maps and printed information for destinations you'll be visiting later in your trip.

Travel Tips

Emergency and Medical Help: In all the countries in this book, dial 112 for police, medical, or other emergencies. If you get sick, do as the locals do and go to a pharmacist for advice. Or ask at your hotel for help—they'll know the nearest medical and emergency services.

Theft or Loss: To replace a passport, you'll need to go in person to an embassy (see page 737). If your credit and debit cards disappear, cancel and replace them (see "Damage Control for Lost Cards" on page 699). File a police report, either on the spot or within a day or two; you'll need it to submit an insurance claim for lost or stolen rail passes or travel gear, and it can help with replacing your passport or credit and debit cards. For more information, see www.ricksteves.com/help.

Time Zones: Norway, Sweden, and Denmark, which share the same time zone as continental Europe, are generally six/nine hours ahead of the East/West Coasts of the US. Finland and Estonia are one hour ahead of Norway, Sweden, and Denmark. The exceptions are the beginning and end of Daylight Saving Time: Europe "springs forward" the last Sunday in March (two weeks after most of North America) and "falls back" the last Sunday in October (one week before North America). For a handy online time converter, try www.timeanddate.com/worldclock.

Business Hours: Banks are generally open weekdays from 9:00 to 15:00 or 16:00. Shops generally open at 10:00 and close between 17:00 and 20:00 on weekdays; bigger stores and malls tend to stay open later, while smaller stores and shops in smaller towns may have shorter hours. On Sundays banks and most shops are closed, and public transportation options are generally fewer. Many museums in Scandinavia are closed on Mondays.

Watt's Up? Europe's electrical system is 220 volts, instead of North America's 110 volts. Most newer electronics (such as laptops, battery chargers, and hair dryers) convert automatically, so you won't need a converter, but you will need an adapter plug with two round prongs, sold inexpensively at travel stores in the US. Avoid bringing older appliances that don't automatically convert voltage; instead, buy a cheap replacement in Europe.

Discounts: While discounts are generally not listed in this book, note that liberal Scandinavia is Europe's most generous corner when it comes to youths (under 18), students (with International Student Identity Cards, www.isic.org), seniors, and families. Children usually sleep and sightsee for half-price or free.

Online Translation Tips: Google's Chrome browser instantly translates websites. You can also paste text or the URL of a foreign website into the translation window at Translate.google.com. The Google Translate app converts spoken English into most European languages (and vice versa) and can also translate text it "reads" with your smartphone's camera.

Money

Here's my basic strategy for using money in Scandinavia:
- Upon arrival, head for a cash machine (ATM) and load up on local currency, using a debit card with low international transaction fees.
- Withdraw large amounts at each transaction (to limit fees) and keep your cash safe in a money belt.
- Pay for most items with cash.
- Pay for larger purchases with a credit card with low (or no) international fees.

PLASTIC VERSUS CASH

In Scandinavia, credit cards are widely accepted, even for small purchases. Generally you can choose to pay with cash if you prefer—except in Sweden (where cash is less common; you can't pay for a tram, metro, or bus ride with cash in Stockholm, for example).

I tend to use my credit card to book and pay for hotel reservations, to buy advance tickets for events or sights, and to cover major expenses (such as expensive meals, car rentals, or plane tickets). While you could use your debit card for some of these expenses, keep in mind that you have greater fraud protection with your credit card. The card you use may depend on which charges the lowest international transaction fees.

I use cash to pay for cheap food, taxis, tips, and local guides. And having a bit of local currency on hand helps you out of a jam if your card randomly doesn't work.

WHAT TO BRING

I pack the following and keep it all safe in my money belt.

Debit Card: Use this at ATMs to withdraw local cash as needed.

Credit Card: Use this to pay for everyday expenses such as meals and sightseeing, and especially for larger items (at hotels,

Exchange Rates

I've priced things in local currencies throughout the book. Denmark, Norway, and Sweden use crowns (*kroner* in Denmark and Norway; *kronor* in Sweden), but crowns from one country are not accepted in the next. Finland and Estonia use euros. (Check www.oanda.com for the latest rates.)

$1 equals about...
6 Danish kroner (DKK)
8 Norwegian kroner (NOK)
8 Swedish kronor (SEK)
0.80 euro (€)

To roughly convert Danish prices into US dollars, divide by 6 (e.g., 15 DKK = about $2.50, 100 DKK = about $16). In Sweden and Norway, divide prices by 8 (100 NOK = about $12.50). So, that 1,000-NOK Norwegian sweater is about $125, and your 360-SEK dinner in Stockholm is about $45. To roughly convert prices in euros to dollars, add 20 percent (€20 = about $24).

larger shops and restaurants, travel agencies, car-rental agencies, and so on).

Backup Card: Some travelers carry a third card (debit or credit; ideally from a different bank), in case one gets lost, demagnetized, eaten by a temperamental machine, or simply doesn't work.

US Dollars: I carry $100-200 US as a backup. While you won't use it for day-to-day purchases, American cash in your money belt comes in handy for emergencies, such as if your ATM card stops working.

What NOT to Bring: Resist the urge to buy the local currency before your trip or you'll pay the price in bad stateside exchange rates. Wait until you arrive to withdraw money. I've yet to see a European airport that didn't have plenty of ATMs.

BEFORE YOU GO

Use this pre-trip checklist.

Know your cards. Debit cards from any major US bank will work in any standard European bank's ATM (ideally, use a debit card with a Visa or MasterCard logo). As for credit cards, Visa and MasterCard are universal, American Express is less common, and Discover is unknown in Europe.

Most credit and debit cards have chips that authenticate and secure transactions. Europeans insert their chip cards into the payment machine slot, then enter a PIN. With a US card, you often provide a signature instead of a PIN number to verify your identity.

Any American card, whether with a chip or an old-fashioned

magnetic stripe, will work at Europe's hotels, restaurants, and shops. For self-service payment machines, you may need a PIN number. I've been inconvenienced a few times by self-service payment machines in Europe that wouldn't accept my card, but it's never caused me serious trouble.

If you're concerned, ask if your bank offers a true chip-and-PIN card. Cards with low fees and chip-and-PIN technology include those from Andrews Federal Credit Union (www.andrewsfcu.org) and the State Department Federal Credit Union (www.sdfcu.org). See "Using Credit Cards," later, for more information.

Report your travel dates. Let your bank know that you'll be using your debit and credit cards in Europe, and when and where you're headed.

Know your PIN. Make sure you know the numeric, four-digit PIN for each of your cards, both debit and credit. Request it if you don't have one and allow time to receive the information by mail.

Adjust your ATM withdrawal limit. Find out how much you can take out daily and ask for a higher daily withdrawal limit if you want to get more cash at once. Note that European ATMs will withdraw funds only from checking accounts; you're unlikely to have access to your savings account.

Ask about fees. For any purchase or withdrawal made with a card, you may be charged a currency conversion fee (1-3 percent), a Visa or MasterCard international transaction fee (1 percent), and— for debit cards—a $2-5 transaction fee each time you use a foreign ATM (some US banks partner with European banks, allowing you to use those ATMs with no fees—ask).

If you're getting a bad deal, consider getting a new debit or credit card. Reputable no-fee cards include those from Capital One, as well as Charles Schwab debit cards. Most credit unions and some airline loyalty cards have low-to-no international transaction fees.

IN EUROPE
Using Cash Machines

European cash machines have English-language instructions and work just like they do at home—except they spit out local currency instead of dollars, calculated at the day's standard bank-to-bank rate.

In most places, ATMs are easy to locate. When possible, withdraw cash from a bank-run ATM located just outside that bank. Ideally use it during the bank's opening hours; if your card is munched by the machine, you can go inside for help.

If your debit card doesn't work, try a lower amount—your request may have exceeded your withdrawal limit or the ATM's limit. If you still have a problem, try a different ATM or come back later—your bank's network may be temporarily down.

Avoid "independent" ATMs, such as Travelex, Euronet, Moneybox, Cardpoint, and Cashzone. These have high fees, can be less secure than a bank ATM, and may try to trick users with "dynamic currency conversion" (see later).

Exchanging Cash

Because Scandinavian countries have different currencies, you'll likely wind up with leftover cash when you're leaving a country. Plan ahead to avoid withdrawing more cash than you'll need. Coins can't be exchanged once you leave the country, so try to spend them before you cross the border. If you do end up with leftover bills, they're easy to convert to the "new" country's currency. When changing cash, use exchange bureaus (easy to find at major train stations and airports—but with crummy rates) rather than banks. Banks in some countries may not exchange money unless you have an account with them.

Using Credit Cards

European cards use chip-and-PIN technology, while many cards issued in the US use a chip-and-signature system. But most European card readers can automatically generate a receipt for you to sign, just as you would at home. If a cashier is present, you should have no problems. Some card readers will instead prompt you to enter your PIN (so it's important to know the code for each of your cards).

At self-service payment machines (transit-ticket kiosks, parking, etc.), results are mixed, as US chip-and-signature cards aren't configured for unattended transactions. If your card won't work, look for a cashier who can process your card manually—or pay in cash.

Drivers Beware: Be aware of potential problems using a credit card to fill up at an unattended gas station, enter a parking garage, or exit a toll road. Carry cash and be prepared to move on to the next gas station if necessary. When approaching a toll plaza, use the "cash" lane.

Dynamic Currency Conversion

Some European merchants and hoteliers cheerfully charge you for converting your purchase price into dollars. If it's offered, refuse this "service" (called dynamic currency conversion, or DCC). You'll pay extra for the expensive convenience of seeing your charge in dollars. Some ATMs also offer DCC, often in confusing or misleading terms. If an ATM offers to "lock in" or "guarantee" your conversion rate, choose "proceed without conversion." Other prompts might state, "You can be charged in dollars: Press YES for dollars, NO for the local currency." Always choose the local currency.

Security Tips

Pickpockets target tourists. To safeguard your cash, wear a money belt—a pouch with a strap that you buckle around your waist like a belt and tuck under your clothes. Keep your cash, credit cards, and passport secure in your money belt, and carry only a day's spending money in your front pocket or wallet.

Before inserting your card into an ATM, inspect the front. If anything looks crooked, loose, or damaged, it could be a sign of a card-skimming device. When entering your PIN, carefully block other people's view of the keypad.

Don't use a debit card for purchases. Because a debit card pulls funds directly from your bank account, potential charges incurred by a thief will stay on your account while the fraudulent use is investigated by your bank.

To access your accounts online while traveling, be sure to use a secure connection (see page 719).

Damage Control for Lost Cards

If you lose your credit or debit card, report the loss immediately to the respective global customer-assistance centers. Call these 24-hour US numbers collect: Visa (tel. 303/967-1096), MasterCard (tel. 636/722-7111), and American Express (tel. 336/393-1111). To make a collect call to the US, dial these numbers:

- From Denmark—800-100-10
- From Estonia—800-12001
- From Finland—0-800-11-0015
- From Norway—800-190-11
- From Sweden—020-799-111

European toll-free numbers (listed by country) can be found at the websites for Visa and MasterCard.

You'll need to provide the primary cardholder's identification-verification details (such as birth date, mother's maiden name, or Social Security number). You can generally receive a temporary card within two or three business days in Europe (see www.ricksteves.com/help for more).

If you report your loss within two days, you typically won't be responsible for unauthorized transactions on your account, although many banks charge a liability fee of $50.

TIPPING

Tipping in Scandinavia isn't as automatic and generous as it is in the US. For special service, tips are appreciated, but not expected. As in the US, the proper amount depends on your resources, tip ping philosophy, and the circumstances, but some general guidelines apply.

Restaurants: Tipping is an issue only at restaurants that have table service. If you order your food at a counter, don't tip. For more details on restaurant tipping, see "Eating," later in this chapter.

Throughout Scandinavia, a service charge is typically included in your bill, and you aren't required to leave an additional tip. But don't assume that the service charge goes to your server—often it goes right to the restaurant owner. In fancier restaurants or whenever you enjoy great service, round up the bill (about 5-10 percent of the total check). Rounding up for good service is especially common in Estonia (though never more than 10 percent).

Taxis: To tip the cabbie, round up. For a typical ride, round up your fare a bit (for instance, if the fare is 85 DKK, pay 90 DKK). If the cabbie hauls your bags and zips you to the airport to help you catch your flight, you might want to toss in a little more. But if you feel like you're being driven in circles or otherwise ripped off, skip the tip.

Services: In general, if someone in the service industry does a super job for you, a small tip (the equivalent of a euro or two) is appropriate...but not required. If you're not sure whether (or how much) to tip for a service, ask your hotelier or the TI.

GETTING A VAT REFUND

Wrapped into the purchase price of your Scandinavian souvenirs is a Value-Added Tax (VAT) of 20-25 percent (among the highest rates in Europe). You're entitled to get most of that tax back if you purchase goods worth more than a certain amount (300 DKK in Denmark, 315 NOK in Norway, 200 SEK in Sweden, €40 in Finland, and €38 in Estonia) at a store that participates in the VAT refund scheme (look for signs in store windows—VAT is called MVA in Norway; MOMS in Denmark, Finland, and Sweden; and *käibemaks* or km in Estonia). Typically, you must ring up the minimum at a single retailer—you can't add up your purchases from various shops to reach the required amount. (If the store ships the goods to your US home, VAT is not assessed on your purchase.)

Getting your refund is straightforward...and worthwhile if you spend a significant amount on souvenirs.

Get the paperwork. Have the merchant completely fill out the necessary refund document. You'll have to present your passport. Get the paperwork done before you leave the store to ensure you'll have everything you need (including your original sales receipt).

Get your stamp at the border or airport. If you've made purchases in Denmark, Sweden, Finland, and/or Estonia, process your VAT document at your last stop in the European Union (such as at the airport) with the customs agent who deals with VAT refunds.

If you've shopped hard in Norway (a non-EU country), get your document(s) stamped at the border or at your point of departure from Norway.

Arrive an additional hour before you need to check in to allow time to find the customs office—and to stand in line. Some customs desks are positioned before airport security; confirm the location before going through security.

It's best to keep your purchases in your carry-on. If they're too large or dangerous to carry on (such as knives), pack them in your checked bags and alert the check-in agent. You'll be sent (with your tagged bag) to a customs desk outside security; someone will examine your bag, stamp your paperwork, and put your bag on the belt. You're not supposed to use your purchased goods before you leave. If you show up at customs wearing your new Norwegian sweater, officials might look the other way—or deny you a refund.

Collect your refund. Many merchants work with services such as Global Blue or Premier Tax Free that have offices at major airports, ports, or border crossings (either before or after security, probably strategically located near a duty-free shop). These services, which extract a 4 percent fee, can usually refund your money immediately in cash, or credit your card (within two billing cycles). If the retailer handles VAT refunds directly, it's up to you to contact the merchant for your refund. You can mail the documents from home, or more quickly, from your point of departure (using an envelope you've prepared in advance or one that's been provided by the merchant). You'll then have to wait—it can take months.

CUSTOMS FOR AMERICAN SHOPPERS

You can take home $800 worth of items per person duty-free, once every 31 days. Many processed and packaged foods are allowed, including: vacuum-packed cheeses, dried herbs, jams, baked goods, candy, chocolate, oil, vinegar, mustard, and honey. Fresh fruits and vegetables and most meats are not allowed, with exceptions for some canned items. As for alcohol, you can bring in one liter duty-free (it can be packed securely in your checked luggage, along with any other liquid-containing items).

To bring alcohol (or liquid-packed foods) in your carry-on bag on your flight home, buy it at a duty-free shop at the airport. You'll increase your odds of getting it onto a connecting flight if it's packaged in a "STEB"—a secure, tamper-evident bag. But stay away from liquids in opaque, ceramic, or metallic containers, which usually cannot be successfully screened (STEB or no STEB).

For details on allowable goods, customs rules, and duty rates, visit www.cbp.gov.

Sightseeing

Sightseeing can be hard work. Use these tips to make your visits to Scandinavia's finest sights meaningful, fun, efficient, and painless.

MAPS AND NAVIGATION TOOLS

A good map is essential for efficient navigation while sightseeing. The maps in this book are concise and simple, designed to help you locate recommended destinations, sights, and local TIs, where you can pick up more in-depth maps. Maps with even more detail are sold at newsstands and bookstores.

You can also use a mapping app on your mobile device. Be aware that pulling up maps or looking up turn-by-turn walking directions on the fly requires an Internet connection: To use this feature, it's smart to get an international data plan (see the "Using a Mobile Phone in Europe" section, later). With Google Maps or City Maps 2Go, it's possible to download a map while online, then go offline and navigate without incurring data-roaming charges, though you can't search for an address or get real-time walking directions. A handful of other apps—including Apple Maps, Off-Maps, and Navfree—also allow you to use maps offline.

PLAN AHEAD

Set up an itinerary that allows you to fit in all your must-see sights. For a one-stop look at opening hours in the bigger cities, see the "At a Glance" sidebars for Copenhagen, Oslo, Bergen, Stockholm, Helsinki, and Tallinn. Most sights keep stable hours, but you can easily confirm the latest by checking with the TI or visiting museum websites.

Don't put off visiting a must-see sight—you never know when a place will close unexpectedly for a holiday, strike, or restoration. Many museums are closed or have reduced hours at least a few days a year, especially on holidays such as Christmas, New Year's, and Labor Day (May 1). A list of holidays is in the appendix—also check online for possible museum closures during your trip. In summer, some sights may stay open late; in the off-season, hours may be shorter.

Going at the right time helps avoid crowds. This book offers tips on the best times to see specific sights. Try visiting popular sights very early or very late. Evening visits (when possible) are usually peaceful, with fewer crowds.

If you plan to hire a local guide, reserve ahead by email. Popular guides can get booked up.

Study up. To get the most out of the sight descriptions in this book, read them before your visit.

AT SIGHTS

Here's what you can typically expect:

Entering: Be warned that you may not be allowed to enter if you arrive 30 to 60 minutes before closing time. And guards start ushering people out well before the actual closing time, so don't save the best for last.

Some important sights have a security check, where you must open your bag or send it through a metal detector. Allow extra time for these lines in your planning. Some sights require you to check daypacks and coats. (If you'd rather not check your daypack, try carrying it tucked under your arm like a purse as you enter.)

Photography: If the museum's photo policy isn't clearly posted, ask a guard. Generally, taking photos without a flash or tripod is allowed. Some sights ban selfie sticks; others ban photos altogether.

Temporary Exhibits: Museums may show special exhibits in addition to their permanent collection. Some exhibits are included in the entry price, while others come at an extra cost (which you may have to pay even if you don't want to see the exhibit).

Expect Changes: Artwork can be on tour, on loan, out sick, or shifted at the whim of the curator. Pick up a floor plan as you enter, and ask museum staff if you can't find a particular item.

Audioguides and Apps: Many sights rent audioguides, which generally offer excellent recorded descriptions in English. If you bring your own earbuds, you can enjoy better sound. To save money, bring a Y-jack and share one audioguide with your travel partner. Museums and sights often offer free apps that you can download to your mobile device (check their websites).

Services: Important sights may have a reasonably priced on-site café or cafeteria (handy places to rejuvenate during a long visit). The WCs at sights are free and generally clean.

Before Leaving: At the gift shop, scan the postcard rack or thumb through a guidebook to be sure that you haven't overlooked something that you'd like to see.

Every sight or museum offers more than what is covered in this book. Use the information in this book as an introduction—not the final word.

Sleeping

I favor hotels that are handy to your sightseeing activities. Rather than list accommodations scattered throughout a city, I choose hotels in my favorite neighborhoods. My recommendations run the gamut, from dorm beds to fancy rooms with all the comforts.

Extensive and opinionated listings of good-value rooms are a major feature of this book's Sleeping sections. I like places that are

PRACTICALITIES

Sleep Code

Hotels are classified based on the average price of a standard double room with breakfast in high season.

	Denmark	Norway	Sweden	Finland/Estonia
$$$$ Splurge Most rooms over:	1,100 DKK	1,500 NOK	2,000 SEK	€225/€110
$$$ Pricier	900- 1,100 DKK	1,200- 1,500 NOK	1,500- 2,000 SEK	€175-225/ €90-110
$$ Moderate	700- 900 DKK	900- 1,200 NOK	1,000- 1,500 SEK	€125-175/ €70-90
$ Budget	500- 700 DKK	600- 900 NOK	500- 1,000 SEK	€75-125/ €50-70
¢ Backpacker Most rooms under:	500 DKK	600 NOK	500 SEK	€75/€50

RS% Rick Steves discount

Unless otherwise noted, credit cards are accepted, hotel staff speak English, and free Wi-Fi is available. Comparison-shop by checking prices at several hotels (on each hotel's own website, on a booking site, or by email). For the best deal, *book directly with the hotel*. Ask for a discount if paying in cash; if the listing includes **RS%**, request a Rick Steves discount.

clean, central, relatively quiet at night, reasonably priced, friendly, small enough to have a hands-on owner or manager and stable staff, and run with a respect for Scandinavian traditions. I'm more impressed by a convenient location and a fun-loving philosophy than flat-screen TVs and a fancy gym. Most places I recommend fall short of perfection. But if I can find a place with most of these features, it's a keeper.

Book your accommodations as soon as your itinerary is set, especially if you want to stay at one of my top listings or if you'll be traveling during busy times. See the appendix for a list of major holidays and festivals in Scandinavia; for tips on making reservations, see page 708.

Some people make reservations as they travel, calling hotels a few days to a week before their arrival. If you anticipate crowds (worst on weekdays at business destinations and weekends at tourist locales) on the day you want to check in, call hotels at about 9:00 or 10:00, when the receptionist knows who'll be checking out and which rooms will be available. Apps such as HotelTonight.com specialize in last-minute rooms, often at business-class hotels in big cities.

RATES AND DEALS

I've categorized my recommended accommodations based on price, indicated with a dollar-sign rating (see sidebar). The price ranges suggest an estimated cost for a one-night stay in a standard double room with a private toilet and shower in high season, include breakfast, and assume you're booking directly with the hotel (not through a booking site, which extracts a commission). Room prices can fluctuate significantly with demand and amenities (size, views, room class, and so on), but relative price categories remain constant.

Room rates are especially volatile at larger hotels that use "dynamic pricing" to set rates. Prices can skyrocket during festivals and conventions, while business hotels can have deep discounts on weekends when demand plummets. Of the many hotels I recommend, it's difficult to say which will be the best value on a given day—until you do your homework.

Once your dates are set, check the specific price for your preferred stay at several hotels. You can do this either by comparing prices on Hotels.com or Booking.com, or by checking the hotels' own websites. To get the best deal, contact my family-run hotels directly by phone or email. When you go direct, the owner avoids the 20 percent commission, giving them wiggle room to offer you a discount, a nicer room, or free breakfast if it's not already included (see sidebar). If you prefer to book online or are considering a hotel chain, it's to your advantage to use the hotel's website.

Some hotels offer a discount to those who pay cash or stay at least three nights. To cut costs further, try asking for a cheaper room (for example, with a shared bathroom or no window) or offer to skip breakfast (if included).

Additionally, some accommodations offer a special discount for Rick Steves readers, indicated in this guidebook by the abbreviation **"RS%."** Discounts vary: Ask for details when you reserve. Generally, to qualify you must book direct (that is, not through a booking site), mention this book when you reserve, show this book upon arrival, and sometimes pay cash or stay a certain number of nights. In some cases, you may need to enter a discount code (which I've provided in the listing) in the booking form on the hotel's website. Rick Steves discounts apply to readers with ebooks as well as printed books. Understandably, discounts do not apply to promotional rates.

TYPES OF ACCOMMODATIONS

Accommodations in Scandinavia are fairly expensive, but normally very comfortable and usually come with a generous breakfast. When budgeting, plan on spending about $180-250 per hotel double in big cities, and $125-150 in smaller towns. Money-conscious

Hotels vs. Booking Websites vs. Consumers

In the last decade it's become almost impossible for independent-minded, family-run hotels to survive without playing the game as dictated by the big players in the online booking world. Priceline's Booking.com and Expedia's Hotels.com take roughly 80 percent of this business. Hoteliers note that without this online presence, "We become almost invisible." Online booking services demand about a 20 percent commission. And in order to be listed, a hotel must promise that its website does not undercut the price on the third-party's website. Without that restriction, hoteliers could say, "Sure, sell our rooms for whatever markup you like, and we'll continue to offer a fair rate to travelers who come to us directly"—but that's not allowed.

Here's the work-around: For independent and family-run hotels, book directly by email or phone, in which case hotel owners are free to give you whatever price they like. Research the price online, and then ask for a room without the commission mark-up. You could ask them to split the difference—the hotel charges you 10 percent less but pockets 10 percent more. Or you can ask for a free breakfast (if not included) or free upgrade.

If you do book online, be sure to use the hotel's website (you'll likely pay the same price as via a booking site, but your money goes to the hotel, not agency commissions).

As consumers, remember: Whenever you book with an online booking service, you're adding a needless middleman who takes roughly 20 percent. If you'd like to support small, family-run hotels whose world is more difficult than ever, book direct.

travelers should consider doubles in hostels and rooms in simple hotels with shared baths—a respectable option in clean and wholesome Scandinavia.

Hotels

Check hotel websites for deals. When a classy, modern $200 place

has a $150 summer special that includes two $10 buffet breakfasts, a dumpy $100 hotel room without breakfast becomes less exciting.

Some hotels can add an extra bed (for a small charge) to turn a double into a triple; some offer larger rooms for four or more people (I call these "family rooms" in the listings). If there's space for an extra cot, they'll cram it in for you. In general, a triple room is cheaper than the cost of a double and a single. Three or four people can economize by requesting one big room.

Some modern Scandinavian hotels have "combi" rooms (singles with a sofa that turns the room into a perfectly good double), which are cheaper than a full double.

Arrival and Check-In: Hotels and B&Bs are sometimes located on the higher floors of a multipurpose building with a secured door. In that case, look for your hotel's name on the buttons by the main entrance. When you ring the bell, you'll be buzzed in.

Hotel elevators are common, though some older buildings still lack them. Elevators are typically very small—pack light, or you may need to send your bags up without you.

When you check in, the receptionist will normally ask for your passport and keep it for anywhere from a couple of minutes to a couple of hours. The EU requires that hotels collect your name, nationality, and ID number. Relax. Americans are notorious for making this chore more difficult than it needs to be.

If you're arriving in the morning, your room probably won't be ready. Check your bag safely at the hotel and dive right into sightseeing.

In Your Room: More pillows and blankets are usually in the closet or available on request. Towels and linens aren't always replaced every day. Hang your towel up to dry.

Most hotel rooms have a TV, telephone, and free Wi-Fi (although in old buildings with thick walls, the Wi-Fi signal doesn't always make it to the rooms; sometimes it's only available in the lobby). Simpler places rarely have a room phone, but will have Wi-Fi.

To guard against theft in your room, keep valuables out of sight. Some rooms come with a safe, and other hotels have safes at the front desk. I've never bothered using one and in a lifetime of travel, I've never had anything stolen from my room.

Checking Out: While it's customary to pay for your room upon departure, it can be a good idea to settle your bill the day before, when you're not in a hurry and while the manager's in. That way you'll have time to discuss and address any points of contention.

Hotelier Help: Hoteliers can be a good source of advice. Most know their city well, and can assist you with everything from public transit and airport connections to finding a good restaurant, the nearest launderette, or a late-night pharmacy.

Hotel Hassles: Even at the best places, mechanical breakdowns occur: sinks leak, hot water turns cold, toilets gurgle and smell, the Wi-Fi goes out, or the air-conditioning dies when you

Making Hotel Reservations

Reserve your rooms as soon as you've pinned down your travel dates. For busy national holidays, it's wise to reserve far in advance (see the appendix).

Requesting a Reservation: For family-run hotels, it's generally cheaper to book your room directly via email or a phone call. For business-class hotels, or if you'd rather book online, reserve directly through the hotel's official website (not a booking agency's site). For complicated requests, send an email. Almost all of my recommended hotels take reservations in English.

Here's what the hotelier wants to know:
- type(s) of rooms you need and size of your party
- number of nights you'll stay
- your arrival and departure dates, written European-style as day/month/year (for example, 18/06/20 or 18 June 2020)
- special requests (such as en suite bathroom vs. down the hall, cheapest room, twin beds vs. double bed, quiet room)
- applicable discounts (such as a Rick Steves reader discount, cash discount, or promotional rate)

Confirming a Reservation: Most places will request a credit-card number to hold your room. If you're using an online reservation form, look for the *https* or a lock icon at the top of your browser. If you book direct, you can email, call, or fax this information.

Canceling a Reservation: If you must cancel, it's courteous—and smart—to do so with as much notice as possible, especially for smaller family-run places. Cancellation policies can be strict;

need it most. Report your concerns clearly and calmly at the front desk. For more complicated problems, don't expect instant results.

If you find that night noise is a problem (if, for instance, your room is over a nightclub), ask for a quieter room in the back or on an upper floor.

Above all, keep a positive attitude. Remember, you're on vacation. If your hotel is a disappointment, spend more time out enjoying the city you came to see.

Short-Term Rentals

A short-term rental—whether an apartment, house, or room in a local's home—is an increasingly popular alternative, especially if you plan to settle in one location for several nights. For stays longer than a few days, you can usually find a rental that's comparable to—and cheaper than—a hotel room with similar amenities. Plus, you'll get a behind-the-scenes peek into how locals live.

Many places require a minimum-night stay, and compared to hotels, rentals usually have less-flexible cancellation policies.

From:	rick@ricksteves.com
Sent:	Today
To:	info@hotelcentral.com
Subject:	Reservation request for 19-22 July

Dear Hotel Central,

I would like to stay at your hotel. Please let me know if you have a room available and the price for:
• 2 people
• Double bed and en suite bathroom in a quiet room
• Arriving 19 July, departing 22 July (3 nights)

Thank you!
Rick Steves

read the fine print or ask about these before you book. Many discount deals require prepayment, with no cancellation refunds.

Reconfirming a Reservation: Always call or email to reconfirm your room reservation a few days in advance. For smaller hotels and B&Bs, I call again on my day of arrival to tell my host what time to expect me (especially important if arriving late—after 17:00).

Phoning: For tips on how to call hotels overseas, see page 720.

And you're generally on your own: There's no hotel reception desk, breakfast, or daily cleaning service.

Finding Accommodations: Aggregator websites such as Airbnb, FlipKey, Booking.com, and the HomeAway family of sites (HomeAway, VRBO, and VacationRentals) let you browse properties and correspond directly with European property owners or managers. If you prefer to work from a curated list of accommodations, consider using a rental agency such as InterhomeUSA.com or RentaVilla.com. Agency-represented apartments typically cost more, but this method often offers more help and safeguards than booking direct.

Before you commit, be clear on the details, location, and amenities. I like to virtually "explore" the neighborhood using the Street View feature on Google Maps. Also consider the proximity to public transportation, and how well-connected the property is with the rest of the city. Ask about amenities (elevator, air-conditioning, laundry, Wi-Fi, parking, etc.). Reviews from previous guests can help identify trouble spots.

The Good and Bad of Online Reviews

User-generated review sites and apps such as Yelp, Booking. com, and TripAdvisor can give you a consensus of opinions about everything from hotels and restaurants to sights and nightlife. If you scan reviews of a hotel and see several complaints about noise or a rotten location, it tells you something important that you'd never learn from the hotel's own website.

But as a guidebook writer, my sense is that there is a big difference between the uncurated information on a review site and a guidebook. A user-generated review is based on the experience of one person, who likely stayed at one hotel in a given city and ate at a few restaurants there (and who doesn't have much of a basis for comparison). A guidebook is the work of a trained researcher who, year after year, visits many alternatives to assess their relative value. I recently checked out some top-rated user-reviewed hotel and restaurant listings in various towns; when stacked up against their competitors, some were gems, while just as many were duds.

Both types of information have their place, and in many ways, they're complementary. If something is well-reviewed in a guidebook, and also gets good ratings on one of these sites, it's likely a winner.

Think about the kind of experience you want: Just a key and an affordable bed...or a chance to get to know a local? There are typically two kinds of hosts: those who want minimal interaction with their guests, and hosts who are friendly and may want to interact with you. Read the promotional text and online reviews to help shape your decision.

Apartments: If you're staying somewhere for four nights or longer, it's worth considering an apartment (shorter stays aren't worth the hassle of arranging key pickup, buying groceries, etc.). Apartment rentals can be especially cost-effective for groups and families. European apartments, like hotel rooms, tend to be small by US standards. But they often come with laundry machines and small, equipped kitchens, making it easier and cheaper to dine in. If you make good use of the kitchen, you'll save on your meal budget.

Rooms in Private Homes: Renting a room in someone's home is a good option for some travelers. Beds range from air-mattress-in-living-room basic to plush-B&B-suite posh. Some places allow you to book for a single night; if staying for several nights, you can buy groceries just as you would in a rental house. While you can't expect your host to also be your tour guide—or even to provide you with much info—some may be interested in getting to know the travelers who come through their home.

Other Options: Swapping homes with a local works for people with an appealing place to offer, and who can live with the idea of having strangers in their home (don't assume where you live is not interesting to Europeans). A good place to start is HomeExchange. To sleep for free, Couchsurfing.com is a vagabond's alternative to Airbnb. It lists millions of outgoing members, who host fellow "surfers" in their homes.

Confirming and Paying: Many places require you to pay the entire balance before your trip. It's easiest and safest to pay through the site where you found the listing. Be wary of owners who want to take your transaction offline to avoid fees; this gives you no recourse if things go awry. Never agree to wire money (a key indicator of a fraudulent transaction).

Hostels

Scandinavian hostels are among Europe's finest. A hostel provides cheap beds in dorms where you sleep alongside strangers. Travelers of any age are welcome if they don't mind dorm-style accommodations and meeting other travelers. Most hostels offer kitchen facilities, guest computers, Wi-Fi, and a self-service laundry. Hostels almost always provide bedding, but the towel's up to you (though you can usually rent one for a small fee). Family and private rooms are often available.

Independent hostels tend to be easygoing, colorful, and informal (no membership required; www.hostelworld.com). You may pay slightly less by booking directly with the hostel. **Official hostels** are part of Hostelling International (HI) and share an online booking site (www.hihostels.com). HI hostels typically require that you be a member or pay extra per night.

Camping

Scandinavian campgrounds are practical, comfortable, and cheap (about $10/person with $20 "Camping Key Europe" discount

card—buy the card at the first campsite you visit or through www.campingkeyeurope.com). This is the middle-class Scandinavian family way to travel: safe, great social fun, and no reservation problems. Campgrounds are friendly, safe, more central and convenient than rustic, and rarely full.

The national tourist office websites have campground listings, but for more comprehensive guides, visit these websites: www.camping.se (Sweden), www.camping.dk (Denmark), and www.

camping.no (Norway). You'll find campgrounds just about everywhere you need them.

Many campgrounds also offer camping cottages *(stugor)* or huts *(hytter)* for wannabe campers with no gear. These normally sleep four to six in bunk beds, and come with blankets and a kitchenette. The toilet and shower may be in a nearby shared washhouse. Because locals typically move in for a week or two, many campground huts are booked for summer long in advance. You can book these ahead as well, or try your chances on the road.

Eating

I look for restaurants that are convenient to your hotel and sightseeing. When restaurant-hunting, choose a spot filled with locals, not tourists. Venturing even a block or two off the main drag leads to higher-quality food for a better price.

Most Scandinavian nations have one inedible dish that is cherished with a perverse but patriotic sentimentality. These dishes, which often originated during a famine, now remind the young of their ancestors' suffering. Norway's penitential food, lutefisk (dried cod marinated for days in lye and water), is used for Christmas and for jokes. Swedes and Norwegians make pickled herring the centerpiece of any buffet (pickling was the best way to preserve the abundant fish back in the Middle Ages). And Finns go for *kalakukko*—a fish-and-bacon hand pie, a convenient portable lunch back in the day.

But contemporary Nordic cuisine has taken several giant steps forward in recent years. Emphasizing pure, fresh ingredients and innovative preparations, Scandinavia's chefs are piling up well-deserved accolades.

BREAKFAST
The vast breakfast buffet that comes with most hotel rooms is a

great way to stock up on calories for a busy day of sightseeing. Plenty of local treats show up on the breakfast table: various herring dishes, hearty breads and crackers, and rich, sweet goat cheese.

You'll also find fruit, cereal, and various milks (look for

words like *skummet* for skim, *let/lavt* for low-fat, *sød/hel* for whole). Grab a drinkable yogurt and go local by pouring it in the bowl and sprinkling your cereal over it. The great selection of breads and crackers comes with jam, butter *(smør)*, margarine (same word), and cheese *(ost)*. And you'll get an array of cold cuts, pickled herring, caviar paste (in a squeeze tube), and boiled eggs (*bløt/blød* is soft-boiled; *hård* is hard-boiled); use the egg cups and small spoons provided to eat your soft-boiled egg Scandinavian-style.

The brown cheese with the texture of earwax and a slightly sweet taste is called *geitost/gede ost* ("goat cheese") or *brunost* ("brown cheese"). It's not really a cheese—it's made from boiled-down, slightly sweetened whey—and often contains a blend of goat and cow's milk. Give this odd but enjoyable dairy product a try—it's a tasty topping on traditional heart-shaped waffles. Swedes prefer a spreadable variety called *messmör*.

For beverages, it's fruit juices and coffee or tea. While it's bad form to take freebies from the breakfast buffet to eat later, many hotels will provide you with the wrappings to pack yourself a lunch, legitimately, for $7-8. Ask for a "packed lunch"—*madpakke* (Danish) *matpakke* (Norwegian), or *packad lunch* (Swedish).

LUNCH

Many restaurants offer cheap daily *(dagens)* lunch specials and buffets. Scandinavians, not big on lunch, often just grab a sandwich and a cup of coffee at their work desk.

Especially in Denmark, you'll find *smørrebrød* shops turning sandwiches into an art form. These open-face delights taste as good as they look. My favorite is the one piled high with shrimp. The roast beef is good, too. And don't be afraid to give herring a try. Shops will wrap sandwiches up for a perfect picnic in a nearby park.

If you want to enjoy a combination of picnics and restaurant meals on your trip, you'll save money by eating in restaurants at lunch (when there's usually a special and food is generally cheaper) and picnicking for dinner.

PICNICS

Scandinavia has colorful markets, economical supermarkets, and take-away delis. Picnic-friendly mini-markets at gas and train stations are open late. Samples of picnic treats: *Wasa* cracker breads (the rye "Sport" flavor is my favorite), packaged meat and cheese, brown "goat cheese" *(geitost)*, drinkable yogurt, smoked fish from markets, fresh fruit and vegetables, lingonberries, squeeze tubes of sandwich spreads (from mustard and mayo to shrimp and caviar), rye bread, and boxes of juice and milk. Most convenience shops offer cheap ready-made sandwiches. If you're bored with sandwiches, some groceries and most delis have hot chicken, salads by the portion, and picnic portables.

DINNER

The largest meal of the Nordic day is dinner. To keep it affordable, alternate between picnic dinners (outside or in your hotel room);

cheap, forgettable, but filling cafeteria or fast-food dinners ($20); and atmospheric, carefully chosen restaurants popular with locals ($40 and up). One main course and two salads or soups fill up two travelers without emptying their pocketbooks. Booze is as pricey as it is heavily taxed; stick to beer instead (although it's not cheap either). Water is usually served free with an understanding smile at most restaurants.

In Scandinavia, a $40 meal in a restaurant is not that much more than a $30 American meal, since tax and tip are included in the menu price.

RESTAURANT PRICING

I've categorized my recommended eateries based on price, indicated with a dollar-sign rating (see sidebar). The price ranges suggest the average price of a typical main course—but not necessarily a complete meal. Obviously, expensive items (like steak and seafood), fine wine, appetizers, and dessert can significantly increase your final bill.

The categories also indicate a place's personality: **Budget** eateries include street food, takeaway, order-at-the-counter shops, basic cafeterias, and bakeries selling sandwiches. **Moderate** eateries are nice (but not fancy) sit-down restaurants, ideal for a straightforward, fill-the-tank meal. **Pricier** eateries are a notch up, with more attention paid to the setting, presentation, and cuisine. This category often includes affordable "destination" or "foodie" restaurants. And **splurge** eateries typically come with an elegant setting, polished service, pricey and intricate cuisine, and an expansive (and

Restaurant Code

I've assigned each eatery a price category, based on the average cost of a typical main course. Drinks, desserts, and splurge items (steak and seafood) can raise the price considerably.

		Denmark	Norway	Sweden	Finland & Estonia
$$$$	**Splurge** Most main courses over:	175 DKK	175 NOK	200 SEK	€25
$$$	**Pricier**	125-175 DKK	125-175 NOK	150-200 SEK	€20-25
$$	**Moderate**	75-125 DKK	75-125 NOK	100-150 SEK	€15-20
$	**Budget** Most main courses under:	75 DKK	75 NOK	100 SEK	€15

In Scandinavia, a hot dog or other takeout spot is **$**; a sit-down café is **$$**; a casual but more upscale restaurant is **$$$**; and a swanky splurge is **$$$$**—though in pricey big cities even casual places come with high prices.

expensive) wine list. Note that in expensive Scandinavian cities, you may pay splurge prices for even more casual meals.

I haven't categorized places where you might assemble a picnic, snack, or graze: supermarkets, delis, ice cream-stands, cafés or bars specializing in drinks, chocolate shops, and so on.

SMÖRGÅSBORD

The *smörgåsbord* (known in Denmark and Norway as the *store koldt bord*) is a Scandinavian culinary tradition. Though locals reserve the *smörgåsbord* for festive times such as the Christmas season, anyone can dig into this all-you-can-eat buffet any time of year at certain hotels and on overnight ferries. While the word originally referred to a spread of cold cuts, the *smörgåsbords* you'll find usually include hot dishes, too.

Seek out a *smörgåsbord* at least once during your trip, just for the high of seeing so much wholesome Nordic food spread out before you.

Follow these simple steps to enjoy a tasty *smörgåsbord*:
1. Browse the buffet before you begin, so you can budget your

stomach space. Think of the *smörgåsbord* as a five- or six-course meal.

2. Don't overload your plate. Instead, make several trips, taking a fresh plate and cutlery each time. To signal the waiter that you're finished with each round, lay your fork and knife side-by-side on the plate. If you're getting up but are not finished with your plate, place your fork and knife in the shape of an *X* on the plate.

3. Begin with the herring dishes, along with boiled potatoes and crispbreads.

4. Next, sample the other fish dishes (warm and cold) and more potatoes. *Gravlax* is salt-cured salmon flavored with dill, served along with a sweet mustard sauce.

5. Move on to salads, egg dishes, and various cold cuts.

6. Now for the meat dishes—it's meatball time! Pour on some gravy as well as a spoonful of lingonberry sauce, and have more potatoes. Reindeer and other roast meats and poultry may also tempt you.

7. Still hungry? Make a point to sample the Nordic cheeses—try creamy Havarti, mild Castello (a soft blue cheese), and in Norwegian buffets, goat cheese. Sample the delicious seasonal fruits and white bread. And there are racks of traditional desserts, cakes, and custards (see "Dessert," later). Cap the meal with coffee.

Smaklig måltid! Enjoy your meal!

DRINKING

Purchasing heavily taxed wine, beer, and spirits in Scandinavia can put a dent in your vacation budget. In Sweden and Norway, spirits, wine, and strong beer (more than 3.5 percent alcohol) are sold in state-run liquor stores: Systembolaget in Sweden, and Vinmonopolet in Norway. Buying a beer or glass of wine in a bar or restaurant in Sweden or Norway is particularly expensive. Therefore, many Scandinavians will have a drink or a glass of wine at home (or in their hotel room) before going out, then limit themselves to one or two glasses at the restaurant. If taking an overnight cruise during your trip, you can get a good deal on a bottle of wine or spirits in the onboard duty-free shop.

Liquor laws are much more relaxed in Denmark, where you can buy wine, beer, and spirits at any supermarket or corner store. Prices are a bit lower as well. Public drinking is acceptable in Denmark, while it is illegal (although often done) in Norway and Sweden. Throughout Scandinavia, drinking and driving is not tolerated.

Some local specialties are *akvavit*, a strong, vodka-like spirit distilled from potatoes and flavored with anise, caraway, or other herbs and spices—then drunk ice-cold (common in Norway, Sweden, and Denmark). *Lakka* is a syrupy-sweet liqueur made from cloudberries, the small orange berries grown in the Arctic (popular in Norway, Sweden, and Finland). *Salmiakka* is a nearly black, licorice-flavored liqueur (Finland, Norway, and Denmark). *Gammel Dansk* can be described as Danish bitters for the adventurous (Denmark only).

DESSERT

Scandinavians love sweets. A meal is not complete without a little treat and a cup of coffee at the end. Bakeries fill their win-

dow cases with all varieties of cakes, tarts, cookies, and pastries. The most popular ingredients are marzipan, almonds, hazelnuts, chocolate, and fresh berries. Many cakes are covered with entire sheets of solid marzipan. To find the neighborhood bakery, just look for a golden pretzel—the classic Scandinavian symbol for a bakery—hanging above the door or windows.

Scandinavian chocolate is some of the best in Europe. In Denmark, seek out Anthon Berg's dark chocolate and marzipan treats, as well as Toms' chocolate-covered caramels (Toms Guld are the best). Sweden's biggest chocolate producer, Marabou, makes huge bars of solid milk chocolate, as well as some with dried fruits or nuts. *Daim* are milk chocolate-covered hard toffees, sold in a variety of sizes, from large bars to bite-size pieces, all in bright red wrappers. The Freia company, Norway's chocolate goddess (named for the Norse goddess Freya), makes a wonderful assortment of delights, from *Et lite stykke Norge* ("A little piece of Norway"—bars of creamy milk chocolate wrapped in pale yellow paper) and *Smil* (chocolate-covered soft caramels sold in rolls) to *Firkløver* (bars of milk chocolate with hazelnuts) and the venerable Kvikk Lunsj, similar to a Kit Kat bar. For those who can't decide on one type, the company sells bags of assorted chocolates called *Twist* and red gift boxes of pricey chocolates called *Kong Haakon*, named after Norway's first king.

While chocolate rules, licorice and gummy candies are also popular. Black licorice *(lakrits/lakris/lakrids)* is at its best here—although *saltlakrits* (salty licorice) is not for the timid. Black licorice flavors everything from ice cream to chewing gum to liqueur. Throughout Scandinavia, you'll find stores selling all varieties of candy in bulk. Fill your bag with a variety of candies and pay by the gram. Look around at the customers in these stores...they aren't all children.

Staying Connected

One of the most common questions I hear from travelers is, "How can I stay connected in Europe?" The short answer is: more easily and cheaply than you might think.

The simplest solution is to bring your own device—mobile phone, tablet, or laptop—and use it just as you would at home (following the tips below, such as connecting to free Wi-Fi whenever possible). Another option is to buy a European SIM card for your mobile phone—either your US phone or one you buy in Europe. Or you can use European landlines and computers to connect. Each of these options is described next, and more details are at www.ricksteves.com/phoning. For a very practical one-hour talk covering tech issues for travelers, see www.ricksteves.com/mobile-travel-skills.

USING A MOBILE PHONE IN EUROPE

Here are some budget tips and options.

Sign up for an international plan. To stay connected at a lower cost, sign up for an international service plan through your carrier. Most providers offer a simple bundle that includes calling, messaging, and data. Your normal plan may already include international coverage (T-Mobile's does).

Before your trip, call your provider or check online to confirm that your phone will work in Europe, and research your provider's international rates. Activate the plan a day or two before you leave, then remember to cancel it when your trip's over.

Use free Wi-Fi whenever possible. Unless you have an unlimited-data plan, you're best off saving most of your online tasks for Wi-Fi. You can access the Internet, send texts, and even make voice calls over Wi-Fi.

Most accommodations in Europe offer free Wi-Fi, but some—especially expensive hotels—charge a fee. Many cafés (including Starbucks and McDonald's) have free hotspots for customers; look for signs offering it and ask for the Wi-Fi password when you buy something. You'll also often find Wi-Fi at TIs, city squares, major museums, public-transit hubs, airports, and aboard trains and buses.

Minimize the use of your cellular network. Even with an international data plan, wait until you're on Wi-Fi to Skype, download apps, stream videos, or do other megabyte-greedy tasks. Using a navigation app such as Google Maps over a cellular network can take lots of data, so do this sparingly or use it offline.

Tips on Internet Security

Make sure that your device is running the latest versions of its operating system, security software, and apps. Next, ensure that your device and key programs (like email) are password- or passcode-protected. On the road, use only secure, password-protected Wi-Fi hotspots. Ask the hotel or café staff for the specific name of their Wi-Fi network, and make sure you log on to that exact one.

If you must access your financial info online, use a banking app rather than accessing your account via a browser. A cellular connection is more secure than Wi-Fi. Avoid logging onto personal finance sites on a public computer.

Never share your credit-card number (or any other sensitive information) online unless you know that the site is secure. A secure site displays a little padlock icon, and the URL begins with *https* (instead of the usual *http*).

Limit automatic updates. By default, your device constantly checks for a data connection and updates apps. It's smart to disable these features so your apps will only update when you're on Wi-Fi, and to change your device's email settings from "auto-retrieve" to "manual" (or from "push" to "fetch").

When you need to get online but can't find Wi-Fi, simply turn on your cellular network just long enough for the task at hand. When you're done, avoid further charges by manually turning off data roaming or cellular data (either works) in your device's Settings menu. Another way to make sure you're not accidentally using data roaming is to put your device in "airplane" mode (which also disables phone calls and texts), and then turn your Wi-Fi back on as needed.

It's also a good idea to keep track of your data usage. On your device's menu, look for "cellular data usage" or "mobile data" and reset the counter at the start of your trip.

Use Wi-Fi calling and messaging apps. Skype, Viber, FaceTime, and Google+ Hangouts are great for making free or low-cost voice and video calls over Wi-Fi. With an app installed on your phone, tablet, or laptop, you can log on to a Wi-Fi network and contact friends or family members who use the same service. If you buy credit in advance, with some of these services you can call any mobile phone or landline worldwide for just pennies per minute.

Many of these apps also allow you to send messages over Wi-Fi to any other person using that app. Be aware that some apps, such as Apple's iMessage, will use the cellular network if Wi-Fi isn't available: To avoid this possibility, turn off the "Send as SMS" feature.

How to Dial

International Calls

Whether phoning from a US landline or mobile phone, or from a number in another European country, here's how to make an international call. I've used one of my recommended Copenhagen hotels as an example (tel. 33 13 19 13).

Initial Zero: Drop the initial zero from international phone numbers—except when calling Italy.

Mobile Tip: If using a mobile phone, the "+" sign can replace the international access code (for a "+" sign, press and hold "0").

US/Canada to Europe

Dial 011 (US/Canada international access code), country code (45 for Denmark), and phone number.

▶ To call the Copenhagen hotel from home, dial 011 45 33 13 19 13.

Country to Country Within Europe

Dial 00 (Europe international access code), country code, and phone number.

▶ To call the Copenhagen hotel from Germany, dial 00 45 33 13 19 13.

Europe to the US/Canada

Dial 00, country code (1 for US/Canada), and phone number.

▶ To call from Europe to my office in Edmonds, Washington, dial 00-1-425-771-8303.

Domestic Calls

Denmark, Estonia, and Norway use a direct-dial system (no area codes). To call anywhere within one of these countries, just dial the number. Sweden and Finland, on the other hand, use area codes (included in my listings). To make domestic calls anywhere within these countries, punch in just the phone number if you're dialing locally (and add the area code if calling long distance).

▶ To call the Copenhagen hotel from anywhere in Denmark (including Copenhagen), dial 33 13 19 13.

▶ To call a recommended hotel in Stockholm from within Stockholm, dial 723-7250. To call the same hotel from Kalmar (in southeast Sweden), dial 08/723-7250.

USING A EUROPEAN SIM CARD

With a European SIM card, you get a European mobile number and access to cheaper rates than you'll get through your US carrier. This option works well for those who want to make a lot of voice calls or need faster connection speeds than their US carrier provides. Fit the SIM card into a cheap phone you buy in Europe (about $40 from phone shops anywhere), or swap out the SIM card

PRACTICALITIES

More Dialing Tips

Scandinavian Phone Numbers: Scandinavian phone numbers may vary in length; for instance, a hotel can have a six-digit phone number and an eight-digit fax number. Note that calls to a European mobile phone are substantially more expensive than calls to a fixed line.

Toll and Toll-Free Calls: Toll calls begin with 90 in Denmark; 70 in Estonia; 0900, 0939, 0944, and 099 in Sweden; Finland has many toll-call prefixes. International rates apply to US toll-free numbers dialed from Scandinavia—they're not free.

More Phoning Help: See www.howtocallabroad.com.

European Country Codes		Ireland & N. Ireland	353 / 44
Austria	43	Italy	39
Belgium	32	Latvia	371
Bosnia-Herzegovina	387	Montenegro	382
Croatia	385	Morocco	212
Czech Republic	420	Netherlands	31
Denmark	45	Norway	47
Estonia	372	Poland	48
Finland	358	Portugal	351
France	33	Russia	7
Germany	49	Slovakia	421
Gibraltar	350	Slovenia	386
Great Britain	44	Spain	34
Greece	30	Sweden	46
Hungary	36	Switzerland	41
Iceland	354	Turkey	90

in an "unlocked" US phone (check with your carrier about unlocking it).

SIM cards are sold at mobile-phone shops, department-store electronics counters, some newsstands, and vending machines. Costing about $5-10, they usually include prepaid calling/messaging credit, with no contract and no commitment. Expect to pay $20-40 more for a SIM card with a gigabyte of data. If you travel

Hurdling the Language Barrier

In Scandinavia, English is all you need; it seems every well-educated Scandinavian speaks it. Still, knowing a few key words in the language of the country you are visiting is good style and helpful.

Each country has its own language, but Danish, Norwegian, and Swedish are so closely related that locals can laugh at each other's TV comedies. These languages add a few extra letters (Æ, Ø, Ö, Å, Ä) that affect pronunciation—and also alphabetizing. If you can't find, say, Årjäng in a map index, look after Z. Finnish and Estonian are vastly different from the other Scandinavian languages; in fact, Finnish has more in common with Hungarian than with Swedish.

Here are a few Swedish, Norwegian, and/or Danish words you'll see and hear a lot: *hej/hei* (hi), *tack/takk/tak* (thanks), *gammal/gammel* (old), *litten/litt/lille* (small), *stor* (big), *slott/slot* (palace), *centrum/sentrum* (center), *gata/gate/gade* (street), and *öl/øl* (beer).

You'll find a list of survival phrases at the end of each country introduction chapter in this book. Give it your best shot. The locals will appreciate your efforts.

with this card to other countries in the European Union, there may be extra roaming fees.

I like to buy SIM cards at a phone shop where there's a clerk to help explain the options. Certain brands—including Lebara and Lycamobile, both of which are available in multiple European countries—are reliable and especially economical. I've also had good luck with Telenor SIM cards in Norway and Comviq cards in Sweden. Ask the clerk to help you insert your SIM card, set it up, and show you how to use it. In some countries—including Norway and Denmark—you'll be required to register the SIM card with your passport as an antiterrorism measure (which may mean you can't use the phone for the first hour or two).

Find out how to check your credit balance. When you run out of credit, you can top it up at newsstands, tobacco shops, mobile-phone stores, or many other businesses (look for your SIM card's logo in the window), or online.

PUBLIC PHONES AND COMPUTERS

It's possible to travel in Europe without a mobile device. You can make calls from your hotel (or the increasingly rare public phone), and check email or browse websites using public computers.

Most **hotels** charge a fee for placing calls—ask for rates before you dial. You can use a prepaid international phone card (available at post offices, newsstands, street kiosks, tobacco shops, and train stations) to call out from your hotel. Dial the toll-free access number, enter the card's PIN code, then dial the number.

You'll see **public pay phones** in a few post offices and train stations. The phones generally come with multilingual instructions; most don't take coins but instead require insertable phone cards (sold at post offices, newsstands, etc.).

Most hotels have **public computers** in their lobbies for guests to use; otherwise you may find them at Internet cafés and public libraries (ask your hotelier or the TI for the nearest location). On a European keyboard, use the "Alt Gr" key to the right of the space bar to insert the extra symbol that appears on some keys. If you can't locate a special character (such as @), simply copy and paste it from a web page.

MAIL

You can mail one package per day to yourself worth up to $200 duty-free from Europe to the US (mark it "personal purchases"). If you're sending a gift to someone, mark it "unsolicited gift." For details, visit www.cbp.gov and search for "Know Before You Go." The postal service works fine throughout Scandinavia, but for quick transatlantic delivery (in either direction), consider services such as DHL (www.dhl.com). You can get stamps at the neighborhood post office, newsstands within fancy hotels, and some minimarts and card shops.

Transportation

For transportation within Scandinavia, consider these factors: Cars are best for three or more traveling together (especially families with small kids), those packing heavy, and those delving into the countryside. Trains, buses, and boats are best for solo travelers, blitz tourists, and city-to-city travelers, and those who don't want to drive in Europe. Intra-European flights are an increasingly inexpensive option. While a car gives you more freedom, trains, buses, and boats zip you effortlessly and scenically from city to city, usually dropping you in the center, often near a TI. Cars are an expensive headache in places like Copenhagen and Stockholm.

TRAINS

With a few exceptions, trains cover my recommended Scandinavian destinations wonderfully.

Schedules and Tickets: Pick up train schedules from stations as you go. While most information is given both in the country's language and in English, it's good to know the word for "delayed"— *forsinket* in Danish and Norwegian, and *försenad* in Swedish.

To study ahead online, check www.bahn.com (Germany's ex-

cellent Europe-wide timetable). Local train companies also have their own sites with fare and timetable information, and online booking; see www.dsb.dk or www.rejseplanen.dk (Denmark), www.nsb.no (Norway), www.sj.se (Sweden), www.vr.fi (Finland), and www.gorail.ee (Estonia).

Rail Passes: One of the great Nordic bargains, the Eurail Scandinavia pass is your best rail pass deal for a trip limited to Denmark, Norway, Sweden, and Finland. Although the pass is

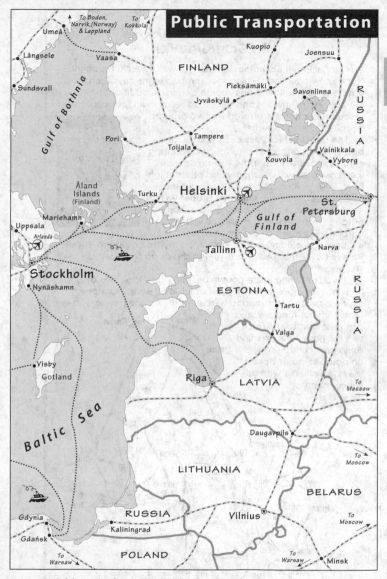

Public Transportation

To Boden, Narvik, (Norway) & Lappland

To Kokkola

Umeå

Långsele

Sundsvall

Vaasa

FINLAND

Kuopio

Joensuu

Pieksämäki

Jyväskylä

Savonlinna

RUSSIA

Gulf of Bothnia

Pori

Tampere

Toijala

Kouvola

Vainikkala

Vyborg

Åland Islands (Finland)

Turku

Helsinki

St. Petersburg

Uppsala

Mariehamn

Gulf of Finland

Arlanda

Tallinn

Narva

Stockholm

Nynäshamn

ESTONIA

Tartu

RUSSIA

Valga

Visby

Gotland

Riga

LATVIA

To Moscow

Baltic Sea

Daugavpils

To Moscow

LITHUANIA

BELARUS

Gdynia

RUSSIA

Vilnius

To Moscow

Gdańsk

Kaliningrad

To Warsaw

POLAND

To Warsaw

Minsk

available only for second-class seats, Scandinavian second class is plenty comfortable (and some trains do not offer first class). All Eurail passes allow up to two kids (ages 4-11) to travel free with an adult.

If your trip extends south of Scandinavia, you could consider a Select Pass, which allows you to choose four adjacent countries connected by land or ferry (for instance, Germany-Denmark-Sweden-Finland)—but the Scandinavia pass is a better value. Single-

Rail Passes and Train Travel in Scandinavia

A regional Eurail **Scandinavia Pass** lets you travel in Denmark, Norway, Sweden, and Finland for three to eight days (consecutively or not) within a one-month period. In addition, single-country rail passes can be a solid value in all four countries. Discounted rates are offered for two or more people traveling together.

The Eurail **Select Pass** costs a little more, but lets you connect two to four neighboring countries over two months, mixing Scandinavian countries with Germany and other neighbors. They're also covered (along with most of Europe) by the classic Eurail **Global Pass.**

Rail passes are best purchased outside Europe (through travel agents or Rick Steves' Europe). For more on the ins and outs of rail passes, including prices, download my **free guide to Eurail Passes** (www.ricksteves.com/rail-guide) or go to www.ricksteves.com/rail.

If you're taking just a couple of train rides, look into buying individual point-to-point tickets, which may save you money over a pass. Use this map to add up approximate pay-as-you-go fares for your itinerary, and compare that to the price of a rail pass. Keep in mind that significant discounts on **point-to-point tickets** may be available with advance purchase.

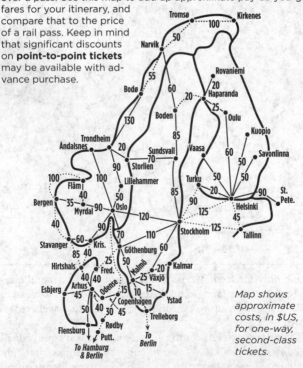

Map shows approximate costs, in $US, for one-way, second-class tickets.

country Eurail passes are also available for Denmark, Norway, Sweden, and Finland.

Rail passes give you discounts on some boat tickets (such as Stockholm to Helsinki, Tallinn, and Riga) and cover almost all trains in the region (though you'll need paid seat reservations for long rides and express trains, including Norway's Myrdal-Flåm ride—part of the Norway in a Nutshell route). If you'll be taking a popular train on a busy day and want to be assured of having a seat, a reservation can be a good investment even if it's not required.

For more detailed advice on figuring out the smartest rail-pass options for your train trip, visit www.ricksteves.com/rail.

BUSES

Don't overlook long-distance buses, which are usually slower but have considerably cheaper and more predictable fares than trains. (In Denmark, however, the train system is excellent and nearly always the better option.) On certain routes, such as between Stockholm and Oslo, the bus is cheaper and only slightly slower than the train. Scandinavia's big bus carriers are Norway's Nor-Way Bussekspress (www.nor-way.no), Denmark's public buses (www.rejseplanen.dk), Sweden's Swebus (www.swebusexpress.se), and Finland's Matkahuolto (www.matkahuolto.fi). Estonia has several carriers, of which Lux Express is the largest (www.luxexpress.ee).

BOATS

Boats are romantic, scenic, and sometimes the most efficient—or only—way to link destinations in coastal Scandinavia. But boats can often be more expensive than other options, although some routes may be covered or discounted if you have a rail pass. Note that short-distance ferries may take only cash, not credit cards.

Advance reservations are recommended for overnight boats, especially in summer or on weekends. The main links are Oslo to Copenhagen (www.dfdsseaways.com), Stockholm to Helsinki (www.vikingline.fi and www.tallinksilja.com), and Stockholm to Tallinn (www.tallinksilja.com).

Several companies speed between Helsinki and Tallinn in 2-3 hours (see the Tallinn chapter). It's possible to connect Norway and Denmark by ferry (Kristiansand and Hirtshals, www.fjordline.com and www.colorline.com). Ferries are essential for hopping between the mainland and Scandinavia's many islands, such as Ærø in central Denmark (drivers should reserve in advance for weekends and summer, www.aeroe-ferry.dk), or Stockholm's archipelago. Boats are both a necessary and spectacular way to travel through Norway's fjords or along its coast (www.fjordtours.no, www.fjord1.no, and www.tide.no). Bergen, in Norway, is a departure point for boats to the Arctic (www.hurtigruten.com).

TAXIS AND UBER

Most European taxis are reliable and cheap. In many cities, couples can travel short distances by cab for little more than two bus or subway tickets. Taxis can be your best option for getting to the airport for an early morning flight or to connect two far-flung destinations. If you like ride-booking services like Uber, these apps usually work in Europe just like they do in the US: You request a car on your mobile device (connected to Wi-Fi or a data plan), and the fare is automatically charged to your credit card.

RENTING A CAR

The minimum age to rent a car varies by country and rental company (you must be 21 in Denmark and Estonia, and 19 in Sweden, Norway, and Finland). Drivers under the age of 25 may incur a young-driver surcharge, and some rental companies do not rent to anyone 75 and over. If you're considered too young or old, look into leasing (covered later), which has less-stringent age restrictions.

Research car rentals before you go. It's cheaper to arrange most car rentals from the US. Consider several companies to compare rates.

Most of the major US rental agencies (including Avis, Budget, Enterprise, Hertz, and Thrifty) have offices throughout Europe. Also consider the two major Europe-based agencies, Europcar and Sixt. It can be cheaper to use a consolidator, such as Auto Europe/Kemwel (www.autoeurope.com—or the often cheaper www.autoeurope.eu), which compares rates at several companies to get you the best deal—but because you're working with a middleman, it's especially important to ask in advance about add-on fees and restrictions.

Always read the fine print or query the agent carefully for add-on charges—such as one-way drop-off fees, airport surcharges, or mandatory insurance policies—that aren't included in the "total price."

For the best deal, rent by the week with unlimited mileage. To save money on fuel, you can request a diesel car. I normally rent the smallest, least-expensive model with a stick shift (generally much cheaper than an automatic). Almost all rentals are manual by default, so if you need an automatic, you must request one in advance; be aware that these cars are usually larger models (not as maneuverable on narrow, winding roads).

Figure on paying about $300 for a one-week rental. Allow extra for supplemental insurance, fuel, tolls, and parking. For trips of three weeks or more, leasing can save you money on insurance and taxes. Be warned that international trips—say, picking up in Copenhagen and dropping off in Oslo—can be expensive if the rental company assesses a drop-off fee for crossing a border.

As a rule, always tell your car-rental company up front exactly which countries you'll be entering. Some companies levy extra insurance fees for trips taken in certain countries with certain types of cars (such as BMWs, Mercedes, and convertibles). Double-check with your rental agent that you have all the documentation you need before you drive off.

Picking Up Your Car: Compare pickup costs (downtown can be less expensive than the airport) and explore drop-off options. Always check the hours of the location you choose: Many rental offices close from midday Saturday until Monday morning and, in smaller towns, at lunchtime.

When selecting a location, don't trust the agency's description of "downtown" or "city center." In some cases, a "downtown" branch can be on the outskirts of the city—a long, costly taxi ride from the center. Before choosing, plug the addresses into a mapping website. You may find that the "train station" location is handier. Returning a car at a big-city train station or downtown agency can be tricky; get precise details on the car drop-off location and hours, and allow ample time to find it.

When you pick up the rental car, check it thoroughly and make sure any damage is noted on your rental agreement. Rental agencies in Europe tend to charge for even minor damage, so be sure to mark everything. Before driving off, find out how your car's gearshift, lights, turn signals, wipers, radio, and fuel cap function, and know what kind of fuel the car takes (diesel vs. unleaded). When you return the car, make sure the agent verifies its condition with you. Some drivers take pictures of the returned vehicle as proof of its condition.

In some cases, I prefer to connect long distances by train or bus, then rent cars for a day or two where they're most useful (I've noted these places throughout this book).

Car Insurance Options

When you rent a car, you are liable for a very high deductible, sometimes equal to the entire value of the car. Limit your financial risk with one of these options: Buy Collision Damage Waiver (CDW) coverage with a low or zero deductible from the car-rental company, get coverage through your credit card (free, if your card automatically includes zero-deductible coverage), or get collision insurance as part of a larger travel-insurance policy.

Basic **CDW** includes a very high deductible (typically $1,000-1,500), costs $15-30 a day (figure roughly 30-40 percent extra), and reduces your liability, but does not eliminate it. When you reserve or pick up the car, you'll be offered the chance to "buy down" the basic deductible to zero (for an additional $10-30/day; this is sometimes called "super CDW" or "zero-deductible coverage").

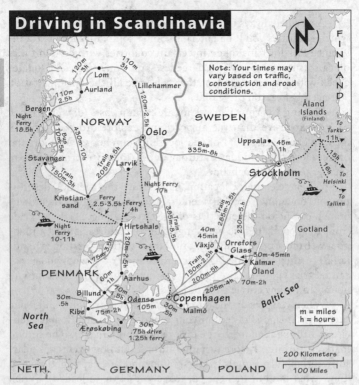

Driving in Scandinavia

Note: Your times may vary based on traffic, construction and road conditions.

m = miles
h = hours

200 Kilometers
100 Miles

If you opt for **credit-card coverage,** you'll technically have to decline all coverage offered by the car-rental company, which means they can place a hold on your card (which can be up to the full value of the car). In case of damage, it can be time-consuming to resolve the charges with your credit-card company. Before you decide on this option, quiz your credit-card company about how it works.

If you're already purchasing a **travel-insurance policy** for your trip, adding collision coverage can be an economical option. For example, Travel Guard (www.travelguard.com) sells affordable renter's collision insurance as an add-on to its other policies; it's valid everywhere in Europe except the Republic of Ireland, and some Italian car-rental companies refuse to honor it, as it doesn't cover you in case of theft.

For more on car-rental insurance, see www.ricksteves.com/cdw.

Leasing

For trips of three weeks or more, consider leasing (which automatically includes zero-deductible collision and theft insurance). By technically buying and then selling back the car, you save lots of money on tax and insurance. Leasing provides you a brand-new car with unlimited mileage and a 24-hour emergency assistance program. You can lease for as little as 21 days to as long as five and a half months. One of many companies offering affordable lease packages is Auto Europe.

Navigation Options

If you'll be navigating using your phone or a GPS unit from home, remember to bring a car charger and device mount.

Your Mobile Device: The mapping app on your mobile phone works fine for navigation in Europe, but for real-time turn-by-turn directions and traffic updates, you'll generally need Internet access. And driving all day while online can be very expensive. Helpful exceptions are Google Maps, Here WeGo, and Navmii, which provide turn-by-turn voice directions and recalibrate even when they're offline.

Download your map before you head out—it's smart to select a large region. Then turn off your cellular connection so you're not charged for data roaming. Call up the map, enter your destination, and you're on your way. View maps in standard view (not satellite view) to limit data demands.

GPS Devices: If you prefer the convenience of a dedicated GPS unit, consider renting one with your car ($10-30/day). These units offer real-time turn-by-turn directions and traffic without the data requirements of an app. Note that the unit may only come loaded with maps for its home country; if you need additional maps, ask. Also make sure your device's language is set to English before you drive off.

A less-expensive option is to bring a GPS device from home. Be aware that you'll need to buy and download European maps before your trip.

Maps and Atlases: Even when navigating primarily with a mobile app or GPS, I always make it a point to have a paper map. It's invaluable for getting the big picture, understanding alternate routes, and filling in when my phone runs out of juice. The free maps you get from your car-rental company usually don't have enough detail. It's smart to buy a better map before you go, or pick one up at a European gas station, bookshop, newsstand, or tourist shop.

Driving

Except for the dangers posed by scenic distractions and moose crossings, Scandinavia is a great place to drive. But never drink and drive—even one drink can get a driver into serious trouble.

Road Rules: Seat belts are mandatory, and children too small to be secure in seatbelts (generally, under 4.5 feet) need a child-safety seat. Be aware of typical European road rules; for example, many countries require headlights to be turned on at all times, and it's generally illegal to drive while using your mobile phone without a hands-free headset. In Europe, you're not allowed to turn right on a red light, unless there is a sign or signal specifically authorizing it, and on expressways it's illegal to pass drivers on the right. Ask your car-rental company about these rules, or check the US State Department website (www. travel.state.gov; search for your country in the "Learn about your destination" box, then click on "Travel and Transportation").

Fuel: Gas is expensive—often more than $6 per gallon. US credit and debit cards likely won't work at pay-at-the-pump stations, but are generally accepted (with a PIN code) at staffed stations. Carry cash just in case. Diesel rental cars are common; make sure you know what type of fuel your car takes before you fill up.

On the Road: Roads are good (though nerve-rackingly skinny in western Norway). Signs and road maps are excellent. Local road etiquette is similar to that in the US. There are plenty of good facilities, gas stations, and scenic rest stops. Snow is a serious problem off-season in the mountains.

Tolls: You'll encounter one-way tolls of up to €60 on major bridges including the Øresund Bridge between Sweden and Denmark, the Svinesund Bridge between Sweden and Norway, and the Storebælt Bridge between the Danish islands of Zealand and Funen. Cities such as Oslo, Bergen, and Stockholm charge tolls for entering the city center.

To minimize tolls in Norway, register as a visitor at www. autopass.no.

Parking: Parking on the street is a headache in major cities, where expensive garages are safe and plentiful. It's usually a good strategy to park on the outskirts and take public transportation into city centers.

Many Scandinavian cities, such as Tallinn and Helsinki, have pay-and-display parking; check signs locally. Denmark uses a parking windshield-clock disk (free at TIs, post offices, and newsstands; set it when you arrive and be back before your posted time limit is up). Even in the Nordic countries, thieves break into cars. Park carefully, use the trunk, and show no valuables.

Signage: As you navigate, you'll find town signs followed by the letters *N, S, Ø* (*Ö* in Sweden), *V,* or *C.* These stand for north *(nord/nor),* south *(sør/söder/syd),* east *(øst/öster),* west *(vest/väster),* and center *(centrum),* respectively; understanding them will save you lots of wrong turns.

FLIGHTS

Copenhagen is usually the most direct and least expensive Scandinavian capital to fly into from the US. Copenhagen is also Europe's gateway to Scandinavia from points south.

This book covers far-flung destinations separated by vast stretches of mountains and water. While boats and trains are more romantic, cheap flights can provide an affordable and efficient way to connect the dots on a Scandinavian itinerary.

The best comparison search engine for both international and intra-European flights is Kayak.com. An alternative is Google Flights, which has an easy-to-use system to track prices. For inexpensive flights within Europe, try Skyscanner.com.

Flying to Europe: Start looking for international flights about four to six months before your trip, especially for peak-season travel. Off-season tickets can be purchased a month or so in advance. Depending on your itinerary, it can be efficient to fly into one city and out of another. If your flight requires a connection in Europe, see our hints on navigating Europe's top hub airports at www.ricksteves.com/hub-airports.

Flying within Europe: If you're considering a train ride that's more than five hours long, a flight may save you both time and money. When comparing your options, factor in the time it takes to get to the airport and how early you'll need to arrive to check in. SAS, the region's dominant airline, operates a low-cost Finnish subsidiary called Blue1 (hubs in Helsinki and Stockholm, www.blue1.com) and is affiliated with Oslo-based Widerøe Air (www.wideroe.no). Other options are Norwegian Airlines (hubs in Oslo and Bergen, www.norwegian.com); and Tallinn-based Estonian Air (www.estonian-air.com). Well-known cheapo airlines include EasyJet and Ryanair. But be aware of the potential drawbacks of flying with a discount airline: nonrefundable and nonchangeable tickets, minimal or nonexistent customer service, pricey and time-consuming treks to secondary airports, and stingy baggage allowances with steep overage fees. If you're traveling with lots of luggage, a cheap flight can quickly become a bad deal. To avoid unpleasant surprises, read the small print before you book. These days you can also fly within Europe on major airlines affordably—and without all the aggressive restrictions—for around $100 a flight.

Flying to the US and Canada: Because security is extra tight for flights to the US, be sure to give yourself plenty of time at the airport. It's also important to charge your electronic devices before you board because security checks may require you to turn them on (see www.tsa.gov for the latest rules).

Resources from Rick Steves

Begin your trip at www.ricksteves.com: My mobile-friendly website is the place to explore Europe. You'll find thousands of fun articles, videos, photos, and radio interviews organized by country; a wealth of money-saving tips for planning your dream trip; monthly travel news dispatches; a video library of my travel talks; my travel blog; and my latest guidebook updates (www.ricksteves.com/update).

Our **Travel Forum** is an immense yet well-groomed collection of message boards where our travel-savvy community answers questions and shares their personal travel experiences—and our well-traveled staff chimes in when they can be helpful (www.ricksteves.com/forums).

Our online **Travel Store** offers travel bags and accessories that I've designed specifically to help you travel smarter and lighter. These include my popular carry-on bags (which I live out of four months a year), money belts, totes, toiletries kits, adapters, other accessories, and a wide selection of guidebooks and planning maps.

Choosing the right **rail pass** for your trip—amid hundreds of options—can drive you nutty. Our website will help you find the perfect fit for your itinerary and your budget: We offer easy, one-stop shopping for rail passes, seat reservations, and point-to-point tickets (www.ricksteves.com/rail).

Small Group Tours: Want to travel with greater efficiency and less stress? We offer more than 40 itineraries and have over 900 departures annually reaching the best destinations in this book... and beyond. Our 14-day Best of Scandinavia tour features the big-city highlights of Stockholm, Copenhagen, and Oslo, as well as quieter Nordic nooks such as the Danish island of Æro and a scenic cruise through the fjords; we also offer a nine-day tour of Tallinn, Helsinki, and St. Petersburg. You'll enjoy great guides, a fun bunch of travel partners (with small groups of 24 to 28 travelers), and plenty of room to spread out in a big, comfy bus when touring between towns. You'll find European adventures to fit every vacation length. For all the details, and to get our Tour Catalog, visit www.ricksteves.com or call us at 425/608-4217.

Books: *Rick Steves Scandinavia* is one of many books in my series on European travel, which includes country guidebooks,

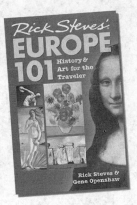

city guidebooks (Rome, Florence, Paris, London, etc.), Snapshot guides (excerpted chapters from my country guides), Pocket Guides (full-color little books on big cities), "Best Of" guidebooks (condensed country guides in a full-color, easy-to-scan format), and my budget-travel skills handbook, *Rick Steves Europe Through the Back Door*. Most of my titles are available as ebooks.

My phrase books—for German, French, Italian, Spanish, and Portuguese— are practical and budget-oriented. My other books include *Europe 101* (a crash course on art and history designed for travelers); *Mediterranean Cruise Ports* and *Scandinavian & Northern European Cruise Ports* (how to make the most of your time in port); and *Travel as a Political Act* (a travelogue sprinkled with advice for bringing home a global perspective). A more complete list of my titles appears near the end of this book.

TV Shows: My public television series, *Rick Steves' Europe*, covers Europe from top to bottom with over 100 half-hour episodes, and we're working on new shows every year. To watch full episodes online for free, see www.ricksteves.com/tv.

Travel Talks on Video: You can raise your travel I.Q. with video versions of our popular classes (including talks on travel skills, packing smart, cruising, tech for travelers, European art for travelers, travel as a political act, and individual talks covering most European countries). See www.ricksteves.com/travel-talks.

Radio: My weekly public radio show, *Travel with Rick Steves*, features interviews with travel experts from around the world. It airs on 400 public radio stations across the US, and you can also listen to it as a podcast on iTunes, iHeartRadio, Stitcher, Tune In, and other platforms. A complete archive of programs (over 400 in all) is available at www.soundcloud.com/rick-steves. Most of this audio content is available for free through my **Rick Steves Audio Europe** app.

APPENDIX

Useful Contacts

Emergency Needs
Police, Fire, and Ambulance: 112 (Europe-wide in English)

US Embassies
Embassies are located in all the capital cities. All passport services are by appointment, and embassies are closed on both American and host country's national holidays.
Denmark: Dag Hammarskjölds Allé 24, Copenhagen, Mon-Thu 9:00-12:00, info tel. 33 41 71 00 (Mon-Fri 8:30-17:00), emergency after-hours tel. 33 41 74 00, https://dk.usembassy.gov
Estonia: Kentmanni 20, Tallinn, Mon-Fri 9:00-12:00 & 14:00-17:00, tel. 668-8100, emergency tel. 509-2129, https://ee.usembassy.gov
Finland: Itäinen Puistotie 14B, Helsinki, info tel. 40/140-5957 (Mon and Wed 14:00-16:00, Tue 15:00-16:00), emergency tel. 09/616-250, https://fi.usembassy.gov
Norway: Morgedalsvegen 36, Oslo, Mon-Fri 8:30-17:00, tel. 21 30 85 40, https://no.usembassy.gov
Sweden: Dag Hammarskjölds Väg 31, Stockholm, info tel.

08/783-5375 (Tue 9:00-11:00), emergency tel. 08/783-5300, https://se.usembassy.gov

Canadian Embassies

Denmark: Kristen Bernikowsgade 1, Copenhagen, Mon-Fri 8:30-12:00 & 13:00-16:30, tel. 33 48 32 00, www.canada.dk

Estonia: Toom-Kooli 13, Tallinn, Mon-Fri 8:30-17:00, tel. 627-3311, www.canada.ee

Finland: Pohjoisesplanadi 25B, Helsinki, Mon-Fri 8:30-11:00 & 14:00-16:30, tel. 09/228-530, www.canadainternational.gc.ca/finland-finlande

Norway: Wergelandsveien 7, Oslo, Mon-Fri 8:30-16:30, tel. 22 99 53 00, www.canadainternational.gc.ca/norway-norvege

Sweden: Klarabergsgatan 23, Stockholm, Mon-Fri 9:00-12:00, tel. 08/453-3000, www.canadainternational.gc.ca/sweden-suede

Holidays and Festivals

This list includes selected festivals, plus national holidays observed throughout Scandinavia. Many sights and banks close down on national holidays—keep this in mind when planning your itinerary. Before planning a trip around a festival, verify the dates with the festival website, city tourist offices (www.goscandinavia.com; for Estonia, www.visitestonia.com), or my "Upcoming Holidays and Festivals" web pages at www.ricksteves.com.

Jan 1	New Year's Day
Jan 6	Epiphany, Sweden and Finland
Feb	Vinterjazz, winter jazz festival (www.jazz.dk), Denmark
Feb 24	National Day, Estonia
March or April	Easter Sunday-Monday
April 30	Walpurgis Night (bonfires, choirs), Sweden and Finland
April or May	Common Prayer Day (fourth Friday after Easter), Denmark
May 1	Labor Day (parades)
Early-Mid-May	MaiJazz (international jazz festival, www.maijazz.no), Stavanger, Norway
May 15	St. Hallvard's Day (theater, concerts), Oslo
May 17	Constitution Day (parades), Norway
Late May-Early June	Bergen International Festival (concerts, ballet, opera, theater; www.fib.no)
May or June	Ascension Day

May or June	Whitsunday and Whitmonday
May-June	Medieval Festival ("Middelalderfestival," www.oslomiddelalderfestival.org), Oslo
June 5	Constitution Day, Denmark
June 6	National Day (parades), Sweden
Early June	Old Town Days (music and parades; http://vanalinnapaevad.ee), Tallinn
Early June	Archipelago Boat Day (steamboat parade, (www.skargardstrafikanten.se), Stockholm
Early June	Taste of Stockholm (outdoor food vendors; www.smakapastockholm.se)
Mid-June	Norwegian Wood Rock Music Festival (www.norwegianwood.no), Oslo
Mid-June	Bergenfest (rock, pop, hip-hop, and folk music; www.bergenfest.no), Bergen, Norway
Mid-June-Mid-Aug	Grieg in Bergen Festival (summer-long concert series; www.grieginbergen.com), Bergen, Norway
June 23	Victory Day, Estonia
June 23	Sankthansaften (St. John's Eve, midsummer festival, Norway and Denmark)
Late June	Midsummer Eve and Midsummer Day (celebrations, bonfires)
Late June-Early July	Roskilde Festival (music and culture, www.roskilde-festival.dk), Roskilde, Denmark
Early July-Early Aug	Savonlinna Opera Festival (www.operafestival.fi), Savonlinna, Finland
Mid-July	Stockholm Jazz Festival (http://stockholmjazz.se)
July	Copenhagen Jazz Festival (www.jazz.dk)
Mid-Late July	International Jazz Festival (www.jazzfest.dk), Aarhus, Denmark
Late July	Food Festival ("Gladmat," www.gladmat.no), Stavanger, Norway
Late July-Mid-Aug	Hans Christian Andersen Festival (www.hcandersenfestspil.dk), Odense, Denmark
Mid-Aug	International Chamber Music Festival (www.kammermusikkfestivalen.com), Stavanger, Norway
Mid-Aug	Chamber Music Festival (www.oslokammermusikkfestival.no), Oslo

Mid-Aug	Jazz Festival (www.oslojazz.no), Oslo
Mid-Late Aug	Helsinki Festival (music, dance, film, theater; www.helsinkifestival.fi)
August 20	Day of Restoration of Independence (celebrates 1991 independence), Estonia
Late Aug-Sept	Aarhus Festival (music, dance, theater; www.aarhusfestuge.dk), Aarhus, Denmark
Mid-Sept	Ultima Contemporary Music Festival (www.ultima.no), Oslo
Mid-Oct	DølaJazz Festival (www.dolajazz.no), Lillehammer, Norway
Mid-Nov-late Dec	Christmas Fair (Tivoli Garden), Copenhagen
Dec 6	Independence Day (candlelit windows), Finland
Dec 10	Nobel Peace Prize Award Ceremony, Oslo and Stockholm
Dec 13	St. Lucia Day (festival of lights), Sweden, Norway, and parts of Finland
Dec 25	Christmas
Dec 26	Boxing Day

Books and Films

To learn about Scandinavia past and present, check out a few of these books and films.

General Scandinavia

A History of Scandinavia: Norway, Sweden, Denmark, Finland, and Iceland (T. K. Derry, 1979). This comprehensive tome weaves together the history of these five countries.

Scandinavia Since 1500 (Byron J. Nordstrom, 2000). Nordstrom presents a readable account of the region's history.

Scandinavian Folk and Fairy Tales (Claire Booss, 1988). This collection of Scandinavian folklore includes illustrations by local artists.

The Vikings (Else Roesdahl, 1987). Roesdahl offers a Scandinavian perspective on this complex Nordic society.

Denmark
Books

Conquered, Not Defeated (Peter Tveskov, 2003). Tveskov combines historical fact with childhood memories of Denmark under German occupation in World War II.

The Fairy Tale of My Life (Hans Christian Andersen, 1975). Andersen's autobiography chronicles everything from his impoverished childhood to encounters with other literary greats.

Hans Christian Andersen: A New Life (Jens Andersen, 2003). The author reveals new dimensions to the man behind many famous childhood stories.

The Little Mermaid (Hans Christian Andersen, 1837). This charming story about a mermaid selling her soul to become a human doesn't end quite as happily in Andersen's original tale as it does in Disney's world. Other beloved stories by the Danish-born Andersen include *The Little Match Girl, The Princess and the Pea,* and *The Steadfast Tin Soldier.*

Music and Silence (Rose Tremain, 1999). Tremain captures Denmark in the 17th century through the eyes of a lute player at court.

Smilla's Sense of Snow (Peter Høeg, 1992). In this thriller set in snowy Copenhagen, Smilla looks into the murder of her six-year-old neighbor (later adapted as a 1997 movie starring Julia Ormond).

We, the Drowned (Carsten Jensen, 2010). This novel covers the wars and adventures of the seafaring men of Marstal, a port town on the island of Ærø—and the angst of the families they leave behind.

Winter's Tale (Isak Dinesen, 1942). Best known for her memoir *Out of Africa,* Isak Dinesen (a.k.a. Karen Blixen) set most of these short stories in her homeland of Denmark.

Film and Television

Babette's Feast (1987). This Oscar winner for Best Foreign Language Film, about a Frenchwoman taking refuge in rural 19th-century Denmark, is the original foodie movie (based on the novel by Isak Dinesen).

Borgen (2010-2013). In this dramatic political TV series, principal character Birgitte Nyborg juggles her ambitions as the first female prime minister of Denmark with her responsibilities as a wife and mother.

The Bridge (Danish: *Broen;* Swedish: *Bron;* 2011-2018). This crime drama, a coproduction of Swedish and Danish TV, follows the cases and personal lives of a brilliant but obsessive-compulsive Swedish detective and her empathetic Danish collaborator.

Italian for Beginners (2000). Thirtysomethings learn Italian in hopes of finding romance in a small Danish town.

Pelle the Conqueror (1988). A Swedish father and son emigrate to Denmark in the 19th century and work to build a new life in this film based on the 1976 book by Martin Andersen Nexø (winner of the 1989 Oscar for Best Foreign Language Film).

Estonia
Books
The Czar's Madman (Jaan Kross, 1992). Accused of insanity, a nobleman from the Livonian region of Estonia is subsequently monitored and scrutinized by his family.

Treading Air (Jaan Kross, 1998). This novel follows the life of protagonist Ullo Paerand, from the 1920s through the Soviet occupation of Estonia.

Truth and Justice (Anton Hansen Tammsaare, 1926). In one of the cornerstones of Estonian literature, Tammsaare draws from his own life to describe Estonia's evolution into an independent state.

Film
Autumn Ball (2007). Based on the novel by Mati Unt, this film explores the isolation of six disparate people living in a Soviet-era apartment complex.

The Singing Revolution (2006). This documentary follows the evolution of Estonian music as a form of peaceful protest and symbol of patriotism.

Spring (1969). Set in a small town boarding school, this coming-of-age story is an Estonian classic.

Tangerines (2013). In this Golden Globe-nominated film, a man in a small village must care for wounded victims during the 1992 war in Abkhazik, Georgia.

Finland
Books
The Adventurer (Mika Waltari, 1950). An orphan drifts through historical events in Europe during the Middle Ages.

Kalevala (Elias Lönnrot, 1835). Regarded as Finland's national epic, *Kalevala* is a compilation of Karelian and Finnish oral folklore and poetry.

My Childhood (Toivo Pekkanen, 1966). Toivo Pekkanen chronicles his family's working-class life in early-20th-century Finland.

Purge (Sofi Oksanen, 2010). Finnish author Sofi Oskanen explores the Soviet occupation of Estonia and postwar suffering in this powerful novel about two women who reconcile their violent pasts.

Seven Brothers (Aleksis Kivi, 1870). In this Finnish classic, young brothers must learn to work hard and become productive members of society.

The Unknown Soldier (Väinö Linna, 1957). This iconic Finnish book candidly captures native soldiers' responses to World War II by delving into each character's psyche.

Film

Hellsinki (2009). Two criminals get caught up in a neighborhood black-market liquor business in 1960s Finland.

The Man Without a Past (2002). In this Academy Award-nominated film, a man is beaten up shortly after arriving in Helsinki, loses his memory, and must start his life anew.

Mother of Mine (2005). A young Finnish boy is evacuated to Sweden during World War II.

Road North (2012). An estranged father and son reunite for a road trip to northern Finland.

Uuno Turhapuro (1973-2006). Many Finnish politicians and celebrities make appearances throughout these 19 classic Finnish comedies about good-for-nothing Uuno, who disrupts and undermines his father-in-law in outlandish situations.

Norway
Books

Beatles (Lars Saabye Christensen, 1984). Four Beatles fans grow up in Oslo in the '60s and '70s.

A Doll's House (Henrik Ibsen, 1879). Ibsen's controversial play questions marriage norms and the role of women in a 19th-century man's world. (Ibsen explores similar themes in *Hedda Gabler*.)

Growth of the Soil (Knut Hamsun, 1917). This epic tale of a man living in backcountry Norway helped Hamsun win the Nobel Prize in Literature in 1920.

The Ice Palace (Tarjei Vesaas, 1993). Two young girls become unlikely friends—until a tragic disappearance shatters one of their lives.

Into the Ice: The History of Norway and the Polar Regions (Einar-Arne Drivenes and Harald Day Jolle, 2006). This comprehensive overview details expeditions, research, and the history of the polar region from the 19th century to the present.

Kon-Tiki (Thor Heyerdahl, 1948). Heyerdahl chronicles his historic 1947 journey from Peru to Polynesia on a balsa-wood raft. Norwegian filmmakers have catalogued his exploits in two films called *Kon-Tiki:* an Academy-Award-winning documentary (1950) and a blockbuster historical drama that was nominated for an Oscar for Best Foreign Language Film (2012).

Kristin Lavransdatter (Sigrid Undset, 1920-1923). This trilogy (also a 1995 movie) focuses on the life of a Norwegian woman in the 14th century.

My Struggle (Karl Ove Knausgaard, 2012). This six-part autobiography of a father and writer from Oslo is hugely popular in Norway and is quickly gaining worldwide recognition.

Out Stealing Horses (Per Petterson, 2005). A widower in remote

Norway meets a neighbor who stirs up memories of a pivotal day in 1948.

Sophie's World (Jostein Gaarder, 1994). A 14-year-old Norwegian girl becomes embroiled in a metaphysical mystery wrapped in the history of philosophy.

The Winter Fortress (Neal Bascomb, 2016). Bascomb uses letters, diaries, and once-secret documents to flesh out the story of the WWII Norwegian commandos who destroyed the heavy water plant at Vemork, striking a blow to the Nazi atomic bomb program.

Film and Television

Cool & Crazy (2001). In this uplifting documentary, a group of Norwegian men find companionship and success when they join an all-male choir.

Elling (2001). After his mother passes away, an autistic man—with a new oddball roommate—struggles to function in society.

The Heavy Water War (2015). This six-part miniseries recounts the sabotage of the heavy water plant at Vemork, part of Hitler's atomic bomb program, and touches on morality and collaboration in wartime.

Insomnia (1997). The midnight sun plays a role in this Norwegian thriller about a police detective investigating a small-town murder.

The Kautokeino Rebellion (2008). Based on the true events of 1852, the Sami people of Norway revolt against their exploitation by Norwegian authorities.

The King's Choice (2016). During the German invasion of April 1940, King Haakon and the royal family escape from Oslo and refuse to surrender to the pursuing Nazis.

Lilyhammer (2012-2014). This dark and humorous Netflix series follows a *Sopranos*-style New York mobster who, under the witness protection program, relocates to Lillehammer and adjusts to Norwegian society the only way he knows how.

Max Manus (2008). Based on real events in the life of WWII resistance fighter Max Manus, this film recounts the exploits of Manus and his comrades in Oslo during the Nazi occupation of Norway.

Nobel (2016). In this eight-part thriller, a Norwegian soldier returns home from Afghanistan only to be entwined in a web of political intrigue and murder surrounding the Nobel Peace Prize.

Occupied (2015-2016). A twisty-turny political thriller in which Norway, after discovering a clean source of energy and shutting down oil production in the North Sea, is occupied by Russia with backing from the EU (two seasons on Netflix).

Pathfinder (1987). Around 1000 A.D., a boy in Lapland must survive and fight against other Norse tribes.

Song of Norway (1970). This musical is based on the life of Norwegian composer Edvard Grieg.

Trollhunter (2010). Trolls wreak havoc in modern-day Norway in this fun fantasy/thriller that explains the real purpose of those power lines in the Norwegian mountains.

Vikings (2013-). This History Channel series centers on the adventures of mythological Viking Ragnar Lothbrok and his sons as they become renowned Norse heroes.

The Wave (2015). A collapsing mountainside sends a 250-foot tsunami roaring down the Geirangerfjord toward the town of Geiranger, leaving residents just 10 minutes to escape.

Sweden
Books

Faceless Killers (Henning Mankell, 1990). This is the first of 10 mysteries featuring inspector Kurt Wallander.

The Girl with the Dragon Tattoo (Stieg Larsson, 2005). The first book in Larsson's *Millennium* trilogy, about a punky computer hacker and a disgraced journalist, put Swedish crime fiction on the map. The Swedish film versions of these books (with Noomi Rapace as Lisbeth) are as compelling as the novels. Hollywood released its own version of *The Girl with the Dragon Tattoo* in 2011, starring Daniel Craig and Rooney Mara.

Hanna's Daughters (Marianne Fredriksson, 1994). This moving novel follows the lives of three remarkable Swedish women from the 1870s through World War II.

A Man Called Ove (Fredrik Backman, 2014). This dark comedy centers on a cranky widower whose life is devoid of joy—until some lively neighbors move into his housing complex (also an Oscar-nominated motion picture).

Pippi Longstocking (Astrid Lindgren, 1945). Kids of all ages love reading about the adventures of the strong-willed and unconventional nine-year-old living in Sweden.

The Red Room (August Strindberg, 1879). This biting satire on Stockholm society made Strindberg a literary giant.

Sweden: The Nation's History (Franklin D. Scott, 1988). Scott provides a comprehensive overview of the history of the Swedish people from feudalism to democracy.

The Wonderful Adventures of Nils (Selma Lagerlöf, 1906). In this fantastical children's novel (winner of the Nobel Prize for

Literature), Nils loves nothing more than eating, sleeping, and tormenting animals—at least until he is shrunken down to their size.

Film and Television

As It Is in Heaven (2004). A famous conductor returns to his village in Sweden, where he finds love and the key to happiness.

Dalecarlians (2005). After living in Stockholm, Mia returns home to her small village and must adjust to the life she left behind.

The Emigrants (1971). A Swedish family faces a rough transition as they move from Sweden to Minnesota in this film starring Max von Sydow and Liv Ullmann (based on the novels by Vilhelm Moberg). The sequel *The New Land* (1972) continues the family's journey.

Let the Right One In (2008). In this Swedish romantic horror film, a lonely boy finds friendship with a vampire girl.

My Life as a Dog (1985). This bittersweet tale from director Lasse Hallström focuses on a young boy in 1950s Sweden.

The Seventh Seal (1957). In this Ingmar Bergman film (set in Sweden during the Black Death), a knight questions the meaning of life. Other masterpieces from the Oscar-winning Swedish director include *Smiles of a Summer Night* (1955), a turn-of-the-century frolic, and *Fanny & Alexander* (1983), about two children overcoming their father's death.

Together (2000). This satirical view of socialist values is set in a 1970s Stockholm commune.

Wallander (2005-2013). Based on the characters in Henning Mankell's Kurt Wallander detective novels, this Swedish crime series is a study in the Scandinavian temperament and culture.

Welcome to Sweden (2014-2015). In this NBC comedy series starring Greg Poehler (who co-produces the show with his sister Amy), an American accountant follows his girlfriend back to her home in Stockholm, where he embarks on crazy adventures with her quirky family.

Conversions and Climate

Numbers and Stumblers

- Europeans write a few of their numbers differently than we do. 1 = 1, 4 = 4, 7 = 7.

- In Europe, dates appear as day/month/year, so Christmas 2020 is 25/12/2020.
- Commas are decimal points and decimals commas. A dollar and a half is $1,50, one thousand is 1.000, and there are 5.280 feet in a mile.
- When counting with fingers, start with your thumb. If you hold up your first finger to request one item, you'll probably get two.
- Scandinavians number their weeks. Instead of saying, "Spring break is the third week in March," they'd say, "Spring break is week 12."
- On escalators and moving sidewalks, Europeans keep the left "lane" open for passing. Keep to the right.

METRIC CONVERSIONS

A **kilogram** equals 1,000 grams (about 2.2 pounds). One hundred **grams** (a common unit at markets) is about a quarter-pound. One **liter** is about a quart, or almost four to a gallon.

A **kilometer** is six-tenths of a mile. To convert kilometers to miles, cut the kilometers in half and add back 10 percent of the original (120 km: 60 + 12 = 72 miles). One **meter** is 39 inches—just over a yard.

1 foot = 0.3 meter	1 square yard = 0.8 square meter
1 yard = 0.9 meter	1 square mile = 2.6 square kilometers
1 mile = 1.6 kilometers	1 ounce = 28 grams
1 centimeter = 0.4 inch	1 quart = 0.95 liter
1 meter = 39.4 inches	1 kilogram = 2.2 pounds
1 kilometer = 0.62 mile	32°F = 0°C

CLOTHING SIZES

When shopping for clothing, use these US-to-European comparisons as general guidelines (but note that no conversion is perfect).

Women: For pants and dresses, add 30 in Scandinavia (US 10 = Scandinavian 40). For blouses and sweaters, add 8 for most of Europe (US 32 = European 40). For shoes, add 30-31 (US 7 = European 37/38).

Men: For shirts, multiply by 2 and add about 8 (US 15 = European 38). For jackets and suits, add 10. For shoes, add 32-34.

Children: Clothing is sized by height—in centimeters (2.5 inches = 1 cm), so a US size 8 roughly equates to 132-140. For shoes up to size 13, add 16-18, and for sizes 1 and up, add 30-32.

Scandinavia's Climate

First line, average daily high; second line, average daily low; third line, average days without rain. For more detailed weather statistics for destinations in this book (as well as the rest of the world), check www.wunderground.com.

J	F	M	A	M	J	J	A	S	O	N	D

DENMARK • Copenhagen

J	F	M	A	M	J	J	A	S	O	N	D
37°	37°	42°	51°	60°	66°	70°	69°	64°	55°	46°	41°
29°	28°	31°	37°	45°	51°	56°	56°	51°	44°	38°	33°
14	15	19	18	20	18	17	16	14	14	11	12

ESTONIA • Tallinn

J	F	M	A	M	J	J	A	S	O	N	D
25°	25°	32°	45°	57°	66°	68°	66°	59°	50°	37°	30°
14°	12°	19°	32°	41°	50°	54°	52°	48°	39°	30°	19°
12	12	18	19	19	20	18	16	14	14	12	12

FINLAND • Helsinki

J	F	M	A	M	J	J	A	S	O	N	D
26°	25°	32°	44°	56°	66°	71°	68°	59°	47°	37°	31°
17°	15°	20°	30°	40°	49°	55°	53°	46°	37°	30°	23°
11	10	17	17	19	17	17	16	16	13	11	11

NORWAY • Oslo

J	F	M	A	M	J	J	A	S	O	N	D
28°	30°	39°	50°	61°	68°	72°	70°	60°	48°	38°	32°
19°	19°	25°	34°	43°	50°	55°	53°	46°	38°	31°	25°
16	16	22	19	21	17	16	17	16	17	14	14

SWEDEN • Stockholm

J	F	M	A	M	J	J	A	S	O	N	D
30°	30°	37°	47°	58°	67°	71°	68°	60°	49°	40°	35°
26°	25°	29°	37°	45°	53°	57°	56°	50°	43°	37°	32°
15	14	21	19	20	17	18	17	16	16	14	14

APPENDIX

Fahrenheit and Celsius Conversion

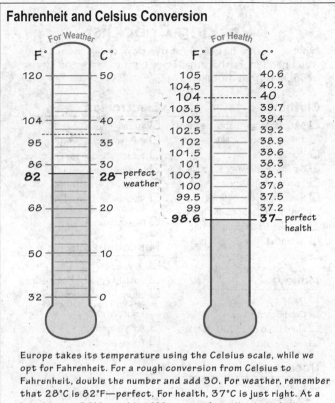

For Weather

F°	C°
120	50
104	40
95	35
86	30
82	**28**—perfect weather
68	20
50	10
32	0

For Health

F°	C°
105	40.6
104.5	40.3
104	40
103.5	39.7
103	39.4
102.5	39.2
102	38.9
101.5	38.6
101	38.3
100.5	38.1
100	37.8
99.5	37.5
99	37.2
98.6	**37**—perfect health

Europe takes its temperature using the Celsius scale, while we opt for Fahrenheit. For a rough conversion from Celsius to Fahrenheit, double the number and add 30. For weather, remember that 28°C is 82°F—perfect. For health, 37°C is just right. At a launderette, 30°C is cold, 40°C is warm (usually the default setting), 60°C is hot, and 95°C is boiling. Your air-conditioner should be set at about 20°C.

APPENDIX

Packing Checklist

Whether you're traveling for five days or five weeks, you won't need more than this. Pack light to enjoy the sweet freedom of true mobility.

Clothing

- ☐ 5 shirts: long- & short-sleeve
- ☐ 2 pairs pants (or skirts/capris)
- ☐ 1 pair shorts
- ☐ 5 pairs underwear & socks
- ☐ 1 pair walking shoes
- ☐ Sweater or warm layer
- ☐ Rainproof jacket with hood
- ☐ Tie, scarf, belt, and/or hat
- ☐ Swimsuit
- ☐ Sleepwear/loungewear

Money

- ☐ Debit card(s)
- ☐ Credit card(s)
- ☐ Hard cash (US $100-200)
- ☐ Money belt

Documents

- ☐ Passport
- ☐ Tickets & confirmations: flights, hotels, trains, rail pass, car rental, sight entries
- ☐ Driver's license
- ☐ Student ID, hostel card, etc.
- ☐ Photocopies of important documents
- ☐ Insurance details
- ☐ Guidebooks & maps

Toiletries Kit

- ☐ Basics: soap, shampoo, toothbrush, toothpaste, floss, deodorant, sunscreen, brush/comb, etc.
- ☐ Medicines & vitamins
- ☐ First-aid kit
- ☐ Glasses/contacts/sunglasses
- ☐ Sewing kit
- ☐ Packet of tissues (for WC)
- ☐ Earplugs

Electronics

- ☐ Mobile phone
- ☐ Camera & related gear
- ☐ Tablet/ebook reader/laptop
- ☐ Headphones/earbuds
- ☐ Chargers & batteries
- ☐ Phone car charger & mount (or GPS device)
- ☐ Plug adapters

Miscellaneous

- ☐ Daypack
- ☐ Sealable plastic baggies
- ☐ Laundry supplies: soap, laundry bag, clothesline, spot remover
- ☐ Small umbrella
- ☐ Travel alarm/watch
- ☐ Notepad & pen
- ☐ Journal

Optional Extras

- ☐ Second pair of shoes (flip-flops, sandals, tennis shoes, boots)
- ☐ Travel hairdryer
- ☐ Picnic supplies
- ☐ Water bottle
- ☐ Fold-up tote bag
- ☐ Small flashlight
- ☐ Mini binoculars
- ☐ Small towel or washcloth
- ☐ Inflatable pillow/neck rest
- ☐ Tiny lock
- ☐ Address list (to mail postcards)
- ☐ Extra passport photos

INDEX

INDEX

INDEX

MAP INDEX

Explore Europe

At ricksteves.com you can browse through thousands of articles, videos, photos and radio interviews, plus find a wealth of money-saving travel tips for planning your dream trip. And with our mobile-friendly website, you can easily access all this great travel information anywhere you go.

TV Shows

Preview the places you'll visit by watching entire half-hour episodes of Rick Steves' Europe (choose from all 100 shows) on-demand, for free.

ricksteves.com

your travel dreams into affordable reality

Radio Interviews

Enjoy ready access to Rick's vast library of radio interviews covering travel

tips and cultural insights that relate specifically to your Europe travel plans.

Travel Forums

Learn, ask, share! Our online community of savvy travelers is a great resource

for first-time travelers to Europe, as well as seasoned pros. You'll find forums on each country, plus travel tips and restaurant/hotel reviews. You can even ask one of our well-traveled staff to chime in with an opinion.

Travel News

Subscribe to our free Travel News e-newsletter, and get monthly updates from Rick on what's happening in Europe.

Audio Europe™

Rick's Free Travel App

Get your FREE **Rick Steves Audio Europe**™ app to enjoy...

- Dozens of self-guided tours of Europe's top museums, sights and historic walks
- Hundreds of tracks filled with cultural insights and sightseeing tips from Rick's radio interviews
- All organized into handy geographic playlists
- For Apple and Android

With Rick whispering in your ear, Europe gets even better.

Find out more at ricksteves.com

Pack Light and Right

Gear up for your next adventure at ricksteves.com

Light Luggage

Pack light and right with Rick Steves' affordable, custom-designed rolling carry-on bags, backpacks, day packs and shoulder bags.

Accessories

From packing cubes to moneybelts and beyond, Rick has personally selected the travel goodies that will help your trip go smoother.

Rick Steves has

Save time and energy

This guidebook is your independent-travel toolkit. But for all it delivers, it's still up to you to devote the time and energy it takes to manage the preparation and logistics that are essential for a happy trip. If that's a hassle, there's a solution.

Rick Steves Tours

A Rick Steves tour takes you to Europe's most interesting places with great

great tours, too!

with minimum stress

guides and small groups of 28 or less. We follow Rick's favorite itineraries, ride in comfy buses, stay in family-run hotels, and bring you intimately

close to the Europe you've traveled so far to see. Most importantly, we take away the logistical headaches so you can focus on the fun.

Join the fun

This year we'll take thousands of free-spirited

travelers—nearly half of them repeat customers—along with us on four dozen different itineraries, from Ireland to Italy to Athens. Is a Rick Steves tour the right fit for your travel dreams? Find out at ricksteves.com, where you can also request Rick's latest tour catalog. Europe is best experienced with happy travel partners. We hope you can join us.

See our itineraries at ricksteves.com

A Guide for Every Trip

BEST OF GUIDES

Full color easy-to-scan format, focusing on Europe's most popular destinations and sights.

Best of England
Best of Europe
Best of France
Best of Germany
Best of Ireland
Best of Italy
Best of Spain

COMPREHENSIVE GUIDES

City, country, and regional guides with detailed coverage for a multi-week trip exploring the most iconic sights and venturing off the beaten track.

Amsterdam & the Netherlands
Barcelona
Belgium: Bruges, Brussels, Antwerp & Ghent
Berlin
Budapest
Croatia & Slovenia
Eastern Europe
England
Florence & Tuscany
France
Germany
Great Britain
Greece: Athens & the Peloponnese
Iceland
Ireland
Istanbul
Italy
London
Paris
Portugal
Prague & the Czech Republic
Provence & the French Riviera
Rome
Scandinavia
Scotland
Spain
Switzerland
Venice
Vienna, Salzburg & Tirol

E BEST OF ROME

, Italy's capital, is studded with
remnants and floodlit fountain
s. From the Vatican to the Colos-
with crazy traffic in between, Rome
erful, huge, and exhausting. The
the heat, and the weighty history

of the Eternal City where Caesars walked
can make tourists wilt. Recharge by taking siestas, gelato breaks, and after-dark
walks, strolling from one atmospheric
square to another in the refreshing evening air.

Pantheon—which
dome until the
2,000 years old
over 1,500).

thens in the Vat-
s the humanistic

diators fought
ther, entertaining

ome ristorante.
ther.
t St. Peter's
ously.

Rick Steves guidebooks are published by Avalon Travel,
an imprint of Perseus Books, a Hachette Book Group company.

POCKET GUIDES

Compact, full color city guides with the essentials for shorter trips.

Amsterdam	Paris
Athens	Prague
Barcelona	Rome
Florence	Venice
Italy's Cinque Terre	Vienna
London	
Munich & Salzburg	

SNAPSHOT GUIDES

Focused single-destination coverage.

Basque Country: Spain & France
Copenhagen & the Best of Denmark
Dublin
Dubrovnik
Edinburgh
Hill Towns of Central Italy
Krakow, Warsaw & Gdansk
Lisbon
Loire Valley
Madrid & Toledo
Milan & the Italian Lakes District
Naples & the Amalfi Coast
Normandy
Northern Ireland
Norway
Reykjavík
Sevilla, Granada & Southern Spain
St. Petersburg, Helsinki & Tallinn
Stockholm

CRUISE PORTS GUIDES

Reference for cruise ports of call.

Mediterranean Cruise Ports
Scandinavian & Northern European Cruise Ports

Complete your library with...

TRAVEL SKILLS & CULTURE

Study up on travel skills and gain insight on history and culture.

Europe 101
Europe Through the Back Door
European Christmas
European Easter
European Festivals
Postcards from Europe
Travel as a Political Act

PHRASE BOOKS & DICTIONARIES

French
French, Italian & German
German
Italian
Portuguese
Spanish

PLANNING MAPS

Britain, Ireland & London
Europe
France & Paris
Germany, Austria & Switzerland
Ireland
Italy
Spain & Portugal

Credits

RESEARCHERS
To help update this book, Rick relied on...

Glenn Eriksen
A solo backpacking trip across Europe and Scandinavia back in the '70s turned out to be Glenn's first step on the road to Rick Steves' Europe. Today, as a guidebook editor and researcher, he indulges his love for the Old Country while helping Rick's readers "keep on travelin'." When not on the road, Glenn lives in Seattle with his wife, Kathy, and enjoys hiking, photography, and keeping in touch with his Norwegian roots.

Cameron Hewitt
Born in Denver and raised in central Ohio, Cameron settled in Seattle in 2000. Ever since, he has spent three months each year in Europe, contributing to guidebooks, tours, radio and television shows, and other media for Rick Steves' Europe, where he serves as content manager. Cameron married his high school sweetheart (and favorite travel partner), Shawna, and enjoys taking pictures, trying new restaurants, and planning his next trip.

Pål Bjarne Johansen
A tour guide and guidebook researcher for Rick Steves' Europe, covering Scandinavia and Spain, Pål grew up in the Norwegian countryside near the Swedish border and has family ties in Denmark. He discovered his passion for travel and adventure at a young age, and has backpacked much of the world since graduating high school. When Pål's not working for Rick Steves, you'll find him skiing the Norwegian woods in the winter, and sailing the seven seas in the summer.

Suzanne Kotz
Suzanne, an editor with Rick Steves' Europe, began her travel career riding in a station wagon with her six siblings from Michigan to Florida for spring break. Since then, she's broadened her destinations to include much of Europe and parts of Asia. A librarian by training and a longtime editor of art publications, she's happiest with a good book in her hands. She lives in Seattle with her husband and son.

CONTRIBUTOR

Gene Openshaw

Gene has co-authored a dozen *Rick Steves* books, specializing in writing walks and tours of Europe's cities, museums, and cultural sights. He also contributes to Rick's public television series, produces tours for Rick Steves Audio Europe, and is a regular guest on Rick's public radio show. Outside of the travel world, Gene has co-authored *The Seattle Joke Book.* As a composer, Gene has written a full-length opera called *Matter,* a violin sonata, and dozens of songs. He lives near Seattle with his daughter, enjoys giving presentations on art and history, and roots for the Mariners in good times and bad.

ACKNOWLEDGMENTS

Thanks to Thor, Hanne, Geir, Hege, and Kari-Anne, our Norwegian family. Special thanks to Jane Klausen for her expertise in all things Danish. Thanks to these translators for their help with the survival phrases: Marita Bergman, Unni-Marie Kvikne, Mati Rummessen, and Christina Snellman. And, in loving memory of Berit Kristiansen, whose house was my house for 20 years of Norwegian travel.

Avalon Travel
Hachette Book Group
1700 Fourth Street
Berkeley, CA 94710

Printed in Canada by Friesens.
15th Edition. First printing June 2018.

ISBN 978-1-63121-816-3

For the latest on Rick's talks, guidebooks, tours, public television series, and public radio show, contact Rick Steves' Europe, 130 Fourth Avenue North, Edmonds, WA 98020, 425/771-8303, www.ricksteves.com, rick@ricksteves.com.

Rick Steves' Europe
Managing Editor: Jennifer Madison Davis
Special Publications Manager: Risa Laib
Assistant Managing Editor: Cathy Lu
Editors: Glenn Eriksen, Julie Fanselow, Tom Griffin, Katherine Gustafson, Suzanne Kotz, Rosie Leutzinger, Carrie Shepherd
Editorial & Production Assistant: Jessica Shaw
Editorial Intern: Kevin Teeter
Researchers: Glenn Eriksen, Cameron Hewitt, Pål Bjarne Johansen, Suzanne Kotz
Contributor: Gene Openshaw
Graphic Content Director: Sandra Hundacker
Maps & Graphics: David C. Hoerlein, Lauren Mills, Mary Rostad

Avalon Travel
Senior Editor & Series Manager: Madhu Prasher
Editor: Jamie Andrade
Editor: Sierra Machado
Copy Editor: Maggie Ryan
Proofreader: Kelly Lydick
Indexer: Stephen Callahan
Production & Typesetting: Krista Anderson, Lisi Baldwin, Rue Flaherty
Cover Design: Kimberly Glyder Design
Maps & Graphics: Kat Bennett, Mike Morgenfeld

Photo Credits
Front Cover: Nyhavn, Denmark, photo by Jan Wlodarczyk, Alamy
Title Page: Boat from Balestrand to Bergen © Rick Steves
Additional Photography: Dominic Arizona Bonuccelli, Tom Griffin, Sonja Groset, Cameron Hewitt, David C. Hoerlein, Lauren Mills, Jennifer Schutte, Rick Steves, Ian Watson, Wikimedia Commons (PD-Art/PD-US)
Additional Credits: p. 41, Photo of Richard Karpen— courtesy of Jack Juliussen
Photos are used by permission and are the property of the original copyright owners

Let's Keep on Travelin'

Your trip doesn't need to end.

Follow Rick on social media!